30 Sept 1985

To Mary Maples Dunn

with compliments & affection

PHE

SWIFT vs. MAINWARING

The Examiner and *The Medley*

This edition presents the text of *The Examiner* as Swift wrote it and John Barber printed it, not as it was revised for publication by George Faulkner in 1738. This edition also juxtaposes for the first time Swift's *Examiners* with Arthur Mainwaring's *Medleys* that replied to them every week. The apparatus includes textual variants for both sets of essays, an introduction providing necessary background, and annotation of the sources and allusions in the text.

The Examiner and *The Medley* are engrossing because they put the reader so close to the *actualités* of London in November 1710– June 1711: the slow discrediting of Marlborough, the sudden stabbing of Harley at a meeting of a council committee, the first leaks in the secret treaty negotiations with France, the first boisterous meetings of the October Club. Together *The Examiner* and *The Medley* constitute a debate about all the questions that were left unanswered in 1688–9— 'a set of alternative interpretations' of what the Revolution really meant.

From the literary point of view *The Examiner* is important, as Irvin Ehrenpreis says, because 'Swift seldom wrote better'. Occasional essays are well-known 'to discover the genuine abilities of an Author, before his more dilatory and accumulated productions', and *The Examiner* is no exception. Even under the pressure of weekly publication Swift was still able to achieve, in Herbert Davis's words, 'an aloofness, as if beyond bias and passion'.

George Parker, the astrologer whom Swift did *not* ridicule, called attention to 'the many Friendly Aspects of the Superior Planets of Saturn and Jupiter' during the early months of Swift's sojourn in London. Within six weeks of his arrival in September 1710 the Queen had granted his petition to remit to the Church of Ireland the tax of first fruits and twentieth parts and Swift in turn had undertaken to defend the new Ministry in print. *The Examiner* is a product of those propitious days before Saturn and Jupiter turned malign. In the end the whole period seemed to Swift to have been a waste of time. He summarized it in two lines of *Horace, Lib. 2. Sat. 6. Part of it imitated* (1714): 'Thus in a Sea of Folly tost, | My choicest Hours of Life are lost'.

The Coffehous Mob, anonymous woodcut

SWIFT
vs.
MAINWARING

The Examiner and *The Medley*

EDITED BY

FRANK H. ELLIS

CLARENDON PRESS · OXFORD

1985

Oxford University Press, Walton Street, Oxford OX2 6DP

London Glasgow New York Toronto
Delhi Bombay Calcutta Madras Karachi
Kuala Lumpur Singapore Hong Kong Tokyo
Nairobi Dar es Salaam Cape Town
Melbourne Auckland

and associated companies in
Beirut Berlin Ibadan Mexico City Nicosia

Oxford is a trade mark of Oxford University Press

Published in the United States
by Oxford University Press, New York

British Library Cataloguing in Publication Data
Swift vs. Mainwaring.
1. Swift, Jonathan — Criticism and interpretation
I. Ellis, Frank H.
828'.509   PR3727
ISBN 0-19-812522-4

Printed in Great Britain
at the University Press, Oxford
by David Stanford
Printer to the University

What a Present is here intended for the future Republick of
Letters!

The Medley, 18 December 1710

If two Men would argue on both Sides, with Fairness, good
Sense, and good Manners; it would be no ill Entertainment
to the Town.

The Examiner, 14 December 1710

Not the *Meddle*, but the *Medley*, you fool!

Journal to Stella, 28 April 1711

PREFACE

THIS book was undertaken mainly for two reasons: (1) to get into print at last *The Examiners* as Swift wrote them in 1710-11, and (2) to juxtapose *The Examiners* with *The Medleys* that responded to each of them. *The Examiner* has already been published twice in this century, but both editions are based on George Faulkner's 1738 text, a whole generation removed from the excitements of 1710-11. *The Medley*, on the other hand, has not been published since the eighteenth century. Readers today may well wonder why, for Mainwaring wields the same weapons as Swift, with some of the same jolting effects. Interspersing *The Medleys* with *The Examiners* puts them in the only context in which they have meaning.

If the work of establishing the text of *The Examiner* had to begin all over again at the beginning, the search for the meaning of *The Examiner* could set out from the high ground reached by the two Scotts, Sir Walter and Temple, who are (gratefully) cited in the footnotes below as E*1814* and E*1922*, respectively.

Seven copies of *The Examiner* and *The Medley* collated for this edition were collected during a visit to England supported by a grant from the American Philosophical Society, for which I am happy to have the opportunity now to say thank you. The support of my own college, in the form of grants for research assistance, proved particularly rewarding in this project, for in recent summers it materialized in the person of a young classics scholar, Dianne E. Miller, whose editorial skills are reflected everywhere in the book.

It is a pleasure as well to thank all those who so patiently and generously responded to my requests for help: D.M. Abbott, Sandra Allen, Amanda J.E. Arrowsmith, Young-Ju Bae, Peter M. Barber, Carey S. Bliss, Evelyn B. Cannon, Mary Ceibert, Eveline Cruickshanks, Alan Downie, Ann C. Farr, Oliver W. Ferguson, Jane G. Flener, the Revd Alister D. Fraser, Judith Gardner-Flint, David Hayton, Cathy Henderson, C.J. Herington, Sue Hodson, Henry Horwitz, the Revd Edward S.O. Jacson, A.C. James, the Revd W.J. Leadbetter, Jennifer B. Lee, Glenise A. Matheson, Howard Nenner,

Major the Revd Robert H. Nesham, Mrs G.C. Parkes, Mary Paul
Pollard, Irène Simon, Harold Skulsky, D.J.H. Smith, Henry L.
Snyder, William A. Speck, Daniel Traister, Mrs M.A. Welch, Neda
Westlake, Reginald Williams, David L.T. Woolley, and Christopher
J. Wright.

Numbering of The Examiners: In every edition since the first
Swift's *Examiners* have been misnumbered. 'The wrong numbering
arose from Mr. Barber's having omitted the original No. 13 (a
paper on *Non-Resistance*), when he first collected the Examiners
into a Volume' (Nichols, *Literary Anecdotes*, ii 156n.). *The
Examiner*, No. 13, was Atterbury's 'violent defence of the doctrine of hereditary right, in its most absurd extent' (p. xxv
below), which the printer, John Barber, for reasons unknown,
failed to include in the duodecimo edition. In the present edition the numbering of the first edition is restored.

Decimal numbers refer to the page and line numbers of the text
of *The Examiner* and *The Medley* in the present edition.

Dates are in the Old Style, according to which the English
calendar by 1710-11 had fallen eleven days behind the Gregorian
calendar used on the Continent. But the year is taken as beginning on 1 January, not on 25 March.

Frank H. Ellis,
Smith College,
Northampton,
Massachusetts

CONTENTS

ILLUSTRATIONS

ABBREVIATIONS AND SHORT TITLES

An Account of the Conduct	[Nathaniel Hook,] *An Account of the Conduct of the Dowager Duchess of Marlborough, from her first coming to Court, to the Year 1710*, London, by James Bettenham for George Hawkins, 1742.
Addison, *Letters*	*The Letters of Joseph Addison*, ed. Walter Graham, Oxford, Clarendon Press, 1941.
Anon.	*The Life and Reign of Her late excellent Majesty, Queen Anne. In which is contained a particular Account of the most Remarkable Transactions during her Majesty's Reign*, London, 1738 (Morgan T31).
APS	*The Acts of the Parliaments of Scotland 1124-1707*, 11 vols. in 12, plus index, Edinburgh, 1844-75.
Bayle, *Dictionary*	Pierre Bayle, *An Historical and Critical Dictionary*, trans. Pierre Desmaizeaux, 4 vols., London, C. Harper *et al.*, 1710.
Beatson	Robert Beatson, *A Political Index to the Histories of Great Britain and Ireland*, 2nd edn., 2 vols., London, for G.G.J. and J. Robinson, 1788.
Bennett	Gareth V. Bennett, *The Tory Crisis in Church and State 1688-1730. The Career of Francis Atterbury Bishop of Rochester*, Oxford, Clarendon Press, 1975.
Biographia Britannica	*Biographia Britannica: Or, The Lives of the Most Eminent Persons*, 6 vols. in 7, London, for W. Innys *et al.*, 1747-66; 2nd edn., edd. Andrew Kippis *et al.*, 5 vols. [A-Fastolf only], London, by W. and A. Strahan for C. Bathurst, 1778-93.
BL	The British Library, Great Russell Street, London.
Bolingbroke, *Letters*	*The Letters and Correspondence, Public and Private, of the Right Honourable Henry St. John, Lord Visc. Bolingbroke*, ed. Gilbert Parke, 4 vols., London, G.G. and J. Robinson, 1798.
Boyer, *Annals*	Abel Boyer, *The History of the Reign of Queen Anne, Digested into Annals*, 11 vols., London, for A. Roper and F. Coggan, 1703-13.
Boyer, *The History*	Abel Boyer, *The History of Queen Anne*, London, T. Woodward, 1735.
Boyer, *The Political State*	Abel Boyer, *The Political State of Great Britain*, 38 vols., London, for J. Baker, 1711-29.
Burnet	Gilbert Burnet, *History of His Own Time*, 2 vols., London, for Thomas Ward *et al.*, 1724-34.
Burnet, 1833	*Bishop Burnet's History of His Own Time: With Notes by the Earls of Dartmouth and Hardwicke, Speaker Onslow, and Dean Swift*, 2nd edn., 6 vols., Oxford, Oxford University Press, 1833.

Churchill's Annals	*Churchill's Annals: Being a Compleat View of the Duke of Marlborough's Life and Glorious Actions, both in the Field and Cabinet*, London, Sarah Popping, 1714.
CJ	*Journals of the House of Commons, 1547-1796*, 51 vols. [London], 1803.
CJ Ireland	*The Journals of the House of Commons of the Kingdom of Ireland*, 2nd edn., 31 vols. in 27, Dublin, by Abraham Bradley *et al.*, 1782-94.
CLU-C	University of California at Los Angeles—William Andrews Clark Memorial Library.
A Collection of the Addresses	*A Collection of the Addresses which have been Presented to the Queen, since the Impeachment of the Reverend Dr. Henry Sacheverell. Whereby it most evidently appears, That the Sense of the Kingdom, whether Nobility, Clergy, Gentry, or Commonalty, is express for the Doctrine of* Passive Obedience *and* Non-Resistance, *and for Her Majesty's* Hereditary Title *to the Throne of Her Ancestors*, 2 vols., London, John Morphew, 1710.
Coxe, *Marlborough*	William Coxe, *Memoirs of the Duke of Marlborough, with his Original Correspondence*, new edn., ed. John Wade, 3 vols., London, George Bell and Sons, 1876.
CSmH	Henry E. Huntington Library, San Marino, California.
CTB	*Calendar of Treasury Books, 1660-1704*, ed. William A. Shaw, 19 vols. in 35, London, HMSO, 1904-38.
CTP	*Calendar of Treasury Papers, 1557-1728*, ed. Joseph Redington, 6 vols., London, Longmans, Green, *et al.*, 1868-89.
CtY	Yale University, New Haven, Connecticut.
Cunningham	Alexander Cunningham, *The History of Great Britain: from the Revolution in 1688, to the Accession of George the First*, 2 vols., London, A. Strahan and T. Cadell, 1787.
Dalrymple	Sir John Dalrymple, Bt., *Memoirs of Great Britain and Ireland*, 5th edn., 3 vols., London and Edinburgh, A. Strahan, T. Cadell, J. Bell, *et al.*, 1790.
Dalton	*English Army Lists and Commission Registers, 1661-1714*, ed. Charles Dalton, 6 vols. in 3, London, Francis Edwards, 1960.
Defoe, *Letters*	*The Letters of Daniel Defoe*, ed. George H. Healey, Oxford, Clarendon Press, 1955.
De La Chesnaye-Desbois	François Alexandre Aubert De La Chesnaye-Desbois et Badier, *Dictionnaire de la noblesse*, 19 vols., Paris, Schlesinger, 1863-76.
Dickson	P.G.M. Dickson, *The Financial Revolution in England. A Study of the Development of Public Credit 1688-1756*, London and New York, Macmillan and St. Martin's Press, 1967.

DNB	*The Dictionary of National Biography*, edd. Sir Leslie Stephen and Sir Sidney Lee, 22 vols., Oxford, Oxford University Press, 1959-60.
Downie	James A. Downie, *Robert Harley and the Press. Propaganda and Public Opinion in the Age of Swift and Defoe*, Cambridge, Cambridge University Press, 1979.
Dunton	John Dunton, *The Life and Errors*, ed. John B. Nichols, 2 vols., London, J. Nichols, Sons and Bentley, 1818.
E½°	*The Examiner*, folio half-sheet edition, 1710-11.
E12°	*The Examiner*, duodecimo edition, 1712.
E*1738*	*Volume V. of the Author's Works*, Dublin, George Faulkner, 1738 (Teerink-Scouten 42, 50).
E*1814*	*The Works of Jonathan Swift, D.D. Dean of St. Patrick's, Dublin*, ed. Walter Scott, 19 vols., Edinburgh, Constable, 1814 (Teerink-Scouten 138).
E*1922*	*The Prose Works of Jonathan Swift, D.D.*, ed. Temple Scott, 12 vols., London, G. Bell and Sons, 1905-25.
Echard	Laurence Echard, *The History of England*, 3 vols., London, Jacob Tonson, 1707-18.
EHR	*The English Historical Review*, London, Longmans, Green, 1886- .
Ehrenpreis	Irvin Ehrenpreis, *Swift the Man, His Works, and the Age*, 3 vols., London, Methuen, 1962-84.
Foxcroft	H.C. Foxcroft, *A Supplement to Burnet's History of My Own Time*, Oxford, Clarendon Press, 1902.
Foxon	David F. Foxon, *English Verse 1701-1750. A Catalogue of Separately Printed Poems with Notes on Contemporary Collected Editions*, 2 vols., London, Cambridge University Press, 1975.
GEC	George E. Cokayne, *The Complete Peerage*, 2nd edn., edd. Vicary Gibbs *et al.*, 13 vols. in 14, London, St. Catherine Press, 1910-59.
Gregg	Edward Gregg, *Queen Anne*, London, Routledge and Kegan Paul, 1980.
Grimblot	*Letters of William III and Louis XIV and their Ministers; Illustrative of the Domestic and Foreign Politics of England ... 1697-1700*, ed. Paul Grimblot, London, Longman, Brown, Green, and Longmans, 1848.
Hamilton	*The Diary of Sir David Hamilton 1709-1714*, ed. Philip Roberts, Oxford, Clarendon Press, 1975.
Harley, 'Plaine English'	Robert Harley, 'Plaine English to all who are honest, or would be so if they knew how', BL MS Portland Loan 29/10/1, edd. W.A. Speck and James A. Downie, *Literature and History*, i (March 1976), 102-9.

Hearne

Remarks and Collections of Thomas Hearne, edd. C.E. Doble *et al.*, 11 vols., Oxford, Clarendon Press, 1884-1918.

Hill

B.H. Hill, 'The change of government and the "loss of the City", 1710-11', *Economic History Review*, xxiv (1971), 395-413.

Hill, *Corr.*

The Diplomatic Correspondence of the Right Hon. Richard Hill, Envoy Extraordinary from the Court of St. James to the Duke of Savoy, ed. W. Blackley, 2 vols., London, John Murray, 1845.

The History and Proceedings of the House of Commons

The History and Proceedings of the House of Commons from the Restoration to the Present Time, 14 vols., London, for Richard Chandler, 1742.

HLQ

The Huntington Library Quarterly, San Marino, California, Henry E. Huntington Library and Art Gallery, 1937- .

HMC *Bath MSS*

Historical Manuscripts Commission, *Calendar of the Manuscripts of the Marquis of Bath Preserved at Longleat, Wiltshire*, 3 vols., London, HMSO, 1904-8.

HMC *Dartmouth MSS*

Historical Manuscripts Commission, Eleventh Report, Appendix, Part V, *The Manuscripts of the Earl of Dartmouth*, London, HMSO, 1887.

HMC *Downshire MSS*

Historical Manuscripts Commission, *The Manuscripts of the Marquess of Downshire. Papers of Sir William Trumbull*, 1 vol. in 2, London, HMSO, 1924.

HMC *Egmont MSS*

Historical Manuscripts Commission, *Report on the Manuscripts of the Earl of Egmont*, 2 vols. in 3, London, HMSO, 1905-9.

HMC *Eighth Report*

The Eighth Report of the Royal Commission on Historical Manuscripts, London, Eyre and Spottiswoode, 1881.

HMC *Frankland-Russell-Astley MSS*

Historical Manuscripts Commission, *Report on the Manuscripts of Mrs. Frankland-Russell-Astley*, London, HMSO, 1900.

HMC *Hope Johnstone MSS*

Historical Manuscripts Commission, *The Manuscripts of J.J. Hope Johnstone, Esq., of Annandale*, London, HMSO, 1897.

HMC *Lords MSS*

Historical Manuscripts Commission, *The Manuscripts of the House of Lords 1678-1714*, 4 vols., London, HMSO, 1887-94; new series, 10 vols., London, HMSO, 1900-53.

HMC *Mar and Kellie MSS*

Historical Manuscripts Commission, *Report on the Manuscripts of the Earl of Mar and Kellie*, London, HMSO, 1904.

HMC *Portland MSS*

Historical Manuscripts Commission, *The Manuscripts of the Duke of Portland*, 10 vols., London, HMSO, 1891-1931.

HMC *Stuart MSS*

Historical Manuscripts Commission, *Calendar of the Stuart Papers Belonging to His Majesty the King*, 7 vols., HMSO, 1902-23.

HMC *Third Report*   *Third Report of the Royal Commission on Historical Manuscripts*, London, Eyre and Spottiswoode, 1872.

Holmes   Geoffrey Holmes, *British Politics in the Age of Queen Anne*, London, Macmillan, 1967.

Horn   *British Diplomatic Representatives 1689-1789*, ed. David B. Horn, Camden Third Series, vol. xlvi, London, Royal Historical Society, 1932.

IU   University of Illinois, Urbana.

Kennett   *A Compleat History of England*, 3 vols., London, B. Aylmer *et al.*, 1706.

L   The British Library, Great Russell Street, London.

Lamberty   Guillaume de Lamberty, *Memoires pour servir à l'histoire du XVIII. siècle*, 14 vols., La Haye and Amsterdam, H. Scheurleer, P. Mortier, *et al.*, 1724-40.

La Mothe le Vayer   François de la Mothe le Vayer, *Oeuvres*, 7 vols., Dresden, Michel Groell, 1756-9.

L'Estrange   Sir Roger L'Estrange, *Fables of Aesop and other Eminent Mythologists*, London, for R. Sare *et al.*, 1692.

Le Vassor   Michel Le Vassor, *Histoire du regne de Louis XIII*, 9 vols. in 18, Amsterdam, Pierre Brunel, 1703-12.

Lillywhite   Bryant Lillywhite, *London Coffee Houses. A Reference Book*, London, Allen and Unwin, 1963.

LJ   *Journals of the House of Lords. 1509-1857*, 89 vols. [London].

Lockhart   George Lockhart, *Memoirs concerning the Affairs of Scotland, from Queen Anne's Accession to the Throne, to the Commencement of the Union of the Two Kingdoms of Scotland and England, in May 1707*, London, 1714.

Lockhart Papers   *The Lockhart Papers*, ed. Anthony Aufrere, 2 vols., London, by Richard and Arthur Taylor for William Anderson, 1817.

LU   London University Library.

Luttrell   Narcissus Luttrell, *A Brief Historical Relation of State Affairs from September 1678 to April 1714*, 6 vols., Oxford, Oxford University Press, 1857.

M½°   *The Medley*, folio half-sheet edition, 1710-11.

M12°   *The Medley*, duodecimo edition, 1712.

Macky   *Memoirs of the Secret Services of John Macky*, ed. Spring Macky, London, 1733.

Macpherson, *Original Papers*   James Macpherson, *Original Papers; Containing the Secret History of Great Britain, from the Restoration, to the Accession of the House of Hannover*, 2nd edn., 2 vols., London, for W. Strahan and T. Cadell, 1776.

Marlborough-Godolphin Corr.   *The Marlborough-Godolphin Correspondence*, ed.

	Henry L. Snyder, 1 vol. in 3, Oxford, Clarendon Press, 1975.
Marlborough-Heinsius Corr.	*The Correspondence 1701-1711 of John Churchill, First Duke of Marlborough, and Anthonie Heinsius, Grand Pensionary of Holland,* ed. B. van 't Hoff, Utrecht, Kemink en Zoon, 1951.
Morgan	William T. Morgan, *A Bibliography of British History (1700-1715),* 5 vols., Bloomington, Indiana University Press, 1934-42.
NQ	*Notes and Queries; for Readers and Writers, Collectors and Librarians,* London, Oxford University Press, 1849- .
NCBEL	*The New Cambridge Bibliography of English Literature,* ed. George Watson, 5 vols., Cambridge, Cambridge University Press, 1969-77.
Nichols, *Literary Anecdotes*	John Nichols, *Literary Anecdotes of the Eighteenth Century,* 9 vols., London, Nichols, Son and Bentley, 1812-15.
Nichols, *Supplement*	*A Supplement to Dr. Swift's Works, Being the Fourteenth in the Collection: Containing Miscellanies in Prose and Verse, by the Dean; Dr. Delany, Dr. Sheridan, Mrs. Johnson, and Others, his Intimate Friends,* London, for J. Nichols and sold by H. Payne and N. Conant, 1779 (Teerink-Scouten 87).
NjP	Princeton University, Princeton, New Jersey.
Noble	Mark Noble, *A Biographical History of England, from the Revolution to the End of George II's Reign,* 3 vols., London, W. Richardson *et al.,* 1806.
NUL	Nottingham University Library.
O	The Bodleian Library, Oxford.
OED	*The Oxford English Dictionary,* edd. James A.H. Murray *et al.,* 15 vols., Oxford, Clarendon Press, 1933- .
Ogg, i-iii	David Ogg, *England in the Reign of Charles II,* 2nd edn., 2 vols., Oxford, Clarendon Press, 1956; *England in the Reigns of James II and William III,* 2nd edn., Oxford, Clarendon Press, 1957.
Oldmixon, *The History*	John Oldmixon, *The History of England, During the Reigns of King William and Queen Mary, Queen Anne, King George I,* London, for Thomas Cox *et al.,* 1735.
Oldmixon, *The History of Addresses*	John Oldmixon, *The History of Addresses,* 2 vols., London, J. Baker, 1709-11.
Oldmixon, *The Life*	John Oldmixon, *The Life and Posthumous Works of Arthur Maynwaring, Esq; Containing several Original Pieces and Translations in Prose and Verse, never before Printed,* London, for A. Bell, 1715.
Oldmixon, *Memoirs*	John Oldmixon, *Memoirs of the Press, Historical and Political, for Thirty Years Past, from 1710 to 1740,* London, for T. Cox, 1742.

Parl. Hist.	William Cobbett, *The Parliamentary History of England from the Earliest Period to the Year 1803*, 36 vols., London, T.C. Hansard *et al.*, 1806-20.
POAS, Yale	*Poems on Affairs of State. Augustan Satirical Verse, 1660-1714*, edd. George deF. Lord *et al.*, 7 vols., New Haven, Yale University Press, 1963-75.
Pope, *Poems*	*The Twickenham Edition of the Poems of Alexander Pope*, edd. John Butt *et al.*, 10 vols. in 11, London and New Haven, Methuen and Yale University Press, 1939-67.
Private Correspondence	*Private Correspondence of Sarah, Duchess of Marlborough, Illustrative of the Court and Times of Queen Anne*, 2nd edn., 2 vols., London, Henry Colburn, 1838.
PRO	Public Record Office, Chancery Lane and Kew, London.
PU	University of Pennsylvania, Philadelphia.
Rushworth	John Rushworth, *Rushworth's Historical Collections of Private Passages of State*, 8 vols., London, for D. Browne, *et al.*, 1721.
Shaw	*The Knights of England*, ed. William A. Shaw, 2 vols., Baltimore, Genealogical Publishing Co., 1971.
Shrewsbury Corr.	*Private and Original Correspondence of Charles Talbot, Duke of Shrewsbury*, ed. William Coxe, London, Longman *et al.*, 1821.
Simms	J.G. Simms, *The Williamite Confiscation in Ireland 1690-1703*, London, Faber and Faber, 1956.
Somers Tracts	*A Collection of Scarce and Valuable Tracts on the Most Interesting and Entertaining Subjects*, 16 vols., London, for F. Coggan, 1748-52.
Speck, *Tory and Whig*	William A. Speck, *Tory and Whig. The Struggle in the Constituencies 1701-1715*, London, Macmillan, 1970.
Speck, *'The Examiner'*	William A. Speck, *'The Examiner* examined: Swift's Tory pamphleteering', *Focus: Swift*, ed. Claude J. Rawson, London, Sphere Books, 1971.
Spence	Joseph Spence, *Observations, Anecdotes, and Characters of Books and Men Collected from Conversation*, ed. James M. Osborn, 1 vol. in 2, Oxford, Clarendon Press, 1966.
SRO	Scottish Record Office, HM General Register House, Edinburgh.
Stanley	Thomas Stanley, *The History of Philosophy*, 3rd edn., London, for W. Battersby *et al.*, 1701.
Statutes of the Realm	*The Statutes of the Realm from Magna Charta to the End of the Reign of Queen Anne*, 11 vols., 1810-28, reprinted London, Dawson's, 1963.

STC

A Short-Title Catalogue of Books Printed in England, Scotland, and Ireland and of English Books printed Abroad, 1475-1640, edd. A.W. Pollard, G.R. Redgrave *et al.*, London, The Bibliographical Society, 1926, 2nd edn., 1976- .

Steele

Tudor and Stuart Proclamations 1485-1714, ed. Robert Steele, 2 vols., Oxford, Clarendon Press, 1910.

Swift, *Corr.*

The Correspondence of Jonathan Swift, ed. Harold Williams, 5 vols., Oxford, Clarendon Press, 1963-5.

Swift, *Discourse*

Jonathan Swift, *A Discourse of the Contests and Dissentions between the Nobles and the Commons in Athens and Rome*, ed. Frank H. Ellis, Oxford, Clarendon Press, 1967.

Swift, *Journal*

Jonathan Swift, *Journal to Stella*, ed. Harold Williams, 1 vol. in 2, Oxford, Clarendon Press, 1948.

Swift, *Poems*

The Poems of Jonathan Swift, ed. Harold Williams, 1 vol. in 3, Oxford, Clarendon Press, 1937.

Swift, *Prose*

The Prose Writings of Jonathan Swift, ed. Herbert Davis, 14 vols., Oxford, Basil Blackwell, 1939-68.

Swift, *Tale*

Jonathan Swift, *A Tale of a Tub to which is added The Battle of the Books and the Mechanical Operation of the Spirit*, edd. A.C. Guthkelch and D. Nichol Smith, 2nd edn., Oxford, Clarendon Press, 1958.

Swift's Library

Harold Williams, *Dean Swift's Library with a Facsimile of the Original Sale Catalogue*, Cambridge, Cambridge University Press, 1932.

Teerink-Scouten

H. Teerink, *A Bibliography of the Writings of Jonathan Swift*, 2nd edn., ed. Arthur H. Scouten, Philadelphia, University of Pennsylvania Press, 1963.

Tilley

Morris P. Tilley, *A Dictionary of the Proverbs in England in the Sixteenth and Seventeenth Centuries*, Ann Arbor, University of Michigan Press, 1950.

Tindal

Paul de Rapin-Thoyras, *The History of England*, trans. and continued by Nicholas Tindal, 3rd edn., 4 vols. in 5, London, for John and Paul Knapton, 1743-7.

Trevelyan

George M. Trevelyan, *England under Queen Anne*, 3 vols., London, Longman, Green, 1930.

The Tryal

The Tryal of Dr. Henry Sacheverell, before the House of Peers, for High Crimes and Misdemeanors; Upon an Impeachment by the Knights, Citizens and Burgesses in Parliament Assembled, London, for Jacob Tonson, 1710.

TxU

University of Texas, Austin.

Vernon

Letters Illustrative of the Reign of William III

from 1696 to 1708 Addressed to the Duke of Shrewsbury by James Vernon, ed. G.P.R. James, 3 vols., London, H. Colburn, 1841.

Wentworth Papers

The Wentworth Papers, 1705-1739. Selected from the Private and Family Correspondence of Thomas Wentworth, Lord Raby, created in 1711 Earl of Strafford, ed. James J. Cartwright, London, Wyman and Sons, 1883.

Wing

Donald G. Wing, *Short-title Catalogue of Books Printed in England, Scotland, Ireland, Wales, and British America*, 2nd edn., New York, Index Committee of the Modern Language Association of America, 1972- .

Wood

Anthony à Wood, *Athenae Oxoniensis. An Exact History of All the Writers and Bishops who have had their Education in the University of Oxford. To which are added the Fasti, or Annals of the said University*, 3rd edn., ed. Philip Bliss, 5 vols., London, F.C. and J. Rivington, 1813-20.

Zedler

Groszes vollständiges Universal-Lexicon aller Wissenschaften und Künste, ed. Johann Heinrich Zedler, 64 vols. and 4 supplements, Halle and Leipzig, Johann-Heinrich Zedler, 1732-54.

INTRODUCTION

1. Harley and Swift

SWIFT'S *Examiners* are thirty-three essays of about 2,000 words
a piece, published every Thursday from 2 November 1710 to 14 June
1711. Each of them was answered by Arthur Mainwaring's *Medley*,
published the following Monday. In the person of a Tory country
gentleman, Swift committed all the resources of his genius to the
cause of party propaganda. Generically, *The Examiner* constitutes
the editorial page (complete with letters to the editor also
written by Swift) of a weekly newspaper of which Abel Roper's
Post-Boy is the news section. Tactically, *The Examiner* constitutes only a part, albeit the showpiece, of Harley's total propaganda programme. Taken together *The Examiner* and *The Medley*
constitute a discourse in the subjunctive mode, 'a set of alternative interpretations'[1] of the main issues of post-Revolution
England: what exactly happened in 1688-9? Was it a constitutional
aberration, or a precedent for future revolutions? What is the
basis for Anne's title to the throne? Where is the *ultima ratio*
in a partly democratic polity? What is to be the position of the
state church in a partly free society?

The best contemporary description of *The Examiner* is that in
John Gay's *The Present State of Wit*, published 3-14 May 1711. At
this time Gay was living on the fringes of Grubstreet, writing
anonymous verse and prose for the periodicals, very much like
young Samuel Johnson a generation later. Gay's enthusiasm for *The
Tatler* and *The Spectator* made him sound like a Whig to Swift, but
Gay himself confessed he 'never cared one Farthing either for
Whig or Tory'. Here is what he wrote:

> *The Examiner* is a Paper, which all Men, who speak without
> Prejudice, allow to be well Writ. Tho' his Subject will admit
> of no great Variety, he is continually placing it on so many
> different Lights, and endeavouring to inculcate the same thing
> by so many Beautiful Changes of Expressions, that Men, who are
> concern'd in no Party, may Read him with Pleasure. His way of
> assuming the Question in Debate, is extremely Artful; and his

[1] Ogg, iii 519.

Letter to *Crassus*, is, I think, a Master-piece.... I presume
I need not tell you that the *Examiner* carries much the more
Sail, as 'tis supposed to be writ by the Direction, and under
the Eye of some Great Persons who sit at the helm of Affairs.
... The reputed Author is Dr. *S---t*, with the assistance,
sometimes, of Dr. *Att-----y*, and Mr. *P---r*.[1]

The story of Swift's recruitment by Harley has been told many
times,[2] but never any better than by Swift himself in his *Journal
to Stella*, his letters to Archbishop King, and his *Memoirs, Relating to that Change which happened in the Queen's Ministry in
the Year 1710*. It was Harley who made the first advance, presumably in 1708-9, when he was out of office and Swift was in London, writing and publishing some powerful high church propaganda:
An Argument against Abolishing Christianity (written *c.*April
1708), *A Letter from a Member of the House of Commons in Ireland
to a Member of the House of Commons in England, concerning the
Sacramental Test* (published *c.*1 January 1709), *A Project for the
Advancement of Religion, and the Reformation of Manners* (published *c.*20 April 1709). The advance must have been made through
an intermediary, presumably Erasmus Lewis. For Swift had not met
Harley when he arrived in London on 7 September 1710 with a commission from the Church of Ireland to solicit a remission of
taxes that the Queen had already granted to the Church of England.
'I will apply to Mr. *Harley*,' Swift wrote to his ecclesiastical
superior, 'who formerly made some Advances towards me, and unless
he be altered, will, I believe, think himself in the Right to use
me well.' Although Harley was chancellor of the exchequer and a
commissioner of the Treasury under the first lord, Swift learned
that 'all Affairs in the Treasury are governed by Mr. *Harley*'.[3]

Furnished with this information, Swift made application to
Harley, again through an intermediary, who was instructed to
represent him as one who, like Harley, had been 'extreamly ill

[1]Swift, *Journal*, p. 269; Gay, *The Present State of Wit, in a Letter to a
Friend in the Country*, London, 1711, pp. 6, 8-10.
[2]Robert W. Babcock, 'Swift's conversion to the Tory party', *Essays and
Studies in English and Comparative Literature*, Ann Arbor, University of Michigan Press, 1932, pp. 133-49; James P. Brawner, 'Swift and the Harley-St. John
ministry', *West Virginia University Bulletin, Philological Studies*, iii (1939),
46-59; Bernard A. Goldgar, *The Curse of Party. Swift's Relations with Addison
and Steele*, Lincoln, University of Nebraska Press, 1961, pp. 50-79; Ehrenpreis,
ii 387-99; Downie, pp. 126-30.
[3]Swift, *Corr.*, i 173.

used by the late Ministry'.[1] At their first meeting on 4 October
1710 Harley set Saturday 7 October as the day on which Swift
should make formal presentation of the petition of the Church of
Ireland. Before this second meeting Swift's friends told him
that Harley 'would do every thing to bring [him] over'.[2]

Harley's behaviour at the meeting exceeded anything that Swift
might have expected, and the comedy of a first minister of Great
Britain shamelessly flattering an Irish parson was duly reported
to Stella: 'All this is odd and comical, if you consider him and
me. He knew my Christian name very well.' It was the next day
that Swift decided he was not so fond of St. James's Coffee-house
as he used to be.[3]

For once Harley was not dilatory. 'In less than a Fortnight he
... treated the Matter four Times with the Queen.' Exactly two
weeks later, on 21 October 1710, he told Swift that 'she had
granted it absolutely', something that Swift's Whig friends had
been unwilling to do for three years. Swift was so surprised that
he did not 'know ... what to make of it, unless to shew the rascals of the other party that they used a man unworthily, who had
deserved better'. It must have been at this meeting of 21 October,
'When the affair of the first fruits was fully dispatched', that
Harley recruited Swift to write *The Examiner*. Swift's assurance
to Stella that when the affair of the first fruits was settled
he would have 'nothing to do here', must have been pure smoke-
screen. But the repetition of this protestation in *Memoirs, Relating to that Change in the Queen's Ministry*, written in October
1714, is curious, for 21 October was the occasion on which Harley
reminded Swift of 'what useful things [he] had written against
the principles of the late discarded faction' in 1708-9 and of
'the want of some good pen, to keep up the spirit raised in the
people, to assert the principles, and justify the proceedings of
the new ministers'.[4]

These words, rather than St. John's *Letter to the Examiner*, published in August 1710, provide the mandate for Swift's *Examiner*.
Harley went on to say 'That this province [*The Examiner*] was in

[1] Swift, *Corr.*, i. 183.
[2] Swift, *Journal*, p. 46. Swift learned later that the new ministers 'were
afraid of none but me; and ... resolved to have me' (ibid., p. 303).
[3] Ibid., pp. 46, 48.
[4] Swift, *Corr.*, i 194; *Journal*, pp. 66-7; *Prose*, viii 123.

the hands of several persons, among whom some [St. John, Atterbury, Freind] were too busy, and others [King, Manley, Prior] too
idle to pursue it; and concluded, that it should be his particular care, to establish me here in England, and represent me to
the Queen as a person they could not be without.' Swift must have
felt that he was walking on air: 'I promised to do my endeavours,
in that way, for some few months; to which he replied, He expected
no more; and that he had other and greater occasions for me.'[1]

The condition that Swift's authorship of *The Examiner* should
remain secret, although consistent with Harley's usual practice,
would have been insisted upon by Swift in any case. The phrases
in the *Journal* of 29 and 30 October, 'I ... am now come home to
write some business ... I ... must go write', refer almost certainly to *The Examiner* of 2 November 1710, the first that Swift
wrote. But the word '*Examiner*' is not even mentioned to Stella
until 1 January 1711 and on 7 March he suggested to her that
Atterbury might be the author. Nothing was said about *The
Examiner* in Swift's letter of 4 November 1710 to Archbishop King
announcing that the Queen had remitted the first fruits and
twentieth parts to the Church of Ireland.[2] And not even some of
the Saturday Club, Harley's kitchen cabinet, knew who wrote *The
Examiner*.[3]

Swift's *Examiner* was Harley's third attempt to provide an effective propaganda vehicle 'to keep up the spirit raised in the
people' by the Sacheverell trial[4] in February-March 1710. Harley
tried first with Abel Roper's *The Moderator*, which in despite of
its title kept up from 22 May to 10 November 1710 a running attack
on the Whig journals, Defoe's *Review*, Ridpath's *The Observator*,
and Steele's *The Tatler*. In the last week of July 1710 Harley
turned Defoe around to write for him again. At about the same time
he recruited an almost unknown writer, Simon Clement (11.20n.),

---

[1]Swift, *Prose*, viii 123.

[2]Since Swift had committed himself to writing *The Examiner* 'for some few
months', his telling his ecclesiastical superior two days after he started,
'I shall obey your Grace's Directions whether my Stay here be further necessary' (*Corr.*, i 190), seems to be an act of sheer bravado.

[3]In February 1711 Lord Rivers, Harley's ambassador to Hanover and a privy
councillor, cursed *The Examiner* to Swift's face 'for speaking civilly of the
duke of Marlborough' (Swift, *Journal*, p. 195). Swift told Archbishop King
only that 'the Ministry have desired me to continue here some Time longer,
for certain Reasons' (Swift, *Corr.*, i 202).

[4]Swift, *Prose*, viii 84.

to present the platform of the government that Harley was slowly
putting together in the spring and summer of 1710. But *The
Moderator* was not a success.[1]

In August 1710, therefore, Harley recruited Dr William King to
undertake a new periodical, *The Examiner*, with the assistance of
Francis Atterbury, Dean of Carlisle, Dr John Freind, Matthew
Prior, Delariviere Manley, and Henry St. John.[2] Despite the
distinction of the writers, Harley could not have been satisfied
with the result. No. 8, of 21 September 1710, for example, under-
mines Harley's effort to form a government of 'moderate Men on
both Sides' in this outrageous fashion: 'A Man of no Party ...
is of *a Party*; but 'tis *such a Party*, as he is *asham'd to own.*'
No. 13, of 26 October, was 'an avowed and violent defence of the
doctrine of hereditary right, in its most absurd extent'.[3]

So it is easy to understand why Harley would have done anything
to 'bring [Swift] over'. In the most worldly terms, Harley bought
Swift's services at the cost of £1,000 a year from the privy
purse. The beneficiary of Anne's generosity was not Swift, of
course. The Queen refused even to give an audience to the man
upon whose petition she remitted £1,000 a year in taxes to the
Church of Ireland and who defended so valiantly the 'motley
comprehensive administration' that she had set her heart on
forming. In return Swift received neither the 'Lean Bishoprick or
... fat Deanery' in England that Harley had promised him nor even
a word of appreciation from the Irish hierarchy for the success
of his mission. 'And this was the first time I began to conceive
some imperfect Idea of Courts and Ministers', Gulliver observed.[4]

But the nice part of the story is the affectionate relationship
that developed between the Lord Treasurer and the vicar of

---

[1]Since Harley kept his propagandists isolated from each other, Roper went
on attacking the *Review* months after Defoe had rejoined Harley, and Defoe in
turn attacked *The Moderator* (*A Supplement to the Faults on Both Sides*, London,
for J. Baker, 1710, pp. 51-2).

[2]Nichols, *Supplement*, pp. 62-3. Nichols does not include Mrs Manley in this
list and attributes *The Examiner*, No. 7, to Dr King. It has been pointed out,
however, that *The Examiner*, No. 49, known to have been written by Mrs Manley
(Swift, *Journal*, p. 402), is a sequel to *The Examiner*, No. 7, and it 'does
seem probable' that Mrs Manley wrote *The Examiner*, No. 7, as well (Gwendolyn
B. Needham, *HLQ*, xii (1948-9), 271-2).

[3]Swift, *Prose*, viii 86; *E1814*, i 128.

[4]Swift, *Corr.*, i 194; *Prose*, viii 146, 124; *Corr.*, i 219; *Prose*, xi 38. It
was finally Ormond who presented Swift with the deanery of St. Patrick's
(*Journal*, p. 567).

Laracor. It began in mutual interest: Harley needed Swift to write *The Examiner*; Swift needed Harley to realize his modest ambition 'to live in England ... with a competence to support [himself] with honour'. But it soon grew into mutual respect and affection. Five months after their first meeting, when Harley lay stabbed and in doubt of his life, Swift was almost distracted. 'I now think of all his kindness to me,' he told Stella. Swift never came to Harley 'without a Whig in [his] sleeve' and only once did Harley refuse to grant the favour. He 'always treated me with the Tenderness of a Parent,' Swift said, which must have seemed to Archbishop King a strange statement for a man of forty-three to make about a man of forty-nine. Never presuming to advise Harley in Harley's trade of politics, Swift was surprised to be outdone by Harley 'in [his] own trade as a scholar'. And twenty-three years after he had seen Harley for the last time, Swift told Harley's son, 'I loved ... your father better than any other Man in the world.'

Harley's affection for Swift manifested itself partly in teasing and allowing himself to be teased: 'I ... rallied him, &c. which he took very well ... he called me Dr. Thomas Swift, which he always does when he has a mind to teaze me ... Lord treasurer calls me now Dr. Martin.'[1]

The reasons why an amiable relationship developed between Harley and Swift are not far to seek. At the Revolution Harley rode out with his father at the head of a troop of horse raised for William of Orange. Swift celebrated William's victory at the Boyne in stiff, pindaric verses. Although publicly committed to the Revolution Settlement, both of them were sure that no office in the state, not even that of village hog reeve, should be entrusted to a non-conformist. 'Where *Sects* are tolerated in a State', Swift said, 'it is fit they should enjoy a full Liberty of Conscience, and every other Privilege of free-born Subjects, *to* which no Power is annexed'. He must have been delighted,

---

[1]Swift, *Corr.*, i 227; *Journal*, pp. 212-13; *Prose*, ix 29; *Corr.*, i 215; *Prose*, ix 28; *Corr.*, v 46; *Journal*, pp. 97, 280, 381. Mr (not Dr) Thomas Swift, Swift's 'little Parson-Cousin' (Swift, *Corr.*, i 166), allowed himself to be thought a co-author of *A Tale of a Tub*. Harley's 'Dr. Martin' seems much more likely to be the moderate Martin of *A Tale of a Tub*, of which the fourth edition had just been published (p. xli, n. 4 below), than the 'sort of swallow' that Swift supposed.

therefore, to learn 'That it was [Harley's] opinion and desire,
that no person should have the smallest employment, either civil
or military, whose principles were not firm for the church and
monarchy'.[1]

Although they called themselves Whigs or Old Whigs, neither
Harley nor Swift was totally committed to the principle of party.
'In K. Wms time [Harley] said Partys in a State are Knavery [and]
in the Church they are hypocrisie.'[2] In the next reign his ambition was to control both parties 'without Subduing either', or
to 'Graft the Whiggs on the Bulk of the Church Party', as he
advised the Queen in May 1710.[3] If Harley could have read *The
Sentiments of a Church-of-England Man, with Respect to Religion
and Government* before it was published in February 1711, he would
have known before he recruited Swift to write *The Examiner* how
similar were their ideas on party. It was not until 1703 that
Swift troubled himself to learn the differences between Whig and
Tory, 'having formerly employed [himself] in other, and ... much
better speculations'. Somewhat belatedly, therefore, Swift discovered that he was a political 'Monster', 'a State Whig, a Church
Tory', like his friend, Archbishop King.[4] In the end Swift came to
see that 'All the struggle [between Whig and Tory] is about Places
... Principles and the Merits of a Cause signify nothing' and to
define a Whig as 'one *who Believed in the late Ministry*' (455.105).
He concluded, just as Harley did, that 'a Prince ought not ... to
be under the Guidance ... of either [party]'.[5]

A third point of agreement was the commitment to the cause of
peace, reached independently long before they met. And finally,
what drew them together in October 1710 was a common sense of
injured merit. Both of them had been badly used by Godolphin and
the Whig Junto. The Greg espionage case had given the Junto an
opportunity to destroy Harley's political career that they

---

[1]Swift, *Prose*, ii 12; viii 125.   [2]NUL MS Pw2 Hy 6620.
[3]BL MSS Portland Loan 29/165 Misc. 97, p. 21; 29/10/19, not foliated; cf.
Defoe, *Letters*, p. 67.
[4]Swift, *Prose*, viii 120; *The Character and Principles of the Present Set
of Whigs*, London, for John Morphew, 1711, p. 31; BL Add. MS 4815, quoted in
Sir Charles Simeon King, Bt., *A Great Archbishop of Dublin: William King,
D.D., 1650-1729*, Longmans, Green, New York, 1908, p. 275. Swift would not
have been thought to be writing *The Medley* had he not been known to be a Whig
(Swift, *Journal*, p. 289).
[5]Swift, *Prose*, ii 24.

eagerly seized. Their success was only prevented by the 'coarse-clad honesty' of a government clerk who refused to save himself from the gallows at the price of perjury (39.127n). Swift's experience was less dramatic. Godolphin simply made it clear to him in June 1708 that the Junto's price for remitting the first fruits and twentieth parts to the Church of Ireland, and indeed of Swift's own advancement in the Church, was his 'Acknowledgment' of (i.e. collaboration in) repeal of the Irish Test Clause.[1]

Much more difficult than the question of what drew them together, is the question of Swift's position in the Harley ministry. A few fictions, however, can be easily disposed of. The most absurd of the fictions, fabricated by Bolingbroke, was that Swift was simply a hired writer: 'the lie of the day ... was coined and delivered out to him, to write Examiners and other political papers upon'.[2] This devastatingly cruel remark by a man Swift loved is totally incompatible with everything that is known about Swift's independence: 'I am of a Temper to think no Man great enough to set me on Work.' It also implies a refinement of organization of which Harley was simply incapable. Weeks went by without Swift even seeing Harley.[3] But the contradictory fiction, apparently originated by John Hawkesworth, is almost equally absurd: 'He dined every *Saturday* at Mr. *Harley*'s, with the lord keeper [Harcourt], Mr. Secretary *St. John*, and lord *Rivers*. ... His intimacy with them was so remarkable that he was thought not only to defend, but in some degree to direct their measures.'[4] Swift could not help it if these great men used him 'like one who was their betters', partly because of his black coat and partly because of his intellectual superiority, but he could not have directed their measures without being Harley.

The great distance between Swift and the hired writers—Clement, Defoe, Dyer,[5] Manley, Roper—can be measured by the fact that

---

[1]Swift, *Prose*, ii 176; *Marlborough-Godolphin Corr.*, p. 965; Swift, *Corr.*, i 85.

[2]Philip Dormer Stanhope, Earl of Chesterfield, *Miscellaneous Works*, 2 vols., London, for Edward and Charles Dilly, 1778, ii 3. Bolingbroke was parroting *The Medley* (237.145-6).

[3]Swift, *Prose*, iii 194; *Journal*, p. 247.

[4]*The Works of Jonathan Swift*, edd. John Hawkesworth *et al.*, 14 vols., London, for C. Bathurst *et al.*, 1755-79, i 10-11.

[5]It is not certain that the Jacobite John Dyer, who produced a widely distributed manuscript newsletter, belongs in this list, but *The Examiner* was advertised in the issue of 30 September 1710 (BL MS 29/321).

Swift, at his own insistence, was *not* paid and by the fact that
he was invited to join the Saturday Club ten days after Harley
had made the generous mistake of offering to pay him. In the
beginning the Saturday Club 'used to discourse, and settle matters of great importance'. But these matters could not have included the content of next Thursday's *Examiner*, for Rivers did
not know that Swift wrote *The Examiner*. Swift himself warned that
'many thought [his attendance at these meetings] to be of greater
consequence than they really were' and a recent authority has
called the legend that Swift wielded power in the Harley ministry
'nonsense'.[1]

Despite his attendance at the meetings of the Saturday Club at
Harley's house in York Buildings, Swift was not an insider. He
knew nothing of the secret peace negotiations with France that
Harley and Shrewsbury had opened in August 1710. The secretary
of state, St. John, only learned of them in April 1711 when Harley was disabled by Guiscard's attack.[2] Swift finally learned of
them in August 1711 'by the little words I hear thrown out by the
ministry'. He knew nothing of whatever talk there may have been
about a second Stuart restoration and refused to believe that
there may have been a plot: 'so I did little Imagine my self', he
said sarcastically, 'to be perpetually in the Company of Tray-
tors'. He did not even know Harley's policy about parliamentary
investigation into alleged mismanagement of the Treasury, for
which the new Tory Members were clamouring in December 1710. 'The
Ministers never tell any Thing,' he complained to Archbishop King.
Even after he asked them, he was 'not altogether satisfied' what
the policy was.[3]

One reason why Swift was not Harley's confidant was that Harley
was incapable of confiding in anyone outside his immediate family.
Swift complained as bitterly as Defoe had done of Harley's lack
of communicativeness. In retrospect he had to number Harley's
'Obstinate Love of Secrecy' among his defects. 'Every man must
have a Light sufficient for the Length of the Way he is appointed
to go,' Swift said. And then he added, with a change of metaphor,

---

[1]Swift, *Journal*, pp. 182, 193; *Prose*, viii 124; cf. *Journal*, p. 241; Speck,
'*The Examiner*', p. 153.
[2]G.M. Trevelyan, *EHR*, xlix (1934), 100-5.
[3]Swift, *Journal*, p. 348; *Prose*, viii 134; *Corr.*, i 201; cf. *Journal*, p. 628.

'Although the main Spring in a Watch [Harley] be out of Sight,
there is an intermediate Communication between it and the smallest Wheel [Swift], or else no true Motion could be performed.'
'How can I help it,' he asked, 'if the Courtiers give me a watch
that will not go right?'[1]

Orrery's slur that Swift 'was employed, not trusted' has already been disposed of by Deane Swift:

> to say *that* DR. SWIFT was employed but not trusted by the earl
> of OXFORD ... is really nothing more than to say that the lord
> treasurer would not communicate to DR. SWIFT some two or three
> of his own secret resolutions

(including, presumably, those mentioned above).[2]

So Swift enjoyed Harley's 'agreeable Conversation in a private
Capacity', but not his 'secret resolutions'. He himself had no
delusions of power and it worried him when his friends suffered
such delusions: 'all that passes *inter nos*, | Might be proclaim'd
at *Charing-Cross*', he warned them. He expressed his opinion when
it was sought, but in the end he came to know that 'people at
[his] level must be content to have their opinion asked, and to
see it not followed'. Harley would have profited if he had followed it more frequently.[3]

Despite his uncommunicativeness, Harley was able somehow to
convey to Swift what he wanted in *The Examiner*. Besides the broad
mandate 'to assert the principles, and justify the proceedings of
the new ministers', Harley managed in the beginning to offer Swift
more particular direction. In his second *Examiner*, No. 15 of 9
November 1710, Swift was prevailed upon 'through *the Importunity
of Friends*, to interrupt the Scheme I had begun in my last Paper'
(20.1-2). Apparently, for reasons that Harley might not have been
able to explain, he suddenly wanted a full-scale attack on Wharton, whom he had removed as lord-lieutenant of Ireland on 26
October:

> it is thought expedient, for some Reasons, that the World
> should be informed of his Excellency's Merit as soon as pos-
> sible.[4]

---

[1]Swift, *Prose*, vii 74; viii 85-6; Nichols, *Literary Anecdotes*, i 400.

[2]John Boyle, Earl of Cork and Orrery, *Remarks on the Life and Writings of
Dr. Jonathan Swift*, London, for A. Millar, 1752, p. 47; Deane Swift, *An Essay
upon the Life, Writings, and Character of Dr. Jonathan Swift*, 2nd edn., London, for Charles Bathurst, 1755, p. 161.

[3]Swift, *Prose*, vii 75; viii 107; *Journal*, p. 241; *Poems*, i 201; *Corr.*,
ii 23.   [4]Swift, *Prose*, iii 184.

Swift obliged with a blistering attack in *The Examiner* of 30
November and followed it up the first week of December with *A
Short Character of His Ex. T. E. of W. L. L. I------* worked up
from facts supplied by Harley's informants.[1]

While Swift acknowledged that *The Examiner* was written with the
'encouragement and direction' of 'the great men', it must not be
supposed that either Harley or St. John (after Swift met him in
November 1710) provided week-by-week direction of *The Examiner*.
When 'the main Spring' was out of sight for weeks, the little
wheel communicated through intermediaries. It is inconceivable
that Swift could spend the evening of 27 March 1711 with Prior
and Dr Freind, talk to Erasmus Lewis about 'business ... relating
to the publick and myself' on 9 April, and have dinner with Prior
and Atterbury on 17 May, without acquiring high-level intelligence, whether or not his informants knew that he was writing *The
Examiner*.[2] As the annotation of the essays discovers, there is
very little inside information in *The Examiner*. Most of the information in *The Examiner* comes from overt sources, mainly from
the ephemeral literature of the period: pamphlets and periodicals.
Swift complains that the demand of weekly publication often forced
him to make use of 'any Materials' he could find (66.8) and it is
very exciting to see a paragraph in William Benson, *A Letter to
Sir J--- B----* (1711), short-circuiting into *The Examiner*, No. 34
of 22 March 1711 (276.126-7n.).

Harley was lucky to have found in Swift someone whose understanding of Harley's propaganda needs was almost clairvoyant. In January 1711, while summarizing the accomplishments of the first
session of Anne's fourth Parliament, Swift does not even mention
the passage through the Commons of the Place Bill (later defeated
in the Lords) because both Harley and St. John 'spoke heartily
against it'.[3] In August 1711, when the government was embarrassed
by the accidental disclosure of Prior's secret diplomatic mission
to Versailles, it was Swift who 'thought of a project to bite the
town' and turn the embarrassment into a joke. A generation later
it seemed that Harley and *The Examiner* were doubles: 'it is impossible to separate them, when one reads the *Examiner*.... The Minister's Designs or Actions were all along forc[efully] told,

[1]Swift, *Journal*, p. 115.   [2]Ibid., pp. 146, 225, 246, 271; *Prose*, viii 86.
[3]SRO GD 220/5/808/12.

explained, or disguised (as might best suit the Purpose) by the
Examiner; and we are sure to expound right, when we expound the
Minister by the *Examiner*, or the *Examiner* by the Minister.'[1]

Swift, however, did not become Harley's *alter ego* by compromis-
ing his own principles. Going to work for Harley required Swift
to change none of his ideas, either in church or state.[2] Even
after he had committed himself to Harley, Swift retained a stubborn independence. Perhaps the best example of this is the *Greenshields* v. *Regina* case that agitated the government early in 1711.
The facts about James Greenshields and his appeal to the House of
Lords from a conviction by the Lords of Session in Edinburgh for
conducting religious services according to the Book of Common
Prayer, are set forth below (262.183n., 277.147n.). Swift, who confessed that he was 'altogether uninform'd in the Particulars of
this Case' (277.148), presumably did not know that the Queen had
participated in every step of the prosecution of Greenshields and
then offered him a benefice in Ireland if he would drop his appeal.[3] Nor may Swift have known that Harley had done everything
in his power to quash Greenshield's appeal, arguing that 'the
Church party in England woud take it ill if [Greenshields] was
not protected, and the Scots Presbyterians wou'd highly resent
any favour he mett with'. But the sentence of the Lords of Session was reversed and the ministry 'intirely baffled'. Whether or
not he knew of Harley's embarrassment, Swift reacted predictably
to the apparent persecution of a fellow churchman and represented
Greenshields in *The Examiner* as a victim. 'If another man's reason fully convinceth me', Swift said, 'it becomes my own reason.'[4]

Since Addison and Steele kept *The Spectator* going for nearly
four years and Defoe wrote the *Review* for more than nine, the
question naturally arises, Why did Swift abandon *The Examiner*
after only eight months? Since Swift himself is ambiguous on this
point, it is not surprising that later writers have contradicted
each other.

[1] Swift, *Journal*, pp. 348-9; *The Grand Accuser the Greatest of all Criminals*,
Part I, London, for J. Roberts, 1735, p. 41.
[2] W.A. Speck, *The World of Jonathan Swift. Essays for the Tercentenary*, ed.
Brian Vickers, Oxford, Basil Blackwell, 1968, p. 83; Downie, p. 128.
[3] Robert Wodrow, *Analecta: or, Materials for a History of Remarkable Provi-
dences*, Edinburgh, for The Maitland Club, 1842-3, i 211-12, 322; Defoe,
Review, 8 October 1709.
[4] *Lockhart Papers*, i 347-8; Swift, *Prose*, i 261.

Mainwaring, of course, took full credit when Delariviere Manley laid down *The Examiner* only six weeks after taking it over from Swift. And Atterbury, who should have known better, thought that Mainwaring's advertisement in *The Medleys* of 2-23 July 1711 exposing Swift's mistake about the Act of Indemnity (475.132-6n.) 'had quite sunk the *Examiner*'.[1] Writing at the time, Swift seems to imply that he did not willingly lay down *The Examiner*: 'in this day's *Examiner* [7 June 1711] the author talks doubtfully, as if he would write no more, so that if they go on they may probably be by some other hand, which in my opinion is a thousand pities; but who can help it?' On the strength of this, one writer has concluded that Swift was forced to lay down *The Examiner*.[2]

But five months later Swift says, 'The author [of *The Examiner*], whoever he was, laid it down on purpose to confound guessers.' Gay had identified Swift as the Examiner in May 1711. Mainwaring finally identified the Examiner as 'the ingenious Divine who writ *the Tale of a Tub*' (486.129-30) only after Swift had laid it down. In October 1714 Swift confirmed that he laid down *The Examiner* on purpose: 'my stile being soon discovered, and having contracted a great number of enemies, I let it fall into other hands'. So another writer's guess that Swift laid down *The Examiner* in order to undertake 'a more important task' is almost certainly correct.[3]

The 'more important task' was writing *The Conduct of the Allies*, the chief weapon in Harley's peace offensive of 1711-12 and one of the most successful works of propaganda in English. The need for *The Conduct of the Allies* was broached to Swift on 29 April 1711. On 17 May the Examiner wondered whether he would 'have any Appetite to continue this Work much longer' (432.143-4). In August 1711 Swift told Stella that 'There is now but one business the ministry wants me for.' He continued to refer to the planning and writing of *The Conduct of the Allies*, in London and Windsor, as 'a great deal of matters', 'some business', 'something I am doing', and 'my large pamphlet', until it was published in November 1711.[4]

[1]BL MS Add. 61461, f. 137ᵛ.
[2]Swift, *Journal*, pp. 291-2; Downie, p. 137.
[3]Swift, *Journal*, p. 402; *Prose*, viii 124; Ricardo Quintana, *The Mind and Art of Jonathan Swift*, London, Oxford University Press, 1936, p. 185.
[4]Swift, *Journal*, pp. 257, 273, 279, 299, 343, 356, 361, 421, 422.

2. Swift's *Examiner*

All of Swift's most successful works are presented as if written
by a 'personated' narrator, as it was called at the time: the
Grubaean Sage of *A Tale of a Tub*, the gentleman-astrologer Isaac
Bickerstaff Esq., the 'modern' MP of *An Argument against abolish-
ing Christianity*, Lemuel Gulliver, the mad sociologist of *A
Modest Proposal*.[1] For *The Examiner* Swift created the character of
a narrator in the first few numbers and then, unaccountably, threw
him away. The character that Swift created is clearly delineated:
he is a literate country gentleman with a steward named Will
Bigamy, a liveried footman named Ned, and a coachman named John.
He is a justice of the peace with two clerks named Charles and
Harry (66.16-67.29) and 'a true Lover of the Church' (135.185).
Since he is not a Member of Parliament, like his predecessor in
some of the pre-Swift *Examiners*, he does not need to sink his
identity into a party and 'say without further examining, *I am
of the side with* Clodius'.[2] The first thing that the 'squire
tells us about himself is that 'It is a Practice I have generally
follow'd, to converse in equal Freedom with the deserving Men of
both Parties' (1.1-2). In politics, therefore, as an impartial
examiner, responsible to no one but himself, he could seek 'the
medium between [the] Extreams' (245.159-60) of Country Tory and
Junto Whig. And he finds the golden mean, of course, in the 'motley comprehensive administration' that Harley had put together in
1710.[3] 'Why should not the present Ministry', he asks, 'find a
Pen to praise them as well as the last?' (214.102-3). So a 'bashful and unexperience'd ... Writer' (82.21) attaches himself to
the Ministry as an anonymous and unpaid volunteer, the Examiner.

Having drawn the character with sufficient definition for it
to gain public notice—Mainwaring calls him 'the "Squire" of his
Parish' (155.35-6)—it is strange that Swift should so soon abandon it.[4] Although he continues upon occasion to revert to country

---

[1] The pioneering study of this much-mooted topic is William B. Ewald, Jr.,
The Masks of Jonathan Swift, Oxford, Blackwell, 1954.

[2] Swift, *Discourse*, p. 122. Swift characterized himself as 'a Strict Examiner'
in a letter of January 1708 (*Corr.*, i 64).

[3] Swift, *Prose*, viii 124.

[4] Irvin Ehrenpreis supplies an answer to this question (*Acts of Implication*,
The Beckman Lectures (Berkeley: University of California Press, 1980), pp.
64-5).

gentleman (199.193, 443.125-6), Swift drops the persona after
December 1710 and projects the Examiner as a disembodied voice.
This anomaly was also noted at the time: 'the *Examiner* ... never
could be prevailed upon to write a Week together in the same
Character, in the same Dress, nor in the same Lodgings'.[1] Perhaps
what happened was that as Swift became more and more captured by
his own rhetoric, the intervenient country gentleman faded out of
his mind until the anonymous Examiner was left to confront his
subject directly. 'The first Proselyte [a man] makes is Himself',
Swift knew, 'and when that is once compass'd, the Difficulty is
not so great in bringing over others', which simply restates a
rule of classical rhetoric (412.125-32). This in turn may explain
why, although 'Swift seldom wrote better than in *The Examiner*',
as a modern critic has said, *The Examiner* is not in a class with
Swift's most successful work.[2]

The voice that Swift projects in *The Examiner* is its most
remarkable literary feature, so remarkable, in fact, that his
opponents describe it quite literally in their attempts to be
ironical. Mainwaring's sneer, that the Examiner 'has wonderfully
the Air and Resemblance of a *Roman* hero in his Triumph' (471.22-
3), can only be read today as literally and exactly true. Buoyed
up by his success in negotiating remission of the first fruits
for the Church of Ireland, by his satisfaction in striking back
at the 'rascals' who had cast him away, by Harley's promise to
keep him in England, and above all by Harley's affection, Swift
is indeed triumphal in *The Examiner*.

Harley's ministry was driven to the right by the results of the
general election in October 1710, by St. John's design, and by
the demands of the October Club. Swift may have felt from the
beginning, as he wrote in May 1714, that Harley's 'moderating
Scheam ... to reconcile both Parties' was 'visionary and impossible'. But in any case, if the Examiner was to continue 'to
assert the principles and justify the proceedings of the new
ministers', he would have to move to the right as well. So the
Examiner became a partisan *malgré lui*.[3]

---

[1][Richard Steele,] *Two Letters concerning the Author of the Examiner*, London, A. Baldwin, 1713), p. 13.
[2]Swift, *Prose*, i 108; Ehrenpreis, ii 409.
[3]Swift, *Prose*, viii 83, 84. Although *The Examiner* attacks some Whigs whom
Swift defended in *A Discourse of the Contests and Dissentions* (1701) and many

Partisanship was a role that brought out all of Swift's natural combativeness and all of his rhetorical resources. The man who thought himself 'to be one appointed by providence for defending a post assigned me, and for gaining over as many enemies as I can', would have felt that any other response was cowardly. So the cool impartiality of the early papers quickly gave way to 'intolerable Bluntness and ill Manners' (415.24). The enemy was quickly identified—the duumvirs, Marlborough and Godolphin, the Whig Junto, the moneyed Men, the 'Papists and Fanaticks'—and then subjected to 'a regular Attack' (379.151).[1] One of Swift's strategies, Mainwaring says, was 'to put the worst Construction upon every thing that happen'd during the late Ministry'. Mainwaring is also the best witness to the contemporary reader's response to this strategy:

> he sometimes gives a kind of weight to what he says, so as to make Impressions of Terrour upon honest Minds.

Indeed it is the threatening, moral tone of Swift's *Examiner* that establishes it as satire, and not as comedy, which is social and conciliatory. At its maximum effectiveness *The Examiner* achieves something like the literary equivalent of terrorism, with words that in their context are unexpected, menacing, and subversive:

> We acted all along as if we believ'd nothing of a God or His Providence; and therefore it was consistent to offer up our Edifices [innuendo: Blenheim Palace and Marlborough House] only to *Those*, whom we look'd upon as *Givers of all Victory*, in his stead (441.52-5).

Swift called these 'hard Words' and George Orwell reminds us that 'Violence and scurrility are part of the pamphlet tradition.'[2]

Swift's phrase for the tone of his papers is 'innocent Boldness' (427.8-9). His opponents agreed with the 'Boldness' but found other modifiers than 'innocent'. The one most frequently recurring, 'authoritative', was also one of the first. An anony-

---

Whig practices of 1690-1710, it attacks only one Whig principle. In December 1703 Swift was 'mightily urged by some great people', presumably Somers and Halifax, to write against the Tories' second bill to prevent occasional conformity. But what he wrote 'came too late by a day' to publish (Swift, *Corr.*, i 39, 44) and by 1711 he had discovered that 'there [was] no Law (beside that of God Almighty) against *Occasional Conformity*' (361.160-1). With this exception, Swift did not 'change any Principles relating to Government, either in Church or State', when he undertook *The Examiner* (Swift, *Prose*, vi 127).

[1] Ibid., ix 262; cf. vii 106.
[2] [Mainwaring,] *Reflections upon the Examiner's Scandalous Peace*, London, for A. Baldwin, 1711, p. 3; *British Pamphleteers*, edd. George Orwell *et al.*, 2 vols., London, A. Wingate, 1948-51, i 8.

mous writer in the first week of December 1710 concluded that
The Examiner was 'publish'd by Authority'[1] and Mainwaring picked
up the term immediately (120.42-3, 351.69, 394.68, 472.47). It
was observed in November 1710 that *The Examiner* was 'a courtly
Paper' and Mainwaring picked up this phrase as well (483.33).
'One would take the Author to be some very great Man,' George
Ridpath sneered. Two weeks later he added, 'He's an Author of
such a Gigantick Size ... that he is able to crush such Pigmies
as you and I with his little finger.'[2] Once again, Mainwaring
carried on the joke: 'I am aw'd, and kept at a distance by the
importance of his Person' (43.6-7). 'They do me too much honour,'
Swift replied. Instead of 'innocence' the Examiner's readers
heard 'Insolence'. But Swift knew what he was doing: 'Mr. Presto,
you are so impudent,' he boasted to Stella. And he did it so well
that in less than a year Harley's ministry became '*the* Examiner'*s*
M------y' and the Tory party became 'the *Examiner*'s Party'.[3]

Once he had committed himself, Swift did not hold back. Addison's joke about the pre-Swift *Examiner*, 'it wou'd have been more
properly entitled the *Executioner*', applies *a fortiori* to Swift's
Examiner.[4] Oldmixon called Thursday the Examiner's '*Periodical*
Day of Slandering' and on those Thursdays when Swift was particularly slanderous he would note that 'the *Examiner* is *Devilish
severe to day*'.[5] On the other hand, Swift was not incapable of
a fast shift from the boldest insolence to a strain of totally
disarming innocence:

> I have been curious enough to look into all the Papers I could
> meet with that are writ against the *Examiner* ... for [no] other
> End, but that of finding an Opportunity to own and rectify my
> Mistakes (319.164-8).

Indeed, the pleasure of reading Swift's *Examiner* derives in large
part from the serene self-confidence with which Swift manipulates
the tone of the essays. This self-confidence is not always reflected in the *Journal to Stella* for the same weeks. But in *The
Examiner* Swift transcends his own quotidian doubts, annoyances,

---

[1] *The Speech of the Lord Haversham's Ghost*, London, 1710, p. 4.
[2] *The Observator*, 1-4, 4-8, 18-22 November 1710.
[3] Swift, *Prose*, iii 187; *Journal*, p. 283; [Mainwaring,] *Reflections upon the Examiner's Scandalous Peace*, 1711, p. 6, quoted in [Abel Boyer,] *An Account of the State and Progress of the Present Negotiation of Peace*, London, 1711, p. 28; *The Observator*, 28 July-1 August 1711.
[4] *The Whig-Examiner*, 14 September 1710.
[5] [Oldmixon,] *A Letter to the Seven Lords of the Committee, Appointed to Examine Gregg*, London, for J. Baker, 1711, p. 11; (280.60).

frustrations, and triumphantly sweeps the reader along with him.
What pleased Swift in the essays was 'the Correctness of the
Style, and a superior Spirit' (414.2).

John Oldisworth, who revived *The Examiner* in December 1711 and
cranked out 216 numbers, called his work 'Essays on Government'.[1]
Mainwaring rallied Swift for referring once to his *'Discourses'*
(105.46), but Swift commonly called the *Examiners* 'Papers' (163.
2, 22; 332.117; 458.177, etc.). There is, however, more structure
in Swift's *Examiners* than might be expected in 'Papers'. In *The
Examiner* of 29 March 1711, for example, the first paragraph takes
up 'Abuses ... the Qu--- ... Peace ... Debts ... Mony' (328.12-
34). A similar series, 'Abuses ... Elections ... Supplies ...
Debts ... Queen' (332.119-22), closes the essay. A later *Examiner*
opens with Whiggish 'Overt-Acts' of derogation in the first paragraph and moves on to Whiggish derogatory 'Words' in the second
(400.11-12, 401.32). Whether deliberate or accidental, the
presence of this kind of subliminal structure helps explain the
impression of flexibility and strength that is gained from reading Swift's *Examiners*.

The style of *The Examiner*, the choice and arrangement of the
words, differs markedly from the style of the *Journal to Stella*
written exactly at the same time. The *Journal* is colloquial,
homely, intimate, private. *The Examiner*, by contrast, is rhetorical, authoritative, abusive, public. It is remarkable how easily
Swift's polemical style falls into allegory, of which there is
none, of course, in the *Journal*. Not only are there the big
sculptured figures of the goddess Political Lying, with her emblem, the mirror (21.60), and false Merit (274.73), and Faction
(285.50), which fill some of the tamest pages in *The Examiner*,
but there are also the little part-time quasi-allegories like
this one: *'Faction*, in order to support it self, is generally
forc'd to make Use of such abominable Instruments ... &c., &c.'
(440.39-441.41). It can only be concluded that abstractions had
a greater reality for Swift than they did for Blake, for example.

---

[1]*The Examiner*, 6-9 February 1713.

3. *The Examiner* as propaganda

'What will not a Man do in a Democracy to gain the People's Affection?'[1] The emphasis in Pierre Bayle's question must fall on
the word 'Democracy'. Oliver Cromwell could afford to trust God
to reconcile his enemies, but Robert Harley evidently thought he
could not. It was Sir Edward Seymour who for a mere £5 a day to
put in his pocket, had sold the rights to publish the Votes of
the House of Commons. This absolutely unprecedented 'appeal to
the Collective Body of the People' was found to be 'of very
dangerous Consequence to the Constitution'.[2]

One consequence was the creation of that monster, public opinion. The first systematic attempt to exploit the monster was that
of Shaftesbury and the Green Ribbon Club. *Swift* vs. *Mainwaring*
has a precedent in Sir Roger L'Estrange's *Observator* vs. Henry
Care's *Weekly Packet of Advice from Rome* (1678-83). Ever since
the monster was begot by Seymour's greed and nourished by Shaftesbury's ambition, it has required a steady diet of propaganda. William Wotton thought that 'Tindal, Collins, De Foe, Tutchin, and
that gang have done the Whigs more harm than good, infinitely'.[3]
But this is not what Swift believed: 'Give me pen, ink, and
paper', he said, 'and ensure me against prosecution, and I will
engage to write down any ministry whatever.'[4] Nor was it what
Mainwaring believed. He did not find it ridiculous when, early in
the Harley regime, he heard two guests at dinner [Addison and
Steele?] say they were 'sure it is possible to scribble these men
down'.[5]

Swift's belief in the power of propaganda was tempered, of
course, by the Christian ethos. Swift saw that *The Examiner* was
necessary because Harley's authority depended not wholly on facts
or what he actually did, but also on opinion, or what he was

---

[1]Bayle, *Dictionary*, ii 884.

[2]*A Dialogue between a Member of Parliament, a Divine, a Lawyer, a Freeholder,
a Shopkeeper, and a Country Farmer*, no place of publication, 1703, pp. 8, 5;
cf. Defoe, *Some Remarks on the First Chapter in Dr. Davenant's Essays*, London, A. Baldwin, [1703], p. 27.

[3]Christ Church MS Wake XVII, quoted by Mary Ransom, *EHR*, lvi (1941), 80.

[4]Sir John Hawkins, *The Life of Samuel Johnson, LL.D.*, 2nd edn., London,
J. Buckland, 1787, p. 54.

[5]Blenheim MS E25, quoted by Henry L. Snyder, *Literatur als Kritik des Lebens.
Festschrift zum 65. Geburtstag von Ludwig Borinski*, edd. Rudolph Haas *et al.*,
Heidelberg, Quelle und Meyer, 1975, p. 127.

popularly perceived to do. 'Authority', Swift said, 'is very much
founded on Opinion' (418.98-9).

But Swift was either mistaken or ironical when he said, 'I am
an Examiner only, and not a Reformer' (229.73-4). A propagandist
is of necessity a reformer—of attitudes and behaviour. Behind
the Examiner stands a priest. What Mainwaring writes sarcastically again may be read as literally true: '[The Examiner's]
Design was to furnish People with good Principles, to inform and
undeceive them, and to set them right in their Opinions.'[1] It is
too bad that Swift's response to the following has not survived:

> the Design of that Paper [The Examiner, No. 17, 23 December
> 1710, the famous balance sheet of Roman gratitude and British
> ingratitude], at this Juncture, and in this Scarcity of Money,
> cou'd be no other, than to direct the Mob to fire [Marl-
> borough's] Houses, and to plunder his Family.[2]

There can be no doubt now that these effects are well within the
capabilities of propaganda. But neither can there be any doubt
that Swift would have been appalled if The Examiner had produced
these effects. A week later he wrote to Stella, 'I really think
they will not do well in too much mortifying that man.' It is
necessary to say this because 'propaganda' is now in such bad
odour. But Dr Jonathan Swift is not a type of Dr Joseph Goebbels.
'The weapons I use', Swift said, 'will do you no hurt.' And he
rated satire along with philosophy and 'The Divine Authority of
Holy Writ' (229.68-9; cf. 391.170-5) as the only effective deter-
rents on human behaviour.[3]

The body of people whom Swift undertook to reform is said to
have been 'mainly' the squirearchy, the country gentlemen, clergy,
and freeholders of Britain.[4] There is much evidence, beginning in
August 1710 before Swift took it over, that The Examiner was read
in the country houses. The Earl of Jersey, from his own house in
Kent, wrote to a friend in London, 'Postboys, Examiners, &c., are
the usual entertainments of the country gentry.' John Oldmixon
heard ugly rumours of the Examiner's 'Libels by Dozens ... bundled
... up with Briefs and Fast-Prayers, and distributed ... by

---

[1]The Medley, 25 June 1711; cf. 83.58-60, 429.40.
[2]The Speech of Lord Haversham's Ghost, 1710, p. 4.
[3]Swift, Journal, p. 145; Corr., iii 367.
[4]Richard I. Cook, Studies in English Literature 1500-1900, ii (1962), 297-
8; Modern Language Quarterly, xxiv (March 1963), 31-41; W.A. Speck, Transactions of The Royal Historical Society, 5th series, xxii (1972), 27.

Apparators gratis to the poorer Vicars and Curates'. And the very thing that Oldmixon feared was happening in Yorkshire. John Hungerford, a Tory member, sent home *The Examiner* every Thursday to Scarborough. *The Examiner* arrived on Sunday 'and after evening service the parson usually invites a good number of his friends to his house, where he first reads over the paper, and then comments on the text; and all the week after carries it about with him to read to such of his parishioners as are weak in the faith.'[1]

But it is as difficult to believe that Swift would deliberately limit his audience to the provinces as it is to believe that he would limit his audience to London 'and some ... Miles about', which he explicitly refused to do. It was Dyer's handwritten newsletter that was 'entirely calculated for Fox-hunters, and works best over a Barrel of Brown Beer'.[2] No one reading a dozen numbers of '*Jack Dyer*'s Letter', as it was called, could confuse it with *The Examiner*. Before he undertook *The Examiner* Swift had observed that no matter how insipid the *Review* and *The Observator* were, they seemed 'to be levelled to the Understandings of a great Number'. And since they had become an indispensable part of coffee-house furniture, they were read by 'Customers of all Ranks'. Five years later Swift still admired the Whig periodical writers for their 'Style and Genius levelled to the Generality of Readers'.[3]

It must have been 'the Generality of Readers', therefore, to whom Swift addressed *The Examiner*. It is probable that he abandoned the lord-of-the-manor persona precisely in order to appeal to the widest possible audience. 'I write to the Vulgar, more than to the Learned', he said, and he could only have been pleased when an anonymous critic cried down his polemical style as 'adapted to the Taste of the Vulgar'.[4] Swift wanted his innuendoes to be

---

[1] HMC *Dartmouth MSS*, Eleventh Report, Appendix, Part V, p. 296; [Oldmixon,] *Remarks upon Remarks: or The Barrier-Treaty and the Protestant Succession Vindicated*, London, for A. Baldwin, 1711, p. 28; HMC *Portland MSS*, iv 641.

[2] Swift, *Prose*, vii 2; *The Infernal Congress: or, News from Below*, 2nd edn., London, for J. Baker, 1713, sig. A3^r.

[3] Swift, *Prose*, ii 113; vii 104.

[4] Swift, *The Works*, 19 vols., Dublin, George Faulkner, 1768, i, p. viii; *The Grand Accuser the Greatest of all Criminals*, Part I, 1735, p. 15. Swift had addressed *A Tale of a Tub* to 'the Learned' reader and had been bitterly disappointed to be misunderstood. The fifth edition with 'An Apology' was

understood and there is much evidence that they were. When he
called attention to 'the manner of Voting on the Bishops Bench'
in the House of Lords, it was understood that what he meant was
that a large majority of the bishops voted Whig. The same reader
also understood that Swift was submitting the voting record of
the episcopal bench 'down to the Judgment of the People', which,
he said, is 'extreamly pernicious'.[1] Swift must have been particularly pleased with this, for the reader was William Wotton,
who had systematically misread *A Tale of a Tub*.

   The kind of ignorance that Swift encountered in 'the Generality
of Readers' of *The Examiner* is illustrated by what Defoe was
reporting to Harley in November 1710: 'the Poor Distracted People
... believe firmly, that the Queen was at the Point to be De-
thron'd and Depos'd, and the Pretender to be Invited over, they
believe the Church was to be Overthrown, and the *Presbyterians* to
take Possession of them'.[2] But not all of the deceived, the misled, and the ignorant whom Swift addressed in *The Examiner* can
have lived in the country. He must have been pleased most of all
by the sarcasm that designated him as 'this Weekly Director of
the whole Kingdom'.[3]

   Both while he was writing *The Examiner* and retrospectively,
Swift insisted that what he wrote was true. And one main line of
Mainwaring's counter-propaganda was to keep repeating that *The
Examiner* was 'neither *True* nor *Probable*' (434.13). But the only
untruths that Mainwaring could cite were the result of misinfor-
mation (72.153n.) or inadvertence (132.146n.).[4] Mainwaring's
failure to uncover deliberate or substantive untruths confirms
Swift's claim that 'My Business in those Papers was to represent

---

published in 1710, presumably just before Swift arrived in London in September (*Corr.*, i 167). Henceforth Swift addressed himself to 'the Ignorant'
(*Prose*, i 117).
   [1]134.79; [William Wotton,] *The Case of the Present Convocation consider'd;
in Answer to The Examiner's Unfair Representations of it*, London, John
Churchill, 1711, p. 20.
   [2]*Review*, 9 November 1710.
   [3]*A Letter to a Member of the October-Club: Shewing, That to yield Spain to
the Duke of Anjou by a Peace, would be the Ruin of Great Britain*, London, for
A. Baldwin, 1711, p. 60.
   [4]Swift, *Journal*, p. 208; *Prose*, vii 105. It has been surmised that Harley
and St. John deliberately misinformed Swift (175.152-5; Ehrenpreis, ii 410),
but there is only one example in the thirty-three *Examiners* (303.110n.). Of
inadvertence there is a rich vein (*The Yearbook of English Studies*, xi
(1981), 58-66).

Facts, and I was as sparing as possible of reflecting upon particular Persons.' The word 'Facts' runs through *The Examiner* like
a leitmotiv: 'Some Facts ... The Fact ... a Fact ... The Fact
... one Fact ... my Facts ... one Fact ... some Facts.' By em-
phasizing facts Swift seems to imply that merely to state the
facts about the late Ministry is to slander them: *dire le vrai
est médire*. 'The Facts ... will ... reflect upon the *Persons* concern'd, as if we had told their Names at length' (67.35-7). This
helps to explain why Swift's polemical style is so full of part-
time allegory. Avarice and Ambition are juxtaposed so often (184.
168; 229.65; 260.132, 261.148; 375.61-2, etc.) that they coalesce
into some kind of two-headed monster Vice. And eventually not
even the most 'Superficial' reader could fail to identify this
allegorical figure, Old Avarice-and-Ambition, as the Duke of
Marlborough.[1] 'My Business in these Papers', Swift recalled, 'was
to represent Facts ... but the Mischief is, that the Readers have
always found Names to tally with those Facts; and I know no
Remedy for this.' What can a poor writer do? Swift undertook *The
Examiner* so that 'the World [not just the squirearchy] should,
from time to time, be Undeceived by true Representations of Persons and Facts'.[2]

This was not, however, the only use that Swift found for his
facts. The Medley discovered rather late that the Examiner also
had a 'Genius for Fiction'.[3] What Oldmixon meant, of course, was
'a genius for telling lies', but inadvertently he described
another reason for the success of *The Examiner*. In it Swift pro-
vides hints of a fictional England almost as satisfying as Lilliput, but which differs from Lilliput in that its satisfactions
are psychological rather than pictorial. Mainwaring, who had a
high reputation as a critic, reminds us that romance-writers 'endeavour'd to give an Air of Truth to their Fictions' (434.15).
Swift manages to give an air of fiction to his facts.

The master fiction is a Virgilian-Renaissance-pastoral vision
of Polyolbion. It boasts 'the Majesty of a Crown, the Honor of
a Nobility, and the Dignity of a Magistracy.... Arts and Sciences
... Bishops and Clergy ... Gentry [living] in a decent hospitable manner ... [and] Hands sufficient for Trade and Manufactures'

---

[1] Cf. Ehrenpreis, *Acts of Implication*, 1980, pp. 61-2.
[2] Swift, *Prose*, iii 190; vii 105.   [3] *The Medley*, 30 July 1711.

(130.95-100). It is all created out of words, a 'Kingdom of
Speech', in Defoe's phrase.[1]

In this fictional world the 'Image of a *Tory* ... serves to
represent the whole Body' (314.13-15). The Medley thought that
the Tories were crazy 'to let the *Examiner* deal in Descriptions
and Images' (294.190). Perhaps they were, but again the Examiner
knew what he was doing. 'A crowd thinks in images', it has been
said,

> and the image itself ... calls up a series of other images,
> having no logical connection with the first.... It accepts as
> real the images evoked in its mind, though they most often
> have only a very distant relation with the observed fact....
> Crowds being only capable of thinking in images are only to
> be impressed by images.[2]

The *point d'appui* of this system is a tripod of fictions:
(1) the fiction of impartiality, by which Swift reassures the
reader that he is above party—'I do not write for a Party ...
I am not Partial' (404.113, 427.2); (2) the fiction of homo-
geneity, i.e. of a homogeneous society, a seamless, frictionless,
organic society;[3] and (3) the fiction of unanimity—'the People's
joining as one Man, to wish, that [the Godolphin] Ministry should
be changed ... Parliament chosen with the universal Applause of
[the] People ... five in six [knights of the shire] are entirely
for the present Measures' (52.71-2, 165.76-7, 181.81-2). The
leitmotiv for the last of these is Swift's reckless but amusing
parody of the new science of political arithmetic: 'nine parts
in ten of the Kingdom ... nine Parts in ten of the Nobility and
Gentry ... nineteen in twenty [Tories]' (68.51-2, 82.27, 278.161-
2, 315.49-50).

The image of Queen Anne that is projected in *The Examiner* is
totally different from that projected in the *Journal to Stella*.
In the *Journal* she is an elusive figure with whom Swift does not
have an audience, who does not invite him to preach before her,
who appears at her levee with her fan in her mouth, and whose
improved health is explained by 'a certain Reason, that she has
done with Braces'.[4] She was not one of Swift's favourites, but
the Examiner idolized her:

[1] *A New Test of the Sence of the Nation*, London, 1710, p. 4.
[2] Gustav Le Bon, *The Crowd*, New York, Viking, 1960, pp. 41, 68.
[3] Ehrenpreis, ii 411.
[4] Swift, *Journal*, pp. 185, 126n., 328, 542.

a QUEEN, who besides all Virtues that can enter into the Composition of a private Person, possesses every Regal Quality that
can contribute to make a People happy. Of great Wisdom, yet
ready to receive the Advice of Her Councellors:[1] Of much
Discernment in chusing proper Instruments, when She follows
Her own Judgment,[2] and only capable of being deceived by that
excess of Goodness which makes Her judge of others by Herself
(167.136-42).

The Queen, in fact, was the Examiner's favourite subject. He

wrapped himself in the panoply of the throne and made himself

invulnerable. The Medley recognized this at once: 'By this means

he gives himself a becoming Advantage ... to fall upon him is

... to insult the Q---n' (191.172-4, 221.63-4).

There were several reasons for Swift to include the Queen in

every *Examiner*. The first was historical and psychological. The

duumvirs and the Junto had the opportunity and the resources to

have celebrated 'the Golden track of *ANNE*'s distinguish'd Reign'

with the Queen herself in the role of Gloriana, 'the *Augustula*

of the *British* Empire'.[3] If the Kit-Cat poets—Garth, Congreve,

Walsh, Addison, Steele, Mainwaring—had been turned loose to

embellish this promising theme, Marlborough might have marched

his regiments into Paris. Instead of this, the Whigs bullied the

Queen. They '*Clip'd* and *Mangl'd*' her prerogative (378.125); they

denied her even a veto of appointments to state offices. They

minced 'into nothing' her style and titles (401.28), until she

'felt that she had been reduced to a cypher'.[4] By 'unctuous

iteration', in the language of the Whig interpretation of his-

tory, Swift put Anne back at 'the centre of power', just as Har-

ley had promised her.[5]

---

[1]Shortly before he wrote this panegyric, Swift learned from Abigail Masham
that the Queen had 'changed' and that 'from the Opinion of having been formerly too much *directed*, fell into the other extream and became difficult to
be *advised*' (*Journal*, p. 433; *Prose*, viii 144).
[2]'In dispensing her Favours, [the Queen] was extreamly cautious and slow;
and after the usuall Mistake of those who think they have been often imposed
on, became so very suspicious that she overshot the Mark and erred in the
other Extream' (ibid., viii 151).
[3]John Hughes, *Poems and Translations by several Hands*, ed. John Oldmixon,
London, for J. Pemberton, 1714, p. 163; Conyers Place, *The True English Revo-
lutionist, or; The Happy Turn, Rightly Taken*, London, for W. Taylor, 1710,
p. 58. Anne sometimes fancied herself as a second Gloriana (352.93n., 448.111-
12n.).
[4]Gregg, p. 296.
[5]*DNB*, i 463; *Miscellaneous State Papers*, ed. Philip Yorke Hardwicke, 2 vols.,
London, for W. Strahan and T. Cadell, 1778, ii 487.

The second reason for invoking the Queen was tactical. By harp-
ing on '*those Indignities offer'd ... to Her M-----y* ... the Insolences offer'd to the Qu---' (240.24-5, 388.85), Swift set up
an unassailable defensive position for himself. As the Examiner's
anonymous critic put it, 'The Charge ... of Insolence towards the
Queen ... was indeed the very best Topick ... her Majesty permitting it to be once openly and directly asserted, no Answer
could possibly be made to it.'[1]

The figure of the Queen projected in *The Examiner* is scaled
down to two dimensions: her care for *all* her subjects and her
generosity to the Church. It is based on such images as these:
'If you did but know what pains she takes in Council every day,
you would wonder; she spends all her time in taking care of her
People.'[2] Access to the Good Queen of romance, the source of all
'Favours' as well as 'the centre of power', the ogrish Whigs
denied to her distracted subjects by 'a huge invisible Net ...
thro' which nothing of Value could pass' (101.139). The villains
of this fictional world are single-character freaks: L'Avare
Marlborough, Sid Hamet Godolphin the Lebanese money-changer, Will
Bigamy Cowper, Defecator Wharton, and the like.

This diminishment is accomplished in the normal fashion of
satire by a system of reductive metaphors. John Toland noticed
that 'one prime Artifice' of *The Examiner* 'is, To talk constantly
of the *Whigs*, as if they were all *Dissenters*'.[3] 'Dissenters', however, is only the least of what the Examiner calls the collec-
tivity of cast ministers. He makes them 'Animals' (21.31),
'Criminals' (83.43), 'Sharper[s]' (99.100), 'Mountebanks' (167.
154), 'Artists' (i.e. illusionists, 'operators') (196.127), '*Robbers*' (457.152).

A few more features of Swift's propaganda method may be mentioned very briefly:

(1) The propaganda masters, Somers and Halifax for the Whigs,
and Harley for the Tories, seem to have believed that it was
necessary to answer every opposing pamphlet and broadside—some-

---

[1] *The Grand Accuser the Greatest of All Criminals*, 1735, p. 16.
[2] *A Dialogue between a Member of Parliament, a Divine, a Lawyer, a Freeholder, a Shopkeeper, and a Country Farmer*, 1703, p. 20.
[3] *The Memorial of the State of England, In Vindication of the Queen, the
Church, and the Administration*, London, 1705, p. 76.

times paragraph by paragraph or even line by line—on the principle of 'unanswer'd (and of consequence taken for granted)'.
Swift, however, knew a better principle: unanswered (and of
consequence forgotten). Answers 'make it sell', he said.[1]

(2) As a consequence, Swift ignored St. John's instruction to
the Examiner to provide 'a Weekly Antidote to the Weekly Poison
of the *Review*, *The Observator*, and *The Tatler*'.[2] He resolved 'to
take very little notice of other Papers' for the very good reason
that 'if it once came to Rejoinder and Reply, we should be all
upon a Level' (36.46-7, 241.61-2).[3]

(3) Swift recognized that the apotropaic function of *The Examiner* absolutely required it to rise high above the level of the
opposition press. His running bill of complaints against the Whig
writers cannot be taken seriously: 'I cannot be angry with those
Gentlemen for perpetually writing against me,' Swift said, 'It
furnishes them largely with Topicks' (211.41-212.43). Better for
Mainwaring, Ridpath, and Steele to 'batter down the *Examiner*' than
to batter down the government (212.53). So, with a delightful
solecism that mocks at their success, the Examiner magnanimously
acquiesces in their clumsy efforts: 'I chose ... to ... suffer
them in quiet to roar on at the *Examiner*' (213.75-9)—as gently
as any sucking dove.

In default of any evidence of size of press runs or numbers of
concealed editions, the success of *The Examiner* can only be
measured by the testimony of contemporaries and quotation of *The
Examiner* by contemporaries. The best evidence is Mainwaring's
grudging admission, 'It did a World of Mischief.'[4] Mainwaring's
concession is confirmed by an anonymous Tory who annotated the
Smith College copy of the duodecimo *Examiner*: 'Swift ... did his
party infinite service and gave the friends of the old ministry

---

[1] Joseph Rawson, *A Letter to the Reverend Dr. Sacheverel. With a Postscript,
concerning the late Vindication of Him; in Answer to Mr. B---t's Modern
Phanatick*, London, for A. Baldwin, 1711, p. 29; Swift, *Prose*, ii 69.
[2] Refusing to reply is of course, a well-known figure of rhetoric; cf.
Delariviere Manley, *Memoirs of Europe*, London, for John Morphew, 1711, p.
231; Defoe, *Review*, 14 December 1710.
[3] Swift found the principle so important that he copied it into his commonplace book (*Prose*, iv 248).
[4] Oldmixon, *The History*, p. 456.

inexpressible disquiet.'[1] Marlborough complained that it stabbed
him to the heart.[2] In a very different tone, there is some amusing testimony to the success of *The Examiner* in this piece of
negative evidence:

> *Guilford* is a Town in *Surrey* ... where they have never yet
> taken in the *Examiner*, and consequently where the Mists before
> the Peoples Eyes must needs be thicker than those of *Old Brent-
> ford.*[3]

Even more impressive, because largely unconscious, is the amount
of quotation of *The Examiner*. As a reformer, Swift is intent to
change the behaviour of his readers. As a propagandist he seems
willing to settle for a change in what they say (373.1-2). 'The
generality of the People', he says, 'know not how to *Talk* or
Think, 'till they have read their *Lesson* in the Papers of the
Week' (35.27-9). He notices that Mainwaring borrows his phrase
'Hedge-Writers'. He quotes the Commons' resolution that
£35,000,000 of the public revenue remained unaccounted for in
Godolphin's management of the Treasury (416.52). Mainwaring
obligingly reports that 'in every Coffee-house and Ale-house ...
I may hear it with confidence asserted ... that *Thirty five Mil-
lions were lost to the Publick, during the late Administration*'.[4]
In *The Examiner* of 23 November 1710 Swift observes that the late
administration remained in office ''till neither God nor Man
could suffer their continuance' (52.74-5). Mainwaring in *The
Medley* (266.81-2, 446.43, etc.) and Oldmixon in *A Letter to the
Seven Lords Appointed to Examine Gregg* (p. 22) repeatedly retort
the phrase upon Swift. A generation later an anonymous reader of
The Examiner complained that 'our present Condition [under Wal-
pole] ... is such ... as to use the *Examiner*'s Words, *No Government in any Age or Country would ever endure*'.[5] Whigs quote *The
Examiner*:

---

[1] It is significant that the annotator paraphrases the Examiner (455.104-5)
while praising him.

[2] *Marlborough-Godolphin Corr.*, iii 1662.

[3] *A True and Faithful Account of the Last Distemper and Death of Tom. Whigg,
Esq;*, Part II, London, 1710, p. 8.

[4] [Mainwaring and R. Walpole,] *A State of the Five and Thirty Millions mention'd in the Report of a Committee of the House of Commons*, London, for
A. Baldwin, 1712, p. 1; cf. 'Whether it be so or no, 'tis enough that it is
so believed' (Swift, *Prose*, vi 132).

[5] *The Grand Accuser the Greatest of all Criminals*, Part I, 1735, pp. 74-5.

Arthur Mainwaring, the Kit Cat portrait by Sir Godfrey Kneller

certain Vices are more or less pernicious, according to the
Stations of those who possess them.
                    (*The Examiner*, 22 February 1711) (261.162-3)

every Passion is more useful or pernicious according to the Circumstances of the Person in whom it reigns.
                    (Richard Steele, *The Medley*, 5 March 1711) (279.18-19)

and Tories quote *The Examiner*:

our *Faction*, (for so with great Propriety of Speech [the Whigs]
call the Queen and Ministry, almost the whole Clergy, and nine
parts in ten of the Kingdom).
                    (*The Examiner*, 5 March 1711) (68.50-2)

The Queen, Her Ministry, and Her Parliament, together with five
parts in six of the whole Kingdom ... must all be distinguish'd
by the Name of a *Faction*.
                    (Joseph Trapp, *The Character and Principles of the present
                    Set of Whigs*, 2nd edn., London, John Morphew, 1711, p. 26)

This kind of resonance—his words ringing down the years—is the
success that Swift hoped for in *The Examiner* (84.98-100). And
since Whiggish sarcasm supplies some of its most reliable contemporary criticism, it may be permissible to quote a Whiggish
sarcasm against *The Conduct of the Allies* (1711) and apply it
literally to *The Examiner*:

> O Noble Leaves! O *Sw-ft*'s Immortal Deed!
> Thee unborn *Tories* shall with Pleasure read,
> And bind *Thy* Sacred Pages with their Creed;
> To future Times *Thou* shalt recorded stand
> The Great *Historian*, who hast sav'd the Land;
> In *Bodley*'s Library shall be inroll'd
> Thy Covers and thy Back be wrought with Gold,
> And live when Drake's *Memorial* lies unsold.[1]

4. Arthur Mainwaring

Arthur Mainwaring (1668-1712) is an interesting and undervalued
figure. 'A Man of the *Belles Lettres*, a Wit, a Declaimer, a Mytho-
logist, a Poet and a Learned Historian',[2] is what one hostile
critic called him, and he was all of these things and more (Fig. II).
He began his political life as a flaming Jacobite. His first published work, *Tarquin and Tullia* (1689), was subsequently described
by Pope as 'that very hot copy of verses against King William and

---

[1]*A Genuine Epistle from M—w P—r, Esq; at Paris, to the Reverend J—n
S—t, D.D. at Windsor*, London, 1714, p. 15.
[2][Simon Clement], *A Vindication of the Faults on both Sides, from the
Reflections of the Medley*, London, 1710, p. 4.

Queen Mary'.[1] It appears that he wrote at least three more copies
of Jacobite verse: *The King of Hearts* (1689), *Suum Cuique* (1689),
and *The Duchess of York's Ghost* (1691). When Jacob Tonson accused
Dryden of writing *The King of Hearts*, Dryden 'disown'd it, saying,
*It was written by an ingenious Young Gentleman ... Nam'd ...
Maynwaring*'. Neither the time nor the circumstances of Mainwaring's conversion to Whiggism have been established, but what
little evidence there is indicates that it occurred about 1700
when he was admitted to the Kit-Cat Club and met the Whig ideo-
logues and propaganda masters, Somers and Halifax.[2]

 Mainwaring's appointment in November 1701 as commissioner of
customs (worth £1,200 a year) cannot have come as a reward for
services, for his first unequivocally Whiggish works are two
copies of verse, *The History and Fall of the Conformity Bill*
(January 1704?) and *An Address to our Sovereign Lady* (April
1704).[3] When he learned that Godolphin believed him to be the
author of Walsh's savage satire on the Tories for whom the accession of Queen Anne had promised a new *'Saturnian* Age of Gold',
Mainwaring characteristically went straight to the Lord Treasurer
and not only convinced him that he was not the author of *The Golden Age Restor'd* (January 1703), but also won an assurance that
he would not be removed from his post in the customs. 'The Lord
Treasurer was extreamly well pleas'd with Mr. *Maynwaring*'s Frankness, Saying, *You may depend upon it*, Sir, *You shall keep your
Place if you please as long as I keep mine*. And from that Time
there grew such an Intimacy between them, that it ended in a mutual
Love, more like that of Brothers than of Friends.'[4] Godolphin was
even better than his word, for in May 1705 he bought one of the
two offices of auditor of the imprests worth £2,000-£7,000 a year
and secured a royal warrant for presenting it to Mainwaring. The
other auditor of imprests was Harley's younger brother, Edward.

 In April 1705, to encourage Whig votes in the general election,
Mainwaring wrote some spirited verses, *The French King's Thanks
and Advice to the Tory M--b-rs and M-n----rs*, to be sung to the
tune of *Lilliburlero*.[5] His first surviving prose pamphlet for the

---

[1]Spence, p. 203.
[2]Oldmixon, *The Life*, p. 14; *The Yearbook of English Studies*, xi (1981), 51-3.
[3]*POAS*, Yale, vii 3, vi 615.   [4]Oldmixon, *The Life*, p. 22.
[5]Foxon F253, reprinted in *A Collection of New Songs. Adapted to the Times*,
no place or date of publication, p. 6, with other poems by Mainwaring.

Whigs, written in July 1705 but not published, was *Remarks on a late Romance, entitled The Memorial of the Church of England; or, The History of the Ten Champions*. This was a reply to Dr James Drake's highly successful attack on 'the Family', as Defoe called them, 'the drift of it pretending to shew that the lord treasurer, dutchesse of Marlborough, &c. are undermining the church, by ... putting [Whigs] into places'.[1]

In December 1706 Mainwaring entered Parliament in a by-election for Preston, Lancs., a seat controlled by James Stanley, Earl of Derby, as Chancellor of the Duchy of Lancaster, and 'upon the scrutiny, carried it by 6' against Henry Fleetwood, the Tory candidate. He was re-elected for Preston in May 1708, and though defeated in the Tory landslide of October 1710, was returned by Bishop Trelawny to one of the seats for West Looe, Cornwall, presumably on Godolphin's recommendation.[2]

But more important than the Treasury post and the seat in Parliament added together was Mainwaring's complicated relationship with another member of 'the Family', the Duchess of Marlborough. This began in 1707, just about the time that the Duchess discovered she had been supplanted in the Queen's affection by her poor relation, Abigail Masham. During the palace revolution precipitated by Harley's 'intrigue to alter the Ministry' in February 1708, Mainwaring wrote two ballads for Sarah to sing to his accompaniment on the harpsichord. Almost the first surviving letter from Mainwaring to the Duchess, dated 3 April 1708, already implies a relationship of some familiarity and complete trust. It enclosed an election pamphlet. 'I took the hint of it', Mainwaring wrote, 'from one of the letters with which your Grace honoured me, wherein you mention the usefulness of raising a cry upon the Jacobites.'[3] By the end of 1708 Mainwaring had become a member of 'the Family'.

When the Duchess was in the country, she liked long letters. So Mainwaring wrote them. He flattered her shamelessly and teased

---

[1]Luttrell, v 574; Mainwaring's pamphlet may have circulated in manuscript, but it was first printed in Oldmixon, *The Life*, pp. 25-39.

[2]Luttrell, vi 125; Robert Walcott, *English Politics in the Early Eighteenth Century*, Oxford, Clarendon Press, 1956, pp. 191, 225.

[3]Swift, *Corr.*, i 69; POAS, Yale, vii 306-21; *Private Correspondence*, i 117. The pamphlet, possibly Mainwaring's first published prose work, was *Advice to the Electors of Great Britain; Occasion'd by the Intended Invasion from France* (19 April 1708) (Henry L. Snyder, *HLQ*, xxix (November 1965), 58-9).

her about her 'lover', the malodorous Marquis of Kent (who was
her nominee as Lord Chamberlain of the Household). But most of
all he wrote about politics and patronage: who gets what and
when, in which it was the Duchess who rode in the whirlwind and
directed the storm. Unlike Swift, who wavered, Mainwaring seems
never to have doubted the value of the two-party system of government. When Vanbrugh's Queen's Theatre in the Haymarket began to
offer competition to the Theatre Royal in Drury Lane, Mainwaring
saw that 'Our Stage is thus an Emblem of the State | ... by Oppo-
sition Great'.[1]

When the Duchess was in lodgings in town, they played piquet,
listened to music together, and plotted propaganda in support of
Godolphin, who remained so oblivious of its importance. So Mainwaring became the Duchess's informant, adviser, co-conspirator,
confidant, and correspondent (as well as accompanist), using the
same cipher that the Duke of Marlborough and Godolphin used in
writing to the Duchess and to each other. It was this relationship that propelled Mainwaring into the role of the Medley.

It has been said that Mainwaring had 'a fatal influence on
Sarah'.[2] And it is true that it was Mainwaring who suggested in
January 1710 that an address be brought into Parliament to remove
Mrs Masham from the Queen's presence, which was a terrible mistake.[3] But part at least of the feverish gaiety and wit that
charmed the Duchess was symptomatic of the consumption that
finally killed Mainwaring in November 1712. The emotional out-
breaks induced by the disease—'I ... have seen him weep at the
dismal Prospects of those Evils, which he ... foresaw'—made him
an implacable enemy, feared even by his closest friends in the
Kit-Cat Club. His conversation and correspondence are full of
violent hyperboles: 'I would freely give half [of my estate] ...
rather than yield up *Spain* to the House of *Bourbon*'; 'I would
rather be buried alive than accused of acting an ill part to
[Godolphin]'.[4] But his correspondence with the Duchess is also

---

[1] [Giovanni Bononcini], *Camilla. An Opera*, trans. Owen Swiney, London,
J. Tonson, 1707, sig. A3^V; Henry L. Snyder, *Philological Quarterly* (October
1971), 615.   [2] Gregg, p. 272.
[3] BL MS Lansdowne 885, f. 78. Anne was so incensed at this proposed invasion
of her prerogative that she summoned Mainwaring to the palace and spoke to
him 'very plain' (100.103n).
[4] Oldmixon, *The Life*, p. 140; id., *The History*, p. 480; *Private Correspondence*, i 283-4.

full of very good advice for dealing with the Queen, which the
Duchess simply chose to ignore. The truth seems to be that no
one could have any influence on the Duchess of Marlborough.

November 1709 to September 1710 was a period of intense propaganda activity for Mainwaring. Although he continued to publish
verse, he turned more frequently now to prose. Besides writing
a speech for Halifax to deliver in the House of Lords and two
drafts of a letter for Marlborough, protesting to the Queen
against the dismissal of Sunderland, he published a pamphlet or
broadside nearly every month during this period, including two
in August and three in September. It was also during this period
that Mainwaring was offered a more important post in the government, one that entailed a seat in the Privy Council. It was presumably treasurer of the Navy, an 'office of great trust, dignity,
and profit'. Oldmixon hints that it 'requir'd a nice Knowledge of
Figures'. But wholly through the interest of the Duchess of Marlborough, the treasurership went to Robert Walpole, whose personal
finances were in perilous straits.[1]

In August 1710 'the old ministry saw it was absolutely necessary to set up a Paper in opposition to the Examiner'. This
thought seems unlikely to have occurred to Godolphin or Marlborough, who despised the press. It may have occurred to Somers or
Halifax, who had functioned as propaganda masters, but the most
likely source is Mainwaring himself and the Duchess of Marlborough. Harley made a last-minute effort to recruit Mainwaring for
his own service. But Mainwaring had already decided that Harley
was 'the most errant tricking Knave in all Britain that no man
alive believes'.[2]

In any case it was finally Joseph Addison whom Mainwaring
settled upon 'to set up a Paper in opposition to the Examiner'.
The paper was called *The Whig-Examiner*, but Mainwaring decided
almost immediately that he had made a mistake. Addison could not
easily adjust his style to the roughhouse of party politics. He
seems to have written only the first two numbers of *The Whig-
Examiner* himself. To the third number, of 28 September 1710,

---

[1]Beatson, i 344; Oldmixon, *The Life*, pp. 129, 141, 306; J.H. Plumb, *Sir
Robert Walpole*, 2 vols., London, Cresset Press, 1956-60, i 151 (where Walpole's thank-you letter of 11 January 1710 to the Duchess is inadvertently
said to be addressed to Mainwaring); *Private Correspondence*, ii 151.

[2]Oldmixon, *Memoirs*, p. 8; id., *The Life*, p. 339; BL MS Add. 61461, f. 66.

Mainwaring contributed 'that excellent Speech of *Alcibiades*' that
Swift imitated in *The Examiner* of 30 November 1710.[1]

By this time Mainwaring must already have decided to replace
Addison, for the first number of *The Medley*, 5 October 1710, be-
gins with *A Letter to the Whig-Examiner* (alluding to St. John's
Letter to the Examiner) that sounds like a friendly dismissal:

> I have read, Sir, your three Papers with a great deal of
> Pleasure; and as you observe in the second, that every Author
> has his *Admirers*, I do assure you very sincerely I am one of
> yours. Yet I cannot help being so much your *Friend*, as to put
> you in mind of a great Error you have been guilty of, &c., &c.

Addison went on to write two more *Whig-Examiners* (5 and 12 October 1710), to which Mainwaring contributed the last half of No. 4
and two important paragraphs of No. 5, and then wrote no more.
During the same weeks Mainwaring wrote *The Medley*, Nos. 1 and 2
(5 and 11 October 1710). The publication date of *The Medley*, No. 3
(16 October 1710), was changed to Monday, and there it remained
to the end.[2]

5. Mainwaring's *Medley*

Despite some self-imposed limitations, Mainwaring's *Medley* was
a success from the start. 'Mr. Tonson sent me another answer to
the first paper', he wrote to the Duchess, 'in which I think it is
said that the author ought to be put in the pillory; so that I
think it is well that nobody but your Grace knows about it'. It
was successful enough to be attributed to Swift, and although
James Grahme, the Tory Member for Westmorland, sent *The Examiner*
to his cousin the Duke of Montrose every week, he also sent *The
Medley*. But the self-imposed limitations were considerable.[3]

The first was the decision to remain on the defensive—Oldmixon
calls it 'the only Intent' of *The Medley*. Mainwaring guessed correctly what the strategy of *The Examiner* was to be: 'if they [the
new ministry] shew no faults in those that went before them, who

---

[1]Oldmixon, *The Life*, pp. 158, 163.

[2]Ibid., pp. 164-7. Oldmixon collaborated with Mainwaring from the beginning
(Oldmixon, *Memoirs*, pp. 9-10, 210), writing part of *The Medley*, No. 2, 11 Oc-
tober 1710. Fortunately he kept a detailed record of his contributions to
The Medley, vol. i, which were largest during Mainwaring's illness in January—
April 1711 (Oldmixon, *The Life*, pp. 169-201). The second volume of *The Medley*
(3 March—7 August 1712) was presumably the work of Oldmixon alone (BL MS
Add. 61461, ff. 155, 160).

[3]*Private Correspondence*, i 393-4; Swift, *Journal*, p. 289; SRO GD220/5/807/9.

can bear their seizing the Government without any pretence of
merit, and dispossessing all those that have deserved so well?'
Swift began by showing the faults of Wharton and Marlborough in
the first numbers that he wrote. By the same strategy *The Medley*
should have taken the offensive, attacking St. John, 'Perfidious,
Noisy, Impudent, and Vain', and Abigail Masham. These two were
extremely vulnerable after the Quebec Expedition and Mainwaring
hated both of them. 'He had a very mean Opinion not only of Mr.
St. John's Honesty, but of his Capacity, where a solid Understanding was necessary' and he habitually referred to Mrs Masham as
'a stinking ugly chamber maid'.[1] But these rich fields were abandoned for the stony ground of 'what is generally understood by
the word *answering*':

> Whatever is said of this poor Paper [Mainwaring wrote], the
> only Intent of it is just the contrary of what the *Examiner*
> has resolv'd on concerning [*The Medley*]. 'Tis to take notice
> of him, to animadvert him, to provide an Antidote for his
> weekly Poisons.[2]

Swift understood that 'if it once came to Rejoinder and Reply,
we should be all upon a Level' (241.61-2). Mainwaring seems to
agree: 'I shou'd be well employ'd indeed', he says sarcastically,
'to argue gravely with him, who shamefully affirms what no body
in his Senses can believe' (120.36-7). But he argues. And Swift,
of course, encourages him: 'If *I* were as *They*,' he says, 'my
chief Endeavour should certainly be to batter down the *Examiner*'
(212.52-3); cf. p. xlvii above.

Swift did not need to know who the Medley was, for he chose to
ignore him. But once it had been decided to limit *The Medley* to
'what is generally understood by the word *answering*', it became
imperative for Mainwaring to find out *whom* he was answering. But
Harley had made this almost impossible by beginning with a committee, or editorial board, of Tory writers, and then turning *The
Examiner* over to a Whig. Mainwaring learned very early that
Atterbury was to be involved: 'If it be true', he wrote to the

---

[1] *POAS*, Yale, vii 35; HMC *Portland MSS*, v 655; Oldmixon, *The History*, p. 456;
Private Correspondence, i 392. The decision to remain on the defensive was
confirmed by Mainwaring as late as May 1711 (437.112-438.115).

[2] *The Medley*, 23 July 1711. Having revealed in 'An Apology' for *A Tale of
a Tub* (September(?), 1710) that Answerers are only 'kept alive by ... Replies'
(Swift, *Prose*, i 4), Swift is careful never to mention Mainwaring by name in
The Examiner and to mention *The Medley* only twice (429.37-8, 42).

Duchess in August or September 1710, 'that Mr. Harley has retained Dr. Atterbury to write a justification of his actions, 'tis
likely that hard task may give occasions for more scribbling.'[1]
Three months after Atterbury had been replaced, Mainwaring continued to believe that it was he who wrote *The Examiner* (173.108-
9). It was yet another month before he decided that it was written by a Tory committee: 'A Poet, sometimes a Priest, sometimes a
Physician, sometimes a silly Academick, and sometimes even an old
Woman' (253.157-254.159). It was not until the first weeks of May
1711 that the Examiner's identity was revealed in Gay's *The
Present State of Wit*. And it was not until 18 June 1711, just
after Swift had abandoned the role, that Mainwaring described the
Examiner as 'the ingenious Divine who writ *the Tale of a Tub*'
(486.129-30). During the entire time that he was *'answering'* Swift,
therefore, Mainwaring was fencing in the dark and his attack was
frequently misdirected. The Examiner, he supposed, 'was retain'd
at first to scribble against the Revolution' (235.52-3). But he
would not have supposed this if he had known that the Examiner
was Swift. For not only was Swift by many years an earlier enthu-
siast for William of Orange and the Glorious Revolution, but he
was known to Mainwaring as a Whig and a protégé of Somers and
Halifax.[2]

Besides these self-imposed limitations, Mainwaring suffered from
several more that were not self-imposed. The first was the in-
tractability of the material. 'The Family' and the Junto were
essentially indefensible. The Examiner concludes his letter to
Crassus/Marlborough by noticing that *'your Friends offer nothing
material in your Defence'* (232.166-7). Indeed, there was nothing
that could be offered in Marlborough's defence. Not one act of
generosity appears on Marlborough's record. The Duchess's 'ungovernable Rage ... haughty Pride, and unsatiable Covetousness'
(375.67-8) are equally indefensible. And the only defence of
Wharton that Mainwaring essayed was a feeble *tu quoque* in a letter
to the Duchess.[3]

---

[1]*Private Correspondence*, i 393.
[2]Swift, *Corr.*, i 150-1. Oldmixon, writing after the fact, said that Mainwaring 'took [Swift] to have the greatest hand in the *Examiner*', but he quotes
Mainwaring saying exactly the same thing about Prior, and I can find no evidence that Mainwaring knew that Swift wrote *The Examiner* at the time Swift
was writing it (cf. 281.87-8).   [3]*Private Correspondence*, i 217-18.

Another unavoidable limitation was Mainwaring's ill health. He discovered that he was 'in Danger of a Consumption' while still a student at the Inner Temple. He was virtually incapacitated by the disease from January to April 1711, 'forc'd to lye all day, upon a Couch,' he told the Duchess, 'tho I still walkd about, till I cou'd walk no longer.' But even when he could no longer write *The Medley*, he sent 'Hints' to Oldmixon and corrected his copy. Hampstead air and horseback riding were prescribed to restore his strength and eventually he could refer to the attack as 'my late insupportable Illness; which ... I am quite cured of', but it was in fact almost the end. He signed his last report as auditor of the imprests on 4 November 1712 and died of tuberculosis at the age of 44 in the arms of his servant, Thomas Wood, eight days later. 'The greatest Lady in *England*, wept often by the side of his Death Bed.'[1]

Mainwaring would have been a more effective answerer of *The Examiner* if *The Examiner* had been written by a high church country Tory and member of the October Club, like Sir John Pakington. Mainwaring's effectiveness was limited in an odd way by the fact that he agreed with Swift on so many issues, and shared so many of Swift's prejudices. 'As for ... Scots,' he wrote to the Duchess, 'it is impossible ... to think worse of them than I do, or to apprehend more mischief from them.' On another occasion he complained that 'The license of the press is too great and I hope some proper way may be found to restrain it', again almost duplicating Swift's words. He did not defend the Palatine refugees when Swift attacked them. And both Mainwaring and Swift would have disagreed violently with Davenant's wish that 'this Kingdom [become] the Asylum for all oppressed and afflicted Persons'.[2] Mainwaring might even have agreed with Swift that a Whig was 'one *who believed in the late Ministry*'.[3] Even his later attacks on Swift as 'that Orthodox Divine, who ... is ... never half so witty upon

---

[1]Oldmixon, *The Life*, pp. 9, 201, 343; BL MS Add. 61461; Thomas Betterton, *The History of the English Stage*, London, E. Curll, 1741, p. [2]28.

[2]*Private Correspondence*, i 396; cf. *POAS*, Yale, vii 283; *Private Correspondence*, i 237; cf. 378.141-2; Charles Davenant, *The Political and Commercial Works*, 5 vols., London, for R. Horsfield *et al.*, 1771, ii 6.

[3]455.104-6. There were sharp differences between Swift and Mainwaring on 'the Civil and Religious Rights' of dissenters (446.35-6, 401.55-402.63) and of course on the war (Mainwaring, *Remarks upon the Present Negotiations of Peace begun between Britain and France* (London, 1711, 8°, p. 34).

any other Subject, as upon that of Religion', lose their force
when measured against Mainwaring's own heterodoxy. He condemns
those hypocrites who crowd into church to 'be in the Queen's
sight', but admits that they have 'no more Religion than myself'.[1]

In spite of all these limitations, *The Medley* was a success because Mainwaring seems to have known instinctively what he had to
do to succeed. This was to turn the Examiner into a comic figure,
the 'Hero ... in a Farce of his own making' (472.35). The title
that Mainwaring chose for the vehicle of this effort allowed him,
as he said, 'to ramble as much as I please from one Subject to
another'; 'Connection wou'd be a Vice in it' (105.42-3, 321.5-6).
The tone that he sought was witty and ironical. And in this, perhaps without knowing it, he was turning Swift's weapons against
himself: 'I endeavour to make my Readers merry with him,' he
said (120.64). That he was successful is attested even by hostile
readers: 'he's admirable at his short Turns of sheer Wit, and has
all manner of Misrepresentation at Command'.[2]

Mainwaring reported to the Duchess that two friends had told
him at dinner that it was 'possible to scribble these men [the
new ministers] down'.[3] And several sympathetic readers thought
that he had done so.[4] It was Samuel Johnson, however, who judged
correctly that 'no man was ever written down but by himself'.[5]
Mainwaring could not have succeeded at all if Swift had not provided him with 'Handles' (208.197). The 'Handles' include several
ineradicable prejudices: a hatred and fear of Dissenters, foreigners, moneyed men. But most of the 'Handles' are inadverten-
cies, slips of the tongue or memory, momentary unawareness of
double meanings, of innuendoes, or of the full spectrum of possible
connotations, like Johnson's pontifical pronouncement that 'The
woman had a bottom of good sense.' To Johnson's question, 'Where's
the merriment?', Henri Bergson finally supplied the answer:

[1]Mainwaring, *The British Academy*, London, 1712, p. 10; BL MS Add. 61459,
ff. 184ᵛ-5.
[2]Simon Clement, *A Vindication of the Faults on both Sides*, 1710, p. 4.
[3]Blenheim MS E25, quoted in Henry L. Snyder, *Festschrift ... Borinski*, 1975
[p. xxxix, n. 5 above], p. 127.
[4]Francis Hare, *The Negociations for a Treaty of Peace, in 1709. Consider'd,
In a Third Letter to a Tory Member*, 2nd edn., London, for A. Baldwin, 1711,
p. 50; *Biographia Britannica*, v 3076.
[5]Samuel Johnson, *A Journey to the Western Islands of Scotland*, ed. R.W.
Chapman, London, Oxford University Press, 1930, p. 344.

The comic is that side of a person which reveals his likeness
to a thing.... Consequently it expresses an individual or collective imperfection which calls for an immediate corrective.
This corrective is laughter.... Thus, absentmindedness is essentially laughable, and so we laugh at anything rigid, ready-made,
mechanical.[1]

The 'Handles' that Swift provided are absentmindedness, rigidities
like xenophobia, and self-deception: 'The universe as a hot chest-
nut.' One of the 'Handles' is a lie. 'I never receiv'd Injury from
the late Ministry,' the Examiner testifies (255.2-3), but Swift
complains to Stella that 'the rascals of the other party ... used
a man unworthily, who had deserved better'.[2] Even without knowing
that the Examiner was lying, the Medley (Oldmixon in this case)
is able to score by pointing out that the Examiner 'railing with
as much Rancour and Scurrility as he cou'd' (293.129-31) against
the ministers who had done him no injury is heartless and un-
christian. Another of the 'Handles' is an inadvertency. Without
bothering to read the Act of Indemnity (7 Ann. c. 22), Swift
learned from an election pamphlet that 'great and many Misa[pro]-
p[riatio]ns were thereby p[asse]d'.[3] He then repeated the accusation twice in *The Examiner* (72.152-4, 389.113-15). The first time
around Mainwaring failed to grab the ring. But, alerted by a letter 'from an unknown Hand' (474.112), he did not fail the second
time around. He scored 'A hit! a hit! a palpable hit!'

There are not many of these, but from this scattered material
Mainwaring is able to fashion a comic figure, the well-intentioned
incompetent, the buffoon. George Ridpath may have originated the
joke, but it was Mainwaring who blew it up into an authentic
freak, The Blunderer, like Old Avarice-and-Ambition in *The Examiner*. Mainwaring's representation of Swift as the 'Hero ... in a
Farce of his own making' (472.35-6), *The Satirist Satiriz'd*, is
the great achievement of *The Medley*. 'When Presto begins to prate,
Give him a rap upon the pate.'[4]

As an opposition writer Mainwaring did not enjoy the virtual
immunity from prosecution that Swift enjoyed. Prosecution for

---

[1]Henri Bergson, *Laughter*, trans. Cloudesley Brereton and Fred Rothwell, London, Macmillan, 1911, pp. 87, 112.
[2]Swift, *Journal*, p. 66.
[3][Francis Atterbury?], *To the Wh--s Nineteen Queries, A Fair and Full Answer,
by an Honest Torie; Purely for the Publick Good of his Country*, London, for
J. Baker, 1710, p. 8.
[4]*The Observator*, 29 November—2 December 1710; Swift, *Journal*, p. 218.

libel was always a real danger and Mainwaring's protestations of
innocence are frequently shrill. The decision in *Bushell's Case*
(1670) had established that intent to damage *was not* an essential
criterion of defamation or libel, but intent to publish the docu-
ment with the defamatory meaning alleged by the plaintiff *was*. The
prosecution therefore consisted largely in charging innuendoes.
For example, He was full of the pox (innuendo: the French pox).
The defence lay in proving another, innocent meaning: he had
small-pox.[1] This is why Mainwaring is so nervous about 'the Guilt
of *Meanings* which others find out for [him]' (437.106-7).

Mainwaring ran great risks to make his meaning clear. Swift
testifies to this in one of his few references to *The Medley*. This
is to *The Medley* of 7 May 1711, in which Mainwaring risked saying
that Harley 'had brought [the] Nation under great Difficulties'
(411.109-10). In high dudgeon but not without a grain of grudging
admiration, Swift responds: 'I do not remember to have seen any
Libel, suppos'd to be writ with Caution and double Meaning, in
order to prevent Prosecution, deliver'd under so thin a Cover'
(431.113-16). That Mainwaring was willing to work under so thin a
cover both excited his readers and made sure that he would not be
misunderstood. A good example of this is recorded in a contemporary pamphlet. Mainwaring with seeming irrelevance mentions the
fact that Harley cites 13 Car. II, Stat. I, c. 1 which made it a
capital offence to levy war against Charles II. One anonymous
reader understood the libellous innuendo very clearly:

> who [he asked] ... acknowledg'd Her Majesties Power and Author-
> ity, as declar'd by a Statute in the 12th [*sic*] of *Her Royal
> Uncle*. Whence one may infer, that, that Person [Harley] by
> quoting a Statute made so many Years before the Revolution, is
> a *French* Partizan, and one who denies the validity of all Laws
> since,

in short, a Jacobite.[2]

If he ran great risks, Mainwaring also took great precautions
to avoid prosecution, or if prosecuted to turn off the innuendoes.
It was Addison who said that Thomas Brown was the first 'to omit
only the Vowels of a great Man's Name, and fall most unmercifully

---

[1] W.S. Holdsworth, *Law Quarterly Review*, xl (1924), 312; xli (1925), 20-1.
[2] Oldmixon, *Memoirs*, pp. 11-12; *Cursory but Curious Observations of Mr. Ab-l
R—er, Upon a late Famous Pamphlet, Entituled, Remarks on the Preliminary
Articles Offered by the F. K. in hopes to procure a General Peace*, London, for
John Morphew, 1711, pp. 9-10.

upon all the Consonants'. Mainwaring did the same. He used 'Abbre-
viations, Dashes, or Initial Letters', as well as the 'Allegories,
Similies, Allusions, &c.' that Defoe prescribed. He learned further from Dr James Drake to hide his argument behind 'cunning
Cyphers and Disguises, (yet so as to be understood)'. By evasive
tactics like these Mainwaring succeeded in avoiding prosecution.
'*Harley* was so irritated against the *Medley*, that he ... marked
several Passages in them and gave them to the Attorney-General.
... The Attorney-General [Sir Edward Northey] brought back the
Papers to Mr. *Harley*, and declared nothing could be made of what
was said therein, for the Reflexions were not on particular Persons and Things, and he apprehended the reducing them to Particulars in *Westminster-Hall*, would not only be a forc'd and unparallel'd *Innuendo*, but would bring Matters into Proof which were
better left, as they were, dark and doubtful'.[1]

6. Opposition vs. Establishment

Mainwaring's limitations, self-imposed and unavoidable, and Swift's
advantages are all summed up in Oldmixon's complaint that 'We can't
attack him without affronting the Government' (191.177-8). Swift
knew what he had to do to write 'in Defence of those whom Her
Majesty employs in her greatest Affairs, and of the Causes they are
engaged in',[2] and he did it in 'a Paper writ with plain Sense, and
in a tolerable Stile' (240.47). But the only semblance of a cause
was the cause of peace. And in *The Examiner* Swift could only adum-
brate the propaganda campaign that began with *The Conduct of the
Allies* (November 1711).

Swift refused to 'play the *Whig* and *Tory* Game'. He scorned 'to
advance an Opinion meerly because it is *That* of the Party':

> To enter into a Party as into an Order of *Fryars* with so resigned
> an Obedience to superiors [he said], is very unsuitable both with
> the civil and religious Liberties, we so zealously assert.[3]

But he could not write *The Examiner* without playing the establishment and opposition game. He defended freedom of speech for the
establishment, but not for the opposition (150.161, 195.93-4;

---

[1]*The Spectator*, 14 July 1714; *Review*, 1 June 1710; Boyer, *Annals*, 1706,
p. 175; Oldmixon, *Memoirs*, pp. 11-12.
[2]Swift, *Prose*, viii 14.
[3]Conyers Place, *The Arbitration: or, The Tory and Whig Reconcil'd*, London,
for J. Baker, no date, p. 10; Swift, *Prose*, ii 24.

275.110-276.125). He defended the right of the Church to be established by law (Swift, *Prose*, ii 78-9, 115), but for the dissenters
he could imagine nothing but acquiescence in civil disability:
'what is left', he asked, 'but to be Silent and Passive?' (361.
158-9). The phrase recalls Dryden's longing for 'a passive aptness
in all subjects'.[1] *Annus Mirabilis* (1667) is unabashed establishment propaganda. John Milton, writing opposition propaganda in *A
Readie and Easie Way to Establish a Free Commonwealth* (1660), can
formulate a better aim for government, namely 'to make the people
flourishing, vertuous, noble and high spirited'.[2]

The cause that is defended in *The Examiner* is not one that Harley was engaged in. It is the hopeless cause of the politics of
nostalgia, 'the old Principles in Church and State' (257.44-5, 359.
65-6); 'the old Constitution' (181.72-3, 318.133, 331.80, 343.1),
'the old Course' (441.43-4), 'the old Sentiments' (314.25-6).
Swift's normal sentimentality about the past must have been exacer-
bated by the empirical politics of Harley: 'He was saying ... some
Days ago', Swift wrote to Archbishop King, 'That Wisdom in publick
Affairs, was not what is commonly believed, the forming of Schemes
with remote Views; but the making Use of such Incidents as happen.'
Swift could take no credit for defending this cause. 'Where is the
Merit', he asked, 'or what Opportunity to discover our Wit, our
Courage, or our Learning' (82.24-5) in defending the cause of the
establishment? Swift complained to Stella 'how my Stile is altered
by living & thinking & talking among these People, instead of my
Canal & river walk, and Willows'. 'Wit and learning', he complained
to Lord Peterborough, 'are crumbled into pamphlets and penny-
papers.' Instead of another *Tale of a Tub* Swift wrote *A Short
Character of His Ex. T. E. of W. L. L. I------* and seven penny
papers of doggerel verse.[3] The advantages of the establishment
writer have to be weighed with the cost to the creative writer.

It has been said that Swift jeopardized his career in the Church
by his persistent support of the Test Act.[4] It may also be said

---

[1] *Annus Mirabilis; The Year of Wonders. 1666* (1667), st. cxli.
[2] *The Readie and Easie Way to Establish a Free Commonwealth*, London, by T.N.
for Livewell Chapman, 1660, p. 17.
[3] Swift, *Journal*, p. 556; Swift, *Corr.*, i 238, 211; 'Swift's seventh penny
paper', *The (London) Times Literary Supplement*, No. 3766 (10 May 1974), 506.
[4] W.A. Speck, *The World of Jonathan Swift. Essays for the Tercentenary*, ed.
Brian Vickers, 1968, p. 71.

that he jeopardized his career as an imaginative writer to support
the Harley ministry and the English establishment. I used to think
that the paragraph in *The Examiner* of 29 March 1711 in which Swift
appeals to the gratitude of posterity (332.113-15) to keep alive
the memory of the third Parliament of Great Britain, was very weak.
How could the writer of the Epistle Dedicatory of *A Tale of a Tub*
seriously invoke the gratitude of posterity? Is it inadvertent
irony? Is it a 'Handle' that Mainwaring overlooked? To both questions the answer must be, Yes. And now I begin to see why Swift
felt that he needed the gratitude of posterity. In the end he
came to feel that the whole period of *The Examiner* had been a
waste of time. He summed it up in two lines of *Horace, Lib. 2.
Sat. 6. Part of it imitated* (1714): 'Thus in a Sea of Folly tost,
| My choicest Hours of Life are lost.'

THE text of *The Examiner* has been established from the evidence of the following witnesses:

$\frac{1}{2}°$ *The Examiner* ... London: Printed for John Morphew, 1710-11 (Teerink-Scouten 525). Copies collated: O^a O^b O^c L LU CtY NjP PU TxU CSmH CLU-C.

12° *The Examiners for the Year 1711. To which is prefix'd, A Letter to the* Examiner, London: for John Morphew and A. Dodd, 1712 (Teerink-Scouten 4). Copies collated: CtY CSmH FHE.

38 *Volume V. of the Author's Works. Containing The Conduct of the Allies, and the Examiners*, Dublin: by and for George Faulkner, 1738 (Teerink-Scouten 42, 50). Copies collated: PU.

The shelfmarks of $\frac{1}{2}°O^{abc}$ are Nich. Newsp. 17-18, Hope Folio 17, and c.9.11.Jr. That of L is 627.m.20. The first Burney copy of L (Burney 148b; *not* collated) includes preliminary matter that was published in *Notes & Queries*, 11 August 1855.[1] Some of the notes by a contemporary hand in the Princeton copy, $\frac{1}{2}°$NjP, are included in the annotation of this volume.

The fact that Swift made stop-press corrections in a later *Examiner*—'I was in the City with my Printer to alter an *Examiner'* (Swift, *Journal*, 31 January 1713)—leads one to suppose that he did the same in 1710-11. The supposition is borne out by the evidence of collation. Swift stopped by John Barber's printing house in Queen's Head Alley the night of 24 January 1711 to delete an offending clause in *The Examiner*, No. 26, and again on the night of 9 May 1711 to rewrite the last sentence of No. 41, creating in both cases two states or issues of the first edition. Other variants among different copies of the first edition, amending obvious errors, can safely be attributed to press correctors. These occur in five *Examiners*, Nos. 19, 24, 31, 37, and 46, so there are two issues created by stop-press corrections of seven of the thirty-three folio half-sheet *Examiners*.

Since it was published by John Morphew, 12° must be an authorized

---

[1] The Burney copies were used by William B. Todd in an ingenious study providing bibliographical evidence of successive reprinting and reimpression of *The Examiner*, Nos. 1-9, 17-18 (*The Library*, 5th series, x (1955), 49-54).

edition, but it is not a substantive edition. It corrects dozens
of errors in ½° (inevitably introducing a few new ones) but includes no variants from ½° that could not have been made by a press
corrector. It was set up from a corrected run of the ½° *Examiners*
and published, without Swift's intervention, on 13 March 1712.
Swift's indifference is reflected in the *Journal* of 25 March 1712:
'The last years Examiners', he tells Stella, 'printed together in
a small Volume [in 'a fair Elzevir Letter', according to Morphew's
advertisement] go off but slowly. The Printer over printd himself
by at least a thousand'.[1]

Although 12° is not itself a substantive edition, it is the
archetype of two substantive editions, 38 8° and 38 12°. The impe-
tus for adding a fifth volume to George Faulkner's 1735 edition of
Swift's works probably came from Charles Ford: 'I know no reason
why, at this distance of time,' he wrote to Swift in November 1733,
'the Examiners ... might not be inserted. I doubt you have been
too negligent in keeping copies; but I have them bound up [12°],
and most of them single besides [½°].'[2] The evidence of collation
indicates that in a copy of 12°—presumably Charles Ford's copy—
Swift undertook a perfunctory revision of *The Examiner* Nos. 14-46.
The revised 12° was then restyled by Faulkner's press corrector,
who systematically expanded

tho/altho'/though	to	although
thro'	"	through
till/'till	"	until
'tis	"	it is
'twas	"	it was
t'other	"	the other
has	"	hath
does	"	doth

etc. It is from this hypothetical volume, 12°α, that 38 8° and
38 12° were set up in succession. After the composition of 38 8°,
12°α must have been subjected to further authorial revision and
further attention by a press corrector. On any other assumption

---

[1]Swift, *Journal*, pp. 523-4. Morphew may have had a premonition of this, for
he published 12° in partnership with A. Dodd.
[2]Swift, *Corr.*, iv 202. Swift was not so negligent of *The Examiner* as Ford
supposed. He gave a set to Jemmy Leigh to carry to Ireland in November 1711
(Swift, *Journal*, p. 402).

it would be difficult to account for the substantive and accidental variants between 38 8° and 38 12°.

   In the following schema, substantive editions appear in bold-
face:

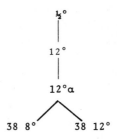

The text of *The Examiner* has been established on the following
principles:

   1. Since the objective was to produce the text intended by
author and printer in 1710-11, all errors in substantives and
accidentals that were corrected in 12° have been incorporated
into the copy-text, ½°CLU-C. After this had been done, only four
editorial emendations were required.

   2. None of the stylistic revisions made in 38 8° 12° has been
adopted.

   3. Seventeenth- and eighteenth-century spellings in the copy-
text have been retained where authority for them can be found in
OED—thus 'Doner' (53.96) was retained but not '*Nonjurers*' (184.
157).

   4. Hundreds of accidental variants created by Faulkner's in-
domitable press corrector and included in the list above have not
been included in the textual notes.

   5. Otherwise all emendations of the copy-text, substantive and
accidental, are recorded in the textual notes.

   The text of *The Medley* has been established from the evidence
of the following witnesses:

½° *The Medley* ... London, Printed and Sold by A. Baldwin, 1710-
    11. Copies collated: O L IU^a IU^b TxU.

12° *The Medleys for the Year 1711. To which are prefix'd, The
    Five Whig*-Examiners, London, Printed by J. Darby, and Sold by
    Egbert Sanger, 1712. Copies collated: IU TxU FHE.

89 *The Lover and Reader: To which are prefixed The Whig-Examiner,*
    and a Selection from The Medley, of Papers written by the
    Principal Authors of The Tatler, Spectator, and Guardian,
    London, Printed by and for John Nichols, 1789. Copies col-
    lated: IU TxU.

The shelfmarks of ½°IU^{ab} are q NICKELL x329.942M46 and x329.
942M46, respectively. 12° is gathered in 12s, but the chain-lines
are vertical and the format may be 24mo. But, as McKerrow said,
'Into the question of 24mo. I cannot enter.'

Authorship of the *Medleys* included in this volume has been
divided between Mainwaring and Oldmixon mainly on the evidence of
Oldmixon's attributions in *The Life and Posthumous Works of Arthur
Maynwaring, Esq;,* pp. 172-98. On this evidence Mainwaring wrote
seventeen of the thirty-three essays himself, collaborated with
Oldmixon on eleven, with Steele on one, and Oldmixon wrote four.
Oldmixon's contribution to some of the collaborations may have
been slight.[1] Even in March and April, when he was too ill to
write, Mainwaring still managed to provide 'Hints for those Papers
he did not write' (Oldmixon, *The Life*, p. 201).

For six of the thirty-three *Medleys* in this volume there are two
issues of the first or folio half-sheet edition: Nos. 6, 7, 18,
21, 29, 31. It can safely be assumed that these resulted from
stop-press corrections, but it need not be assumed that they are
authorial. It is difficult to imagine Mainwaring interrupting the
press run to make the dubious 'corrections' in Nos. 6 and 7 (11.19,
14.82, 26.4). And even the decision not to call Sacheverell 'an
Anabaptist Tory' (372.216) may have been made by an Anabaptist
pressman in Ann Baldwin's shop.

The strain of writing even 2,000 words a week is attested by
both writers. Swift expresses it openly: 'I Begin to be heartily
weary of my Employment as *Examiner* (328.1) ... I know not whether
I shall have any Appetite to continue this Work much longer (432.
143-4).' Mainwaring simply writes less. This is reflected in the

---

[1] Oldmixon says his contribution to No. 9, 27 November 1710, was only 'some
pleasant Notes' upon the ridiculous acrostic upon Harley. But to these notes,
he says, Mainwaring 'made some Additions and Alterations'. In the case of No.
25, 19 March 1711, Oldmixon says Mainwaring wrote 'only that Part ... which
relates to *Guiscard*', but this is the whole essay after the first paragraph
(Oldmixon, *The Life*, pp. 178, 193). For these reasons I have interpreted Oldmixon's 'almost all' and 'for the most part' as the work of Mainwaring.

larger type sizes used in the later numbers of *The Medley*. Nos.
6-29 are printed in a 10-point type called long primer in the
eighteenth century.[1] For Nos. 30-1 an 11-point type, called small
pica, was used. Nos. 32-3 revert to long primer, but Nos. 34-8 are
set in a 12-point type called pica. This enabled Mainwaring to
fill both sides of a folio half-sheet with 1,600 words.

Mainwaring intended that the entire profit of 12° should go to
Oldmixon. He planned an edition 'in great and small Paper' of
which 500 copies on 'Imperial Paper' were to have been sold by
subscription at two guineas. This Oldmixon 'look'd on as a handsome Gratuity, and such an Edition', as he says, 'I accordingly
prepar'd'.[2]

It might be inferred from this that Oldmixon was responsible for
the very extensive rewriting that appears in some of the duodecimo
Medleys. But such may not be the case. It was Mainwaring whom Dryden called upon to read Congreve's first play, *The Old Bachelor*
(1693); it was Mainwaring to whom William Walsh brought *The Golden
Age Restor'd* (1703) to be 'corrected and improv'd', and it was Mainwaring who 'altered and amended' Francis Hare's four letters on
The Management of the War 'so much, that they might, indeed, have
well past for his own'.[3] So it is unlikely, indeed inconceivable,
that John Oldmixon would have ventured to rewrite for the duodecimo edition Mainwaring's *Medley*s Nos. 10 and 31. And if it was
Mainwaring who rewrote his own essays, the simplest assumption is
that it was also Mainwaring who 'altered and amended' three of
Oldmixon's *Medley*s (Nos. 27, 28, and 29) 'so much, that they might,
indeed, have well past for his own', and that it was 'Mr. *Manwaring*' who prepared the copy for the duodecimo edition.

The volume was published, not by Ann Baldwin, but by Egbert
Sanger, at the end of March 1712. Swift's guess that *The Medley*

---

[1] It is possible to be certain on this point because the long primer in Ann
Baldwin's shop is identical with the long primer type specimen in James Watson, *The History of the Art of Printing*, Edinburgh, 1713, p. xl. Ann Baldwin's
11-point type is smaller than Watson's pica (p. xxxviii), so I have called it
small pica, but in design it is much closer to Watson's long primer than to
Watson's pica. All these types were probably Dutch and it is interesting to
observe that the capital A in the long primer is notched in the manner that
became characteristic of William Caslon's designs.

[2] Oldmixon, *Memoirs*, pp. 13-14.

[3] BL MS Add. 4221, f. 341, quoted in Hugh Macdonald, *John Dryden: A Bibliography*, Oxford, 1939, p. 54n.; Oldmixon, *The Life*, p. 21; Oldmixon, *Memoirs*,
p. 20.

in duodecimo 'perhaps may sell better' than *The Examiner* in duodecimo was proved right in 1714 when the duodecimo Medley achieved
a second edition (of which there are copies in The British Library
and Williams College Library). The edition called the third on the
title-page is simply unsold copies of the second edition with a
new title-page.

But Oldmixon failed to realize his 'handsome Gratuity'. At the
very moment that 500 large-paper copies were ready for delivery
to White's Chocolate-house, whence they were to be forwarded to
subscribers,

> a Rumour [was] maliciously and industriously spread by the Sup-
> porters of *The Examiner*, that the Subscription was for Mr. *Man-*
> *waring*'s own Use, which so shocked him, that he would not hear
> it named afterwards, nor indeed would I press it, whereby my
> Hopes of the Subscription were stifled, and the whole Impression
> I was to make what I could of, and was oblig'd to sell the large
> Paper Books at the same Price as the small (Oldmixon, *Memoirs*,
> p. 14).[1]

Since 1714 *The Medley* has not been reprinted, although two and
a half *Medleys*, Nos. 23, half of 32, and 38, were included in John
Nichols's edition of Steele's *The Lover* and *The Reader*. This edition has, of course, no authority but 89 is included in a number
of textual notes to indicate that Nichols correctly took $\frac{1}{2}°$ as his
copy-text.

The copy-text for the present edition, $\frac{1}{2}°O$, has been emended
according to the following principles:

1. Since the objective was to produce the text intended by
author and printer to be published in 1710-11, all errors in substantives and accidentals that were corrected in 12° have been
incorporated into the copy-text.

2. For the same reason none of the stylistic revisions made in
12° have been adopted.

3. Seventeenth- and eighteenth-century spellings have been retained where authority for them can be found in *OED*, viz. 'timerous' (110.182). Otherwise, the spelling has been normalized.

---

[1] The format of the large-paper edition (of which there are copies in The
British Library, Columbia, The Library Company of Philadelphia, Indiana, and
The Huntington Library) is not 12° but 8°: A^8a-b^8d^2 B-2H^{8}2I^6. And the size of
the sheet (approximately $20\frac{1}{2}$" × $16\frac{1}{2}$") is not now called Imperial (26" × 21"
to 36" × 24") but Half Imperial ($21\frac{1}{2}$" × $14\frac{1}{4}$" to $23\frac{1}{2}$" × $16\frac{1}{2}$") (E.J. Labarre,
Dictionary and Encyclopaedia of Paper and Paper-making, 2nd edn., London,
Oxford University Press, 1952, p. 130).

4. All emendations of the copy-text, in accidentals as well as in substantives, are recorded in the textual notes.

Numbering of The Examiners. In every edition since the first Swift's *Examiners* have been misnumbered. 'The wrong numbering arose from Mr. Barber's having omitted the original No. 13 (a paper on *Non-Resistance*), when he first collected the Examiners into a Volume.'[1] *The Examiner*, No. 13, was Atterbury's 'violent defence of the doctrine of hereditary right, in its most absurd extent' (p. xxv above), which the printer, John Barber, for reasons unknown, failed to include in the duodecimo edition. In the present edition the numbering of the first edition is restored.

[1]Nichols, *Literary Anecdotes*, ii 156n.

The EXAMINER.

Longa est Injuria, longæ
Ambages, sed summa sequar fastigia rerum.

IT is a Practice I have generally follow'd, to converse in equal
Freedom with the deserving Men of both Parties; and it was never
without some Contempt, that I have observ'd Persons wholly out
of Employment, affect to do otherwise: I doubted whether any Man
could owe so much to the side he was of, though he were retain'd   5
by it; but without some great point of Interest, either in Possession or Prospect, I thought it was the Mark of a low and narrow Spirit.

'Tis hard, that for some Weeks past, I have been forc'd in my
own Defence, to follow a Proceeding that I have so much con-   10
demn'd in others. But several of my Acquaintance among the
declining Party, are grown so insufferably Peevish and Splenatick, profess such violent Apprehensions for the Publick, and
represent the State of Things in such formidable Idea's, that I
find my self dispos'd to share in their Afflictions, though I   15
know them to be groundless and imaginary, or, which is worse,

5 though] altho' 38 8°   although 38 12°   9 'Tis] It is 38 8°   IT is
38 12°   12-13 Splenatick] Splenetick 38 12°

Motto Virgil, *Aeneid*, i 341-2: The Tale is intricate, perplex'd, and long,
Hear then, in short, the Story of her Wrong. The translations of the epigraphs
appeared first in Faulkner's 1760 edition of *The Works of Jonathan Swift*
(Teerink-Scouten 51A).
  2 *both Parties*: For an Irish parson worth £200 a year, Swift's acquaintance
with the great of both parties was indeed remarkable. *A Discourse of the Contests and Dissentions* (1701) gained him the acquaintance of Somers, Halifax,
and Burnet in 1702, but it was *A Tale of a Tub* (1704) that kept up the interest. 'If it had not been for that,' he told Stella, 'I should never have been
able to get the access I have had.' By 1708 he could boast, 'I converse in full
Freedom with many considerable Men of both Parties' (*Prose*, viii 119; *Journal*,
p. 47; *Prose*, ii 2).
  12-13 *Peevish and Splenatick*: Upon returning to London in September 1710,
Swift found Godolphin 'over-run with Spleen and Peevishness' and Steele 'very
low'. Even when Swift disclosed his plan to save Steele's employment in the
stamped paper office, Addison seemed negative and suspicious and they 'parted
very dryly' (Swift, *Corr.*, i 173; *Journal*, pp. 46, 67-8).

purely affected. To offer them Comfort one by one, would be not
only an endless, but a disobliging Task. Some of them, I am convinc'd wou'd be less Melancholy, if there were more Occasion. I
20   shall therefore, instead of hearkning to further Complaints, employ some part of this Paper for the future, in letting such Men
see, that their natural or acquir'd Fears are ill-grounded, and
their artificial ones as ill-intended. That all our present Inconveniencies, are the Consequence of the very Counsels they so
25   much admire, which wou'd still have encreas'd, if those had continu'd: And that neither our Constitution in Church or State,
could probably have been long preserv'd, without such Methods
as have been lately taken.
      THE late Revolutions at Court (Fig. III), have given room to
30   some specious Objections, which I have heard repeated by well-
meaning Men, just as they had taken them up on the Credit of
others, who have worse Designs. They wonder the Queen wou'd chuse
to change Her Ministry at this Juncture, and thereby give Uneasiness to a General who has been so long successful abroad; and
35   might think himself Injur'd, if the entire Ministry were not of
his own Nomination. That there were few Complaints of any Consequence against the late Men in Power, and none at all in Parlia-

24 Counsels] Councils ½°   28 lately] already 38 8°+12°

---

27 *Methods*: Ridpath pretends not to 'understand his meaning when he says,
without such Methods &c.' (*The Observator*, 1-4 November 1710), but these words
introduce a major propaganda theme: the change of ministry was necessary to
preserve the constitution.
      29 *Revolutions*: Shrewsbury replaced Kent as Lord Chamberlain on 13-14 April
1710. Dartmouth replaced Sunderland as Secretary of State (southern) on 15
June. Poulett nominally replaced Godolphin on 11 August, but Harley, as Chancellor of the Exchequer, assumed management of the Treasury. On 21 September
Rochester replaced Somers as Lord President of the council, St. John replaced
Boyle as Secretary of State (northern), and the Queen dissolved Parliament and
ordered a general election. Sir John Leake replaced Orford at the admiralty
board on 4 October. Harcourt replaced Cowper as Lord Keeper on 19 October. And
finally, on 26 October Ormond replaced Wharton as Lord-Lieutenant of Ireland.
Except Shrewsbury all of the new leaders were Tories, but Harley retained in
office many Whigs (including Marlborough and Newcastle), for his objective was
a ministry that would exclude neither party, 'a motley comprehensive administration', as Swift called it (*Prose*, viii 124).
      34 *General*: This opens what must have been intended simply as a warning to
Marlborough to curb his demands for patronage, for as late as 29 December 1710
Harley hoped to win Marlborough's support for his administration (HMC *Portland
MSS*, ii 224). George Ridpath, however, found this 'a terrible Charge'. 'It
looks like the beginning of a very heavy Impeachment,' he said (*The Observator*,
1-4 November 1710).

A True
LIST

Of the NAMES of those that are turn'd out at C----t, and of those that are put in their Places.

ROom, Room, I say, make Room and out; get you out, you phanatical Low-Church Party; who upon the Account of a good Post or Place of Preferment, can occasional Conform for your own Interest, not out of any true Principal to support the old *English* Constitution; but like Sharks, can fish in any troubled Waters, to the utter Destruction of our antient Hereditary Right of *Great Britain*, and the Church of *England* as by Law Established; to prevent which, our most gracious S―――n, has by the Advice of her C――l, taken that effectual Care, that she finds it necessary for her own Support, and the Churches true interest, to turn out, and put in, the Persons hereafter mentioned, *viz.*

The 6th of *June* 1710 On *Sunday* Night her Majesty was graciously pleased to confer the Honour of Knighthood on *William Oldes*, Esq; and at the same time he was made Gentleman-Usher of the Black Rod, in the Room of Sir *David Mitchell* lately deceased.

The 15th of *June*, Yesterday the Right Honourable the Earl of *Sunderland* resigned his Place, as one of her Majesty's principal Secretary of State.

The 22d of *June*, Yesterday the Right Honourable the Lord *Darthmouth*, being appointed one of her Majesty's principal Secretaries of State, came this Day, being the first time he came to his Office, at the *Cock Pit* at *White Hall*.

The 29th of *June*, The Earl of *Potemore* is appointed to command her Majesties Forces in *Portugal*, in the Room of the Earl of *Galloway*.

The 6th of *July*, Doctor *Laurence Broderick*, Chaplain to the Honourable the House of Commons, is made one of the Prebends of *Westminster-Abby*, in the Room of the Reverend Doctor *Burch*, lately deceased.

The 11th of *July*, The Right Honourable the Earl of *Anglesey*, is made Pay-Master of her Majesty's Forces in *Ireland*, in the Room of my Lord *Cunningsby*.

The 13th of *July*. *James Cressel*, Esq; was appointed Envoy Extraordinary to the Elector of *Hannover*, and to the Duke of *Wolfembustle*.

The 15th of *July*, *Clement Cottrell*, Esq; Son to the late Sir *Charles Cottrell*, was sworn Master of the Ceremonies, in the Room of his Father deceased.

The 18th of *July*. Collonel *Corbet* is now made Governour of *Mary-Land*, according to her most Excellent Majesty's appointment.

The 25th *Ditto*, The Earl of *Portland* was made Captain of her Majesties first Troop of Guards, in the Room of the Earl of *Albermarle*.

The 27th *Ditto*, We have an Account from *Oxford*, that Sir *Simon Harcourt*, and several other Gentlemen, are made Justices of the Peace for the said County.

The 3d of *August*, The Queen has been graciously pleased to constitute Collonel *Francis Gore*, a Brigadier General of her Majesty's Forces.

Ditto, We are informed that *Adam Coburne*, Esq; has resigned his Place of Chief Justice's Clerk in *Scotland*, and that the Right Honourable the Earl of *Marr's* Brother succeeds him in that Post

The 10th of *August*, On *Thursday* last the Right Honourable the Earl of *Godolphin*, resigned his Place of Lord High Treasurer of *Great-Britain*.

Ditto, And that Mr *Smith*, Chancellor of the Exchequor, and under Treasurer, has resigned those Places, and we hear that the Right Honourable, *Robert Harley* Esq; succeeds him in the same.

Ditto, 'Tis likewise said, that the Lord C―――r of G――t B――n, who is also will also resign the same.

Ditto, A Commission is passing the Seals, appointing the Lord *Archibald Hamilton*, Governor of *Jamaica*, and *Robert Lowther* Esq; Governor of *Barbadoes*.

The 12th of *August*, Her Majesty has appointed the Earl of *Rivers* her Envoy Extraordinary to the Court of *Hannover*, in the Room of *James Cressel* Esq; deceased.

Ditto, A Commission is passing the Seals, appointing the Right Honourable *Robert Harley* Esq; to be Chancellor of the Exchequor, and under Treasurer.

Ditto, Her Majesty has been pleased to appoint the Right Honourable the Earl of *Pawlet*, the Right Honourable *Robert Harley* Esq; the Right Honourable *Henry Pagit* Esq; Sir *Thomas Mansell* Barronett, and *Robert Benson* Esq; Commissioners for executing the Office of Lord High-Treasurer of *Great-Britain*, in the Room of the Lord *Godolphin*.

'Tis also confidently reported, that Sir *Symon Harcourt*, Justice *Powell*, and Baron *Price*, are to be appointed Lords Commissioners of the C―――y of G――t B――r, in the Room of the L―d H―h C―――r.

LONDON: Printed for *J. Smith*, near *Fleet-street*. 1710.

A True List of the Names of those that are turn'd out at C---t, and of those that are put into their Places . . . London, for J. Smith, 1710, folio halfsheet

ment; which on the contrary, pass'd Votes in favour of the chief
Minister. That if Her Majesty had a mind to introduce the other
Party, it wou'd have been more seasonable after a Peace, which   40
now we have made desperate, by Spiriting the *French*, who rejoice
at these Changes, and by the fall of our Credit, which unqualifies
us for continuing the War. That the Parliament so untimely dissolv'd, had been diligent in their Supplies, and dutiful in their
Behaviour. That one Consequence of these Changes appears already   45
in the fall of the Stocks: That we may soon expect more and worse:
And lastly, that all this naturally tends to break the Settlement
of the Crown, and call over the *Pretender*.

These and the like Notions are plentifully scatter'd abroad,
by the Malice of a ruin'd Party, to render the Queen and Her   50
Administration odious, and to inflame the Nation. And these are
what, upon Occasion, I shall endeavour to overthrow, by discovering the Falshood and Absurdity of them.

It is a great Unhappiness, when in a Government Constituted
like ours, it should be so brought about, that the continuance   55
of a War, must be for the Interest of vast Numbers (Peaceable
as well as Military) who would otherwise have been unknown as
their Original. I think our present Condition of Affairs, is admirably describ'd by two Verses in *Lucan*,

56 Peaceable] Civil 38 8°+12°   57 would otherwise] otherwise would 38
8°+12°

---

38 *Votes*: This was the session of Parliament (November 1709—April 1710)
that voted record-breaking supplies of £6,726,555 and the impeachment of Henry
Sacheverell, at Godolphin's insistence (Swift, *Prose*, viii 115).

42 *the fall of ... Credit*: 'The most artful Method by which the late Ministry endeavour'd to support their tottering Power, was by suggesting and
propagating the Notion, that the Credit of the Nation wholly depended upon
the Lord Treasurer' (Boyer, *Annals*, 1711, p. 231). On 3 August 1710 the Bank
of England tried to precipitate a financial crisis and save Godolphin from
dismissal by refusing to lend money to the Government 'by reason of the sinking of credit' (*HLQ*, iii (1939-40), 228).

46 *Stocks*: Between mid April and November 1710 rumours of a dissolution of
Parliament and the uncertainties attendant upon Harley's new appointments
caused losses of 'full Three Millions in the Article of Stocks'. Bank stock
fell from 121 to 99, United East India Company from 136¼ to 113¾, and Million
Bank from 76 to 68 (Charles Davenant, *Sir Thomas Double at Court, and in High
Preferments*, London, for J. Morphew, 1710, p. 84; *The British Mercury*, 12-14
April 1710, 30 October—1 November 1710).

59 *Lucan*: *The Civil War*, i 181: [From bribery and corruption] came devour-
ing usury and interest that looks greedily to the day of payment; credit was
shattered, and many found their profit in war (trans. J.D. Duff).

60
Hinc usura Vorax, avidumq; in tempore fœnus,
Hinc concussa fides, & multis utile bellum.

which without any great Force upon the Words, may be thus translated,

Hence are deriv'd those Exorbitant Interests and Annuities;
65   *hence those large Discounts for Advances and prompt Payment;*
hence Publick Credit is shaken, and hence great Numbers find
their Profit in prolonging the War.

'Tis odd, that among a free Trading People, as we take our
selves to be, there shou'd so many be found to close in with
70   those Counsels, who have been ever averse from all Overtures towards a Peace. But yet there is no great Mystery in the Matter.
Let any Man observe the Equipages in this Town; he shall find
the greater number of those who make a Figure, to be a Species
of Men quite different from any that were ever known before the
75   Revolution, consisting either of Generals and Colonels, or of
such whose whole Fortunes lie in Funds and Stocks: So that *Power*,

---

68-9 take our selves to be] call ourselves 38 8°   call our selves 38 12°
70 Counsels] Councils ½°

---

64 *Interests and Annuities*: To encourage loans to the Government, Godolphin offered premiums and discounts and paid unheard-of interest rates, 'such
as 14 *per Cent. per Annum* upon Annuities ... [and] 7 *per Cent.* upon Exchequer
Bills' (Defoe, *An Essay upon Loans*, London, 1710, p. 9).

72 *Equipages*: This was a common complaint: 'how many make a good Figure,
keep a Coach and a Miss, who not long since were Men of nothing' (Guy Miège,
The Present State of Great Britain, London, by J.H. for J. Nicholson *et al.*,
1707, pp. 142-3).

76 *Funds*: The funds, short for 'publick Funds of Interest', were created in
the 1690s when taxes on leather, malt, etc., instead of being applied to current Government expenses, were used to pay high returns on perpetual and
ninety-nine-year annuities. This *'Dutch'* practice, as Swift scornfully and
correctly called it, enabled Godolphin to finance wars with France by deferring payment even into the nineteenth century. This was done, as Defoe explained, 'by Establishing Annual Receipts of limited or perpetual Interests
for such Summs, as might be borrowed upon the Credit of the Nation, the Principal to sink in the Hands of the Publick. These were call'd FUNDS.' Deficits
in the funds, when the tax revenue was insufficient to cover payments on the
annuities, created the first national debt, which reached £5,143,459 by 1697
(Swift, *Prose*, vii 68-9; Dickson, pp. 46-62, 354; Defoe, *An Essay upon Loans*,
London, 1710, p. 9). As in the phrase 'Fortunes ... in Funds', the term was
also beginning to assume its twentieth-century meaning, 'Government obligations as a medium of investment'. A complete list of funds in this sense is
included in *Publick Securities: Or, The Parliamentary Fund Established for
Paying the Annuities, or other Interests granted to Private Persons or Commu-
nities for Moneys at several times advanc'd the Publick Service*, London, for
Timothy Childe, 1712.

which according to the old Maxim, was us'd to follow *Land*, is now
gone over to *Money*; and the Country Gentleman is in the Condition
of a young Heir, out of whose Estate a Scrivener receives half
the Rents for Interest, and hath a Mortgage on the whole, and is   80
therefore always ready to feed his Vices and Extravagancies
while there is any Thing left. So that if the War continues some
Years longer, a Landed Man will be little better than a Farmer at
a rack Rent, to the Army, and to the publick Funds.

It may perhaps be worth inquiring from what Beginnings, and by   85
what Steps we have been brought into this desperate Condition:
And in search of this, we must run up as high as the Revolution.

Most of the Nobility and Gentry who invited over the Prince of
Orange, or attended him in his Expedition, were true Lovers of
their Country and its Constitution, in Church and State; and were   90
brought to yield to those Breaches in the Succession of the Crown,
out of a regard to the Necessity of the Kingdom, and the Safety

82 continues] continue 38 8°+12°

---

78 *Money*: Since there were no taxes on dividends or interest, but a twenty
per cent per annum tax on land, the creditors of the Government were easily
perceived as the mortagees of the kingdom: 'every new Summ that was lent [to
the Government by the "Money'd Men"], took away as much Power from the Landed
Men, as it added to theirs' (Swift, *Prose*, vii 70). Apart from the most successful general and the most successful physician of the day, Marlborough and
Dr John Radcliffe, who loaned Mainwaring £4,000 to £5,000 on a bankrupt estate,
these 'Friends to the Government at Thirty *per Cent*.' included a large minority
of Jews and recent Dutch and French immigrants. The coming into existence of
a 'cosmopolitan mercantile plutocracy', therefore, created an economic, eth-
nic, and geographic schism in English society (Oldmixon, *The Life*, p. 347;
Anthony Hammond, *Considerations upon Corrupt Elections of Members to Serve in
Parliament*, London, 1701, p. 4; Dickson, pp. 262-7, 278-81).
92 *Necessity*: Filmer had argued that 'no Necessity' could justify a breach
of the natural law of primogeniture. But the law of primogeniture had been
breached in December 1689 in the Bill of Rights which excluded from the succession James Francis Edward, the infant son of James II. So Locke agreed that
'Children ... have a Right of Inheritance to their Fathers Property ... But
Government being for the benefit of the Governed ... cannot be inherited by
the same Title ... If the Agreement and consent of Men first gave a Scepter
into any ones hand, or put a Crown on his Head, that also must direct its
descent and conveyance' (*Two Treatises of Government*, London, for Awnsham and
John Churchill, 1698, vol. i, §§ 93-4). And Swift concurred. As a High Churchman Swift is intent here upon stating his belief in the revolution principle
very carefully and in terms not very different from those of the deist Matthew
Tindal, who had said 'upon extraordinary occasions, it will always be lawful
to break thro the ordinary Rules ... [which] cou'd have no other reason for
their Institution, than the common Safety, that Supreme Law of Nature and
Nations' (*The Jacobitism, Perjury, and Popery of High-Church Priests*, London,
for J. Baker, 1710, p. 6).

of the People, which did, and could only, make them lawful; but
without Intention of drawing such a Practice into Precedent, or
95 making it a standing Measure by which to proceed in all times to
come; and therefore we find their Counsels ever tended to keep
Things as much as possible in the old Course. But soon after, an
under Sett of Men, who had nothing to lose, and had neither born
the burthen nor heat of the Day, found means to whisper in the
100 King's Ear, that the Principles of Loyalty in the Church of *England*, were wholly inconsistent with the *Revolution*. Hence began
the early Practice of caressing the Dissenters, reviling the Universities, as Maintainers of Arbitrary Power, and reproaching the
Clergy with the Doctrines of Divine-Right, Passive-Obedience and
105 Non-Resistance. At the same time, in order to fasten wealthy
People to the New Government, they propos'd those pernicious Expedients of borrowing Money by vast *Premiums*, and at exorbitant
Interest: A Practice as old as *Eumenes*, one of *Alexander*'s Cap-
tains, who setting up for himself after the Death of his Master,
110 persuaded his principal Officers to lend him great Sums, after
which they were forc'd to follow him for their own Security.

    96 Counsels] Councils ½°   98 under Sett] underset ½° 12°   under set
    38 12°

---

    98 *Sett*: 'a Set of Upstarts, who had little or no part in the *Revolution*,
but valued themselves by their Noise and pretended Zeal when the Work was
over, were got into Credit at Court, by the Merit of becoming Undertakers and
Projectors of Loans and Funds: These, finding that the Gentlemen of Estates
were not willing to come into their Measures, fell upon those new Schemes of
raising Mony, in order to create a Mony'd-Interest, that might in time vie
with the Landed, and of which they hoped to be at the Head' (Swift, *Prose*,
vi 10). More particularly the reference is to Godolphin and Halifax, who,
between them (with short intervals), managed the Treasury from November 1690
to August 1710 and conferred upon mankind the benefits of an infinitely ex-
pansible national debt and an easily inflatable paper currency.
    98-9 *born ... Day*: Matt. 20:12.
    107 *Premiums*: In 1691-3 the Treasury had to pay an additional interest or
premium of two per cent to induce lenders to make short-term loans at six per
cent (Dickson, p. 343).
    108 *Eumenes*: Plutarch, *Life of Eumenes*, xiii 6; cf. 'the Designs then on
Foot: ... *Run into Debt, and create remote Funds, 'twill engage the People to
you*' (Davenant, *New Dialogues upon the present Posture of Affairs*, London,
for J. Morphew, 1710, p. 67; 'the true Reason for [borrowing Millions upon
Funds of Interest], was the Security of a new Prince, not firmly settled on
the Throne; People were tempted to lend, by great Premiums and large Interest,
and it concerned them nearly to preserve that Government, which they trusted
with their Money' (Swift, *Prose*, vi 10).

This introduced a Number of new dextrous Men into Business and
Credit: It was argued, that the War could not last above two or
three Campaigns, and that it was easier for the Subject to raise
a Fund for paying Interest, than to tax them annually to the full   115
Expence of the War. Several Persons who had small or encumber'd
Estates, sold them, and turn'd their Money into those Funds to
great Advantage: Merchants, as well as other monyed Men, finding
Trade was dangerous, pursued the same Method: But the War continuing, and growing more expensive, Taxes were encreased, and   120
Funds multiplied every Year, till they have arrived at the monstrous height we now behold them. And that which was at first a
Corruption, is at last grown necessary, and what every good Subject must now fall in with, tho' he may be allowed to wish it
might soon have an End; because it is with a Kingdom, as with a   125
private Fortune, where every new Incumbrance adds a double
weight. By this means the Wealth of the Nation, that used to be
reckoned by the Value of Land, is now computed by the Rise and
Fall of Stocks: And altho' the Foundation of Credit be still the
same, and upon a Bottom that can never be shaken; and though all   130
Interest be duly paid by the Publick, yet through the Contrivance
and Cunning of *Stock-jobbers*, there has been brought in such a
Complication of Knavery and Couzenage, such a Mystery of Iniquity,

127 the Nation] a Nation 38 8°+12°

---

112 *new dextrous Men*: These included Thomas Neale, promoter of state lot-
teries, William Paterson, projector of tontine loans and the Bank of England,
Sir John Foch, perpetrator of the poll tax, and Mordecai Abbott, originator
of exchequer bills (Dickson, p. 52).

116 *Several Persons*: Davenant says that those who 'sold ... Mannors to buy
into the Funds' were 'few' (*Sir Thomas Double at Court, and in High Preferments*, 1710, p. 93).

121-2 *monstrous height*: Harley's brother Edward, auditor of the imprests
(together with Mainwaring), describes Harley's prospect: 'When he came into
the Treasury he found the Exchequer almost empty, nothing left for the subsistence of the Army, but some tallies upon the third general mortgage of the
customs; the Queen's civil list near 700,000*l*. in debt; the funds all exhausted, and a debt of 9,500,000*l*., without any provision of Parliament;
which had brought all the credit of the Government to a vast discount ... Besides these difficulties, the Bank, stock jobbers, and moneyed men of the city
were all engaged to sink the credit of the Government, which they did so effectually that Navy bills and others were sold at forty and forty-five per
cent. discount' (HMC *Portland MSS*, v 650).

123-4 *every good Subject*: Swift urged Stella to buy Bank stock on 26 October when it had fallen thirty per cent and on 13 November he himself bought
Bank stock on margin at £93 a share (*Journal*, pp. 74, 135).

and such an unintelligible Jargon of Terms to involve it in, as
135 were never known in any other Age or Country of the World. I have
heard it affirmed by Persons skill'd in these Calculations, that
if the Funds appropriated to the Payment of Interest and Annuities, were added to the Yearly Taxes, and the Four-Shilling Aid
strictly exacted in all Counties of the Kingdom, it would very
140 near, if not fully, supply the Occasions of the War, at least
such a Part, as in the Opinion of very able Persons, had been at
that time Prudence not to exceed. For I make it a Question,
whether any wise Prince or State, in the Continuance of a War,
which was not purely Defensive, or immediately at his own Door,
145 did ever propose that his Expence should perpetually exceed what
he was able to impose annually upon his Subjects? Neither if the
War lasts many Years longer, do I see how the next Generation
will be able to begin another, which in the Course of Human Affairs, and according to the various Interests and Ambition of
150 Princes, may be as necessary for them as it has been for us. And
had our Fathers left us as deeply involved as we are like to
leave our Children, I appeal to any Man, what sort of Figure we
should have been able to make these twenty Years past. Besides,
neither our Enemies, nor Allies, are upon the same Foot with us
155 in this Particular. *France* and *Holland*, our nearest Neighbours,
and the farthest engaged, will much sooner recover themselves

142 Prudence] prudent 38 8°+12°   147 lasts] last 38 8°   151 had our
Fathers] if our Fathers had 38 8°+12°

---

134 *unintelligible Jargon*: This is the country gentleman's disdain for
trade. Swift understood the jargon, but his pretence that he does not begins
to create the *ingénu* role of the Examiner. It also reflects the Tory's suspicion of words. Swift's predecessor-Examiner complains of 'the *fallacy* and
emptiness of *popular Phrases*' and 'this unaccountable *Witchcraft* of *Words*'
(*The Examiner*, 21 September 1710).
137-42 *if ... exceed*: Swift seems to be quoting Harley, either directly,
or indirectly through *Faults on both Sides*, which was written 'under the
direction of Mr. *Harley*' (*Faults on both Sides*, 2nd edn., London, 1710, p. 19;
Burnet, 1833, vi 14n.).
137-8 *Annuities*: Godolphin floated the first, a life annuity paying fourteen per cent a year, in 1693. From 1704 to 1708 he raised £8,191,427 through
the sale of ninety-nine-year annuities paying between six and seven per cent
a year (Dickson, pp. 53, 59-62).
138 *Four-Shilling Aid*: This was the land tax, assessed at the rate of
four shillings per pound on an assessment made in 1660-1. It yielded
£1,900,000 a year and was the Treasury's principal resource.
155-6 *France ... will much sooner recover*: Defoe repeats this argument in
the *Review*, 8 February 1711.

after a War. The first, by the absolute Power of the Prince, who
being Master of the Lives and Fortunes of his Subjects, will
quickly find Expedients to pay his Debts: And so will the other,
by their prudent Administration, the Greatness of their Trade,   160
their wonderful Parsimony, the Willingness of their People to
undergo all kind of Taxes, and their Justice in applotting as
well as collecting them. But above all, we are to consider that
France and Holland fight in the Continent, either upon, or near
their own Territories, and the greatest part of the Money circu-   165
lates among themselves; whereas ours crosses the Sea either to
Flanders, Spain, or Portugal, and every Penny of it, whether in
Specie or Returns, is so much lost to the Nation for ever.

   Upon these Considerations alone, it was the most prudent Course
imaginable in the Queen, to lay hold of the Disposition of the   170
People for changing the Parliament and Ministry at this Juncture,
and extricating Her self, as soon as possible, out of the Pupil-
age of those who found their Accounts only in perpetuating the
War. Neither have we the least Reason to doubt, but the ensuing
Parliament will assist Her Majesty with the utmost Vigor, till   175
Her Enemies again be brought to sue for Peace, and again offer
such Terms as will make it both honourable and lasting; only with

169 Course] Conrse ½°

---

160 *prudent Administration*: cf. Defoe, *A Speech without Doors*, London,
for A. Baldwin, [April] 1710, pp. 7-8: 'the *Dutch* ... have ... a wise Oeconomy
and frugal Administration'. The favourable attitude towards the Dutch reflects
Harley's opinion, not Swift's (*Prose*, vii, *passim*; Speck, '*The Examiner*',
p. 146).
168 *Returns*: Merchandise 'which comes back (to one) in exchange for merchandise sent out as a trading venture' (*OED*).
176-8 *again* ... *again* ... *again*: 'put in *Italick* for our greater Notice'
(Leslie, *The Good Old Cause, Further Discuss'd*, London, 1710, p. 14; cf.
Swift, *Tale*, p. 107). On 28 May 1709 the allies signed a treaty of peace with
France that they had negotiated at Gertruydenberg, near The Hague, with Jean-
Baptiste Colbert, marquis de Torcy, Louis XIV's Secretary of State. On 4 June
Louis gave his 'final Answer' (Burnet, ii 529). He agreed to all of the forty
articles but one: he refused to accept Article IV, which required him to use
French troops to drive his grandson, Philippe IV, from the throne of Spain.
He offered instead to hire mercenary troops for the same purpose and when
this offer was refused it was impossible to believe that the English plenipo-
tentiaries, Marlborough and Townshend, wanted peace (Anon., pp. 330, 472-81).
'The Tories contended, that a clause so harsh and unnatural, was only inserted
by the Duke of Marlborough, in order to break off the treaty, and secure himself in his power and emoluments as commander-in-chief' (E*1814*, iii 323-4).

this difference, that the Ministry perhaps will not *again* refuse
them.

180   *Audiet pugnas vitio parentum*
                              Rara Juventus.

180-1 *Audiet ... Juventus*: Horace, *Odes*, i 2 24: Our children, made fewer
by their sire's sins ... shall hear of battles.

No. 6 [Mainwaring]   6 November 1710

                          The MEDLEY.
           The Usefulness of History.
           What our Orators shou'd do with the History of the Rebellion.
           An Extract from Monsieur Le Vassor.

A Renown'd *French* Critick lays down this Maxim, in the Preface to
his Reflections upon History: *Politicks*, he says, *are the most
vain of all Sciences.* I have seen of late such lively Instances
of it, in the Writings of our High-Church, Militant at this time,
5 and *knocking* down all before them, that I have resolv'd to quit
that Science for the present. My last presented to the Reader a
short Moral Essay: This shall humbly offer a small Sketch of History. It will be needless to recommend that Study to my Fellow-
Subjects: The great use of it has been set forth by Antients and
10 Moderns; nor wou'd the World have preserv'd so many Volumes, if
there had not been something in it, equally pleasant and profitable. But I am rather for copying what is already well written
in that kind, than for attempting any thing my self. There was
once a History so famous among the *Grecians*, that the greatest
15 Orator they ever had, writ it over eight times: I wish all our

    1 *Critick*: René Rapin, *Oeuvres diverses*, 2 vols., Amsterdam, Abraham Wolf-
gang, 1686, ii 226.
    7 *Essay*: To *The Medley* of 30 October 1710 Mainwaring had contributed a
moral essay in doggerel verse about the ungrateful hind that grazed on the
sheltering vine tree and exposed herself to the hunters.
    14 *History*: The orator is Demosthenes, who wrote out Thucydides' *The His-
tory of the Peloponnesian War* eight times in order to memorize it (Rapin,
Oeuvres diverses, 1686, ii 301).

English Orators, that are so fond of our *History of the Rebellion*, wou'd resolve for their Improvement to write it over as
often: And that they may still like it better hereafter, I wou'd
advise them no longer to call it a History, which it no way resembles, but to give it the more agreeable Title of *Faults on*   20
both sides. How much better wou'd their Pens be employ'd in this
Labour, than in writing vile Histories of their own? *Lucian* says,
There was a time when most of his Countrymen were mad: and one
of the great Symptoms of their Disease was, That they cou'd not
forbear writing *Histories*. We have been of late so much infested   25
with the same Malady, that there's hardly any considerable Per-
son for Quality or Merit, Male or Female, Dead or Living, whose
Life is not written by some body that knows nothing of them. But
if ever I shou'd turn Historian, I wou'd certainly follow *Bocca-
line*'s Advice, to *write nothing but what I have seen, and not let*   30
it be publish'd till I am dead: Naturally dead, I mean, and not
in the Sense that some Authors are defunct. Or if I meddled with

19 way] ½° O L IU^a   ways Σ   23 There] there ½°

17 *History of the Rebellion*: In his prefaces to the three volumes of
Clarendon's *The History of the Rebellion and Civil Wars in England* (1702-4),
Rochester attempted to appropriate the work for the Tory party: '*a truth it
is which cannot be controverted, That the Monarchy of* England *is not now
capable of being Supported, but upon the Principles of the Church of* England'
(ii, sig. a2^v).
20 *Faults*: *Faults on both Sides: Or, An Essay upon the Original Cause,
Progress, and Mischievous Consequences of the Factions in this Nation* (1710)
professes impartiality while making anti-party propaganda for Harley (White
Kennett, *The Wisdom of Looking Backward, To Judge the Better of One Side and
T'Other*, London, for J. Roberts, 1715, p. 60). It had 'a prodigious Run'
(Oldmixon, *The Life*, p. 171) and was said to have been written 'by one
Clements, under the direction of Mr. Harley'. But it was also 'supposed to be
penned by my Ld Pet---h and the accurate Mr. [Andrew?] Fletcher' (Berkshire
RO MS Trumbull (Alphabetical Series) 54, Item 37). The author was finally
identified by Henry L. Snyder (*Philological Quarterly*, lvi (1977), 266-71).
He is Simon Clement (*c*.1652-after 1724), a trader to New England who suffered
bankruptcy and began to write pamphlets for the Whigs in the 1690s (Wing
C4637-38A; *CTB 1702*, p. 768). Harley took him up, as he did Toland, Defoe,
and others, when Clement was in trouble (Downie, p. 121). For writing *Faults
on both Sides* (1710) and *A Vindication of the Faults on both Sides* (1710),
Clement was appointed secretary to Peterborough in his embassy to the Empire
and remained in Vienna from April 1711 to March 1715 as chargé d'affaires
(Horn, p. 32).
22 *Lucian*: How to write History, 2.
29-30 *Boccaline*: René Rapin, *Oeuvres diverses*, 1686, ii 239.
32 *defunct*: Mainwaring had reported that the Examiner was 'already dropping into his Grave' in *The Medley*, No. 1, 5 October 1710, and pronounced him
'Defunct' in No. 2, 11 October 1710. Swift had made this game popular in the
Partridge papers (1708-9).

any thing that I had not seen my self, I wou'd follow the example
of *Polybius*, who says he relates all such matters upon the Credit
35 of honest People, that he knows were Eye-Witnesses of them. And
if I shou'd chuse to write the Life of any *English* Man or Woman,
my Ambition wou'd lead me to the most deserving, whether in
Favour or Disgrace. I had ever an abhorrence of the Ingratitude
of those Republicans the *Athenians*, of whom we read, that as soon
40 as *Themistocles* was disgrac'd, all the small Authors wrote
against him, tho he had every where beaten the *Barbarians*. This
in a Monarchy wou'd be intolerable; and to rail at any body that
had taken twenty seven Towns, and won eight Battels, wou'd with
us be thought base and detestable. But this is foreign to the
45 Business I am going upon; which is to collect out of the two
first Tomes of Monsieur *le Vassor*'s excellent History a short Extract of the Story of the Marquiss *D'Ancre* and his Wife *Galigai*.

In which the Reader will observe the Danger of Foreigners having Interest with a Sovereign, and the Misfortunes that such
50 People must bring upon a State and themselves. He will observe
likewise the ill Consequences of removing Able and Successful
Ministers, to put others in their places of less Experience and
Reputation. He will also see the Reflections which this impartial
Historian makes upon the Ingratitude of that Age and Country to

34 *Polybius*: *The Histories*, iii 4 13; iv 2 2, quoted in Le Vassor, i, sig.
*12^r.

40 *Themistocles*: Plutarch, *Life of Themistocles*, xxi 4-5.

42 *rail*: cf. 2.33-37.

47 *the Story*: The story of the Florentine Concino Concini, 'le plus grand
fourbe du monde', and his wife Leonora Dori, called Galigai, whose insolence
'ne contribuoient pas peu à irriter les Princes et les grands Seigneurs
contre son mari', is the story of Shrewsbury and his Italian wife, Adelida
Roffeni née Paleotti. The first draft of the story, preserved in BL MS 61462,
pp. 1-27, was written after April 1710, when Shrewsbury was appointed Lord
Chamberlain and when Mainwaring believed that he was to become the first minister of the new Government. During the minority of Louis XIII (1610-17), Concini was the favourite of the regent, Maria de' Medici, whose benefactions to
him included the marquisate of Ancre in Picardy, the office of first gentleman of the bedchamber, and the baton of a marshal of France 'sans avoir servi
à la guerre' (Le Vassor, i 321, 459, ii 465). Ridpath mentions 'Madam *Conchini*, or *Galigai* the It---n' in *The Observator*, 1-4 November 1710.

54 *Ingratitude*: 'Quelle bassesse dans les grands Seigneurs de France de
souffrir une pareille indignité [imprisonment in the Bastille of Henri de
Bourbon, prince de Condé]! Tel est le genie des François. Chacun pense à ses
interêts particuliers' (Le Vassor, ii 782). The modern instance was England's
ingratitude towards Marlborough, one of the main Whig propaganda themes in
1710-11: 'by their vile Endeavours I may see, | Their wonted Gratitude to
mine and me' (*Bellisarius a great Commander; and Zariana his Lady*, London,
J. Morphew, 1710, p. 7).

Persons of high Merit: Only some of his Expressions have been   55
soften'd in the Translation, to make them pass better with the
English Reader. For the rest, I have not added one Sentence of
my own; nor is there an Expression in the whole, which is not
copy'd and translated from the Original. But the Reader must not
expect to find it all together; because divers other matters are   60
mix'd with it in the Body of the Work. The Author himself gives
the Reasons in his Preface why it is in vain to expect a true
History of the present Ministers of State in *France*. Wholly employ'd about their own Fortunes, they will take care, he says, of
giving an exact and faithful Account of the Intrigues of the   65
Cabinet, and of the Court. *Will they go themselves*, says he, *to
acquaint the Public with their own Frauds and Wickedness? Will
they speak sincerely of the Passions of a Prince, to whom they
owe their Rise and Employments?* This is one of the Motives he
gives for chusing to write of what happen'd in a former Age: and   70
this little Abridgment which I have made from him, may be of some
Use and Instruction to the present; especially to those, who,
according to the same Author, know how to read History, as they
ought to do: To reflect on the Unruliness and Injustice of human
Passions: To discern solid and real Virtue, from that which only   75
consists in the false Opinion of the World: To make useful Remarks on Peoples good or ill Qualities; and to profit by the

68 *Passions*] *shameful and criminal Passions* 12°

---

56 *Translation*: Mainwaring worked from the second edition of the French
text. He did not use the English translation by Jean de Fonvive (1700-2). His
translation is literal but his method includes splicing together two passages
thirty pages apart with an 'and' and then skipping over 106 pages for the
next sentence. His propaganda purposes are revealed in his omissions and additions to the French text. He translates 'Epernon [Marlborough] s'en plaignoit
avec sa hauteur acoutumée' (ii 437) as 'The Duke had complain'd of this'
(17.181-2), omitting the qualifying phrase (despite its obvious appropriate-
ness) as foreign to his purposes. He translates 'La haine que le peuple de
Paris témoignoit tout publiquement à Conchini' (ii 468) as 'The Hatred which
the People of *Paris* publickly express'd against the Marquiss *D'Ancre*, for
occasioning the Duke *D'Epernon*'s Retirement' (18.208-10), adding the partici-
pial phrase (for which there is no suggestion in the text) to make the application to Marlborough.
  63-9 *Wholly ... Employments*: Le Vassor, i, sig. *12.
  68 *Prince*: The allegorical counterpart of Maria de' Medici is of course
Queen Anne. Mainwaring mentions the Queen's 'shamefull passion' for Mrs
Masham in a letter of 30 April 1710 to the Duchess of Marlborough (BL MS Add.
61461, f. 27ᵛ; cf. *POAS*, Yale, vii 309).
  76-7 *To ... Qualities*: Le Vassor, i, sig. *8ʳ.
  77-80 *to ... Modern*: Ibid., i, sig. *9ʳ.

Examples that are prais'd and recommended, and to avoid the
Faults that are censur'd and condemn'd. Such Persons as these, he
80 says, can only reap the true Fruit of History, Antient or Modern;
and to Minds thus prepar'd, I recommend the following Epitome.

When *Marie de Medicis* was Queen Regent of *France*, just a hundred years ago, the Marquiss *d'Ancre*, who had marry'd an *Italian*
Woman call'd *Galigai*, was made first Gentleman of the Chamber
85 [*Anno* 1610.] Not long after his Preferment he fell out with
Bellegarde the *Grand Ecuier*, or Master of the Horse; and the History says, the Quarrel between these two Men gave a great deal of
Disturbance. The Marquiss *d'Ancre* did not at the bottom love
Bellegarde, believing that he who had been longer at Court might
90 hinder his own growing Favour: Besides, *Bellegarde* was not easy
to live with, or to be reconcil'd, being one that pretended to
support himself independent of the other Ministers or Favourites.
The other was also a proud Man, and blown up with his new Favour: However in one thing they agreed, which was to act in con-
95 cert with some others about the Queen, to remove the Duke of
Sully, Intendant of the Finances. This they brought about in a
very short time; and, as the Historian says, the Duke of *Sully*
was the Victim of their Agreement: Upon whose Removal the Duke
of *Rohan*, in his excellent Memoirs, observes, That his Services
100 had procur'd him the ill Will of so many People; for, says he,
eminent Virtue, such as his was, accompany'd with Favour, is

82 *Marie*] ½° O L IU[a] *Mary* Σ   84-5 Chamber [*Anno* 1610.]] Chamber, *Anno*
1610. 12°

---

86 *Bellegarde*: The English counterpart of Roger de Saint-Lary, duc de
Bellegarde, Henri III's *grand écuyer*, is Charles Seymour, 'the proud Duke' of
Somerset, Queen Anne's Master of the Horse. Somerset was a Whig and one of
the seven lords appointed to examine Greg. He threatened to resign if Harley
were not removed in February 1708, but quarrelled with the Junto and allowed
himself to expect to be first minister in Harley's new Government (Swift,
Prose, vii 13-14). When he learned that Harley was to play this role, he
turned back to the Whigs only to find that neither party trusted him
(*Marlborough-Godolphin Corr.*, p. 1644).
87-96 *the ... Sully*: Le Vassor, i 100-1.
96 *Sully*: Maximilien de Béthune, duc de Sully, 'un des plus grands hommes
et le plus habile Ministre de son siècle' (De La Chesnaye-Desbois, iii 104),
was Henri IV's *surintendant des finances*. He was dismissed by Maria de'
Medici in July 1611. His English counterpart is Godolphin, Lord Treasurer,
whom Anne dismissed in August 1710.
97-8 *the ... Agreement*: Le Vassor, i 109.
99-116 *his ... Kingdom*: Henri de Rohan, duc de Montbazon, *Mémoires*, 2nd
edn., Amsterdam, Elsevier, 1646, pp. 2-4.

subject to Envy; which is an Evil as frequent among Men, as it is
unworthy of those that make Profession of Honour. Many therefore
were inclin'd to lay him aside, and for divers Reasons; some to
fix their own Authority in the Government of the State, and to   105
remove from among them a Man so exact in his Office, who gave
them reason to be asham'd of themselves; some from a particular
ill Will which they bore to him; the Marquiss *d'Ancre*, from a
fear that he wou'd prove a hinderance to his ambitious Designs;
the rest, because they thought him too good a Manager of the Pub-   110
lick Treasure. At last, says the same Author, Experience shew'd
that this prov'd the Ruin of the State; the Treasures were
drain'd, the Stores squander'd, and the Comparison of the miserable Condition of *France* soon after, to the flourishing Estate in
which the Duke of *Sully* left it, too plainly demonstrated how   115
prejudicial his Removal from Affairs was to the Kingdom.
  But the Historian goes on thus, *B.2. p.* 318. The Marquiss
d'Ancre had form'd a Design to change all things at Court, to
remove the Ministers *of the late King*, and to put in their Places
Men that wou'd depend entirely upon himself. He thought therefore 120
next of removing the Chancellor: He took great Pains to do this,
being, as the Author says, the *greatest Cheat in the whole World*.
  The first thing he endeavour'd was, to make the Chancellor lose
his Reputation with the Queen, in which he labour'd with more
Success than all the rest; and a sudden Affair happen'd, which   125
gave *d'Ancre* an occasion to do the Chancellor ill Offices with
her Majesty. There was something to be *seal'd*, to which the Chancellor *made a difficulty of putting the Seals*. D'*Ancre* complain'd
of this to the Queen, who grew dissatisfy'd with him upon it,
and express'd her Displeasure, *pag.* 353. And the Marquiss   130
d'Ancre, and his Wife, had said so much to the Queen against all
the Ministers, and particularly against the Chancellor, that she

109 Designs] Designt ½° O L IU[a]   117 2] 3 ½°

117-20 *The ... himself*: Le Vassor, i 318 (½° corrected).
121 *Chancellor*: Nicolas Brulart, marquis de Sillery, keeper of the seal
and chancellor of France, was removed in 1616. His English counterpart is
Cowper, Lord Keeper (1705) and Lord Chancellor (1707), who was removed in
October 1710.
122-5 *the ... rest*: Le Vassor, i 321 (½°).
127-9 *the ... it*: Ibid., i 323 (½° corrected).
130-5 *express'd ... her*: Ibid., i 353-4 (½°).

began to keep them out of the Secret of Affairs. *Galigai* had the
Insolence to say a thousand offensive things, in which *Mary de*
135   *Medicis* indulg'd her. *That Creature*, says the Author, *forgot her-*
self to such a degree, that she did not keep even the Measures of
Decency. All the World was shock'd at her, and her Manners did
not a little contribute to set People against her Husband; who
gave also himself great occasion of Offence, by offering very
140   dangerous Advice at that time. The Queen was then engag'd in a
War, and he was not only for granting to her Enemies the greatest
part of their Demands, but he was also one of those that made the
People of *Paris* rise in open Rebellion, and insolently demand the
Conclusion of the Peace.
145   The Marquiss *d'Ancre* had never out of his view the Design he
had form'd from the first day he was about the Queen, to remove
from Court the Duke *d'Epernon*, as well as the other Ministers
that he might be sole Master of Affairs, *B.7 p*. 310. And by a
secret Conspiracy between him and some others, he did not despair
150   of forcing the Queen to sacrifice the Duke *d'Epernon*. *Mary de*
Medicis knew very well their Intrigue, but she dissembled it: the
Duke *d'Epernon was too necessary to be laid aside in the present*
Conjuncture. But the Marquiss *d'Ancre* persuaded her, that Measures were taking in the Court of *Madrid* prejudicial to her
155   Government, and that the Duke *d'Epernon* was in the Management.
Mary de Medicis believ'd this the more readily, because she her
self was jealous of that Court, which she thought had already
too much Influence in all Matters that were transacted in the
Court of *France*, and which was likely to have much more here-

153 *Conjuncture*] *Conjecture* 12°   154 taking] taken 12°

135-8 *That ... Husband*: Le Vassor, i 459 (½°)
142-3 *was ... Rebellion*: Ibid., ii 311.
145-60 *The ... Appearances*: Ibid., ii 310-12.
147 *Epernon*: Jean-Louis de Nogaret de la Valette, duc d'Épernon, the
mignon of Henri III, conspired against Henri IV and seized the regency for
Maria de' Medici but was banished from her court in 1618. His English counterpart is Marlborough.
152 *Epernon ... too necessary to be laid aside*: Mainwaring emphasizes
Marlborough's importance by italicization and by quoting the French text in a
side note (Le Vassor, ii 312 [½° corrected]).
154 *Madrid*: The antitype is Hanover, where Marlborough regularly paid his
court to the elector, Georg Ludwig, visiting there in December 1704, December
1705, May 1707, and April 1708.

after, according to all Appearances, as the Historian himself   160
expresses it. Persuaded at last of all that the Marquiss *d'Ancre*
and his Wife *Galigai* repeated to her without ceasing, the Queen
took a Resolution to sacrifice the Duke *d'Epernon*, as soon as the
State of her Affairs wou'd permit it; and *Galigai* had so much
Artifice, that she found means every day to increase her Hus-   165
band's Power. The Queen began to have a strange Distrust of the
Duke *d'Epernon*, and to look upon him as an Enemy, tho he sur-
mounted with Ease all the Difficulties that her Enemies cou'd
occasion to her Affairs. Upon this Subject a *French* Nobleman at
that time made a judicious Remark, which may be seen, *B.7. p.*   170
315. *When particular Resentments*, said he, *are more regarded,*
than the true Interest and Service of the Sovereign, this always
produces great Misfortunes to the State. The Duke *d'Epernon* dissembled as well as he cou'd the Mortification he was under for
the Loss of the Queen's Favour, tho he knew that the Artifices   175
which the Marquiss *d'Ancre* and his Wife made use of to ruin him,
succeeded to admiration. Publick Marks (says the Author, *Book* 8.)
of the Queen's Alteration towards him, fully convinc'd him that
his Disgrace was resolv'd upon. The Refusal of some Favours,
which the Duke had earnestly desir'd for his Friends, had made   180
him sensible before that he was not so well at Court. The Duke
had complain'd of this; and the Queen not concern'd to manage him
any longer, took that occasion of his Discontent to call him no
more to her Council. That last Proof of the Displeasure, or at
least Indifference, of the Queen, was enough to mortify a Man   185
that had less Merit: And he resolv'd to prevent the Order he expected wou'd be sent him, to leave the Court. Behold him there-

162-73 *the ... State*: Le Vassor, ii 311-15.
173-87 *The ... Court*: Ibid., ii 437-8.
179 *Refusal*: The death of Algernon Capel, 2nd Earl of Essex, in January
1710 left two military posts vacant, for Essex had been constable of the
Tower of London and colonel of the fourth regiment of dragoons. Both posts,
although theoretically at the disposal of the Crown, were in practice part of
Marlborough's patronage as Captain-General of the army. Marlborough had in
mind George Fitzroy, Duke of Northumberland, for the first post and Lieutenant-
General Thomas Meredith for the second. Anne, however, with Harley's encouragement, decided to make Richard Savage, Earl Rivers, her constable of the Tower
and 'honest JACK HILL', Abigail Masham's brother, colonel of the fourth
dragoons. Marlborough was tricked into acquiescing in Rivers's appointment,
but dug in his heels over the promotion of Hill, whose incompetence was well
known. The impasse was resolved when Anne dropped her insistence upon Hill and
appointed Meredith instead (Swift, *Prose*, viii 117).
187-207 *Behold ... him*: Le Vassor, ii 438-9.

fore now, says the Historian, taking leave of his Friends, and
declaiming against the Usage he met with, and the ungrateful
190 Returns for his most important Services. He affected not to shew
any Civility to those that he knew to be his Enemies, how distinguish'd soever they were by their Birth, their Rank, or their
Credit. The Duke made no difficulty to provoke them more against
him. He thought it became him to revenge himself for their Ill-
195 Offices, by insulting them with a noble Contempt: *D'Epernon*, says
the Author of his Life, did not follow those shameful Court-
Maxims, which teach Men to dissemble their Resentment, and basely
to return Actions of Grace for Injuries receiv'd. A Stoical In-
sensibility seem'd to him out of season; persuaded, as he was,
200 that a due Concern for having lost the fruit of all his Services,
was not unworthy of a great Mind. When he took leave, *Mary de
Medicis* receiv'd his Compliments with an affected Coldness. But
tho a Treatment so little deserv'd, made him not lose Respect;
yet he knew how, says the Author, upon this occasion to shew a
205 just Sense of it, and to convince her Majesty in a decent manner,
that she wou'd perhaps be one day under a necessity of having
again recourse to him.

The Hatred which the People of *Paris* publickly express'd
against the Marquiss *D'Ancre* for occasioning the Duke *D'Epernon*'s
210 Retirement, gave him great Uneasiness: But ought he to have been
surpriz'd, says Monsieur *le Vassor*, that the *French* bore impa-
tiently any one that pretended to lessen the Chief Peers of the
Realm, and those that fill'd the first Places in the Ministry
with such great Reputation? So many Persons, distinguish'd by
215 their Birth, by their Employments, and by their Services, could
not fail of having Friends and Creatures who wou'd animate the
People against the Marquiss *D'Ancre*. This he took as a Presage
of his Fall, and never ceas'd from that time to represent to his
Wife, *Galigai*, that it wou'd be better for them to retire imme-
220 diately into *Italy*. In the middle of these Distractions, he kept
up, says the Author, I know not what weak Sentiments of Religion;
which the Misfortunes, that came one after another upon him,
contributed not a little to revive in him. He had certain Fits of

196 *Author*: Guillaume Girard, *Histoire de la vie du duc d'Epernon*, Paris,
A. Courbé, 1655, p. 282, quoted in Le Vassor, ii 438-9.
208-17 *The ... Ancre*: Le Vassor, ii 468; cf. 13.56n.
217-42 *This ... good*: Ibid., ii 470-3.

Devotion, or rather of *Superstition*, which on such occasions lay
hold of ambitious Courtiers, when they have not quite shook off   225
the Yoke. He fancy'd that God gave him notice of his approaching
Ruin, and that he ought to get out of *France* as soon as he cou'd,
lest the Hand of the Lord shou'd fall heavy upon him in a manner
yet more insupportable. He throws himself down at his Wife's
feet, and presses her with all possible Earnestness to take a   230
Resolution of retiring with him: *You are a Scoundrel and an un-*
grateful Wretch, reply'd *Galigai* to him in a fierce disdainful
Tone; *Is it not the most unworthy, the basest thing in the*
world, that you can have so much as a Thought of abandoning the
Queen, who has heap'd her Benefits upon us? How dare you make   235
such a Proposal to me? This Obstinacy in her, which at the same
time had a certain Air of Courage and Constancy, broke his Resolution: yet he said to *Bassompierre, If I cou'd with Honour quit*
a Wife to whom I have SUCH GREAT OBLIGATIONS, I wou'd soon be in
a place where the Lords and Commons of France *wou'd not come to*   240
look for me. And we shall see, says the Historian, before the
next Year is past, that his Inspiration was good. [The remaining Part of this History shall be continu'd in my next.]

No. 15 [Swift]   9 November 1710

The EXAMINER

> *E quibus hi vacuas implent Sermonibus aures,*
> *Hi narrata ferunt alio: mensuraq; ficti*
> *Crescit, & auditis aliquid novus adjicit autor,*
> *Illic Credulitas, illic temerarius Error,*
> *Vanaq; Lætitia, est, consternatiq; Timores,*
> *Seditioq; recens, dubioq; autore susurri.*

Motto Ovid, *Metamorphoses*, xii 56-61:

> With idle Tales this fills our empty Ears;
> The next reports what from the first he hears;
> The rolling Fictions grow in Strength and Size,
> Each Author adding to the former Lies.
> Here vain Credulity, with new Desires,
> Leads us astray, and groundless Joy inspires:
> The dubious Whispers, Tumults fresh design'd,
> And chilling Fears astound the anxious Mind.

I Am prevailed on, through *the Importunity of Friends*, to interrupt the Scheme I had begun in my last Paper, by an Essay upon
the Art of *Political Lying*. We are told, *The Devil is the Father
of Lies*, and *was a* Liar *from the beginning*; so that beyond Con-
5   tradiction, the Invention is old: And which is more, His first
Essay of it was purely *Political*, employ'd in undermining the
Authority of his Prince, and seducing a third Part of the Subjects from their Obedience. For which he was driven down from
Heaven, where (as *Milton* expresseth it) he had been VICEROY of a
10 great *Western Province*; and forced to exercise his Talent in Inferior Regions among *other fallen Spirits*, or *poor deluded Men*,
whom he still daily tempts to *his own Sin*, and will ever do so
'till he is *Chain'd in the bottomless Pit*.
    But though the Devil be the Father of *Lies*, he seems, like
15 other great Inventers, to have lost much of his Reputation, by
the continual Improvements that have been made upon him.
    Who first reduc'd *Lying* into an Art, and adapted it to *Poli-
ticks*, is not so clear from History, though I have made some
diligent Enquiries: I shall therefore consider it only according
20 to the modern System, as it has been cultivated these twenty
Years past in the Southern Part of our own Island.
    The Poets tell us, That after the Giants were overthrown by
the Gods, the *Earth* in revenge produced her last Offspring, which
was *Fame*. And the Fable is thus interpreted; that when Tumults
25 and Seditions are quieted, Rumours and false Reports are plentifully spread through a Nation. So that by this Account, *Lying* is
the last Relief of a *routed, earth-born, Rebellious Party* in a
State. But here, the Moderns have made great Additions, applying
this Art to the gaining of Power, and preserving it, as well as
30 revenging themselves after they have lost it: As the same

13 is] be 38 8°+12°

---

2 *Scheme*: 'letting ... Men see, that their natural or acquir'd Fears [of
changes in the ministry] are ill-grounded' (2.21-2).
    3-4 *The ... beginning*: John 8:44.
    7 *third Part*: *Paradise Lost*, ii 692, v 710.
    9 *VICEROY*: The phrase is not Milton's but Swift's. Satan's antitype is
Wharton, Lord-Lieutenant of Ireland (December 1708–October 1710).
    13 *Chain'd ... Pitt*: Rev. 20:1-3. See the excellent article by Clayton D.
Lein, *Studies in English Literature*, xvii (1977), 407-17.
    15 *Inventers*: The popes and John Calvin (Swift, *Prose*, i 65-76, 120-31).
    22 *Poets*: Virgil, *Aeneid*, iv 178-80; Ovid, *Metamorphoses*, xii 56-61.

Instruments are made use of by Animals to feed themselves when
they are hungry, and bite those that tread upon them.

But the same Genealogy cannot always be admitted for *Political*
Lying; I shall therefore desire to refine upon it, by adding
some Circumstances of its Birth and Parents. A *Political Lie* is   35
sometimes born out of a discarded Statesman's Head, and thence
delivered to be nursed and dandled by the Mob. Sometimes it is
produced a Monster, and *lickt* into Shape; at other times it
comes into the World compleatly formed, and is spoiled in the
licking. It is often born an Infant in the regular way, and re-   40
quires Time to mature it: And often it sees the Light in its full
growth, but dwindles away by degrees. Sometimes it is of Noble
Birth; and sometimes the Spawn of a Stock-jobber. *Here*, it
screams aloud at opening the Womb; and *there*, it is delivered
with a *Whisper*. I know a *Lie* that now disturbs half the Kingdom   45
with its Noise, which tho' too proud and great at present to own
its Parents, I can remember in its *Whisper-hood*. To conclude the
Nativity of this Monster; when it comes into the World without a
Sting, it is still-born; and whenever it loses its *Sting*, it dies.

No wonder, if an Infant so miraculous in its Birth, should be   50
destined for great Adventures: And accordingly we see it has been
the *Guardian Spirit* of a *prevailing Party* for almost twenty Years.
It can conquer Kingdoms without Fighting, and sometimes with the
loss of a Battle: It gives and resumes Employments; can sink a
Mountain to a Mole-hill, and raise a Mole-hill to a Mountain; has   55
presided for many Years at Committees of Elections; can wash a
Blackamore white; make a Saint of an Atheist, and a Patriot of a
Profligate; can furnish *Foreign Ministers* with Intelligence, and
raise or let fall the Credit of the Nation. This Goddess flies
with a huge *Looking-glass* in her Hands, to dazzle the Crowd, and   60

---

36 Statesman's] Stateman's ½°   37 Mob] Rabble 38 8°+12°   49 dies]
dieth 38 12°   60 *Looking-glass*] Lookinglass ½°

---

43 *Stock-jobber*: 'A low wretch who gets money by buying and selling
shares in the funds' (Samuel Johnson, *A Dictionary of the English Language*,
2 vols., London, by Strahan for J. and P. Knapton *et al.*, 1755.
47 *Whisper-hood*: This Dickensian whimsy is unworthy of Swift.
57 *Atheist*: probably Somers. During the attempt to impeach him in 1701,
Sir Edward Seymour 'reflected on ... his religion, that he was a Hobbist'
(Vernon, iii 13).
58 *Profligate*: Wharton (70.127-72.143 below).

make them see, according as she turns it, their Ruin in their
Interest, and their Interest in their Ruin. In this Glass you
will behold your best Friends clad in Coats poudred with *Flower-
de-Luce's* and *Tripple Crowns*; their Girdles hung round with
65 *Chains*, and *Beads*, and *Wooden Shoes*: And your worst Enemies
adorned with the Ensigns of *Liberty, Property, Indulgence*, and
Moderation, and a *Cornucopia* in their Hands. Her large Wings,
like those of a flying Fish, are of no use but while they are
moist; she therefore dips them in *Mud*, and soaring aloft scatters
70 it in the Eyes of the Multitude, flying with great swiftness; but
at every turn is forced to stoop in *dirty Ways* for new Supplies.
     I have been sometimes thinking, if a Man had the Art of the
Second Sight for seeing *Lies*, as they have in *Scotland* for seeing

66-7 and *Moderation*] Moderation 38 8°+12°   71 *Ways*] *way* ½° 12°

---

    63 *poudred*: 'In heraldry and decorative art: To strew with a multitude of
(isolated) small objects or figures' (*OED*).
    63-5 *Flower-de-Luce's ... Shoes*: The emblems of 'Popery, Slavery, and the
Pretender' (35.18-19).
    66 *Indulgence*: Like Sacheverell, Swift uses this word, with its connota-
tions of reluctant concession, rather than the more usual word 'toleration'
(*The Perils of False Brethren, both in Church, and State*, London, for Henry
Clements, 1709, p. 19; Benjamin Hoadly, *A Collection of Several Papers Printed
in the Year 1710*, London, for James Knapton, 1718, p. 19). When the Queen in
her address from the throne at the opening of Parliament on 27 November 1710
said, 'I am resolved ... to maintain the Indulgence, by Law allowed to scrupulous Consciences,' 'Some Reflexions were made that the Queen did not use the
old word *Toleration* but the new one *Indulgence*: nor the old epithet *Tender*
but *Scrupulous*, the terms used by Dr. *Sacheverell*' (*CJ*, xvi 403; BL MS Lansdowne 1024, f. 235ᵛ). St John explained why 'Indulgence' was used: 'First,
because [it] is the term in law; secondly, because, in truth, dissenters are
not tolerated: the penalty of the law is only suspended, and they, by consequence, only indulged. And, thirdly, because some have been of late years so
hardy as to assert, that being tolerated by act of parliament, amounts to a
legal establishment; and that therefore they are on as good a foot as the
church of England' (Bolingbroke, *Letters*, i 43).
    67 *Moderation*: The word was 'very ambiguous' (Defoe, *The Master Mercury*,
8 August 1704) even before it became a party shibboleth. Harley adopted it as
an election slogan in 1705 and Defoe publicized it in the *Review*. In clerical
circles the moderates formed the bulk of the Low Church party, while in
Parliament the moderates tended to follow the 'managers', Godolphin and Harley, rather than the party leaders like the Tory Earls of Nottingham and
Rochester or the Whig Junto. The Whigs boasted of moderation. The Tories used
it as a term of abuse meaning 'nothing but Getting *Money*, and *Preferment*' in
politics and 'nothing but Lukewarmness in Religion' (Sacheverell, *The Perils
of False Brethren, Both in Church, and State*, 1709, p. 11; James Drake, *The
Memorial of the Church of England*, London, 1705, p. 27). As 'A Whig and one
that wears a Gown' (*Poems*, p. 121), Swift undertook to defend Harley's moderation in politics while attacking the Junto's moderation in religion.

Spirits, how admirably he might entertain himself in this Town;
to observe the different Shapes, Sizes and Colours, of those   75
swarms of *Lies* which buz about the Heads of *some People*, like
Flies about a Horse's Ears in Summer: Or those Legions hovering
every Afternoon in *Popes-head Ally*, enough to darken the Air; or
over a Club of discontented Grandees, and thence sent down in
Cargo's to be scatter'd at Elections.   80

   There is one essential Point wherein a *Political Liar* differs
from others of the Faculty; That he ought to have but a short
Memory, which is necessary according to the various Occasions
he meets with every Hour, of differing from himself, and Swearing to both sides of a Contradiction, as he finds the Persons   85
dispos'd, with whom he has to deal. In describing the Virtues and
Vices of mankind, it is convenient upon every Article, to have
some Eminent Person in our Eye, from whence we copy our Description. I have strictly observ'd this Rule; and my Imagination this
minute represents before me a certain *Great Man* famous for this   90
Talent, to the constant Practice of which he owes his twenty
Years Reputation of the most skilful Head in *England*, for the
management of nice Affairs. The Superiority of his Genius consists in nothing else but an inexhaustible Fund of *Political
Lies*, which he plentifully distributes every minute he speaks,   95
and by an unparallel'd Generosity forgets, and consequently contradicts the next half-hour. He never yet consider'd whether any
Proposition were True or False, but whether it were convenient
for the present Minute or Company to affirm or deny it; so that
if you think to refine upon him, by interpreting every thing he   100
says, as we do Dreams by the contrary, you are still to seek, and
will find your self equally deceiv'd, whether you believe him or
no: The only Remedy is to suppose that you have heard some inarticulate Sounds, without any Meaning at all. And besides, That
will take off the Horror you might be apt to conceive at the   105

  78 *Popes-head Ally*] *Exchange-Alley* 12° 38 8°+12°   85 finds] find ½° 12°
102 him] *om.* 38 8°+12°   103 have] *om.* 38 12°

---

  78 *Popes-head Ally*: When the stockjobbers left the Royal Exchange *c.*1697
they moved across the street to Bridges' coffee-house in Pope's Head Alley and
Garraway's and Jonathan's in Exchange Alley (Lillywhite, pp. 131, 219, 306).
  95 *Lies*: 'Honest Tom Wharton', as he was called, understood that 'a lie
well believed is as good as if it were true' (Burnet, 1833, v 234).

Oaths wherewith he perpetually Tags both ends of every Proposition: Tho' at the same time I think he cannot with any Justice be
tax'd for Perjury, when he invokes *God* and *Christ*, because he has
often fairly given publick Notice to the World, that he believes
110 in neither.

Some People may think that such an Accomplishment as this, can
be of no great Use to the Owner or his Party, after it has been
often Practis'd, and is become Notorious; but they are widely
mistaken: Few *Lies* carry the Inventor's Mark; and the most
115 prostitute Enemy to Truth may spread a thousand without being
known for the Author. Besides, as the vilest Writer has his
Readers, so the greatest *Liar* has his Believers; and it often
happens, that if a *Lie* be believ'd only for an Hour, it has done
its Work, and there is no farther occasion for it. Falshood
120 *flies*, and Truth comes *limping* after it; so that when Men come
to be undeceiv'd, it is too late, the Jest is over, and the Tale
has had its Effect: Like a Man who has thought of a good Repar-
tee, when the Discourse is chang'd, or the Company parted: Or,
like a Physician who has found out an infallible Medicine, after
125 the Patient is dead.

Considering that natural Disposition in many Men to *Lie*, and
in Multitudes to *Believe*, I have been perplex'd what to do with
that Maxim, so frequent in every Bodies Mouth, That *Truth will at
last prevail*. Here, has this Island of ours, for the greatest
130 part of twenty Years, lain under the Influence of such Counsels
and Persons, whose Principle and Interest it was to corrupt our
Manners, blind our Understandings, drain our Wealth, and in time
destroy our Constitution both in Church and State; and we at last
were brought to the very brink of Ruin; yet by the means of per-
135 petual Misrepresentations, have never been able to distinguish

116 *Writer*: cf. 'I Never yet knew an Author that had not his Admirers'
(Addison, *The Whig-Examiner*, 21 September 1710).
128 *Truth*: proverbial (Tilley T579).
133 *Constitution*: 'Several concurring circumstances tended by degrees to
imprint an opinion in the body of the Gentlemen & People, that there was an
intention of altering in time the constitution in Church & State' (Huntington
MS ST 57, vol. iv, p. 114, quoted in *HLQ*, iii (1939-40), 237). Article IV of
the impeachment of Sacheverell began: 'the said *Henry Sacheverell*, in his said
Sermons and Books, doth falsely and maliciously suggest, *That Her Majesty's
Administration* [i.e. the Godolphin ministry], *both in Ecclesiastical and Civil
Affairs, tends to the Destruction of the Constitution*' (*The Tryal*, p. 9).

between our Enemies and Friends. We have seen a great part of the
Nation's Mony got into the Hands of those, who by their Birth,
Education and Merit, could pretend no higher than to wear our
Liveries. While others, who by their Credit, Quality and Fortune,
were only able to give Reputation and Success to the Revolution,   140
were not only laid aside, as dangerous and useless; but loaden
with the Scandal of Jacobites, Men of Arbitrary Principles, and
Pensioners to *France*; while Truth, who is said to *lie in a Well*,
seem'd now to be buried there under a heap of Stones. But I
remember, it was a usual Complaint among the *Whigs*, that the bulk   145
of Landed-Men was not in their Interests, which some of the
Wisest lookt on as an ill Omen; and we saw it was with the utmost difficulty that they could preserve a Majority, while the
Court and Ministry were on their Side; 'till they had learn'd
those admirable Expedients for deciding Elections, and influ-   150
encing distant Buroughs by *powerful Motives* from the City. But
all this was meer Force and Constraint, however upheld by most
dextrous Artifice and Management: 'Till the People began to
apprehend their Properties, their Religion, and the Monarchy it
self in Danger; then we saw them greedily laying hold on the   155
first Occasion to interpose. But of this mighty Change in the
Dispositions of the People, I shall discourse more at large in
some following Paper; wherein I shall endeavour to undeceive
those deluded or deluding Persons, who hope or pretend, it is
only a short Madness in the Vulgar, from which they may soon   160

158 undeceive] undeceive or discover 38 8°+12°

136-9 *We ... Liveries*: A Whig reader both applied these lines more narrowly than Swift may have expected and unintentionally exposed one of Swift's
most successful satiric tactics: 'I cannot but take notice of a rude and un-
mannerly Reflection of the *Examiner* ... Language fit for a Livery, which no
one out of it shou'd use. *That Author* first *makes* the *late Ministry* no Gentlemen, as far as He can; and then treats them *as such*' (Joseph Rawson, *A Letter
to the Reverend Sacheverel*, London, for A. Baldwin, 1711, pp. 23-4).
139 *others*: Swift may have had in mind *A List of One Unanimous Club of
Members of the Late Parliament, Nov. 11. 1701. that met at the Vine-Tavern in
Long-Acre* (1701), variously called the Whig Black List and the Vine Tavern
Queries, in which Harley and other Old Whigs in the present administration
are called Tories, Jacobites, and French pensioners.
143 *Truth*: proverbial (Tilley T582).
150 *Expedients*: 'that detestable Art of ... corrupting the Members of the
House of Commons with Gifts, Places and Preferments' (*Faults on both Sides*,
2nd edn., 1710, p. 20).
156 *Occasion*: the general election of October 1710.

recover. Whereas I believe it will appear to be very different
in its Causes, its Symptoms, and its Consequences; and prove a
great Example to illustrate the Maxim I lately mention'd, That
Truth (however sometimes late) *will at last prevail.*

No. 7 [Mainwaring]   13 November 1710

The MEDLEY

A Continuation of the Story of the Marquiss D'Ancre *and his Wife* Galigai.

WE now present the Reader, according to Promise, with the remaining part of the Story of the Marquiss *D'Ancre* and his Wife
Galigai.
    The next thing we heard of, says the Historian, was an Alliance
5 of all those in the Court and the Parliament that wish'd ill to
the Marquiss *D'Ancre*, and a Rising of the very People of *Paris*
against him; and his Ruin was only defer'd for some months. The
Queen had, at his Sollicitation, made more Changes in the Ministry: *Du Vair*, Keeper of the Seals, was remov'd; and the Seals
10 were given to a Man of an ill Character, call'd *Mangot*. All good
Persons murmur'd, that a Magistrate of extraordinary Reputation
and Merit shou'd be disgrac'd, in order to raise an unworthy
Creature of the Marquiss *D'Ancre*. *Du Vair* suffer'd his Disgrace
with a Greatness of Soul which was not suspected of Affectation:
15 The World knew he had no way sought that eminent Dignity of the
Robe; content to do Justice, with an Integrity very rare in his

4 heard] ½° O IU[a]   hear Σ

4-7 *an ... months*: Le Vassor, ii 474.
7-21 *The ... Kingdom*: Ibid., ii 606-7.
9 *Du Vair*: Guillaume du Vair (1556-1621), cleric, jurist, philosopher, and
prose stylist, was president of the *parlement* of Provence under Henri IV. He
was forced to resign as keeper of the seals in 1616. His English antitype is
Cowper, who was forced to resign as Lord Chancellor in October 1710 (Oldmixon,
The Life, p. 174).
10 *Mangot*: Claude Mangot was Henri IV's master of requests. In November
1616 the marquis d'Ancre appointed him keeper of the seals to succeed du Vair.
His English antitype is Sir Simon Harcourt, whom Harley appointed to succeed
Cowper (but with the title of Lord Keeper) in October 1710. Harcourt's 'ill
Character' was his susceptibility to bribery (*POAS*, Yale, vi 336-7, vii 33).

corrupt Age: He had taken no pains to establish himself at Court,
whither he had been call'd against his Will, and where he scorn'd
to support himself by Flattery and base Complaisance. But his
Justice and Probity were not at all agreeable to those that now   20
govern'd the Kingdom. *Barbin*, a little Country Gentleman and
Partisan, was made Intendant to the Queen, and Comptroller-
General of the Finances. They wou'd no longer make use of any
able Minister, experienc'd in Affairs and Negotiations: This must
needs have been inconvenient to the Marquiss *D'Ancre*, who pre-   25
tended to govern all with three of his Creatures, and to direct
whatever concern'd the Policy, the War, and the Treasury.

About this time there was a Letter prepar'd to be sent to the
Queen, from an unknown Hand. The Author of it was made to speak
like a Man inspir'd. He exhorted, he threaten'd, in the name of   30
God. He had a mind to make the Queen believe that the Letter was
written by some Holy Man, that had the Blessing of an intimate
Communication with God. Her Majesty was humbly beseech'd to read
it in private, to consider attentively the Importance of it, to
communicate it to no body whatsoever; and above all, not to men-   35
tion it to him that was the principal Subject of it: that is to
say, to the Marquiss *D'Ancre*. How gross and impertinent is all
this, says *Le Vassor?* And yet continues he, it is one of the best
Machines in the Tragedy; the Catastrophe of which prov'd so fatal
to the Marquiss *D'Ancre* and *Galigai*. It was hop'd, that the   40
Superstitious Queen wou'd fall into this Snare, and that the
Fear of the Devil, with whom she was threaten'd, wou'd make her
consent to the Removal of the Marquiss *D'Ancre* and his Wife. The
unknown Saint remonstrated to her Majesty the blind and guilty
Obedience which she paid to the Counsels of certain Persons, who   45
thought of nothing but to raise their own Fortune upon the Ruins

---

21 *Barbin*: Claude Barbin, 'a little Country Gentleman' from Champagne, was
farmer-general of the salt tax under Henri IV. During the regency he ingra-
tiated himself with Leonora Galigai, who secured him appointment as intendant
of the household. He became the confidant of the marquis d'Ancre and exercised
great authority over Maria de' Medici. In May 1616, when the former ministers
of Henry IV were disgraced, he succeeded as comptroller-general of finances.
Barbin's English antitype is Harley.
21-7 *Barbin ... Treasury*: Le Vassor, ii 608.
28-33 *a ... God*: Ibid., ii 610.
33-40 *Her ... Galigai*: Ibid., ii 611.
40-84 *It ... Minister*: Ibid., ii 613-15.

of the State, and of her Majesty herself, whom these People betray'd. The Persons were not nam'd, but the Marquiss *D'Ancre* and
Galigai were so well describ'd, that it was impossible to mistake
50 them. The Author represented afterwards many Faults committed in
the Administration of Affairs; the Disorders they had occasion'd,
and the great Evils that wou'd infallibly follow, if not prevented by speedy and effectual Remedies. These Remedies so necessary, were particularly mark'd: And the better to conceal the
55 Fraud, in making *Mary de Medicis* believe that this wholesome
Advice came from some good and holy Professor of Religion, hid in
the bottom of a Cloyster, he exhorted her Majesty to double her
Acts of Devotion, to be more fervent in Good-Works, to ordain publick Prayers for forty Hours, particularly in the Churches of
60 *Paris*; to employ little Children of twelve years old, or under
to appease the Anger of God, by lifting their innocent Hands to
Heaven, and to make them march very devoutly in a publick and
solemn Procession. If you do this, said the Writer of the Letter,
copying to a miracle the Stile of the new Prophets, your Majesty
65 will avert those Misfortunes with which your Person is threaten'd:
But if you neglect the Advice which I give you in the name of
God, you will soon feel the terrible Effects of his Anger, justly
provok'd against you. Have regard to what I have said to you: 'Tis
the surest way to bring down the Blessings of Heaven upon your
70 self and all *France*. How ridiculous soever this may appear, it was
not ill imagin'd to shake and trouble the Mind of *Mary de Medicis*,
who was very ignorant, and falsly devout. If your Majesty, says
he, does not obey the Order of Heaven, you will plunge your self
into the greatest Misfortunes. And in short, there is but one
75 Remedy to prevent it; which is, to send the Marquiss *D'Ancre* and
his Wife to *Italy*: those two Occasions of Scandal, who cause a
general Discontent in the State. This pretended Interpreter of

47 these] the ½°

---

64 *new Prophets*: the Camisars, Protestant peasants of the Cévennes in
southern France, whose religious enthusiasm took the form of glossolalia and
trance states. After their suppression in 1704 some of the survivors escaped
to London where their feats continued to attract attention and to encourage
local imitators (Hearne, ii 243).

72 *very ignorant, and falsly devout*: 'A praying, godly idiot' was what
the Duchess of Marlborough called Queen Anne, Maria de' Medici's English antitype (Burnet, 1833, v 454n.).

the Orders of Heaven, endeavour'd to soften the Grief which so
severe an Order must needs raise in the good Queen, by permitting
her to give them any new Gratifications, provided they wou'd go   80
and enjoy them out of the Kingdom. But, said he, if your Majesty
persists in keeping them, you will have the mortification to see
them perish miserably, and to feel the Effects of these Threats,
which God denounces against you by me his Minister.

This Letter was deliver'd to the Queen, which she was desir'd   85
to keep extreme secret. She promis'd to read it when she went to
bed, and to reflect upon it very seriously. But as great a Secret
as it was, she cou'd not help shewing it to her Confessor, and
to *Galigai*. They took upon them to shew the Cheat, and to make
a Jest of it; and the Queen was presently cur'd of the Scruples   90
and the Fear which somebody had endeavour'd by this Stratagem to
raise in her.

When this wou'd not do, many Intrigues were set on foot, and
the common Arts of Courtiers were employ'd on the one side to
remove the Marquiss *D'Ancre*; whilst on the other, he himself,   95
with his Creatures *Mangot* and *Barbin*, were as busy in forming
Designs to increase their Power, to ruin the divers Cabals that
were form'd against them, and to establish their own Fortune.
They resolv'd to push things to an Extremity, and openly to
attack any Party that shou'd rise against them. *Barbin*, the most   100
intimate Confident of the Marquiss *d'Ancre*, a bold enterprizing
Man, exhorted him to this with more vehemence, because he cou'd
support himself by no other way, than by absolutely ruining all
Opposers. *Mangot* was in the same Case, and whenever the Queen
shew'd a Disposition to follow right measures, the artificial   105
Insinuations of *Barbin* soon turn'd her from that Resolution,
which was but weakly taken. The Marquis *d'Ancre* frighted with the
Storm that was gathering over his Head, often press'd his Wife to
go back with him to *Italy*; but *Galigai* had more Courage, or less
Prudence than her Husband: And since he cou'd not get the better   110
of her Obstinacy, he wou'd not abandon her. In the mean time many
Accusations were publish'd against them by their Enemies, in
Papers dispers'd for that very purpose; and these Reports, most
of which were true, did set Peoples Minds strangely against the

85-98 *This ... Fortune*: Le Vassor, ii 616-18.
99-118 *They ... France*: Ibid., ii 640-2.

115 Marquis *d'Ancre*, and his Ministry. All the World complain'd of
     the Administration; and every body, according to his Passion or
     Interest, made frightful Descriptions of the Misfortunes that
     threaten'd *France. Are these Men*, said they, *fit to make their
     Creatures Mareschals of* France, *and Generals of Armies? To take
120 away, and to give the Seals? To turn out Secretaries of State,
     and put others in their Places? And shall* Barbin, *a worthless
     Man*, Homme de neant, as 'tis in the Original, *be made Comptroller
     of the Finances?* These Murmurs and Clamours increas'd, as the
     opposite Party grew weaker; and it was fear'd that these Ministers
125 wou'd be still more insupportable, when their Enemies were all
     oppress'd. New Expedients therefore were propos'd to ingage the
     Queen to send the Marquis *d'Ancre* and his Wife to *Italy*: And
     since she had rejected the Advice which the pretended Servant of
     God had given her, to send them out of the Kingdom, a real Divine
130 and Bishop of the Church was ingag'd to make a new Experiment,
     and to propose their Banishment, as a thing absolutely necessary
     in the present Situation of the Kingdom. The Prelate acquitted
     himself of his Commission with great Dexterity: And *Mary de
     Medicis* being mov'd by his Remonstrances, declar'd frankly to
135 *Galigai*, that she, with her Husband, wou'd do well to get imme-
     diately out of the Kingdom. The Woman being assur'd of her Hus-
     band's ready Compliance, who had press'd her more than once,
     throwing himself down upon his Knees before her, to avoid the
     Storm that had so long threaten'd them, prepar'd herself in good
140 earnest to leave the Kingdom. Their Moveables begun to be packing
     up, and the Bankers gave them Letters of Credit for *Florence*: And
     the Marquis *d'Ancre* was angry at his Wife, who being more ambi-
     tious and obstinate than himself, wou'd not consent to go out of
     France, till they had receiv'd this positive Order from their
145 Mistress.

     In the mean time their Enemies did not fail to represent, that

---

118-26 *Are ... oppress'd*: Le Vassor, ii 661-2.
126-45 *New ... Mistress*: Ibid., ii 673-5.
132 *Prelate*: Although allegory has by this time passed into prophecy and
Wunschphantasie (the Duchess of Shrewsbury 'shav'd for a Witch', 33.210),
Mainwaring had in mind 'a reall devine' (BL MS Add. 61462), probably John
Sharp, Archbishop of York, whom he designates '*Archimitrato Boreius*, who had
a great sway with the Empress in matters relating to the other World' (*The
Impartial Secret History of Arlus, Fortunatus, and Odolphus, Ministers of
State to the Empress of Grand-Insula*, no place of publication, 1710, p. 34).

these pretended Preparations for retiring out of *France* were only
a Feint and Disguise: And after many Expedients offer'd, in order
to get quite rid of them, one was bold and wicked enough to speak
the thing out. There is nothing remains, said he, to examine, but   150
which of these two ways her Majesty ought to chuse, either to
command one of her good and faithful Subjects to kill the Marquiss *d'Ancre*, after which *Galigai* may be clapt up in Prison, if
it be not thought expedient to send her into *Italy*; or else to
put them both into the hands of the Parliament, and to proceed   155
against them according to the Forms. Many People were shock'd at
the first Proposition; upon which one said, the second Expedient
was best: Let every thing be done in the ordinary Forms of Justice; let their Papers be seiz'd, the Parliament will find there
indisputable Proofs of the *strict Correspondence which they hold*   160
with the antient Enemies of the Crown. But others were so bent
upon *d'Ancre*'s Destruction, that nothing wou'd satisfy them, but
having him assassinated: And when that Tragedy was acted, and an
imprudent Servant came to the Queen, and said, no body knew how
to tell so sad a piece of News to *Galigai*, desiring her Majesty   165
wou'd please to tell it herself: She answer'd angrily, If no body
can tell her that her Husband is murder'd, it ought to be sung
in her Ears. Let no body talk to me any more of those People, I
told them long enough ago that they wou'd do well to return to
Italy.   170

157 which] ⁀, ½°

149-61 *one ... Crown*: Le Vassor, ii 681-2.
160 *Correspondence*: Mainwaring's suspicion that Shrewsbury, a great Whig
and favourite of William III, was also corresponding with Saint-Germain,
probably dates from 1694-5, when Matthew Smith, the informer, insinuated that
Shrewsbury had failed to warn the King of the Assassination Plot and Sir John
Fenwick insinuated that Shrewsbury himself was involved in the Plot (Mainwaring, *The Impartial Secret History of Arlus, Fortunatus, and Odolphus*, 1710,
p. 33). Mainwaring further believed that Shrewsbury had committed himself to
the Pretender's restoration during his residence at Rome (1702-5) (Dorothy H.
Somerville, *The King of Hearts. Charles Talbot, Duke of Shrewsbury*, London,
Allen and Unwin, 1962, pp. 76-80, 122-3; *POAS*, Yale, vii 549).
161-3 *But ... acted*: Le Vassor, ii 690, 707-8.
163 *Tragedy*: The marquis d'Ancre was assassinated in April 1617 on the
orders of Louis XIII, aged sixteen. Mainwaring projected a similar fantasy in
1708 in which Queen Anne turned out Abigail Masham 'And hang'd up *Machiavell*
[Harley]' (*POAS*, Yale, vii 316).
163-70 *an ... Italy*: Le Vassor, ii 715.

The old Ministers were now sent for to Council, and the new
Ones and Creatures of the Marquiss *d'Ancre* were so frighted with
the News of his Death, that not one of them thought himself safe
at home. *Mangot*, Keeper of the Seals, and *Barbin* immediately hid
175   themselves, being in great Disquiet, and very uncertain what to
do. After having deliberated some time together, they sent one
of their Close Cabal call'd *Brageloni*, whose Imployment the Historian does not name, but I suppose he was some Secretary, to
beg the Queen's Protection. *Mary de Medicis*, in a great deal of
180   Disorder and Apprehension, gave however good words to *Barbin*,
whom she lov'd better than the rest, but was in some doubt
whether she shou'd be able to save him, or not. *Mangot* having
less to hope for, took a Resolution of going to Court, to see the
end of his Destiny. He went strait towards the Queen's Apartment,
185   having before taken two or three Turns alone in the Court, under
great Disorder: People were not very fond of keeping him Company, who was then in a Place where every body turns presently
his Back upon those that lose their Credit and Imployments. The
disconsolate *Mangot* waited a good while, expos'd to the Rail-
190   leries of all the World, till an Officer came, in the Queen's
Name, and took away the Seals from him. *Barbin* had still worse
Usage than this: Men were commission'd to go to his House, to
seize him, to make an Inventory of his Papers and Movables, and
to bring away his Seal also. The Commissioners did not find him
195   at home; Bailiffs therefore had Orders to lay hold of him, and
carry him away. All his Papers were taken from him, not excepting those that he had in his Pocket. A List was made of them, and
they were all seal'd up. Thinking to make his Court, *Barbin* fell
to railing at the Marquiss *d'Ancre*, with whom he had been most
200   intimate; and said, he had often desir'd the Queen's Leave to
retire, which she had refus'd him, because she was afraid of
being abandon'd by her true Servants. Such is the Genius of Courtiers: *Barbin* ador'd the Marquiss *d'Ancre* yesterday, to day he
publickly speaks ill of him. But what better cou'd be expected
205   from a Man that was void of honest, generous Principles? *Barbin*
was kept close Prisoner at home, till he was remov'd to a Prison
call'd *Fort l'Eveque*.

171-91 *The ... him*: Le Vassor, ii 725-8.
191-210 *Barbin ... false*: Ibid., ii 730-3.

Galigai had been seiz'd a good while before *Barbin*. The Soldiers
plunder'd all she had, and then put her into Prison. There was a
Report that she was shav'd for a Witch, but that was false.   210

Thus was the whole Face of Affairs chang'd; every body made
Court to those that came into Power: Upon which the Duke of *Rohan*
made this Observation, *That there are few Souls so well made, and
so generous, to follow in Adversity those that they honour'd in
Prosperity*, tho he himself was one of those well-made Souls. And   215
others had now some Compassion for *Galigai*, and said, she was
not guilty of the Disorders in the State; the Fault ought only
to be imputed to the Ambition of her Husband: yet at last she was
condemn'd and suffer'd; having without any Distinction of Birth,
Beauty, or Wit, rais'd herself to the Quality of being a Lady   220
about the Queen. So far the Historian, from whom I will borrow
one Remark more, and so conclude. He says, *It is a miserable
thing indeed, that such People as these shou'd ever have it in
their Power, by base Intrigues, and often by black Calumnies, to
remove and deprive of their Employments those that have usefully*   225
serv'd their Country.

210 shav'd] shew'd ½°

211-15 *Thus ... Souls*: Le Vassor, ii 753-4.
215-18 *And ... Husband*: Ibid., ii 784.
219 *condemn'd and suffer'd*: Ibid., ii 794-6.
    without any Distinction: Adelida, daughter of Andrea, marchese Paleotti
of Bologna, and a widow with one daughter and no dowry, abjured Catholicism
in order to marry Shrewsbury in August 1705. 'Tis not to be conceivd',
Davenant said, 'what ground [the Duke] has Lost in the Minds of Men by his
Marriage' (BL MS 4291, f. 66). The 'Masculine Dutchess', as Mainwaring called
her, was a large woman of indeterminate age who still pretended to have love
affairs (*POAS*, Yale, vii 549; *Wentworth Papers*, pp. 214, 283). Queen Anne was
amused by her, but refused to make her a lady of the bedchamber (Somerville,
The King of Hearts, 1962, pp. 222, 292).
219-21 *without ... Queen*: Le Vassor, ii 797.
222-6 *It ... Country*: Ibid., ii 790.

No. 16 [Swift]   16 November 1710

The EXAMINER.

Medioq; ut limite curras,
Icare, ait, moneo: ne si demissior ibis,
Unda gravet pennas, si celsior, ignis adurat.

IT must be avow'd, that for some Years past, there have been few
Things more wanted in *England*, than such a Paper as this ought to
be; and such as I will endeavour to make it, as long as it shall
be found of any Use, without entring into the Violences of either
5 Party. Considering the many grievous Misrepresentations of Persons and Things, it is highly requisite, at this Juncture, that
the People throughout the Kingdom, shou'd, if possible, be set
right in their Opinions by some impartial Hand, which has never
been yet attempted: Those who have hitherto undertaken it, being
10 upon every Account the least qualify'd of all Human-kind for such
a Work.

    We live here under a limited Monarchy, and under the Doctrine
and Discipline of an excellent Church: We are unhappily divided
into two Parties, both which pretend a mighty Zeal for our Reli-
15 gion and Government, only they disagree about the Means. The
Evils we must˙ fence against are, on one side, Fanaticism and Infidelity in Religion; and Anarchy, under the name of a Common-

---

Motto Ovid, *Metamorphoses*, viii 203:
                              My Boy, take care
            To wing thy Course along the middle Air,
            If low, the Surges wet thy flagging Plumes,
            If high, the Sun the melting Wax consumes.
    4-5 *without ... the Violences of either Party*: What Harley wanted was a
paper that would gain support of the moderates of both parties. In theory
Swift agreed, for he could not 'conceive it possible to go far towards the
Extreams of either, without offering some Violence to his Integrity or
Understanding'. But in practice Swift had already decided that when the political nation was completely polarized, 'it seems every Man's Duty to chuse
one of the two Sides'. So Swift became more Tory than Harley. And when Harley
had fallen, Swift saw that he had been right, for Harley's 'moderating scheme
... put him upon innumerable difficulties, and some insuperable' (Swift,
Prose, ii 1, 2; viii 116-17).
    10 *the least qualify'd*: The reference is almost certainly to Abel Boyer,
whose claim to impartiality (*Annals*, 1703, sigs. A1^r, A4^v) had become his
trademark.

wealth, in Government: On the other side, Popery, Slavery, and
the Pretender from *France*. Now to inform and direct us in our
Sentiments, upon these weighty Points; here are on one side two   20
stupid, illiterate Scribblers, both of them *Fanaticks* by Profession; I mean the *Review* and *Observator*. On the other side we have
an open *Nonjuror*, whose Character and Person, as well as good
Learning and Sense, discover'd upon other Subjects, do indeed
deserve Respect and Esteem; but his *Rehearsal*, and the rest of   25
his Political Papers, are yet more pernicious than those of the
former two. If the generality of the People know not how to *Talk*
or *Think*, 'till they have read their *Lesson* in the Papers of the
Week, what a Misfortune is it that their Duty shou'd be convey'd
to them thro' such *Vehicles* as those? For let some Gentlemen   30
think what they please, I cannot but suspect, that the two *Wor-
thies* I first mention'd, have in a degree done Mischief among us;
the mock authoritative manner of the one, and the insipid Mirth
of the other, however insupportable to reasonable Ears, being of
a level with great numbers among the lowest part of Mankind. Nei-   35
ther was the Author of the *Rehearsal*, while he continu'd that
Paper, less Infectious to many Persons of better Figure, who

33 authoritative] authorative ½°

---

21 *Scribblers*: Defoe had been writing the *Review* since February 1704.
George Ridpath, who was both a dissenter and a Scot, took over *The Observator*
after Tutchin's death in September 1707 (Bodl. MS Ballard 25, f. 78; *The
Thoughts of an Honest Whig, upon the Present Proceedings of that Party*, London, 1710, p. 12). Harley sponsored the *Review* (404.124n.); Ridpath's em-
ployers were said to be Scots, 'either Mr. [James] *J*[ohnsto]*n*[e], D. [of]
H[amilto]*n*, or others' (Defoe, *Letters*, p. 289; William Atwood, *The Scotch
Patriot Unmask'd*, London, for J. Nutt, 1705, p. 25). Defoe replied to this
attack in the *Review* of 14 December and 16 December 1710.
23 *Nonjuror*: Charles Leslie (1650-1722), a Jacobite and non-juror, wrote
The Rehearsal, a spirited counterstroke to the *Review* and *The Observator*, from
August 1704 to March 1709. In *The New Association. Part II* (1703) he attacked
Swift's *Discourse of the Contests and Dissentions*, which he attributed to
Burnet. The Princeton copy of the *Examiners* in half-sheet is annotated by the
kind of reader whom Swift could not possibly have 'set right': 'The Revd Mr
Lesly a continu[al] Advocate in the best of Causes And his weekly Rehearsals
(whatever the Examiner may say) did baffle all the [scribb]lers of the [Whig]
Party and expose their dark designs, and did open the notorious forgeries and
falsehoods they impos'd upon the world. Mr. Examiner had been more honest if
he had not cast any Reflections upon that worthy Author who has done the
Church and Crown so much service by his unwearied Pains as [by ...] Arguments.'
30 *Vehicles*: cf. Swift, *Prose*, i 97.
33 *the mock authoritative manner*: 'So grave, sent ntious, dogmatical a
Rogue, that there is no enduring him' (Swift, *Prose*, ii 113).

perhaps were as well qualified, and much less prejudic'd, to
judge for themselves.

40   It was this Reason, that mov'd me to take the matter out of
those *rough*, as well as those *dirty* Hands, to let the remote and
uninstructed part of the Nation see, that they have been misled
on both sides, by mad, ridiculous Extreams, at a wide distance on
each side from the Truth; while the right Path is so broad and
45 plain, as to be easily kept, if they were once put into it.

      Further, I had lately entered on a Resolution to take very
little notice of other Papers, unless it were such, where the
Malice and Falshood, had so great a mixture of Wit and Spirit, as
would make them dangerous; which in the present circle of
50 Scribbles, from Twelvepence to a Halfpeny, I could easily foresee
would not very frequently occur. But here again, I am forc'd to
dispense with my Resolution, tho' it be only to tell my Reader,
what Measures I am like to take on such Occasions for the future.
I was told that the Paper call'd the *Observator*, was twice fill'd
55 last Week with Remarks upon a late *Examiner*. These I read with
the first Opportunity, and to speak in the News-Writers Phrase,
they gave me *Occasion for many Speculations*. I observ'd with
singular Pleasure, the Nature of those *Things*, which the Owners
of them, usually call *Answers*; and with what dexterity this match-
60 less Author had fallen into the whole Art and Cant of them. To
transcribe here and there three or four detacht Lines of least
weight in a Discourse, and by a foolish Comment mistake every
Syllable of the meaning, is what I have known many of a superior
Class, to this formidable Adversary, entitle an *Answer*. This is
65 what he has exactly done in about thrice as many Words as my
whole Discourse; which is so mighty an Advantage over me, that
I shall by no means engage in so unequal a Combat; but as far as

      50 foresee] forsee ½°

---

      43 *Extreams*: cf. 'Parties ... have prov'd to us like a Whip-saw, which
soever Extream is pull'd, the Nation is still miserably sawn between them'
(*Faults on both Sides*, 2nd edn., 1710, p. 55).
      54 *Observator*: Ridpath, who had 'never taken any notice of the *Examiner*'
before, devoted parts of two numbers of *The Observator* (1-4 November and
4-8 November 1710) to Swift's first *Examiner*, parts of the next two numbers
of *The Observator* (8-11 November and 11-15 November 1710) to Swift's second
Examiner, and kept up the attack through *The Observator* of 2-6 December 1710.
      64 *an Answer*: Swift provides an example below (143.5).

I can judge of my own Temper, entirely dismiss him for the
future; heartily wishing he had a Match exactly of his own Size
to meddle with, who should only have the odds of Truth and   70
Honesty; which as I take it, would be an effectual way to silence
him for ever. Upon this Occasion, I cannót forbear a short Story
of a Fanatick-Farmer, who liv'd in my Neighbourhood, and was so
great a Disputant in Religion, that the Servants in all the
Families thereabouts, reported, how he had confuted the Bishop   75
and all his Clergy. I had then a Footman who was fond of reading
the Bible, and I borrow'd a Comment for him, which he studied so
close, that in a Month or two I thought him a match for the Farmer. They disputed at several Houses, with a Ring of Servants and
other People always about them, where *Ned* explain'd his Texts so   80
full and clear, to the Capacity of his Audience, and shew'd the
Insignificancy of his Adversary's Cant, to the meanest Understanding, that he got the whole Country of his side, and the Farmer
was cur'd of his Itch of Disputation for ever after.

The worst of it is, that this sort of outragious Party-writers   85
I have above spoke of, are like a couple of Make-bates, who inflame small Quarrels by a thousand Stories, and by keeping Friends
at distance hinder them from coming to a good Understanding, as
they certainly would, if they were suffer'd to meet and debate
between themselves. For let any one examine a reasonable honest   90
Man of either side, upon those Opinions in Religion and Government, which both Parties daily buffet each other about, he shall
hardly find one material Point in difference between them. I would
be glad to ask a Question about *two Great Men* of the late Ministry, how they came to be *Whigs*? and by what figure of Speech,   95
half a dozen others lately put into great Employments, can be
call'd *Tories*? I doubt, whoever would suit the Definition to the
Persons, must make it directly contrary to what we understood it
at the time of the Revolution.

93 *difference*: cf. 'the Difference of their Opinions ... is not so great
as they are made to believe' (*Faults on both Sides*, 2nd edn., 1710, p. 4).
94 *two Great Men*: Marlborough and Godolphin 'only became Whigs through
the necessity of identifying their own principles with that of the party
which supported their power' (E*1814*, iii 335).
96 *half a dozen*: The point that Swift is straining to make is that three
of the half a dozen lately put into 'great Employments'—Shrewsbury, Ormond,
and Harley—actively supported William of Orange in the 'dark disputes' of
1688 (hence Whigs), while Godolphin remained loyal to James II (hence Tory).

100   In order to remove these Misapprehensions' among us, I believe
it will be necessary upon Occasion, to detect the Malice and
Falshood of some popular Maxims, which those Idiots scatter from
the Press twice a Week, and draw an hundred absurd Consequences
from them.

105   For Example, I have heard it often objected as a great piece of
Insolence in the Clergy and others, to say or hint that the *Church
was in danger*, when it was Voted otherwise in Parliament some
Years ago: And the Queen Her self in Her last Speech, did openly
condemn all such Insinuations. Notwithstanding which, I did then,
110   and do still believe, the Church has, since that Vote, been in
very imminent Danger; and I think I might then have said so, without the least Offence to her Majesty, or either of the two Houses.
The Queen's Words, as near as I can remember, mention'd the Church
being in danger *from Her Administration*; and whoever says or
115   thinks That, deserves, in my Opinion, to be hang'd for a Traitor.
But that the Church and State may be both in danger under the
best Princes that ever Reign'd, and without the least Guilt of
theirs, is such a Truth, as a Man must be a great Stranger to
History or common Sense, to doubt. The wisest Prince on Earth may
120   be forced, by the Necessity of his Affairs, and the present Power
of an unruly Faction, or deceived by the Craft of ill designing
Men: One or two Ministers, most in his Confidence, may *at first*
have good Intentions, but grow corrupted by Time, by Avarice, by
Love, by Ambition, and have fairer Terms offer'd them, to gratify
125   their Passions or Interests, from *One Set of Men* than another,

107 *Voted*: On 8 December 1705 the House of Commons voted 212 : 162 that
'Whoever goes about to suggest ... that the Church is in danger under her
Majesty's Administration, is an Enemy to the Queen, the Church, and the Kingdom' (*CJ*, xv 58).
108 *Queen*: In her speech upon the prorogation of 5 April 1710 Anne insisted
that it was 'very injurious ... to insinuate that the Church is in any Danger
from My Administration' (*LJ*, xix 145).
116-19 *But ... doubt*: This was Sacheverell's argument in his reply of 7
March 1710 to the charges against him: 'I hope I may say without Offence, that
the *Church* may be in Peril from *other Causes*, without any Reflection upon Her
Majesty's Government, or any Contradiction to *Her Royal Proclamation*, and the
Resolution of *both Houses of Parliament*, four Years ago' (*The Tryal*, p. 339);
cf. *A True Defence of Henry Sacheverell, D.D. in a Letter to Mr. D---n*, London, for W. Dolphin, 1710, p. 13.
122 *Ministers*: It is Marlborough who was corrupted by avarice, Godolphin
by 'his Passion for the Dutchess [of Marlborough]' (Swift, *Prose*, vii 9), and
both by time and opportunity.
125 *Set*: the Whig Junto, formed in 1694-5: Somers, Halifax, Orford, Whar-

'till they are too far involv'd for a Retreat; and so be forc'd
to take *Seven Spirits more wicked than themselves*. This is a very
possible Case; and will not *the last state of such Men be worse
than the first?* that is to say, will not the Publick, which was
safe at first, grow in Danger by such Proceedings as these? And   130
shall a faithful Subject, who foresees and trembles at the Consequences, be call'd *Disaffected*, because he delivers his Opinion,
tho' the Prince declares, as he justly may, that the Danger is
not owing to his Administration? Or, shall the Prince himself be
blam'd, when in such a Juncture he puts his Affairs into other   135
Hands, *with the universal Applause of His People?* As to the Vote
against those who shou'd affirm the Church was in Danger, I think
it likewise referr'd to Danger from or under the Queen's Administration, (for I neither have it by me, nor can suddenly have
recourse to it;) but if it were otherwise, I know not how it can   140
refer to any Dangers but what were past, or at that time present;
or how it could affect the future, unless the Senators were all
inspir'd, or at least that Majority which voted it. Neither do I
see any Crime further than ill Manners, to differ in Opinion from
a Majority of either or both Houses; and that ill Manners, I must   145
confess I have been often guilty of for some Years past, tho' I
hope I never shall again.

Another Topick of great use to these weekly Inflamers, is the

---

ton, to which Charles Spencer, 3rd Earl of Sunderland, was added in Anne's
reign.
127 *Spirits*: Matt. 12:43-5. The 'Spirits more wicked' than Godolphin and
Marlborough were the seven members of the parliamentary committee appointed
in February 1708 to examine William Greg: Somerset, Devonshire, Bolton, Wharton, Townshend, Somers, and Halifax. Greg was a clerk in Harley's office who
began in October 1707 to sell secret documents to the French. Harley discovered his practices in December 1707 (HMC *Portland MSS*, iv 469). Greg made
a full confession, pleaded guilty to the charge of high treason, and was condemned to death in January 1708 (Luttrell, vi 258, 259). For ninety days,
while he lay in Newgate, the parliamentary committee tried to bribe him to
implicate Harley in his treasonable acts. But not even the promise of his
life and £200 a year could induce him to commit perjury. He was executed on
28 April 1708 and his head set up on Westminster Hall, one of the true heroes
of the age of Queen Anne (HMC *Portland MSS*, v 648; Swift, *Prose*, iii 252;
Luttrell, vi 297).
132 *Disaffected*: It was Sacheverell who was called disaffected for insisting that the Church was in danger (*The Observator*, 3 July 1710).
136 *with ... People*: paraphrasing Commons' reply to Anne's speech from the
throne of 29 November 1710 (*CJ*, xvi 405). The Tory landslide in the general
election of October 1710 appeared to confirm Anne's choice of new ministers.

young *Pretender* in *France*, to whom their whole Party is in a high
150 Measure indebted for all their Greatness; and whenever it lies in
their Power, they may perhaps return their Acknowledgments, as
out of their Zeal for *frequent Revolutions*, they were ready to do
to his supposed Father: Which is a Piece of *Secret History*, that I
hope will one Day see the Light; and I am sure It shall, if ever
155 I am Master of it, without regarding *whose Ears may tingle*. But
at present, the Word *Pretender* is a Term of Art in *their* Possession: A Secretary of State cannot *desire leave to resign*, but the
Pretender is at bottom: The Queen cannot dissolve a Parliament,
but it is a Plot to dethrone herself, and bring in the *Pretender*.
160 Half a Score Stock-Jobbers are playing the Knave in *Exchange-
Alley*, and there goes the *Pretender* with a *Sponge*. One would be
apt to think they bawl out the *Pretender* so often, to take off
the Terror; or tell so many Lies about him, to slacken our Caution, that when he is really coming, *by their Connivance*, we may
165 not believe them; as the Boy serv'd the Shepherds about the *coming of the Wolf*. Or perhaps they scare us with the *Pretender*,
because they think he may be like some Diseases, that *come with a
Fright*. Do they not believe that the Queen's present Ministry
love her Majesty, at least as well as *some others* lov'd the

---

151 Acknowledgments] Acknowledgment 38 12°   153 *Secret*] *secret* ½°

---

149 *Pretender*: James Francis Edward Stuart (1688-1766) was recognized by
Louis XIV as James III in September 1701 and called the chevalier de St George
in France. In England he was called Perkin and eventually 'the Old Pretender'.
'"The Pretended Prince of Wales", as he is styled in several Acts of Parliament, was first called "the Pretender" in Queen Anne's speech to Parliament
on March 11th, 1707/8' (E*1922*, ix 260).
152 *ready*: Swift's assumption that Defoe and Ridpath were ready to 'return
their Acknowledgments' to James II for his Declaration of Indulgence of April
1687 is reasonable (because both of them were dissenters), but Defoe denied
the charge: 'I protested openly', he said, 'against the Addresses of Thanks
to [James II] for his Illegal Liberty of Conscience, founded upon the Dispensing Power' (*Review*, 24 November 1711).
153 *a Piece of Secret History*: If written, it is not now known.
161 *Sponge*: As part of the Whig effort to sink public credit, 'Lord [Godol-
phin?]' suggested to Defoe the possibility that the new Harley ministry might
simply repudiate the national debt, 'take *a Parliament-Spunge* and wipe it all
out'. This possibility appalled Defoe, who reverted to it repeatedly (*Review*,
13 July, 27 July, 12 August 1710; *POAS*, Yale, vii 471). Ridpath picked it up
in *The Observator*, 19-22 July 1710, Clement in *Faults on both Sides* (August
1710), ridiculing the 'Spunge that shall wipe out all the publick Debts, and
cancel the appropriated Funds' (p. 44), and Addison in *The Spectator*, 3 March
1711.

Church? And why is it not as great a Mark of *Disaffection* now to   170
say the *Queen is in Danger*, as it was some Months ago to affirm
the same of the *Church?* Suppose it be a false Opinion, that the
Queen's Right is hereditary and *indefeasible*; yet how is it possible that those who hold and believe that Doctrine, can be in
the *Pretender*'s Interest? His Title is weaken'd by every Argument   175
that strengthens hers. 'Tis as plain as the Words of an Act of
Parliament can make it, That her present Majesty is Heir to the
Survivor of the late King and Queen her Sister. Is not that an
Hereditary Right? What need we explain it any further? I have
known an *Article of Faith* expounded in much looser and more   180
general Terms, and that by an Author whose Opinions are very much
follow'd by a certain Party. Suppose we go further, and examine
the Word *Indefeasible*, with which some Writers of late have made
themselves so merry: I confess it is hard to conceive, how any
Law which the supream Power makes, may not by the same Power be   185

170 a] *om.* ½°   174 that] such a 38 8°+12°

---

173 *hereditary*: For Whig extremists Anne was 'the *Queen of the Revolution*',
'a good behaviour Queen', appointed by Parliament *durante bene placito* (*The
Observator*, 24-6 October 1704; University of Leeds MS Brotherton Lt.11,
p. 134). For Tory extremists she was a divine right monarch. Sacheverell
preached that Anne's title 'Devolv'd upon Her, by a Long Succession of Her
Royal Ancestors ... Proclaim'd ... by the *Voice of God* in the Universal Joy,
Satisfaction, and Unanimity of Her Subjects' (*A Defence of Her Majesty's Title
to the Crown*, 2nd edn., London, for Henry Clements, 1710, p. 10). For moderate
Whigs and Tories Anne's title was 'both ... Hereditary and Parliamentary'
(*Faults on both Sides*, 1710, p. 47): Anne was queen by virtue of the basic law
of primogeniture as amended to exclude Catholic candidates.
176 *Act*: After the Bill of Rights (December 1689) had excluded from the
succession all persons holding communion with the Church of Rome (including of
course the eighteen-month-old Pretender-to-be), the Act of Settlement (June
1701) named as successor to William III, 'in default of issue of his Majesty',
the Princess Anne, James II's second daughter.
181 *Author*: Gilbert Burnet, whose *Exposition of the Thirty-Nine Articles*
(1699) was censured by the Lower House of Convocation in 1701. 'They did not
like a latitude of sense', Burnet said, 'in which I had expounded the
Articles chiefly those that related to Predestination' (Foxcroft, p. 508).
183 *Indefeasible*: If the law of succession in the male line literally
cannot be set aside, then the Pretender had succeeded as James III and VIII
in September 1701 upon the death of his father. Defoe makes merry with 'Indefeasible' when he argues that 'if *Jure Divino* comes upon the Stage, the
Queen has no more Title to the Crown than my Lord Mayor's Horse' (*Review*, 6
September 1705). These words were quoted by his lawyer in defence of Sacheverel-
ell's claim that church and state were in danger from such 'impious Doctrines'
(*The Tryal*, p. 309).

repeal'd: So that I shall not determine, whether the Queen's Right
be *indefeasible* or no. But this I will maintain, that whoever
affirms it so, is not guilty of a Crime. For in that Settlement
of the Crown after the Revolution, where Her present Majesty is
190   named in Remainder, there are (as near as I can remember) these
remarkable Words, *To which we bind our selves and our Posterity*
for ever. Lawyers may explain this, or call them words of Form,
as they please: And Reasoners may argue that such an Obligation
is against the very Nature of Government; but a plain Reader, who
195   takes the Words in their natural Meaning, may be excus'd, in
thinking a Right so confirm'd, is *indefeasible*; and if there be
an Absurdity in such an Opinion, he is not to answer for it.

P.S. When this Paper was going to the Press, the Printer brought
me two more *Observators*, wholly taken up in my *Examiner* upon Ly-
200   ing, which I was at the pains to read; and they are just such an
Answer, as the two others I have mention'd. This is all I have to
say on that Matter.

191-2 *To ... ever*: In default of heirs of William and Mary, the Bill of
Rights named the Princess Anne as their successor, to which the Parliament
did submit 'themselves their Heires and Posterities forever' (*Statutes of the*
Realm, vi 144).

No. 8 [Mainwaring and Oldmixon]   20 November 1710

The MEDLEY.

The Examiner's *Skill in Painting, but base Ingratitude.*
A Picture of a Court, copy'd from Tacitus.
Of Courage, and Generals of Armies.
And of Credit.

I Have resolv'd never to say any thing to the *Examiner*, unless a
word or two by chance in passing: He gave his Reasons, in his last
Paper, why he wou'd have nothing to do with the *Review* and *Obser-*
vator, because of *their authoritative Manner, and insipid Mirth.*
5   I do not pretend to have the same Reasons for not arguing with

4 *authoritative ... Mirth*: 35.33-4.

him; far be it from me: But I am aw'd, and kept at a distance by
the importance of his Person, which he sets forth in three Instances. First, he says, *it must be avow'd there have been few
things more wanted in* England, *than such a 'Paper as his.* Secondly,
he says, *he keeps a Footman,* and that his name is *Ned,* and that   10
he is a pretty *Disputant in Religion.* Thirdly, he gives hopes,
That a Piece of Secret History shall one day see the Light, which
will make some Peoples *Ears tingle.* I am not so fool-hardy to
quarrel with such a Man as this is, but shall leave him to the
two Weekly Authors before-mention'd, whom he modestly calls in   15
one place, *Two stupid illiterate Scriblers,* and in another,
Idiots: And at last, adds this Postscript, *When this Paper,* says
he, *was going to the Press, the Printer brought me two more* Observators, *wholly taken up in my* Examiner *upon Lying.* They were well
imploy'd indeed! But whatever Remarks the *Observator* may make   20
upon him, he shall fight his own Battel for me, I will be so wise
to keep on the stronger Side: And if this *Examiner* does not prove
too hard for all that shall attack him, I will never more believe
what any Man shall say of himself. I know the Criticks find numberless Faults with him, but they are an envious Generation; and   25
I defy any of them to shew me an Author that has one Perfection
in a higher degree than he has, I mean the Talent of Painting or
Drawing a Character: A pregnant Proof of this may be seen in his
Piece of *November* the 9th, where he has given us a Picture to the
Life of a very great Friend of his, that first set him to work,   30
and in all likelihood pays him his Wages. He had been speaking
of *a Political Lyar,* and then proceeds to this lively Description:

11 gives] has 12°

8-9 *it ... his:* 34.1-3.
10 *a Footman ... Ned:* 37.76, 80.
12-13 *a ... tingle:* 40.153-5.
16-17 *Two ... Idiots:* 35.20-1, 38.102.
17-19 *Postscript ... Lying:* 42.198-200.
24 *Criticks:* 36.54 above. After the number of 2-6 December 1710, Ridpath
devoted part of one number of *The Observator* each week to answering *The
Examiner* and kept this up until the last number of *The Observator,* 30 July
1712.
30 *Friend:* Mainwaring turns Swift's attack on Wharton (20.9) against
Harley. 'Could any one but an idiot call him honest', Mainwaring asked the
Duchess of Marlborough. He is 'the most errant tricking knave in all Britain
that no man alive believes, any more than an Oates or a Fuller', he told her
(*Private Correspondence,* i 238, 392).

In describing the Virtues and Vices of Mankind, it is convenient,
upon any Article, to have some eminent Person in our Eye, from
35 *whence we copy our Description. I have strictly observ'd this*
Rule, and my Imagination this Minute represents before me a cer-
tain Great Man famous for this Talent: The Superiority of his
Genius consists in nothing else, but in an inexhaustible Fund of
Political Lyes, which he plentifully distributes every Minute he
40 *speaks, and by an unparallel'd Generosity forgets, and conse-*
quently contradicts, the next half hour. He never yet consider'd
whether any Proposition was true or false, but whether it were
convenient for the present Minute, or Company to affirm or deny
it; so that if you think to refine upon him, by interpreting every
45 *thing he says, as we do Dreams by the contrary, you are still to*
seek, and will find your selves equally deceiv'd, whether you
believe him or no: The only Remedy is to suppose, that you have
heard some inarticulate Sounds, without any meaning at all.

Shew me in any Writer, Antient or Modern, a Character better
50 drawn than this: Shew me at Sir *Godfrey Kneller*'s, who is fam'd
for taking a Likeness, any Picture that has so strong a Resemblance. But what did the Painter mean by calling it the Picture
of a Vice-Roy of a *Western* Province? What one Feature is there in
this Piece of any Vice-Roy, but that of *R-----r*? This was a poor
55 Disguise to cover so malicious a Satyr. But I lately noted before
the Ingratitude of this Age; and here is a new Instance of it,
slily working in a dark uncommon manner; and plainly demonstrat-
ing, that some People will never leave off falling upon their best
Friends and Patrons.

53 Province] Prince ½°

33-48 *In ... all*: 23.86-104.
50 *Kneller*: Godfrey Kneller, anglicized from Göttfried Kniller, was born
in Lübeck, studied under Ferdinand Bol in Amsterdam, and emigrated to London
in 1675, where he became the most successful portrait painter of the period.
Mainwaring sat for Kneller for his Kit-Cat Club portrait some time after
1703. Kneller painted the Duchess of Marlborough twice: once in 1691-2 as one
of the Hampton Court Beauties and again in 1705. In 1710 he painted the Duke
of Marlborough (Michael Morris, Lord Killanin, *Sir Godfrey Kneller and His
Times 1646-1723*, London, Batsford, 1948, pp. 98, 99, 103).
54 *R-----r*: Rochester was appointed Lord-Lieutenant of Ireland in December
1700 and retained by Anne. But his reluctance to resume his post required
Anne to replace him in February 1703.
56 *Ingratitude*: 12.54 above.

I know no body that comes near the *Examiner* for this Gift of   60
describing and drawing Characters, except a *Latin* Author call'd
Tacitus; and he gives a Description of a Court, which is almost
as natural as the *Examiner*'s Character of a single Person. He was
speaking of *Agricola*, the General at that time, and of the vile
Wretches that cou'd not bear his Merit, and that gave him mali-   65
cious Commendations, in order to draw him into Ruin, under pretence of doing him Honour; and then concludes with these words:
Agricola was in his Absence accus'd of many things to his Sover-
eign, without the least Ground or Foundation. He was brought into
imminent Danger, not for any Fault he had committed, nor upon   70
the Complaint of any body that he had injur'd; but the occasion
of his Troubles were these: The Offence which the Prince took at
his shining Vertues, the Glory of the Man himself, and the
Malice of some People who treacherously prais'd him, and who are
always the worst sort of Enemies. Whilst every good Man, for the   75
Love which he bore to the Publick; and every bad Man, out of Envy
and Ill-will, was for pushing him on to new Dangers; *Agricola, by*
his own Vertues, and the Vices of others, was still carry'd to
greater Difficulties, which yet always turn'd to his Honour.

Such have been the Condition and the Circumstances of most   80
Courts in the World: And *Macchiavel* seems to have found out some
reason for it, which was always too deep for me, and I never
cou'd comprehend why he said so. But his words are these: *It is*
impossible for Princes to be grateful to such as have got great
Victories. If 'tis impossible, there's no remedy; and the Generals 85
must bear with it. But since 'tis certain, that Valour and Conduct are something, and not to be found together every day; I
shou'd think, that when People are in War, they shou'd not too
much discourage a Man that has those Qualities, but shou'd give
him good Words and good Usage, at least while he is doing their   90
business. The *Romans* were wiser in this respect than some other
People that I cou'd name: They did not make it impracticable for
Scipio to serve, till such time as *Carthage* was destroy'd. When
that was done, and a Peace was made, then indeed they sent him to

68-79 *Agricola ... Honour*: Tacitus, *Agricola*, 41.
83-5 *It ... Victories*: Machiavelli, *Discourses*, i 29.
93 *Scipio*: After he had reduced Carthage to rubble, Lucius Scipio Africanus was tried on trumped-up charges and retired to his villa at Literninum
(Livy, xxxviii 50-2).

95 his Villa, and seem'd not to care what became of him: And that was
     soon enough in all conscience. If there were any young sprightly
     Officer, equally fit to command, there might be less Inconveni-
     ence in laying aside an old one. But alas! *Philip de Comines*,
     who was a very wise Man, observ'd long ago, That *let a Man*
100 *have ever SO GREAT A GENIUS FOR CONQUEST, if he wants good Sense,*
     his other Qualities will avail him nothing. A warm Heart can do
     little without a cool Head: But where they meet together, the
     Success of such a General is the just Reward of his Merit. I know
     a certain Party that attribute all this to Fortune, who by them
105 is prefer'd both to Valour and Conduct: And 'tis not to be won-
     der'd at; for why shou'd we not give our selves up to her abroad,
     as well as at home, where we seem so entirely to depend upon her?
     Or if these worthy Gentlemen allow that any thing else has con-
     tributed to our Successes, they never make those Concessions with-
110 out a Sting in the Tail of them. If our Generals fight, they are
     ambitious and rash, and value not the Lives of the Men: If they
     besiege, they are dilatory and trifling, and do it only to spin
     out the time: If they beat the Enemy again and again, 'tis not
     with the least intent of concluding the War: And if they shou'd
115 extend their Conquests to the very Suburbs of *Paris*, it wou'd be
     only for the sake of raising Contributions. Thus, who knows but
     Courage may in time become as scandalous as Wealth; and to Con-
     quer be as sure a way to Disgrace, as to be Rich?
         It is impossible to mention that last Word, without thinking of
120 the present State of our Mony and Credit. The Nation has been
     losing these six months, and yet some People wou'd persuade us,
     That we never were in so thriving a Condition; That Peace and
     Plenty are coming upon us, when we expect nothing but Poverty and
     War: and in short, That all which has been done, is for the bet-
125 ter. Which puts me in mind of the Story of a Quack, who affected

     99-101 *let ... nothing*: Philippe de Comines, *Cronique & histoire*, Paris,
     Galliot du Pré *et al.*, 1546, f. 59^v.
      104 *Fortune*: Marlborough is called Fortunatus in Colley Cibber's *The
     Secret History of Arlus and Odolphus* (7 November 1710), to which Mainwaring
     wrote a reply, *The Impartial Secret History of Arlus, Fortunatus and Odolphus*
     (1710).
      111 *Lives*: 231.155-232.156.
      116 *Contributions*: 56.176.
      120 *Credit*: 3.42.
      125 *Story of a Quack*: Oldmixon evidently recalls Aesop's fable of The Doc-
     tor and his Patient (L'Estrange, p. 89), but the joke is a commonplace that

an unlucky Phrase, and at every turn cry'd, *So much the better.*
The Doctor visited a Patient of his almost in the Agony, and
ask'd him, *How he slept that Night?* Not a Wink, Sir: *So much the
better*, cries the Doctor. He then inquir'd, *How his Fever was?*
O Lord! says the Patient, I burn as if I were on fire: *So much*   130
the better, quoth the Quack. *How does your Cough?* I spit up my
very Lungs, reply'd the Sickman: *So much the better still*, answers
the Quack. Ah! dear Doctor, quoth the Patient, what pity 'tis a
Man shou'd go out of the World with all these fine Symptoms about
him! And a few hours after he gave up the Ghost. We hear, we see,   135
we feel, we taste, but we must not believe our Senses. Thus, while
the *Whigs* are nibbling at the Presbyterian Principle of *Revolu-*
tion, some *Tories* are imposing on us the Romish Doctrine of Tran-
substantiation; which is as easily reconcil'd to our Senses, as
that we have lost nothing of late, and that 'tis not all owing to   140
them. But *Credit*, they say, *depends upon no Thing or Person.* This
may possibly be true, as impossible as it appears; and I have
nothing to urge against it, but a little Experience and a plain
Fact. Now so it is, that before some late Matters happen'd, a
good many People, both Natives and Foreigners, had great Sums of   145
Mony in the Exchequer, which they thought was so carefully
manag'd, that it wou'd never be so well again, unless in the same
Hands, or Hands of the same Reputation; the contrary of which they
foolishly fancy in the present Case. Upon this, it naturally follow'd, that when those Hands were remov'd, they wou'd be alarm'd,   150
and think of withdrawing their Effects, without staying to see
how the Managers that were put in wou'd behave themselves: Interest being the most impatient, as well as the most timorous thing
in nature. Hold, Gentlemen, cry the Tories, *Credit depends upon*
no Thing, and no Body: and you are as safe now as ever. I beg   155
your pardon as to that, say the Lenders: We thought our Estates
secure before, and if we think otherwise now, we shall certainly
remove them. Now, who can help all this? And what matter who have
been the cause of it? Where has been the great Loss as yet? What's

he could have read in Montaigne, *Essais*, ii xxxvii ('De la ressemblance des
enfans aux peres'), Savinien de Cyrano de Bergerac, *Satyrical Characters*,
London, for Henry Herringman, 1658, p. 115, or Molière, *Le Médecin malgré*
lui (1666), ii iv.
    141 *Credit ... Person:* [Defoe, *An*] *Essay [upon Publick Credit*, London,
1710], p. 22 (½°).

160 30 *per Cent.* for five or six Millions? and how is that worth
     taking notice of? Or what mighty Load is this upon those that are
     to answer for it? All that vexes me in this whole matter, is that
     they wou'd persuade us we are just where we were: For this indeed
     is a little too imposing, and too hard an Affront to be offer'd
165 to common Sense. If they wou'd say, that we may carry on the War
     without Mony, for that I cou'd bring them no less an Authority
     than *Macchiavel*, whom I have once mention'd already, and who says
     expresly in his *Decads* of *Livy*, p. 11. cap. 10. *There's no Opinion
     more false, than that Mony is the Sinew of War.* And he gives you
170 an Instance in the *Venetians*, who, he says, were driven out of
     their *Terra Firma*, at a time when their Coffers were full. So
     that full Coffers are not so much to be minded as some imagine;
     since those that have not Mony, may do as well as those that have:
     which alone decides the Controversy, and makes us immediately all
175 of an Opinion as to this point. Again, if they wou'd say that our
     Trade is of no importance, for that also I cou'd produce an
     Authority from one of their Authors, the late Earl of *Castlemain*,
     who in a Narrative publish'd forty Years ago says; England *can
     subsist without Trade, which is not at all necessary: We remember
180 by our Histories when it began here. The* Venetians, *the* Genoese,
     the Flemings, *and the* Jews, *were us'd to bring us Superfluities,
     and manag'd the Traffick of the Nation: However, 'twas then we
     conquer'd* France. Thus in either of these Cases it were easy to
     help them out with Precedents. The Papists and Tories cou'd never
185 endure Trade and Credit: The former endeavour'd to render Trade
     as superfluous, as the latter wou'd make Credit chimerical. But
     when they go about to persuade us, that notwithstanding the 30
     per Cent. aforesaid, *&c.* we are just in as good a Condition as
     before; I know not what in the world to say for them upon this
190 head: but must confess to their shame, they are a little ungener-

---

160 Millions?] ~; ½°   179 *subsist*] consist 12°   189 upon] on 12°

---

160 *Millions*: The capital of the Bank of England was 'Five or Six Millions'
(*Faults on both Sides*, 2nd edn., 1710, p. 38). If the stock had fallen thirty
per cent, the paper loss would have been the enormous sum of £1,650,000.
    168-9 *There's ... War*: Machiavelli, *Discourses*, ii 10. (½°).
    170-1 *the ... full*: Ibid.
    178-183 *England ... France*: Roger Palmer, Earl of Castlemaine, *A Short and
True Account of the Material Passages in the Late War between the English and
Dutch*, London, for H. Herringman, 1671, pp. 89-90.

ous in their Proceedings, since they seem not to care how much
they abuse poor CREDIT, because she is one of *the Ruin'd Party*.

192   *Ruin'd Party*: Oldmixon(?) scores here by equating credit with Whig,
and ruined credit with 'ruin'd Party', in Swift's phrase (3.50).

No. 17 [Swift]   23 November 1710

The EXAMINER

*Qui sunt boni cives? qui belli, qui domi de patria bene merentes, nisi qui
patriæ beneficia meminerunt?*

I Will employ this present Paper upon a Subject, which of late
hath very much affected me, which I have consider'd with a good
deal of Application, and made several Enquiries about, among
those Persons who I thought were best able to inform me; and if
I deliver my Sentiments with some Freedom, I hope it will be for-   5
given, while I accompany it with that Tenderness which so nice a
Point requires.

   I said in a former Paper (Numb. 14.) that one specious Objection to the late removals at Court, was the fear of giving Uneasiness to a General, who has been long successful abroad: And   10
accordingly, the common Clamour of Tongues and Pens for some
Months past, has run against the Baseness, the Inconstancy and
Ingratitude of the whole Kingdom to the Duke of *M---------*, in
return of the most eminent Services that ever were perform'd by
a Subject to his Country; not to be equal'd in History. And then   15
to be sure some bitter stroak of Detraction against *Alexander* and
Cæsar, who never did us the least Injury. Besides, the People
that read *Plutarch* come upon us with Parallels drawn from the

18 that] who 38 8°+12°
_____

Motto Cicero, *Pro Cn. Plancio*, 80: Who is the good and laudable Citizen?
Who in Peace, or who in War hath merited the Favour of his Country? Who but
that Person who with Gratitude remembereth and acknowledges the Favours and
Rewards he hath already received.
9-10 *giving ... abroad*: 2.34-5.
13 *Ingratitude*: 12.54.
18 *Parallels*: This may be a reference to *The Medley* (12.39-40).

Greeks and *Romans*, who ungratefully dealt with I know not how
20   many of their most deserving Generals: While the profounder Politicians, have seen Pamphlets, where *Tacitus* and *Machiavel* have
been quoted to shew the danger of too resplendent a Merit. Should
a Stranger hear these furious Out-cries of Ingratitude against
our General, without knowing the particulars, he would be apt to
25   enquire where was his Tomb, or whether he were allow'd Christian
Burial? Not doubting but we had put him to some ignominious Death.
Or, has he been tried for his Life, and very narrowly escap'd?
Has he been accus'd of High Crimes and Misdemeanors? Has the
Prince seiz'd on his Estate, and left him to starve? Has he been
30   hooted at as he passed the Streets, by an ungrateful Mob? Have
neither Honours, Offices nor Grants, been confer'd on Him or his
Family? Have not he and they been barbarously stript of them all?
Have not he and his Forces been ill pay'd abroad? And does not
the Prince by a scanty, limited Commission, hinder him from pur-
35   suing his own Methods in the conduct of the War? Has he no Power
at all of disposing Commissions as he pleases? Is he not severely
us'd by the Ministry or Parliament, who yearly call him to a
strict Account? Has the Senate ever thank'd him for good Success,

---

22-3 Should a Stranger] If a Stranger should 38 8°+12°   27 has] Has 12°
hath 38 8°   Hath 38 12°   30 Mob] Rabble 38 8°+12°   36 pleases] pleaseth 38 8°+12°

21-2 *Tacitus and Machiavel ... quoted*: 45.62, 81.
29   *Estate*: Delariviere Manley imitates this in *The D. of M---h's Vindication: In Answer to a Pamphlet lately Publish'd, call'd [Bouchain ...]*, London,
for J. Morphew, 1711, p. 5: 'Who, after this, would not conclude the D. of
M--- had been turn'd out of all, his Estate confiscated, and himself under
the most rigid Sentence?'
33   *pay'd*: Immediately upon taking office in August 1710 Harley borrowed
£400,000 from a consortium of Tory bankers headed by Richard Hoare and sent
£350,000 to Marlborough (Hill, p. 403). Marlborough replied that 'the Army
was never better paid' (BL MS Portland Loan 29/52, f. [1ᵛ]).
34   *Commission*: As Commander-in-Chief of the confederate army, Marlborough
was said to have had 'a more deciding influence' even than William III (*Biographia Britannica*, v 3563n.). Mrs Manley also imitated this detail in *The D.
of M---h's Vindication*, 1711, p. 7: 'Was his Commission limited? Had he not
Power to advance or retreat?'
35   *Power*: 17.179n.
38   *Account*: Marlborough was not called upon to account for his expenditures
until the summer of 1711.
       thank'd: Except for the year 1703, voting thanks to the Duke of Marl-
borough for his glorious victories was, from 1702 to 1709, as regular an
activity of Parliament as voting the supply. Extracts from the Journals are
conveniently collected in *The Sense of the Nation concerning the Duke of Marlborough, As it is express'd in several Acts of Parliament* (1712).

and have they not always publickly censur'd him for the least Miscarriage? Will the Accusers of the Nation join issue upon any of   40
these Particulars, or tell us in what Point, our damnable Sin of
Ingratitude lies? Why, 'tis plain and clear; For while he is Commanding abroad, the Queen Dissolves her Parliament, and changes
Her Ministry at home: In which *universal Calamity*, no less than
two Persons allied by Marriage to the General, have lost their   45
Places. Whence came this wonderful Simpathy between the Civil and
Military Powers? Will the Troops in *Flanders* refuse to Fight, unless they can have *their own* Lord Keeper, *their own* Lord President of the Council, *their own* chief Governor of *Ireland*, and
their own Parliament? In a Kingdom where the People are free, how 50
came they to be so fond of having their Councils under the Influence of their Army, or those that lead it? who in all well-
instituted States, had no Commerce with the civil Power, further
than to receive their Orders, and obey them without Reserve.

When a General is not so Popular, either in his Army or at   55
Home, as one might expect from a long course of Success; it may
perhaps be ascribed to his *Wisdom*, or perhaps to his Complexion.
The possession of some one *Quality*, or a defect in *some other*,
will extremely damp the Peoples Favour, as well as the Love of
the Souldiers. Besides, this is not an Age to produce Favourites   60
of the People, while we live under a Queen who engrosses all our
Love, and all our Veneration; and where the only way for a great
General or Minister, to acquire any degree of subordinate Affection from the Publick, must be by all Marks of the most *entire*
Submission and Respect, to Her Sacred Person and Commands; other- 65
wise, no pretence of great Services, either in the Field or the
Cabinet, will be able to skreen them from universal Hatred.

But the late Ministry was closely join'd to the General, by
Friendship, Interest, Alliance, Inclination and Opinion, which

43 Dissolves] dissolveth 38 8°   dissolves 38 12°   changes] changeth 38
8°+12°   61 engrosses] engrosseth 38 8°+12°   62 where] ~, ½° 12° 38 8°

---

45 *two Persons*: Godolphin, father-in-law to Marlborough's eldest daughter, Henrietta, and Sunderland, husband of Marlborough's second daughter,
Anne.
65 *Submission*: Marlborough was said to have lost all credit with the Queen
when he forced her 'much against her Inclination' to accept Harley's resignation in February 1708 (BL MS Lansdowne 885, f. 62^V; Swift, *Prose*, vii 73).

70 cannot be affirm'd of the present; and the Ingratitude of the
    Nation, lies in the People's *joining as one Man*, to wish, that
    such a Ministry should be changed. Is it not at the same time
    notorious to the whole Kingdom, that nothing but a tender regard
    to the General, was able to preserve that Ministry so long, 'till
75 neither God nor Man could suffer their continuance? Yet in the
    highest Ferment of Things, we heard few or no Reflections upon
    this great Commander, but all seem'd unanimous in wishing he
    might still be at the Head of the Confederate Forces; only at the
    same time, in case he were resolv'd to resign, they chose rather
80 to turn their Thoughts somewhere else, than throw up all in Des-
    pair. And this I cannot but add, in defence of the People, with
    regard to the Person we are speaking of, that in the high Station
    he has been for many Years past, his *real Defects* (as nothing
    Human is without them) have in a detracting Age been very
85 sparingly mention'd, either in Libels or Conversation, and all
    his *Successes* very freely and universally applauded.

       There is an active and a passive Ingratitude; applying both to
    this Occasion, we may say, the first is, when a Prince or People
    returns good Services with Cruelty or ill Usage: The other is,
90 when good Services are not at all, or very meanly rewarded. We

       71 lies] lieth 38 8°

---

    71 *joining as one Man*: Swift's phrase for the general election of October
    1710 (39.136).
    78 *Head*: Until 29 December 1710 Harley hoped to be able to keep Marl-
    borough as Commander-in-Chief (*POAS*, Yale, vii 555). It has been said that
    Marlborough refused to collaborate with Harley unless he could be Prime Mini-
    ster himself (Cunningham, ii 363).
    80 *somewhere else*: It had been known since February 1708 that if it became
    necessary Harley would replace Marlborough with Ormond (*POAS*, Yale, vii 305).
    85 *sparingly mention'd*: The first references to Marlborough's avarice were
    unpublished. In January 1699 Tallard, the French ambassador, expressed sur-
    prise that the vice had 'so much power over him' (Grimblot, ii 235) and in
    privately circulated verses there are references to 'sly Avaro' (University
    of Leeds MS Brotherton Lt.11, p. 164). It was in the third edition of William
    Shippen's *Faction Display'd* (1705) that Marlborough was publicly exposed as
    Penurio (*POAS*, Yale, vi 798) and in [Colley Cibber,] *The Secret History of
    Arlus and Odolphus*, London, 1710, p. 9, he is said to have 'had from his
    Youth an irresistible *Tendre*' for money. But these were only the scattered
    drops of the storm that was soon to break.
    87 *Ingratitude*: By misreading Swift's text, this paragraph was applied to
    another Whig propaganda theme, England's ingratitude towards William III (*A
    Letter to the Eldest Brother of the Collegiate Church of St. Katherine, In
    Answer to his Scurrilous Pamphlet Entitul'd The Modern Fanatick*, London, for
    J. Baker, 1711, p. 38).

have already spoke of the former; let us therefore in the second
place, examine how the Services of our General have been rewarded;
and whether upon that Article, either Prince or People have been
guilty of Ingratitude?

Those are the most valuable Rewards which are given to us from   95
the certain Knowledge of the Doner, that they *fit our Temper best*:
I shall therefore say nothing of the Title of *Duke*, or the *Garter*,
which the Queen bestow'd the General in the beginning of her
Reign; but I shall come to *more Substantial* Instances, and mention nothing which has not been given in the Face of the World.   100
The Lands of *Woodstock*, may, I believe, be reckoned worth 40000 *l.*
On the building of *Blenheim* Castle 200000 *l.* have been already
expended, tho' it be not yet near finish'd. The Grant of 5000 *l.*
per An. on the Post-Office, is richly worth 100000 *l.* His Principality in *Germany* may be computed at 30000 *l.* Pictures, Jewels,   105
and other Gifts from Foreign Princes, 60000 *l.* The Grant at the
Pall-mall, the Rangership, &c. for want of more certain Knowledge,
may be call'd 10000 *l.* His own, and his Dutchess's Employments at

96 Doner] Donor 38 8°+12°   98 beginning] begining ½°

---

101 *Woodstock*: In February 1705 Parliament passed legislation (3 & 4 Ann.
c. 4) to enable Anne to bestow upon Marlborough and his heirs for ever the
royal manor of Woodstock and the hundred of Wootton. Anne then undertook construction of Blenheim Palace entirely at her own expense. She chose as her
architect Captain John Vanbrugh, who gave full rein to his comic genius in the
design of the edifice. Since the park is eight miles around, £40,000 is probably a low estimate.
103 *Grant*: In January 1707 further legislation was passed (6 Ann. c. 7)
enabling Anne to pay Marlborough a pension during her lifetime of £5,000 a
year out of post office revenues.
104-5 *Principality*: In August 1704, in recognition of the victory at Schel-
lenberg and Blenheim, Emperor Leopold made Marlborough a Prince of the Empire,
and in November 1705 the new Emperor, Joseph, conferred upon him the principality of Mindelheim in Suabia, worth about £2,000 a year (Peter Barber,
British Library Journal, viii (1982), 54, 67-8).
106 *Gifts*: Swift again errs on the low side: 'The Emperor gave this year
[1705] to the value of 50000libs. besides what was presented by the King of
Prussia, the Elector of Hannover, & other Courts' (Hearne, i 162). Other gifts
included gold plate from the Elector of Hanover and a diamond-encrusted sword
from the Emperor (GEC, viii 496).
106-7 *Grant at the Pall-mall*: the lease at a nominal rent of the Friary,
4 acres of Crown land adjacent to St. James's Palace, on which Marlborough
House, designed by Sir Christopher Wren, had just been erected (1709-10)
(HMC *Portland MSS*, iv 506).
107 *Rangership*: In March 1702 Anne appointed Lady Marlborough ranger of
Windsor Park, worth £1,500 a year, and the occupancy of Windsor Lodge, which
became the Marlboroughs' favourite residence.

five Years Value, reckoning only the known and avow'd Sallaries,
110 are very low-rated at 100000 *l*. Here is a good deal above half a
Million of Money, and I dare say, those who are loudest with the
Clamor of Ingratitude, will readily own, that all this is but
a Trifle in comparison with what is *untold*.

The reason of my stating this Account is only to convince the
115 World, that we are not quite so ungrateful either as the *Greeks*
or the *Romans*. And in order to adjust this matter with all Fairness, I shall confine my self to the latter, who were much the
more generous of the two. A Victorious General of *Rome* in the
Height of that Empire, having *entirely subdued his Enemy*, was re-
120 warded with the larger Triumph; and perhaps a Statue in the *Forum*,
a Bull for a Sacrifice, an embroidred Garment to appear in: A
Crown of Lawrel, a Monumental Trophy with Inscriptions, sometimes
five hundred or a thousand Copper Coins were struck on occasion
of the Victory, which doing Honour to the General, we will place
125 to his Account; And lastly, sometimes, tho' not very frequently,
a Triumphal Arch. These are all the Rewards that I can call to
mind, which a victorious General received after his return from
the most glorious Expedition, conquered some great Kingdom,
brought the King himself, his Family and Nobles to adorn the

---

113 a Trifle] a mere Trifle 38 12°   with] of 38 8°   119 *Enemy*] Enemies 12° 38 8°+12°

---

109 *Sallaries*: The estimated annual income of the Duke and Duchess was
£62,325. The salaries from English sources were £37,325, so Swift's estimate
of £20,000 a year is 'very low' indeed (*The D--e and D---s of M---h's Loss;
Being An Estimate of their former Yearly Income*, 1712) (E1922, ix 96).
113 *untold*: The Duke's kickbacks, rake-offs, and '*private Perquisites*'
(56.173) were partly told in 1711: Sir Solomon Medina, for example, paid him
£6,000 a year for exclusive advance news of the outcome of battles. The
Duchess's defalcations, however, have never been counted. She was 'a bold
frontless woman who knew how to make the most of her opportunities', as Johnson said, and it was widely known that she trafficked in the 'Sale of Offices
and Places of Trust' (Boswell, *The Journal of a Tour to the Hebrides*, edd.
Frederick A. Pottle and Charles H. Bennett, New York, McGraw-Hill, 1961,
p. 141; William Pittis, *The Case of the Church of England's Memorial Fairly
Stated*, London, 1705, p. 36).
114 *Account*: The balance sheet device is not original with Swift. It had
been used recently at least twice: Defoe, *Review*, 23 April 1709; *The Divine
Rights of the British Nation and Constitution Vindicated*, London, for J. Baker,
1710, pp. 121-4.
119 *subdued*: The indispensable condition for a triumph, that the enemy had
been totally defeated, had not been met in November 1710.

Triumph in Chains, and made the Kingdom either a *Roman* Province,   130
or at best a poor depending State, in humble Alliance to that
Empire. Now of all these Rewards, I find but two which were of
real Profit to the General; The *Lawrel Crown*, made and sent him
at the Charge of the Publick, and the *Embroidred Garment*; but I
cannot find whether this last were paid for by the Senate or the   135
General: However, we will take the more favourable Opinion, and
in all the rest, admit the whole Expence as if it were ready
Money in the General's Pocket. Now according to these Computations
on both sides, we will draw up two fair Accounts, the one of *Roman*
Gratitude, and the other of *British* Ingratitude, and set them   140
together in ballance.

A Bill of *Roman* Gratitude

Imprimis.	l.	s.	d.
For			
Franckincense			
and Earthen			
Pots to burn			
it in	4	10	0
A Bull for Sa-			
crifice	8	0	0
An Embroi-			
dred Garment	50	0	0
A Crown of			
Lawrel	0	0	2
A Statue	100	0	0
A Trophy	80	0	0
A thousand			
Copper Me-			
dals value			
halfpence a			
piece	2	1	8

A Bill of *British* Ingratitude

Imprimis.	l.	s.	d.	
Woodstock	40000	0	0	
Blenheim	200000	0	0	145
Post-Office				
Grant	100000	0	0	
Mildenheim	30000	0	0	
Pictures,				
Jewels, &c.	60000	0	0	150
Pall-mall				
grant, &c.	10000	0	0	
Employ-				
ments	100000	0	0	
				155
				160

135 were] was 38 12°   138 General's] Geral's ½°   151-2 *Pall-mall*
grant] *Pall-mall-grant* ½°

130 *Province*: It was later enacted that triumphs should only be decreed to
those who had enlarged the empire, another condition that had not been met
(Quintus Valerius Maximus, *Romae antiquae descriptio*, London, by J. C. for
Samuel Speed, 1678, p. 89).

	A Triumphal		
	Arch	500 0 0	
	A Triumphal		
165	Carr, valu'd		
	as a Modern		
	Coach	100 0 0	
	Casual Char-		
	ges at the Tri-		
170	umph	150 0 0	
	Sum Total	994 11 10	540000 0 0

     This is an Account of the visible Profits on both sides; and if
the *Roman* General had any *private Perquisites*, they may be easily
discounted, and by more probable Computations, and differ yet more
175 upon the Ballance. If we consider, that all the Gold and Silver for
Saufguards and *Contributions*, also all *valuable Prizes* taken in the
War were openly expos'd in the Triumph, and then lodged in the
Capitol for the Publick Service.
     So that upon the whole, we are not yet quite so bad at *worst*, as
180 the *Romans* were at *best*. And I doubt, those who raise this hideous
Cry of Ingratitude, may be mightily mistaken in the Consequence
they propose from such Complaints. I remember a saying of *Seneca*,
Multos ingratos invenimus, plures facimus; We find many ungrate-
ful Persons in the World, but we *make* more, by setting too high a
185 Rate upon our Pretensions, and undervaluing the Rewards we receive.
When unreasonable Bills are brought in, they ought to be Taxed,

---

     176 also] and 38 8°   181 Consequence] Consequences 38 8°   182 *Seneca*]
Senaca ½° 12°

---

     176 *Saufguards and Contributions*: The extortion of money to protect a place
from pillage or from the quartering of soldiers is common military practice.
Safeguards, signed by the commanding officer, were issued after contributions
had been levied and paid (*OED*). 'What with the Moneys arising from *Safe-
Guards*, [and] his Share of the *Contributions*, which are more and more extended
into the Enemies Country ... his Grace [Marlborough] does not lay by less than
80000*l*. a Campaign' (H. S., *Reasons why the Duke of Marlborough cannot lay
down his Commands*, London, J. Baker, 1710, p. 6). Another source put it at
£2,000 a day (*Wentworth Papers*, p. 74).
     183 *Multos ... facimus*: a slight misquotation of 'Multos experimur in-
gratos, plures facimus' (Seneca, *De beneficiis*, i 1 4).
     185 *Pretensions*: As early as June 1705 Marlborough was complaining of 'the
base ingratitude of [his] countrymen' (*Marlborough-Godolphin Corr.*, p. 448).

or cut off in the middle. Where there have been long Accounts between two Persons, I have known one of them perpetually making
large Demands and pressing for Payments, who when the Accounts
were cast up on both sides, was found to be Debtor for some   190
Hundreds. I am thinking if a Proclamation were issued out for
every Man to send in his *Bill of Merits*, and the lowest Price he
set them at, what a pretty Sum it would amount to, and how many
such Islands as this must be sold to pay them. I form my Judgment
from the Practice of those who sometimes happen to *pay themselves*, 195
and I dare affirm, would not be so unjust to take a farthing more
than they think is due to their Deserts. I will instance only in
one Article. A Lady of my Acquaintance, appropriated twenty six
Pounds a Year out of her Allowance, for certain uses, which her
Woman received, and was to pay to the Lady or her Order, as it   200
was called for. But after eight Years, it appeared upon the
strictest Calculation, that the Woman had paid but four Pound a
Year, and sunk two and twenty for her own Pocket; 'tis but supposing instead of twenty six Pound, twenty six thousand, and by
that you may judge what the Pretensions of *Modern Merit* are,   205
where it happens to be its own Paymaster.

190 Debtor] Creditor ½° 12° 38 12°   199 her Allowance] her own Allowance 38 8°   202 Pound] Pounds 38 8°+12°   204 Pound] Pounds 38 8°

---

198 *Lady*: Upon her accession Queen Anne made Lady Marlborough Mistress of
the Robes (£1,500 a year), Groom of the Stole (£1,000 a year), First Lady of
the Bedchamber, and Keeper of the Privy Purse (£2,000).
200 *Woman*: The Duchess of Marlborough admired this 'witty comparison'. One
grant from the Queen, she said, 'occasioned the witty comparison that was
made between me and the lady's woman, who out of her mistress's pin-money of
26*l*. put twenty two into her own pocket. The matter was this.' The Duchess
recalls that she refused grants of £2,000 that the Queen repeatedly urged her
to charge against the privy purse, but when she was dismissed, 'I wrote ... to
ask her MAJESTY whether she would allow me to charge in the privy-purse accounts, which I was to send her, that yearly sum from the time of the offer,
amounting to 18,000*l*. Her MAJESTY was pleased to answer, that I might charge
it. This therefore I did' (*An Account of the Conduct*, pp. 293-5). Walter Scott
observes that the anecdote does the Duchess 'more discredit than she seems to
be aware of' (E*1814*, iii 348).
204 *twenty six thousand*: The yearly allowance for the privy purse was in-
creased from £20,000 to £26,000 in 1708 (*An Account of the Conduct*, p. 282).

No. 9 [Mainwaring and Oldmixon]   27 November 1710

The MEDLEY.

The Vanity óf the Whigs.

An Acrostick, *with Notes.*

Danger from Flatterers.

Translation of La Fontaine.

Of the Sausage-Maker in Aristophanes.

THERE is certainly no Creature in the World so vain as a *Whig*:
None but his Generals have Courage; none but his Ministers have
Probity or Politicks; none but his Patriots Principles; none but
his Bank has Mony; none but his Ladies Beauty; none but his Au-
5 thors Learning, and none but his Poets Wit. I shall not go about
to prove the Vanity of these Pretences, the matter being so very
notorious, especially with respect to Wit; in which the Tories
every day distinguish themselves more and more, and make new
Acquisitions: so that they will soon have all the Wit on their
10 side, almost as soon as they will have the Places. If there were
any Mortal living, that cou'd be suppos'd to question this, how
many Instances cou'd I produce to demonstrate it? *Examiners,
Doubles, Atalantis's*, Men and Women, all Authors of a size, might
be fairly shewn together, in order to make it good: But I shall
15 satisfy my self at this time with one Instance only. Indeed, 'tis
an extraordinary one: An *Acrostick*, handed about by Persons of
Distinction of that side with great Applause, and not at all un-

La] *Le* ½° 12°   3 Principles;] ∼, ½°

---

13 *Doubles*: Davenant had been called Tom Double since *The True Tom Double,
or An Account of Dr. Davenant's Late Conduct and Writings, Particularly with
Relation to the XIth Section of his Essay on Peace at Home, and War Abroad*
(1704). His latest work, *Sir Thomas Double at Court and in High Preferment*,
had been published on 3 October 1710 (*The Medley*, 5 October 1710).
   Atalantis's: The two volumes of Delariviere Manley's *Secret Memoirs and
Manners of Several Persons of Quality, of Both Sexes. From the New Atlantis*
and the two volumes of her *Memoirs of Europe, Toward the Close of the Eighth
Century ... done into English by the Translator of the New Atalantis*, called
collectively *The New Atlantis*, were published between May 1709 and November
1710 (*HLQ*, xii (May 1949), 264).

deserv'd, as will be seen immediately. The name of the Author I
cou'd not learn, but the Gentleman who gave me his Verses, assur'd
me he was *tam Marte quam Mercurio*, the very same that Sir *Walter*   20
Raleigh was: And tho he is so modest as to conceal himself, his
Fame will out-do every thing that has been heard of in *Parnassus*,
since Mr. *Quarles* flourish'd.

                  The Acrostick *is this:*

          Hail! Bright Asserter of our Free-born State!   25
          Active, tho still, like our approaching Fate:
          Rousing the Spirit of our lethargick Isle,
          Lingring beneath a most destructive Smile.
          Eager of Right, Britannia *undeceiv'd,*
          Yea, Glorious Anna's *perfect Ease retriev'd.*   30

Tho this Acrostick is modern, there are certain mysterious Expressions in it, that will hinder its being so intelligible to Posterity, as might be wish'd: For which reason, a small Comment
upon it will not be very impertinent, nor I hope unacceptable to   35
the Courteous Reader.

Hail! is a word of great Antiquity: The Jews us'd it, as every
one knows, when they were doing the most wicked thing that ever
was done in the world. 'Tis also met with in Chorus's on the
Stage, and has a fine Effect in *Incantations*, which signify   40
charming, and singing, or chirping, as well as enchanting and

---

19 Gentleman] ~, ½°

---

18 *Author*: 'Major General C---r' (Oldmixon, *The Life*, sig. Aa4^r). There
are only two candidates for this dubious distinction: George Carpenter, promoted major-general in September 1708, and Thomas Crowther, promoted major-
general in 1710 (Dalton, vi 17, 18). As a future Whig Member of Parliament
(Whitchurch 1715-22, Westminster 1722-7), Carpenter is more likely to have
been known to Oldmixon (GEC, iii 54).
20 *tam Marte quam Mercurio*: George Gascoigne included a portrait of himself
in armour with this motto on the verso of the title-page of *The Steel Glas. A
Satyre* (1576) (Wood, i 435-6). Raleigh wrote commendatory verses for the same
volume and after Gascoigne's death the motto was 'assumed by, or appropriated
to', Raleigh himself (*Biographia Britannica*, v 3467n.).
23 *Quarles*: Francis Quarles (1592-1644), the emblemist and archetypal bad
poet (John Pomfret, *Poems on Several Occasions*, 3rd edn., London, for Edward
Place, 1710, sig. π2^v).
37 *The Jews us'd it*: Mark 15:18.

bewitching; tho all those Interpretations are very applicable to
this Author and his Poem.

    Bright Asserter. *Dark* Asserter is never us'd by the best
45   Writers; for *Asserters* are always *bright.* However, there are
several sorts of Asserters: King *William* was an Asserter, but
that was of Liberty only: The last Parliament were Asserters, but
that was worse still, for they were only Asserters of King *William*
and the Revolution. What kind of Asserter is here meant (since
50   there never was an Asserter of nothing) appears by the next words,
which are,

    Free-born State. But here it will be necessary to add a Restric-
tion, lest those words shou'd be taken in any *Antimonarchical*
Republican Meaning; for doubtless the Poet intends them in a good
55   Church-Sense, That our State is as *Free,* as *Indefeasible* and
Hereditary can make it: which is surely free enough, and proves
it to be well born, and bless'd with Original Freedom, without
any regard to that foolish accidental Liberty which it receiv'd
at the Revolution.

60   *Active, tho still*: A pretty Image that! and borrow'd, as I suppose, from the late Circumstances of the Church, which was at the
same time both in danger and safe. *Active, tho still!* Nothing can
be more just or clear. But mind the Simile that follows—

    Like our approaching Fate. Here the Criticks will have it, that
65   our Author has some meaning that is not so well; and that he mix'd
a little touch of Satyr to give his Thing a relish. But if I am to
speak my Conscience, I think his Friends are to blame, if they are
angry at him for any Meaning, of which they ought not to suspect
him.

70   *Rousing the Spirit of our Lethargick Isle.* Here he seems to

    60 *Active,*] ~∧ ½°   62 *Active,*] ~∧ ½°

---

55 *Free ... Indefeasible*: Mainwaring scores here by pointing out an anomaly
in Swift's argument. If succession to the throne is *'Indefeasible'*, as Swift
did not deny (42.187), then 'the People' are not 'Free', as Swift claimed
(51.50), i.e., they are not free to alter the succession, as Parliament did
in 1689.
    61-2 *Church ... in danger and safe*: 38.109-19.
    70 *Lethargick Isle*: 'This State Lethargy is such an Apoplectick Symptom, as
is commonly the Forerunner of Death to the Body Politick' (Davenant, *Essays*
upon: I. The Ballance of Power. II. The Right of making War, Peace, and Alli-
ances. III. Universal Monarchy, London, for J. Knapton, 1701, p. 1; cf. Swift,
Prose, i 30).

compare *Great Britain* to Something that's asleep; but he rightly
observes, that she's almost awake now: Her Eyes are opening, and
her *Spirit* will doubtless *be rouz'd* e'er long. This needs no
Interpretation.

Lingring beneath. This shou'd seem again to be satyrical, as if   75
the Island were *wasting under* a Consumption. But the next words
clear the Point; which are these:

A most destructive Smile. Yet here the Allegory, by being a
little too frequently vary'd, is grown somewhat obscure. It does
not appear by the Poet, who it is that smiles: Only 'tis probable   80
he means some *Syren*, that is now pleas'd, and in good-humour, because he says the Smile is destructive; for I never read of any
Smiles that were destructive, but the Smiles of these ugly
Creatures, that were half Women, half Fish, and yet were us'd to
bewitch People. This will puzzle the Commentators of the next   85
Age, for even in ours we can hardly guess at it.

Eager of Right. A strong Expression! tho not very intelligible;
but there can be no harm in it. Eagerness is always commendable,
when a Person is sure that what he is eager for belongs to him,
and is his Right: as for example; If our Poet shou'd be eager to   90
assert his Title to this Acrostick.

Britannia undeceiv'd; not quite yet, as I noted before, but in
a very fair way to it.

Yea; a very fine Affirmative, most antient and sonorous: And
those that think it was only added to tag out the last Letter in   95
the Acrostick, know nothing of the force of Monosyllables, nor of
the true Spirit of Poetry.

Retriev'd: A word not much in use among the Writers of Verse;
but it was chosen, I suppose, by this Author, because of the
great Importance of it eight Years ago, and was now transplanted,   100

96 *Monosyllables*: cf. Pope, *Poems*, i 278.
98 *Retriev'd*: In October 1702 the Tory majority in the House of Commons
voted that Marlborough had 'by his Conduct of the Army [in the campaign of
1702], retrieved the ancient Honour and Glory of the *English* Nation', 'the
word *Retrieved*', as Burnet explained, 'implying that it was formerly lost'
(*CJ*, xiv 85, 87; Burnet, ii 334). The Whigs resented this insinuation that
William's victories were 'tarnished with the frequency of his defeats', but a
motion to remove the word was defeated (Dalrymple, iii [2]244). The poets kept
the word alive (William Walsh, *The Golden Age Restor'd* (January 1703), *POAS*,
Yale, vi 495; Samuel Cobb, *Honour Retriev'd. A Poem. Occasion'd by the late
Victories obtain'd over the French and Bavarians by the Forces of the Allies,
under the Command of his Grace the Duke of Marlborough* (1705)).

by Poetical Licence, out of the Vote of Parliament into this
Acrostick. A strange Fate has attended this word from the time it
was reviv'd with such great Propriety of Speech. It was in full
force, and many good Speeches were made for it by admirable
105 *British* Orators, when nothing had been done, and it cou'd have no
signification; and now, after forty Towns and Battles won, it is
all of a sudden grown obsolete again. But I think our Author has
taken care at last to provide for its Immortality; and by chusing
it for the very lowest and most weighty word of his whole Acros-
110 tick, he has fix'd it in a Place where it shall for ever stand,
as the Foundation or Bottom of his well-built Poem, when Votes,
and even Acts of Parliament, shall be quite forgotten.

   I shall not mind what People may say to me for making these few
useful Criticisms on the foregoing Verses; I value an Author for
115 his Love of Poetry, as much as some value a Poet for his Art: And
may this Person write in quiet the remainder of his days, as soon
as the War is ended,

                    --------*And chuse for his Command,*
                    Some peaceful Province in Acrostick Land.
120   Mac Fleckno

   The only Danger to a Great Man from such Incense as this, is,
That such immoderate Praises often spoil and corrupt the good
Habits of the Mind; nor is it always in his power to distinguish
between the false Attempts of a Flatterer, and the honest Commen-
125 dations of a Friend. The *Greeks* said, Flatterers were like so many
Ravens, croaking about High Ministers; and that they never lifted
a Man up, but as the Eagle does the Tortoise, in order to get
something by the Fall of him. It is very hard to know the Hearts
of Men; but if Ministers will be doing prodigious and extra-

103 Speech.] ~, ½°

───────

   105 *nothing*: Marlborough's first campaign (May-October 1702) accomplished
little. The Dutch strategists vetoed his plan to engage the French army under
Boufflers, but successful sieges of Venlo, Roermond, and Liège cleared the
French out of the Meuse valley, the traditional invasion route between France
and the Netherlands.
   112 *Acts of Parliament*: 53.101n., 103n.
   118-9 *And ... Land*: [Dryden,] *Mac Fleckno* [205-6] (½°).
   127 *Eagle ... Tortoise*: L'Estrange, p. 192.

ordinary things, they must expect to be commended for their Ac-   130
tions: And I shou'd think this Author as unlikely to have Guile
or Design, as most that I have met with. I shall now shew you on
the other side what sorry Poets the Whigs are; they have nothing
of their own, and are therefore forc'd to borrow of the *French*,
whom they pretend to hate so much. One of them shew'd me some   135
Verses of *la Fontaine*'s, with a new Translation:

> *Un Intendant? qu'est que cette chose?*
> *Je definis cette estre, un Animal,*
> *Qui, comme on dit, scait pecher en eau trouble &c.*

> An Intendant! What is he?   140
> Here his true Description see:
> He's an Animal, that seems
> Pleas'd to fish in troubled Streams:
> Let the Publick sink or swim,
> 'Tis the self-same thing to him.   145
> If you say the State and Crown,
> In his Hands are tumbling down:
> *Come have Patience, Sir*, he cries,
> *Funds shall fill, and Stocks shall rise.*
> If you ask him *How*, or *Why*?   150
> Straight you have in one Reply,
> All the Reason he can tell;
> *Phoo! I warrant things go well.*

Aristophanes has an odd Whim in one of his Comedies: 'He introduces a chief Person of his Play, endeavouring to persuade a Man   155
that made Sausages to resolve upon meddling with Affairs of State.

139 *en*] *in* ½°
_____

136 *Verses*: The verses are a translation of lines 188-97 of *Belphegor*.
Mainwaring quotes from Jean de La Fontaine, *Contes et nouvelles en vers*, 2
vols., Amsterdam, Pierre Brunel, 1699, i 187.
154 *Aristophanes*: *In Equitibus, Act*. I. *Sc*. 2. (½°). Like Swift, Mainwaring seems to have used editions with parallel translations in Latin, for the
Greek editions lack act-scene divisions (Aristophanes, *Veteres Comoediae*,
trans. N. Frischlin, Frankfurt, Ioannes Spies, 1586, ff. 91ᵛ-94ᵛ).
155-6 *Man that made Sausages*: 'That wonderful talent Mr. HARLEY possessed,
in the supreme degree, of confounding the common sense of mankind' was noticed
by the Duchess of Marlborough (*An Account of the Conduct*, p. 218).

The Man was surpriz'd at his Discourse, and ask'd, why he wou'd
despise and laugh at a poor Fellow, who had never imploy'd his
Thoughts or Time in any thing but making Sausages. Upon which the
160 Poet instructs his other Person to speak thus; Behold all these
Ranks of People, you shall be a great Leader and Chief among them;
you shall tread upon the Senate, and tie up the Hands of our
Generals. Who I? says the Sausage-maker: Yes, you shall do it,
quoth the other Person. Get upon this Table where you make your
165 Puddings, and look all about you: Do you see in that Scene the
Custom House, and all those Ships that are laden there with Mer-
chandize? See them! yes, says the Fellow; what then? Why all those
things shall be sold by you; the Oracle says you shall be a very
great Man. How shou'd that be for God's sake, cry'd the Fellow?
170 How shou'd I be a Great Man, that am but a Pudding-maker? Because,
said he, you are bold and wicked. But I think my self unworthy of
Greatness, said the Fellow. What does that signify, answer'd the
other? Do you think your self a good or an ill Man? Nay, for that
matter, said he, I am bad enough. I wish you Joy, reply'd the
175 other, you will find your self so much the better qualify'd when
you come to do Business, for our Commonwealth has nothing now to
do with Men of Learning and Probity, but is wholly govern'd by
the Ignorant, Impure and Immoral; therefore do not despise what
the Gods tell you by their Oracles, which prophesy very great
180 Honours that will be done to Persons of your Trade. But how, said
he, is it possible that I shou'd govern the People? With all the
Ease in the World, answer'd the other: Do only what you are us'd
to do; MIX, JUMBLE, DISTURB AND CONFOUND ALL MATTERS; feign and
invent any thing to please and delude the Rabble: for the rest
185 you have a great many Talents that are proper to gain their
Favour. You have a false Tongue, and a mischievous unlucky Understanding; you have some little smattering also in the Law: In
short, you have all the Qualities that our Republick wants at this
time, and that are necessary to make you a very Great Person.'
190   Monsieur *le Clerc*, taking notice of this Scene, says, 'The

---

187 *smattering*: There is an element of self-satire in this, for Mainwaring
shared Harley's 'smattering'. Harley was admitted to the Middle Temple in
March 1682 and Mainwaring to the Inner Temple five years later, but neither
of them was called to the bar.
190-7 *The ... Senate*: [Jean Le Clerc,] *Parrhas[iana ou pensées diverses sur*

Character was drawn for *Cleon*, who was a troublesom Orator, an
Enemy to the best Men of the Country, and to the greatest Generals
of that Government. He says the Poet very justly expos'd this
Person in his Play; who having never given the least Proof of his
Sincerity, or Love of his Country, had yet made himself consider-   195
able, by affecting a false Zeal for the Interest of the People,
and by living at open variance with the Nobility and the Senate.'
Monsieur *Le Clerc* says further, 'That the *Greek* and *Roman* Histories have many illustrious Examples of Great Men, to whom their
Country had infinite Obligations, ruin'd or banish'd; not for   200
having been found guilty of any Crime, but only for having been
accus'd by such Orators as this *Cleon*. Those that sought the
great Employments, and were resolv'd to get them, had need, *he*
says, but of two things; one was, to affect an Air of Popularity,
which was easily enough maintain'd: The other was, to affirm any   205
thing boldly, that suited with the present Taste of the Multitude.
Provided they had these two Qualities, no Vice, *he says*, of their
own cou'd hurt them: It was no matter if they were Ignorant, Malicious, Saucy, Revengeful, Violent and Cruel; they cover'd all
these Faults under the specious Veil of Zeal for the Publick   210
Good; their ready Gift of Speaking pass'd for Sense and Understanding in the Minds of the Multitude, who had still less Knowledg then themselves. And tho in reason they ought to have made
themselves odious by the Falshood of their Accusations, and the
Violence of their Prosecutions, the blind and credulous People   215
did not find it out; but took their most invenom'd Passions for
an extraordinary Regard to the Safety of the State.' And doubtless it was this very same *Cleon* that *Plutarch* mentions in his
Political Precepts, *who had a hundred Heads of fawning Flatterers*
licking about him, as the Comedian speaks, *and who debas'd him-*   220
self to court the Favour of the Multitude" doing all things to
humour them, and joining himself with the worst and most distem-
per'd of the People against the best. God preserve all Countries
from such *Cleons*, and such Sausage-makers.

des matières de critique, d'histoire, de morale et de politique, 2 vols.,
Amsterdam, Henri Schelte, 1701], ii 169 (½° corrected).
    198-217 *That ... State*: ibid., ii 167-8.
    219-23 *a ... best*: Plutarch, *Moralia*, 806F-807A. Plutarch quotes Aristopha-
nes, *Peace*, 756.

No. 18 [Swift]   30 November 1710

The EXAMINER

Quas res luxuries in flagitiis, avaritia in rapinis, superbia in contumeliis
efficere potuisset; eas omnes sese hoc uno Prætore per triennium pertu-
lisse, aiebant.

WHEN I first undertook this Paper, I was resolv'd to concern my
self only with *Things*, and not with *Persons*. Whether I have kept
or broken this Resolution, I cannot recollect; and I will not be
at the Pains to examine, but leave the matter to those little
5   Antagonists, who may want a Topick for Criticism. Thus much I
have discover'd, that it is in Writing as in Building; where,
after all our Schemes and Calculations, we are mightily deceiv'd
in our Accounts, and often forc'd to make use of any Materials we
can find, that the Work may be kept a going. Besides, to speak my
10 Opinion, the *Things* I have occasion to mention, are so closely
link'd to *Persons*, that nothing but *Time* (the Father of *Oblivion*)
can separate them. Let me put a parallel Case: Suppose I should
complain, that last Week my Coach was within an Inch of overturning, in a smooth, even Way, and drawn by very gentle Horses; to
15 be sure, all my Friends would immediately lay the Fault upon
John, because they knew, he then *Presided* in my Coach-Box. Again,
suppose I should discover some Uneasiness to find my self, I knew
not how, over Head-and-Ears in Debt, tho' I was sure my Tenants
paid their Rents very well, and that I never spent half my Income;
20 they would certainly advise me to turn off Mr. *Oldfox* my *Receiver*,

18 was] were 38 8°   19 half] all 38 8°

Motto Cicero, *In Q. Caecilium divinatio*, i 3: These things were the Effects
of his scandalous and unbounded Luxury, his insatiable Avarice, his contume-
lious Insolence. These were the Sufferings of that unhappy Nation for three
Years under his oppressive Government.
16 *John*: Walter Scott supposed that John Churchill, Duke of Marlborough, was
intended (E*1814*, iii 351), but 'Presided' does not suggest military command.
Mainwaring and Ridpath both understood that Swift meant John Somers, late Lord
President of the Privy Council (105.50); *The Observator*, 2 December 1710).
18 *Debt*: 7.121-2n.
20 *Oldfox*: L. Godolphin (E*1738*). Godolphin was called Volpone in Shippen's
Faction Display'd (April(?) 1704) and in Mrs Manley's *The Secret History of*

and take another. If, as a Justice of Peace, I should tell a
Friend that my Warrants and *Mittimus*'s were never drawn up as I
would have them; that I had the Misfortune to send an Honest Man
to Goal, and dismiss a Knave; he would bid'me no longer trust
Charles and *Harry*, my two *Clerks*, whom he knew to be ignorant,   25
wilful, assuming and ill-enclin'd Fellows. If I should add, that
my Tenants made me very uneasy with their Squabbles and Broils
among themselves; he would counsel me to Cashier *Will Bigamy*, the
Seneschal of my Mannor. And lastly, if my Neighbour and I happen'd to have a Misunderstanding about the *delivery of a Message*,   30
what could I do less than strip and discard the *blundering* or
malicious Rascal that carry'd it?

It is the same Thing in the Conduct of Publick Affairs, where
they have been manag'd with Rashness or Wilfulness, Corruption,
Ignorance or Injustice; barely to relate the Facts, at least,   35
while they are fresh in Memory, will as much reflect upon the
Persons concern'd, as if we had told their Names at length.

I have therefore since thought of another Expedient, frequently
practic'd with great safety and success by Satyrical Writers:
Which is, That of looking into History for some Character bearing   40
a Resemblance to the Person we would describe; and with the
absolute Power of altering, adding or suppressing what Circumstances we please, I conceiv'd we must have very bad Luck, or

32 that] who 38 8°+12°

Queen Zarah, and the Zarazians (1705). But the nickname received the widest
currency in the sermon, *The Perils of False Brethren, both in Church, and State*
(40,000 copies sold), for which Sacheverell was impeached when Godolphin foolishly 'applyed [it] to himself' (Swift, *Prose*, vii 9).

25 *Charles and Harry*: E. Sunderland, *and Harry* Boyle, [*late*] *Secretaries of
State* (E*1738*).

28 *Will Bigamy*: L. Chancellor Cowper (E*1738*). The story of Cowper's relationship with his ward, an orphan named Elizabeth Cullen or Culling, by whom
he had two children (Hearne, i 57; *The English Traveller: Giving a Description
of ... England and Wales*, 3 vols., London, T. Read, 1746, i 315; *Biographia
Britannica*, 2nd edn., iv 338-9), is told at large by Delariviere Manley under
the names of Hernando and Louisa (*Secret Memoirs*, 1709, i 214-44). Subsequently,
in 1688, Cowper married Judith Booth, the daughter of a London merchant.

32 *Rascal*: 'Horatio Walpole, secretary to the English Embassy at the treaty
of Gertruydenberg. Swift, in the Conduct of the Allies [*Prose*, vi 50], accuses
him of misleading the nation, by falsely stating that the French had willingly
acceded to the preliminary articles, and would even have made farther concessions, when he must have known the contrary' (E*1814*, iii 352).

42 *altering, adding or suppressing*: 13.56n.

very little Skill to fail. However, some Days ago in a Coffee-
45 House, looking into one of the Politick Weekly Papers; I found
the Writer had fallen into this Scheme, and I happen'd to light
on that part, where he was describing a Person, who from small
Beginnings grew (as I remember) to be Constable of *France*, and
had a very *haughty, imperious Wife*. I took the Author for a Friend
50 to our *Faction*, (for so with great Propriety of Speech they call
the Queen and Ministry, almost the whole Clergy, and nine parts
in ten of the Kingdom) and I said to a Gentleman near me, that
although I knew well enough what Persons the Author meant, yet
there were several Particulars in the *Husband*'s Character, which
55 I could not reconcile. For that of the *Lady*, was just and adequate enough; but it seems I mistook the whole Matter, and apply'd
all I had read to a couple of Persons, who were not at that time
in the Writers Thoughts.

Now to avoid such a Misfortune as this, I have been for some
60 time consulting *Livy* and *Tacitus*, to find out the Character of a
Princeps Senatus, a *Prætor Urbanus*, a *Quæstor Ærarius*, a *Cæsari
ab Epistolis*, and a *Proconsul*; but among the worst of them, I cannot discover One from whence to draw a Parallel, without doing
Injury to a *Roman* Memory: So that I am compel'd to have recourse
65 to *Tully*. But this Author relating Facts only as an Orator, I
thought it would be best to observe his Method, and make an Extract from six Harangues of his against *Verres*, only still preserving the Form of an Oration. I remember a younger Brother of
mine, who Deceas'd about two Months ago, presented the World with

49 *a ... Wife*: 'Swift insinuates, with justice, that the character of Galigai [16.135-8] would better have suited the Duchess of Marlborough' (E*1814*,
iii 352).
50 *Faction*: cf. Durfey, *Belisarius and Zariana. A Dialogue*, '⌐...on, for
J. Morphew, 1710, p. 3: 'The Faction ... lessen those they wou1! remove | That
their vile Projects might effectual prove.'
67 *Harangues*: Cicero's Verrine orations consist of the *actio prima* and five
books of the *actio secunda*. Since Verres absconded during the trial, the *actio
secunda* did not need to be delivered in court. Verres, whose name means hog,
undertook the systematic spoliation of Sicily during his term as propraetor.
His antitype, Wharton, undertook something similar in Ireland during his term
as Lord-Lieutenant (December 1708-October 1710).
68-9 *Brother ... Deceas'd*: Addison, who laid to rest *The Whig-Examiner* after
No. 5 of 12 October 1710. Thus Swift makes the retort courteous to Mainwaring's
quip modest (11.32). Ridpath kept the joke going, announcing the death of the
Examiner's 'Brother the *Moderator*' in *The Observator*, 29 November-2 December
1710. Abel Roper's *The Moderator*, a predecessor of *The Examiner*, ceased publication with No. 50 of 6-10 November 1710.

a Speech of *Alcibiades* against an *Athenian* Brewer: Now, I am told   70
for certain, that in those days there was no Ale in *Athens*; and
therefore that Speech, or at least a great part of it, must needs
be Spurious. The difference between Me and my Brother is this; he
makes *Alcibiades* say a great deal more than he really did, and I
make *Cicero* say a great deal less. This *Verres* had been the *Roman*   75
Governor of *Sicily* for three Years, and on return from his Government, the *Sicilians* entreated *Cicero* to impeach him in the Senate,
which he accordingly did in several Orations, from whence I have
faithfully Translated and Abstracted that which follows.

My Lords,   80

'A Pernicious Opinion hath for some time prevail'd, not only at
Rome, but among our neighbouring Nations, that a Man who has
Money enough, tho' he be ever so guilty, cannot be condemn'd in
this Place. But however industriously this Opinion be spread, to
cast an Odium on the Senate, we have brought before your Lord-   85
ships *Caius Verres*, a Person, for his Life and Actions, already
condemn'd by all Men; but as he hopes, and gives out, by the Influence of his Wealth, to be here absolved. In condemning this
Man, you have an Opportunity of belying that general Scandal, of
redeeming the *Credit lost by former Judgments*, and recovering the   90
Love of the *Roman* People, as well as of our Neighbours. I have
brought a Man here before you, my Lords, who is a Robber of the
Publick Treasure, an Overturner of Law and Justice, and the

92 a Man here] here a Man 38 8°

---

70 *Speech*: In the general election of October 1710 James Stanhope, a Whig
general fresh from victories in Spain, contested one of the Westminster seats
against Thomas Crosse, a local Tory brewer. In *The Whig-Examiner* for 28 September 1710 Addison included a pretended speech of Alcibiades against one
Taureas, an anachronistic Athenian brewer: 'Is it then possible, O ye *Athenians*
... That I who have overthrown the Princes of *Lacedaemon*, must now see myself
in Danger of being defeated by a Brewer?... Let it not avail my Competitor,
that he has been tapping his Liquors while I have been spilling my Blood; that
he has been gathering Hopps for you, while I have been reaping Lawrels. Have I
not born the Dust and Heat of the Day, while he has been Sweating at the Furnace?' Scott calls attention to the difference between 'the light and comic
style of Addison's parody, [and] the fierce, stern, and vindictive tone of
Swift's philippic against the Earl of Wharton' (*E1814*, iii 353-4). Scott would
have been even more admiring if he had known that Swift wrote 'light and comic'
verses on the Westminster election (*POAS*, Yale, vii 480) as well as the stern
philippic against Wharton.
81-106 *A ... corrupt*: Cicero, *In C. Verrem*, i 1 (§1)-2 (§4).

Disgrace, as well as Destruction, of the *Sicilian* Province: Of
95   whom, if you shall determine with Equity and due Severity, your
Authority will remain entire, and upon such an Establishment as
it ought to be: But if his great Riches will be able to force
their way through that Religious Reverence and Truth, which become so awful an Assembly, I shall, however, obtain thus much,
100 That the Defect will be laid where it ought, and that it shall not
be objected that the Criminal was not produced, or that there
wanted an Orator to accuse him. This Man, my Lords, has publickly
said, That Those ought to be afraid of Accusations who have only
robb'd enough for their own Support and Maintenance; but that *He*
105 has plunder'd sufficient to bribe Numbers, and that nothing is so
High or so Holy which Money cannot corrupt. Take that Support
from him, and he can have no other left. For what Eloquence will
be able to defend a Man, whose Life has been tainted with so many
scandalous Vices, and who has been so long condemned by the uni-
110 versal Opinion of the World? To pass over the foul Stains and
Ignominy of his Youth, his corrupt Management in all Employments
he has born, his Treachery and Irreligion, his Injustice and Oppression, he has left of late such Monuments of his Villanies in
Sicily, made such Havock and Confusion there, during his Govern-
115 ment, that the Province cannot by any Means be restored to its
former State, and hardly recover it self at all under many Years,
and by a long Succession of good Governours. While this Man
governed in that Island, the *Sicilians* had neither the Benefit of
our Laws, nor their own, nor even of common Right. In *Sicily*, no
120 Man now possesses more than what the Governour's Lust and Avarice
have overlook'd, or what he was forced to neglect out of meer
Weariness and Satiety of Oppression. Every thing where he presided,
was determin'd by his arbitrary Will, and the best Subjects he
treated as Enemies. To recount his abominable Debaucheries, would
125 offend any modest Ear, since so many could not preserve their
Daughters and Wives from his Lust. I believe there is no Man who
ever heard his Name, that cannot relate his Enormities. We bring

101 objected that] objected, 38 8°   106 so Holy] Holy 38 8°+12°
120 possesses] possesseth 38 8°+12°

106-27 *Take ... Enormities*: Cicero, *In C. Verrem*, i 3 (§10)-5 (§15).
127-47 *We ... &c.*: Except for phrases 'DEFILERS OF ALTARS ... *Priesthood*'
etc., the rest of the oration is Swift's, not Cicero's.

before you in Judgment, my Lords, a Publick Robber, an Adulterer,
a DEFILER OF ALTARS, an Enemy of Religion, and of all that is
Sacred; he sold all Employments in *Sicily* of Judicature, Magi-   130
stracy, and Trust, Places in the Council, and the *Priesthood* it
self, to the highest Bidder; and has plunder'd that Island of
forty Millions of Sesterces. And here I cannot but observe to
your Lordships, in what manner *Verres* pass'd the Day: The Morning
was spent in taking Bribes, and selling Employments, the rest of   135
it in Drunkenness and Lust. His Discourse at Table was scandalously unbecoming the Dignity of his Station; Noise, Brutality,
and Obsceneness. One Particular I cannot omit, that in the high
Character of Governor of *Sicily*, upon a solemn Day, a Day set
a-part for Publick Prayer for the Safety of the Commonwealth; he   140
stole at Evening, in a Chair, to a marry'd Woman of infamous

129 of] to 38 12°   130 he sold all Employments in *Sicily*] in *Sicily* he
sold all Employments 38 8°+12°

---

129 *DEFILER OF ALTARS*: Verres defiled temples by removing the statuary for
his private collection. Wharton's pollutions were of a different kind. In
August 1682 he desecrated the church at Great Barrington, on the Windrush, near
Burford, Oxon.: besides other acts too gross to mention in the nineteenth century, 'the bells were rung backwards, the ropes cutt, the bible torn, the cover
of the font and the desk of the pulpit broaken' (David Royce, *The History and
Antiquities of Stow*, Stow-on-the-Wold, T. Clift, 1861, pp. 34-7). Then, during
a debate in the House of Lords in December 1705, when Wharton ridiculed the
idea that the Church was in danger, the old Duke of Leeds stood up and said,
'If there were any that had pissed against a communion table, or done his other
occasions in a pulpit, he should not think the church safe in such hands. Upon
which lord Wharton was very silent for the rest of that day' (Burnet, 1833,
v 242).
130 *sold ... Employments*: 'So long as Verres was praetor no man could become a senator unless he had first paid Verres money. The same thing may be
said of magistracies, directorships [*curationes*], and priesthoods' (*In C. Verrem*, ii 2 50 (§§125-6)). During his propraetorship of Ireland Wharton is said
to have 'gained ... five and forty thousand Pounds by the most favourable Computation' (Swift, *Prose*, iii 181).
131 *Priesthood*: Verres' crony, whom he illegally appointed a high priest of
Jupiter, was one Theomnastus (*In C. Verrem*, ii 2 51). The antitype of Theomnastus may be Ralph Lambert, whom Wharton in November 1708 appointed a vice-
regal chaplain, a post vaguely coveted by Swift, for which, however, he 'made
no manner of application' (Swift, *Corr.*, i 113). In May 1709 Lambert was
appointed Dean of Down (Henry Cotton, *Fasti Ecclesiae Hibernicae*, 2nd edn., 5
vols., Dublin, Hodges and Smith, 1848-60, iii 227).
136 *Discourse*: Verres' dinner parties 'were celebrated with loud shouts and
cries of abuse, and sometimes ... an actual hand-to-hand fight' (*In C. Verrem*,
ii 5 11 (§28)). 'Bawdy, Prophaneness and Business, fill up [Wharton's] whole
Conversation' (Swift, *Prose*, iii 180).
141 *Woman*: Wharton's 'infamous Intrigues with Mrs. *Coningsby*' are mentioned
in *A Continuation of A Short Character of Thomas, Earl of Wharton* (Swift,

Character, against all Decency and Prudence, as well as against
all Laws both Humane and Divine. Didst thou think, O *Verres*, the
Government of *Sicily* was given thee with so large a Commission,
145   only by the Power of That to break all the Bars of Law, Modesty,
and Duty, to suppose all Mens Fortunes thine, and leave no House
free from thy Rapine, or Lust? &c.'

This Extract, to deal ingenuously, has cost me more Pains than
150   I think it is worth, having only served to convince me, that
modern Corruptions are not to be parallel'd by ancient Examples,
without having recourse to Poetry or Fable. For instance, I never
read in Story of a Law enacted to take away the Force of all Laws
whatsoever; by which a Man may safely commit upon the last of
155   *June,* what he would infallibly be hang'd for if he committed on
the first of *July*; by which the greatest Criminals may escape,
provided they continue long enough in Power to antiquate their
Crimes, and by stifling them a while, can deceive the Legislature
into an *Amnesty*, of which the Enacters do not at that Time fore-
160   see the Consequence. A cautious Merchant will be apt to suspect,
when he finds a Man who has the Repute of a cunning Dealer, and
with whom he has old Accounts, urging for a general Release. When
I reflect on this Proceeding, I am not surprised, that those who
contrived a Parliamentary *Sponge* for their *Crimes*, are now afraid
165   of a new Revolution *Sponge* for their *Money*: And if it were

Prose, iii 240). The 'day of public fast ... for pardon and blessing' that
brought Wharton to Mrs Coningsby in the spring was 15 March 1710, during the
Sacheverell trial (Steele, i 531).
    153   *Law*: An Act for the Queens most gracious general and free Pardon (7
Ann. c. 22) received the royal assent on 21 April 1709. 'The Act was made
chiefly to skreen [the Whig ministry] in case of a Change in the Administration, which the Conduct of some of them no doubt induced them to apprehend'
(Anon., p. 466). 'The Earl of Wharton himself profited by this Act. A Mr.
George Hutchinson gave Wharton £1,000 to procure his appointment to the office
of Register of the Seizures. This was proved before the House of Commons in
May, 1713, and the House resolved that it was "a scandalous Corruption," and
that as it took place "before the Act of her Majesty's most gracious, general,
and free, Pardon; this House will proceed no further in that Matter" [*CJ*,
xvii 356]' (E*1922*, ix 105-6; cf. Swift, *Journal*, p. 249). Swift's misinforma-
tion about the terms of the Act of Indemnity, which enabled Mainwaring to
score heavily when he discovered it in June 1711 (474.113-21), may derive from
[Atterbury?] *To the Wh--s Nineteen Queries, A Fair and Full Answer by an
Honest Torie*, London, for J. Baker, 1710, p. 8.
    162   *Release*: 'Remission of a debt' (*OED*).
    165   *Sponge*: 40.161.

possible to contrive a *Sponge* that could only affect those who
had need of the other, perhaps it would not be ill employ'd.

No. 10 [Mainwaring]   4 December 1710

The MEDLEY.

Of the falsest Paper that ever was printed.
Two Accounts stated and ballanc'd, arising from one in a late Examiner.
The Praises of our General in bad Verse.
A Defence of changing Sides.

THE *Examiner* has appear'd all along to be a Person of profound
Judgment, and has been justly admir'd for it: But he seem'd even
to excel himself, in the Choice of a Subject, when he writ about
Political Lying, and expos'd the only Secret by which his Party
have prevail'd, and the only Great Man that was to pay him for   5
his Labour. His own Side began then to be offended at his Ignorance and Folly: Some of them said, he was certainly bewitch'd:
Others said, his Paper shou'd be totally suppress'd; since no
Good was to be expected from one that writ at random, and cou'd
not distinguish what was proper to touch upon, and what not; but   10
wou'd saucily put down whatever enter'd into his rambling Imagination. I am still for helping him out as far as 'tis possible,
rather than for making things worse with him than they are: And
must needs therefore declare, that I don't think he intended at
that time to abuse his Patron or his Party, however he blunder'd   15
upon it; but that he had quite another meaning in view, which he
since has discover'd to the World. All the best Authors, who writ
in former Ages, convey'd their Instructions by Precepts and
Examples: Now the *Examiner*, having it in his Thoughts to publish
the falsest, as well as most impudent Paper that ever was printed,   20
writ a previous Discourse about Lying, as a necessary Introduction to what was to follow. The first Paper was the Precept, and
the second was the Example. By the falsest Paper that ever was

---

5 *Man*: 43.30.
20 *Paper*: the balance sheet of Roman gratitude and British ingratitude
(55.142).

printed, I mean the *Examiner*, *Numb*. 17. in which he pretends to
25 give an Account of what the D. of *M*. has got by his Services. It
were easy to shew that in every Article, except the Pension upon
the Post-Office, he grosly enhances the Account: This might as
plainly be prov'd, as that the Grant of *Mindelheim* was not an
English Bounty, but given as a just Return for an Empire wonder-
30 fully sav'd. It were easy also to shew, that the Person ingeni-
ously meant, in the pretty Tale of the *Lady's Woman*, was the most
faithful and just Servant that ever any Lady had, tho she happen'd
to be strangely supplanted by the Chambermaid.

   But all this shall be past over for the present, because I will
35 have no Difference with the *Examiner:* or to use the words of his
own ingenious Friend, that writ the Letter to him, *pag*. 5. *I will
allow all this, not because 'tis true; for the contrary shall one
time or other be made out to the World, when the true State of
our present Condition will be set in a clearer Light.* Allowing
40 therefore the *Examiner's* honest Account to be right, he brings in
the D. of *M*.

	He is Creditor on the other Side;
Debtor to Great Britain.	which part of the Account our
	Examiner forgot.
45 By Grants.	*By the Battles of* Schellenberg, *and*
Employments.	Blenheim.

   28 *Mindelheim*] *Mildenheim* ½°

---

   31 *Tale*: 57.198-200.
   33 *Chambermaid*: After Abigail Hill had been installed as bedchamber woman
to the Princess Anne, 'She learned the Arts of a Court, and observed the
Queen's Temper, with so much Application, that she got far into her Heart: And
she imployed all her Credit, to establish *Harley* in the supreme Confidence with
the Queen, and to alienate her Affections from the Dutchess of *Marlborough*'
(Burnet, ii 487). Mainwaring had called her 'A Dirty Chamber-Maid' in 1708
(*POAS*, Yale, vii 309).
   36 *Letter*: 'It was not long after the *Examiner* was publish'd [3 August
1710], that a Letter came out, directed to the Author, containing Instructions
how he should behave himself in it; that Letter no Body doubts, was a Production of Mr. *St. J--n's*, and Mr. *Maynwaring* cou'd not suffer so much Insolence
to pass, without Animadversion. The Author [Addison] of a Paper, call'd the
Whig Examiner [No. 2, 21 September, and No. 4, 5 October 1710], undertook it,
by Direction from him; if he was not himself that Author, which I never presum'd to ask him' (Oldmixon, *The Life*, p. 158).
   36-9 *I ... Light*: [Henry St. John, *A Letter to the Examiner, Containing a
View of Foreign and Domestic Affairs*, London, 1710] Pag. 5 (½°).

Pictures bought, or given by   *Forcing the* French *Lines twice.*
    Foreigners.   Ramellies, Oudenarde, Mons, &c.
Jewels the same.   *And by Twenty Seven Towns taken,*
Mindelheim, by the Emperor.   *which being reckon'd at* 300000 *l.*
    a Town (the Price that Dunkirk *was*   50
    sold at before it was fortify'd)
    amounts in all, throwing in the
    Battles, and the Fortifications,
Amounting in all to   *to*
    540000 *l.*   8,100,000 *l.*   55

                    Ballance on the Credit-Side,
                          7,560,000 *l.*

This is the State of the Credit, a word not improperly us'd
upon this occasion. Now, according to the *Examiner*'s Account, tho
monstrously false in every Particular but one, he has had something more than 15000 *l.* for every Battle and Town, one with
another; and taking the whole according to this groundless absurd   60
Calculation, he has done all this after the Rate of Three Pence
for every Pound, which our Enemies wou'd have given to prevent it:
Not to mention the Contributions, which wou'd have been made for
him by some of their Friends in other Places, to hinder such unlucky Conquests as he has still been unmercifully pursuing: For   65
it ought to be known to every gentle Reader, that he has done no
less than *cut off the very Legs and Arms of the* French *King.* Such
that Monarch himself accounted *Lisle* to be, with some other Places
that have been taken from him, as appears by the Duke of *Montagu*'s
Letter of *Decemb.* 29. 1677. lately printed. But knowing not how   70
to rate *those Legs and Arms of the Enemy,* I will throw them into
this general Account, without any particular Value set upon them.
    This Account being fairly stated, I will now cast up another of
a different kind with the *Examiner.* I need not tell him whose
Account it is, but the State of it is thus.   75

---

46 *twice: Churchill's Annals,* pp. 12, 20.
50 *Dunkirk:* sold to France in 1662 for 500,000 French crowns, or £125,000
(*CTB 1660-7,* pp. 459, 493).
67 *cut ... King:* 'Mais il faut tout hazarder plus tost que de me Laisser
couper bras & Jambes que sont les Places [Valenciennes, Condé, Tournai, Courtrai]
qu l'on me demande', was what Louis XIV said (*Copies & Extracts of some Letters
Written to and from the Earl of Danby (now Duke of Leeds) in the Years 1676,
1677, and 1678,* London, for John Nicholson, 1710, pp. 41-2).

Debtor.	*Creditor.*

By sinking the Publick Credit in
K. William's *Reign*; *reckoning the*   By Services in the late King's Reign,
Effect it had on the Bank, East-   ------- *A Land Bank.*
80   India *Company*, *Navy-Bills*, *Ordnance*,
Debentures, *Tallies upon all the*   By *Ditto*, in the Present,
Funds,   ------- *A new Scheme.*
      --Five Millions and a Half.
By Ditto, *since that time*, *according*
85   *to the lowest Computation*,
                  -------The same Sum.   Amounting in both,
            In both Eleven Millions.   To ----00 00 00
               Ballance yet to be accounted for,   11,000,000

Thus you see the Difference between the Charge of Commanding
90   Abroad, and of Scheming at Home: The first comes to Five Hundred
and Forty Thousand Pounds, according to the utmost Stretch of
Malice and Invention; the other to Eleven Millions, according to
the lowest Computation.

So much for the *Examiner*'s accounting at Home, I will now con-
95   sider his Comparison between *Roman* and *British* Gratitude. He has
shewn, with his usual Strength of Reason, that we are now about
five hundred times more grateful than the *Romans* were; having
given the D. of *M.* five hundred times as much as ever the *Romans*
gave their Generals; which was but one thousand Pounds, making

   85 *Computation*] *Compution* ½°

---

   77 *sinking the Publick Credit*: The National Land Bank was created by a bill
(7 & 8 Gul. III c. 31) that Harley got through Parliament in April 1696. The
Bank was authorized to borrow £2,564,000 at seven per cent interest secured by
the taxes on salt, glass, earthenware, and clay pipes. The capital was then to
have been invested in land and mortgages, 'calculated ... to advance the
Landed-Men's Interest, in Opposition to the growing Power of Money'd-Men'
(Boyer, *The History of King William the Third*, 3 vols., London, for A. Roper
et al., 1702-3, iii 164) and to break the Bank of England's monopoly of loans
to the Government. But only £7,000 was subscribed and the ignominious failure
of the scheme precipitated a financial crisis, including a run on the Bank of
England (J. Keith Horsefield, *British Monetary Experiments 1650-1710*, Cambridge, Mass., Harvard University Press, 1960, 196-208).
   82 *new Scheme*: If this is a reference to Harley's South Sea Co. scheme
(468.105), it occurs three to four months before the presently accepted date
of origin (J.G. Sperling, *Historical Journal*, iv (1961), 192). The failure of
the South Sea Co. in 1720 was even more spectacular than that of the National
Land Bank (Dickson, pp. 90-156).

the most of it. This is so Historical, that one wou'd think not   100
a word cou'd be said against it. Every Reader, from the Probability of the matter, must needs be satisfy'd that it was SO; and
just as it appears by his two Columns of Addition. All the mistake
is, that in his *Roman* Account he has put down but one Article, the
Charge of a Triumph; which, according to his Bill of Parcels,   105
amounted in the Sum Total to no more than nine hundred ninety
four Pounds, eleven Shillings and ten pence. But he has sunk all
the other Articles of the Account, all the great Advantages of
Roman Generals, who, you must know, had their Pensions, Lands,
Houses, Contributions, *&c.* as well as other People; and even   110
their Proconsulates, such as *Asia, Africa, Spain, &c.* But these
things he took no notice of, I suppose out of Partiality to the
D. of *M.* to shew how much better 'tis to command an Army now,
than it was in the days of *Lucullus* and *Pompey.* And it was doubtless for the same reason that he reduc'd the whole Profits of a   115
Roman Conqueror to a Crown bought for Two-pence, which he must
know is not half so much as a Halter comes to now-a-days; which
will cost him, at the lowest rate, Four-pence. As to the *Embroi-*
der'd Coat, he says, *he can't find who paid the Embroiderer,*
whether the Senate or the General himself. You see how nice he is   120
in History: Nor will he allow so much as the *Earthen Pots,* the
Bull, the *Halfpenny Medals,* the *Triumphal Chariot,* &c. to be *of*
real Profit to the General; who seems by this Reckoning to have
no more Right to such things, than my Lord Mayor has to the
Pageants on a Show-day: upon whom and his Great Horse the City of   125
London has often been at twice the Expence, that the *Romans,*
according to this Author, bestow'd on *a Victorious General in the*
Height of that Empire, having subdu'd his Enemy, conquer'd some
great Kingdom, and brought the King himself, his Family and Nobles,
to adorn the Triumph in Chains. Is not this very odd? If I had   130
not his Word for it, I shou'd as soon have believ'd, that because
a White Staff is worth but Six-pence, therefore that is the full
value of it in the hands of a Lord Chamberlain; as that the
Advantages of a *Roman* General were to be calculated by a Crown

119-20 *can't ... General*: 55.135-6.
122-3 *of ... General*: 55.132-3.
127-30 *a ... Chains*: 54.127-55.130.

135 bought of an Herb-woman. We read, That one of 'em cou'd afford to
     spend a Thousand Crowns a day, and have besides his Rooms of
     extraordinary Expence, settled at four, five, ten, and twenty
     thousand Crowns a night: That he at one time lent a Prætor four
     hundred embroider'd Robes, and had as great an Income as some
140 Northern Kings. The *Roman* History is full of magnificent Accounts
     of their Statues, Arches, Portico's, vast Edifices, &c. And even
     in that sneaking covetous Commonwealth of *Athens*, it is said,
     That more of this kind was done in the Days of *Pericles*, than was
     to be seen in *Rome* before the *Cæsars*. However, *Pericles* often
145 wore a Garland of Flowers, which I believe was not rated by him,
     according to the prime Cost in the Market. And yet after all, it
     must be confess'd, that the *Examiner* is not so much out upon this
     occasion, as he has been upon some others. For I do not believe,
     that a Triumph us'd to cost much above a hundred times more than
150 he makes it; which I think is very fair for him: tho he might as
     well have charg'd the D. of *M.* with only what the Publick pays
     for his Passage from *Holland* in the Yacht, as have brought no
     more to the Account of a *Roman* Conqueror than what is set forth
     in his *Bill of* Roman *Gratitude.*

155   I cannot help applauding, in the next place, the Raillery of
     the same Author, at which he is excellent. He is troubled that
     the D. of *M--------*'s Services shou'd be call'd *the most Eminent
     that ever were perform'd by a Subject to his Country, not to be
     equal'd in History. And then,* quoth he, *to be sure some bitter
160 Stroke of Detraction against* Alexander *and* Cæsar, *who never did
     us the least injury.* He has an infinite deal of Wit, that's cer-
     tain: But for all his Jest, *Cæsar* invaded and enslav'd us; if he
     looks upon Invasion and Slavery as Injuries. He takes the same
     General to be highly oblig'd, That *he has not been try'd for his
165 Life, and very narrowly escap'd: That He has not been accus'd of
     High Crimes and Misdemeanours: That the Prince has not seiz'd his
     Estate, and left him to starve: That He has not been hooted at*

     135 *one:* Plutarch, *Life of Lucullus,* xxxix 5.
     142 *said:* Plutarch, *Comparison of Pericles and Fabius,* iii 5.
     157-61 *the ... injury:* 49.13-17.
     162 *Cæsar:* In his second raid across the Channel (54 BC), Caesar captured
     the camp of Cassivelaunus, imposed tribute, and took hostages back to Gaul
     (*De Bello Gallico,* v 11-12).
     164-8 *he ... Streets:* 50.27-30.

as he pass'd the Streets: That He has not been strip'd of All:
That his Defects have been sparingly mention'd, and all his Suc-
cesses very freely applauded. This is another sort of Reckoning,   170
which he is the first Author of. However, the last words put me
in mind of great Compliments that were once paid him in a most
stupid Poem; some of which I will now transcribe, to shew the
different Turn of Mens Thoughts.

> *Great Thanks, O Captain great in Arms! receive*   175
> *From thy Triumphant Country's publick Voice:*
> *Thy Country greater Thanks can only give*
> *To* Anne, *to her who made those Arms her Choice.*
> *Recording* Schellenberg's *and* Blenheim's *Toils,*
> *We dreaded lest thou should'st those Toils repeat:*   180
> *We view'd the Palace charg'd with* Gallick *Spoils,*
> *And in those Spoils we thought thy Praise compleat:*
> *For never* Greek, *we deem'd, nor* Roman *Knight,*
> *In Characters like these did e'er his Acts indite.*
>
> *There* Ister *pleas'd, by* Blenheim's *glorious Field,*   185
> *Rolling shall bid his Eastern Waves declare*
> Germania *sav'd by* Britain's *ample Shield;*
> *And bleeding* Gaul *afflicted by her Spear:*
> *Shall bid them mention* Marlbro' *on that Shore,*
> *Leading his Islanders, renown'd in Arms,*   190
> *Thro Climes, where never* British *Chief before,*
> *Or pitch'd his Camp, or sounded his Alarms.*

I have but one Difficulty upon me, for having transcrib'd these
Verses; which is, That if it shou'd ever be prov'd that the very
Person who dully writ these Truths in Verse, has since publish'd   195
so many Fictions in Prose, I shou'd have much ado to speak in his
defence for the future. People wou'd be sure to fall upon him

172-3 in ... Poem] by a friend of the *Examiner*'s 12°   193-6 I ... many]
Since one of the *Examiner*'s own Party has publish'd such Truths as these in
Verse, I wonder he is not asham'd of his own 12°   196-204 I ... Friend]
om. 12°

---

168 *he ... All:* 50.32.
169-70 *his ... applauded:* 52.83-6.
173 *Poem:* Matthew Prior's *An Ode, Humbly Inscrib'd to the Queen* (July 1706)
(*POAS*, Yale, vii 174), of which lines 171-80 and 301-8 are quoted.

without mercy; to say, That he had expos'd himself beyond Redemption; and to maintain, That the infamous Punishments inflicted by
200 a Government, are nothing to the Reproaches that a Man brings
upon himself by such Behaviour. As you are surer that any one is
guilty, who confesses it himself, than he who is only condemn'd
by other People; a great deal of this stuff wou'd be urg'd against
my Friend. Those that are learned, and have read *Demosthenes*,
205 wou'd call to mind a Saying of his; That *such Wretches as flatter
a Man in Prosperity, and abuse him in Adversity, are like old Rup-
tures, Cramps and Pains in the Body, which fall upon it terribly
upon every Turn of Humours, or even Change of Weather*. And those
who are not such deep Scholars, wou'd yet quote a Saying of Sir
210 *Benjamin Rudyard's*, which is mention'd somewhere by *Old Double*;
That *there's nothing in Court-Preferments worth being a Knave for*.
But to that I cou'd easily answer in his behalf, That this is no
better than an old Puritan Principle, wholly irreconcilable with
modern Practice. Besides, 'tis not a small matter that makes a
215 Courtier a Knave: Things change their nature there, and Tricking
and Fraud become Policy and Dexterity. I cou'd shew also a great
many Examples of other People that have deserted the very same
Cause, and endeavour'd to sacrifice their best Friends, as well
as the *Examiner*. Where then can be the Knavery in all this? Use
220 makes that honourable, which might otherwise perhaps be thought
base and wicked. Is it not done every day? And was it not always
done? It wou'd be fine Times indeed, if People might not change
as often as they pleas'd, and be of what side they pleas'd, as
well now as in former Ages. If it had never been done before,
225 something might be said: But Sir *William Temple* informs us, That

204-5 Those ... his] Has he never read a Saying of *Demosthenes*; 12°
205-6 *flatter ... and*] *om*. 12°   206 *him*] a Man 12°   208-9 And ... a]
Or has he never heard of a plain blunt 12°   209 Sir] honest Sir 12°
210 which ... *Double*] *om*. 12°   212 But] *om*. 12°   cou'd ... behalf] know
he will answer 12°   214-25 Besides ... But] And that for his part, he's
resolv'd to make the best of the present Times, and get what he can; the
rather because Alterations are so frequent among us; which has long been observ'd all the World over: 12°   225 informs us] observing 12°

205-8 *such ... Weather*: source unknown.
211-12 *there's ... for*: Davenant, *An Essay upon the Probable Methods of
making a People Gainers in the Ballance of Trade*, London, for James Knapton,
1699, p. 264.

nothing better was expected from us abroad in his days: Monsieur
De Wit being us'd to tell him, *That ever since the Reign of Queen*
Elizabeth *there had been such a Fluctuation in the Counsels of*
England, *they cou'd not be depended upon for two years together.*
From which Remark however, we may draw this good Conclusion; That   230
when we are in the wrong, we shall not continue so for ever; but
may justly hope, from *De Wit*'s Observation, to be right again in
a year or two. In the mean while I hope to see something done for
my Friend the *Examiner*: And that till such time as he is provided
for, we shall not think of enacting here a barbarous Law among   235
the *Indians*, that we read of in *Philostratus* by which they
declar'd every Man uncapable of bearing an Office, that cou'd
be prov'd to have been guilty of telling a Lye.

226 Monsieur] And that Monsieur 12°   227 being] was 12°   229 *for*]
om. 12°   233-4 hope ... *Examiner*] wish my Friend the *Examiner* all possible success at this Court, being in great hope that something will speedily
be done for him 12°

227-9 *ever ... together*: Sir William Temple's *Letters* [2 vols., ed. Jonathan Swift, London, for J. Tonson, 1700-3, i 162] (½°).
236 *Philostratus*: [*Life of Apollonius*,] lib. 2. c. 30 (½° corrected).

No. 19 [Swift]   7 December 1710

The EXAMINER.

Quippe ubi fas versum atq; nefas : tot bella per orbem:
Tam multæ Scelerum facies

I Am often violently tempted to let the World freely know who the
Author of this Paper is; to tell them my Name and Titles at
Length; which would prevent abundance of inconsistent Criticisms
I daily hear upon it. Those who are Enemies to the Notions and
Opinions I would advance, are sometimes apt to quarrel with the   5
Examiner as defective in point of Wit, and sometimes of Truth.
At other Times they are so generous and candid, to allow, it is

Motto Virgil, *Georgics*, i 505: Where sacred Order Fraud and Force confound;
| Where impious Wars and Tumults rage around.

written by a Club, and that very great *Hands* have *Fingers* in it.
As for those who only appear its Adversaries in Print, they give
10 me but very little Pain: The Paper I hold lies at my mercy, and
I can govern it as I please; therefore, when I begin to find the
Wit too bright, the Learning too deep, and the Satyr too keen for
me to deal with, (a very frequent Case no doubt, where a Man is
constantly attack'd by such shrewd Adversaries) I peaceable fold
15 it up, or fling it aside, and read no more. It would be happy for
me to have the same Power over People's Tongues, and not be
forced to hear my own Work railed at and commended fifty times a
day, affecting all the while a Countenance wholly unconcerned,
and joining out of Policy or good Manners with the Judgment of
20 both Parties: This, I confess, is too great a Hardship for so
bashful and unexperienc'd a Writer.

But, alas, I ly under another Discouragement of much more
weight: I was very unfortunate in the Choice of my Party when I
set up to be a Writer; where is the Merit, or what Opportunity to
25 discover our Wit, our Courage, or our Learning, in drawing our
Pens for the Defence of a Cause, which the QUEEN and both Houses
of Parliament, and nine parts in ten of the Kingdom, have so
unanimously embraced? I am cruelly afraid, we Politick Authors
must begin to lessen our Expences, and lye for the future at the
30 mercy of our Printers. All hopes now are gone of writing our
Selves into Places or Pensions. A certain starvling Author who
workt under the late Administration, told me with a heavy Heart,
above a Month ago, that he and some others of his Brethren had
secretly offered their Service dog-cheap to the present Ministry,
35 but were all refus'd, and are now maintain'd by Contribution,
like *Jacobites* or *Fanaticks*. I have been of late employ'd out of

14 peaceable] peaceably 38 8°+12°   36 *Jacobites*] *Jacobits* ½°

---

8 *Club* ... *very great Hands*: 'the *Examiner* ... is publish'd by Authority
... that *Club* charges [Marlborough] with the Receipt of 240000 Pounds of the
Publick Money' (*The Speech of the Lord Haversham's Ghost*, London, 1710, p. 4).
31 *Author*: Perhaps only a notional Grub Street hack, like the narrator of
A Tale of a Tub, with his 'Quill worn to the Pith in the Service of the State,
in *Pro*'s and *Con*'s ... and *Prerogative*, and *Property*, and *Liberty of Conscience*, and *Letters to a Friend*' (Swift, *Tale*, p. 70), but possibly Richard
Steele, who edited *The London Gazette* until October 1710 and who may have
offered his services 'dog-cheap' during an interview with Harley in December
1710 (Swift, *Journal*, p. 128).

perfect Commiseration, in doing them good Offices: For, whereas
some were of Opinion that these hungry Zealots should not be suffered any longer in their malapert way to snarl at the present
Course of publick Proceedings; and whereas, others propos'd, that   40
they should be limited to a certain Number, and permitted to
write for their *Masters*, in the same manner as Councel are
assign'd for *other* Criminals; that is, to say all they can in
Defence of their Client, but not reflect upon the Court: I humbly
gave my Advice, that they should be suffered to write on, as they   45
used to do; which I did purely out of Regard to their Persons:
For I hoped it would keep them out of Harms-way, and prevent them
from falling into evil Courses, which tho' of little Consequence
to the Publick, would certain be *fatal to themselves*. If I have
room at the bottom of this Paper, I will transcribe a Petition to   50
the present Ministry, sent me by one of these Authors, in behalf
of himself and fourscore others of his Brethren.

   For my own part, notwithstanding the little Encouragement to be
hoped for at this time from the Men in Power, I shall continue my
Paper 'till either the World or my self grow weary of it: The   55
latter is easily determined; and for the former, I shall not
leave it to the Partiality of either Party, but to the Infallible
Judgment of my Printer. One principal End I design'd by it, was
to undeceive those well-meaning People, who have been drawn un-
aware into a wrong Sense of Things, either by the common Preju-   60
dices of Education and Company, the great personal Qualities of
some Party-leaders, or the foul Misrepresentations that were constantly made of all who durst differ from them in the smallest
Article. I have known such Men struck with the Thoughts of some
late Changes, which, as they pretend to think, were made without   65
any Reason visible to the World. In Answer to this, it is not
sufficient to alledge, what no Body doubts, that a Prince may
chuse his own Servants without giving a Reason to his Subjects;
because it is certain, that a wise and good Prince will not

---

52 others] *om.* 38 8°+12°   67-8 what no Body doubts, that a Prince may
chuse his own Servants] that a good and wise Prince may be allowed to change
his Ministers 38 8°+12°   69-70 certain, that a wise and good Prince will
not change his Ministers] probable that he will not make such a Change 38
8°+12°

---

37 *Offices*: 1.12-13n.
65 *Changes*: 2.29.

70 change his Ministers without very important Reasons; and a good
    Subject ought to suppose, that in such a Case there are such
    Reasons, tho' he be not appris'd of them, otherwise he must in-
    wardly tax his Prince of Capriciousness, Inconstancy, or ill
    Design. Such Reasons indeed, may not be obvious to Persons preju-
75 diced, or at great distance, or short Thinkers; and therefore, if
    they be no Secrets of State, nor any ill Consequences to be appre-
    hended from their publication; it is no uncommendable Work in any
    private Hand to lay them open for the Satisfaction of all Men.
    And if what I have already said, or shall hereafter say of this
80 kind, be thought to reflect upon *Persons*, tho' none have been
    named, I know not how it can possibly be avoided. The Queen in
    her Speech mentions, *with great Concern*, that the *Navy and other*
    Offices are burthened with heavy Debts, and *desires that the like*
    may be prevented for the time to come. And, if it be *now* possible
85 to prevent the continuance of an Evil that has been so long grow-
    ing upon us, and is arrived to such a height, surely those Cor-
    ruptions and Mismanagements must have been great which first
    introduced them, before our Taxes were eaten up by Annuities.
    If I were able to rip up, and discover in all their Colours,
90 only about eight or nine Thousand of the most scandalous Abuses,
    that have been committed in all Parts of publick Management for
    twenty years past, by a certain Set of Men and their Instruments,
    I should reckon it some Service to my Country, and to Posterity.
    But to say the Truth, I should be glad the Authors Names were
95 convey'd to future Times along with their Actions. For tho' the
    present Age may understand well enough the little Hints we give,
    the Parallels we draw, and the Characters we describe, yet this
    will all be lost to the next. However, if these Papers, *reduced*
    into a more durable Form, should happen to live 'till our Grand-
100 children are Men, I hope they may have Curiosity enough to con-

    100 are] be 38 8°+12°

    _____

    78 *lay ... open*: cf. 'to ... display by Incision ... I take ... to be the
    last Degree of perverting Nature' (Swift, *Tale*, pp. 67, 173).
    82-4 *with ... come*: the speech from the throne at the opening of Parlia-
    ment, 27 November 1710 (*CJ*, xvi 403).
    88 *Annuities*: In November 1710 the carrying charges on existing annuities
    stood at £913,065 (Davenant, *New Dialogues upon the Present Posture of Affairs*,
    1710, p. 84).
    92 *Set*: 6.98.

sult Annals, and compare Dates, in order to find out what *Names*
were then intrusted with the Conduct of Affairs, in the Consequences whereof, themselves will so deeply share; like a heavy
Debt in a private Family, which often lies an Incumbrance upon an
Estate for three Generations.   105

But leaving the Care of informing Posterity to better Pens, I
shall with due Regard to Truth, Discretion, and the Safety of my
Person from the Men of *the new-fangl'd Moderation*, continue to
take all proper Opportunities of letting the misled part of the
People see how grosly they have been abus'd, and in what Particu-   110
lars: I shall also endeavour to convince them, that the present
Course we are in, is the most probable Means, with the Blessing
of God, to extricate our selves out of all our Difficulties.

Among those who are pleas'd to write or talk against this
Paper, I have observ'd a strange manner of Reasoning, which I   115
should be glad to hear them explain themselves upon. They make no
Ceremony of exclaiming upon all Occasions against a Change of
Ministry, in so critical and dangerous a Conjuncture. What shall
we, who heartily approve and join in those Proceedings, say in
defence of them? We own the Juncture of Affairs to be as they   120
describe: We are push'd for an Answer, and are forc'd at last
freely to confess, that the Corruptions and Abuses in every
Branch of the Administration, were so numerous and intollerable,
that all Things must have ended in Ruin, without some speedy
Reformation. This I have already asserted in a former Paper; and   125
the Replies I have read or heard, have been in plain Terms to
affirm the direct contrary; and not only to defend and celebrate
the late Persons and Proceedings, but to threaten me with Law and
Vengeance, for casting Reflections on so many great and honourable Men, whose *Birth, Virtue and Abilities, whose Morals and*   130

102-3 Consequences] Consequence 38 8°+12°   111 shall also] also shall
38 8°+12°   130 *Virtue*] Virtues 38 8°+12°   *and*] and ½°   *whose*] whose ½°

---

108 *new new-fangl'd Moderation*: Whig principles plus the desperation of
politicians out of office; '*incensed Moderation*' (273.41-2); cf. 'the Whigs
... admit no Principles to be Moderate, but what will suffer them to engross
the whole Management' (Davenant, *New Dialogues upon the Present Posture of
Affairs*, 1710, p. 37).

125 *a former Paper*: No. 14, 2 November 1710.

128 *Law*: The Examiner was threatened with law in *The Observator* of 4-8
November, 15-18 November, and 22-5 November 1710.

Religion, whose Love of their Country and its Constitution in
Church and State, were so universally allow'd; and all this set
off with odious Comparisons reflecting on the present Choice. Is
not this in plain and direct Terms to tell all the World that the
135   Qu--- has in a most dangerous Crisis turn'd out a whole Set of
the best Ministers that ever serv'd a Prince, without any manner
of Reason, but her Royal Pleasure, and brought in others of a
Character directly contrary? And how so vile an Opinion as this
can consist with the least pretence to Loyalty or good Manners,
140   let the World determine.

I confess my self so little a Refiner in the Politicks, as not
to be able to discover, what other Motive besides Obedience to
the Queen, a Sense of publick Danger, and a true Love of their
Country, join'd with invincible Courage, could Spirit those great
145   Men, who have now under Her Majesty's Authority undertaken the
Direction of Affairs. What can they expect but the utmost Efforts
of Malice from a Set of enraged domestick Adversaries, perpetually
watching over their Conduct, crossing all their Designs, and using
every Art to foment Divisions among them, in order to join with
150   the weakest upon any Rupture? The Difficulties they must encounter
are nine times more and greater than ever; and the Prospects of
Interest, after the *Reapings* and *Gleanings* of so many Years, nine
times less. Every Misfortune at Home or Abroad, tho' the necessary Consequence of former Counsels, will be imputed to them; and
155   all the good Success given to the Merit of former Schemes. A
Sharper has held your Cards all the Evening, plaid Booty, and
lost your Mony, and when things are almost desperate, you employ
an Honest Gentleman to retrieve your Losses.

___

144 Spirit] spirit up 38 8°+12°   150 upon] upou ½°0^{b} L NjP CLU-C

___

131-2 *Love ... State*: 'how can the *Examiner* give the Character of true
Lovers of their Country and its Constitution in Church and State, to the
Nobility and Gentry that invited over the Prince of *Orange*' (*The Observator,*
4-8 November 1710).
150 *Difficulties*: 7.121-2n.
152 *Reapings*: 55.142-56.171, 57.198.
156 *Sharper*: Godolphin, Burnet said (i 478), 'loved gaming the most of any
man of business I ever knew'. Mrs Manley imagines him with 'The Affairs of a
Nation in his *Head*, [and] a pair of *Cards*, or a Box of *Dice* in his *Hand*'
(*Secret Memoirs*, 1709, ii 114).
        plaid Booty: 'To join with confederates in order to ... victimize
another player' (*OED*).
158 *Gentleman*: Harley.

I would ask whether the Queen's Speech does not contain Her Intentions, in every Particular relating to the Publick, that a   160
good Subject, a *Britain* and a Protestant can possibly have at
Heart? *To carry on the War in all its Parts, particularly in*
Spain, with the utmost Vigour, in order to procure a safe and
honourable Peace for us and our Allies; To find some Ways of pay-
ing the Debts on the Navy; to support and encourage the Church of   165
England; *to preserve the* British *Constitution according to the*
Union; *To maintain the Indulgence by Law allow'd to Scrupulous*
Consciences; and to employ none but such as are for the Protestant
Succession in the House of Hanover. 'Tis known enough, that
Speeches on these Occasions, are ever digested by the Advice of   170
those who are in the chief Confidence, and consequently that
these are the Sentiments of Her Majesty's Ministers, as well as
Her own; and we see, the two Houses have unanimously agreed with
Her in every Article. When the least Counterpaces are made to any
of these Resolutions, it will then be time enough for our Malecon-   175
tents to bawl out *Popery, Persecution, Arbitrary Power,* and *the*
Pretender. In the mean while, it is a little hard to think, that
this Island can hold but six Men of Honesty and Ability, enough
to serve their Prince and Country; or that our Safety should depend upon their Credit, any more than it would upon the Breath in   180
their Nostrils. Why should not a *Revolution* in the Ministry be
sometimes necessary as well as a *Revolution* in the Crown? It is
to be presum'd, the former is at least as lawful in it self, and
perhaps the Experiment not quite so dangerous. The *Revolution* of
the *Sun* about the *Earth* was formerly thought a necessary Expedi-   185
ent to solve Appearances, tho' it left many Difficulties unanswer'd; 'till Philosophers contriv'd a better, which is that of
the *Earth's Revolution* about the *Sun.* This is found upon Experience to save much Time and Labour, to correct many irregular
Motions, and is better suited to the Respect due from a *Planet*   190
to a *Fix'd Star.*

161 at] a ½°0[b] CLU-C   162 *on*] of 38 8°+12°

162-9 *To ... Hanover:* CJ, xvi 403.
167 *Indulgence:* 22.66n.
174 *Counterpaces:* 'A movement or step against something' (*OED*); counter-
measures.
178 *six Men:* the Junto and Godolphin.

No. 11 [Mainwaring]   11 December 1710

The MEDLEY.

Of the Power of Numbers.

Of an Excellent Parallel drawn by the Examiner.

Part of one of Cicero's *Orations.*

FROM Political Lying, the Subject of my last Paper, 'tis an easy,
and not unnatural Transition, to Political Numbers; the latter
being often the Effect or the Consequence of the former. Much has
been said both by Antients and Moderns of the Command of Reason,
5   and the Force of Eloquence; but in my mind, nothing can compare
to the Power of Numbers, taken in any sense whatsoever. Of these
there are three sorts, which are chiefly consider'd; *Poetical,*
Mathematical, and *Political.* The Power of Poetical Numbers is
such, that Woods have danc'd, and Rivers chang'd their Course in
10   obedience to them. That of Mathematical Numbers is so invincible,
that if we believe Bishop *Wilkins,* there's never an Oak in
Windsor-Forest that can resist a Hair, dispos'd of to the most
Geometrical Advantage. And the Political Numbers come so little
short of either the one or the other, that even Law and Reason
15   submit and fall down before them. Did they not in *Athens* vote
Heroick Virtue into Faction, and Publick Merit into Treason? Did
they not drive the Best Men into Banishment, at one time for
having sav'd, at another for having reform'd the State? Did they
not in *Rome* at one time take the Power from *Cato* for his Virtue,
20   and at another time give it to *Clodius* for his Vice? What they

2 *Numbers*: Mainwaring appears to imitate, or parody, *A Tale of a Tub* (Swift,
Tale, pp. 2, 57-8).
11 *Wilkins*: 'by these Mechanicall contrivances ... it is possible ... for
any man to lift up the greatest Oak by the roots ... to pull it up with a
hair' (John Wilkins, *Mathematicall Magick. Or, The Wonders that may be per-*
formed by Mechanicall Geometry, London, by M.F. for Sa. Gellibrand, 1648,
p. 96); cf. Swift, *Tale,* p. 237.
16 *Merit into Treason*: cf. Swift, *Discourse,* pp. 94-5.
19 *Cato*: Marcus Porcius Cato Uticensis, 'the Conscience of Rome' (and hero
of Addison's tragedy in 1713), was removed from power in 58 BC when the triumvirate sent him on a diplomatic mission to get him out of the way.
20 *Clodius*: Publius Clodius Pulcher, who profaned the mysteries of the Bona
Dea to gain access to Caesar's wife, and who manipulated the Roman mob in
Caesar's behalf, was illegally adopted into a plebeian gens so he could be
elected tribune in 58 BC.

have done since, is so well known, I need not repeat it. For
there is this great Inconvenience in Political Numbers, as well
as others, that they may be put to an ill use, as often as to a
good one: Nay, it frequently happens, that the Ambitious make
use of these Numbers to the destruction of those that compose   25
them. The truth is, there has been nothing extravagantly foolish,
and prodigiously wicked, but has been of their doing: Had not
Caiaphas a Majority at *Jerusalem*, and *Cromwel* in *England*? So that
the Power of Political Numbers has in all Ages been as wonderful,
as ever it can be in ours; and 'tis hop'd, much more mischievous.   30
What is it that those Numbers have not done for and against the
Church, in Councils and Convocations? And for and against Liberty,
in Senates and Conventions? By the one Superstition, by the
other, Tyranny, have been alternately abolish'd and establish'd.
So prodigious is the Force of a Majority! In the *North* indeed   35
this Power has not been well employ'd of late: In *Denmark* and
Sweden it has made Slaves of Free Nations, and dissolv'd the
Constitution of their Limited Governments. But then in *England*,
it abdicated King *James*, after having *vigorously withstood him*:
It set aside his pretended Heir, and settled the Protestant Suc-   40
cession: It also threw out the Tack, and lately asserted the

28 *Caiaphas*: Caiaphas, the high priest, 'and all the council, sought false
witness against Jesus' (Matt. 26.59).
    Majority: 'the Tyranny of the Majority' is a major theme of Swift's *Dis-
course of the Contests and Dissentions* (Swift, *Discourse*, pp. 87, 97, 106,
108-9, 116).
36-7 *Denmark and Sweden*: Denmark and Sweden were transformed from constitutional monarchies on the 'Gothick' model, like England, into absolute monarchies, like France, within the space of twenty years. The ancient constitution
of Denmark was abandoned in 1660 when the rule of Frederick III was made
hereditary. In 1661 a new constitution, the Kongelov, translated into law the
most extreme forms of absolute rule (Robert Molesworth, *An Account of Denmark,
as It was in the Year 1692*, 3rd edn., London, for Timothy Goodwin, 1694,
pp. 44-68). Sweden's evolution began in 1680 during the rule of Charles XI
when the Riksråd decreed that all estates of any value should revert to the
Crown. The Riksråd was then renamed the Kungliga Råd and Charles XI undertook
to rule by decree, which it became the sole function of the Kungliga Råd to
ratify (René Aubert, abbé de Vertot, *The History of the Revolutions in Sweden*,
trans. J. Mitchel, 2nd edn., London, for A. Swall and T. Child, 1696; John
Robinson, *An Account of Sueden: Together with an Extract of the History of
that Kingdom*, London, for Tim. Goodwin, 1694, pp. 92-116.
39 *abdicated*: 367.93n.; cf. *An Address to the Church of England Clergy,
concerning Resistance*, London, S. Popping, 1710, p. 21: ''Tis true, he did
Abdicate. But before he *Abdicated* ... he was resisted.'
41 *the Tack*: The gravest parliamentary crisis of the first half of Anne's
reign occurred on 28 November 1704 when 134 high Tories (136 including the
tellers) voted to attach the third bill to prevent occasional conformity to

Revolution and Toleration: It has done a great many good things
for us, and will one time or other do a great many more; for its
Power in *England* has generally been exerted on the right side,
45   tho sometimes also on the wrong. It has carry'd on Occasional
Bills: It has Abhor'd and Address'd: It has petition'd for a new
Parliament, and it has also petition'd again for a Dissolution.
For the good things it has done, have been generally the Work of
Reflection, and dear-bought Experience. And several other Matters
50   are necessary to give due weight to Political Numbers, or the
Credit will never go with the Power. This Hint, and all the rest,
are only given here as general Heads, of which some Use and
Application may possibly be made hereafter. But I must hasten
now to my Friend the *Examiner*.
55   This excellent Writer will have reason at last to think himself
Somebody, since he is taken so much notice of in Print. But the
particular Reason of my Compliments to him at this time, is to
return him Thanks for the Countenance he has given to my poor

---

the land tax bill. Frustrated by the defeat in the House of Lords of two previous bills to prevent occasional conformity, the Tackers intended to force
the third bill through the upper house, since by tradition the Lords could
not amend a money bill but only pass or reject it intact. The loss of the land
tax bill might have forced the allies 'to accept of such terms as *France*
would offer them' (Burnet, ii 401-2), for the war could not have been continued without it. But 251 moderate Tories and Whigs voted against the tack
(Boyer, *Annals*, 1705, p. 173) and the land tax bill was sent up to the Lords
without it.
    asserted: in the first two articles of Sacheverell's impeachment (*CJ*,
xvi 258, 261).
    45-6 *Occasional Bills*: The Tory majority in the House of Commons passed the
first two bills to prevent occasional conformity in November 1702 and November
1703. The bills would have imposed penalties on dissenters who received the
sacrament according to the rites of the Church of England in order to qualify
for office under the Crown or in local government and then resumed attendance
at a dissenting chapel. The first two bills were defeated in the House of
Lords in January 1703 and December 1703 (Boyer, *Annals*, 1703, pp. 145, 154-5,
172-204; *Annals*, 1704, pp. 171-89). Mainwaring wrote a 'merry Ballad', *The
History and Fall of the Conformity-Bill*, against the second of these (*POAS*,
Yale, vii 3) and then quoted a stanza of it in *The Medley*, 16 October 1710.
    46 *Abhor'd and Address'd*: Charles II prorogued the newly elected second
Whig Parliament in October 1679. The first petition to convene the Parliament
was carried up to him in December 1679 by seventeen Opposition lords. This was
backed up by a flood of similar addresses to the throne from all over England.
The reaction came in February 1680 in a wave of counter-addresses of 'abhorrence' of the Opposition tactics, 'which were almost every where promoted by
the Clergy' (Oldmixon, *The History of Addresses*, i 13-14). In 1680 'the names
of Abhorrer and Petitioner were changed for those of Tory and Whig' (George M.
Trevelyan, *England under the Stuarts*, 17th edn., London and New York, Methuen
and Putnam's Sons, 1938, p. 411).

manner of applying old Stories, in his late Elegant Oration
against *Verres*; being, as he assures us, faithfully translated   60
and abstracted from *Cicero*. *Lucian* laughs, in his agreeable manner, at a foolish Man of his Acquaintance, who took it into his
head to write after *Thucydides*: And *Cicero* mentions another that
comes nearer the Case before us, who endeavour'd to copy *Demos-*
thenes in those places only where he least excel'd. Just such an   65
Imitator is my unlucky Friend of *Cicero*; who in the Rhapsody he
has printed, and calls a Translation from him, has added more
rude Reflections of his own than are to be found in that Author,
whose only fault is his falling too much into such Reflections.
Such a Piece indeed it is, taken all together, that I wonder what   70
his merry Friends of the High-Church, Lords or Commons, who may
have heard by chance that *Cicero* was as good a Speaker as most of
their Party, must think of the Eloquence of this Famous *Roman*, as
it appears in the Dress of our *British Examiner*, and in the only
Language that they take any pleasure in reading. However, I am   75
told they have all been instructed to apply this Speech mighty
right: And a lucky Parallel it is, as ever was drawn sure, between *Verres* who was detested and complain'd of by the whole
Island that he enslav'd, and a certain Lord, who lately left a
Government with the universal Regret of the People whom he   80
govern'd: Of the People, I mean, who are for the Protestant Interest in that Island, and for the Interest of the Illustrious House
of *Hanover* in *Great Britain*: And of the People, who frequently by
the Declarations of their Representatives, gave hearty and

78 detested] detected ½°   the] a 12°

---

59 *Oration*: 69.80-72.147.
61 *Lucian*: *How to write history*, 19.
63 *Cicero*: *Brutus*, lxxxiv 289.
68 *Reflections of his own*: 70.127n.
84 *Declarations*: On 27 August 1709 the Irish House of Commons voted an
address to Wharton in which they gratefully acknowledged 'her Majesty's more
particular Care ... in appointing your Excellency our Chief Governor' and
three days later the speaker expressed 'the profound Honour they bear the
Vicegerent, whom Her Princely Goodness hath been pleas'd to place over them'
(Boyer, *Annals*, 1710, pp. 192-4). Mainwaring was anticipated by *The Observator*,
2-6 December 1710: 'it appear'd upon the Records of the Senate of *Sicily*, that
they were very well satisfy'd with the Conduct of their Proconsul'. But Mainwaring confided to the Duchess his true estimate of Wharton's competence as
Lord-Lieutenant of Ireland: 'my Lord and Lady Wharton are landed. They have
left a bad character behind them, and it is certain that my Lord is not equal

85 repeated Thanks to her Majesty, for having plac'd over them a
    Governour, who with indefatigable Industry, and very great Abili-
    ties, had steddily pursu'd all his life the true Interest of his
    Country, and had always shewn the *warmest Zeal for supporting the*
    Revolution, and the Government founded upon it. And is not this
90 now the Character of a Man, extremely resembling that of *Verres*,
    who stands upon Record in the *Roman* Story, for a vile stupid
    Wretch, and as great an Enemy to the Liberty of *Rome*, as his
    small Capacity wou'd suffer him to be? Such a nice Discerner is
    the *Examiner*, that I am only afraid his Friends will silence him,
95 who to blacken a Man of *the ruin'd Party*, as he calls it, has
    confounded opposite Characters, misrepresented Facts, and jumbled
    notorious Falshoods and Inconsistences together; not doubting,
    but by his *Island* and his *Governor*, the only two words that have
    the least relation to the Person he wou'd insult, he might impose
100 upon such Readers as he generally meets with, and might indear
    himself still more to their Favour or Contributions, by the Impu-
    dence of the Scandal, and the Leudness of the Picture. But in-
    stead of entering into a particular Examination of his Speech,
    I will humbly offer another, taken from the same Author, and per-
105 haps as ill translated as his: Only I will be warn'd by his sad
    Fate, not to add one Thought or Expression of my own. It is part
    of *Cicero*'s Oration in the Senate, when there was a Question
    there about recalling *Cæsar* from his unfinish'd Conquests in
    France.
110   'My Friend here that interrupts me, says, I have reason to be
    an Enemy to *Cæsar*. I will answer him first, by professing, that
    I shall always have more regard to the Publick Good, than to my
    own Sufferings; and I can justify what I now contend for, by the
    Example of our bravest and most illustrious Citizens. Did not
115 *Tiberius Gracchus* get immortal Honour, when he alone of all the
    Tribunes supported *Lucius Scipio*, tho he was an Enemy profest
    both to *Lucius* and his Brother *Africanus*? When he swore in the
    Senate, that he was not reconcil'd to them; but he thought it
    below the Dignity of the *Roman* Empire, that *Scipio* shou'd be

to such a post. He would make a very good miner' (*Private Correspondence*,
i 217).
    95   *the ruin'd Party*: 3.50.
    110-99   *My ... Conduct*: Cicero, *De Prov*[*inciis*] *Consul*[*aribus*, viii 18-
xiv 35, with large omissions] (½°).

carry'd to the same Place, whither the Generals of their Enemies   120
had been often led in his Triumphs. Who had more Adversarys than
Caius Marius? yet they were so far from voting to recal him from
France, that having particular regard to the Circumstances of
that War, they decreed to him the Command of it in a manner extraordinary.   125

'A very great War has been now carry'd on with *France*, and that
great People have been subdu'd by *Cæsar*; but they are not yet
bound by any Laws or Treaties, nor by any settled Peace. We see
a War very far advanc'd; or, that I may speak truly, almost
ended; yet so, that if the same Person who began it is suffer'd   130
to proceed, we may soon expect a good Conclusion of the whole:
But if any other Man is appointed in his room, there may be
danger of hearing that the Remains of this vast War may be repair'd, and pursu'd with new Vigour. I therefore considering my
self as a Senator, tho an Enemy, if you please, to the Man, ought 135
to be what I always was, a Friend to the Commonwealth. But how
can I be an Enemy to him, by whose Letters, Fame, or Expresses,
my Ears are every day gratify'd with new Names of People conquer'd, or of Places taken?

'Believe me, my Lords, I burn (as you your selves do, and I   140
hope believe the same of me) with an inexpressible Love of my
Country; and this Disposition of my Mind, which I ever had, and
always shall have, reconciles me to *Cæsar*, and restores him to my
Friendship. People may think, or suspect what they please of me;
but I can be no Man's Enemy that deserves so well of the Publick.   145
For if I have not only declar'd an Enmity, but have denounc'd War
against those that are bringing Fire and Sword upon us, tho some
of them were my familiar Acquaintance; why shou'd not the same
Publick Good, that cou'd provoke me against my Friends, appease
me towards my Enemies? What Hatred have I to *Publius Clodius*, but 150
that I think him a Man pernicious to his Country? You have decreed Honours to *Caius Cæsar*, so many in number, as no Man ever
receiv'd in any War: So great in themselves, and in the manner of

141 believe] you think 12°   142 my Mind] Mind 12°

---

132 *other Man*: It had been known since February-March 1708 that if Harley
had to replace Marlborough, '*Ormond* had been sent to head the War' (*POAS*,
Yale, vii 305).

bestowing them, as is quite beyond Example. Yet nothing governs
155   me in this Debate, but the Reason and Necessity of the War, and
the Good and Safety of my Country. If I only consider'd *Cæsar*,
what reason can he have to wish to stay Abroad, but that he may
perfect the Service which he has far advanc'd? Wou'd his Return
to his Country offend any body? It cannot be the People that sent
160   him, nor the Senate that applauded him: Nay, if any there are
that hate the Man, there can be no reason even for them to call
him Home; they call him Home to Glory, to a Triumph, to publick
Congratulations, to the highest Honour of the Peers, to the
Favour of the Commons, and to the Joy and Affection of the
165   People.

'But if he is content to stay Abroad for the Good of the Commonwealth, and to defer the Enjoyment of his Fortune till the War
is ended; what Opinion shou'd I be of, who if *Cæsar* were otherwise inclin'd, ought only to consult the Advantage of my Country,
170   especially at a time when we are so near a Peace? Before *Cæsar*
commanded, we rather endeavour'd to stop the Conquests of the
French, than to carry the War into their Country: Other Generals
thought those People were rather to be repel'd than attack'd. But
Cæsar has proceeded after quite another manner: He thought it not
175   only his Business to conquer those that were in Arms, but to reduce their Country.

'No body had ever right Notions of our Government from its
first Foundation, but he thought the *French* were most formidable
to it; who may now be oblig'd, in one Campaign or two, to accept
such Terms, as will be firm for ever. But if things unfinish'd
180   and imperfect shall be left in that Condition, tho their Strength
be broken now, they will certainly rise again, and revive to
prosecute another War. Wherefore let *France* continue under his
Care, to whose Valour, Fidelity and Fortune it was committed.
For if he that is adorn'd with the greatest Gifts of Fortune,
185   were no longer willing to trust to that Goddess; if he were in
haste to return to our Country, to our Altars, to that High Rank
which he must always bear among us, and to his most delightful
Children: If, lastly, he were apprehensive of an ill Event, which
wou'd now take more from his Glory, than any new Conquests cou'd
190   add to it; yet in all these Cases it were our Interest to wish,
that he alone might have the finishing of this War, who has

hitherto conducted it with such wonderful Success. But when he
who has long since done enough for his own Glory, tho not yet
quite enough for our Safety, had rather enjoy more late the
Fruits of his Labours, than not fully acquit himself of his Duty   195
to his Country; surely we ought neither to recal to Affairs at
Home a General, that will have reason to resent such Usage; nor
to disturb and interrupt our War with *France*, of which we may
soon hope to have so good an Account from his Conduct.'

No. 20 [Swift]   14 December 1710

The EXAMINER

Sunt quibus in Satyra videar nimis acer, & ultra
Legem tendere opus: sine nervis altera, quicquid
Composui, pars esse putat.

WHEN the Printer came last Week for his Copy, he brought along
with him a Bundle of those Papers, which in the Phrase of *Whig*
Coffee-houses have *swinged off* the *Examiner*, most of which I had
never seen nor heard of before. I remember some time ago in one
of the *Tatlers* to have read a Letter, wherein several Reasons are   5
assigned for the present Corruption and Degeneracy of our Tast,
but I think the Writer has omitted the principal one, which I
take to be the Prejudice of Parties. Neither can I excuse either
side of this Infirmity; I have heard the arrantest Drivellers *Pro*
and *Con* commended for their *Smartness* even by Men of tolerable   10
Judgment; and the best Performances exploded as Nonsense and

---

  4 nor] or 38 8°+12°   10 *Smartness*] Shrewdness 38 8°+12°

Motto Horace, *Satires*, ii 1 1:
              There are to whom too poignant I appear,
              Beyond the Laws of Satire too severe.
              My Lines are weak, unsinew'd, others say,
              A Man may spin a thousand such a Day.
  1 *Printer*: John Barber.
  2 *Papers*: *The Observator*, 1-4 November, 15-18 November 1710, *The Medley*, 20
November, 4 December 1710.
  4-5 *one of the Tatlers*: No. 230, 26-8 September 1710, written by Swift himself 'about the corruptions of style and writing' (Swift, *Journal*, p. 22).

Stupidity. This indeed may partly be imputed to Policy and Prudence; but it is chiefly owing to that Blindness, which Prejudice
and Passion cast over the Understanding: I mention this because
15 I think it properly within my Province in quality of *Examiner*.
And having granted more than is usual for an Enemy to do, I must
now take leave to say, that so weak a Cause, and so ruin'd a Faction, were never provided with Pens more resembling their Condition, or less suited to their Occasions.

20   *Non tali auxilio, nec defensoribus istis*
                Tempus eget

This is the more to be wondred at, when we consider they have
the full Liberty of the Press, that they have no other way left
to recover themselves, and that they want not Men of excellent
25 Parts to set their Arguments in the best Light they will bear.
Now if two Men would argue on both sides with Fairness, good
Sense, and good Manners, it would be no ill Entertainment to the
Town, and perhaps be the most effectual means to reconcile us.
But I am apt to think that Men of a great Genius are hardly
30 brought to prostitute their Pens in a very odious Cause; which
besides, is more properly undertaken by Noise and Impudence, by
gross Railing and Scurrility, by Calumny and Lying, and by little
trifling Cavils and Carpings in the wrong Place, which those
Whifflers use for Arguments and Answers.
35   I was well enough pleased with a Story of one of these Answerers,
who in a Paper last Week found many Faults with a late Calculation
of mine. Being it seems more deep learned than his Fellows, he was
resolved to begin his Answer with a *Latin* Verse, as well as other
Folks: His Business was to look out for something against an
40 *Examiner* that would pretend to *tax* Accounts; and turning over
Virgil, he had the luck to find these Words, *Fugiant Examina*
taxos; so down they went, and out they would have come, if one of
his unlucky *Prompters* had not hindred it.
I here declare once for all, that if these People will not be
45 quiet, I shall take the Bread out of their Mouths, and answer the

20-1 *Non ... eget*: Virgil, *Aeneid*, ii 521: Not such the aid nor these the
defenders the hour craves.
36 *Paper*: *The Medley*, 4 December 1710.
41-2 *Fugiant Examina taxos*: Virgil, *Eclogues*, ix 30: swarms of bees shun
the yews.

Examiner my self; which I protest I have never yet done, though
I have been often charged with it; neither have those Answers
been written or published with my privity, as malicious People
are pleased to give out; nor do I believe the common *Whiggish*
Report, that the Authors are hired by the Ministry to give my   50
Paper a value.

But the Friends of this Paper have given me more Uneasiness
with their Impatience, than its Enemies by their Answers. I heard
my self censur'd last Week by some of the former, for promising
to discover the Corruptions in the late Administration, but never   55
performing any Thing. The latter on the other side, are thundring
out their Anathema's against me for discovering so many. I am at
a loss how to decide between these Contraries, and therefore shall
proceed after my own Way, as I have hitherto done: My Design being
of more Importance than that of writing only to gratify the Spleen   60
of one Side, or provoke that of the Other, tho' it may occasionally have both Effects.

I shall therefore go on to relate some Facts that in my humble
Opinion were no Hindrance to the Change of the Ministry.

The first I shall mention, was That of introducing certain new   65
Phrases into the Court Style, which had been very seldom or never
made use of in former Times. They usually ran in the following
Terms: *Madam, I cannot serve you while such a one is in Employment: I desire humbly to resign my Commission, if Mr. ------ continues Secretary of State: I cannot answer that the City will*   70
lend Money, unless my L--d ------- be Pr------t of the C----il.
I must beg leave to surrender, except --------- has the Staff.
I must not accept the Seals, unless --------- comes into t'other

---

65-76 *introducing ... Nation*: quoted in *The Observator*, 13-16 December 1710,
with the comment: 'Has the Crown no Attorny General '.

68-70 *Madam ... State*: These words were directed to the Queen by Marlborough
on 6 February 1708 (Coxe, *Marlborough*, ii 191). Swift was anticipated in the
use of these 'new Phrases' by Colley Cibber (*The Secret History of Arlus and
Odolphus*, 1710, pp. 19, 25).

70-1 *I ... C----il*: These words might have been Godolphin's, before 25
November 1708, when Somers succeeded Pembroke as Lord President of the council.
The Queen had an aversion to Somers 'upon account of his having disobliged the
Prince' (*Private Correspondence*, i 156); 'upon the Queen's refusing [Somers]
the Lord Treasurer offered his white staff to her Majesty, which she refused'
(HMC *Portland MSS*, iv 507).

71 *I ... Staff*: These might have been Godolphin's words in February 1708,
before Sir Thomas Mansell resigned the staff of comptroller of the household.

73-4 *I ... Office*: These words might have been spoken by Sunderland, 'who

Office. This has been the Language of late Years from Subjects to
75 their Prince. Thus they stood upon Terms, and must have their own
Conditions to ruin the Nation; Nay, this dutiful manner of capi-
tulating, had spread so far, that every Under-strapper began at
length to perk up and assume: *He expected a Regiment*; or *His Son
must be a Major*; or *His Brother a Collector*, else he threatned to
80 Vote *according to his Conscience*.

Another of their glorious Attempts, was the Clause intended in
the Bill for the Encouragement of Learning; for taking off the
Obligation upon Fellows of Colledges in both Universities to
enter upon Holy Orders: The Design of which, as I have heard the
85 Undertakers often confess, was to remove the Care of educating
Youth out of the Hands of the Clergy, who are apt to infuse into
their Pupils too great a Regard for the Church and the Monarchy.
But there was a farther Secret in this Clause, which may best be
discovered by the first Projectors, or at least the *Garblers* of
90 it; and these are known to be *C-ll-ns* and *Tindal*, in conjunction

82 for] by 38 8°+12°

---

had refus'd to come into the Secretary's Office, before Mr. *Harley* was remov'd
from thence; and who was suppos'd to have been the Promoter of the ... Address,
for Removing Mrs. *M[asham]* from Her Majesty's Bed-Chamber' (Boyer, *An Essay
towards the History of the Last Ministry and Parliament*, London, for J. Baker,
1710, pp. 34-5).

81 *Clause*: Following a petition by sixteen London publishers for a copy-
right law, the Whig lawyer Spencer Compton brought in a bill, of which a
much-amended Act for the Encouragement of Learning (8 Ann. c. 21) received the
royal assent on 5 April 1710 (*CJ*, xvi 240, 339, 394, 396). The rejected clause
to which Swift refers is reflected in Ralph Bridges' letter of 3 March [1709]:
'A little paper has been industriously handed about to make way for a Bill to
break in upon the Statutes of Colleges in both Universities. It arose from the
Warden of All Souls putting in execution the Statutes against such as refused
Holy Orders' (HMC *Downshire MSS*, i 2 871). White Kennett complained that
taking off the requirement of holy orders would conduce only 'to the breeding
up Sparks and Beaux instead of grave Divines' (Bodl. MS Ballard 7, f. 124).

88 *a farther Secret*: innuendo: repeal of the Test Act(?).

89 *Garblers*: 'One who garbles or mutilates (literary works, statements,
&c.)' (*OED*, citing this line).

90 *C-ll-ns*: Anthony Collins (1676-1729) was a gentleman-scholar, a disciple
of Locke, who left him £200 in his will, and something of a stricken deer,
whom Swift had not yet singled out from 'the whole Herd of ... Deists'
(257.37-8) as he was to do in *Mr. C---ns's Discourse of Free-Thinking, Put
into Plain English, by way of Abstract, for the Use of the Poor* (1713).

Tindal: Matthew Tindal (1657-1733) graduated DCL from Exeter College,
Oxford, and in November 1685 began to practise in doctors' commons, the ecclesiastical, probate, and admiralty courts. Thereafter Dr Tindal, as he was
called, divided his time between Oxford, where he was a fellow of All Souls,
and London, where he was 'a noted Debauchee' (Hearne, i 237). The work that

with a most *pious Lawyer* their Disciple.

What shall we say to their prodigious skill in *Arithmetick*,
discover'd so constantly in their Decision of Elections; where
they were able to make out by the *Rule of False*, that *three* were
more than *three and Twenty*, and *Fifteen* than *Fifty*? Nay 'twas a   95
Maxim which I never heard any of them dispute, that in determining Elections, they were not to consider where the Right lay, but
which of the Candidates was likelier to be true to the *Cause*.
This they used to illustrate by a very apt and decent Similitude,
of Gaming with a Sharper; if you cannot Cheat as well as he, you   100
are certainly undone.

made him famous was one that he knew 'would make the clergy mad'. It was
called *The Rights of the Christian Church Asserted. Against the Romish, and
All Other Priests who Claim an Independent Power over it* (1706), but what it
asserted was that the Church of England has no rights, and no power but what
is granted to it by the state. More than twenty replies were made to this book,
including one by Swift, who described Tindal as 'an old neglected Man, who hath
long lain under the Extreams of Obloquy, Poverty and Contempt' (Swift, *Prose*,
ii 73). What Swift refers to here is another of Tindal's anti-clerical tirades
in which he argues that the constitution in Church and state cannot be defended
'if they who have the Education of the Gentry and Nobility ... instil into 'em
such Principles as must oblige 'em to endeavour its destruction' (*The Jacobitism, Perjury, and Popery of High-Church Priests*, 1710, p. 14).
   91 *Lawyer*: John Asgill (1659-1738) was called to the bar from the Middle
Temple in 1692. He was a Whig Member of Parliament for Bramber, Sussex (1699-
1700, 1702-7), and for Enniscorthy in the Irish Parliament (1703). In July
1700, however, he published *An Argument Proving, that according to the Covenant
of Eternal Life Revealed in the Scriptures, Man may be Translated from Hence
into that Eternal Life, without Passing through Death*, for which he was expelled successively from both Parliaments. 'I can't still but wonder', he said,
'that a Man should be expel'd two Houses of Commons in two Christian Kingdoms,
for professing his Faith in Jesus Christ according to the Scriptures' (*Mr.
Asgill's Defence upon his Expulsion from the House of Commons of Great Britain
in 1707*, London, by A. Baldwin, 1712, p. 57). Swift was not alone in making
him out to be a deist: '*Tolandists* and *Asgilites*, | ... form new Articles
Divine, | Exceeding far our Thirty Nine' (*POAS*, 1704, iii 401). But Asgill's
zaniness was quite independent of the deists. 'I knew *Asgyl*,' Oldmixon said,
'and his Whims seem'd to qualify him more for *Bedlam*, than a House of Commons' (Oldmixon, *The History*, p. 308).
   93 *Elections*: Swift refers to two notorious cases resulting from the
general election of May 1708, in which Tories with more votes were set aside
by the Committee on Elections in the House of Commons in favour of Whigs with
fewer votes. These same cases are queried in an election broadside of October
1710: 'Whether in Voting Sir *Simon Harcourt*, Sir *Charles Blois*, and Twenty
more, not duly Elected, the Charters of Corporations were not *sweetly* Preserved? And whether the Gentlemen, who Counted Nine to be a greater Number
than Thirteen, and Three more than Twenty Seven, ought not to study the Rules
of Arithmetick and Honesty, before they come again to Parliament?' (*The Gun-
Smiths Queries*, no place of publication, 1710; cf. Burnet, ii 517).
   99 *Similitude*: 'if you think it fair | Amongst known cheats to play upon
the square, | You'll be undone' (Rochester, *A Satyr against Reason and Mankind*,
lines 161-3); cf. 86.155-6.

   Another Cast of their Politicks was that of endeavouring to
impeach an innocent *L-dy*, for no Reason imaginable, but her faithful and diligent Service to the Q----, and the Favour Her M------
105 bore to her upon that Account, when others had acted contrary in
so shameful a manner. What else was the Crime? Had she *treated*
Her Royal Mistress with Insolence or Neglect? Had she *enrich'd*
her self by a long Practice of Bribery, and obtaining Exorbitant
Grants? Had she *engross'd Her M-----y's Favours, without admitting*
110 *any Access but through her Means?* Had she *heaped Employments upon*
her self, her Family and Dependants? Had she *an imperious, haughty*
Behaviour? Or, after all, was it a perfect Blunder and Mistake of
one Person for another? I have heard of a Man who lay all Night
on a rough Pavement; and in the Morning, wondring what it could
115 possibly be, that made him rest so ill, happen'd to see a *Feather*
under him, and imputed the uneasiness of his Lodging to That. I
remember likewise the Story of a Giant in *Rablais*, who us'd to
feed upon *Wind-mills*, but was unfortunately choak'd with a small
lump of *fresh Butter*, before a warm Oven.
120   And here I cannot but observe how very refin'd some People are
in their Generosity and Gratitude. There is a certain great
Person (I shall not say of what Sex) who for many Years past, was
the constant Mark and Butt, against which our present Malecontents
us'd to discharge their Resentment: Upon whom they bestow'd all

   103 *L-dy*: During the patronage crisis of January 1710 Mainwaring urged Marlborough 'to insist positively upon the removal of Abigail [Masham]' (BL MS Add.
61462) and Sunderland undertook to draft such an address to Parliament (Boyer,
An Essay towards the History of the Last Ministry and Parliament, 1710, pp. 8,
34). When Anne learned of this threat, 'She sent for several persons of both
houses in her service, declared with great Spirit and Courage against it ...
among these is said to be ... Manwaring to whom she spoke very plain'
(Leicestershire RO MS Finch DG7, Bundle 23).
   106-12 *treated ... Behaviour*: All this was being said of the Duchess of
Marlborough both in prose and verse: 'She'll give him a place, if he'll give
her a Snack' (Leeds University MS Brotherton Lt.11, p. 84); 'I guesse the
dutchesse of Marleborough did it [appoint Daniel Pulteney ambassador to Den-
mark]' (BL MS Add. 4291, f. 72); Delariviere Manley, *Secret Memoirs*, 1709,
ii 152-3; *Memoirs of Europe*, 1710, ii 280; Cibber, *The Secret History of Arlus
and Odolphus*, 1710, pp. 21-3.
   117 *Giant*: Bringuenarilles (Rabelais, *Gargantua et Pantagruel*, iv xvii).
   122 *Person*: Daniel Finch, second Earl of Nottingham, still a Tory, was expressing his resentment at being left out of Harley's ministry by stirring up
demands for impeaching Godolphin and the Junto in order to upset Harley's
'wild and unwarrantable scheme of balancing parties', as Nottingham called it
(Henry Horwitz, *Revolution Politicks. The Career of Daniel Finch Second Earl
of Nottingham, 1647-1730*, Cambridge, Cambridge University Press, 1968, p. 228).

the Terms of Scurrility, that Malice, Envy and Indignation cou'd   125
invent; whom they publickly accus'd of every Vice that can possess
a Human Heart: Pride, Covetousness, Ingratitude, Oppression, Treachery, Dissimulation, Violence and Fury, all in the highest Extreams: But of late, they have chang'd their Language on a
suddain; That Person is now the most faithful and just that ever   130
serv'd a Prince; That Person, originally differing from them in
Principles, as far as East and West, but united in Practice, and
falling together, they are now reconcil'd, and find twenty
Resemblances between each other, which they could never discover
before. *Tanti est ut placeam tibi perire.*   135
   But to return: How could it be longer suffer'd in a free Nation,
that all Avenues to Preferment should be shut up, except a very
few, when one or two stood constant *Centry*, who dockt all Favours
they handed down; or spread a huge invisible Net, between the
Prince and Subject, thro' which nothing of Value could pass? And   140
here I cannot but admire at one Consequence from this Management,
which is of an extraordinary Nature: Generally speaking, Princes
who have ill Ministers are apt to suffer in their Reputation, as
well as in the Love of the People: But it was not so with the
Q----. When the Sun is overcast by those Clouds he exhales from   145
the Earth, we still acknowledge his Light and Influence, and at
last find he can dispel and drive them down to the Horizon. The
Wisest Prince, by the necessity of Affairs, the misrepresentations
of designing Men, or the innocent Mistakes, even of a good Predecessor, may find himself encompass'd by a Crew of Courtiers,   150
whom Time, Opportunity and Success, have miserably corrupted. And
if he can save himself and his People from Ruin, under the *worst*
Administration, what may not his Subjects hope for, when with
their universal Applause, he changes Hands, and makes use of the
best?   155
   Another great Objection with me against the late Party, was the
cruel Tyranny they put upon *Conscience*, by a barbarous *Inquisition*,

---

   139 they] *om.* 38 8°+12°   154 changes] changeth 38 8°+12°   makes]
maketh 38 8°+12°

---

   135 *Tanti ... perire:* Martial, viii 69: It is worth while to perish that
I may give you pleasure (E*1922*, ix 119).
   138 *Centry:* 100.109-10 above.

refusing to admit the least *Toleration* or *Indulgence*. They impos'd a Hundred *Tests*, but could never be prevail'd with to *dis-*
160 *pense* with, or *take off* the smallest, nor even admit of *Occasional*
Conformity; but went on Daily (as their Apostle *Tindal* expresseth
it) *narrowing their Terms of Communion*; pronouncing nine Parts in
ten of the Kingdom *Hereticks*, and shutting them out of the Pale
of their Church. These very Men, who talk so much of a *Comprehen-*
165 *sion in Religion* among us, how came they to allow so little of it
in *Politicks*, which is *Their Sole Religion*? You shall hear them
pretending to bewail the Animosities kept up between the Church
of *England* and Dissenters, where the Differences in Opinion are
so few and inconsiderable; yet these very Sons of *Moderation* were
170 pleased to *excommunicate* every Man who disagreed with them in the
smalest *Article* of their *Political Creed*, or who refus'd to receive any new *Article*, how difficult soever to digest, which the
Leaders impos'd at Pleasure to serve their own Interest.

I will quit this Subject for the present, when I have told one
175 Story. 'There was a great King in *Scythia*, whose Dominions were
bounded to the North, by the poor, mountainous Territories of a
petty Lord, who paid Homage as the King's Vassal. The *Scythian*
Prime Minister being largely *Brib'd*, indirectly obtain'd his
Master's Consent to suffer this Lord to built Forts, and provide
180 himself with *Arms*, under pretence of preventing the Inroads of
the *Tartars*. This little depending Sovereign, finding he was now
in a Condition to be troublesome, began to insist upon Terms, and

160 nor] or 38 8°+12°

---

162 *narrowing ... Communion*: Tindal, *The Rights of the Christian Church*
Asserted, 4th edn., London, 1709, p. 346. This edition, Tindal said, is 'more
correct' (p. lxxxix).
169 *Moderation*: 85.108.
175 *Story*: 'These Facts', Swift said, 'are well enough known to the whole
Kingdom' (Swift, *Prose*, viii 49) and indeed the story is told in substantially
the same terms by Abel Boyer, *An Essay towards the History of the Last Ministry*
and Parliament, 1710, p. 47: 'an *Act of Indemnity* [72.153n.] was procured to
skreen a Great Man [Godolphin], who is shrewdly suspected of having lavish'd
away near a Million *Sterling*, to bring about the *Union*; with no other design
than to retrieve a False step [advising the Queen to assent to the Scottish
Act of Security], for which he might have lost his Head.'
178 *Brib'd*: In 1714 Swift moderated the charge: 'by *the Weakness* or Corruption of a certain Minister ... an Act of [Security] was obtained for the
Scots, which gave them leave to arm themselves' (Swift, *Prose*, viii 49, italics
added).

threaten'd upon every occasion to unite with the *Tartars*: Upon
which, the *Prime Minister*, who began to be in pain about his
Head, propos'd a *Match* betwixt his Master, and the only Daughter   185
of this Tributary Lord, which he had the good Luck to bring to
pass; and from that time, valu'd himself as Author of a most
glorious *Union*, which indeed was grown of absolute Necessity by
his Corruption. This Passage, cited literally from an old History
of *Sarmatia*, I thought fit to set down, on purpose to perplex   190
little smattering Remarkers, and put them upon the Hunt for an
Application.

190 thought] though ½°

---

188 *Union*: 'the Union was of no other service to the nation, than by giving
a remedy to that evil, which my Lord Godolphin had brought upon us, by per-
suading the Queen to pass the Scotch act of security' (Swift, *Prose*, viii 114).
189-90 *History of Sarmatia*: cf. Swift, *Tale*, p. 272.

No. 12 [Mainwaring]   18 December 1710

The MEDLEY.

Of Beauty and Assemblies.
Of the Examiner*'s Bashfulness.*
Of Informers and Suborners among the Romans.
Of the Mischief they did in the Macedonian *Army.*

IT was not thought so strange, that Valour, Wisdom, and Wealth
were out of fashion, as that Beauty shou'd be also in Disgrace;
and that the Fair shou'd grow into Contempt as fast as the Great:
For Beauty is the Growth of British *Ground*, as the Poet sings;
and ill Faces were formerly reckon'd Contraband Goods, and were   5
not suffer'd to be imported. What harm Beauty has done since, is
hard to discover. I never heard that it contributed to the Danger
of the Church, at least it was never complain'd of by the Doctor.

2 *Beauty*: 'The first part is a complaint on the Torys that they will not
admitt of the d. of M[arlborough]'s daughters to be toasts any more' (SRO
GD 220/5/807/119).
4 *For ... Ground*: source unknown.
5 *ill Faces*: Possibly a reference to the Duchess of Shrewsbury (33.219n.).

It has always been famous for *good Principles*, a great Encourager
10 of *Passive-Obedience*, and not a little pleas'd to turn *Subjects*
into *Slaves*. All the World owns it is of *Divine Institution*: And
I cou'd give a plain Proof, in a certain Family, that it has *an
Hereditary Right*: And, to recommend it still more to the Humour
of some People, it has always delighted in *Variety and Change of
15 Servants*. In *China* we are told it is in such Repute, that the Men
of Quality are not suffer'd to marry ugly Women: And in *England*
it was once so fortunate (I mean in the days of Queen *Elizabeth*)
that no Servants were incourag'd but such as were handsom. It has
since that time made a very great Figure among us, and our Court
20 was as bright at Home, as our Army was glorious Abroad. It added
Lustre to the Throne it surrounded; it charm'd every Mortal that
approach'd; it was the Grace of our Triumphs, the Pride of our
Nation, and the Envy of our Enemies. *Italians* a thousand years
ago were so far from being admir'd here, that on the contrary a
25 Pope made a Latin Pun upon our People, and said, they shou'd not
be call'd *English*, but *Angels*; [*non Angli sed Angeli*.] What a
wonderful Change has been here since those days! nor is it less
surprizing, that at a time when Beauty is eclips'd, there shou'd
be any body so idle as to set up *an Assembly*. Those Entertain-
30 ments are generally design'd for Foreigners: But what Diversion
can Strangers have in any Place, where by the Company they meet,
they will have reason to think themselves at Home? How much better did the *French* Ladies imploy their time, when Funds were first
scarce in that Country? It is well known to the Curious, that many
35 of that Sex turn'd Projectors; and that the Tax upon *Coats of Arms*

26 *non*] not ½° 12°

---

10 *Passive-Obedience*: During the Sacheverell trial the doctor was 'visited
daily ... by a great Company of Passive-Obedience and Non-Resisting Ladies'
(Oldmixon, *The Life*, p. 124; cf. *The History of Dr. Sacheverell; Faithfully
Translated from the Paris-Gazette*, London, for A. Baldwin, 1711, p. 4).
14 *Variety*: cf. 'Le vrai plaisir d'aimer est dans le changement' (Molière,
Le Festin de pierre (1677), i 2).
25 *Pope*: Gregory I (590-604) (Bede, *Historia ecclesiastica gentis anglorum*,
ii 1). There is another version of the legend in the anonymous *Life of Gregory
the Great* (ed. Bertram Colgrave, Lawrence, University of Kansas Press, 1968,
p. 90): 'Cumque responderent, "Anguli dicuntur, illi de quibus sumus," ille
dixit, "Angeli Dei".'
29 *Assembly*: 'The City Ladies Visiting-day ... is a familiar Assembly, or
a general Council of the fair and charming Sex' (*The Works of Mr. Thomas
Brown*, 4 vols., London, for Sam Briscoe, sold by J. Morphew, 1708, iii 80).

was found out by the Dutchess of *Roquelaure*. If some of our
Ladies wou'd follow this Example, and had not an Abhorrence for
the Ways and Means of *France*, what a Comfort at this time might
they be to their Friends? But I never heard that a Basset-Table
carry'd on a War, or that an *Assembly* contributed to the Support   40
of Publick Credit.

The Title, as well as Design of this Paper, allows me to ramble
as much as I please from one Subject to another, and I am now
going to make the strangest Transition that I believe was ever
seen; it is from Beauty and Credit to the *Examiner*. There is a   45
Passage in one of his late *Discourses*, as he calls them, that
shou'd be written in Letters of Gold; it is that where he stiles
himself a *Bashful Author*. This I must own transported me extremely: If a Man that is in hopes of some small Office, shou'd
have a mind beforehand to hire some Domesticks, and shou'd pitch   50
upon a late Lord President, a Treasurer, Chancellor, and two
Secretaries (all of them, I will venture to say, the best and
ablest in their several Stations that ever serv'd at one time) to
be his Coachman, his Receiver, his Steward, and his two Clerks;
wou'd not all the World say, that this is a very modest *bashful*   55
Person? With his *John*, his *Oldfox*, his *Will*, his *Charles*, and his
Harry; not to mention his *blundering malicious Rascal*, that he
keeps to carry Messages? This is one Instance therefore of my
Friend's *Bashfulness*. I cou'd give a hundred others, but will
mention no more than one more, which shews his good Fortune as   60
well as his Modesty: It is in the same Paper, where he says, he
has *so little Power over Peoples Tongues, that he is forc'd to*
hear his own Work commended fifty times a day. To this I can only
answer, that he has much better Luck than I have had. I have

60 no more than] only 12°

---

36 *Roquelaure*: Marie-Louise de Montmorency-Laval (d. 1735) married in 1683
the duc de Roquelaure, who was 'très mal dans ses affaires'. She managed to
make him one of the richest peers in France by various devices, one of which
was the enregistering of arms, which Louis XIV made compulsory in 1696 (De La
Chesnaye-Desbois, xvii 652; *Mémoires de Saint Simon*, ed. A. de Boislisle, 2nd
edn., 41 vols., Paris, Hachette, 1879-1928, ii 249, xiii 183, xxiv 173).
46 *Discourses*: 36.62, 66. Swift commonly calls them 'Papers' (p. xxxviii).
48 *Bashful*: 82.21.
50 *Domesticks*: 66.16 ff.
57 *Rascal*: 67.32.
62-3 *Power ... day*: 82.15-18.

65 heard indeed several brisk genteel young Men of his Party, those
    I mean among them that have the most Wit and Judgment, cry up to
    the Skies *Abel Roper* and *John Dyer*. Some of them wou'd swear,
    that *Abel had laid about him purely*; others, that *Dyer had maul'd
    the Whigs plaguily*: But I can safely affirm, that from the time
70 my Friend took Pen in hand, I never heard one Person of his own
    side speak the least kind word of him, or his Performers. On the
    contrary, I have heard them often rail at him, and cry, This Fel-
    low can't keep a Secret: There's no Sense or good Policy in him;
    he has little Wit, and less Judgment. He always lets our Enemies
75 know beforehand what we are about: If he is order'd to publish
    any notorious Lyes, he begins with a Treatise of Political Lying.
    If he has a Friend who is faulty that way, or any other, he imme-
    diately draws his Picture. If there's a Design upon any Body's
    Estate, out it comes, say they; if this Blunderer has but the
80 least notice of it, the first thing he does, is to make a dull
    Speech about *Verres*. Yet after all these Discouragements, this
    bashful unexperienc'd Author expresses a great Desire, that his
    *Papers, reduc'd into a more durable Form, shou'd live till our
    Grandchildren are Men*. What a Present is here intended for the
85 future Republick of Letters! The *Examiner* and our Grandchildren
    nam'd together in the same Paragraph! What fine Work is here like
    to be! Well! I have always been his Friend, and will shew it now
    upon this difficult occasion, by telling him the only means that
    can convey his Papers *to our Grandchildren*; and I will confirm

---

67 *Roper*: the proprietor of *The Post Boy*, a Tory newspaper for which Swift
and St. John wrote occasional paragraphs (*Wentworth Papers*, p. 212; Swift,
Journal, pp. 237, 446, 574; *Tory Annals Faithfully Extracted out of Abel
Roper's Famous Writings*, London, 1712, sig. A4^r).
    Dyer: the proprietor of a factory-produced manuscript newsletter that
had wide circulation among the Tory gentry (Henry L. Snyder, 'Newsletters in
England, 1689-1715: with special reference to John Dyer', *Newsletters to News-
papers: Eighteenth Century Journalism*, edd. D.H. Bond and W.R. McLeod, Morgan-
town, The School of Journalism, West Virginia University, 1977, pp. 3-19).
    77 *Friend*: 43.30.
    79 *Estate*: 50.29.
    Blunderer: Mainwaring's central seed image for the Examiner, probably
borrowed—'[The Examiner] makes such Blunders against common Sense ... his
Blunders' (*The Observator*, 25-9 November, 29 November-2 December 1710)—finds
unexpected confirmation: 'Did you ever see such a blundering goose-cap as
Presto?' (Swift, *Journal*, p. 245).
    81 *Speech*: 69.80-72.147.
    83-4 *Papers ... Men*: 84.98-100. Swift's sentence is not optative but con-
ditional. Mainwaring omits the words 'happen to'.

what I say by an Example. There was a Writer of great Solidity in   90
the last Age, who went by the name of *Tom Coryat*: This grave, yet
sometimes pleasant and romancing Author, writ several *Discourses*,
and gave them a Title which may serve another Work: He call'd
them his *Crudities*. And he having at last an Inclination, like my
Friend's, to print all his strange Stuff together *in a durable*   95
Form, for the use of his Grandchildren, there was a Humour
among abundance of People at that time to send a great many Verses to be put before the Book, in praise of honest *Tom*. These
Mock-Commendations made it sell then prodigiously, and have kept
it alive ever since. The same Method I earnestly recommend to   100
the *Examiner*, or rather to his Bookseller: and I dare answer, he
will have as many Copies of Verses given him, as ever *Tom* had, to
print before his Discourses; with the Pictures and Characters of
Himself and his Chief Patrons, to adorn the Frontispiece of his
Work. Therefore the more haste he makes *to reduce it to a durable* 105
Form, the better: For all these Ornaments will certainly be ready
at a Week's warning. I will now make another strange and wonderful Transition; which shall be from the *Examiner* to Informers.

   The two most infamous Characters among the *Romans*, were those
of *Informers* and *Suborners*: And I have read of a Law of theirs,   110
which I thought so reasonable that it shou'd always be remember'd.
It was a Law, by which the *Informer* was oblig'd to produce his

   95 Friend's] Friend 12°

---

   93 *Title: Coryats Crudities hastily gobled up in five Moneths travells*
(1611) was introduced by about seventy-five commendatory verses in Greek,
Latin, Celtic, French, Spanish, Italian, macaronics, and the language of
Utopia, as well as English. There was one by Ben Jonson and two by John Donne.
   110 *Informers and Suborners: Delatores & Mandatores* (½°). 'That Part ...
which relates to *Informers*, *Suborners* ... was occasion'd by the barbarous
Usage of Lieutenant General *Meredith*, Lieutenant General *Maccartney*, and
Colonel *Honeywood*, who for a Toast in their Merriment disagreeable to the new
Ministers, were all three discarded on the Information of a General, as famous
for his *Amorous* as his Martial Exploits' (Oldmixon, *The Life*, p. 189). The
amorous general may be Ormond, the threatened replacement for Marlborough
(*POAS*, Yale, vi 440, vii 298; Macky, p. 10). Mainwaring believed that another
of the informers was Charles Ross of Balnagowan, the younger son of George
Ross, 11th Lord Ross, and colonel of the Fifth Regiment of Dragoons (Dalton,
ii 212). Upon Ross's promotion to Colonel-General of Dragoons in May 1711,
Mainwaring told the Duchess of Marlborough that 'he deserved it richly, being
one of [the] Informers against the poor Gentlemen that were broke' (BL MS Add.
61461, f. 124^V).
   112 *Law: Callistratus de Jure Fisci*, i 2 (½°) [Justinian, *Corpus iuris*
civilis, Pandectis ad florentinum archetypum expressis, Institutionibus,

Suborner: and if he did not do it immediately, he was doom'd to
be ty'd Neck and Heels. But this, as the Law further declares,
115 was not intended to skreen the *Informer* from Punishment, if he
cou'd prove that he was *suborn'd*; but that they might both be
punish'd together, and share the same Fate which they deserv'd.
These Creatures were always number'd among the Calamities of the
Age they liv'd in; rewarded in bad Times, and suppress'd in good.
120 So that we read of a famous Saying even of *Domitian*, that wicked
Emperor, in the beginning of his Reign: *The Prince*, said he, *that
does not punish, encourages Informers*. This Expression was
applauded by all his Subjects, and gave them ground to hope for
a better Government than that which soon after oppress'd them.
125 And the same Author, among the Praises of that Good Prince *Vespasian*, reckons, as one of the chief, his manner of punishing these
Offenders. 'Among the other Misfortunes of the Times, says he,
there were still *Informers* and *Suborners*. These, the Emperor
order'd to be daily beaten and slash'd in the Marketplace with
130 Cudgels, Whips, and Scourges; and to be led ignominiously thro
the Amphitheatre in the face of the People, crouded into Seats
and Scaffolds to behold the Prizes. And as soon as this last
Scene of their Infamy was perform'd, he gave directions, that
some of them shou'd be publickly sold for Slaves, and that others
135 shou'd be carry'd to those barren unfrequented Islands, whither
notorious Criminals were often sent to perish: Hoping, *says the
Author*, by this Severity to restrain Men from attempting such
Villanies hereafter.' A great deal more to the same purpose might
be collected from others; but I will rather observe, what care
140 the *Roman* Laws took to protect Men from such Inquisitions, whenever Justice cou'd be heard among them.

Those Laws did not rashly give every Man that pleas'd a Power
to accuse another. One of their Authors says, We shall know *who*

*Codice et Novellis, addito textu graeco, ut & in Digestis & Codice, legibus &
constitutionibus graecis, cum optimis quibusque editionibus collatis*, 2 vols.,
ed. Simon van Leeuwen, Amsterdam, Joannes Blaeu, 1663, i 752; *Digestorum*,
xlix 14 2 (§5)].
    121-2 *The ... Informers*: Sueton[ius, *Domitianum*,] 1. 8 [c. 9] (½°).
    127-38 *Among ... hereafter*: [Suetonius, *Divus Titus*,] 1. 8. c. 8 (½°).
Vespasian is an error for *Titus*.
    143 *One of their Authors*: [C. Licinius] Macer. *de Accusationibus* (½°).
    143-6 *who ... Pay*: Justinian, *Corpus iuris civilis*, 1663, i 750; *Diges-
torum*, xlviii 2 8. The insinuation that Ormond received '*Pay*' gains credibility
from the fact that although his annual rent-roll was about £25,000 (Irish), he

have the Right of Accusing, by first considering *who have it not.*
Among these he reckons such Men as are *Infamous*, and such as *re-*   145
ceive Pay. On the other side, there were some Persons that cou'd
not be accus'd; and among these were all such Men, as were *abroad*
in the Service of their Country; in favour of whom, there was a
particular Law enacted. There was also a certain Form of Proceeding settled, for such Persons as were allow'd to accuse. Every   150
Man in that case was oblig'd to appear before the Prætor, and to
give in the Name of the Person he accus'd. Then he swore to his
Information: And part of the solemn Oath was, That he had no
Design of Calumny. And the Informer was oblig'd by word of mouth,
or by Writing, publickly to declare the Offences of the accus'd   155
Person. When all this was done, the Prætor might either receive
or reject the Information, as he saw good: And if he receiv'd it,
he appointed a certain Day in which the Informer and the Person
accus'd shou'd appear face to face. Lastly, If the accus'd Person
was found guilty, he was punish'd according to the nature of his   160
Offence: If he was acquitted, the Informer was punish'd for his
Calumny or false Accusation. And the Punishment he was condemn'd
to, was to be shamefully burnt in the Forehead.

These were the Precautions which that Wise People took, to defend themselves from such dark irreparable Injuries. And yet when   165
they lost their Liberty, and fell under the Dominion of bad Em-
perors, Informations and Subornations rag'd to such a height,

---

was so extravagant that he always needed money (*The Letters of Thomas Burnet*
to George Duckett, ed. D. Nichol Smith, Oxford, Roxburghe Club, 1914, p. 5;
Cunningham, ii 281).

146-8   *that ... Country*: Val[erius] Max[imus, *Dictorum Factorumque Memo*]*:-*
bilium Libri IX]. 1. 3 [vii §9] (½°).

149   *Law*: *Lex Memmia* (½°). The cashiered officers were in winter quarters
in Flanders.

151-4   *appear ... Calumny*: Livy, 1. 44. [Cicero] *Epist*[*ulae ad*] *fam*[*iliares*].
Caelius ad Cic. 1. 8 [vi] (½°). The first reference is wrong.

154-6   *the ... Person*: *Ulpian. de Accus*[*ationibus*]. lib. 7 [*Corpus iuris*
civilis, 1663, i 719-20; *Digestorum*, xlviii 2 7 (§§1-2)]. *Seneca in Ludo* (½°).
The latter refers to Seneca's *Apocolocyntosis*, in which the Emperor Claudius
is posthumously brought to trial before Aeacus in the underworld. Although the
accusations against Claudius are publicly recorded, Aeacus condemns him without hearing his defence. In most manuscripts and all editions before 1557 the
work is called *Ludus de morte Claudi* or simply *Ludus*.

162   *Punishment*: Plin[y]. *Pan*[*egyricus*, 35. 2] (½°). Pliny says only that
Trajan rounded up the most notorious informers and ordered them to be cruci-
fied. The error seems to have been picked up in *The Observator*, 20-3 December
1710: 'Pliny and others tell us [the punishment] was by branding ... on the
Forehead.'

that I do not remember to have read of so many in other Nations,
unless it were once, for a very short time, in the *Macedonian*
170   Army; of which Calamities among those *Grecians, Plutarch* speaks
so warmly and so sensibly, that I can't forbear copying his words.
    'The Philosopher *Bias* being ask'd, says *Plutarch*, what Animal
he thought was the most hurtful? reply'd, That of Wild Creatures,
a *Tyrant*; and of Tame ones, a *Flatterer*. But *Plutarch* says, He
175   might have answer'd better, by only distinguishing between Flatterers of two kinds: For some of them indeed he thinks may be
reckon'd tame Creatures, such as are those *Shirks* that ply about
Great Tables: But for those that with *their Calumnies and secret
Malice reach the very Closets and Bedchambers of Ladies*, these,
180   he says, are properly to be call'd wild and savage Animals; who
contribute only to make us indiscreetly angry, or envious, difficult, stingy, sour, timerous and jealous, with several idle malicious Stories, Hints and Conjectures, always fastning upon some
Distemper of the Mind, and growing like a Botch or Boil upon its
185   inflam'd and putrid part. Are you angry? Revenge your self, say
they. Do you suspect this or that? Believe it without more enquiry. Do you love any thing? Enjoy it, whatsoever it costs you,
whether in Fame or Honour. If at any time you have made a Promise
to a Friend, and upon second thoughts have a mind to break it,
190   but are asham'd of so scandalous an Action; these Flatterers,
says *Plutarch*, are sure to put their Advice in the worse Scale,
and incline the Balance to the side you like. These light and
empty Counterfeits, he says, finding they want Weight, when put
into the Balance against a real substantial Friend, endeavour to
195   remove him as far as they can: Or not compassing always that
Design, they then proceed to Compliment and Ceremony, pretending
outwardly to admire him, whilst by private Whispers they blacken
and undermine him: Taking the Advice of *Medius*, that chief Para-
site among the *Macedonians*, who taught his Disciples to slander
200   boldly, and to push home their Calumnies: For tho the Wound
might be cur'd and skin'd over, yet the Teeth of Slander wou'd

182 timerous] timorous 12°   192 and] aud ½°

172-91 *Bias ... Scale:* [Plutarch,] *How to know a Flatterer from a Friend.*
Mor[alia, 61-2] (½°).
192-204 *These ... Philotas: Moralia,* 65.

not fail to leave a Scar behind them. By these Scars, says *Plu-tarch*, or (to speak more properly) Gangrenes and Cancers of false Accusations, fell the Brave *Callisthenes, Parmenio,* and *Philotas*.'

204 *the Brave*: 107.110.

No. 21 [Swift]   21 December 1710

The EXAMINER.
Pugnacem scirent sapiente minorem.

I Am very much at a loss how to proceed upon the Subject intended in this Paper, which a new Incident has led me to ingage in: The Subject I mean, is that of *Soldiers* and the *Army*; but being a matter wholly out of my Trade, I shall handle it in as cautious a manner as I am able.   5

It is certain, that the Art of War hath suffer'd great Changes, almost in every Age and Country of the World; However, there are some Maxims relating to it, that will be eternal Truths, and which every reasonable Man will allow.

In the early times of *Greece* and *Rome*, the Armies of those   10
States were compos'd of their Citizens, who took no Pay, because the Quarrel was their own; and therefore the War was usually de-cided in one Campaign; or, if it lasted longer, however in Winter the Soldiers return'd to their several Callings, and were not dis-tinguish'd from the rest of the People. The *Gothick* Governments   15
in *Europe*, tho' they were of Military Institution, yet observ'd almost the same Method. I shall instance only here in *England*. Those who held Lands in *Capite* of the King, were oblig'd to attend him in his Wars with a certain number of Men, who all held Lands from them at easy Rents on that Condition. These fought   20

9 will] must 38 8°+12°   13 however] yet 38 8°+12°   17 here] *om.* 38
8°+12°

Motto Ovid, *Metamorphoses*, xiii 354.
                Arms to the Gown the Victory must yield.
   2 *Incident*: 116.149.

without Pay, and when the Service was over, return'd again to
their Farms. It is recorded of *William Rufus*, that being absent
in *Normandy*, and engag'd in a War with his Brother, he order'd
twenty thousand Men to be rais'd, and sent over from hence to
25   supply his Army; but having struck up a Peace before they were
embark'd, he gave them leave to disband, on Condition they would
pay him ten Shillings a Man, which amounted to a mighty Sum in
those Days.

Consider a Kingdom as a great Family, whereof the Prince is the
30   Father, and it will appear plainly thac Mercenary Troops are only
Servants Arm'd, either to awe the *Children* at home; or else to
defend from Invaders, the Family who are otherwise employ'd, and
chuse to contribute out of their Stock for paying their Defenders,
rather than leave their Affairs to be neglected in their Absence.
35   The Art of making Soldiery a Trade, and keeping Armies in Pay,
seems in *Europe* to have had two Originals. The first was Usurpation, when popular Men destroy'd the Liberties of their Country,
and seiz'd the Power into their own Hands, which they were forc'd
to maintain by hiring Guards to bridle the People. Such were an-
40   ciently the *Tyrants* in most of the small States in *Greece*, and
such were those in several Parts of *Italy*, about three or four
Centuries ago, as *Machiavel* informs us. The other Original of
Mercenary Armies, seems to have risen from larger Kingdoms or
Commonwealths, which had subdu'd Provinces at a distance, and
45   were forc'd to maintain Troops upon them, to prevent Insurrec-
tions from the Natives: Of this sort were *Macedon, Carthage* and
Rome of old; *Venice* and *Holland* at this Day; as well as most

40 in *Greece*] of *Greece* 38 8°+12°

---

22 *recorded*: Matthew [of] Paris[, *Flores historiarum*, ed. Henry R. Luard,
3 vols., London, HMSO, 1890, ii 27] (E*1922*, ix 123).
29 *Kingdom as a great Family*: not a simple metaphor, but the basis, in
opposition to Locke, of Tory belief in divine right and passive obedience:
'the title of Prince or King was more significant to express the power of him
who succeeds only to the right of that fatherhood which his ancestors did
naturally enjoy' (Sir Robert Filmer, *Patriarcha*, ed. Peter Laslett, Oxford,
Blackwell, 1949, p. 61).
31 *Servants ... Children*: Sir William Temple, 'An Essay upon the Original
and Nature of Government' (*Miscellanea. The First Part*, 3rd edn., London, for
Jacob Tonson *et al.*, 1691, p. 71).
42 *Machiavel*: *The Works of the Famous Nicolas Machiavel*, London, for
R. Clavel *et al.*, 1695, p. 21.   —

Kingdoms of *Europe*. So that Mercenary Forces in a free State,
whether Monarchy or Commonwealth, seem only necessary, either for
preserving their Conquests, (which in such Governments it is not   50
prudent to extend too far) or else for maintaining a War at distance.

In this last, which at present is our most important Case,
there are certain Maxims that all wise Governments have observ'd.

The first I shall mention is, That no *private* Man should have   55
a Commission to be *General for Life*, let his Merit and Services
be ever so great. Or, if a Prince be unadvisedly brought to offer
such a Commission in one Hand, let him (to save Time and Blood)
deliver up his *Crown* with the other. The *Romans* in the Height and
Perfection of their Government, usually sent out one of the new   60
Consuls to be General against their most formidable Enemy, and
recall'd the old one, who often return'd before the next Election,
and according as he had Merit was sent to command in some other
part, which perhaps was continued to him for a second, and sometimes a third Year. But if *Paulus Æmilius*, or *Scipio* himself, had   65
presum'd to move the *Senate* to continue their *Commissions for
Life*, they certainly would have fallen a Sacrifice to the Jealousy
of the People. *Cæsar* indeed (between whom and a *certain General*,
some of late with much Discretion have made a Parallel) had his
Command in *Gaul* continued to him for five Years, and was after-   70
wards made *perpetual Dictator*, that is to say, *General for Life*,
which gave him the Power and the Will of utterly destroying the

51-2 at distance] at a Distance 38 8°+12°   60 the] their ½°

---

56 *General for Life*: Marlborough asked Anne not once but three or four
times to appoint him to the non-existent and unconstitutional post of Captain-
General for life, like Baby Doc, Président à Vie de la République d'Haiti.
'His chief Motive', Swift said, 'was the Pay and Perquisites by continuing
the War.' The second time that Anne refused, Marlborough expressed his 'Displeasure' by writing her an angry letter (Henry L. Snyder, *Journal of the
Society for Army Historical Research*, xlv (1967), 68, 73-4; Swift, *Prose*,
vii 7; viii 114).

65 *Paulus Æmilius*: 'Æmilius Paulus, the celebrated Roman general, and conqueror of Macedonia, was twice consul, and died B.C. 160' (E*1922*, ix 1ˆ'j.

Scipio: 'Scipio Africanus, the greatest of Roman generals and the conqueror of Carthage, who died *c.* B.C. 184' (E*1922*, ix 124).

69 *Parallel*: Walter Scott cites the suppressed paragraph of *The Tatler*,
5 July 1709 (E*1814*, iii 377), but Swift refers to *The Medley*, 11 December 1710
(92.110-95.199). Ridpath obligingly describes the propaganda effect of these
lines: 'frightning [the nation] with the Designs of our General's acting the
part of another *Julius Caesar*' (*The Observator*, 23 December 1710).

Roman Liberty. But in his time the *Romans* were very much degener-
ated, and great Corruptions crept into their Morals and Disci-
75 pline. However, we see there still were some Remains of a noble
Spirit among them; For when *Cæsar* sent to be chosen *Consul*, notwithstanding his Absence, they decreed he should come in Person,
give up his Command, and *petere more majorum*.

It is not impossible but a General may desire such a Commission
80 out of *Inadvertency*, at the *Instigation of his Friends*, or perhaps of his *Enemies*, or meerly for the *Benefit and Honour of it*,
without intending any such *dreadful Consequences*; and in that
Case, a wise Prince or State may barely refuse it without shewing
any marks of their Displeasure. But the Request in its own Nature
85 is highly Criminal, and ought to be entred so upon Record, to
terrify *others* in time to come from venturing to make it.

Another Maxim to be observ'd by a free State engaged in War, is
to keep the Military Power in absolute Subjection to the Civil,
nor ever suffer the former to influence or interfere with the
90 latter. A General and his Army are *Servants hired* by the Civil
Power to Act as they are directed from thence, and with a Commission large or limited as the Administration shall think fit; for
which they are largely pay'd in Profit and Honour. The whole System by which Armies are Govern'd, is quite *alien* from the peace-
95 ful Institutions of States at Home; and if the Rewards be so
inviting as to tempt a *Senator* to take a Post in the Army, while
he is there on his Duty, he ought to consider himself in no other
Capacity. I know not any sort of Men so apt as Soldiers are, to
reprimand those who presume to interfere in what relates to their
100 Trade. When they hear any of us in a Coffee-House, wondring that
such a Victory was not pursued, complaining that such a Town cost

74 Corruptions crept] Corruptions had crept 38 8°+12°   96 while] whilst
12° 38 8°+12°

76-8 *when ... majorum*: Florus, *Epitomae*, ii 13 (§16).
88 *Subjection*: While the right of making war and peace was a part of the
royal prerogative that Parliament was only beginning to challenge, a measure
of civilian control was exerted through the annual military estimates.
101 *Victory*: The victory was that at Oudenarde (July 1708), which left open
the road to Paris. Marlborough was inclined to march, but Prince Eugene and
the Dutch were afraid (*Marlborough–Godolphin Corr.* ii 1038), so the victorious
army spent the rest of the campaign mired in the suburbs of Lille.
Town: cf. 'a single Town is hardly purchased with less than the Lives
of fifteen Thousand brave Fellows, and six or seven Million Sterling' (*The*

more Men and Mony than it was worth to take it; or that such an
opportunity was lost, of fighting the Enemy; they presently reprove us, and often with Justice enough, for medling in Matters
out of our Sphere, and clearly convince us of·our Mistakes in   105
Terms of Art that none of us understand. Nor do we escape so; For
they reflect with the utmost Contempt of our Ignorance, that we
who sit at Home in Ease and Security, never stirring from our
Fire-sides, should pretend from Books, and general Reason, to
argue upon Military Affairs; which after all, if we may judge   110
from the share of Intellectuals in some who are said to excel
that way, is not so very profound or difficult a Science. But if
there be any Weight in what they offer, as perhaps there may be a
great deal; surely these Gentlemen have a much weaker Pretence to
concern themselves in Matters of the Cabinet, which are always   115
either far above, or much beside their Capacities. Soldiers may
as well pretend to prescribe Rules for Trade, to determine Points
in Philosophy, to be Moderators in an Assembly of Divines, or
direct in a Court of Justice, as to misplace their Talent in
examining Affairs of State, especially in what relates to the   120
Choice of Ministers, who are never so likely to be ill chosen as
when approved by them. It would be endless to shew how pernicious
all Steps of this nature have been in many Parts and Ages of the
World. I shall only produce two at present; one in *Rome*, and
t'other in *England*. The first is of *Cesar*, when he came to the 125
City with his Soldiers to *settle the Ministry*, there was an end
of their Liberty for ever. The second was in the Great Rebellion
against King *Charles* the First. The King and both Houses were
agreed upon the Terms of a Peace: But the Officers of the Army
(as *Ludlow* relates it) set a Guard upon the House of Commons,   130

---

105 of our Mistakes] *om.* 38 8°+12°.   107 of] on 38 8°+12°   130 set]
sets ½° 12°

History of the Life and Reign of Her Late Majesty Queen Anne, London, 1740,
p. 272).
  103 *opportunity ... lost*: cf. 'The greatest Fault [of Henri Massue de
Ruvigny, Earl of Galway, commander-in-chief of the English forces in Spain]
consisted in ... not falling upon the Enemies Flank, which might have easily
been done' (*A Detection of the Earl of Gallway's Conduct at Almanza*, London,
for J. Morphew, 1711, p. 15).
  106 *Terms of Art*: 8.134.
  125 *Cesar*: Cicero, *De Officiis*, iii 84.
  130 *Guard*: Edmund Ludlow, *Memoirs*, 3 vols., Vivay [i.e. London], 1698-9),
i 270 (E1922, ix 126).

took a List of the Members, and kept all by Force out of the
House, except those who were for bringing the King to a Tryal.
Some Years after, when they erected a Military Government, and
ruled the Island by *Major-Generals*, we received most admirable
135   Instances of their Skill in Politicks. To say the Truth, such
formidable Sticklers can have but two Reasons for desiring to
interfere in the Administration; the first is that of *Cesar* and
Cromwell, of which, God forbid, I should accuse or suspect any
body; since the second is pernicious enough, and that is, *To pre-*
140   *serve those in Power who are for perpetuating a War, rather than*
see others advanced, who they are sure will use all proper means
to promote a safe and Honourable Peace.

Thirdly, Since it is observed of Armies, that in the present
Age they are brought to some degree of Humanity, and a more regu-
145   lar demeanor to each other and to the World, than in former Times;
It is certainly a good Maxim to endeavour preserving this Temper
among them, without which they would soon degenerate into *Savages.*
To this End, it would be prudent among other Things, to forbid
that detestable Custom of *drinking to the Damnation or Confusion*
150   of any Person whatsoever.

Such desperate Acts, and the Opinions infused along with them,
into Heads already inflamed by Youth and Wine, are enough to
scatter Madness and Sedition through a whole Camp. So seldom *upon*
their Knees to *Pray*, and so often to *Curse*! This is not properly
155   Atheism, but a sort of *Anti-religion* prescribed by the Devil, and
which an Atheist of common Sense would scorn as an Absurdity. I
have heard it mention'd as a common Practice last Autumn, *some-*
where or other, to *drink Damnation and Confusion*, (and this with
Circumstances very aggravating and horrid) to the *New Ministry*,

134   *Major-Generals*: Ludlow, *Memoirs*, ii 519, 559-60, 580-2.
136   *Sticklers*: 'The judges of the field in a formal duel, whose duty it was
to interfere when the rules of judicial combat were violated, were called
sticklers, from the wooden truncheons which they held in their hands' (E*1814*,
ix 381).
137   *the first*: Marlborough's ambition is reflected in his nicknames: 'King
John the Second' and 'the Sovereign' (Hearne, ii 265; Coxe, *Marlborough*, ii
490).
149   *drinking*: '[Lieutenant-Generals] Meredith, Macartney, and colonel
Honeywood, are obliged to sell their commands at half value, and leave the
army, for drinking Destruction to the present ministry, and dressing up a hat
on a stick, and calling it Harley; then drinking a glass with one hand, and
discharging a pistol with the other at the maukin, wishing it were Harley himself' (Swift, *Journal*, p. 120).

and to those who **hà any Hand** in turning out the *Old*; that is to   160
say, to those Persons whom Her Majesty has thought fit to employ
in her greatest Affairs, with something *more than a Glance against
the Qu--- her Self*. And if it be true that these *Orgyes* were
attended with certain *doubtful Words* of *standing by their G-----l*,
who without Question abhorred them; let any Man consider the Con-   165
sequence of such Dispositions, if they should happen to spread.
I could only wish for the Honour of the Army, as well as of the
Qu--- and Ministry, that a Remedy had been applied to the Disease,
in the *Place* and *Time* where it grew. If Men of such Principles
were able to propagate them in a Camp, and were sure of a *General*   170
for Life, who had any Tincture of Ambition, we might soon bid
farewel to Ministries and Parliaments, whether new or old.
    I am only sorry such an Accident has happened towards the Close
of a War, when it is chiefly the Interest of those Gentlemen who
have Posts in the Army, to behave themselves in such a manner as   175
might encourage the Legislature to make some Provision for them,
when there will be no further need of their Services. They are to
consider themselves as Persons by their Educations unqualified
for many other Stations of Life. Their Fortunes will not suffer
them to retain to a Party after it's *Fall*, nor have they Weight   180
or Abilities to help towards it's *Resurrection*. Their future
Dependance is wholly upon the Prince and Parliament, to which
they will never make their Way, by *Solemn Execrations of the
Ministry*; a Ministry of the Qu---'s own Election, and fully
answering the Wishes of her People. This unhappy step in some of   185
their Brethren, may pass for an uncontrollable Argument, that
Politicks are not their Business or their Element. The Fortune of
War hath raised several Persons up to Swelling Titles, and great
Commands over Numbers of Men, which they are too apt to transfer
along with them into *Civil Life*, and appear in all Companies as   190
if it were at the Head of their Regiments, with a sort of Deport-
ment that ought to have been dropt behind, in that short Passage
to *Harwich*. It puts me in mind of a Dialogue in *Lucian*, where

177 Services] Service 38 8°+12°   191 it] they 38 8°+12°

---

180 *retain to*: 'To ... be attached, or be a retainer to. *Obs.*' (*OED*).
186 *uncontrollable*: 'Incontrovertible, indisputable' (*OED*).
193 *Lucian*: *The Dialogues of the Dead*, xx 368.

Charon wafting one of their *Predecessors* over *Styx*, ordered him
195   to strip off his *Armor* and *fine Cloaths*, yet still thought him
too heavy; *But* (said he) *put off likewise that Pride and Presumption, those high swelling Words, and that Vain-Glory*; because
they were of no use on *t'other side the Water*. Thus if all that
Array of Military Grandeur were confined to the proper Scene, it
200   would be much more for the *Interest* of the Owners, and less
offensive to their Fellow Subjects.

No. 13 [Mainwaring]   25 December 1710

The MEDLEY.

Of the Examiner's *Challenge to Fair Argument.*
Reasons for not accepting it.
His own Objections not yet answer'd by him.
A Symbol of Pythagoras.
Trajan's *Opinion of his Soldiers, and Punishment of Informers.*
A Passage out of Diodorus Siculus, *B.* 12.

THE *Examiner* seems to have a mind that somebody wou'd gravely
dispute with him: *If two Men*, says he, *wou'd argue on both sides
with Fairness, Good Sense, and Good Manners; it wou'd be no ill
Entertainment for the Town.* I shall give some Reasons in this
5   Paper why nobody shou'd accept his Challenge. And first, Who
wou'd argue with a Man gravely, who says a great many Things in
every Paper that he does not believe himself? Of this I cou'd
give a thousand Instances, if I wou'd be at the drudgery of reading his Works. What he says of the *Value of our General's Grants,*
10   of his Intention to *make himself Protector*; of the *Lady's Woman,*
that sunk above Twenty Thousand Pounds a Year; of the Design
which the late Ministers had to *perpetuate the War*: All this, as

12 Ministers] Ministry 12°

2-4   *If ... Town*: 96.26-8.
9   *Value*: £540,000 (56.71).
10   *Protector*: 113.56.
     Lady's Woman: 57.198.
12   *perpetuate the War*: 116.140.

harden'd as he is, he cou'd not put into print without Remorse.
What he adds in other places, That *the People join'd as one Man,
to wish the Ministry chang'd: That neither God nor Man cou'd suf-*   15
*fer their Continuance: That all things must have ended in Ruin,
without a speedy Reformation: That a Sharper had held the Cards,
play'd Booty, and lost the Mony; and when things were almost
desperate, an Honest Gentleman was employ'd:* All this likewise,
the poor Man that affirms it, does not believe one word of. He   20
knows that every Man of Business or Intelligence in *Great Britain*
was alarm'd at the late Changes, and sure they are some *of the
People*: He knows that God bless'd the Endeavours of the last
M-----y for the publick Service with unparallel'd Success; and he
knows also, that *He who held the Cards* is no *Sharper*, tho he   25
play'd them better than any body will ever do again: And for the
Character of the *Honest Gentleman* that holds them now, I refer
him to the Opinion of his Friends of the High-Church. But since
he delights in this pretty Figure of *holding the Cards*, I can't
help observing one thing to him; That in all my Experience at   30
Play, I never knew but one Instance, that any body threw away
the Cards who was in Luck. The Losers indeed often press for new
Cards, and are always glad when they get them: Of which I wish

---

14-16 *the ... Continuance*: 52.71-5.
16-17 *That ... Reformation*: 85.124-5.
17-19 *a ... employ'd*: 86.155-8.
22 *alarm'd*: 'I cannot but think 'tis dangerous to have a *Whigg* Constitution
administred upon *Tory* Principles' (Defoe, *A Supplement to the Faults on Both
Sides*, London, for J. Baker, 1710, p. 52).
26 *better*: recalls the title of a pamphlet, *Seldom comes a Better: or, A
Tale of a Lady and Her Servants* (1710), defending Godolphin's management of
the Treasury. Although he did not write this pamphlet, which attacks Harley in
Mainwaring's phrases (p. 6), Defoe was also defending Godolphin at this time:
'the Credit of the Nation ... is ... absolutely Dependant upon him' (*Review*,
15 July 1710). And in retrospect it was recalled that Godolphin 'frequently
had ... vast Sums of Money from the City, upon the Strength of his own Credit'
and that it was not 'only at Home that he had so glorious a Reputation;
Foreigners during his whole Ministry pour'd in their Money into our Country'
(William Stoughton(?), *The Secret History of the Late Ministry; From their Admission, to the Death of the Queen*, London, for J. Baker, 1715, p. 69).
27 *Honest Gentleman*: 'a cunning Fellow, a Pettifogger ... that never was
true to any Cause he ingag'd in' (*Seldom comes a Better*, London, 1710, p. 6);
cf. 86.158. Harley was equally distrusted by Tory extremists like William
Shippen: 'Of Canting Parents, sprung this Child of Grace. | In Show a *Tory*,
but a *Whig* in Heart' (*POAS*, Yale, vii 31).
32-3 *new Cards*: cf. 'The natural expedient to men that are uneasy is to
change; if these cards are unkind they will take another pack' (PRO SP 29/266,
f. 152).

the *Examiner* Joy, and all his Friends *here* and *elsewhere*. This is
35 therefore one of my Reasons against *arguing*. I shou'd be well employ'd indeed, to argue gravely with him, who shamefully affirms
what no body in his Senses can believe.

Another Reason against Disputing with him, is, the Excess of
his Power, if you will take his own word for it. He plainly
40 represents himself, as the sole Person into whose hands the Care
of the Present M------y is committed: And his Libels come out
with such an Air, that one wou'd think they were publish'd by
Authority. When he rails at the best Ministers that ever serv'd a
Prince, and promises to discover *only about eight or nine Thou-*
45 *sand of their most scandalous Abuses*, without pretending to discover one; and when he audaciously reviles a General, whose
Services have been the Wonder both of Friends and Enemies, and
whose Actions are an Honour even to his wretched Countrymen that
wou'd destroy him: all this he calls *defending the Cause of the*
50 *Q---- and both Houses of Parliament, and nine Parts in ten of the*
Kingdom. Now here wou'd be a new Difficulty upon me, if I were
inclin'd to argue. This Great Man, who seems to be Master of the
Press, and who has hitherto with impunity made use of the Q----'s
Name to countenance his base Invectives, may safely say any thing
55 that he thinks or does not think of the late Ministers: but I am
not so sure that it wou'd be convenient for me to say all that I
think of the new ones. And therefore tho he says this Ministry,
which is of the Q----'s own Election, fully answers the Wishes of
her People; I shall not so much as presume to differ with him:
60 Only observe, that a Twelve-month hence will be a better time to
make a Judgment of these matters, and that some People will think
he's a little too hasty.

These are some of my Reasons why I am not for arguing with the
Examiner, tho I endeavour to make my Readers merry with him: And
65 therefore he may do, what he threatens to do, for me; I mean,
answer his Papers himself, and take the Bread out of his Adver-
sarys mouths, as he neatly expresses it: Nor is there another Man

44-5 *only* ... *Abuses*: 84.90.
47 *the Wonder*: 'Malbro', in himself Wonders contains' (William Atwood, *A*
Modern Inscription to the Duke of Marlboroughs Fame (1706), *POAS*, Yale, vii 206)
49-51 *defending* ... *Kingdom*: 82.26-27.
57-9 *Ministry* ... *People*: 117.184-5.
66-7 *answer* ... *mouths*: 96.45-97.46.

in *England* so equal to such a Work; tho he protests he never did
it yet. *I have often been charg'd*, says he, *with answering the*
Examiner my self. I protest I never did it; nor were those   70
Answers written with my privity, as malicious People give out;
nor do I believe the Ministers hire the Authors to give my Paper
a Value. See what a Wag he is, and what a smart Man at Raillery!
I fancy, if we had more of this, and less arguing, his Papers
wou'd pass never the worse: But that's none of my business. In   75
the mean time, till he can get somebody else to argue with him
gravely, there is a dear Friend of his and mine, call'd *The*
Examiner, whom I wish he wou'd debate with a little more to the
purpose than he has done. This Ingenious Person made some Objections a good while ago, which I am very sure he has not yet   80
answer'd to the satisfaction of any impartial Reader. I beg leave
to transcribe them as they stand in the *Examiner*, Numb. 14. *Well-*
meaning Men wonder the Q---- wou'd chuse to change her Ministry
at this juncture, and thereby give Uneasiness to a G----al, who
has been so long successful abroad. There are few Complaints of   85
any consequence against the late Men in Power, and none at all in
Parliament; which, on the contrary, past Votes in favour of the
Chief Minister. If her M-------- had a mind to introduce the
other Party, it wou'd have been more seasonable after a Peace,
which now we have made desperate, by spiriting the French, *who*   90
rejoice at these Changes; and by the Fall of our Credit, which
unqualifies us for continuing the War. The Parliament, so untimely
dissolv'd, had been diligent in their Supplies, and dutiful in
their Behaviour. One Consequence of these Changes appears already
in the Fall of the Stocks, and we may soon expect more and worse;   95
and, lastly, all this tends to break the Settlement of the Crown,
and call over the Pretender. I durst not have said half so much
for ten times the *Examiner*'s Preferments, nor can I imagine how
he came to be allow'd to do it: And if any one thinks he has
answer'd all this, I am still left to wonder, that such *specious*   100
Objections, as he calls them, shou'd ever be trusted to such

69-73 *I ... Value*: 97.47-51.
82-97 *Well-meaning ... Pretender*: 2.30-3.48. Mainwaring scores here, for
Swift was foolish to give so much space to Whig propaganda.
98 *Preferments*: Mainwaring assumes that the Examiner is Francis Atterbury,
archdeacon of Totnes, prebendary of Exeter Cathedral, and Dean of Carlisle.
100-1 *specious Objections*: 2.30.

Answerers. How much better wou'd it be for his Party, if they
confin'd him only to Panegyricks, at which he lately shew'd his
Skill (*Numb.* 18.) where he concludes his Flattery to an *Innocent*
105 *Lady*, as he stiles her, with a greasy and not improper Image of a
Lump of Fresh Butter? yet this had been harmless, as well as
natural and expressive, if he had let it rest so; but the Minute
he grew serious, he blunder'd worse than ever, and fell to talk
of *Somebody that engross'd her M-------'s Favour, without admit-*
110 *ting any Access but thro her Means.* The Man is certainly bewitch'd! Does he think those Lords and Great Persons, that serve
in Commissions, or otherwise, are not sensible enough upon what
foot they are, and upon how large a bottom the M------y stands,
but this incorrigible Wretch must be still talking of it?
115   When I gave a Hint in my last, that my Friend was little better
than an *Informer*, I did not think he wou'd so soon have made it
out; but he always proves kinder than one can expect upon such an
occasion as this: And in his very next Paper (*Numb.* 21.) he shews
himself an *Informer at second hand*; giving an account of something
120 he has heard *somewhere or other, about drinking Healths the last*
Autumn. It is very hard for those, that have been in any Company,
to report truly what was said in it: the Circumstances, the Manner and Humour, in which any words are spoken, quite alter the
meaning of them, and can't be fairly related. What then will you
125 say of one that speaks of such things by *Hearsay*? *I have heard,*
says my Friend, *it was a common Practice,* &c. But I see there is

114 Wretch] Man 12°

104-5 *Innocent Lady*: 100.103.
106 *Butter*: 100.119. The connection in Mainwaring's mind is through his
image of Mrs Masham as 'A Dirty Chamber-Maid' (*POAS*, Yale, vii 309).
109-10 *engross'd ... Means*: 100.109-10; cf. 'The Important Pass of the
Back-Stairs | Was put into her hand; | And up she brought the greatest Rogue |
Grew in this fruitful Land' (*POAS*, Yale, vii 310). Mainwaring scores again
here, for Swift was not always unmindful of Harley's means of access to the
Queen in 1709-10 (Swift, *Prose*, viii 116).
113 *bottom*: The entire Harley ministry embarked upon Mrs Masham's large
bottom, which was 'As hard as *Alablaster*' (*POAS*, Yale, vii 320), makes a telling image.
115 *Hint*: Even though he did not have the Examiner in mind when he wrote
The Medley of 18 December 1710, Mainwaring is now able to conflate Ormond the
alleged informer (107.110) and the Examiner because *The Examiner* or 21 December 1710 (116.149-50) made the Examiner 'an *Informer at second hand*' (122.119).
120-1 *heard ... Autumn*: 116.156-7.
125-6 *I ... Practice*: ibid.

no Drudgery that he must not pass thro, and am now inclin'd to
pity him; He has sold his Soul to cruel Masters. A very good
Author, treating of the mystical Symbols of *Pythagoras*, says,
The Use and Instruction that may be had from them is very great;   130
and that Princes shou'd mind, above all the rest, that which
directs us *not to be familiar with Swallows*. By which, he says,
is meant Backbiters, and Tale-bearing Whisperers: Swallows being
little Creatures, that chatter and are noisy, that feed on Flesh,
that devour harmless Musical Grashoppers, and that fly near the   135
Surface of the Earth to pick up little Animals. They make no
Return for their Entertainment, fly away upon change of Weather,
and naturally hate Mankind. If Princes, says he, take into their
Familiarity such trifling Bablers, or prating Knaves, as are intended by this Symbol, what wonder if things go very ill with   140
their People? Of how different a Temper was the good Emperor
Trajan, of whom *Pliny* gives this honourable Character, That he
was a Prince *who never wou'd believe his Soldiers design'd
against himself, what they only intended against his Enemies?*
Therefore if any one had come to tell him Lyes of them, 'tis   145
probable he wou'd have answer'd such a Person, as *Lysimachus* of
Thrace did *Philippides*; *What have I*, said *Philippides, that I may
impart to you, Oh my Prince!* To which *Lysimachus* answer'd, *Any
thing that you please, my Friend, except your Secrets.* If any Spy
out of Company had brought an Information to *Trajan*, he wou'd   150
presently have sent him on board some Vessel. Of which Punishment
Pliny makes a lively Description: 'What a Sight was that, says
he, when the Ships that were laden with Informers were committed
to the Winds, and forc'd to open their Sails to the Tempests, and
to follow the angry Waves to whatever Rocks they carry'd them?   155
What a Pleasure was it, to behold those Vessels dispers'd or
broken as soon as they were out of Port? We cou'd not help, says
he, even then giving Thanks to our Prince, who, that he might
preserve his own native Clemency, committed to the Gods of the
Sea the Revenge of injur'd Men.'   160

130-41 *The ... People*; Lil[ii Gregorii] Gyrald[i, Philosophi Pythagorae
Symbolorum Interpretatio, *Opera Omnia*, 2 vols., Liège, Hack *et al.*, 1696,
ii 646] (½°).
143-4 *Prince ... Enemies*: Pliny, *Panegyricus*, xviii 3.
147-9 *What ... Secrets*: Plutarch, *Moralia*, 508C.
152-60 *What ... Men*: Pliny, *Panegyricus*, xxxv 1.

This were a right and glorious Precedent to be follow'd in any
other Nation; Soldiers were always the Care of Great Princes:
Cyrus cou'd call every Man he had by his Name. And I have read of
a King of *Sicily*, who binding up with his own Handkerchief the
165 Wound of a common Trooper, ty'd, says the Author, by the same
Knot the Hearts of all the rest to his Service. The *Romans*,
whilst they were a Free People, decreed particular Privileges to
Men that had serv'd twenty Years. It was not in the power of Informers to cancel the Merit of their Services; a fair and open
170 Tryal was the least that wou'd have been granted. They knew that
the Safety and Preservation of Government depended on Success in
War; and therefore, even in Peace, they cherish'd and rewarded
their Soldiers, that they might always have it in their power to
repel and conquer their Enemies.
175 Nor were the *Grecians* less tender of those that had well serv'd,
till they came to be run down by some prevailing Faction. And one
of their Historians has a remarkable Passage in praise of a certain War it self, which I humbly recommend to the Reader. This
Author taking notice, That nothing which Men account Good is per-
180 fectly so; and that nothing which is reckon'd Bad, is absolutely
Evil, without some mixture of Profit and Advantage: he says, 'The
War of the Great and Powerful King of *Persia* with *Greece*, which
terrify'd and wasted the *Grecians*, and had almost enslav'd them,
prov'd at last, beyond all expectation, a means of their future
185 Glory and Prosperity. For fifty years together, he says, after
that time, Riches flow'd upon them, Arts and Sciences were cultivated, Military Discipline was improv'd, many excellent Commanders
flourish'd, and the *Grecian* Name was honour'd thro all Parts of
the World, for having not only routed the mighty Army of the
190 *Persians* by Sea and Land, but for having also compel'd that
strong Empire to free, by a lasting Treaty, both their own Country, and the Cities upon the Continent of *Asia* that were in Alliance with them.' The same Event was justly expected from another
War, of a later Date than this, and the Disappointment can only
195 be accounted for in the words of a *Roman* Author, us'd upon

163 *call* ... *Name*: Xenophon, *Cyropaedia*, v 3 47-50; La Mothe le Vayer,
i [1]103.
164 *King of Sicily*: Alfonso V de Aragón (La Mothe le Vayer, i [1]104).
181-93 *The ... them*: Di[o]dorus Siculus. B. 12 [1-2] ($\frac{1}{2}$°).

another occasion: *At that time,* said he, *the Commonwealth of the*
Romans seem'd of all others the most to be pity'd: for when they
had conquer'd every thing that appear'd against them, and might
have enjoy'd Safety and Riches, which Mortals think the greatest
Blessings; there were yet, says he, *some Citizens among them,*   200
that were obstinately bent to destroy both themselves and the
Republick.

196-202 *At ... Republick:* Sallust. *Bel[lum] Cat[ilinae,* xxxvi 4] (½°).

No. 22 [Swift]   28 December 1710

The EXAMINER.

Nam &, majorum instituta tueri sacris, cæremonisq;
    retinendis, sapientis est.

                                        Ruituraq; semper
              Stat (mirum!) moles _____

WHoever is a true Lover of our Constitution, must needs be pleas'd
to see what successful Endeavours are Daily made to restore it in
every Branch to its ancient Form, from the languishing Condition
it hath long lain in, and with such deadly Symptoms.

  I have already handled some Abuses during the *late Management,*   5
and shall in convenient time go on with the rest. Hitherto I have
confin'd my self to those of the *State;* but with the good leave
of those who think it a matter of small Moment, I shall now take
Liberty to say something of the *Church.*

  For several Years past, there hath not I think in *Europe,* been   10

8 those] some 38 8°+12°

_____

  Motto Cicero, *De Divinatione,* ii 148; Lucan, *The Civil War,* iv 455: A wise
man will protect and defend the Rights of the Church; which, in Spite of the
Malice of its Enemies, although tottering, and on the Brink of Destruction,
standeth secure, to the Admiration of all Men.
  3 *languishing Condition:* cf. 'Religion now does on her deathbed lie, |
Heart-sick of a high fever and consuming atrophy' (*Ode to Dr. William San-*
croft (1691-3?), Swift, *Poems,* p. 42).
  5 *Abuses:* 97.65-102.173.

any Society of Men upon so unhappy a Foot, as the *Clergy* of *England*, nor more hardly treated, by those very Persons from whom
they deserv'd much better Quarter, and in whose Power they
chiefly had put it to use them so ill. I would not willingly mis-
15   represent Facts; but I think it generally allow'd by Enemies and
Friends, that the bold and brave Defences made before the *Revolution* against those many Invasions of our Rights, proceeded principally from the Clergy; who are likewise known to have rejected
all Advances made them to close with the Measures at that time
20   concerting; while the *Dissenters*, to gratify their Ambition and
Revenge, fell into the basest Compliances with the Court,
approv'd of all Proceedings by their numerous and fulsom Addresses, and took Employments and Commissions by virtue of the dispensing Power, against the direct Laws of the Land. All this is

12 nor] or 38 8°+12°

---

11 *Clergy*: Hostility was so widespread that it is difficult to bring into
focus. Three aspects of it uppermost in Swift's mind are Tindal's anticlerical
propaganda: *The Rights of the Christian Church Asserted* (1706), *The Merciful
Judgments of High-Church Triumphant on Offending Clergymen, and Others, in the
Reign of Charles I* (1710), *The Jacobitism, Perjury and Popery of the High-
Church Priests* (1710); the explosion of anticlericalism in the Sacheverell
trial: 'never were the *Ministers of Christ* so *abus'd* and *vilify'd*', Sacheverell
said, 'I have been ... treated ... with a degree of *Scorn* and *Indignity*, from
which I hop'd my *sacred Profession* ... might have screen'd me' (*The Tryal*,
pp. 339, 336); and 'the *Observator* and *Review* ... charging the whole Body of
the Clergy with the most odious Crimes and Opinions' (Swift, *Prose*, iii 189).
    16-17 *Defences ... of our Rights*: for which the clergy of the Church of
England received a vote of thanks in February 1689 (*CJ*, x 16) and which not
even the Whigs denied (*The French King's Reasons against Peace, in His Speech
in Council*, London, J. Baker, 1710, p. 2; Toland, *The Memorial of the State of
England*, London, 1705, p. 22).
    20 *Dissenters*: 'The dissenters were at first disposed to make common cause
with the Catholics in favour of the dispensing power claimed by James II.; and
an address from the Presbyterians went so far as to praise the king for having
"restored to God his empire over conscience"' (*E1814*, iii 385). James II's
declarations of indulgence (April 1687 and April 1688) also precipitated an
outburst of anti-episcopal verse, including *Dr. Wild's Ghost* (1687), *The Clerical Cabal* (1688), and *The Sentiments* (1688), of which the first may be one of
Defoe's first published works.
    22-3 *Addresses*: 'The *Dissenters* were generally fond and proud of this
Declaration, and caught greedily at the Bait ... They ... presented *Addresses
of Thanks* so flattering and so fulsome, that some of them were thought offensive to the very Ears of the King' (Kennett, iii 489; cf. Swift, *Prose*, xii
269). The most fulsome are included in Oldmixon, *The History of Addresses*,
i 105-55.
    23-4 *dispensing Power*: James II's assumption of a power to suspend the laws
of church and state 'as it was the most illegal Action ... not warranted by
our Constitution, so it had the most fatal Consequences by detaching the Church

so true, that if ever the *Pretender* comes in, they will, next to   25
those of his own Religion, have the fairest Claim and Pretensions
to his Favour, from their Merit and eminent Services to his suppos'd Father, who, without such Encouragement, would probably
never have been misled to go the Lengths he did. It should likewise be remembred to the everlasting Honour of the *London* Divines, 30
that in those dangerous Times, they Writ and Publish'd the best
Collection of Arguments against *Popery*, that ever appear'd in the
World. At the Revolution, the Body of the *Clergy* join'd heartily
in the common Cause (except a few, whose Sufferings perhaps have
atton'd for their Mistakes) like Men who are content to go about,   35
for avoiding a Gulph or a Precipice, but come into the old strait
Road again as soon as they can. But another Temper had now began
to prevail. For as in the Reign of K. *Charles* the First, several
well-meaning People were ready to join in reforming some Abuses;
while others who had deeper Designs, were still calling out for a   40
thorow Reformation, which ended at last in the Ruin of the Kingdom; so after the late King's coming to the Throne, there was a

25 comes] come 38 8°+12°   27 his Favour] Favour 38 12°

---

of *England* from his Interest' (Bevil Higgons, *A Short View of the English History*, The Hague, by T. Johnston, 1727, pp. 355-6). James used his assumed
power to issue Declarations of Indulgence (April 1687 and April 1688) suspend-
ing the Test Acts that excluded non-conformists from 'Employments and Commissions'.

30   *the London Divines*: Mainwaring lists them (159.127-30).

34   *a few*: William Sancroft, Archbishop of Canterbury, four more bishops,
and about 400 of the inferior clergy, including George Hickes, Jeremy Collier,
and Charles Leslie, having taken the oaths of allegiance and supremacy to
James II, found it impossible to take the oaths to William of Orange and were
deprived of their benefices in 1690. Swift's sympathy with the non-jurors is
reflected in his *Ode to Dr. William Sancroft* (1691-3?).

35   *go about*: The remainder of the estimated 9,743 beneficed clergymen
(Swift, *Tale*, p. 41) took the oaths to William and Mary, deviating, Swift
says, from 'the old strait Road' of passive obedience by the necessity of
resisting the authority of James II in order to avoid the 'Gulph or ... Precipice' of Roman Catholicism; cf. 5.92n.

41   *thorow Reformation*: The dissenters' demand for 'all the degrees of
Reformation' was based on the assumption that the Reformation in England had
been only 'partial and pompous' (Defoe, *A Serious Inquiry into this Grand
Question; Whether a Law to prevent the Occasional Conformity of Dissenters,
Would not be Inconsistent with the Act of Toleration, and a Breach of the
Queen's Promise*, London, 1704, p. 24; Defoe, *A Short View of the Present State
of the Protestant Religion in Britain*, Edinburgh, 1707, p. 17); cf. '*Strip,
Tear, Pull, Rent, Flay off all, that we may appear as unlike the Rogue* Peter,
as it is possible' (Swift, *Tale*, p. 139).

restless Cry from Men of *the same Principles*, for a *thorow Revo-*
lution, which as *some* were carrying it on, must have ended in the
45 Destruction of the Monarchy and Church.

What a violent Humour hath run ever since against the Clergy,
and from what corner spread and fomented, is, I believe, manifest
to all Men. It lookt like a set Quarrel against *Christianity*, and
if we call to mind several of the *Leaders*, it must in a great
50 Measure have been actually so. Nothing was more common in Writing
and Conversation, than to hear that Reverend Body charg'd in
gross with what was utterly Inconsistent: Despis'd for their
Poverty, hated for their Riches; reproacht with Avarice, and taxt
with Luxury; accus'd for promoting arbitrary Power, and resisting
55 the Prerogative; Censur'd for their Pride, and scorn'd for their
meanness of Spirit. The Representatives of the lower Clergy
rail'd at for disputing the Power of the Bishops, by the known
abhorrers of Episcopacy; and abus'd for doing nothing in the Convocations, by those very Men who help'd to bind up their Hands.
60 The Vice, the Folly, the Ignorance of every single Man, were laid
upon the Character. Their Jurisdiction, Censures and Discipline
trampl'd under Foot, yet mighty Complaints against their excessive Power. The Men of Wit employ'd to turn the Priesthood it

58 the] their ½° 12°

---

43 *Men*: Among the Whig Members of William III's first Parliament were un-
reconstructed republicans like John Hampden, the grandson of Charles I's great
antagonist, and Major John Wildman, who plotted to assassinate Charles II.
49 *Leaders*: '*Tindal, Toland, Coward, Collins, Clendon,* and all the Tribe of
Free-Thinkers' (149.134-5).
58 *abhorrers of Episcopacy*: cf. Toland, *The Memorial of the State of Eng-*
land, 1705, pp. 21-2: 'the *High-Churchmen* ... Their Rage is sharpn'd in a
special manner against the *Bishops*, whom they revile, bespatter, and abuse in
a strain neither becoming *Priests* nor *Gentlemen*'; Tindal, *New High-Church*
Turn'd Old Presbyterian, London, for B. Bragg, 1709, p. 13: 'Now nothing can
be plainer, than that the Presbyters in the Lower-House of Convocation, claim
in their late disputes a Co-ordinate Power with the Bishops in the Upper-House
... If their Malice had not blinded them, they should not censure the Bishops
for exalting their Episcopal Power too high.'
63 *The Men of Wit*: 'The boldest, and the most insolent *Book* of that sort,
is [Tindal's] the *Rights of the [Christian] Church*' (Wotton, *The Case of the*
Present Convocation Consider'd; In Answer to the Examiner's Unfair Representa-
tion of it, and Unjust Reflections upon it, London, for John Churchill, 1711,
p. 6).
63-4 *The ... Ridicule*: Swift's high church rhetoric about impiety and
irreligion is not unlike Sacheverell's; cf. 'the *Church of England* ... Her
Holy Communion ... *Rent*, and *Divided* by *Factions* ... Her *Pure Doctrin* ... *Cor-*

self into Ridicule. In short, groaning every where under the
Weight of Poverty, Oppression, Contempt and Obloquy. A fair Re-   65
turn for the Time and Money spent in their Education to fit them
for the Service of the Altar; and a fair Encouragement for worthy
Men to come into the Church. However, it may be some Comfort for
Persons of that Holy Function, that their Divine Founder as well
as His *Harbinger*, met with the like Reception. John *came neither*   70
eating nor drinking, and they say he hath a Devil; the Son of Man
came eating and drinking, and they say, behold a Glutton and a
Wine-bibber, &c.

In this deplorable State of the *Clergy*, nothing but the Hand of
Providence, working by its glorious Instrument, the QUEEN, could   75
have been able to turn the Peoples Hearts so surprizingly in
their Favor. This Princess, destin'd for the Safety of *Europe*,
and a Blessing to Her Subjects, began Her Reign with a noble
Benefaction to the Church; and it was hoped the Nation would have
follow'd such an Example, which nothing could have prevented, but   80
the false Politicks of a Set of Men, who form their Maxims upon
those of every tottering Commonwealth, which is always strugling
for Life, subsisting by Expedients, and often at the Mercy of any
powerful Neighbour. These Men take it into their Imagination,
that Trade can never flourish unless the Country becomes a common   85

---

78 a Blessing] Blessing ½°   83 any] every 38 8°+12°

---

rupted, and *Defil'd*; Her *Primitive Worship* ... *Prophan'd*, and *Abus'd*; ... Her
Priests ... *Calumniated, Misrepresented*, and *Ridicul'd*' (Sacheverell, *The
Perils of False Brethren*, 1709, p. 7).
   70-73 *John ... Wine-bibber*: Matt. 11:18-19.
   79 *Benefaction*: In February 1704 Anne informed Parliament of her wish to
grant the entire revenue of a tax on the clergy, the first fruits and tenths,
appropriated to the Crown in 1534, to augment the maintenance of the clergy in
poor parishes (*CJ*, xiv 325). This benefaction, worth £16,000-£17,000 a year in
1704, became known as Queen Anne's Bounty. Swift had just negotiated the same
grant for the Church of Ireland (Swift, *Corr.*, i 189-90).
   81 *Set*: 6.98n.
   85-6 *a common Receptacle*: An Act for naturalizing Foreign Protestants (7
Ann. c. 5) received the royal assent on 23 March 1709. Based on the erroneous
premiss that 'the Increase of People is a Means of advancing the Wealth and
Strength of a Nation', it allowed anyone to become a British subject who would
take the oaths of allegiance and supremacy, receive the sacrament in 'some
Protestant or reformed Congregation', and pay a fee of one shilling. It precipitated one of the great *Völkerwanderungen* of the eighteenth century. Within
weeks of the passage of the Act, the Protestant subjects of the Catholic Elector Palatine of the Rhine began to arrive in London. On Sunday, 22 May 1709,
300 of them received the sacrament in the chapel of the Prussian ambassador in

Receptacle for all Nations, Religions and Languages; a System
only proper for small popular States, but altogether unworthy,
and below the Dignity of an Imperial Crown; which with Us is best
upheld by a Monarch in possession of his just Prerogative, a
90   Senate of Nobles and of Commons, and a Clergy establish'd in its
due Rights with a suitable Maintenance by Law. But these Men come
with the Spirit of *Shop-keepers* to frame Rules for the Administration of Kingdoms; or, as if they thought the whole Art of Government consisted in the Importation of *Nutmegs*, and the curing of
95   *Herrings*. Such an Island as ours can afford enough to support the
Majesty of a Crown, the Honor of a Nobility, and the Dignity of
a Magistracy; we can encourage Arts and Sciences, maintain our
Bishops and Clergy, and suffer our Gentry to live in a decent,
hospitable manner; yet still there will remain Hands sufficient
100   for Trade and Manufactures, which do always indeed deserve the

100 Manufactures] Manafactures ½°

---

the Savoy. By 16 June 'upwards of 6000' had arrived (Luttrell, vi 446, 453).
By 18 July 10,000 had arrived and the summer was only half over (*A View of the
Queen and Kingdom's Enemies, in the Case of the Poor Palatines*, London, 1709,
p. 3). The arrival of so many 'when there was no flagrant Persecution ... was
a great Surprize' (Defoe, *A Brief History of the Poor Palatine Refugees,
Lately Arriv'd in England*, London, J. Baker, 1709, p. 1). Tent cities had to
be erected at Camberwell, Blackheath, and Greenwich. Since most of the refugees 'understood no Trade or Handicraft, yet rather chose to Beg than Labour' (466.70-2), the cost of 'stocking the Kingdom with *imported Beggars*' in
'a time of Dearth and Scarcity' (*The Examiner*, 5 October 1710; Burnet, ii 539)
turned out to be £135,775. 18s. 0½d. plus £100 a day that the Queen contributed (William Cunningham, *Alien Immigrants to England*, London and New York,
S. Sonnenschein and Macmillan, 1897, p. 253; *Wentworth Papers*, p. 96). A parliamentary committee of enquiry formed in January 1711 found that Sunderland,
late Secretary of State, could 'let them into the whole Mystery of the Affair'.
On 14 April 1711 the House of Commons considered their report and resolved
'That whosoever advis'd the bringing over the poor *Palatines* into this Kingdom, was an Enemy to the Queen, and this Kingdom' (*A View of the Queen and
Kingdom's Enemies, in the Case of the poor Palatines*, 1709, p. 9; *CJ*, xvi 598;
H.T. Dickinson, 'The poor Palatines and the parties', *EHR*, lxxxii (1967), 464).
    92   *the Spirit of Shop-keepers*: It was the Dutch, not the English, who
were a nation of shopkeepers in the early eighteenth century and this phrase
was recognized immediately as an attack on them (Wotton, *The Case of the
Present Convocation Consider'd*, 1711, p. 24). So strong was the Vergilian-
Renaissance-pastoral vision of little England that even Charles Davenant, an
economist, believed that 'Trade ... is ... a necessary *Evil*' (Davenant, *An
Essay upon the Probable Methods of Making a People Gainers in the Ballance of
Trade*, London, for James Knapton, 1699, pp. 154-5; italics added). 'It may
likewise deserve to be inquired, whether a great nation ought to be totally
commercial?' (Samuel Johnson, *A Journey to the Western Islands of Scotland*,
ed. Mary Lascelles, New Haven, Yale University Press, 1971, p. 91).

best Encouragement, but not to a degree of sending every living
Soul into the *Warehouse* or the *Workhouse*.

This Pedantry of Republican Politicks hath done infinite Mischief among us; To this we owe those noble Schemes of treating
Christianity as a System of *Speculative Opinions*, which no Man   105
should be bound to believe; of making the *Being* and the Worship
of God, a *Creature* of the State. In consequence of these, that
the Teachers of Religion ought to hold their Maintenance at pleasure, or live by the Alms and charitable Collection of the People,
and be equally incourag'd of all Opinions: That they should be   110
prescrib'd what to teach, by those who are to learn from them;
and, upon default, have a *Staff* and a *Pair of Shoes* left at their
Door; with many other Projects of equal Piety, Wisdom, and good
Nature.

But, God be thanked, they and their Schemes are vanish'd, and   115
their Places *shall know them no more.* When I think of that
Inundation of Atheism, Infidelity, Prophaneness and Licentiousness which were like to overwhelm us, from what Mouths and Hearts
it first proceeded, and how the People join'd with the Queen's
Endeavours to divert this Flood, I cannot but reflect on that   120
remarkable Passage in the *Revelations*, where *the Serpent with*

105 *Speculative Opinions*: 'The Nature of *Church-Government*, the Modes or
Circumstances of *Worship*, the *Prescience* and *Decrees* of God, with certain
other *Speculative Opinions*, of no concern to a *Christian Life*' (Toland, *The
Memorial of the State of England*, 1705, p. 101; cf. Tindal, *The Rights of the
Christian Church Asserted*, 4th edn., 1709, p. 14).

107 *God, a Creature of the State*: 'These Men (who from a Learned Physician
of that Opinion were since called *Erastians*) thought the Government of the
Church did not differ from that of the *State*' (Toland, *The Memorial of the
State of England*, 1705, p. 7). Swift suffered no such delusions: 'the Church
of *England*', he said, 'is no Creature of the Civil Power, either as to its
Polity or Doctrines. The Fundamentals of both were deduced from Christ and
his Apostles, and the Instructions of the purest and earliest Ages' (Swift,
Prose, ii 79).

111 *prescrib'd*: 'Let the *Clergy* ... be oblig'd to preach *Liberty of Conscience*' (Toland, *The Memorial of the State of England*, 1705, p. 53).
Sacheverell suspected that 'the avow'd Design of my *Impeachment* is ... *to have
the Clergy directed what Doctrines they are to Preach*' (*The Tryal*, p. 334).

112 *a Staff and a Pair of Shoes*: 'in the wise Republick of *Holland*, a Staff
and a Pair of Shoes for his Journey, are sent to any *Ecclesiastick* that pre-
sumes to meddle with *State Affairs*' (ibid., p. 104; cf. Tindal, *The Rights of
the Christian Church Asserted*, 4th edn., 1709, p. 214).

116 *their ... more*: Job 7:10.

117 *Inundation*: cf. Sacheverell in his own defence at his trial: 'that
Deluge of *Prophaneness* and *Immorality*, which overspreads the *whole Kingdom* ...
that *Torrent* of *Lewdness, Irreligion*, and *Atheism*' (*The Tryal*, pp. 339, 346).

121-6 *the ... Mouth*: Rev. 12:3, 15-16. Mainwaring interprets the allegory
correctly at 171.59-172.67.

SEVEN Heads cast out of his Mouth Water after the Woman *like a*
Floud, that he might cause Her to be carry'd away of the Floud:
But the EARTH helpt the Woman, *and the Earth open'd her Mouth,*
125   *and swallow'd up the Floud which the Dragon had cast out of his*
Mouth. For the Queen having chang'd her Ministry suitable to her
own Wisdom, and the Wishes of her Subjects, and having call'd a
Free Parliament; at the same time summon'd the Convocation, by
her Royal Writ, *as in all times had been accustomed,* and soon
130   after their Meeting, sent a most gracious Letter to the Archbishop of *Canterbury,* to be communicated to the Bishops and
Clergy of his Province; taking notice of *the loose and prophane*
Principles which had been openly scatter'd and propagated among
her Subjects: That the Consultations of the Clergy were particu-
135   *larly requisite to repress and prevent such daring Attempts, for*
which her Subjects, from all Parts of the Kingdom, have shewn
their just Abhorrence. She *hopes, the Endeavours of the Clergy,*
in this respect, will not be unsuccessful; and for her part, is
ready to give them all fit Encouragement, to proceed in the dis-
140   *patch of such Business as properly belongs to them; and to grant*
them Powers requisite to carry on so good a Work. In conclusion,
earnestly recommending to them, to avoid Disputes, and determin-
ing to do all that in her lies to compose and extinguish them.

It is to be hop'd, that this *last* Part of Her Majesty's Letter,
145   will be the *first* she will please to execute; for, it seems, this
very Letter created the first Dispute. The Fact whereof is thus

146 is] was 38 8°+12°

128-9 *summon'd ... accustomed*: Swift is quoting Anne's letter of 12 December 1710 that had been written by Atterbury (William Pittis, *The History of*
the Present Parliament and Convocation, London, for John Baker, 1711, p. 114;
Bennett, p. 130).
132-43 *loose ... them*: Pittis, *The History of the Present Parliament and*
Convocation, 1711, pp. 114-15.
146 *The Fact*: Swift is mistaken in saying (1) that the Upper House 'sent'
the Queen's letter and the address of the Upper House in reply 'together' to
the Lower House, and (2) that the Upper House 'excused' not mentioning the
letter in their address. Otherwise his account, probably 'related' to him by
George Smalridge, is correct. Archbishop Tenison, who 'was furious that he had
been given no prior notice of it', read the Queen's letter to both Houses
assembled in the Jerusalem Chamber of Westminster Abbey on 13 December 1710.
Tenison *told* Atterbury, prolocutor of the Lower House, that he and the bishops
'had agreed to an Address, to wch they desired the concurrence of the Lower
house and so put it into the Hands of the Prolocutor and promisd to send down
a Copy of the Queen's Letter to Him'. The Lower House then adjourned to Henry

related: The Upper House having form'd an Address to the QUEEN,
before they receiv'd Her Majesty's Letter, sent both Address and
Letter together, to the Lower House, with a Message, excusing
their not mentioning the Letter in the Address, because *this* was   150
formed before the *other* was receiv'd: The Lower House return'd
them, with a Desire, That an Address might be form'd, with due
Regard and Acknowledgments for the Letter. After some Difficulties, the same Address was sent down again with a Clause inserted,
making some short mention of the said Letter. This the Lower   155
House did not think sufficient, and sent it back again with the
same Request: Whereupon the Archbishop, after a short Consultation with *some* of his Brethren, immediately adjourn'd the Convocation for a Month, and no Address at all was sent to the QUEEN.

I understand not Ecclesiastical Affairs well enough to comment   160
upon this Matter; but it seems to me, that all Methods of doing
Service to the Church and Kingdom, by means of a *Convocation*, may
be at any time *eluded*, if there be no Remedy against such an
Incident. And if this Proceeding be agreeable to the Institution,
spiritual Assemblies must needs be strangely contriv'd, very   165

VII's Chapel, went through the address clause by clause, and agreed to every
paragraph without amendments 'Provided their Ldships should make some *Addition*
to it wherein due Notice might be taken of her Majties Letter and Thanks
return'd for it'. When it was received, the bishops' addition, a single clause
in the penultimate paragraph, was voted not to contain '*Sufficient Notice of
the Queen's most gracious* Letter' and a committee was elected to draft a
notice that would be sufficient (Bennett, p. 130; BL MS Lansdowne 1024, ff.
239^V-240^V; Lambeth Palace MS Conv I/1/17, pp. 78-9; Conv I/2/11, ff. 2^V-3).

158 *adjourn'd*: At the next meeting of the Lower House on 15 December 1710
George Smalridge read the committee's proposal for a notice of thanks to the
Queen, but the House was badly divided in the ensuing debate and no vote was
taken. Instead, Atterbury and the committee 'offered the New Additions to the
ABp; and returnd with this Answer that their Ldshps would adhere to their
Address without further Additions ... and while [the Lower House was] at a
great Loss the Schedule was brought in by wch the ABp had prorogued the Convocation to Wednesday the 17th of January' (BL MS Lansdowne 1024, ff. 241^r-
243^r). Since his right to do so had been repeatedly challenged by the Lower
House, the Archbishop's action failed 'to compose and extinguish' the dispute
between the Houses, as the Queen's letter desiderated (Pittis, *The History of
the Present Parliament and Convocation*, 1711, p. 118). No address of thanks
was returned to the Queen, but the Archbishop ordered the intended address of
the Upper House to be published (Morgan M149).

165 *strangely contriv'd*: Swift is assuming Atterbury's argument that the
Lower House of Convocation is an independent body, 'a *Spiritual House of Commons*' (Atterbury, *The Rights, Powers, and Privileges of an English Convocation, Stated and Vindicated*, 2nd edn., London, for Tho. Bennet, 1701, p. 503;
Wotton, *The Case of the Present Convocation Consider'd*, 1711, pp. 14-16). On
this assumption, the subordination of the Lower House to the president of the

different from any *Lay* Senate yet known in the World. Surely,
from the Nature of such a Synod, it must be a very unhappy Circumstance, when the Majority of the Bishops draws one way, and
that of the Lower Clergy another. The latter, I think, are not at
170   this time suspected for any Principles bordering upon those professed by Enemies to Episcopacy; and if they happen to differ
from the greater part of the *present Set* of Bishops, I doubt it
will call *some Things* to mind, that may turn the Scale of general
Favour on the Inferior Clergies side, who with a profound Duty to
175   Her Majesty, are perfectly pleas'd with *the present Turn of Af-*
fairs. Besides, *curious People* will be apt to enquire into the
Dates of *some Promotions*, to call to mind what *Designs* were then
upon the Anvil, and from thence make *malicious Deductions*. Perhaps they will observe the manner of Voting on the Bishops Bench,
180   and compare it with what shall pass in the Upper House of

Upper House, the Archbishop, is as 'strangely contriv'd' as if the House of
Commons should be subordinate to the Lord Chancellor, who presides over the
debate of the Lords.
   170 *suspected*: Matthew Tindal said that Tenison was an atheist (*New High-*
Church turn'd Old Presbyterian, 1709, p. 14).
   172 *Set*: William III had to fill twenty-one of the twenty-six seats on the
episcopal bench. Their names are listed in *King William's Affection to the*
Church of England Examin'd, 1703, p. 19, and it cannot be denied, as Defoe
said, 'but that many of them [were] Men of Latitudinarian Principles' (ibid.,
p. 23). Only one of 'King William's bishops', John Sharp, voted Tory in
Anne's reign. The nine others who survived into this reign invariably voted
Whig (*Letters of Eminent Men Addressed to Ralph Thoresby*, 2 vols., London,
Colburn and Bentley, 1832, i 436; Holmes, pp. 434-5).
   173 *some Things*: 'King William's bishops' voted against the bills to prevent occasional conformity in 1702 and 1703 and for the impeachment of
Sacheverell in 1710 (*POAS*, Yale, vi 510, vii 413).
   178 *malicious Deductions*: If 'Designs' (134.177) refers to the Bill of Comprehension introduced into the House of Lords on 11 March 1689 (*LJ*, xiv 145),
the 'malicious Deduction' may be that Gilbert Burnet was nominated Bishop
of Salisbury on 9 March 1689 to help ensure passage of the bill that 'instead of shutting the Church against *Dissenters*', was intended, as Swift believed, 'to open it to *all Comers*, and *break down its Walls*' (147.93-4). If
'Designs' has a more general reference, it may mean simply that 'King William's bishops' were nominated to increase the Court majority in the House of
Lords. In the case of the Place Bill of 1692-3, for example, the bill was
defeated when Burnet, 'who had earlier spoken strongly for the bill, "went
away" before the [final] vote [on 3 January 1693] and as many as eleven [other
bishops] appear as *new voters on the Court side*' (Eveline Cruickshanks, David
Hayton, Clyve Jones, *Bulletin of the Institute of Historical Research*, liii
(May 1980), 72; italics added).
   179 *manner of Voting*: Wotton understood that what Swift meant was that the
bishops 'voted wrong in the *House of Lords*' (*The Case of the Present Convoca-*
tion Consider'd, 1711, p. 19), but Swift may have meant that the bishops vote
as they are told to do by the Junto (135.190-1). And the 'malicious Deduction'
may be that they vote the same way in the Upper House of Convocation.

Convocation. There is, however, one comfort, that under the
present Dispositions of the Kingdom, a dislike to the Proceedings
of any of their Lordships, even to the number of a *Majority*, will
be purely *Personal*, and not turn'd to the Disadvantage of the
Order. And for my part, as I am a true Lover of the Church, I had   185
rather find the Inclinations of the People favourable to Episcopacy in general, than see a Majority of Prelates cry'd up by
those who are *known Enemies* to the Character. Nor, indeed, hath
any thing given me more Offence for several Years past, than to
observe how *some* of that Bench have been caressed by *certain Per-*   190
sons; and *others* of them openly celebrated by the infamous Pens
of Atheists, Republicans and Fanaticks.

Time and *Mortality* can only remedy these Inconveniencies in the
Church, which are not to be cur'd like those in the State, by a
Change of Ministry. If we may guess the Temper of a *Convocation*,   195
from the Choice of a *Prolocutor*, as it is usual to do that of a
House of Commons by the *Speaker*, we may expect great things from
that Reverend Body, who have done themselves much Reputation, by
pitching upon a *Gentleman* of so much Piety, Wit and Learning, for

186 favourable] favourarable ½°   198 Reputation] Repuation ½°

---

188 *known Enemies*: cf. 'We have therefore great reason to be very thankful
to God in this respect, as having never enjoy'd before, a Set of more Learned,
Moderate, or Orthodox *Bishops*' (Toland, *The Memorial of the State of England*,
1705, p. 104).
190-1 *certain Persons*: On 25 November 1703, during the debate on the second
bill to prevent occasional conformity, a Tory member bantered the Archbishop
of Canterbury for opposing the bill: 'I did wonder', he said, 'to hear so
many B[ishop]s against this Bill, but that wonder ceas'd, when I consider'd
whom they ow'd their Preferment to. The A. B---p of C---y, I think, was promoted to that See by my Lord S[underlan]d's interest; and being ask'd what
Reasons he had against this Bill, Replyed, he had not well consider'd the Bill,
but that my Lord S[ome]rs told him it ought not to pass' ([Sir John Pakington]
A Speech for the Bill against Occasional Conformity, no place or date of
publication, pp. 2-3).
193 *Time and Mortality*: Swift must have been delighted with the interpretation that Wotton put on this phrase: 'the *Examiner* wou'd infer, That he that
knocks these Bishops on the Head, does ... the Church a real piece of Service'
(*The Case of the Present Convocation Consider'd*, 1711, p. 4).
196 *Prolocutor*: Francis Atterbury was elected prolocutor on 25 November
1710 'a longè majori parte' over Richard Willis, a rank Whig (Lambeth Palace
MS Conv i/1/17, p. 33).
197 *Speaker*: William Bromley of Baginton (*c*.1663-1732), a High Churchman
and a Tacker, was elected Speaker on 25 November 1710 without opposition. He
expected to collaborate in the Anglican counter-revolution that Atterbury
intended to effect (Gareth V. Bennett, *Studies in Church History*, edd. G.J.
Cuming and Derek Baker, Cambridge, Cambridge University Press, 1971, p. 313).

200   that Office; and one who is so thoroughly vers'd in those Parts
       of Knowledge which are proper for it. I am sorry that the *Three*
       Latin Speeches, deliver'd upon presenting the *Prolocutor*, were
       not made publick; they might perhaps have given us some Light
       into the Dispositions of each House: And besides, *One* of 'em is
205   said to be so peculiar in the Stile and Matter, as might have
       made up in *Entertainment* what it wanted in *Instruction*.

202 *Speeches*: On 6 December 1710, in Henry VII's Chapel, Smalridge 'made a
long Speech in good Latine well delivred, extremely much in Commendation of
Dr. Atterbury and his writing and preaching ... [Atterbury] spoke as freely in
the Praises of Dr. Smallridge ... After this the Absp read a shorter speech,
commending Peace & Unity, and observing that some spoke for Peace, who had not
the Principles or Practice of it' (BL MS Lansdowne 1024, f. 237). Smalridge's
speech was eventually published in Latin and English (*A Speech to the Upper
House of Convocation, upon the Presentment of the late Prolocutor*, London, for
J. Roberts, 1714).
    204 *One*: Tenison's style was said to have had 'all the good qualities of a
tailor's goose, which were, being very hot and heavy' (Burnet, 1833, iv 244n.).

No. 14 [Mainwaring and Oldmixon]   1 January 1711

                          The MEDLEY.

The Examiner*'s Good-Will to the Army.*

His Loyalty prov'd by his own Sarmatian *Story.*

A Fable out of Cælius Rhodiginus.

An Answer to part of a pretended intercepted Letter from the Elector of
    Bav-----*'s Minister at* Par-- *to his Master.*

       A Late Historian says, *We live in a Country, where we may not*
       only think and speak, but also safely write what we believe to be
       the Truth, to which all Mankind owe Allegiance. And a greater
       Historian than he, call'd *Polybius*, says, 'That Truth shou'd be
5   consider'd as a Great Goddess, that will always take care to ap-
       pear in her proper Light, and that naturally triumphs over Fals-

1-3 *We* ... *Allegiance*: The 'Late Historian' has not been identifi--, but
the gist of the quotation is in Matthew Tindal, *Reasons against Restraining
the Press*, London, 1704, p. 13: 'the chief Happiness ... of rational Creatures,
consists in having the liberty of thinking on what Subject they please, and of
as freely communicating their Thoughts'; cf. 394.71-2n.
    4-8 *That* ... *Persecution*: Polybius, xiii 5 4.

hood, notwithstanding the infinite number of Persons that take
pleasure in her Persecution.' I am not of the Opinion of either
of these Authors: I believe a great many things to be true, which
I know not whether I shou'd do well to write; and I think Fals-   10
hood has so far got the better of Truth, that the latter is
hardly to be met with any where now but in *Plato's intelligible*
World, which he invented in opposition to the *sensible* World we
live in: placing Truth in the former, upon a height unaccessible
to Mortals; and nothing but Opinion, Doubt and Error in the   15
latter, with an utter Loss of Discernment, and a Confusion of
Right and Wrong, of Virtue and of Vice. Read but any of my Friend
the *Examiner's* Papers, and you will fancy him Chief Secretary of
this *sensible* World I have mention'd: For he not only writes
whatever he believes or knows to be false, but plainly shews 'tis   20
his Business and Duty to do so, and that this alone is the Merit
of his Service. After having vilify'd the late Ministers, and
the General of the Army, he at last fell upon the Army it self,
comparing it very fairly to that which destroy'd the Commonwealth
of *Rome*, and to that which erected one in *England*: Either wou'd   25
do, and one as well as the other. Thus while our Troops were victorious in the Cause of Liberty Abroad, they were insulted and
treated with Contempt by this desperate Author at Home. Besides,
he says, *The Officers are by their Education unqualify'd for*
other Stations of Life: Their Fortune will not suffer them to   30
retain to a Party after its Fall, nor have they Weight and Abili-
ties to help towards its Resurrection: They appear in all Com-
panies as if they were at the Head of their Regiments; but they
must now, he says, *throw off their lac'd Coats*; and if so, he
promises it shall *be much more for their Interest*. What a Tool   35
is here! That with a dash of his Pen can strip that Army, which
was not to be disarm'd by all the Power of *France*! But I shall
make no further Remarks now upon his Good-Will to the Army,

17 of Vice] Vice 12°   35 *more*] *om.* 12°   Tool] Hero 12°   36 That]
who 12°   38 Remarks] Rermarks ½°

12-13 *Plato's intelligible World*: 'You surely apprehend the two types, the
visible and the intelligible?' (Plato, *The Republic*, 509D).
19-20 *writes ... false*: cf. 118.5-7.
24 *comparing*: 115.125-116.138.
29-35 *The ... Interest*: 117.178-118.201.

designing in this Paper to recommend another of his Virtues.
40   Among all the Instances I have shewn of his good Morals and
Behaviour, I do not remember to have given any Demonstration yet
of his Duty to the Q---n, which he seems to value himself extremely upon, and to abhor the Want which he will fancy there is
of it in other People. I shall not fetch my Evidence from her
45 Maj----'s Declaration, that *the Church was not in Danger* during
the last Ministry; notwithstanding which, this humble and loyal
Subject says in plain Terms, *I did then, and do still, believe*
the Church has been in very imminent Danger. This is not the
Proof I design to go upon at this time: But all the World knows
50 her Maj----y very often declar'd, that she had nothing more at
heart than the Union of the two Kingdoms, and that she thought it
a very great Happiness that such a Work was perform'd in her
Reign. Now you shall see the Account which this excellent Author
gives of our Union, and of the *Scots* Nation in general, out of
55 an old *Sarmatian* History, which he was so witty to invent a Week
ago, and which I beg leave to translate out of that barbarous
Language for the benefit of the *English* Reader.

England *being bounded on the* North *by a poor mountainous People*
call'd Scots, *who were Vassals to that Crown, and the* English
60 *Prime Minister, being largely brib'd, obtain'd the Q----'s Con-*
sent for the Scots *to arm and exercise themselves; and they find-*
ing they were not in a Condition to be troublesome, began to
insist upon Terms, and threaten'd upon every occasion to join
with the French. *Upon which the Prime Minister, who began to be*
65 *in pain about his Head, set on foot a Treaty to unite the two*
Kingdoms, which he had the good Luck to bring to pass, and from
that time valu'd himself as Author of a most Glorious Union,
which indeed was grown of absolute necessity by his Corruption.

45 *Declaration*: 38.107.
47-8 *I ... Danger*: 38.109-11.
51 *Union*: In her speech of 6 March 1707 giving assent to the Act of Union,
Anne said 'I cannot but look upon it as a peculiar Happiness, that in my Reign
so full a Provision is made for the Peace and Quiet of my People' (*CJ*, xv 327).
58-68 *England ... Corruption*: 102.175-103.191). What he seems to gain by
exposing Swift's variance from Anne's 'Happiness' in the Union, which Swift
called 'a monstrous Alliance' (*POAS*, Yale, vii 283), Oldmixon loses here by
giving wider currency to Swift's 'old *Sarmatian* History' of Godolphin's skul-
duggery.

I am confident my Friend will neither disown the Faithfulness
of this Translation, nor be sorry to see his Story put into *Eng-*   70
lish by another Hand: He is too well with the Enemies of the
Union, to be under any Concern on that Score; but I will be content to submit my Reason and Veracity to his, which I believe
wou'd be thought a very hard Fate for me or any Man, if in all
the scurrilous Libels that have been printed, there is such   75
another Instance to be found of Contempt and Disobedience to her
Maj---y's Royal Pleasure, and of Scorn and Hatred to our united
Countrymen, *those poor mountainous People*, that were *Vassals* and
paid Homage. And the Account he gives of the Reason of *our most*
glorious Union, as he calls it, is admirable: He says, *It was*   80
indeed grown of absolute Necessity by the Corruption of a Great
Minister. One never reads his Papers, without being inform'd and
made wiser: He always takes care to say something that no body
else will, and now he has shewn that Corruption does good sometimes, and that we owe a very great Blessing to it. He is only a   85
little unlucky in the Person he has chosen to fix a Bribe upon,
who is as unsuspected of Bribery, as my Friend is of Truth, and
who defies and despises the poor and harmless Malice of him and
all his Masters; who make him again, in this Instance, boldly
affirm, what they in their Consciences know to be false.   90

   The Characters and Actions of these Men put me in mind of a
certain Fable that I have read in a *Latin* Author; who observing
that Fables were invented not so much for Pleasure as Instruction,
says, there is one in particular from which good Knowledg may be
had; and which is as follows. They report, says he, that *Minerva*, 95
Neptune and *Vulcan*, disputing one day among themselves about the
Greatness of their Art, and the Wonders they cou'd perform; *Nep-*
tune immediately, for Trial-sake, produc'd a Bull, *Minerva* a
House ready furnish'd, and *Vulcan* a Man. *Momus* was the Judg that
was to decide their Contest. He diligently survey'd them all: 100
What Faults he found in the two first, are needless to mention,

89 *Masters*: 'These Masters of the *Examiner* were always thought by him
[Mainwaring] to be the ... Treasurer [Harley], Chancellor [Harcourt], and
Secretary [St. John], the first and last he took to be most concern'd in the
Matter, and that the Secretary wrote himself several of those scandalous
Papers' (Oldmixon, *The Life*, pp. 189-90).
92 *Author*: [Lodovico Ricchieri, *aka* Lodovicus,] Cael[ius] Rhodogin[us,
Lectionum antiquarum libri xxx, Basle, per Hieronymum Frobenium et Nicol.
Episcopium, 1542], 1. 9. c. 21 (½°).

but he said there was one in the new-made Man; which was, That
Vulcan ought certainly to have set Windows to his Breast, that so
it might be plain to every body what he desir'd, what he thought,
105 and whether he spoke Truth or not. The Reason of this Fable, says
the Author, is set forth in *Aristotle*'s seventh Book of Morals,
where it is said, There are some Men so abounding in ill Qualities, that they are a thousand times more mischievous than Brutes;
their Nature being, as *Cicero* says, *wrap'd up in a Cloak of De-*
110 *ceit, or cover'd with a Veil of Dissimulation: Their Foreheads,*
Eyes, and Countenance often lye, but most of all their Speech.
I have been thinking, if there were such Windows as these to some
Breasts in the World, what a sight wou'd be presented to all innocent Spectators. What a Reproach wou'd it be to Human Kind to look
115 into Minds where Fraud and Guile preside; where the Names of all
Things and Persons are chang'd, and the common Notices of Good
and Evil lost; where Prosperity is call'd dangerous, and Poverty
advantageous; where Conquests are stamp'd Treason, and Honesty
Corruption: in short, from whence plain Truth before-mention'd
120 has been banish'd twenty Years? If there be any Persons alive that
are found in this manner, the *Egyptians,* according to a very good
Author, wou'd have punish'd them with Death, as impious towards
God, and destructive of Mankind, by taking away the mutual Trust
which is necessary to Civil Society. And *Marcus Antoninus* himself,
125 that mild Emperor and Philosopher, wou'd have made no scruple to
pronounce them *Impious*: Laying it down for a Maxim in the beginning of his ninth Book, That it is impossible *to lye without Im-*
piety, and without offending Nature, and that first Original Truth
which is the Soul of the Universe: *The good Order of which*, he
130 says, *an Impostor always troubles; and always confounds the right*
Measures of things as far as he is capable of doing it.
    I can't end this Paper without saying one word more to my Friend
the *Examiner*: He having been pleas'd to revive very seasonably the
Dispute between the Upper and Lower House of Convocation, *That he*

116 chang'd,] ~; ½°   121 found] form'd 12°

109-11 *their ... Speech*: [Cicero] *Epist*[*ulae*] *ad* [*Quintum*] *Fratr*[*em*,
i 1 15] (½°).
120 *twenty Years*: 84.92.
121-4 *Egyptians ... Society*: Diod[orus] Sicul[us]. lib. I [77 2] (½°).
127-31 *it ... it*: Marcus Aurelius Antoninus, *Meditations*, ix 1.
134-7 *That ... Affairs*: 134.173-6.

may turn, as he says, *the Scale of General Favour on the Inferior*   135
Clergy's side, assures the World they *are perfectly pleas'd with*
the present Turn of Affairs. I shall not trouble the Reader with
observing what incomparable Judges the lower Clergy are of State-
Affairs; let their own Actions in Convocation speak for them,
which are recorded to their everlasting Honour. So that it must   140
needs be an infinite Satisfaction to those that wish well to the
Religion and Liberty of their Country, to know that such peaceable well-dispos'd Christians are so highly satisfy'd with the
Advantages we have gain'd by some late Proceedings of ours.

Some People in Town, who for a Month past have been handing up   145
and down a pretended intercepted Letter from the Elector of
*Bav----'*s Minister at *Par--* to his Master, will be apt to tell my
Friend upon this occasion, that there are others in the World as
well pleas'd with those Proceedings as the *Inferior Clergy*. The
Letter-Writer will have it, the *French* King was overjoy'd at the   150
News from *England*, and *did not defer one moment to give him*
notice of it. That the French *Court were of opinion the Opportu-*
nity was come, and that use ought to be made of this favourable
Conjuncture: For the Allies, says the pretended Author, *will*
never be able to continue united after this. And he wishes it   155
might bring them to those Ends they hope for from it. I don't
believe one word of all this. Some sour Whigs indeed make a great
noise about it; and I wou'd have printed the Letter at length,

---

158 printed] pirnted ½°

138 *Clergy:* cf. 'Does not all History shew, that they are thoughtless,
precipitant, troublesome, bungling and wretched *Politicians?*' (Toland, *The*
Memorial of the State of England, 1705, p. 103).
139 *Convocation*: The lower clergy regularly elected the most militant High
Churchmen to represent them in Convocation. As a result both William and Anne
were reluctant to summon the Convocation. In 1689-99, 1708-9 there was none,
and in 1701 the session was prorogued amid 'scenes of unbelievable disorder'
(Thomas Lathbury, *A History of the Convocation of the Church of England*, 2nd
edn., London, J. Leslie, 1853, pp. 325-406; Gareth V. Bennett, *Britain after*
the Glorious Revolution, 1689-1714, ed. Geoffrey Holmes, London, Macmillan,
1969, p. 166).
146 *Letter*: 'The entire intercepted Letter from the Elector of *Bavaria's*
Minister to his Master, was by [Mainwaring's] order Printed in *French* and
English, translated by himself, and privately dispers'd' (Oldmixon, *The Life*,
p. 190).
152-6 *the French ... it*: Mainwaring, *A Letter from the E. of Bav---'s Mini-*
ster at Versailles to his Master, Both in French and English, Amsterdam, 1711,
pp. 3, 5, 7. Mainwaring includes the French in footnotes.
156 *Ends*: Restoration of the Pretender?

both in *French* and *English,* but that I look upon it to be a Trick
160 of the *Ruin'd Party.* Who shou'd one hearken to, one's Friends or
one's Enemies, supposing there was something in it? But 'tis
plain this cou'd never come from any Minister of the Elector of
Bav----: 'Tis impossible he shou'd be pleas'd with a Tory
M-------y in *England,* because he has already found he has no
165 Interest in that Side. For 'tis well known, that when a new War
was expected upon the Death of the last King of *Spain,* and we had
then such a M--------; the Elector of *Bav----* cou'd get them to
do nothing for him, tho he sent over an Envoy on purpose to them,
to promise he wou'd keep *Flanders* till the War was declar'd: But
170 they minded not a word he said, having nothing in their thoughts
but a new Parliament, which was to take vigorous Resolutions
after *Christmas.* How therefore shou'd this Elector be pleas'd
with Tory M-------rs now? I know the sour *Whigs* before-mention'd
wou'd answer to this, that he was on our side then, but is now on
175 the *French,* to which those Measures of our Court in the last
Reign drove him: But these I take to be no better than Cavils,
and shall therefore leave to be answer'd by my Friend the *Examiner*; which he can do as easily as ever he did any thing in his
life.

160 *the Ruin'd Party*: 3.50.
167 *M-------*: the short-lived Tory ministry of 1701.
      Elector of Bav----: The Elector of Bavaria was governor of the Spanish
Netherlands when Carlos II died in October 1700. He sent an envoy to London
offering to hold the Spanish Netherlands for the late allies, Holland, England,
and the Empire. 'The Refusal of the ... Proposals to secure *Flanders* ... was
imputed to the *Tory*-Faction.' When the envoy returned to Brussels 'with a
melancholy Account of Expectations from *England* ... the Elector of *Bavaria* ...
made his Bargain with [Louis XIV]' and French troops occupied the strong
points from which ten campaigns of the War of the Spanish Succession failed to
dislodge them completely (Oldmixon, *The History*, pp. 216, 224).
177 *to be answer'd*: The Examiner did not rise to the bait.

No. 23 [Swift]   4 January 1711

The EXAMINER.

*Nulla sunt occultiores insidiæ, quam eæ quæ latent in simulatione officii,
aut in aliquo necessitudinis nomine.*

*THE following Answer is written in the true Style, and with the usual Candour of such Pieces; which I have imitated to the best of my Skill, and
doubt not but the Reader will be extremely satisfied with it.*

The Examiner cross-examin'd, *or
A full Answer to the last* Examiner.   5

IF I durst be so bold with this Author, I would gladly ask him a
familiar Question; *Pray, Sir, Who made you an Examiner?* He talks
in one of his insipid Papers, of *eight or nine thousand Corruptions*, while *We* were at the Head of Affairs, yet, in all this
time he has hardly produc'd fifty: *Parturiunt montes, &c.* --- 10
Hor. But I shall confine my self, at present, to his last Paper.
He tells us, *The Queen began Her Reign with a noble Benefaction
to the Church.* Here's *Priestcraft* with a witness; this is the
constant Language of your *High Flyers*, to call those who are
hired to teach *the Religion of the Magistrate* by the Name of the 15
Church. But this is not all; for, in the very next Line he says,
It was hoped the Nation wou'd have follow'd this Example. You see
the Faction begins already to *speak out*; this is an open Demand
for the *Abby-Lands*; this furious Zealot wou'd have us *Priest-*

Motto Cicero, *In C. Verrem*, ii 1 15 39: It is extremely difficult to explore those Designs which are conceived under the Veil of Duty, and lie hid
under the Pretence of Friendship.
4   *The Examiner cross-examin'd*: parodying a series of titles including *The
Review Review'd* (1707) and *The Rehearsal Rehears'd* (1706).
8-9   *eight or nine thousand Corruptions*: 84.90.
10-11   *Parturiunt montes, &c.* --- *Hor.*: Swift ridicules Mainwaring's pedantry
in citing sources for his quotations.
12-13   *The ... Church*: 129.77-9.
15   *the Religion of the Magistrate*: cf. 'It is grown a mighty Conceit ...
to melt down the Phrase of a *Church established by Law*, into that of *the Religion of the Magistrate*' (Swift, *Prose*, ii 115).
17   *It ... Example*: 129.79-80.
18   *the Faction*: 68.50-2.
19   *Abby-Lands*: These were the vast properties transferred from the Church

20 *ridden* again, like our *Popish* Ancestors: But, 'tis to be hop'd
    the Government will take timely care to suppress such audacious
    Attempts, else we have spent so much Blood and Treasure to very
    little purpose, in maintaining *Religion* and *Revolution*. But what
    can we expect from a Man, who at one Blow endeavours to ruin our
25 Trade? *A Country* (says he) *may flourish* (these are his own Words)
    *without being the common Receptacle for all Nations, Religions
    and Languages*. What! We must immediately banish or murder the
    Palatines; forbid all Foreign Merchants, not only the *Exchange*,
    but the Kingdom; persecute the Dissenters with Fire and Faggot,
30 and make it High-Treason to speak any other Tongue but *English*.
    In another Place he talks of a *Serpent with seven Heads*, which is
    a manifest Corruption of the Text; for the Words *Seven Heads*, are
    not mentioned in that Verse. However, we know what *Serpent* he
    would mean; a *Serpent* with *fourteen Legs*; or, indeed, no *Serpent*
35 at all, but Seven great Men, who were the *best Ministers*, the
    truest Protestants, and the most *disinteressed Patriots* that ever
    serv'd a Prince. But nothing is so inconsistent as this Writer;
    I know not whether to call him a Whig or a Tory, a Protestant or
    a Papist: He finds fault with Convocations; says, *they are Assem-
40 blies strangely contriv'd*; and yet lays the Fault upon Us, that
    we *bound their Hands*: I wish we could have bound their *Tongues*
    too; but as fast as their *Hands* were bound, they could make a
    shift to hold their *Pens*, and have their share in the Guilt of
    ruining the hopefullest Party and Ministry that ever *prescrib'd*
45 to a Crown. This captious Gentleman is angry to *see a Majority of*

to the Crown by the dissolution of the monasteries (27 Hen. VIII c. 28) in
1536. By 1710 many of these estates had fallen into private hands so that any
suggestion that they be restored to the Church was unsettling to Whig magnates
like the Duke of Bedford, who owned the demesne of Woburn Abbey. Charles
Leslie had just been publicly charged with advocating 'the Clergy ... being
restor'd to all the Church-Lands' (*The Observator*, 20-3 December 1710), but
in his works, such as *Now or Never* (1696) which was republished in 1710 with
the title, *Now or Never; or, A Project under God to Secure the Church and
Monarchy of England*, where such a demand might be expected, it is not made;
cf. Toland, *The Memorial of the State of England*, 1710, p. 10.

    25-7 *Country ... Languages*: 129.85-130.86.
    28 *Palatines*: 129.85-6n.
    31 *Serpent with seven Heads*: 131.121-132.122.
    35 *Seven great Men*: 39.127.
        best Ministers: 120.43.
    39-40 *Assemblies strangely contriv'd*: 133.165.
    41 *bound ... Hands*: 128.59.
    45-6 *see ... Character*: 135.187-8.

Prelates cry'd up by those who are Enemies to the Character; now
I always thought, that the Concessions of Enemies were more to a
Man's Advantage than the Praise of his Friends. *Time and Mortal-
ity*, he says, *can only remedy these Inconveniencies in the Church.*
That is, in other Words, When certain Bishops are dead, we shall   50
have others of our own Stamp. Not so fast; You are not yet so
sure of your Game. We have already got one *comfortable Loss* in
Spain, though by a G-----l of our own. For Joy of which, our
J-----to had a merry Meeting at the House of their great Proselyte,
on the very day we receiv'd the happy News. One or two more such   55
Blows would, perhaps, set us right again, and then we can employ
Mortality as well as others. He concludes with wishing, that *three
Letters, spoke when the Prolocutor was presented, were made publick.* I suppose he wou'd be content with *One*, and that is more
than we shall humour him to grant. However, I hope he will allow   60
it possible to have *Grace*, without either *Eloquence* or *Latin*,
which is all I shall say to his malicious *innuendo*.

Having thus, I hope, given a *full satisfactory Answer* to the
Examiner's last Paper, I shall now go on to a more important

62 *innuendo.*] ~, ½°

48-9 *Time ... Church*: 135.193-4.
52 *comfortable Loss*: The news of the disaster at Brihuega, sixty miles
north-east of Madrid, on 29 November/9 December 1710 did not reach London until 26 December (Luttrell, vi 669). Lieutenant-General James Stanhope, in command of an English column covering the retreat of the archduke Charles from
Madrid, allowed himself to lose contact both with the enemy, a Spanish-French
force including 10,000 cavalry, and with the allied column on his right. As
a result he was surrounded and his entire force of more than 5,000 killed or
captured. Although it was the end of the allied effort in Spain (Trevelyan,
iii 85-7, 334-5), the loss was 'comfortable' to the Whig Cross-examiner because he hoped that 'One or two more such *Blows*' might knock out the Harley
ministry. As a Whig member for Cockermouth (1702-13), Stanhope was the most
violent of the managers of the impeachment proceedings against Sacheverell.
54 *Proselyte*: 'Probably the Earl of Nottingham' (E*1814*, iii 395). Although
rumours had made him Secretary of State in June, First Lord of the Admiralty
in September, and Lord Privy Seal in December 1710, Nottingham had been excluded from Harley's ministry and was 'as sour and fiercely wild as ... anything ... that has lived long in the desert' (Luttrell, vi 633, 667; HMC
Portland MSS, v 119). As late as November 1711 Harley was still trying to win
his support and his defection to the Whigs was not publicly known until December 1711. The irony of celebrating a defeat in Spain at Nottingham's house in
Gerrard Street was that Nottingham had long argued that Spain should be the
principal theatre of war, 'for that in Flanders we might war to eternity and
never come to anything decisive' (HMC *Egmont MSS*, ii 220).
57-9 *three ... publick*: 136.201-3. Is the mistake, '*Letters*' for '*Speeches*',
made deliberately to provide an example of 'mangl'd Quotation' (335.163-4)?
59 *One*: 136.204.

65 Affair; which is, To prove, by several undeniable Instances, that
    the late M----ry, and their Abettors, were true Friends to the
    Church. It is yet, I confess, a Secret to the Clergy, wherein
    this Friendship did consist. For Information therefore of that
    Reverend Body, that they may never forget their Benefactors, as
70 well as of all others who may be equally ignorant, I have deter-
    min'd to display *Our* Merits to the World upon that weighty Article.
    And I could wish, that what I am to say were to be written in
    Brass, for an eternal Memorial; the rather, because for the future,
    the Church must endeavour to stand unsupported by those Patrons,
75 who expired in doing it their *last good Office*, and will never
    rise to preserve it any more.
        Let us therefore produce the pious Endeavours of these Church-
    Defenders, who were its Patrons by their Power and Authority, as
    well as Ornaments of it by their Exemplary Lives.
80   *First.* St. *Paul* tells us, *There must be Heresies in the Church,*
    that the Truth may be manifest; and therefore, by due course of
    Reasoning, the more Heresies there are, the more *manifest* will the
    Truth be made. This being maturely consider'd by these Lovers of
    the Church, they endeavour'd to propagate as many Heresies as they
85 could, that the Light of Truth might shine the clearer.
        Secondly. To shew their Zeal for the Church's Defence, they took
    the care of it intirely out of the Hands of *God Almighty* (because
    that was a *foreign Jurisdiction*) and made it their own *Creature*,
    depending altogether upon them; and issu'd out their Orders to
90 *Tindal*, and others, to give publick Notice of it.
        Thirdly. Because *Charity* is the most celebrated of all Christian
    Vertues, therefore they extended theirs beyond all Bounds; and

    74 *Patrons*: presumably the nine members of the House of Commons, of the
    twenty who managed the impeachment proceedings against Sacheverell (*CJ*, xvi
    241-2, 305), who were not re-elected in October 1710: Henry Boyle, Spencer
    Compton, Thomas, lord Coningsby, Spencer Cowper, John Dolben (who died in May
    1710), Robert Eyre, Sir John Hawles, Sir John Holland, Sir Thomas Parker (who
    was appointed a Lord Chief Justice in March 1710 and therefore could not stand
    in the election).
        80-1 *There ... manifest*: 1 Cor. 11:19.
        82 *more Heresies*: cf. '*Diversity of Religions* is so far from being danger-
    ous, that it ought rather to be counted beneficial' (Toland, *The Memorial of
    the State of England*, 1705, p. 52). In these lines one of Swift's most deeply
    held beliefs comes close to the surface, viz., that truth, virtue, and health
    are one and uniform, while falsehood, vice, and sickness are various and multi-
    form.
        88 *Creature*: 131.107; cf. 102.162.

instead of shutting the Church against *Dissenters*, were ready to
open it to *all Comers*, and *break down its Walls*, rather than that
any should want room to enter. The Strength of a State, we know,   95
consists in the number of People, how different soever in their
Callings; and why should not the Strength of a Church consist in
the same, how different soever in their *Creeds*? For that reason,
they charitably attempted to abolish the Test, which ty'd up so
many Hands from getting Employments, in order to protect the   100
Church.

I know very well that this Attempt is objected to us as a Crime,
by several *malignant Tories*, and denied as a Slander by many unthinking People among our selves. The latter are apt in their
Defence to ask such Questions as these; *Was your Test repeal'd?*   105
Had we not a Majority? Might we not have done it if we pleased?
To which the others answer, *You did what you could; you prepared*
the way, but you found a fatal Impediment from that Quarter,
whence the Sanction of the Law must come, and therefore to save
your Credit, you condemn'd a Paper to be burnt which your selves   110

96 consists] consisteth 38 8°+12°

---

96 *number*: cf. Toland, *The Memorial of the State of England*, 1705, p. 64;
Defoe, *A Brief History of the Poor Palatine Refugees*, 1709, p. 3: 'the Greatness, Wealth, and Strength of a Country consist in the Number of its Inhabitants.' Swift demolishes this argument (*Prose*, vii 94-5).

99 *abolish the Test*: cf. 'repealing the Sacramental Test ... is the most
infallible Method of preserving the *National Church*' (Toland, *The Memorial of*
the State of England, 1705, p. 54). Swift replied that 'if once we repeal our
Sacramental Test ... I do not see how we can be said to have any Established
Church remaining' (Swift, *Prose*, ii 115). In November 1708, when Wharton was
appointed Lord-Lieutenant of Ireland, the Anglo-Irish 'were under great apprehensions at his first coming that He woud drive directly at repealing the
Test' (Addison, *Letters*, p. 134) as a trial balloon for abolishing it in England (Swift, *Corr.*, i 114-15). It was this fear that motivated *An Argument* ...
[against] *the Abolishing of Christianity in England* (written 1708, published
1711) and *A Letter from a Member of the House of Commons in Ireland to a Mem-*
ber of the House of Commons in England, Concerning the Sacramental Test (1708).

100 *Employments*: cf. 'the *Church of England* ... is nothing besides the
Hierarchy and the *Ceremonies*, but especially the *Revenues* and the *Monopolizing*
of Offices by the Sacramental Test' (Toland, *The Memorial of the State of Eng-*
land, 1705, p. 100).

110 *a Paper*: After the Whig victories in the election of 1705, 'it was
privately discours'd, that the great Design of that Party, in the approaching
Session, would probably be *to abrogate the Sacramental Test*; and ... a Bill
was actually drawn for repealing the *Test*, and the Scots were underhand encouraged to insist upon it, as one of the Terms of the *Union*, with Assurance that
it would be well accepted here' (Charles Hornby, *The Fourth and Last Part of*
a Caveat against the Whiggs, London, J. Morphew, 1712, pp. 112-13). When repeal

had brought in. But alas! the miscarriage of that noble Project for
the Safety of the Church, had another Original; the knowledge where
of depends upon a piece of secret History that I shall now lay open
   These Church-Protectors had directed a *Presbiterian Preacher* to
115 draw up a Bill for repealing the *Test*; it was accordingly done
with great Art, and in the Preamble, several Expressions of
Civility to the *establisht Church*; and when it came to the Quali-
fications of all those who were to enter on any Office, the Compiler had taken special care to make them large enough for all
120 *Christians* whatsoever, by transcribing the very Words (only form'd
into an Oath) which *Quakers* are oblig'd to profess by a former Act
of Parliament; as I shall here set them down. *I* A. B. *profess*
Faith in God the Father, and in Jesus Christ his eternal Son, the
true God, and in the Holy Spirit one God blessed for ever more;
125 *and do acknowledge the holy Scriptures, of the Old and New Testa-*
ment to be given by Divine Inspiration. This Bill was carried to
the chief Leaders for their Approbation, with these terrible
Words turn'd into an Oath: What should they do? Those few among
them who fancy'd they believed in *God*, were sure they did not
130 believe in *Christ*, or the *Holy Spirit*, or one Syllable of the
Bible; and they were as sure that every Body knew their Opinion
in those Matters, which indeed they had been always too sincere
to Disguise; how therefore could they take such an Oath as that,

112 knowledge] knowlege ½° 12°

---

of the Test Act was not included in the Act of Union, there was published *A*
Letter from a Gentleman in Scotland to his Friend in England, against the
Sacramental Test; as Inconsistent with the Union (1708). Temple Scott's attri-
bution of this work to Charles Leslie (E*1922*, ix 141) is impossible, for the
author, who signed himself C. H. in the second edition (1709), is identified
in the Princeton Theological Seminary copy as John Humfrey, the ejected vicar
of Frome Selwood, Somersetshire, and minister to a dissenting congregation in
London. Swift's statement that the pamphlet was condemned by the House of Commons to be burnt by the hangman in January 1710 is confirmed (William Bisset,
A Dialogue between the Eldest-Brother of St. Katharine's, and a London-Curate,
London, for John Morphew, 1711, p. 17; Edmund Calamy, *An Historical Account of*
My Own Life, ed. John T. Rutt, 2nd edn., 2 vols., London, Henry Colburn *et al.*,
1830, i 371, ii 143-4).
   114 *a Presbiterian Preacher*: Humfrey was 'ordain'd by a classis of presbyters in 1649' (*DNB*, x 235).
   122-6 *I ... Inspiration*: 1 Gul. & Mar. c. 18 (*Statutes of the Realm*, vi
76), the so-called Act of Toleration.

without ruining their Reputation with *Tindal, Toland, Coward, Collins, Clendon*, and all the Tribe of *Free Thinkers*, and so *give*   135
a scandal to weak Unbelievers. Upon this nice point of Honour and Conscience the Matter was husht, the Project for repealing the *Test* let fall, and the *Sacrament* left as the smaller Evil of the two.

134 *Tindal*: 98.90.
   Toland: John Toland (1670-1722), the deist, was born near Londonderry, the 'Son of an *Irish* Priest by a *French* Cook' (Luke Milbourne, *A Letter from Tom o'Bedlam to the B--- of B---r's Jesuit*, London, J. Morphew, 1717, p. 5). Raised a Catholic, he became a Protestant before he was sixteen and was sent by some 'eminent dissenters' to the University of Glasgow. There he became a student activist, 'a Principal Man at Heading the Mob, and *Hallooing* them at the Clergy' (Charles Leslie, *Cassandra. (But I Hope not)*, No. II, London, 1704, p. 64; cf. *Original Letters of Eminent Literary Men*, ed. Sir Henry Ellis, London, for The Camden Society by J.B. Nichols and Son, 1843, p. 227). From Glasgow he proceeded to Leyden for two years and then to Oxford, where his behaviour was 'so publick and notorious' that he was ordered to depart. 'Evidence was ... offered upon Oath, of his Trampling on the Common prayer book, talking against the Scriptures, commending Commonwealths, justifying the murder of K. C[harles] 1st, railing against Priests in general, with a Thousand other Extravagancys' (*N&Q*, xiii (4 January 1862), 7). In September 1697 he was banished from Ireland and his most famous book, *Christianity not Mysterious* (1696), was ordered to be burnt by the common hangman. Harley put him to work writing against a standing army and sent him on a diplomatic mission to Hanover in the summer of 1701 (Swift, *Discourse*, pp. 36-42). In 1705, with Harley's 'encouragement', he wrote *The Memorial of the State of England* in reply to James Drake's *The Memorial of the Church of England* (1705) (*A Collection of Several Pieces of Mr. John Toland*, 2 vols., London, for J. Peele, 1726, ii 228). He returned to England in 1710 after several years on the continent, wrote against Sacheverell, and tried unsuccessfully to be employed again by Harley as a secret agent or propaganda writer. In the latter role he rated himself superior to Swift, whom he characterized—not inaccurately—as 'remarkable ... for his levity' (ibid., ii 222; cf. J.G. Simms, *Irish Historical Studies*, xvi (1968-9), 304-20).
   Coward: William Coward (1657?-1725) graduated MD from Merton College, Oxford, in 1687. In 1694 he was obliged to abandon his practice in Northampton on account of crim. con. 'with some Woman' and remove to London, where he resumed practice in Lombard Street. He wrote 'some Heterodox Books, about the Nature of the Soul', *Second Thoughts concerning the Human Soul* (1702) and *The Grand Essay; or A Vindication of Reason and Religion* (1704), that were ordered to be burnt by the common hangman on 17 March 1704 (Hearne, i 305; *CJ*, xiv 380).
135 *Collins*: 98.90.
   Clendon: John Clendon (d. 1719) of the Inner Temple, 'a common-Lawyer, and an old Villain', as Hearne called him, achieved notoriety by a single book, *Tractatus philosophico-theologicus de persona; Or, A Treatise of the Word Person* (1710), intended 'to expose and render mean and ridiculous the Doctrine of the Trinity'. It was ordered to be burnt by the common hangman on 25 March 1710, along with Tindal's *The Rights of the Christian Church Asserted* (1706), as a 'scandalous, seditious, and blasphemous' libel (Hearne, ii 367; *CJ*, xvi 385). The prosecution of Clendon failed through a fault in the indictment (Luttrell, vi 600).

140   *Fourthly*, These Pillars of the Church, because *the Harvest was*
       great, and the Labourers few, and because they would ease the
       Bishops from that grievous Trouble of *laying on Hands*; were will-
       ing to allow that Power to all Men whatsoever, to prevent that
       terrible Consequence of *unchurching* those, who thought a Hand
145   from under a *Cloak* as effectual as from *Lawn Sleeves*. And indeed,
       what could more contribute to the Advancement of true Religion,
       than a Bill of General *Naturalization for Priesthood*?

       Fifthly, In order to fix Religion in the Minds of Men, because
       Truth never appears so fair as when confronted with Falshood;
150   they directed Books to be Publish'd, that denied the being of a
       God, the Divinity of the *Second* and *Third Person*, the Truth of
       all Revelation, and the Immortality of the Soul. To this we owe
       that great Sense of Religion, that Respect and Kindness to the
       Clergy, and that true love of Virtue so manifest of late Years
155   among the Youth of our Nation. Nor could any Thing be more Dis-
       creet, than to leave the Merits of each Cause to such wise impar-
       tial Judges, who might otherwise fall under the Slavery of
       believing by *Education* and *Prejudice*.

       Sixthly, Because nothing so much distracts the Thoughts, as too
160   great a variety of Subjects; therefore they had kindly prepar'd
       a Bill, to prescribe the Clergy what Subjects they should Preach
       upon, and in what manner, that they might be at no loss; and this
       no doubt, was a proper Work for such Hands, so thoroughly vers'd
       in the Theory and Practice of all Christian Duties.

165   *Seventhly*, To save Trouble and Expence to the Clergy, they con-
       triv'd that *Convocations* should meet as seldom as possible; and
       when they were suffer'd to assemble, would never allow them to
       meddle with any Business; because they said, the Office of a

       168 with] w'th ½°

   140-6 *the ... few*: Matt. 9:37.
   145 *Cloak*: '*contemptuously* for: A Presbyterian or Independent minister'
   (*OED*).
   161 *Clergy*: 'it has been more than hinted by the Managers of the House of
   Commons, That the Clergy ought to be directed by the Civil Power, what Doctrine they should teach' (*The Life, Birth, and Character, of Joh. L[ord]*
   Haversham. With his Last Speech in ... Parliament, London, 1710, p. 5). Out-
   standing among these managers of Sacheverell's prosecution was James Stanhope,
   who argued that 'this Case ... shall determine what Doctrines ... shall or
   shall not be preached' (*The Tryal*, p. 112).
   166 *Convocations*: 141.139.

Clergyman was enough to take up the *whole Man*. For the same
Reason they were very desirous to excuse the Bishops from sitting   170
in Parliament, that they might be at more leisure to stay at Home
and look after the Clergy.

I shall mention at present but one more Instance of their pious
Zeal for the Church. They had somewhere heard the Maxim, that
Sanguis Martyrum est Semen Ecclesiæ; therefore, in order to *sow*   175
this Seed, they began with *Impeaching a Clergyman*: And that it
might be a true Martyrdom in every Circumstance, they proceeded
as much as possible against common Law, which the *long-Robe Part*
of the *Managers* knew was in a hundred Instances directly contrary
to all their Positions, and *were sufficiently warn'd of it before*   180
hand; but their Love of the Church prevail'd. Neither was this
Impeachment an Affair taken up on a suddain. For, a certain great
Person (whose Character has been lately Publish'd by some stupid
and lying Writer) who very much distinguish'd himself by his Zeal
in forwarding this *Impeachment*, had several Years ago endeavour'd   185

172 the] their ½° 12°   175 *Ecclesiæ*] *Eclesiæ* ½°

---

175 *Sanguis ... Ecclesiae*: Tertullian, *Apologeticus*, L 13.

176 *Clergyman*: Henry Sacheverell (1674-1724) was impeached by the House of
Commons (14 December 1709), tried before the House of Lords (27 February-20
March 1710), found guilty, and sentenced (23 March 1710) for 'a Wicked, Malicious and Seditious Intention to Undermine and Subvert Her Majesty's Government' in his sermon *The Perils of False Brethren, both in Church, and State*
(1709).

178 *Law*: Before publication Sacheverell took the precaution of submitting
his sermon to three lawyers, who assured him that it was not actionable at
ecclesiastical or civil law. This was also the opinion of the Government lawyers, so it was decided to proceed by an act of impeachment in the House of
Commons where the Whigs had a safe 2:1 majority (*Wentworth Papers*, pp. 99-100).

the *long-Robe Part*: Of the twenty members of the committee to impeach
Sacheverell, eleven were lawyers: Spencer Cowper, Sir David Dalrymple, John
Dolben, Robert Ayre, Sir John Hawles, Sir Joseph Jekyll, Sir Peter King,
Nicholas Lechmere, Sir Thomas Parker, Sir James Montagu, and William Thompson.

180-1 *were ... before hand*: These may be the words of Somers, who told Swift
that he had 'earnestly, and in vain endeavoured, to dissuade' Godolphin from
proceeding against Sacheverell by impeachment (Swift, *Prose*, viii 115). He
warned that unless they could be sure that the Lords would impose a heavy
sentence on Sacheverell, the ministers should resort to the courts of law
(Cunningham, ii 276-8). The Lords, of course, imposed a ridiculously light
sentence and confirmed Sacheverell as a popular martyr (*POAS*, Yale, vii 439).

184 *Writer*: Swift published *A Short Character of His Ex. T[he] E. of W[har-
ton]* in December 1710 (Swift, *Journal*, p. 115).

185 *Impeachment*: Sacheverell's impeachment was 'principally pushed on' by
Wharton and his aggressiveness during the trial was so well known that the
London mob threatened to pull down his house (Burnet, 1833, v 435; Boyer,
Annals, 1710, p. 266). Equally well known was his 'incomparable *witty* Jest ...

to persuade the late King to give way to just such another Attempt. He told his Majesty, there was a certain Clergyman preach'd
very dangerous Sermons, and that the only way to put a stop to
such Insolence, was to Impeach him in Parliament. The King en-
190   quir'd the Character of the Man; *O, Sir*, said my Lord, *the most
violent, hot, positive Fellow in* England; *so extreamly wilful,
that I believe he would be heartily glad to be a Martyr.* The King
answer'd, *Is it so? Then I am resolv'd to disappoint him*; and
would never hear more of the Matter; by which that hopeful Project
195   unhappily miscarried.

I have hitherto confin'd my self to those Endeavours for the
good of the Church, which were common to all the Leaders and
Principal Men of *Our* Party; but if my Paper were not drawing towards an end, I could produce several Instances of particular Per-
200   sons, who by their Exemplary Lives and Actions have confirm'd the
Character so justly due to the whole Body. I shall at present mention only two, and illustrate the Merits of each by a matter of
Fact.

That worthy Patriot, and *true Lover* of the Church, whom a *late
205   Examiner* is supposed to reflect on under the Name of *Verres*, felt
a pious impulse to be a Benefactor to the Cathedral of *Gloucester*,
but how to do it in the most decent, generous manner, was the
Question. At last he thought of an Expedient: One Morning or Night
he stole into the Church, mounted upon the Altar, and there did
210   that which in cleanly Phrase is called *disburthening of Nature*:

204 a] the ½° 12°

In calling Church-men *Cats*, and hurrying on | His wide-mouth'd *Non-Con* Beagles
to worry 'em' (*A Collection of Poems, For and Against Dr. Sacheverell*, 4 vols.,
London, 1710-11, i 8).
    187 *Clergyman*: probably William Sherlock (1641?-1707), whose heterodox ser-
mons on the Trinity scandalized his contemporaries in the 1690s. When one of
his disciples, Joseph Bingham, a fellow of University College, preached this
heterodoxy in St. Mary's, the University responded by condemning it as 'Falsa,
Impia, & Heretica'. Wharton's intervention in the affair is not otherwise
known, but William III resolved it, not by impeachment, but by ordering to be
published *Directions to Our Arch-Bishops and Bishops, for the Preserving of
Unity in the Church, and the Purity of the Christian Faith, Concerning the
Holy Trinity*, dated 3 February 1695/6.
    205 *Verres*: 71.129n. The fine for 'the great offense' that Wharton committed
in the church of Great Barrington was reduced to £40 and applied by the Bishop
of Gloucester, Robert Frampton, to the repair of Stow church, then 'decrepit
and unserviceable' (Bodl. MS Carte 103, f. 277; David Boyce, *The History and
Antiquities of Stow*, Stow-on-the-Wold, T. Clift, 1861, pp. 34-6).

He was discover'd, prosecuted, and condemn'd to pay a thousand
Pounds, which Sum was all employ'd to *support the Church*, as, no
doubt, the *Benefactor* meant it.

There is another Person whom the same Writer is thought to
point at under the Name of *Will Bigamy*. This Gentleman, knowing   215
that Marriage Fees were a considerable Perquisite to the Clergy,
found out a way of improving them *Cent. per Cent.* for the *good of
the Church*. His Invention was to marry a second Wife while the
first was alive, convincing her of the Lawfulness by such Arguments, as he did not doubt would make others follow the same   220
Example: These he had drawn up in Writing with intention to publish for the *general Good*; and it is hoped he may *now* have leisure
to finish them.

215 *Will Bigamy*: 67.28.
221 *Writing*: Delariviere Manley thought it was 'Mr. Sambrook of *New Forest*
[who] wrote the Defence of *Polygame*' (*The Key to Atalantis, Part I*). Jeremy
Sambrook, who succeeded as fifth baronet in 1740, was Elizabeth Culling's
neighbour at Gobions, once the estate of Sir Thomas More.

No. 15 [Mainwaring]   8 January 1711

The MEDLEY.

A Passage out of one of Cicero's *Orations.*
The Behaviour of the Examiner's *Clergy before and after the Revolution.*
An Answer to some Parts of his Paper, Numb. 22.

AFTER being much tir'd with reading the last *Examiner* but one, I
went into my Study for some Relief, and by a lucky Chance, the
first thing I look'd into, was an Oration of *Cicero*'s in which
there are some Passages that I cou'd not help taking particular
notice of. The whole Oration is chiefly design'd against one   5
Publius Clodius, whose Character perhaps every Reader does not
know: But in short he was one of the Chiefs in a Conspiracy to
overturn the Liberties of *Rome*, and had been a great Fomenter of

6 *Clodius*: Clodius (88.20), the 'embodiment in human form ... of all crime
and enormity' (Cicero, *De domo sua ad pontifices*, xlviii 126), may have suggested Sacheverell to Whig readers.

the Tumults and Rebellions *at that time*, and of the rifling and
10 burning of Houses; and had actually burnt *Cicero*'s own House.
This Man was design'd for one of the *then* new M-----y; and by
many Passages in this Oration, tho he was an Enemy to all good
Men, and a Friend to the worst, he appears to have been a High-
Churchman of those days: for he cover'd his Wickedness with a
15 specious Pretence of Zeal for Religion; and upon the very ground
where he had fir'd *Cicero*'s House, he immediately built a Temple.
Upon this Occasion the Orator has a noble Passage, which my
Friends are desir'd to see in the Original, and which I have
translated as well as I can, for the Use of the Gentlemen of the
20 other Side. *It is your Business*, says he, speaking to those that
had the Care of their Religion, *to decide this Day, whether you
will strip these mad and desperate Magistrates of their Guard of
wicked Citizens, or whether you will arm them with the Religion
of the Immortal Gods. For if this Blemish, this Incendiary of the*
25 *Commonwealth, is to defend his Pestilent and Deadly Ministry by
the Sacred Name of Divine Religion, when 'tis impossible for him
to do it by Human Equity; 'Tis high time to look out for other
Ceremonies, other Ministers of the Immortal Gods, and other Inter-
preters of Religion. But if by your Authority and Wisdom those*

12 this] his 12°   27 *Equity;*] ~: ½°

---

9 *Tumults*: On 27 February 1710, when Sacheverell's trial began in Westminster Hall, 'great Numbers of the Mobility attended him thither, and conducted
him back to his Lodgings in the *Temple*, with loud Huzzas ... The next Day, the
Mobb was still more numerous and louder about Dr. *Sacheverell*'s Coach, and, in
the Heighth of their petulant Zeal, oblig'd all Persons they met to pull off
their Hats to him, and abus'd those that refus'd to comply ... The same Evening, the Rioters went to the *Presbyterian* Meeting-House of Mr. *Burgess*, in a
Court near *Lincoln's-Inn-Fields*, of which they broke the Windows; and committed several other Outrages and Disorders ... On the 1st of *March* their Fury
being encreas'd with their Numbers, they advanc'd to greater Enormities, and
even *Overt-Acts* of Rebellion: For after they had attended upon Dr. *Sacheverell*
as usual, they repair'd to the *Meeting-House* before-mention'd; broke it open,
pull'd down the Pulpit, Pews, Benches, Wainscot, Sconces, Casements, in short,
all that was combustible, and having carried all these Materials into *Lincoln's-Inn-Fields* made a Bonfire of them, with repeated Cries of, *HIGH-CHURCH*
and *SACHEVERELL*' (Boyer, *Annals*, 1710, p. 265).
20-34 *It ... Citizens*: [Cicero, *De*] *domo sua ad pontifices* [i 2] (½°).
24 *Incendiary*: The Duchess of Marlborough remembered Sacheverell as 'an
ignorant, impudent incendiary' (*An Account of the Conduct*, p. 247). Defoe
called him 'Dr. *Firebrand*' (*Review*, 22 December 1709; cf. *A Character of Don
Sacheverellio, Knight of the Firebrand; In a Letter to Isaac Bickerstaff, Esq;
Censor of Great Britain* (no place or date of publication).

things shall be annul'd, that have been done by the Rage of   30
wicked Men, in this miserable Commonwealth, by some oppress'd, by
some deserted, and by others betray'd; then indeed we shall have
just reason to applaud the Prudence of our Ancestors, in settling
the Priesthood in the hands of our Chief Citizens. I wou'd not have
any little ignorant hot-headed Clergyman, or the 'Squire' of his   35
Parish, imagine that the *Roman* Orator was a Deist, or a Latitudinarian, or a Socinian; his Character is sufficiently establish'd
as to his Religion: And every body knows his Opinion of the Immortality of the Soul, which is deny'd by that Pillar of the
High-Church, Mr. *Dodwell. If in this I err, says Cicero, that I*   40
think the Souls of Men immortal, I err with Pleasure; nor will
ever, whilst I live, be forc'd out of an Opinion with which I am
so much delighted. So that one may almost say of him, that he was
a better Christian than some of our High-Churchmen. And what he
meant in the Passage I have translated, was no more than this;   45
That if their Priests, to whom he spoke, suffer'd undeserving Men
to shelter themselves under the Holy Cloak of their Religion; if
Burnings, Plunderings, Perjuries, Immoralities, Seditions, Tumults, and traitorous Attempts to destroy the Senate it self,
were to be countenanc'd by them, they wou'd soon be hated by the   50
People, and bring a Scandal upon Religion it self, when it appear'd, that *their Hearts had all along accompany'd their Fellow-*

---

35 *Clergyman*: Atterbury, 'A little ... man' (Swift, *Journal*, p. 156).
40 *Dodwell*: Henry Dodwell (1641-1711), born in Dublin and educated at
Trinity College, Dublin, became a distinguished medieval historian and a leading lay non-juror. He resigned a fellowship at Trinity College rather than
take orders, and the Camden Professorship of History at Oxford rather than
take the oaths to William and Mary. In February 1706 he published *An Episto-*
lary Discourse concerning the Soul's Immortality, arguing that the 'natural'
soul was made immortal at the moment of baptism, which 'shock'd the very
Foundation of Christianity' (Sir John St. Leger(?), *The Managers Pro and Con:*
Or, An Account of what is said at Child's and Tom's Coffee-Houses For and
Against Dr. Sacheverell, 3rd edn., London, A. Baldwin, 1710, p. 30).
40-3 *If ... delighted*: [Cicero,] *De senectut[e*, xxiii 85] (½°).
48 *Immoralities*: Sacheverell's private life is the subject of William Bisset, *The Modern Fanatick. With a Large and True Account of the Life, Actions,*
Endowments, &c. of the Famous Dr. Sa——l, of which two parts were published
in 1710.
52-3 *their ... Rome*: By changing '*England*' to 'Rome' Mainwaring is enabled
to quote the opening words of the address of the Bishop and clergy of London
and Westminster presented to the Queen on 22 August 1710, in the context of
Clodius' Roman mob (*A Collection of the Addresses*, ii 29). This is the address
that Mainwaring presumably 'Paraphras'd' in lively satirical verses (*POAS*,
Yale, vii 454).

Subjects, the Genuine Sons *of the Churches of* Rome at that time,
in their Attempts against the Liberties of the People and Author-
55   ity of the Senate.

There is no Man can doubt the Truth of this, and therefore I am
at a loss to know what my worthy Friend the *Examiner* means, by
putting us in mind of the Behaviour of the Violent Clergy before
the Revolution. I will not disoblige him for a small matter, and
60   therefore we will recollect all the fine Sermons that they
preach'd for Absolute Monarchy, the Surrenders of Charters, which
they influenc'd, the Abhorrences which they sign'd, and the
Guineas which the two famous Universities of our Land, *Oxford* and
Cambridge, contributed to Sir *Roger L'Estrange*, for writing on
65   the side of Arbitrary Power. I will grant too, that when they had
by all these Means betray'd King *James* into his Mismanagements,
they turn'd against him, and came into the Revolution. But how
did they come? Aukwardly, Ill-favour'dly: Their Oaths had like to
have stuck in their throats; and their Pupils have been instructed
70   since, to thank God they had no hand in it.

I need not say, I mean all this only of the *Examiner*'s Clergy:
There are in *England*, and were then, many Learned, Temperate,

---

60 *Sermons*: Mainwaring is replying to 127.31-2.

61 *Charters*: In 1682, Burnet says (i 527-8), 'The Court was every where
triumphant ... The Cities and Boroughs of *England* were invited, and prevailed
on, to demonstrate their loyalty, by surrendring up their Charters, and
taking new ones modelled as the Court thought fit ... So that it looked like
a strange degeneracy, when all these were now delivered up; and this on design
to pack a Parliament that might make way for a Popish King ... Yet no part of
it was so unaccountable, as the high strains to which ... most of the Clergy
were carried.' 'And what is more strange,' Rapin adds (Tindal, ii 734), 'the
English themselves surrendered to *Charles* II. those very Rights and Privileges
which they had defended with so much passion ... against the attempts of
Charles I.'

62 *Abhorrences*: 90.46.

64 *L'Estrange*: Sir Roger L'Estrange (1616-1704) was *chef de propagande* and
licenser of the press for Charles II and James II, famous for his printing-
house raids '*with his little Pack of inferiour Crape-gown-Men yelping after
him*' (Thomas Shadwell, *Some Reflections upon the Pretended Parallel in the
Play called The Duke of Guise*, London, for Francis Smith, 1683, p. 8). His
most effective propaganda appeared in *The Observator*, in which he kept up a
relentless attack on dissenters and the first Whigs from April 1681 to March
1687. In June 1681 Luttrell records that 'the masters and graduates' of Cambridge collected £200 'as an acknowledgment of [Sir Roger's] good services'
(Luttrell, i 93). Mainwaring himself, who was an undergraduate student at
Christ Church from 1683 to 1687, is sufficient authority for Oxford.

69 *Pupils*: This may be another recollection of Mainwaring's undergraduate
days. At that time it would have seemed to him a most appropriate instruction.

Worthy Men of that Order; and many of the *London* Clergy were de-
servedly made Bishops. The present Archbishop is one of those who
made a noble Figure in defence of the Church of *England*: But does   75
that protect him from being an Object of this·Writer's Virulence?
His Predecessor's Learning, Eloquence, and Piety were an Honour
to the Age he liv'd in; but have they been able to skreen him
from the Malice of these superfine Churchmen? Tho if it had not
been for his Arguments against Popery, and his Labours in *the*   80
first Conversion of a certain Nobleman, they had at this time
wanted a very great Head of their Party.

   But tho I never thought of being serious with my Friend, this
Argument is of so much importance, that I can't help answering
some Parts of his Paper more distinctly: How little regard soever   85
is due to him, there can't be too much shewn to the Cause and the
Men that he attacks. I shall therefore pass over his Politicks
for this time, which grow so furiously silly, that I believe they
will obtain a general Derision by their own Weight: I shall not
say a word of his Method, *to maintain our Bishops and Clergy*, and   90
yet *SUFFER our Gentry to live in a decent hospitable manner*: Nay,
I shall not so much as congratulate him upon his *Herrings* and
Nutmegs, and his Jingle of a *Warehouse* and a *Workhouse*; but shall

---

   73 *Clergy*: Of the eight pre-Revolution London divines mentioned below
(159.127-30), seven were made bishops: Wake (Lincoln, July 1705), Tillotson
(Canterbury, April 1691), Tenison (Lincoln, October 1691; Canterbury, December
1694), Stillingfleet (Worcester, September 1689), Patrick (Chichester, September 1689; Ely, April 1691), Kidder (Bath and Wells, July 1691), Grove (Chichester, April 1691).
   77 *Predecessor*: John Tillotson. One of·the 'superfine Churchmen' is Stephen
Nye, who accused Tillotson of being a Socinian (*Considerations on the Explica-
tions of the Doctrine of the Trinity. Occasioned by Four Sermons Preached by
His Grace the Lord Arch-bishop of Canterbury*, London, 1694, p. 43). Another is
George Hickes, who quotes a witty lord, Charles Sackville, Earl of Dorset, who
called Tillotson 'Mr *Hobs* in the Pulpit' (*Some Discourses upon Dr. Burnet and
Dr. Tillotson*, London, 1695, p. 48).
   81 *Conversion*: Charles Talbot (1660-1718) succeeded as 12th Earl Shrewsbury in March.1668. The family had always been Catholic but the young earl was
converted to the Church of England by Tillotson in 1679-81 'when Popery began
very much to prevail in *England*' (*The Life and Character of Charles Duke of
Shrewsbury*, London, for J. Roberts, 1718, pp. 4-5; HMC *Frankland-Russell-
Astley MSS*, p. 42). Shrewsbury's reconversion to Catholicism was rumoured to
have occurred during his residence in Rome (November 1701 to the Spring of
1705) (*POAS*, Yale, vii 549). Mainwaring calls him 'A Double convert' in some
verses preserved in BL Add. 61462.
   90-1 *maintain ... manner*: 130.97-9.
   92-3 *Herrings and Nutmegs*: 130.94-5.
   93 *Warehouse and ... Workhouse*: 131.102.

make a few Remarks on his more grave Absurdities and Falshoods.

For several years past, he says, *there hath not, I think, in*
95 Europe *been any Society of Men upon so unhappy a foot as the*
Clergy of England, *nor more hardly treated by those very Persons,*
from whom they deserv'd much better Quarter, &c. This is plainly
the *Foot* of the Revolution, so very *unhappy* to *his Clergy*; and
the *Persons* who have so *hardly treated* them, must be the Princes
100 and Ministers ever since that time. Very decent Gratitude! When
all the Clergy (except Non-Jurors) have not only shar'd in the
common Blessings of the Revolution, but have had their particular
Benefits in it; and the very boldest of them can't say, they are
depriv'd of any thing but the Power of persecuting others.

105   *The Clergy,* he says, *are known to have rejected all Advances*
made them to close with the Measures at that time concerting (he
means before the Revolution) *while the Dissenters, to gratify*
their Ambition and Revenge, fell into the basest Compliances, &c.
This may be true of *Persons,* but shou'd not be affirm'd of
110 whole *Parties;* for the *Clergy* did not All *reject the Advances,*
nor did *All* the Dissenters gratify those Passions of Ambition
and Revenge. There was a *Cartwright,* a *Parker,* and *Hall* among the

94-7 *For ... Quarter:* 125.10-126.13.
104 *persecuting:* cf. Swift, *Prose,* ii 122.
105-8 *The ... Compliances:* 126.18-21.
110 *whole Parties:* Mainwaring scores here, for Swift knows that 'it is ill
arguing from Particulars to Generals' (299.38-9), but he frequently forgets it.
112 *Cartwright:* Thomas Cartwright (1634-89) was 'ambitious and servile,
cruel and boisterous' (Burnet, i 695). Although not a Catholic himself, he was
a secret conspirator to re-establish Catholicism in England and was nominated
Bishop of Chester in December 1686. He served on the court of high commission
for ecclesiastical causes and managed the illegal proceedings against the
President and fellows of Magdalen College, Oxford. He extorted an address from
the clergy in his diocese answering the seven bishops—the seven golden candle-
sticks of the church (*POAS,* Yale, iv 215)—who refused to read James's second
Declaration of Indulgence (April 1688). As a result he became so unpopular
that he had to flee with James and died, appropriately, of dysentery in Dublin (*DNB,* iii 1141).
     Parker: Samuel Parker (1640-88), raised a strict Presbyterian, ordained
in the Church of England, and an active collaborator with Roman Catholics in
the reign of James II, was consistent only in his belief that the best body
of divinity is 'that which would help a Man to keep a Coach and six Horses'
(*Somers Tracts,* ii 509). James nominated him Bishop of Oxford in August 1686
and President of Magdalen College in August 1687.
     Hall: Timothy Hall (1637?-90), 'one of the meanest and most obscure of
the City-Divines ... had indeed no Merit but that of Reading the King's
Declaration [of Indulgence]' (Kennett, iii 491). He was consecrated Bishop of
Oxford in October 1688, but the canons of Christ Church refused to install him
(*DNB,* viii 976).

New Prelates, and some *Ecclesiastical Commissioners* among the Old;
and a small number of the Inferior Clergy, who read the *Declara-*
tion for dispensing with the Laws. Yet this is no Reproach to the   115
whole *Order*, that a few in comparison were faulty: The Misfortune
is, that those very Men came into the Revolution with all their
Reluctances about them, and have been ever since both uneasy and
unfaithful.

  It shou'd likewise be remember'd, he says, *to the everlasting*   120
Honour of the London *Divines, that, in those dangerous Times,*
they writ and publish'd the best Collection of Arguments against
Popery that ever appear'd in the World. ----But here the *World*
shou'd be told, that those Writers were not the *Divines* to whom
he intends any present Honour; not one of the now Parochial   125
Clergy in or about *London*, whom he dignifies with being *perfectly*
pleas'd with the present Turn of Affairs, but the *Tillotson's,*
Stillingfleet's, Patrick's, Kidder's, Grove's, Sherlock's, who
died before these happy Changes, with the *T-n-s--'s, Ll--d's,*
Bu---t's, W-k-'s, and others, who now live under the Displeasure   130
of this Writer and his Party.

  At the Revolution the Body of the Clergy join'd heartily in the
Common Cause. Here he might have stopt; but he delighted to go

113 *Ecclesiastical Commissioners*: James II instituted an ecclesiastical
commission in July 1686 'to exercise visitatorial jurisdiction over ecclesiastical or semi-ecclesiastical persons and institutions' (Ogg, iii 176). Its
original members were three 'Old' prelates (i.e. created by Charles II): William Sancroft, Archbishop of Canterbury (who refused to serve and was replaced
by Cartwright), Nathaniel Crew, Lord Crew, Bishop of Durham, Thomas Sprat,
Bishop of Rochester, and four laymen: Lord Chancellor Jeffreys, Robert Spencer,
Earl of Sunderland, Lord President of the Council, Lord Chief Justice Sir
Edward Herbert, and Laurence Hyde, Earl of Rochester, Lord Treasurer. 'Issueing
and causeing to be executed a Commission under the Great Seale for Erecting a
Court called The Court of Commissioners for Ecclesiasticall Causes' was one of
the charges against James II in the Bill of Rights (1689) (*Statutes of the*
Realm, vi 142).
  114-15 *Declaration*: 126.23-4n.
  118 *Reluctances*: The most celebrated 'Reluctance' was that of William Sherlock. His hesitation in taking the oaths of supremacy and allegiance to William
and Mary, and his reasons for finally doing so, pleased no one and earned him
the nickname of Dr Weasel (*POAS*, Yale, v 245).
  120-3 *It ... World*: 127.29-33.
  126-7 *perfectly ... Affairs*: 134.175-6.
  129 *Changes*: 2.29. Mainwaring points out the irony that some of the '*Lon-*
don Divines' of the time of James II of whom the Examiner approves (127.30)
are now Whig bishops (Tenison, Wake) under the Examiner's disapproval. The
point is obscured by the fact that Lloyd and Burnet were not '*London* Divines'
in the time of James II.
  132-3 *At ... Cause*: 127.33-4.

on, and said, *except a few, whose Sufferings perhaps have aton'd*
135   *for their Mistakes*; and they who join'd heartily did it *like Men,*
who are content to go about for avoiding a Gulph or Precipice,
but come into the old strait Road as soon as they can. Well!
granting the *Sufferings* of the Non-Jurors to exceed their *Mis-*
takes; yet, in his own meaning, the Clergy, who first *join'd*
140   *heartily*, and then went back, or round about again to what he
calls the *old strait Road*, were a little more cowardly, and have
put us into greater Confusion, than they who had the sturdiness
to give no ground, in spite of *Gulph and Precipice*.

What a violent Humour, he says, *hath run ever since against the*
145   *Clergy*: He means again since the Revolution. And one of the Proofs
he gives of this violent Humour, is, That *the Representatives of*
the Lower Clergy have been rail'd at for disputing the Power of
the Bishops; and that *by such Persons as are the known Abhorrers*
of Episcopacy. But I wou'd be glad to know when it was, that any
150   Abhorrers of Episcopacy have at all meddled in this Controversy
between the two Houses of Convocation; and whether, if they
enter'd into that Dispute, it wou'd not be more natural for the
Abhorrers of Episcopacy to take part with the *Lower Side* reviling
their Bishops, than to rail at the Inferior Clergy, for disputing
155   the Power of their Diocesans. Not but in the mean time, they may
be a little tempted to *abhor* the Hypocrisy of Men, who brought in
a Declaration of *the Divine Right of Episcopacy* in one hand,
whilst at the same time they thrust the other into the Faces of

134-7 *except ... can*: 127.34-7.
144-5 *What ... Clergy*: 128.46.
146-9 *the ... Episcopacy*: 128.56-8
157 *Declaration*: In the Convocation of 1702-3 the Lower House drafted the
following Declaration and submitted it to the bishops for their concurrence:
'Whereas the Clergy of the Lower House of Convocation have bin by the discourses and writings of several persons very Malitiously, and Scandalously
misrepresented, as if they were favourers of presbytery in Opposition to Episcopacy, and were Enemys to the just Rights, privilidges, prerogatives, and
Jurisdiction of Bishops over the presbyters, as they are Established by the
Laws of God, and of this Land ... Wee ... doe hereby declare, That wee acknowledge the Order of Bishops as Superior to presbyters to be of Divine Apostoli-
call Institution, and that wee [claim no] other Rights ... than [those] ...
necessary to the very Being of the Lower House of Convocation' (Lambeth Palace
MS Conv. I/2/8, f. 22). This was really 'a party trick ... to entrap the
bishops into a decision of a question which it was not competent for them to
decide, since to have done so would have been an infringement of the Act of
Submission' (Lathbury, *History of the Convocation*, 1853, p. 380; cf. Burnet,
ii 346-7).

the Archbishop and Bishops; and in prejudice to their Persons,
deny'd them those Rights, on the Preservation and Exercise of   160
which the very Being of an Episcopal Church depends; I mean the
Superiority of Bishops, and the Subordination of Presbyters. As
to the Complaint in general of this *violent Humour* that has long
run against my Friend's Clergy, I am sorry for it; but let him
not talk of *Leaders that incourag'd it*, nor *of Men of Wit im-*   165
ploy'd about it. They that broach such Doctrines as the Mortality
of the Soul, and the Independency of the Clergy on the State:
They that absolve for High Treason, and damn for Separation; and
the Authors of those Cart-Loads of Rubbish that are written in
the Stile of the condemn'd Doctor: These are the Leaders that   170
have occasion'd this Humour against them; and they are so far
from being ridicul'd by Men of Wit, that, God knows, they are not
Wits that do it; they ridicule themselves.

What my Friend says, of a *Staff and a Pair of Shoes to be left*
at the Door of our Clergy, with his rude Application of a Text in   175
the *Revelation* to her Majesty, shall be consider'd in my next.
Nor will I forget, by that time, to inform my self of the matter
of Fact he reports, concerning what lately pass'd between the two
Houses of Convocation; which I will venture to say beforehand is
misrepresented by him, knowing my Friend's natural Aversion to   180

---

176 *Revelation*] *Revelations* ½°

---

161 *the very Being*: Mainwaring mocks the lower clergy by repeating the
words of their declaration (160.157n.).
163 *violent Humour*: 128.46.
165 *Leaders*: 128.49.
165-6 *Men ... imploy'd*: 128.63.
167 *Soul*: 155.39.
        Clergy: cf. 'The Inferiour Clergy ... claim an equal and co-ordinate
Power with their Bishops, an Exemption from the Queen's Supremacy, and an absolute Independency of the Church from the State' (Mainwaring, *Four Letters to
a Friend in North Britain, upon the Publishing the Tryal of Dr. Sacheverell*,
London, 1710, p. 18).
168 *Treason*: The reference may be to the Tories in both Houses of Parliament in 1696 who voted solidly against a bill of attainder of the Jacobite
conspirator, Sir John Fenwick (1645?-97), who was unquestionably involved in a
plot to assassinate William III. Harley was particularly opposed to the bill
(Oldmixon, *The History*, pp. 156-8).
180 *misrepresented*: Swift's account of the opening of Convocation is
accurate except in one detail (173.108n.), but it fails, not unexpectedly, to
represent Archbishop Tenison's point of view. Anne's letter to the Archbishop
of 13 December 1710, drafted by Atterbury, includes two errors: it claims
that Convocations have 'in all Time' been coterminous with Parliament, which

Truth, and unmerciful Temper towards Men of Moderation, whether
they be Ecclesiastical or Civil.

But, he says, God be thank'd, they and their Schemes are
vanish'd, and their PLACES SHALL KNOW THEM NO MORE. One of their
185 certain *Schemes* was to reduce the Exorbitant Power of *France*, and
to restore the Monarchy of *Spain*: and I dare say they wou'd not
have this *Scheme vanish* under any Administration whatsoever; but
will join heartily with any sort of Hands to carry it on, and if
possible to compleat it. And as to *themselves*, what if their
190 PLACES KNOW THEM NO MORE, they will still, like honest Men, pursue the true Interest of their Country; and for that most desirable End, they will bear being thus insulted, in Remnants of
Scripture. But that is a Liberty which none but my Friend and his
Churchmen are wicked enough to make use of; and therefore I shall
195 confine my self, upon this occasion, to another Passage of *Cicero*
in the same Oration: which not only shews that People may be
driven from their Places, and restor'd to them again, let the
Conspirators be ever so powerful; but also gives an Account of
the different Condition of Affairs upon his own Banishment and
200 Return: *Whereas*, says he, *at my Departure there succeeded Poverty,*
Famine, Devastation, Burning, Rapines, Impunity of Wickedness,
Flight, Fear and Discord: So at my Return, by the Favour of the
Immortal Gods, Fruitful Fields, Plenteous Harvests, Hopes of
Leisure, Tranquillity of Mind, JUSTICE, the Laws, Agreement among
205 *the People, and the Authority of the Senate; all these Blessings*
seem to return with me.

To the former part of this Description, other People have seen
a Parallel; whether there will ever be one to the latter, Time
only can shew.

is not true, and it invokes both Houses to lay aside disputes about 'Unnecessary Forms and Methods of Proceeding'. Since the 'Forms and Methods' of con-
vening and proroguing the Lower House were the crux of the difference between
the two Houses, the Archbishop could not believe that his right to convene
and prorogue the Lower House was 'Unnecessary'. 'The very nature of an *Eccle-*
siastical Synod requires it shou'd be convened [and prorogued] in some such
way' (Wotton, *The Case of the Present Convocation Consider'd*, 1711, p. 16).
    183-4 *But ... MORE*: 131.115-16.
    200-6 *Whereas ... me*: Cicero, *De domo sua ad pontifices*, vii 17.

No. 24 [Swift]   11 January 1711

The EXAMINER.   .

Bellum ita suscipiatur, ut nihil aliud nisi Pax quæsita videatur.

I Am satisfy'd, that no reasonable Man of either Party, can justly
be offended at any thing I said in one of my Papers relating to
the Army; from the Maxims I there laid down, perhaps many Persons
may conclude, that I had a mind the World should think, there had
been occasion given by some late Abuses among Men of that Call-   5
ing; and they conclude right. For my Intention is, that my Hints
may be understood, and my Quotations and Allegories applied; and
I am in some pain to think, that in the *Orcades* on one side, and
the *Western* Coasts of *Ireland* on the other, the *Examiner* may want
a *Key* in several Parts, which I wish I could furnish them with.   10
As for the *French* King, I am under no Concern at all; I hear he
has left off reading my Papers, and by what he has found in them,
dislikes our Proceedings more than ever, and intends either to
make great Additions to his Armies, or propose new Terms for a
Peace: So false is that which is commonly reported, of his mighty   15
Satisfaction in our Change of Ministry: And I think it clear that
his late Letter of Thanks to the *Tories* of *Great Britain*, must
either have been extorted from him against his Judgment, or was
a Cast of his Politicks to set the People against the present
Ministry, wherein it has *wonderfully* succeeded.   20
    But tho' I have never heard, or never regarded any Objections
made against that Paper, which mentions the Army; yet I intended
this as a sort of Apology for it. And first, I declare, (because
we live in a mistaking World) that in hinting at some Proceedings,
wherein a few Persons are said to be concern'd, I did not intend   25

Motto Cicero, *De officiis*, i 23: In all free Governments War should be
undertaken only with a View to procure a solid and lasting Peace.
    5 *occasion*: 116.149n.
    16 *Satisfaction*: 141.150.
    17 *Letter*: Hoadly, *The French King's Thanks to the Tories of Great-Britain*,
London, for A. Baldwin, 1710 (E1922, ix 145-6).
    21 *Objections*: Swift ignores 137.22-138.39.
    25 *not intend*: Swift seems to defend himself for falling into the inductive
fallacy (158.109) by denying the intention.

to charge them upon the Body of the Army. I have too much detested
that barbarous Injustice among the Writers of a late Party, to be
ever guilty of it my self; I mean the accusing Societies for the
Crimes of a few. On the other side, I must take leave to believe,
30   that Armies are no more exempt from Corruptions than other Numbers of Men. The Maxims propos'd were occasionally introduced by
the Report of certain Facts, which I am bound to believe is true,
because I am sure, considering what has passed, it would be a
Crime to think otherwise. All Posts in the Army, all Employments
35   at Court, and many others, are (*or ought to be*) given and resumed
at the meer Pleasure of the Prince; yet when I see a great Officer
broke, a Change made in the Court or the Ministry, and this under
the most just and gracious Princess that ever reign'd, I must
naturally conclude it is done upon prudent Considerations, and
40   for some great Demerit in the Sufferers. But then; is not the
Punishment sufficient? Is it Generous or Charitable to trample on
the Unfortunate, and expose their Faults to the World in the
strongest Colours? And would it not suit better with Magnanimity
as well as common Good-nature, to leave them at quiet to their
45   own Thoughts and Repentance? Yes without Question, provided it
could be so contriv'd that their very Names, as well as Actions,
might be forgotten for ever; *such* an Act of Oblivion would be for
the Honour of our Nation, and beget a better Opinion of us with
Posterity; and then I might have spar'd the World and my self the
50   trouble of *Examining*. But at present, there is a cruel *Dilemma* in
the Case: The Friends and Abettors of the late Ministry are every
Day publishing their Praises to the World, and casting Reflections
upon the present Persons in Power. This is so barefac'd an Aspersion upon the Q----, that I know not how any good Subject can
55   with Patience endure it, tho' he were ever so indifferent with
regard to the Opinions in Dispute. Shall they who have lost all
Power and Love of the People, be allow'd to scatter their Poison;
and shall not those, who are, at least, of the strongest side,
be suffer'd to bring an Antidote? And how can we undeceive the
60   deluded Remainder, but by letting them see, that those discarded
Statesmen were justly laid aside, and producing as many Instances
to prove it as we can? Not from any personal Hatred to them, but

31 *Maxims*: 113.55-6, 114.87-90, 116.146-50.

in Justification to the best of Queens. The many Scurrilities I
have heard and read against this poor Paper of mine, are in such
a strain, that considering the present State of Affairs, they   65
look like a Jest. They usually run after the following Manner:
What? Shall this insolent Writer presume to censure the late
Ministry, the ablest, the most faithful, and truest Lovers of
their Country, and its Constitution, that ever serv'd a Prince?
Shall he reflect on the best H---- of C------ that ever sate   70
within those Walls? Has not the Queen chang'd both for a Ministry
and Parliament of Jacobites *and* High-flyers, *who are selling us*
to France, *and bringing over the* Pretender? This is the very Sum
and Force of all their Reasonings, and this their Method of complaining against the *Examiner*. In *Them* it is humble and loyal to   75
reflect upon the Q---- and the Ministry, and Parliament she has
chosen with the universal Applause of her People; in *Us* it is
insolent to defend Her Majesty and Her Choice, or to answer their
Objections, by shewing the Reasons why those Changes were necessary.   80

  The same Style has been used in the late Case relating to some
Gentlemen in the Army; such a Clamor was raised by a Set of Men,
who had the Boldness to tax the Administration with Cruelty and
Injustice, that I thought it necessary to interfere a little, by
shewing the ill Consequences that might arise from some Proceed-   85
ings, tho' without Application to particular Persons. And what do
they offer in Answer? Nothing but a few poor Common-places against
Calumny and *Informers*, which might have been full as just and
seasonable in a Plot against the Sacred Person of the Q----.

  But, by the way; why are these idle People so indiscreet to   90
name those *two Words*, which afford occasion of laying open to the
World such an infamous Scene of *Subornation* and *Perjury*, as well
as *Calumny* and *Informing*, as I believe is without Example: When
a whole *Cabal* attempted an *Action*, wherein a *condemn'd Criminal*

67 *What? Shall*] *What shall* ½° 12°   69 *Constitution,*] ~⌃ ½°   81 relating to] concerning 38 8°+12°

---

68 *ablest*: 119.26n.
81 *Case*: 116.149n.
87 *Common-places*: 107.109-111.204.
94 *Cabal*: 39.127.
    Criminal: Greg (E1738).

95   refus'd to join with them for the Reward of his Life? Not that I
     disapprove their Sagacity, who could foretel so long before, by
     what *Hand* they should one day fall, and therefore thought any
     Means justifiable by which they might prevent it.

         But waving this at present, it must be own'd in Justice to the
100 Army, that those Violences did not proceed so far among them as
     some have believed; nor ought the Madness of a *few* to be lay'd at
     their Doors. For the rest, I am so far from denying the due
     Praises to those victorious Troops, who did their Part in procur-
     ing so many Victories for the *Allies*, that I could wish every
105 Officer and private Soldier had their full share of Honour in
     proportion to their Deserts; being thus far of the *Athenian*'s
     Mind, who when it was propos'd that the Statue of *Miltiades*
     should be set up *alone* in some publick place of the City, said
     they would agree to it, *whenever he conquer'd alone*, but not be-
110 fore. Neither do I at all blame the Officers of the Army, for
     preferring in their Hearts the late Ministry before the present;
     or, if wishing alone could be of any use, to wish their Continu-
     ance, because then they might be secure of the Wars continuance
     too: Whereas, since Affairs have been put into other Hands, they
115 may perhaps lie under some apprehensions of a Peace, which no
     Army, especially in the course of Success, was ever inclin'd to,
     and which all wise States have in such a Juncture, chiefly en-
     deavour'd. This is a Point wherein the Civil and Military Poli-
     ticks have always disagreed. And for that Reason, I affirm'd it
120 necessary in all free Governments, that the latter should be
     absolutely in Subjection to the former; otherwise, one of these
     two Inconveniencies must arise, either to be perpetually in War,
     or to turn the *Civil* Institution into a *Military*.

         I am ready to allow all that has been said of the Valor and
125 Experience of our Troops, who have fully contributed their Part
     to the great Successes abroad; nor is it their *Fault*, that those
     important Victories had no better Consequences at Home, tho' it
     may be their *Advantage*. War is their Trade and Business: To im-
     prove and cultivate the Advantages of Success, is an Affair of

        108 City,] ∼∧ ½° L LU NjP PU TxU CSmH CLU-C   ∼; 38 8°+12°

        _____

        106 *the Athenian*: Sophanes of Decelea (Plutarch, *Life of Cimon*, viii 1).
        119 *affirm'd*: 114.87-8.

the Cabinet; and the neglect of this, whether proceeding from   130
Weakness or Corruption, according to the usual Uncertainty of
Wars, may be of the most fatal Consequence to a Nation. For, pray
let me represent our Condition in such a Light, as I believe both
Parties will allow, though perhaps not the Consequences I shall
deduce from it. We have been for above nine Years, blest with a   135
QUEEN, who besides all Virtues that can enter into the Composition of a private Person, possesses every Regal Quality that can
contribute to make a People happy. Of great Wisdom, yet ready to
receive the Advice of Her Councellors: Of much Discernment in
chusing proper Instruments, when She follows Her own Judgment,   140
and only capable of being deceived by that excess of Goodness
which makes Her judge of others by Herself. Frugal in Her Management in order to contribute to the Publick, which in proportion
she does, and that voluntarily, beyond any of Her Subjects; but
from Her own Nature, generous and charitable to all that want or   145
deserve; and in order to exercise those Virtues, denying Herself
all Entertainments of Expence which many others enjoy. Then if we
look abroad, at least in *Flanders*, our Arms have been crown'd
with perpetual Success in Battles and Sieges, not to mention
several fortunate Actions in *Spain*. These Facts being thus stated, 150
which none can deny, 'tis natural to ask how we have improv'd
such Advantages, and to what Account they have turned? I shall use
no discouraging Terms. When a Patient grows daily worse by the
tampering of Mountebanks, there is nothing left but to call in
the best Physicians before the Case grows desperate: But I would   155
ask, whether *France* or any other Kingdom, would have made so
little use of such prodigious Opportunities, the Fruits whereof
could never have fallen to the Ground, without the extreamest
degree of Folly and Corruption, and where those have lain, let
the World judge: Instead of aiming at Peace, while we had the   160
Advantage of the War, which has been the perpetual Maxim of all
wise States, it has been reckon'd Factious and Malignant even to

131 Weakness] Weekness ½°   145 that] who 38 8°+12°   160 judge:] ~?
½° 12°

143 *contribute*: Besides Queen Anne's Bounty (129.79n.), Anne gave £100,000 to
the Palatine refugees, spent £200,000 building Blenheim, and contributed
£100,000 to the expense of the war (Burnet, ii 628).
154-5 *Mountebanks ... the best Physicians*: cf. 'A Sharper ... an honest
Gentleman' (86.155-8).

express our Wishes for it; and such a Condition impos'd, as was
never offered to any Prince who had an Inch of Ground to dispute;
165 *Quæ enim est conditio pacis; in qua ei cum quo pacem facias,
nihil concedi potest?*

It is not obvious to conceive what could move Men who sate at
home, and were call'd to consult upon the Good of the Kingdom,
to be so utterly averse from putting an end to a long expensive
170 War, which the Victorious, as well as Conquer'd side, were
heartily weary of. Few or none of them were Men of the Sword;
they had no share in the Honour; they had made large Fortunes,
and were at the Head of all Affairs. But they well knew by what
Tenure they held their Power; that the Qu--- saw thro' their
175 Designs; that they had entirely lost the Hearts of the Clergy;
that the Landed Men were against them; that they were detested by
the Body of the People; and that nothing bore them up but their
Credit with the Bank and other Stocks, which wou'd be neither
formidable nor necessary when the War was at an end. For these
180 Reasons they resolved to disappoint all Overtures of a Peace,
'till they and their Party should be so deeply rooted as to make
it impossible to shake them. To this end, they began to precipitate Matters so fast, as in a little time must have ruin'd the
Constitution, if the Crown had not interpos'd, and rather ven-
185 tur'd the accidental effects of their Malice, than such dreadful
Consequences of their Power. And indeed, had the former Danger
been greater than some hoped or fear'd, I see no difficulty in
the Choice, which was the same with his, who said, *he had rather
be devoured by Wolves than by Rats.* I therefore still insist that
190 we cannot wonder at, or find Fault with the Army, for concurring
with a Ministry who was for prolonging the War. The Inclination
is natural in them all, pardonable in those who have not yet made

175 Designs;] ~, ½° 12°   186 had the former Danger] if the former
Dangers had 38 8°+12°

163 *Condition*: 9.176-8n.
165-6 *Quae ... potest*: Cicero, *Philippics*, xii 4 11: For what kind of
peace is that where no concession can be made to the men with whom you make
peace?
188-9 *he ... Rats*: cf. the German version: 'Better to be devoured by the
wolf than the fleas' (*A New Dictionary of Quotations on Historical Principles
from Ancient and Modern Sources*, ed. H.L. Mencken, New York, Knopf, 1976,
p. 1312).

their Fortunes, and as lawful in the rest, as Love of Power or
Love of Mony can make it. But as natural, as pardonable, and as
lawful as this Inclination is, when it is not under check of the   195
Civil Power, or when a corrupt Ministry joins in giving it too
great a Scope, the Consequence can be nothing less than infallible
Ruin and Slavery to a State.

After I had finish'd this Paper, the Printer sent me two small
Pamphlets, call'd *The Management of the War*, written with some   200
Plausibility, much Artifice, and abundance of Misrepresentation,
as well as direct Falshoods in point of Fact. These I have
thought worth *Examining*, which I shall accordingly do when I find
an Opportunity.

200 *Pamphlets*: *The Management of the War. In a Letter to a Tory-Member*
(1710) and *The Management of the War. In a Second Letter to a Tory-Member*
(1710) were written by Francis Hare, Chaplain-General to the army in Flanders
and a confidant of Marlborough. Mainwaring 'revis'd and corrected them ... so
much, that they might, indeed, have well past for his own' (Oldmixon, *Memoirs*,
p. 20).

No. 16 [Mainwaring]   15 January 1711

The MEDLEY.

Further Remarks on the Examiner, Numb. 22.

His Account of what pass'd in the Convocation, disprov'd.

Of Synods and Councils, Antient and Modern.

I Promis'd in my last to take further notice of some Passages in
the *Examiner, Numb.* 22.

Among the *Republican Politicks*, he represents it to be one of
the *noble Schemes*, that the Clergy *shou'd be prescrib'd what to
teach, by those who are to learn from them, and upon default, to*   5
have a Staff and a Pair of Shoes left at their Door. Set down
this Wit, as borrow'd from a late Tryal, and then add to the

1 *Promis'd*: 161.174-6.
3-6 *Republican ... Door*: 131.103-13.
7 *Wit*: Swift's witticism appears to have been borrowed from Toland and
Tindal (131.112n.), but it does recur in the literature of the Sacheverell trial
(*The Jacobite Plot: Or The Church of England in no Danger. To which is Annex'd
Tom's New Declaration to all the Gentlemen of the Broomstick and Mopstaff Regiments*, [London], 1710, p. [16]).

Account, that in all Christian States and Kingdoms whatsoever, if
the Clergy did not confine themselves to the Truths of the Gospel,
10 but wou'd break out into meddling with publick Persons and
Affairs; then the Prince or People restrain'd them within their
former Bounds, and justly punish'd those who went beyond them.
Nor can the Peace of any Government be otherwise maintain'd. The
contrary *Liberty of Prophesying* wou'd put it into the power of
15 any one *Crumholt*, or other Doctor, to disturb a City, and shake
all the Foundations of Trade and Credit in it. All our Kings, and
Queens, and Parliaments, since the Reformation, have acted upon
this restraining Principle; and the *Examiner*, Great Man! ought to
have known, that the Queen her self has *now* follow'd the Example
20 of her wisest Predecessors, in sending an *Admonition* to all her
own Chaplains, that they shou'd preach no more Politicks before
her Majesty. And there never was a Juncture when this Command
more deserv'd to be put into a Law, that it might be a check upon
many other Preachers, especially within the City; where, from the
25 Arraignment of *Sach-------l*, there has been most intemperate,
seditious, nay blasphemous Preaching: for the Sufferings of our
Saviour have been apply'd to magnify those of that vile Incendiary. But whatever the High Clergy thinks to get by this, 'tis
certain Religion suffers by it: The Interest of both, it seems,
30 can't be advanc'd together; which plainly shews that they are not
the same. And therefore I am afraid the Church will be in *real
Danger* at last, unless more regard be had to those unfashionable

---

15 *Crumholt*: Christian Krumbholtz (1663-1725) was pastor of St. Petri's in
Hamburg. His sermons so excited the burghers against the magistrates that he
was tried for treason, found guilty, and in October 1710, just before the
Sacheverell trial, sentenced to be deprived of his benefices and imprisoned
for life (Zedler, xv 1989; Luttrell, vi 642).

20 *Admonition*: may not have been published; cf. [Henry Compton, Bishop of
London,] *Seasonable Advice to the Ministers of the Church of Great Britain,
(Especially to those in and about the City of London) Not to meddle, as some
have done, with Matters of State, or Controversial Preaching*, London, R. Hal-
sey, 1710. This is a verbatim reprint of Compton's *The Bishop of London's
Seventh Letter of the Conference with his Clergy, held in the Year 1686* (1690),
which in turn is based on James II's *Directions concerning Preachers* (1685).

26 *Preaching*: 'The Clergy did generally espouse *Sacheverel*, as their
Champion' and sermons were preached everywhere exhorting the people to demon-
strate in his favour (Burnet, ii 540). One of the Queen's chaplains, Benjamin
Parker, was suspended by the Bishop of London on the Queen's orders 'for pray-
ing for Dr. *Sacheverell*'s Deliverance from Persecution in her Majesty's
Chapelle' (Hearne, ii 356).

27 *Saviour*: cf. 172.81n.

Divines, who, under a Load of Reproach for Moderation, are content to preach up Peace.

His next Wit and Manners are bestow'd upon her Majesty, in a   35
remarkable Passage, as he calls it, quoted from the *Revelation,*
where the Serpent with seven Heads cast out of his Mouth Water
after the WOMAN like a Flood, that he might cause her to be
carry'd away of the Flood: But the Earth help'd the WOMAN, and
the Earth open'd her Mouth, and swallow'd up the Flood which the   40
Dragon had cast out of his Mouth. For the Queen having chang'd
her Ministry, &c. My Friend was so pleas'd with this Quotation,
and in such fear lest his meaning shou'd be mistaken, that in his
next Paper, *Numb.* 23. he explains it himself in these words: That
it is true indeed, this is a *manifest Corruption of the Text; for*   45
the words seven Heads *are not mention'd in that Verse.* However,
we must needs *know what Serpent he wou'd mean, a Serpent with*
fourteen Legs, or indeed no Serpent at all, but seven Great Men.
And thus he goes on archly, in that most ingenious Paper before-
mention'd, where he *Cross-examines* himself, which I think the   50
finest of all his Writings, and recommend to every Reader that
desires to see Humour in Perfection. This shew'd how wrong an
Interpretation others had given of his Passage, who wou'd needs
have it, that by his Serpent with seven Heads he meant seven
excellent Prelates, who had the Misfortune in a certain Tryal not   55
to vote as he wou'd have had them. And this they insisted upon
as a natural Reflection for my Friend to make, out of his singular Love to the *Inferior Clergy*: But he soon convinc'd them of
their Error. However, it must be confess'd, that this happy Interpreter of Prophecies gives a new Key to the 12th Chapter of the   60
Revelation, and dropping *Rome* and Antichrist, roundly makes the

---

34 *Peace:* Amid a 'Rage and Fury of ... Party' worse than Clement had ever
seen (*A Vindication of the Faults on both Sides,* 1710, p. 29), the voices
calling for peace were those of unfashionable Low Church divines: John England,
Pray for the Peace of Jerusalem; a Sermon (1710), Swift's 'little parson cousin', Thomas Swift, *Noah's Dove: an Exhortation to Peace set forth in a Ser-*
mon (1710), the historian of the reformation of manners. Josiah Woodward, *The*
Christian Peacemaker: being an affectionate Vote for Mutual Love and Good Will
amongst Protestants (1710).
37-42 *the ... Ministry:* 131.121-132.126.
45-8 *a ... Men:* 144.31-5.
55 *Prelates:* The seven bishops who voted Sacheverell guilty were Gilbert
Burnet of Salisbury, William Talbot of Oxford, John Moore of Ely, Richard
Cumberland of Peterborough, William Fleetwood of St. Asaph, Charles Trimnell
of Norwich, and William Wake of Lincoln.

Serpent with seven Heads to have been some late prevailing Monster, consisting of seven Great Men; and by the *Woman*, he very
decently means the Queen (civil and well bred!) and the *Earth* he
65   supposes to be the multitude of People or the Mob, and the drying
up of the *Flood* is the fulfilling of the Prophecy, or Alteration
of the M-------y, which is the same thing: And I wonder he did
not proceed, and copy what is written in the 6th Verse, That *the
Woman was forc'd to fly into the Wilderness*. The Parallel had
70   been as exact in that, as in any other Particular: But some of
his Acquaintance stop'd him there, otherwise I am confident he
wou'd have blunder'd on. But after all, what an idle Man is my
Friend grown, to touch the Scriptures with his profane Hands, and
to offer in earnest or in jest to interpret them, and to acknow-
75   ledg the adding of his own words to the Text? This rallying in
Scripture-Phrases is not only a gross Impiety, but the dullest
Insolence and Rudeness that can be committed. To do it either in
the serious or in the ludicrous Vein, if the matter does by no
means bear it, is an equal Contempt of God and of his Word. There
80   were too many of these Airs in a late Speech recited by a Doctor
in *Westminster-Hall*, where Scripture-Expressions and Allusions
came roundly in, with no Truth, and very little Likeness of it.
The same wicked Humour has defil'd many of the publick Papers
written on the same side, and breaks out at last in this *Examiner*.
85   But I am troubled to find he is dabbling in the *Revelation*, because a very learned and witty Man of his own High-Church, laid
it down for a Maxim, That *he never knew any Writer meddling with
that Book, but it found him mad, or left him so*. Indeed my Friend
may better be trusted to follow that Study, than most others,
90   having in his Composition a certain Antidote against Madness, as

75-6 *rallying in Scripture-Phrases*: 131.121-132.126.
   80 *Speech*: Sacheverell's answer on 7 March 1710 to the articles of impeachment was a long speech that he read 'in a very haughty and assuming Stile'
(Burnet, ii 540). One auditor '*really expected ... a Thunder-Bolt from Heaven
to strike him dead*' (Bisset, *The Modern Fanatick*, 1710, p. 23). Mainwaring
believed that it was written by three chaplains-in-ordinary to the Queen:
Atterbury, Smalridge, and Dr Robert Moss (Oldmixon, *The Life*, p. 112). The
speech is now accepted as the work of Atterbury, whom Mainwaring also believed
to be the Examiner.
   81 *Scripture*: The peroration of Sacheverell's answer is a pastiche of
'Scripture-Expressions' from the Pauline epistles and the Acts of the Apostles
to suggest that Sacheverell himself is another type of suffering apostle.
   87-8 *That ... so*: Robert South, *Twelve Sermons Preached upon several Occasions*, 3 vols., London, by J.H. for Thomas Bennet, 1692-8, ii 569.

every body may find that looks into his Papers; in which he de-
cays so sensibly every Week, that they put me in mind of a Story
I have heard of Mr. *Dryden*. When a Gentleman came from one of Mr.
D'Urfey's Plays, the first Night it was acted, and said, *Was
there ever such stuff! I cou'd not have imagin'd that even this*   95
Author cou'd have written so ill: Oh! Sir, reply'd the Old Bard,
you don't know my Friend Tom *so well as I do; I'll answer for
him, he shall write worse yet.*

I come now to the *Matter of Fact*, relating to the Convocation,
which I undertook to enquire into, and have found my Friend's   100
Account of it exactly answers my Expectation: For in order to
fall upon the Archbishop and Bishops, he shamefully represents
some things, and supplies others from his own Invention: *The
Upper House*, he says, *having form'd an Address to the Queen, before they receiv'd her Majesty's Letter, sent both Address and*   105
*Letter together to the Lower House, with a Message excusing their
not mentioning the Letter in the Address, because this was form'd
before the other was receiv'd.* Positively not so: the *Pious Prolocutor* knows, that he and the Lower House were first sent for up
to the Archbishop and Bishops, where the Archbishop in due   110
respect to the Queen's Letter, read it himself standing, and
keeping the Letter as directed only to him, promis'd to send a
Copy of it to the Lower House. And so the Upper House did not
send both Address and Letter together. No! The Prolocutor carry'd
down the *Address* himself, and after reading and debating on it,   115
then came the Copy of the *Letter*. Nor again, did the Upper House
send any *Message excusing their not mentioning the Letter in the
Address*: The Archbishop told them (as they say) by word of mouth,

92 *Story*: In the last decade of the seventeenth century, when Mainwaring
was much in Dryden's company, Durfey wrote twelve plays (*NCBEL*, ii 762).
103-8 *The ... receiv'd*: 133.147-51.
108 *not so*: The Examiner said that the Lower House received the Queen's
letter and the bishops' address in reply 'both ... together' (133.148-9) on 13
December 1710. Mainwaring says correctly that the Lower House received a copy
of the letter while they were debating the address (Lambeth Palace MS Conv.
I/2/11, f. 2^V).
112 *directed*: 'Her Majesty's Letter was directed to the *Archbishop* alone,
as *President of the Convocation of the Province of* Canterbury' (Wotton, *The
Case of the Present Convocation Consider'd*, 1711, p. 11).
117-8 *Message ... Address*: 133.149-50. 'The Bishops did not excuse their
not mentioning the Queen's Letter in the *Address* which [the Prolocutor carried]
down to the Lower House; because they knew his Grace wou'd wait upon Her
Majesty on purpose about that Matter' (ibid., p. 12).

That tho the Address was drawn up before they receiv'd the Queen's
120 Letter, yet he hop'd the Address might seem to answer to some
Parts of it; or to that effect.

His Relation of Fact goes on thus: *The Lower House return'd
them (*i.e.* the Address and the Letter) *with a Desire that an
Address might be form'd, with due Regard and Acknowledgements for
125 *the Letter.* I am more rightly inform'd, that the *Lower House* did
not *return them.* For they did not meddle with any Return of the
Copy of the Queen's Letter, unless they return'd it to *Abel R.*
who put it the next day into his *Post-Boy.* Nor did the Lower
House *desire that an Address might be form'd with due Regard and*
130 *Acknowledgments for the Letter*: But only, that in the same Address
there might be some Addition, taking notice of that Gracious Letter. And to this Motion their Lordships did agree, and made an
additional Amendment to that purpose. The Clause was this: *Your*
Majesty's most Gracious Letter to the Lord Archbishop of Canter-
135 bury *our President, has been by Him communicated to Us; for which*
We return our most Humble and Dutiful Thanks. But this *Mention,*
says the *Examiner*, the *Lower House did not think sufficient*, and
sent it back again: And he complains, that by this means no
Address at all was sent to the Queen; not considering that this
140 casts Imputation upon the Lower House, who did finally reject it,
tho some of the Members in that House pleaded heartily for it.
He says, That *hereupon the Archbishop, after a short Consultation*
with SOME of his Brethren, immediately adjourn'd the Convocation
for a Month. I presume, he consulted with all his Brethren; tho
145 this *Examiner*, out of Love and Kindness, wou'd distinguish *Some*

122-5 *The ... Letter*: 133.151-3. The quibble on 'return' is intended to
introduce the leak to *The Post-Boy*. What Atterbury carried to the Upper House
was the agreement of the Lower House to the address 'Provided an Addition be
made thereto in which Due Notice shall be taken of her Majties most Gracious
Letter' (Lambeth Palace MS Conv.I/2/11, ff. 3^V-8).
128 *Post-Boy*: The Queen's letter was leaked to *The Post-Boy*, 16 December
1710. It appears from this detail, recorded in similar terms in White Kennett's diary (BL MS Lansdowne 1024, f. 241^V), that Kennett was Mainwaring's
source in the Convocation. The Queen's letter was reprinted in *The British*
Mercury, 18 December 1710, and in *The Daily Courant*, 19 December 1710.
129-30 *desire ... Letter*: This is another quibble, for the Examiner's
'Acknowledgments for the Letter' is identical with Mainwaring's 'Addition'.
133-6 *Your ... Thanks*: Lambeth Palace MS Conv. I/2/11, f. 8^r.
136-44 *this ... Month*: 133.155-9.
144 *all*: Fifteen of the twenty-two members of the Upper House were present
on 15 December 1710 when Tenison prorogued the Convocation to 17 January
(Lambeth Palace MS Conv. I/1/17, p. 89).

of them. By their Consent his Grace did prorogue the Convocation
to the Middle of *January*, as it had been usual, to have some
Recess at *Christmas*, that the Clergy might attend their own Cures
and Families. But this my Friend is angry at: And to all this
foul Representation, he adds but one Truth; which is, That *he*   150
understands not Ecclesiastical Affairs well enough to comment
upon this Matter: Yet they who are thought to assist him understand them better, and must have better inform'd him, if they had
not purposely left *him* in the dark, to conceal their *own Appear-*
ance with him. Thus much at least is certain, that he himself   155
understood nothing of the matter, and therefore humbly suffer'd
himself to be impos'd upon. Let his Assistants answer for so imposing upon the World: For as to what concerns himself, there
seems to be no possibility of Amendment; and therefore 'tis in
vain to hope by any Detection of this kind to inform the Ignor-   160
ance, or reprove the Malice of this unhappy Writer.

My Friend, who is so well pleas'd with the present Face of
Affairs, because 'tis new, and not like the Prospect we had a
Year ago, wou'd be strangely disgusted if I shou'd talk to him of
such old things as Synods and Councils: Of the first *Lateran*   165
Council, for example, where there were a thousand Bishops at once,
and not one *Inferior Clergyman*, who did not own them to be their
Heads. Where there was no Desire of Superiority, no Claim of
Independency: in short, where there were no Rebellious Sons to
the Fathers of the Church; but they were all the most Peaceable,   170
Obedient, Meek, Moderate, and Charitable People in the Universe.
What dull times were these! And how different were such Synods
from those, that one of the Fathers gives an account of! *From*
which, he says, *he never saw any Good come, nor any Remedy of*
Evil in the Church, but rather an Increase: For, he adds, *their*   175
Contentions and Desire of Lording, no Tongue is able to express.

151-2 *understands ... Matter*: 133.160-1.
162 *pleas'd*: 167.135-50.
165-6 *first Lateran Council*: Mainwaring or his source has conflated two
ecumenical councils, the first Lateran Council (1123), said to be attended by
over 300 bishops, and the second Lateran Council (1139), attended by about
1,000.
173 *one*: Nazianzen (½°).
174-6 *never ... express*: Jean Le Clerc, *The Lives of Clemens Alexandrinus,*
Eusebius Bishop of Caesarea, Gregory Nazianzen, and Prudentius the Christian
Poet, London, for Richard Baldwin, 1696, p. 269.

But every body is sensible there is none of that Spirit in the
World at this time. And therefore I know not why the *Examiner* is
in so terrible a Concern, lest *all Methods of serving the Church*
180 *and Kingdom, by means of a Convocation, shou'd come to nothing.*
If nothing has been done by it these Hundred Years, to reason
from thence that nothing will be done hereafter, is an unfair way
of arguing. Besides, every body is convinc'd, that if some People
were let alone, enough wou'd be done in all conscience. But his
185 Fear, I believe, arises from this: It is our misfortune to have
an *Upper House* and a *Lower House*; and the Upper House must needs
have its Privileges as well as the Lower, which is a very hard
Case, especially when the Inferior Clergy have *the Scale of*
General Favour on their side. And this is the true Reason, I sup-
190 pose, why he cannot see how any Good can be done by such an Assembly. But I will tell him further, that his *Inferior Clergy* themselves are a little to blame. I have often thought it a great
pity, that since they have it so much in their power to set all
Matters to rights, they shou'd waste any part of their precious
195 Minutes in Disputes who shou'd *Adjourn* them, and in whom that
Supream Power is lodg'd, which is by some of 'em reckon'd to be
above the *Supream Head*; whether 'tis lodg'd in *Upper* or *Lower*, or
rather *Lower* and *Upper*, according to the Humour we are every
where in to turn things upside down. For tho these Disputes are
200 of vast importance, 'tis true, yet considering how much his *In-*
ferior Clergy have Reformation of Manners at heart, I wonder they

186 Upper House must] Upper must 12°

179-80 *all ... nothing*: 133.161-3.
188-9 *the ... side*: 134.173-4.
195 *Adjourn*: 133.158n.
197 *Supream Head*: By the Act of Supremacy (1534) the king was declared to
be 'the onely supreme hede in erthe of the Churche of England' (*Statutes of*
the Realm, iii 492); cf. 161.167n.
201 *Reformation of Manners*: The Society for the Reformation of Manners had
been founded by 'Five or Six Private Gentlemen of the Church of *England*' (John
Dunton, *The Post-Angel*, December 1701, p. 457; BL MS Add. 30000D, f. 277), but
it was taken up and expanded largely by dissenters. Sacheverell had railed
against it almost from the beginning: 'the ... Duties of *Peace*, and *Quietness*,
Forbearance, and *Forgiveness* ... command us not to ... meddle with those Concerns that do not belong to us, or under the *Sanctify'd Pretence* of *Reforma-*
tion of Manners, to turn *Informer*, assume an Odious and Factious Office,
arrogantly intrench upon Other's *Christian Liberty*' (James Owen, *Moderation*
a Virtue: or, The Occasional Conformist justify'd from the Imputation of

shou'd engage in such debates, rather than think of stopping
that *Inundation of Atheism, Profaneness, and Licentiousness,*
which the *Examiner* says, *are overwhelming us*: The rather because,
as unequal as the *Scale of Favour* is, the *Upper* wou'd most cer-   205
tainly go heartily to work with the *Lower*, in giving any reasonable Check to such Corruptions. And therefore I begin to suspect
at last, that no Decrees of this kind are intended; but that they
are in extream want of some other new Articles and Canons, there
being not above one or two at present which those Fanaticks the   210
Dissenters refuse subscribing to. But this is a Grievance hard to
be redress'd under the present Set of Bishops; or, to use the
words of my Friend, which no body can be weary of, *Time and Mor-*
tality can only remedy these Inconveniences in the Church, which
are not to be cur'd like those in the State by a Change of   215
Ministry. In the mean while I will venture to affirm thus much,
That if at any time hereafter the Inconveniences in the Church
shall be as happily cur'd as those in the State are, we may with
Comfort and Confidence affirm, that they will Both be safe for
ever.   220

Hypocrisy, London, for A. Baldwin, 1703, p. 15; Sacheverell, *The Communication*
of Sin: A Sermon preach'd at the Assizes held at Derby, August 15th, 1709,
1709, p. 8).
   203-4   *that* ... *us*: 131.116-18.
   210   *one or two*: '*Dissenters* ... disagree about the *Use* of *Godfathers and*
Godmothers, and the *Marking* with the *Sign* of the *CROSS* in *Baptism*. They are
against *Kneeling* in the receiving of the *Sacrament*' (John Greenwood, *The Mis-*
chief of Prejudice; or Some Impartial Thoughts upon Dr. Sacheverell's Sermon,
London, J. Baker, 1710, p. 14). The exceptionable practices, however, are
prescribed not by the Articles on Baptism (XXVII) or Holy Communion (XXVIII-
XXXI), but by the prayer book (*The Book of Common Prayer*, London, by the
Assigns of John Bill *et al.*, 1683, sigs. 12^{r}, 19^{r}).
   213-16   *Time* ... *Ministry*: 135.193-5.

No. 25 [Swift]   18 January 1711

The EXAMINER.

Parva momenta in spem metumq; impellunt animos.

HOPES are natural to most Men, especially to sanguine Complexions, and among the various Changes that happen in the Course of publick Affairs, they are seldom without some Grounds: Even in desperate Cases, where it is impossible they should have any Foundation,
5 they are often affected, to keep a Countenance, and make an Enemy think we have some Resource which they know nothing of. This appears to have been for some Months past the Condition of those People, whom I am forc'd, for want of other Phrases, to call the *Ruin'd Party*. They have taken up since their Fall, some real, and
10 some pretended Hopes. When the E. of *S-------d* was discarded, they *hoped* Her M------ would proceed no farther in the Change of Her Ministry (Fig. IV), and had the Insolence to misrepresent Her

7 some] several 38 8°+12°

Motto Livy, xxvii 45 5: The meerest Trifles influence the human Mind and impel it to Hope or Fear.
  11 *no farther ... Change*: Upon Sunderland's dismissal (14 June 1710), the Whigs' 'next Attempt was to play the Bank upon Her Majesty' (*Faults on both Sides*, 1710, p. 37). Four Whig directors of the Bank of England, Sir Gilbert Heathcote, Sir William Scawen, Francis Eyles, and John Gould, represented to the Queen the ill effects of any further changes: 'all credit would be gone, stock fall, and the Bank be ruined' (Luttrell, vi 594; HMC *Portland MSS*, iv 545; Defoe, *Review*, 13 July 1710). People were shocked at the spectacle of 'Directors of a Bank attempting to be Directors of National Affairs' (*The Gun-Smiths Queries*, no place of publication, 1710).
  12-13 *misrepresent ... to Foreign States*: The first response of *'Joab* [Marlborough], and *Vulp* [Godolphin]' to Sunderland's dismissal was to involve the Allies ([Atterbury,] *To the Wh--s Nineteen Queries, A Fair and Full Answer, by an Honest Torie; Purely for the Publick Good of his Country*, London; for J. Baker, 1710, p. 4). Accordingly, before the end of June, Martinus van Vrijbergen, the Dutch envoy, delivered a memorial complimenting the Queen upon her decision to make no more changes in the ministry or to dissolve Parliament. Anne was furious (*Marlborough—Godolphin Corr.*, pp. 1520, 1532, 1548), but Mainwaring pursued the attack in a folio half-sheet of July 1710 which was not only '*Hawked* about the Streets' of London, but also 'with great industry, dispers'd in *Holland*', making the Queen say '*She would make no farther Alterations in her Ministry*' ([Leslie,] *Beaucoup de Bruit pour une Aumelette, Or, Much a Do about Nothing*, London, 1710, p. 14; [Boyer,] *An Essay towards the History of the Last Ministry and Parliament*, 1710, p. 22; [Mainwaring,] *A Letter from Monsieur Pett--m to Monsieur B-ys. Faithfully Translated from the French Original*, London, 1710; cf. *The Examiner*, No. 1, 3 August 1710).

THE
B---k of ENGLAND's

Most Loyal

ADDRESS to Her M----y.

WE your M----y's most Audatious, Imperious, Directing, and Commanding Subjects, the Governour and Royal Company of the B--k of *England*, assembled at G----H----, in the City of *London*, on the 20th of *June* 1710.

Do unwilling and most sorrowfully imbrace, the unfortunate Opportunity of giving your M----y our unnatural, and unhearty Assurances, and non-performances; and that we are not willing, nor I doubt at this Juncture, shall not be very ready to Sacrifice our Lives and Fortunes, and all things else that is near and dear to us, in the Defence of your most sacred Prerogative, Person and Government against the *French* King, his Grand-son and the Pretender to your Crown and Dignity, unless your M---- will give Us leave to direct You and your great Council of the Nation, what Persons in your Government are most fitting at this critical time to be employ'd and intrusted in Offices, and State Affairs.

And if your M--- and your Council should turn out the Low-Church Party, those peaceful and moderate Gentlemen without our Advice, we shall take upon us to say, and to make your M--- sensible, that your P--------y Funds are already low, and will be very Deficient; so shall also the Credit of this Great and Noble B--k follow in an instant, if such Honourable Persons, whose known Loyalty to the Crown, and great Interest and Stock in it are displaced.

And therefore if your Most Gracious M---- will have our true and faithful Obedience to your Person, and our hearty Assistance to your Government; with our Hands, Hearts, and Purses, 'tis but reasonable ; and we think fit to Advise, to keep in such as we are very well assured are fit to be intrusted by your most Gracious M----

If not, we do assure your M----, that our zealous Brethren will be true to their own Interest, and are resolved to stand by one another, and will draw their Stock out of the B--k of *England*, and then it will be shut up as the Exchequor was in King *Charles* the Second time; and then what will be the consequence of that, you may very easily guess.

Then 'twill be no doubt, good Night Madam to your Great Q---- S----, and to the Money in the B--k, which otherwise might have carried on the Wars against *France* and *Spain*; and then you may also hoop for your Assistance, either by the P----, or your D---- h A----.

This is the most true, sense, and harty Advice, which we present unto your most Gracious M----, from them that has been very Instrumental in making You (and now wou'd unmake you) Q---- of G---- B----.

To which most humble and loyal Address, Her M---- was most Graciously pleas'd to make this Reply

Gentlemen,

I Have a greater Regard to the publick Credit of the Nation, than any of my Subjects ; And I design to have those about me, that I can Confide in ; and I shall Discountenance those, that Contribute to make my Reign Uneasie.

FINIS.

LONDON: Printed in the Year, 1710.

Vet. A4 a. 4 (44)

The B--k of England's Most Loyal Address to Her M-----y . . . London, 1710, folio halfsheet

Words to Foreign States. They *hoped*, no Body durst advise the
Dissolution of the Parliament: When this was done, and further
Alterations made at Court, they *hoped* and endeavour'd to ruin   15
the Credit of the Nation. They likewise *hoped* that we should have
some terrible Loss abroad, which would force us to unravel all,
and begin again upon their Bottom. But, of all their *Hopes*,
whether real or assum'd, there is none more extraordinary than
that which they now would seem to place their whole Confidence   20
in: That this great Turn of Affairs was only occasion'd by a
short Madness of the People, from which they will recover in a
little time, when their Eyes are open, and they grow cool and
sober enough to consider the Truth of Things, and how much they
have been deceived. It is not improbable, that some few of the   25
deepest sighted among these Reasoners, are well enough convinc'd
how vain all such *Hopes* must be: But for the rest, the wisest of
them seem to have been very ill Judges of the Peoples Dispositions, the want of which Knowledge was a principal Occasion to
hasten their Ruin; for surely had they suspected which way the   30
popular Current inclined, they never would have run against it
by that *Impeachment*. I therefore conclude, they generally are so
blind, as to imagine some Comfort from this fantastical Opinion,
that the People of *England* are at present distracted, but will
shortly come to their Senses again.   35
    For the Service therefore of our Adversaries and Friends, I
shall briefly *Examine* this Point, by shewing what are the Causes

23 open] opened 38 12°

---

14 *Dissolution*: 'Trouble not your self about that' (Defoe, *Review*, 4 July
1710). Anne dissolved the Parliament on 21 September 1710 (Luttrell, vi 633).
15-16 *ruin the Credit*: cf. 'we hop'd to occasion the Appearance of a full
Stop in Publick Credit' (Davenant, *Sir Thomas Double at Court, and in High
Preferment*, 1710, p. 84).
17 *terrible Loss abroad*: cf. 'you [Englishmen] seemed at present to flag
under a Satiety of Success, as if you wanted Misfortune as a necessary Vicissitude' (Steele, *The Tatler*, 20 June 1710). The loss that was hoped for in
June 1710 came in November (145.52n.).
22 *short Madness*: cf. '*They* [the Godolphin ministry] *were of Opinion, That*
Mr. *H---y* calling in to his Assistance the Hot Tory Party ... would run himself a Ground, plunge the Government into insuperable Difficulties, and so
the Queen ... would be forced to have recourse to the Whiggs, to set all to
rights again' (Defoe, *Eleven Opinions about Mr. H---y; With Observations*,
London, for J. Baker, 1711, p. 30).
32 *Impeachment*: 151.176n.

and Symptoms of a People's Madness, and how it differs from their
natural Bent and Inclination.

40   It is *Machiavel*'s Observation, that the People when left to
their own Judgment, do seldom mistake their true Interests; and
indeed they naturally love the Constitution they are born under,
never desiring to change but under great Oppressions. However,
they are to be deceiv'd by several Means. It has often happen'd
45 in *Greece*, and sometimes in *Rome*, that those very Men who have
contributed to shake off a former Tyranny, have, instead of
restoring the old Constitution, deluded the People into a worse
and more ignominious Slavery. Besides, all great Changes have
the same Effect upon Commonwealths that Thunder has upon Liquors,
50 making the *Dregs* fly up to the Top: The lowest *Plebeans* rise to
the Head of Affairs, and there preserve themselves by representing the Nobles and other Friends to the Old Government, as Enemies
to the Publick. The encouraging of new Mysteries and new Deities,
with the Pretences of further Purity in Religion, hath likewise
55 been a frequent Topick to mislead the People. And, not to mention
more, the promoting false Reports of Dangers from abroad, hath
often serv'd to prevent them from fencing against real Dangers at
home. By these and the like Arts, in Conjunction with a great
Depravity of Manners, and a weak or corrupt Administration, the
60 Madness of the People hath risen to such a height as to break in
pieces the whole Frame of the best instituted Governments. But
however, such great Frenzies being artificially rais'd, are a perfect Force and Constraint upon Human Nature, and under a wise
steddy Prince, will certainly decline of themselves, settling like
65 the Sea after a Storm, and then the true Bent and Genius of the
People will appear. Ancient and Modern Story are full of Instances

65 Sea] Seas 38 8°+12°

40-1 *People ... Interests*: Machiavelli, *Discourses*, i 4.
45 *Greece ... Rome*: cf. Swift, *Discourse*, pp. 91-111.
50 *Dregs fly up*: cf. 'it is with Human Faculties as with Liquors, the
lightest will be ever at the Top' (Swift, *Tale*, p. 183).
54 *further Purity in Religion*: '[They were] call'd *Puritans*, because
they set up for a greater Purity of Worship' (Defoe, *A New Test of the Church
of England's Loyalty: Or, Whiggish Loyalty and Church Loyalty Compar'd*, no
place of publication, 1702, p. 9).
62 *Frenzies ... artificially rais'd*: cf. '*Religious Enthusiasm* ... as it is
purely an Effect of Artifice and *Mechanick Operation*' (Swift, *Tale*, p. 269).

to illustrate what I say. In our own Island we had a great Example
of a long Madness in the People, kept up by a thousand Artifices
like intoxicating Medicines, till the Constitution was destroy'd;
yet the malignity being spent, and the Humour exhausted that   70
serv'd to foment it; before the Usurpers could fix upon a new
Scheme, the People suddenly recover'd, and peaceably restor'd the
old Constitution.

   From what I have offer'd, it will be easie to decide, whether
this late Change in the Dispositions of the People were a new   75
Madness, or a Recovery from an old One. Neither do I see how it
can be prov'd that such a Change had in any Circumstance the
least Symptoms of Madness, whether my Description of it be right
or no. 'Tis agreed, that the truest way of judging the Dispositions of the People in the Choice of their Representatives, is by   80
computing the County-Elections; and in these, 'tis manifest that
five in six are entirely for the present Measures; altho' the
Court was so far from interposing its Credit, that there was no
Change in the Admiralty, nor above one or two in the Lieutenancy,
nor any other Methods us'd to influence Elections. The free un-   85
extorted Addresses sent some time before from every part of the

   84 nor] not ½° 12°

---

   84 *Admiralty*: There were in fact changes—Sir John Leake replaced Orford
as First Lord of the Admiralty on 4 October 1710—but they were made too late
to swing the patronage of the Navy behind the new ministry's candidates.
   Lieutenancy: Of the thirty-nine lord-lieutenants only three Whigs were
replaced (by Rochester, Henry Somerset, 2nd Duke of Beaufort, and James Douglas, 4th Duke of Hamilton, in Cornwall, Hampshire, and Lancashire, respectively)
and complaints were made that the court had done so little (Davenant, *New Dialogues upon the Present Posture of Affairs*, 1710, p. 26; *Lockhart Papers*,
i 319).
   85 *Elections*: During the election Swift had been told 'that Mr. Harley himself would not let the Tories be too numerous, for fear they should be insolent, and kick against him', but later Swift decided that 'The parliament ...
had been chosen without any endeavours from the court, to secure elections ...
For, the trial of Doctor Sacheverel had raised, or discovered, such a spirit
in all parts, that the ministers could very safely leave the electors to themselves, and thereby gained a reputation of acting by a free parliament' (Swift,
Journal, p. 44; *Prose*, viii 126).
   86 *Addresses*: The surprise ending of the Sacheverell trial (264.34n.) precipitated a wave of loyal addresses to the throne. 'These addresses asserted
the doctrines of passive obedience and non-resistance, and acknowledged the
absolute power of the crown. They condemned, as antimonarchical and republican, all doctrines which allowed subjects to resist their sovereigns in any
instance, and declared the defenders of these doctrines to be advocates of
blasphemy and impiety: they affirmed that the Queen acceded to the throne by a

Kingdom, plainly shew'd what sort of Bent the People had taken,
and from what Motives. The Election of Members for this great
City, carry'd contrary to all Conjecture, against the united
90 Interest of those two great Bodies, the *Bank* and *East-India-
Company*, was another convincing Argument. Besides, the *Whigs*
themselves have always confessed, that the Bulk of Landed Men in
England was generally of *Tories*. So that this Change must be
allow'd to be according to the natural Genius and Disposition of
95 the People, whether it were just and reasonable in it self or not.
    Notwithstanding all which, you shall frequently hear the *Parti-
sans* of the late Men in Power, gravely and decisively pronounce,
that the present Ministry cannot possibly stand. Now, they who
affirm this, if they believe themselves, must ground their
100 Opinion upon the Iniquity of the *last* being so far establish'd,
and deeply rooted, that no Endeavours of honest Men, will be able
to restore Things to their former State. Or else these Reasoners
have been so misled by twenty Years Mismanagement, that they have
forgot our Constitution, and talk as if our Monarchy and Revolu-
105 tion began together. But the Body of the People is wiser, and by

    95 not] no 38 8°+12°   100 Opinion] ~, ½°   104-7 talk ... and] *om.*
    38 12°

---

hereditary, and not by a precarious parliamentary right or election: they entreated a dissolution of the present parliament, and contained assurances that
none should be chosen in a new election, but such as should be loyal to the
sovereign and zealous for the church' (Macpherson, *Original Papers*, ii 176).
    88 *Election*: In the general election of October 1710 the Whig candidates
for the City were Sir Gilbert Heathcote, governor of the Bank of England,
James Bateman, director of the Bank, John Ward, director of the United East
India Company, and Sir William Ashurst, director of the Bank. The Tory candidates won 'By a vast majority', which set off wild bell-ringing, bonfires, and
window-breaking in the City (Edward Hatton, *A New View of London*, 2 vols.,
London, for R. Chiswell *et al.*, 1708, ii 596, 604; Luttrell, vi 641; BL MS
Portland Loan 29/321, 17 October 1710 newsletter).
    98 *Ministry cannot possibly stand*: Upon his dismissal in August 1710
'Lord Godolphin at a meeting at the Duke of Devon's House, where were present
the Ld Cowper, Mr. Secretary Boyle and others,. haveing laid before them the
Present State of the Treasury, whereby it appear'd that the Civil List was
then in debt 70000 *l.*, and that there was a debt upon the Navy and other
Offices of 9 Millions five hundred thousand pound, and that the Funds were
exhausted and all credit sunk, and that besides under these circumstances the
new Treasury must find pay for above 255000 men which were then in the Queen's
service, and he added to all this his Dream, that he saw Mr. Harley in a
sculler alone rowing against Wind and Tide without any Person to assist him;
and then he left it to those Lords to determine how long it was possible for
one Man to support an Administration surrounded with such difficulties' (BL
MS Portland Loan 29/52/8).

the Choice they have made, shew they *do* understand our Constitution, and would bring it back to the old Form; which if the new
Ministers take care to maintain, they will and ought to stand,
otherwise they may fall like their Predecessors. But I think we
may easily foresee what a Parliament freely chosen, without   110
Threatning or Corruption, is likely to do, when no Man shall be
in any Danger to lose his Place by the Freedom of his Voice.

But, who are those Advancers of this Opinion, that the present
Ministry cannot hold? It must be either such as are afraid to be
call'd to an Account, in case it should hold; or those who keep   115
Offices, from which others, better Qualify'd, were remov'd; and
may reasonably apprehend to be turn'd out, for worthier Men to
come into their Places, since perhaps it will be necessary to
make some Changes, that the publick Business of the Nation may
go on: Or lastly, *Stock-jobbers*, who industriously spread such   120
Reports that Actions may fall, and their Friends buy to Advantage.

Yet these Hopes, thus freely expressed, as they are more sincere, so they are more supportable, than when they appear under
the Disguise and Pretence of Fears. Some of these Gentlemen are
employ'd to shake their Heads in proper Companies; to doubt   125
where all This will end; to be in mighty Pain for the Nation; to
shew how impossible it is, that the Publick Credit can be supported: To pray that all may do well in whatever Hands; but very
much to doubt that the *Pretender* is at the bottom. I know not any
thing so nearly resembling this Behaviour, as what I have often   130
seen among the Friends of a Sick Man, whose Interest it is that
he should dye: The Physicians protest they see no Danger; the
Symptoms are good, the Medicines answer Expectation; yet still
they are not to be Comforted; They whisper, he is a gone Man; it
is not possible he should hold out; he has perfect Death in his   135
Face; they never liked this Doctor: At last the Patient recovers,
and their Joy is as false as their Grief.

I believe there is no Man so Sanguin, who did not apprehend

118 into] in ½° 38 12°   130 nearly] near 38 12°   131-4 whose ...
Man] *om.* 38 12°

127 *Publick Credit*: This fear received the widest currency in the *Review*
and *The Observator* during the weeks before Godolphin's dismissal (8 August
1710).

some ill Consequences from the late Change, though not in any
140 Proportion to the good Ones: But it is manifest, the former have
prov'd much fewer and lighter than were expected, either at Home
or Abroad, by the Fears of our Friends, or the Hopes of our
Enemies. Those Remedies that stir the Humours in a Diseased Body,
are at first more painful than the Malady it self; yet certain
145 Death is the Consequence of deferring them too long. Actions have
fallen, and the Loans are said to come in slowly. But beside,
that something of this must have been, whether there had been any
Change or no; beside, that the surprize of every Change, for the
better as well as the worse, is apt to affect Credit for a while;
150 there is a further Reason, which is plain and scandalous. When
the late Party was at the Helm, those who were call'd the *Tories*,
never put their Resentments in Ballance with the Safety of the
Nation, but cheerfully contributed to the Common Cause. Now the
Scene is chang'd, the fallen Party seems to act from very differ-
155 ent Motives: They have *given the Word about*; they will keep their
Mony and be passive; and in this Point stand upon the same Foot
with *Papists* and *Nonjurors*. What would have become of the Publick,
if the present great Majority had acted thus, during the late
Administration? Had acted thus, before the others were Masters of
160 that Wealth they have squeez'd out of the Landed Men, and with
the Strength of that, would now hold the Kingdom at defiance?

Thus much I have thought fit to say, without pointing Reflections upon any particular Person; which I have hitherto but
sparingly done, and that only towards those whose Characters are
165 too profligate, that the managing of them should be of any Consequence: Besides as it is a Talent I am not naturally fond of,
so, in the Subjects I treat, it is generally needless. If I display the Effects of Avarice and Ambition, of Bribery and Corruption, of gross Immorality and Irreligion, those who are the least

157 *Nonjurors*] *Nonjurers* ½° 12°

---

145 *Actions*: Although stocks fell sharply during the summer of 1710 (3.46n.),
they had been mixed since November: Bank stock rose from 99¾ to 103¼ and
United East India Company from 114¼ to 121, but Million Bank fell from 69 to
66¼ (*The British Mercury*, 30 October-1 November 1710, 17-19 January 1711).
168 *Avarice and Ambition*: innuendo: Marlborough.
168-9 *Bribery and Corruption*: innuendo: Godolphin.
169 *Immorality and Irreligion*: innuendo: Wharton.

Robert Morden, *Gloucestershire* . . . [London], sold by Abel Swale, Awnsham & John Churchill, [1690]. The parish of Great Barrington is at the upper right, on the border of Oxfordshire and Gloucestershire.

conversant in Things, will easily know where to apply them. Not   170
that I lay any weight upon the Objections of such who charge me
with this Proceeding: 'Tis notorious enough that the Writers of
the other side were the first Aggressors. Not to mention their
scurrilous Libels many Years ago, directly levelled at particular Persons; how many Papers do now come out every Week, full of   175
rude Invectives against the present Ministry, with the first and
last Letters of their Names to prevent Mistakes? It is good sometimes to let these People see, that we neither want Spirit nor
Materials to retaliate; and therefore in this Point *alone*, I
shall follow their Example, whenever I find my self sufficiently   180
provok'd; only with one Addition, that whatever Charges I bring,
either general or particular, shall be religiously true, either
upon avow'd Facts which none can deny, or such as I can prove
from my own Knowledge.

Being resolv'd publickly to acknowledge any Mistakes I have   185
been guilty of; I do here humbly desire the Readers Pardon for
one of mighty Importance, about a Fact in one of my Papers, said
to be done in the Cathedral of *Gloucester*. A whole *Hydra* of
Errors in two Words: For as I am since inform'd, it was neither
in the Cathedral, nor City, nor County of *Gloucester*, but some   190
other Church of that Diocess (Fig. V). If I had ever met any
other Objection of equal weight, tho' from the meanest Hands, I
should certainly have answer'd it.

170 where] were ½°   185 acknowledge] confess 38 8°+12°

---

171 *Objections*: cf. 'He [the Examiner] has openly accus'd the Duke of
Marlborough with aiming at little less than the Royal Power' (*The Observator*,
10-13 January 1711) (cf. 113.56n.).
189 *Errors*: 152.205-153.213. The parish of Great Barrington in the diocese of
Gloucester, and now in Gloucestershire, straddled the border between Gloucestershire and Oxfordshire and was a part of Berkshire (Robert Morden, *Gloucestershire*, London, Abel Swale *et al.*, [1695]).

No. 17 [Mainwaring and Oldmixon]   22 January 1711

The MEDLEY.

Of Nobility in general.
Of the Advantages receiv'd from it.
The sad State of the Senate of Rome.
Some few Remarks on the Examiner.

ARISTOTLE says, *That Nobility, wherever we find it, is a Proof of*
the Virtue of Ancestors. And 'tis but just that we shou'd continue to their Posterity the Respect that was paid to them; because we often receive the Fruits of their Good Actions many Ages
5   after they are dead. But some People here will make a Distinction,
and say, 'Tis very true indeed that all manner of Regard is due
to such Persons as have the Merit as well as Titles of their Predecessors, but that 'tis extremely difficult to shew the same
Respect to others that inherit none of their Virtues. For my own
10   part, I can't help being of that Opinion, and thinking that the
Honour of Parents can never be convey'd to those that descend
from them. When we see the Son, or the Grandson of some very
Great Man, the first Motions of our Minds are full of Tenderness
and Duty, occasion'd by the Memory of his Ancestor: But when we
15   discover afterwards, that this same Person, notwithstanding his
High Birth, is Violent, Partial, Ignorant, and Unjust, we begin
by degrees to consider him in his own just Value, and to have no
more Regard for him at last, than if he sprung from the Dregs of
the People. *Why,* says *Epictetus, shou'd we value a Man because he*
20   *is the Son of a Consul, or some other Great Person, if he has*
nothing of his own that shou'd make us esteem him? But *Socrates*
carry'd this Reflection too far, declaring against Nobility in
general, and maintaining that there is nothing in it truly honourable; but that 'tis often the Original and Occasion of great
25   Evils. And yet the Writer of his Life goes still further, and

---

1-2 *Nobility ... Ancestors*: [Aristotle,] *Polit[ica]*. 1. 5. c. 1 (½°).
19-21 *Why ... him*: Arrian. [*Discourses of Epictetus,*] lib. 3. c. 14
(½°).
23-5 *there ... Evils*: Diogenes Laertius, *Lives*, ii 31.

affirms, That a great Title *is frequently nothing else but an Excuse for doing Ill, and a Cover for Injustice.* After all, I think upon the whole matter, that Author was only in the right, who said, *The Glory of Ancestors appears as a. Light to their Posterity; giving a clearer View of either their Good or their Ill Qualities.* If a Nobleman has many Vices, they seem greater in him, than they wou'd in another Man: If he has many Virtues, his Rank, his Circumstances, and the Hereditary Honour of his Family, make them shine with greater Lustre. The *Romans,* who never fail'd to build a Temple upon every great Occasion, had one in their Capitol, which particularly directed them to look back to their Original. It was a Temple in which there were Altars erected to a certain Goddess, call'd by them *Fortuna Primigenia* whose Assistance they were instructed to implore, that they might always weigh and consider things past as well as present, remember from whom they were descended, and *who they were*; and reflect on their State and Condition in the World, and on the Quality that at their Birth they had receiv'd from their Predecessors. This was perhaps a necessary Admonition in those Times of Paganism, but we have the good fortune to live in an Age, when we see every day, that without such Instructions, those Persons that are truly Noble, know how to make use of the Advantages of their Birth. How happy therefore are those Nations where there is a Majority of such Persons as I have last mention'd, who being the last Resort in all Proceedings, will be sure to judg impartially, without Violence or Prepossession, and according to the strict Rules of Justice? Who will always take care to hear Both Sides, and to receive whatever shall be offer'd in Vindication of accus'd Persons: Who will protect the Unfortunate from the Prosecutions of wicked Men, will inform themselves exactly of the Truth of past Transactions, will prevent the stifling of any Evidence that is material, and above all things will take care that the Facts are

30

35

40

45

50

55

---

38 *Fortuna Primigenia*] [*Fortuna Primigenia*] ½° 12°   43-4 was perhaps]
perhaps was 12°

26-7 *is ... Injustice*: Diog[enes] Laer[tius] (½°, apparently a wrong reference).
29-31 *The ... Qualities*: Sallust. *de Bello Jug[urthino,* lxxxv 23] (½°).
35 *one*: [Johannes] Rosin[us]. *Antiq[uitatum] Rom[anarum Corpus Absolutissimum]. L.* 2. *c.* [16] *de Fortunâ.* [Geneva, Jacob Stoer, 1641, p. 222] (½°).

rightly stated, and that the Ground and Foundation of their Judgment is right. Such a Court as this, must needs be the Ornament,
60 Support and Blessing of any Nation: Nor is it strange that other
Kingdoms shou'd desire to incorporate with such a People; where
their Fortunes and Honours will always be preserv'd; and where
they will neither be hir'd by Interest, nor tempted by Ambition
to enter into dark Designs, in order to oppress the Innocent.
65   The Senate of *Rome*, as it is describ'd by *Cicero*, was very different from such a one as I have been commending. 'There are two
kinds of Men, says he, that have endeavour'd to distinguish themselves in our Commonwealth; one sort of them may properly be
call'd *Populares*, the other *Optimates*. The first are those that
70 in all their Words and Actions desire only to please the Multitude: The second are those that behave themselves in such a manner, as if they wish'd for nothing but the Approbation of Good
Men. They are such Persons, says he, as are neither guilty of
Crimes, nor wicked by Nature, nor mad, nor of *ruin'd* Fortunes.
75 What therefore is the great End of these Fathers of their Country? What are their Views? And what is the Course they steer?
These are the Fundamentals, these the Parts which are maintain'd
by such Leaders, even with the hazard of their Lives: Religion,
the Power of Magistrates, the Authority of the Senate, the Laws
80 and the Customs of our Ancestors; Justice, Jurisdiction and Publick Faith; our Provinces, our Allies, the Glory of our Government, the Business of the War, and of the Treasury. To be the
Patrons and Defenders of these things, so many in number, and so
weighty in themselves, is only the Work of Great Souls, indu'd
85 with Understanding and Constancy: For there is a multitude of Men
among us, says he, who either from a Fear of Punishment, being
conscious of their own Offences, promote new Disturbances and
Changes in the Commonwealth; or who, from an inborn Frensy of

60-1 *other Kingdoms*: innuendo: Scotland and Ireland. In the first session of
Anne's first Parliament in Ireland the Members petitioned for a 'firm and
strict Union with your Majesty's Subjects of *England*'. The Queen returned a
cold answer: 'her Majesty can give no particular Answer at present, but will
take [it] into her Consideration' (*CJ Ireland*, iii 54, 123). In 1707, upon
ratification of the Act of Union with Scotland, Swift observed that 'The
Queen has lately lost a Part | Of her entirely-*English* Heart'. The part of
her heart that she lost was Ireland (*POAS*, Yale, vii 284; cf. *The Story of
the Injured Lady*, Swift, *Prose*, ix 3).
66-93 *There ... Republick*: Cicero, *Orat*[*io*] *pro Sextio*. [xlv 96-9] (½°).
74 *ruin'd*: 3.50, 96.17.

their Minds, are delighted with Discord and Sedition; or who from
the perplex'd Condition of their own Affairs, had rather fall in   90
the general Ruin, than alone. When such Men as these, says he,
have got others to act, and to put in execution their own Designs
and Wickedness, great Commotions are stir'd in the Republick.' As
Lucretius observ'd long ago, that it is pleasant to behold from
a safe Shore the Distresses of Men at Sea; not that we are   95
pleas'd with the Misfortunes of others, but that we are glad to
feel that we our selves are out of them: Even so, when I read of
these Distractions and publick Calamities in other Ages and Countries, I feel a secret Joy in reflecting on our present Condition,
and on the Justice and Prosperity of our own Times and Nation.   100

   I observ'd in some of my former Papers, that the *Examiner* was
at the same time *pert* and *dull*; but now I perceive his Pertness
was a temporary Quality only: 'Twas a new thing to him to be an
Author, a Politician, and a Favourite to Great Men. It made him
look up and speak out with a sort of Air, which conceal'd a   105
little his other native Quality, that appear'd as soon as the
first false Glaring was worn off. And ever since he has been seen
so often in his true Colours, that were he not so much in the
good Graces of some Folks, for whom every one must have an extravagant Veneration, on account of the wonderful things they   110
have done for us, there wou'd be no enduring him. And yet it must
be own'd the Man is very industrious, he writes and answers himself, examines and cross-examines, invents and steals, flatters
and slanders unmercifully. His Masters especially have all the
reason in the World to cherish him, not so much for the Falshoods   115
he writes on their Side, as for those against the *discarded*
M-----y, in which there cannot but be a great deal of Merit, tho
he shou'd do it more grosly still, as 'tis likely he will if he
can; which makes me remember with pleasure his words in the last
Examiner: '*How many Papers do now come out every Week, full of*   120

114 have] shew ½°

94-7 *it ... them*: Lucretius, *De rerum natura*, ii 1-4.
101 *observ'd*: not in any of the earlier *Medleys*.
105 *Air*: 'his Libels come out with such an Air, that one wou'd think they
were publish'd by Authority' (120.41-3).
112-13 *answers himself*: 143.5.
116 *discarded*: 164.60.
120-6 *How ... provok'd*: 185.175-81.

rude Invectives against the present Ministry, with the first and
last Letters of their Names to prevent Mistakes? It is good sometimes to let these People see, that we neither want Spirit nor
Materials to retaliate; and therefore in this point ALONE I shall
125   follow their Example, whenever I find my self sufficiently provok'd.' How is it possible to read this, without thinking my
worthy Friend bewitch'd? I do not know that any one *of the other*
Side, as he calls it, ever points out any Persons by the first and
last Letters of their Names: I am sure, for my own part, I never
130   thought of doing it. But this honest Gentleman has seldom printed
one Paper without using that ingenious Method; and at the very
beginning of this, in which he says, *That he shall be provok'd in*
this Point ALONE to follow their Example, there appear these very
Letters fairly printed, *the E--- of S-------d*. So that his mean-
135   ing is, that he shall be provok'd at last to do what he has done
ever since he writ, and particularly in that very Paper where he
threatens the terrible Effects of his Provocations. Was there
ever such a Man known or heard of in the World! But what follows
is better still; *Whatever Charges I bring*, says he, *whether*
140   *General or Particular, shall be religiously true*: And this he
affirms very gravely, as if nothing had happen'd, after having
been detected of notorious Falshoods in every Paper he has publish'd; and particularly in his *Religious* Account of the Convocation, in which he ought to have been more exact, than in most
145   other Subjects. Yet even all this I cou'd bear from my Friend,
knowing so perfectly as I do, that he can't help it. But his pretending, with a slovenly Pen, to draw a Character of the Q---n,
is intolerable. *Alexander* wou'd never suffer any bungling Painter
to attempt drawing his Picture. And when a Man, call'd *Aristobu-*
150   *lus*, who was, I suppose, such another Penman as my Friend, had
been writing dull Praises of that Monarch, and wou'd needs be
reading them to him as he sail'd down the River *Hydaspes*;

127-8 *of the other Side*: 97.56.
131 *Method*: In the twelve *Examiners* that Swift had written the first and
last letters of proper names are used only once (178.10). In the thirteen
pre-Swift *Examiners* this is done seven times.
139-40 *Whatever ... true*: 185.181-2.
143-4 *Convocation*: 173.108n.
147 *Q---n*: 167.135-50.

Alexander being justly provok'd by such nauseous Flattery,
snatch'd the Papers out of the Scribler's Hand, and threw them
into the Water: By which, says the Historian, he gave the Author   155
to understand, that he deserv'd the same Fate himself. But my
Friend appears to be so secure against all manner of Punishment
for his Insolence, that on the contrary he seems to think all the
Ground about him Holy, as if he were got within a Circle, that
cou'd not be invaded without Profanation. When he rails at the   160
late M------rs, with the utmost stretch of his Malice and Invention, he assures you, 'tis not out of any personal Hatred to them,
but in Justification of the best of Queens. If we offer any
Reasons in behalf of those poor unsuccessful Mi-----rs, tho with
all possible Decency and Respect, he says, *We reflect on the*   165
Q---n. When we condemn Calumny, Informers and Suborners, he protests, *We are in a Plot against her M-----y's Person:* And if we
bestow one word of Pity on any unhappy Men that have lost their
Employments, he says, *'Tis a barefac'd Aspersion on the Q---n.*
This, and much more of the same nature, you have in his last   170
Examiner but one, and will without doubt have it as long as he
writes; for when that Pretence ceases, he is gone. By this means
he gives himself a becoming Advantage over all that dare oppose
him. Whatever we say, tho with all due regard to Sincerity and
Truth, is factious and seditious; whereas the vilest and falsest   175
Invectives he can think of to oblige those that set him to work,
are the pure Effects of his Loyalty and Duty. We can't attack him
without affronting the Government; the Tables are turn'd upon us,
and all we have been doing to prove our selves good Subjects for
these eight years, ends in making us just the same People that   180
the Tories have been so long, and some fourteen years longer. For
all which Misfortunes there is no Remedy, unless the Rule of a
French Critick was to be observ'd, who says, *No body shou'd ever*

183 was] were 12°

153-6 *Alexander* ... *himself*: René Rapin, *Oeuvres diverses*, 1686, ii 299;
cf. Lucian, *How to write history*, 12.
162-3 *not* ... *Queens*: 164.62-165.63.
165-6 *We* ... *Q---n*: 165.76.
167 *We* ... *Person*: 165.89.
169 *'Tis* ... *Q---n*: 164.53-4.
183-5 *No* ... *Actions*: René Rapin, *Oeuvres diverses*, 1686, ii 299.

be otherwise commended, than by a faithful Report of their good
185   *and commendable Actions.* But this Rule wou'd be the entire Ruin
of my Friend, and all his Fellow-Labourers in the same good
Cause; and therefore I am against it.

No. 26 [Swift]   25 January 1711

The EXAMINER.

Διαλεξάμενοί τινα ἡσυχῇ, τὸ μὲν σύμπαν ἐπί τε τῇ δυναστείᾳ καὶ κατὰ τῶν
ἐχθρῶν συνώμοσαν.

*Summissa quædam voce collocuti sunt; quorum summa erat de dominatione sibi
confirmanda, ac inimicis delendis conjuratio.*

NOT many Days ago I observ'd a Knot of discontented Gentlemen
cursing the *Tories* to Hell for their Uncharitableness, in affirming, that if the late Ministry had continu'd to this Time, we
should have had neither *Church* nor *Monarchy* left. They are usu-
5   ally so candid as to call That the Opinion of a Party, which they
hear in a Coffee-house, or over a Bottle from some warm young
People, whom it is odds but they have provok'd to say more than
they believ'd, by some Positions as absurd and ridiculous of
their own. And so it prov'd in this very Instance: For, asking
10 one of these Gentlemen, what it was that provok'd those he had
been disputing with, to advance such a Paradox? he assur'd me in
a very calm manner, it was nothing in the World, but that himself
and some others of the Company had made it appear, that the
Design of the present P-----t and M-----y, was to bring in *Popery*,

8 absurd] absur'd ½°

Motto: Dio Cassius, xlvi 55 2: They meet, they whisper together, and their
whole Design is to establish themselves in their ill-gotten Power upon the
Ruin of their Enemies. Swift's copy, which he annotated, was the 1592 folio
with parallel texts in Greek and Latin published at Geneva by Henri Estienne
(*Swift's Library*, item 95).
4 *neither Church nor Monarchy left*: cf. 'Several concurring circumstances
tended by degrees to imprint an opinion in the body of the Gentlemen & People,
that there was an intention of altering in time the constitution in Church &
State' (James Brydges to John Drummond, 24 August 1710, Huntington Library MS
ST 57, vol. 4, pp. 109-19, reprinted *HLQ*, iii (1939-40), 237).

Arbitrary Power, and the *Pretender*: Which I take to be an Opinion   15
fifty times more improbable, as well as more uncharitable, than
what is charged upon the *Whigs*: Because I defie our Adversaries
to produce one single reason for suspecting such Designs in the
Persons now at the Helm; whereas I can upon Demand produced
twenty to shew, that some late Men had strong Views towards a   20
Commonwealth, and the Alteration of the *Church*.

'Tis natural indeed, when a *Storm* is over, that has only un-
tiled our Houses, and blown down some of our Chimneys, to consider what further Mischiefs might have ensu'd, if it had lasted
longer. However, in the present Case, I am not of the Opinion   25
above-mention'd; I believe the Church and State might have lasted
somewhat longer, tho' the late Enemies to both had done their
worst: I can hardly conceive how Things would have been so soon
ripe for a new *Revolution*. I am convinced, that if they had
offer'd to make such large and sudden Strides, it must have come   30
to Blows, and according to the Computation we have now reason to
think a right one, I can partly guess what would have been the
Issue. Besides, we are sure the Q---n would have interpos'd before they came to Extremities, and as little as they regarded the
Regal Authority, would have been a Check in their Career.   35

But instead of this Question; What would have been the Consequence if the late Ministry had continu'd? I will propose another,
which will be more useful for us to consider; And that is, *What
we may reasonably expect They will do, if ever they come into
Power again?* This, we know, is the Design and Endeavour of all   40
those Scribbles that daily fly about in their Favour; of all the
false, insolent, and scandalous Libels against the present Administration; and of all those Engins set at work to sink the *Actions*,

41 that] which 38 8°+12°

---

31 *Computation*: 'almost the whole Clergy, and nine parts in ten of the
Kingdom' (68.51-2).
43 *Engins*: cf. 'I commanded [*c*.June 1710] the *Observator* and the *Review*,
to descant upon the Publick Credit, and to shew, that by the Talk of a Dissolution, and of Changes in the Ministry, *England* had lost full Three Millions
in the Article of Stocks ... At the same Instant, I sent all the dismal
Accounts I could rake together, piec'd out with Inventions of my own, to all
my Correspondents in *Holland*, in hopes to raise the like Alarms there, and
create the same Fears' (Davenant, *Sir Thomas Double at Court, and in High
Preferments*, 1710, p. 84).

and blow up the Publick Credit. As for those who shew their In-
45 clinations by writing, there is one Consideration, which I wonder
does not sometimes affect them: For how can they forbear having
a good Opinion of the Gentleness and Innocence of those, who permit them to employ their Pens as they do? It puts me in mind of
an insolent pragmatical Orator somewhere in *Greece*, who railing
50 with great Freedom at the chief Men in the State, was answer'd by
one who had been very instrumental in recovering the Liberty of
the City, That *he thank'd the Gods they had now arriv'd to the
Condition he always wish'd them, when every Man in that City might
securely say what he pleas'd.* I wish these Gentlemen would how-
55 ever compare the Liberty they take with what their Masters us'd to
give: How many *Messengers* and *Warrants* would have gone out against
any that durst have open'd their Lips, or drawn their Pens,
against the Persons and Proceedings of their *Junto's* and *Cabals?*
How would their weekly Writers have been calling out for *Prosecu-*
60 *tion* and *Punishment?* We remember when a poor *Nick-name*, borrow'd
from an old Play of *Ben Johnson*, and mention'd in a *Sermon* without any particular Application, was made use of as a Motive to
spur an *Impeachment*. But after all, it must be confest, they had
Reasons to be thus severe, which their Successors have not: *Their*
65 Faults would never endure the Light; and to have expos'd them
sooner, would have rais'd the Kingdom against the Actors, *before
the Time.*

But, to come to the Subject I have now undertaken; which is to
Examine, what the Consequences would be, upon Supposition that the
70 *Whigs* were now restor'd to their Power. I already imagine the
present *free* P--------t dissolv'd, and another of a *different
Epithet* met, by the Force of Money and Management. I read immediately a dozen or two stinging Votes against the Proceedings of
the *late Ministry*, with Addresses to *remove them from Her*
75 *M-----y's Presence and Councils for ever.* The Bill now to be

54 *he*] *they* ½° 12°   57 that] who 38 8°+12°   63 spur an] spur on an
38 8°+12°   67 *the Time*] the proper Time 38 8°+12°   74-5 *Ministry*, ...
ever] ½° 0^b CtY NjP *Ministry* Σ

52-4 *he ... pleas'd*: Cornelius Nepos, *Life of Timoleon*, c. 5.
60 *Nick-name*: 66.20n.
75 *Bill*: A Bill to repeal the Act for a general Naturalization was read
the second time on 23 January 1711 (*CJ*, xvi 464). The Naturalization Act

repeal'd would then be re-enacted, and the Birth-right of an
Englishman reduc'd again to the Value of *twelve Pence*. But to
give the Reader a stronger Imagination of such a Scene; let me
represent the Designs of some Men, lately endeavour'd and projected, in the Form of a Paper of Votes.   80

Order'd, *That a Bill be brought in for repealing the* Sacramental Test.

A Petition of T--d-l, C-ll--s, Cl--d-n, C-w--d, T-l-nd, *in behalf of themselves and many Hundreds of their Disciples, some of
which are Members of this Honourable H----, desiring that Leave*   85
be given to bring in a Bill for qualifying Atheists, Deists *and*
Socinians, *to serve their Country in any Employment.*

Order'd, *That Leave be given to bring in a Bill according to
the Prayer of the said Petition, and that Mr.* L--h--re *do prepare
and bring it in.*   90

Order'd, *That a Bill be brought in for removing the Education
of Youth out of the Hands of the Clergy.*

Another, to *forbid the Clergy preaching certain Duties in Religion, especially* Obedience to Princes.

Another, to *take away the Jurisdiction of Bishops.*   95

Another, for *constituting a General* for Life; *with Instructions*

76 Birth-right] ½° 0^b CtY NjP 12° 38 8°+12° Birth right Σ   87 *Employ-*
ment] Employment, *Ecclesiastical, Civil, or Military* 38 8°+12°

reduced 'the Birth-right of an *Englishman* ... to ... Twelve-pence' because it
required the applicant for naturalization to pay a fee of one shilling (129.
85-130.86).
   82 *Test*: cf. 'Repealing the *Test* ... would level the Church Established,
with every sniveling Sect in the Nation.' In a different frame of mind Swift
said that if the Test is repealed, 'I do not see how we can be said to have
any Established Church remaining' (Swift, *Prose*, vi 130, ii 115).
   83 *T--d-l ... T-l-nd*: 'the Tribe of *Free-Thinkers*' (149.134), who would
of course have been admitted into all civil and military employments by repeal
of the Test Act.
   87 *Socinians*: a sect founded (or appropriated) by an Italian, Fausto Soz-
zini, in Poland in 1588 and introduced into England before 1609. The Socinians
were excluded from the Toleration Act because they preached and wrote against
the Trinity. By 1702 they had begun to call themselves Unitarians (*The Diary
of John Evelyn*, ed. Esmond S. de Beer, 6 vols., Oxford, Clarendon Press, 1955,
v 494).
   89 *L--h--re*: Nicholas Lechmere (1675-1727), the youngest son of one of the
oldest families in England, first achieved fame for his 'Garret-Leap' jail
break in February 1705 (*POAS*, Yale, vii 450). In March 1710, as a Whig Member
of Parliament for Appleby, Westmorland, he summarized the case against
Sacheverell and even his nephew said that he was 'violent, proud, and impracticable' (*The Tryal*, pp. 173-7; Pope, *Poems*, vi 224).
   91 *removing*: 98.85.   96 *General for Life*: 113.56.

to the Committee, that Care may be taken to make the War last as
long as the Life of the said General.

A Bill *of Attainder against* C. D. *of* Sh. J. D. *of* B. L. E. *of*
100   R. *Sir* S. H. *Kt.* R. H. H. S. *Esqs*; A. M. *Spinster, and others,*
for High Treason against the J-nto.

Resolv'd, *That* S--h, D. *of* M. *hath been a most dutiful, just,*
and grateful Servant to Her M-----y.

Resolv'd, *That to advise the Dissolution of a* W--g *Parliament,*
105   *or the Removal of a* W--g *Ministry, was in order to bring in*
Popery *and the* Pretender; *and that the said Advice was High*
Treason.

Resolv'd, *That by the* Original Compact *the Government of this*
Realm is by a Junto, *and a* K--- *or* Qu---; *but the* Administration
110   *solely in the* Junto.

Order'd, *That a Bill be brought in for further limiting the*
Prerogative.

Order'd, *That it be a standing Order of this* H---- *that the*
Merit of Elections be not determin'd by the Number of Voices, or
115   *Right of Electors, but by Weight; and that one* Whig *shall weigh*
down ten Tories.

A Motion being made, and the Question being put, that when a
Whig *is detected of manifest Bribery, and his Competitor being a*
Tory, *has Ten to One a Majority, there shall be a new Election;*
120   *it pass'd in the Negative.*

Resolv'd, *That for a* K. *or* Q. *of this Realm, to Read or*
Examine a Paper brought them to be Sign'd by a J--to *Minister, is*
arbitrary and illegal, and a violation of the Liberties of the
People.

125   These and the like Reformations would, in all probability, be
the First fruits of the Whigs Resurrection; and what Structures
such able Artists might in a short Time build upon such Founda-

99 C. *D. of* Sh.] James *Duke of* Ormonde; 38 8°+12°   100 H. S.] William
Shippen, 38 8°+12°   A. M. *Spinster*] Abigail Masham 38 8°+12°   101 J-nto]
J--n--to ½° Junta 38 8°+12°   108 Compact] Contract 38 8°+12°   111-
12 Order'd ... Prerogative.] *om.* 38 8°+12°   122 J--to] J--t--o ½° J---to
12° Junta 38 8°+12°

100 *Spinster*: Abigail Hill was not a spinster. She married Samuel Masham
in June 1707 in Kensington Palace (GEC, viii 540).
114 *Elections*: 99.93-5.

tions, I leave others to conjecture. All Hopes of a *Peace* cut
off; the Nation *industriously* involved in further Debts to a
Degree, that none would dare undertake the Management of Affairs,   130
but those whose Interest lay in ruining the Constitution. I do
not see how the wisest Prince under such Necessities could be
able to extricate himself. Then, as to the *Church*, the Bishops
would by degrees be dismiss'd, first from the Parliament, next
from their Revenues, and at last from their Office; and the   135
Clergy, instead of their idle Claim of *Independancy* on the State,
would be forc'd to depend for their daily Bread on every Individual. But what System of future Government was design'd; whether
it were already digested, or would have been left for Time and
Incidents to mature, I shall not now *Examine*. Only upon this   140
Occasion I cannot help reflecting on a Fact, which it is probable,
the Reader knows as well as my self. There was a Picture drawn
some time ago, representing *five Persons* as large as the Life,
sitting in Council together like a *Pentarchy*. A void space was
left for a Sixth, which was to have been the Qu---, to whom they   145
intended that Honour: But Her *M-----y* having since fallen under
their Displeasure, they have made a shift to crowd in *two better*
Friends in Her Place, which makes it a compleat *Heptarchy*. This
Piece is now in the Country, reserv'd 'till *better Times*, and
hangs in a Hall, among the Pictures of *Cromwell, Bradshaw,*   150
Ireton, and some other *Predecessors*.

I must now desire leave to say something to a Gentleman, who
has been pleas'd to publish a Discourse against a Paper of mine
relating to the *Convocation*. He promises to *set me right, without*

---

144 in] at ½°   154 promises] promiseth 38 8°+12°

133 *Bishops*: 151.170.
136 *Independancy*: While the high-flying clergy were making extravagant
claims (161.167), there was no confusion in Swift's mind about Church and
state. He knew that 'the Legislative Power, which in all Government must be
absolute and unlimited', could if it wished abolish Christianity (Swift,
Prose, ii 5, 16, 105). He also knew that the clergy were required to 'perform
those Offices, which are assigned to [them] by our Saviour and his Apostles'.
Within the Church the power of the state was permissive, not effective: it
could for example authorize bishops to consecrate a priest or withhold author-
ization. But it could not consecrate a priest (Swift, *Prose*, ii 77, 104).
144 *Pentarchy*: The Whig Junto, or 'the five tyrannising lords', as Anne
called them (Coxe, *Marlborough*, ii 292).
148 *Friends*: the duumvirs, Marlborough and Godolphin.
154-5 *set ... Language*: Wotton, *The Case of the Present Convocation*

155 *any undue Reflections or undecent Language.* I suppose he means in
     Comparison with others, who pretend to answer the *Examiner*: So
     far he is right; but if he thinks he has behav'd himself as be-
     comes a candid Antagonist, I believe he is mistaken. He says, in
     his Title-Page, my *Representations are unfair, and my Reflections*
160 *unjust.* And his Conclusion is yet more severe, where he *doubts I*
     and my Friends are enrag'd against the Dutch, *because they pre-*
     serv'd us from Popery and Arbitrary Power at the Revolution; and
     since that time, from being over-run by the exorbitant Power of
     France, *and becoming a Prey to the* Pretender. Because this Author
165 seems in general to write with an honest meaning, I would seri-
     ously put him the Question, whether He thinks *I and my Friends*
     are for *Popery, Arbitrary Power, France* and the *Pretender?* I omit
     other Instances of smaller Moment, which however do not suit in
     my Opinion with *due Reflection or decent Language.* The Fact relat-
170 ing to the *Convocation,* came from a good Hand, and I do not find
     this Author differs from me in any material Circumstance about it.
     My Reflections were no more than what might be obvious to any
     other Gentleman, who had heard of their late Proceedings. If the
     Notion be right which this Author gives us of a lower House of

     162 *Arbitrary*] *Arbritary* ½°

Consider'd, 1711, p. 3. Wotton, '*to whom our Author never gives any Quarter*'
(Swift, *Tale*, p. 128), was Sir William Temple's adversary and Burnet's
protégé. Since he was not a member of Convocation, his source may have been
Burnet.
     160-4 *doubts ... Pretender*: Wotton wrote: 'without their [the Dutch] Assis-
tance in 1688, *Popery* and *Arbitrary Power*, must ... have over-run us; and
that even since that Time, we must have sunk under the *Exorbitant Power of*
France, and our Church and Queen must have been a Prey to a Pretender impos'd
upon us by this *Exorbitant Power*, if that *Tottering Commonwealth*, as our
Author, *wisely* calls it, had not heartily join'd with us, in bearing the
Burthen of this Calamitous and Bloody War. But I forget my self, and I doubt,
allege those very things in their Favour, for which the *Examiner* and his
Friends, are the most enrag'd against them' (Wotton, *The Case of the Present*
Convocation Consider'd, 1711, p. 24).
     168 *Instances*: such as the Jacobite slur in the last sentence (198.160-
4).
     169 *Fact*: 132.146n. The differences between Swift's account and Wotton's
account of the Convocation are summarized by Walter Scott, who observes, 'It
is obvious, that these and other verbal cavils leave the general truth of the
Examiner's statement unimpeached' (E*1814*, iii 358).
     174 *lower House*: Wotton's limited 'Notion' of the Lower House is implied
most clearly in his definition of the prolocutor, 'the *Referendary* of the
Lower House, *i.e.* one who is to carry Messages and Admonitions from the *Upper*
House to the *Lower*, and to represent their Sense, and to carry their Petitions

Convocation, it is a very Melancholy one, and to me seems utterly   175
inconsistent with that of a Body of Men whom he owns to have a
Negative; and therefore, since a great Majority of the Clergy
differs from him in several Points he advances, I shall rather
chuse to be of their Opinion than his. I fancy, when the *whole
Synod met in one House*, as this Writer affirms, they were upon a   180
better Foot with their Bishops, and therefore whether this Treatment so extreamly *de haut en bas*, since their Exclusion, be suitable to Primitive Custom or Primitive Humility towards Brethren,
is not my Business to enquire. One may allow the Divine or Apostolick Right of *Episcopacy*, and their great Superiority over   185
Presbyters, and yet dispute the Methods of exercising the latter,
which being of *Human Institution*, are subject to Encroachments
and Usurpations. I know, every Clergyman in a Diocess has a good
deal of Dependance upon his Bishop, and owes him Canonical Obedience; But I was apt to think, when the whole Representative of   190
the Clergy met in a Synod, they were consider'd in another Light,
at least since they are allow'd to have a *Negative*. If I am mistaken, I desire to be excus'd, as talking out of my Trade: Only
there is one Thing wherein I entirely differ from this Author.
Since in the Disputes about Privileges, *one side must recede*;   195
where so very few Privileges remain, 'tis a Hundred to One odds,
the Encroachments are not on the Inferior Clergy's Side; and no
Man can blame them for insisting on the small Number that is left.
There is one Fact wherein I must take Occasion to set this Author

---

178 advances] advanceth 38 12°   181 whether] whither ½°   190 think,]
think, that 38 8°+12°   196 odds,] odds, that 38 8°+12°

---

to the *Upper'* (*The Case of the Present Convocation Consider'd*, 1711, p. 14).
Atterbury claimed that the prolocutor was the president of the Lower House,
with the power to convene and adjourn (Kennett, *A Reconciling Letter, upon
the late Differences about Convocational Rights and Proceedings*, London, for
R. Sare, 1702, p. 5).
  177 *Negative*: 'the Lower House ... have a final Negative upon every thing
that the Upper House wou'd have pass into an Ecclesiastical Constitution'
(Wotton, *The Case of the Present Convocation Consider'd*, 1711, p. 18).
  179-80 *whole ... House*: ibid., p. 14.
  181-2 *Treatment so extreamly de haut en bas*: of which Tenison's peremptory
adjournment of the Convocation on 15 December 1710 (133.158) is an example.
  193 *out of my Trade*: 133.160-1. The Examiner of course is a country
gentleman and a justice of the peace (67.21), who speaks jokingly of his
'Trade of *Examining*' (328.6).

200   right; that the *Person* who first mov'd the QUEEN to remit the
       First-fruits and Tenths to the Clergy, was *an eminent Instrument*
       in the late Turn of Affairs; and as I am told, has lately pre-
       vail'd to have the same Favour granted for the Clergy of *Ireland*.
       But I must beg leave to inform the *Author*, that this Paper is
205   not intended for the Management of Controversy, which would be of
       very little Import to most Readers, and only mispend Time, that
       I would gladly employ to better Purposes. For where it is a Man's
       Business to entertain a whole Room full, 'tis unmannerly to apply
       himself to a particular Person, and turn his Back upon the rest
210   of the Company.

          204   the ... this] this ... my 38 8°+12°

       _____

          200 *Person*: Wotton claims that Queen Anne's Bounty was 'first set on Foot
       by a Great MINISTER [Godolphin] in the Last Reign' (*The Case of the Present
       Convocation Consider'd*, 1711, p. 23). Swift replies that it was Harley. It
       seems, however, to have been Burnet (Burnet, ii 370; Tindal, iii 641-2).
          203 *same Favour*: '*This was done by the Author's Sollicitation*' (E*1738*).
       Swift was commissioned by the bishops of the Church of Ireland in 1707 to
       secure remission of the taxes known as first fruits and twentieth parts (Louis
       A. Landa, *Swift and the Church of Ireland*, Oxford, Clarendon Press, 1954, pp.
       52-5). Negotiations in London with Godolphin and the Junto in 1707-9 and Sep-
       tember 1710 came to nothing, but Harley secured it from the Queen in October
       1710 (Swift, *Journal*, p. 66).

No. 18 [Mainwaring and Oldmixon]   29 January 1711

                              The MEDLEY.

       Of Paper-Credit and Stocks, in answer to the Vindication of Faults on both
          Sides, *and* Old Double's New Dialogues.
       His Project for a Fund to carry on the War.
       Some Remarks on the Examiner.

       I Shou'd not have had a word more to say to the Author of *Faults*
       on both Sides, had he not, in his witty way, cruelly attack'd me
       in his *Vindication* lately publish'd, wherein he tells the World
       all at once, *The Medley has been meddling, but is more a Medler*

          1 *Author*: Simon Clement (11.20n.).
          4-5 *The ... Maker*: *A Vindication of the Faults on both Sides, from the*

than a Maker; which is so very ingenious, that if I let him go   5
off so, I shou'd give him too much Advantage over me. He says I
was in a Mistake when I took him for *some Great Man*: I am very
ready to own it, having since had thorow Information of him; but
truly by the Writings his *Great Men* publish every day, a Man may
easily enough be drawn into such an Error, and mistake a small   10
Jobber of *New England* for a Courtier and Statesman. Their Genius
and Performances are so much on a Level, that a better Judg than
I may very well be puzled to tell who is the greater Man, the
Essayer on Credit, or himself. As for their *Reasonings* and *Argu-*
ments, I defy any one to tell me which are best, unless he can   15
prove that one nothing is better than another. The *Fault-Finder*,
in his *Vindication*, complains I dislike him, both when he com-
mends the *Whigs*, and censures the *Tories*; and the reason is,
because he does it so aukardly, that he neither obliges the one,
nor offends the other. I think it vain in him to expect we shou'd   20
return *Argument* and *Conclusions* to such an Antagonist as he; or
that any thing he, or the Writers of the Party he has espous'd
have said, is worth being serious for; when from the first of 'em
to the last, from the *Letter-Writer* to the *Examiner*, there's not
an Author of theirs who is not daily publishing as errant Contra-   25
dictions, as those of the *Revolution* and *Passive-Obedience*, the
Hereditary Right and the *Protestant Succession*, on which Basis

  25 theirs] their's ½°

Reflections of The Medley, the Specimen-Maker, and a Pamphlet, Entituled, Most
Faults on one Side ... By the Author of the Faults on both Sides, London,
1710, p. 4. The witticism depends on the proverbial phrase 'neither meddle nor
make' (Tilley M852).
  7 *some ... Man*: ibid., p. 4. Oldmixon had written, 'What Great Man is this,
that has written so *learnedly* of these Faults on both sides! ... he can be
no body less than a Chief Minister [Harley]' (*The Medley*, 30 October 1710).
  14 *Essayer*: Harley. Defoe also attributed *An Essay upon Publick Credit*
(August 1710) to Harley, presumably upon Harley's instructions (*A Supplement*
to the Faults on Both Sides, 1710, p. 69), but there can be no doubt that
Defoe wrote it under Harley's direction: 'The Town does me too much Honour,
in Supposeing it well Enough done to be your Own', he told Harley (Defoe,
Letters, pp. 276-7).
  17 *complains*: *A Vindication of the Faults on both Sides*, 1710, p. 4.
  21 *Argument ... Conclusions*: ibid., p. 4.
    such an Antagonist: 'Mr. *Maynwaring* thought of taking him to task him-
self, but upon my acquainting him, who the Author was, he ... would not con-
descend to Answer him' (Oldmixon, *The Life*, p. 171).
  24 *Letter-Writer*: St. John (74.36n.).

all that has been lately done by 'em is built: and 'twou'd be
very merry to answer such *Concluders* and *Arguers* in a grave Tone,
30 as our *Fault-Finder* wou'd have us. If I had not known him and his
Merits, I shou'd have had a fair Temptation to enter the Lists
with him as a *Trafficker*, for his positive Assertion, that Trade
can be carry'd on without Paper-Credit. Just such another is that
where he says, the Value of Stocks was *imaginary*, and that when
35 they were 136, they were really but 100. This is all right, it
makes 'em all of a piece; and truly on the foot they stand, I
expect no other kind of *arguing* from them. If they shou'd assert
'tis *Midsummer*, 'twou'd not be more extravagant than what they
have already asserted about *Non-Resistance, Jure Divino, Credit*,
40 and the *late Ministry*. Does not *Hudibras* say,

> What is the Worth of any Thing?
> Just so much Mony as 'twill bring.

But then he did not understand Trade, he went only by Reason and
Common Sense, which these Gentlemen wou'd banish from *Business* as
45 well as from *Politicks*. Old *Double*, who knows as much of these
matters as our *Finder of Faults*, says, *Stocks rise in Value,
according as they are wisely or weakly manag'd*; and that they
are fallen, only because the *Bank* concern'd themselves in the
choice of Parliament-Men, and not for the *Changes at Court*: which

---

32-3 *Trade ... Credit*: What Clement says is that 'Paper-Credit' (Bank notes
and Exchequer bills circulating as money) adds no more to trade than if all
transactions were settled *in specie* (*A Vindication of the Faults on both
Sides*, 1710, p. 10), which is true of one transaction but ignores volume of
trade. Oldmixon sees that 'Paper-Credit' 'creates new Species' (204.86-7),
which increases volume of trade.
34 *imaginary*: 'As to the falling of Stocks [3.46n.], there's nothing strange
nor unreasonable in it, they were run up to an imaginary Value much above
their real Worth' (*A Vindication of the Faults on both Sides*, 1710, p. 15);
cf. 'The true Standard of the worth of any thing is it's intrinsick Value, if
a higher Price be set upon it, that is but imaginary not real worth' (*Faults
on both Sides*, 1710, pp. 39-40).
41-2 *What ... bring*: Butler, *Hudibras* (1678), ii 1 465-6.
46-7 *Stocks ... manag'd*: 'the Price of [stocks] partly depending on Opinion,
their Value is high or low, accordingly as they are seen to be wisely or
weakly manag'd' (Davenant, *New Dialogues upon the Present Posture of Affairs*,
1710, p. 114).
48 *Bank*: 'when ... you pretend to interpose ... in the highest Matters,
you are regarded as dangerous ... To some Steps of this kind ... I rather
attribute the Fall of your Stock than to the Changes at Court' (ibid., pp.
113-14).

is so like his way of arguing, that had he not set his Mark to   50
his *New Dialogues*, we shou'd soon have found the Father out by
the Features of his Offspring. The *Fault-Finder* is, on the contrary, of Opinion, Stocks are not worth more than is paid in, and
he's a Fool or Madman with him that gives a Penny more for them.
He does not think good Management can improve them, or that a   55
constant Interest of seven and eight *per Cent*. besides other Advantages, makes One Hundred Pounds worth a Farthing more, tho
secur'd by Act of Parliament. On the other hand *Double* acknowledges, *That a good Understanding, and mutual good Offices of
Assistance, between the Old Ministry and the Bank, have helpt to*   60
extend Paper Credit. Our Finder of Faults denies every thing like
it: *Paper-Credit*, says he, *adds nothing to the Increase of* Trade;
and unless the Bank of *England* and all Goldsmiths *keep Mony enough
by them to answer all their Bills, Paper is a precarious Credit,
which ought to be look'd upon as a common Cheat.* Old *Double*, who   65
is imploy'd by the same Masters, takes *it for granted, that Gold
and Silver shou'd be left for the Market, and other common Uses,
and that the Bulk of Trade and Business shou'd be carry'd on by
Paper.* You see how finely they agree among themselves: but it will
always be so in defending a Cause that's grounded only on Non-   70
sense and Inconsistency. The *Fault-Finder* will not allow the
Bank or Bankers to make use of a Penny, for they give Bills for
all that's paid; and they must, quoth he, keep enough by them to
answer all, which wou'd make their Business wonderfully beneficial. If they have any Mony of their own, they may trade with it;   75
but if they touch a Shilling of what they have given Notes for,
'tis a Cheat. *This is the Man that is to rectify our Judgments,
and reform our erroneous and superficial Ideas in Trade*: This is

---

53 *Stocks*: 'if ... Men should again suffer themselves to be drawn into the
Cheats of Stock-Jobbers, and will part with their Money to buy Stocks at an
Over-value ... let them never more lay the Blame upon the Change of Court-
Ministers' (*A Vindication of the Faults on both Sides*, 1710, p. 16).
    59-61 *a ... Paper Credit*: [Davenant,] *New Dial[ogues upon the Present
Posture of Affairs*, 1710]. p. 118 (½°).
    63-5 *the ... Cheat*: [*A Vindication of the Faults on both Sides*, 1710] pag.
13 (½°).
    66-9 *Gold ... Paper*: [Davenant, *New Dialogues upon the Present Posture of
Affairs*, 1710] pag. 176 (½°).
    77-80 *rectify ... Attention*: *A Vindication of the Faults on both Sides*, 1710,
pp. 5, 17.

he who is sollicitous that *ingenuous Men wou'd investigate his
Notions with more Attention*; tho I perceive nothing even of the
Merchant in him, but his *Altumal* Cant, a Mark of his poor Traffick and Tar-Education. What shifts are his *Great Men* put to, to
hire such hands to do their Work for them? He will not admit of
Bank or Bankers depending on the Improbability of a general Call
on them, and on that dependance to make use of part of the Cash
paid into them, which is answer'd by Paper; and as long as Credit
is good, creates a new Species, of great Ease and Convenience to
Commerce, as is daily experienc'd, or Traders wou'd not risk
their Estates so freely as they have done, and may in better
times do again. I don't think it extraordinary that these Men are
so angry at Credit, and so industrious to lessen her Reputation.
They have lately disoblig'd her so much, that 'tis likely she
will have as little to do with 'em as she can; and they are not
such Fools as not to see she is not at all in their Interest. All
the Writers against her give themselves Airs of Authority: The
Examiner does as good as tell the World, one can't touch him
without being guilty of Sedition; and the *Finder of Faults* threatens us, that *he's better provided to maintain any thing he has
said than we are aware of*. 'Tis our hard Fate to have nothing but
Truth and Reason on our side; whereas that Author is so plain, as
to say in another place, *The M------y approve of his Performance.*
In this Case 'tis not hard to guess whom he means. And having had
a full Account of the Man and his Hopes, I am extremely surpriz'd
to meet with any such Expressions as these in his Book. *Would you
have the World believe, that if a Great Man has Interest enough
with his Party to get himself thank'd, and to save him from being
censur'd, that he's therefore fairly acquitted of all that has*

79 *ingenuous*] *ingenious* 12°

81-2 *Altumal Cant ... Tar-Education*: the language of petty traders and
sailors ... education at sea (*OED*, citing this line). Oldmixon is mocking
Clement, whose coinage this is (*A Vindication of the Faults on both Sides*,
1710, p. 19).
97 *Sedition*: 'Scurrilities ... against this poor Paper of mine ... reflect
upon the Queen, and the Ministry, and Parliament' (165.63-77).
98-9 *better ... aware*: [*A Vindication of the Faults on both Sides*, 1710]
pag. 20 (½°).
101 *The ... Performance*: [ibid.,] pag. 42 (½°).
104-8 *Would ... him*: [ibid.,] pag. 18 (½°).

been charg'd against him? &c. There's nothing so plain as the
Methods they take to insinuate that all things are for the better, and that none are Losers. Our Author pretends that Bank-   110
Stock is but really 100 *l.* or thereabouts in Value: now 115 *l.* is
actually paid, and 7½ *per Cent.* only to be deduc'd; so that the
original Payment is 107½, and the Stock no more than 103½; which
he makes 3½ above its Value. But so it is with 'em in all cases,
and we must be satisfy'd in this as well as in others. I shou'd   115
not have troubled my self and the Reader so much about such a
Writer, had he not been so far impos'd on by the Applause given
his *Faults on both sides*, on account of its mistaken Author, as
to flatter himself he deserv'd it; and for the sake of what's
true in his Book, I was loth he shou'd be so deceiv'd: the Man   120
being, I believe, willing to be honest, if the Point he has in
view cou'd be gain'd by being so; otherwise he will, like the
rest of the Faction, confound *Whig* and *Tory*, by dividing the
Whigs into *Old* and *Modern*; a wicked Distinction invented by their
Enemies to ruin those by *Divisions*, they cou'd never have con-   125
tended with without them.

I have mention'd a new Work of *Old Double*'s, duller even than
his last; and 'tis probable we shall hear no more from him. The

---

112 deduc'd] deducted ½° L IU^b TxU

110-11 *Bank-Stock ... really 100 l.*: 'it may not be said that One Hundred
Pounds Stock is really worth One Hundred and Twenty' (ibid., p. 16).
118 *mistaken Author*: Harley (201.7n.).
124 *Old and Modern*: The first Whigs (1679-81) were of course an Opposition
party. The second generation (1694-1700) were 'Court Whigs' and 'this strange
Metamorphosis of Principles' was widely recognized at the time (*A Letter to
a Modern Dissenting Whig concerning the present Juncture of Affairs; with a
Comparison between the former Principles, and the present Practices of that
Party*, London, for M. Fabian and B. Lintot, 1701, p. 25). 'The late Modern
Distinction of *Old* Whiggs and *New* Whiggs' (Oldmixon, *The History of Addresses*,
i, sig. A7^v) was made in 1693-4 when the Junto (New Whigs) gradually took
over the Government and the Old Whigs, Robert Harley, Paul Foley, and their
followers, went into Opposition. The distinction was kept up by Harley's
propaganda writers (Davenant, *Sir Thomas Double at Court, and in High Preferments*, 1710, p. 35; Clement, *A Vindication of the Faults on both Sides*, 1710,
p. 26).
127 *new Work*: *New Dialogues upon the Present Posture of Affairs, the
Species of Mony, National Debts, Publick Revenues, Bank and East-India Company, and the Trade now carried on between France and Holland*, London, for
John Morphew, 1710, was advertised as 'Publish'd this Day' in *The Examiner*,
4 January 1711.
128 *last*: *Sir Thomas Double at Court, and in High Preferment, in Two*

Party wou'd be mad, if they shou'd suffer him to write for them
130 again. Who but such a blundering Projector as he, wou'd have
offer'd such a Proposal as he has done to raise Mony, at a time
when we are at our wits end for want of it? It looks as if he had
so little an Opinion of his Patrons himself, as to banter 'em; tho
as matters go, that wou'd be barbarous, and I shou'd not forgive
135 him my self, if I thought he intended it. I rather chuse to believe it comes from the Simplicity of his Heart, and the same
sound Judgment that fifteen or sixteen years ago propos'd the shutting up the Exchequer (or, what's all one, stopping the Payment of
old Debts, and beginning a-new) to the then Ministry. I shall not
140 give the Reader all his notable Design to fill the Tr-----y, only
mention some of the most remarkable Branches of his Fund.

Old Double*'s Project to raise Mony.*

A Tax on Auctions of Books and Pictures.
On Quack-Bills, Almanacks, and Plays.

136 and] and from 12°

---

*Dialogues between Sir Thomas Double and Sir Richard Comeover alias Mr. Whiglove,
the 27th of September 1710*, London, for J. Morphew, 1710, was published 3 October 1710 (*The Examiner*, 28 September 1710; *The Medley*, 5 October 1710).
131 *Proposal*: '*Rook*. I see what you aim at. You would lay a Duty upon Sales
at the Candle, or by Auction ... of ... Books, Pictures, and other Goods ...
Sir Richard Comeover. I suppose you think it would be proper to charge all
printed Bills of Empericks, or Quack-Physicians ... *Rook*. The Common People
also waste much of their Time and Substance in *Play-Houses, Cock-Pits, Bowling-
Greens* ... *Shovel-Boards, Billyard-Tables* ... *Musick-Booths* ... *Strong-Water
Shops*, and the Exposers of *Sights* and *Shews* ... *Sir Thomas Double*. I think
Vintners and Retailing *Wine-Coopers*, may raise something by a Stamp ...
Trueman. Mr. *Rook*, you have been lately in the Country, and have sometimes
Horses at Livery-Stable, and I believe you find by your Bills, that these sort
of Men ... may pay something for a Stamp'd-License. *Sir Richard Comeover*. Pray
for the Sake of my Friend Esq; *Bickerstaff*, let us not forget the Undertaker
of Funerals, which is one of the greatest Modern Cheats ... *Trueman*. I look
upon *Chocolate* and *Coffee-houses*, to be great Wasters of People's Time ...
they may well bear a Tax by Stampt-License, proportion'd to the Rent of their
respective Houses or Rooms. *Rook*. Since you are for charging Vice and Luxury,
methinks you should not forget Cards, which would well bear a Penny Stamp *per*
Pack ... Why should not the *Jews* contribute their Share in the present Exigencies ... their Wealth chiefly consists in Money, which the Law has not hitherto
been able to reach and charge' (Davenant, *New Dialogues upon the Present Posture of Affairs*, 1710, pp. 198-201) (½°).
138   *stopping* ... *Payment*: So far from proposing another stop on the Exchequer, Davenant was afraid 'that the Laws have not made it Criminal enough
to stop Payments in the Exchequer ... A Stop there would at once pull down all
our Civil Rights' (*An Essay upon the Probable Methods of making a People
Gainers in the Ballance of Trade*, 1700, p. 172).

On Cockpits, Bowling-Greens, Ninepin-Alleys.   145
Shovelboards, Billiard-Tables, Musick-Booths.
Strongwater-Shops and Raree-Shews.
On Vintners, Wine-Coopers, Jockeys and Undertakers.
On Chocolate-Houses and Coffee-Houses.
On Cards, and upon the Jews.   150

All which is so very plausible, that out of the extream Passion
I have for the publick Service, let it be under what Management
it will, I cannot but recommend it also to the Consideration of
such whose Heads are full of those matters.

I have often taken notice of the *Examiner*'s Impropriety of   155
Speech, in calling his good Friends the Whigs the *Ruin'd Party*.
I always consider'd them as a great Body of Men zealous for Civil
and Religious Liberty, hearty Enemies to *France* and the Pretender, and Loyal Subjects to the Queen, not disputing any of her
Majesty's Titles, especially that which descends to the House of 160
Hanover: and I thought it very odd that he shou'd term such Men
the *Ruin'd Party*, because it look'd as if Men of the contrary
Principles were only rising and flourishing; which even he sure
has not the face to affirm or insinuate, tho he dares do as much
in that way as any body, when he is set upon't. I cou'd not   165
imagine that Men who are possess'd of so considerable a Part of
the Wealth of the Nation cou'd properly be call'd *Ruin'd*; for I
know the Tale of the Spunge to be a Fiction invented by a Fanatical Writer, who has since aton'd for his Fault. And till some
such Misfortune happen'd, I had no manner of Apprehension such   170
a Party as that cou'd ever be *ruin'd*. And I perceive my Friend
the *Examiner*, as full as he is of the Success of *the Frenzies*

171 ever] *om.* 12°

---

156 *Whigs*: 1.1-15.
    the Ruin'd Party: Partly by repeating it and partly by Mainwaring's and
Oldmixon's mistake in taking it up (92.95, 142.160), Swift was able to make
his term stick.
168 *Spunge*: 40.161.
169 *Writer*: After Defoe went back to work for Harley (Defoe, *Letters*, p.
272) he called the 'Parliament Spunge to wipe out our Scores, and Cancel the
Debts ... a Notion destructive of Parliaments and the Constitution' (*Review*,
12 August 1710).
172-3 *Frenzies ... rais'd*: 180.62.

artificially rais'd, had no other reason for using the Term so
often as he has done, but, as he owns, *for want of other Phrases.*
175 There's no other Epithet, it seems, in his Lexicon, for that
Administration, which for so many years serv'd the Queen and
Nation with so much Wisdom and Glory. These Gentlemen, utterly
undone as they are, have however flatter'd themselves with some
vain Hopes, which he has confuted, as he can do anything he
180 pleases. *They hop'd for some terrible Loss abroad*; and that the
Madness of the People occasion'd his *Great Turn.* They have always
been so *chagrin* at any good News from *Flanders* and *Spain*, that to
be sure they wanted some bad now to comfort them; since, *as they
hop'd and endeavour'd*, says my Friend, *they cou'd not ruin the*
185 *Credit of the Nation.* Now there's not a Tory living, who knows
there are such things as *Stocks, Funds, &c.* but knows also that
the *Ruin'd Party* have at least seven Parts in Ten; and it must be
the most spiteful thing in the world for them *to hope and endeavour to ruin Credit*, which was then above one third Part of their
190 Estates, the Value of the *Funds* and *Stocks* depending upon it.
They did not care; the E. of S. was discarded, and they will lose
10000 *l.* a Man to have him in again. There never was such an
obstinate headstrong sort of People as these *Whigs*, and the
Examiner can never maul 'em enough for it. What! out of a pique
195 beggar themselves and their Families! 'Tis not to be vindicated.
I have more than once observ'd my Friend is very unhappy in his
Expressions, and gives his Adversaries too many Handles to take
hold of him. What does he mean when he says, *All great Changes
have the same effect upon Commonwealths that Thunder has upon
200 Liquors, making the Dregs fly up to the Top?* Nor is what comes
afterwards more justifiable: *The Madness of the People hath risen*

174 *for ... Phrases*: 178.8.
180 *They ... abroad*: 179.16-17.
181 *Madness ... Turn*: 179.21-2.
183-5 *they ... Nation*: 179.15-16. The 'not' is the Medley's addition.
187 *seven Parts*: cf. '[Total investments in all corporations, public and
private] Amount to little less than sixty Millions Sterling ... Of this above
seven Tenths they compute to be in the Hands of the Whigs' (*Review*, 23 November 1710).
198-200 *All ... Top*: The Medley scores here, for Harley and Shrewsbury are
hardly dregs (*Yearbook of English Studies*, xi (1981), 63).
201-3 *The ... Governments*: Swift was probably thinking of 'the Madness' of
1641-9. The Medley scores by applying the words to the termination of Godolphin's Government.

to such a height, as to break in pieces the whole Frame of the
best instituted Governments. For tho all good Men are fully convinc'd, that we never had nor ever shall have any such doings in
Britain; yet since Malice is apt to make the worst of every   205
thing, one wou'd not put words into an Enemy's mouth. I'm sure
I durst not have said half so much, tho with all the Softnings
and Explanations imaginable. He may say and do what he will, and
Old or *New* 'tis all one to him. He has prov'd by many strong
Arguments that the nine in ten is no false Muster: His Proofs are   210
the Shire-Elections, the free and *unextorted* Addresses, and the
16 in 7000 in *London*. There's no more contending with them than
with *Old Double*; who, in his *Dialogues*, says he has examin'd the
very Poll-Book, and finds they have the *Weight* as well as *Number*;
that is, the *Blacksmiths* weigh heavier than the *Mercers*. 'Tis   215
the same with my Friend; when he's bent upon proving a thing, it
must be given up to him: and if he had had a fancy to have made
it 99 in 100, he cou'd as easily have done it; for certainly
there's nothing too hard for him. Who cou'd expect such words as
these to drop from his Pen? *I believe*, quoth he, *there is no Man*   220
so sanguine, who did not apprehend some ill Consequences from the
late Change. For how pitifully does he come off, by saying, *It is*

209 *Old or New*: 181.75-6.
210 *nine in ten*: 68.51-2, 82.27.
211 *Addresses*: 181.86. Mainwaring had already written at least one pamphlet and the spirited verses, *The Humble Address of the Clergy of London and
Westminster, Paraphras'd* (POAS, Yale, vii 454) about the 'Addressing Madness'
(*Review*, 18 May 1710) of April-November 1710. He had remarked that many of
the High Church addresses seemed to originate in London: 'Copies or Patterns
of Addresses were sent down to the more dark and ignorant Parts of the Land,
such as *Wales, Somersetshire, Oxford-shire*, &c. ... But to Countries [counties]
more enlightned ... they only transmitted some particular Heads to work upon.'
Mainwaring also supposed that this was the work of 'Harlequin' [Harley] (*Four
Letters to a Friend in North Britain, upon the Publishing The Tryal of Dr.
Sacheverell*, 1710, pp. 18, 22; *The High Church Mask pull'd off: or, Modern
Addresses anatomized*, London, for A. Baldwin, 1710, pp. 3-4).
212 *16 in 7000*: Swift did not mention (182.88-91) that the Whig, John Ward,
polled only sixteen votes less than the Tory, Col. John Cass, out of nearly
7,000 votes cast (Luttrell, vi 641).
213-14 *he ... Poll-Book*: 'the Church of *England* Interest ... at the City-
Poll ... exceeded you [Whigs] in Substance as well as in Numbers, as will more
evidently appear from the Poll-Books, which ... will be shortly publish'd'
(Davenant, *New Dialogues upon the Present Posture of Affairs*, 1710, p. 159).
*The Poll of the Livery-men of the City of London, at the Election for Members
of Parliament*, London, for John Morphew, 1710, was advertised in *The Examiner*
of 14 December for publication on 18 December 1710.
220-4 *I ... expected*: 183.138-184.141.

manifest they have prov'd much fewer and lighter than were ex-
pected? Loyal Men shou'd not own there were ever any Apprehen-
225 sions at all, much less that there were any the least ill
Consequences; sure I am, I know of none. Every one is extremely
well pleas'd: Every thing is florid and thriving. We may have
a Peace when we will; and there's no fear now of having the War
perpetuated, or Mens brains knock'd out against Stone-Walls, for
230 Towns not worth taking.

> 228 *War*: 116.140.
> 230 *Towns*: 114.101.

No. 27 [Swift]   February 1 1711

The EXAMINER.

Ea autem est gloria, laus recte factorum, magnorumq; in Rempublica meri-
torum: Quæ cum optimi cujusque, tum etiam multitudinis testimonio compro-
batur.

I Am thinking, what a mighty Advantage it is to be entertain'd as
a Writer to a *ruin'd Cause*. I remember a *Fanatick* Preacher, who
was inclin'd to come into the *Church*, and take Orders; but upon
mature Thoughts was diverted from that Design, when he consider'd
5   that the Collections of the *Godly* were a much heartier and
readier Penny, than he could get by wrangling for *Tythes*. He certainly had Reason, and the two Cases are Parallel. If you write
in Defence of a fallen Party, you are maintain'd by Contribution
as a necessary Person, you have little more to do than to carp
10 and cavil at those who hold the Pen on the other side; you are
sure to be celebrated and caressed by all your Party, to a Man.
You may affirm and deny what you please, without Truth or Probability, since it is but loss of Time to contradict you.

> Motto Cicero, *Philippics*, i 29: That is real Honour and true Praise for
> glorious Actions to a meritorious State, when they gain the Commendation and
> Esteem of the Great, and, at the same Time, the Love and Approbation of the
> common People.
> 2 *ruin'd Cause*: 207.156.

Besides, *Commiseration* is often on your side, and you have a Pretence to be thought honest and disinterested, for adhering to   15
Friends in Distress. After which, if your Party ever happens to
turn up again, you have a strong Fund of *Merit* towards making
your Fortune. Then, you never fail to be well furnish'd with
Materials, every one bringing in his *Quota*, and Falshood being
naturally more plentiful than Truth. Not to mention the wonder-   20
ful Delight of libelling Men in Power, and hugging your self in
a Corner with mighty Satisfaction for what you have done.
    It is quite otherwise with Us, who engage as Volunteers in the
Service of a Flourishing Ministry, in full Credit with the Q---n,
and belov'd by the People, because they have no sinister Ends or   25
dangerous Designs, but pursue with Steddiness and Resolution the
true Interests of both. Upon which account they little want or
desire our Assistance; and we may write till the World is weary
of reading, without having our Pretences allow'd either to a
Place or a *Pension*: Besides, We are refus'd the common *Benefit of*   30
the Party, to have our Works cry'd up of course; the Readers of
our own side being as ungentle and hard to please, as if we writ
against them; and our Papers never make their way in the World,
but barely in proportion to their Merit. The Design of *Their* Labours who write on the conquer'd side, is likewise of greater   35
Importance than *Ours*; They are like Cordials for dying Men, which
must be repeated; whereas ours are, in the Scripture-Phrase, but
Meat for Babes: At least, all I can pretend, is to undeceive the
Ignorant and those at distance; but their Task is to keep up the
sinking Spirits of a whole Party.   40
    After such Reflections, I cannot be angry with those Gentlemen

---

14 Besides,] *om.* 38 8°+12°   16 Party] Friends 38 8°+12°

---

21 *Delight*: cf. 'What shall we say of the pleasure that is taken in the
reading of a Defamatory Libel?' (Bayle, *Dictionary*, iv[2], p. xxvi).
    30 *Place*: Swift and the Examiner must be distinguished here. Swift expected
'a *Place*', but he also feared that 'all ministries [are] alike' and he was
determined not to be disappointed if he got nothing (Swift, *Journal*, pp. 126,
167). 'My new friends are very kind,' he told Stella, 'and I have promises
enough, but I do not count upon them ... However, we will see what may be
done, and if nothing at all, I shall not be disappointed' (ibid., p. 173). The
Examiner, as a gentleman-volunteer unknown to the ministers (214.105-11),
could expect nothing.
    38 *Meat for Babes*: 'Ye have need that one teach you again ... and are
become such as have need of milk, and not of strong meat' (Heb. 5:12).

for perpetually writing against me: It furnishes them largely
with Topicks, and is besides, their proper Business: Neither is
it Affectation, or altogether *Scorn*, that I do not reply. But as
45 Things are, we both act suitable to our several Provinces: Mine
is, by laying open some Corruptions in the late Management, to
set those who are ignorant, right in their Opinions of Persons
and Things: It is theirs to cover with *Fig-Leaves* all the Faults
of their Friends, as well as they can: When I have produc'd my
50 Facts, and offer'd my Arguments, I have nothing farther to advance; It is their Office to deny and disprove; and then let the
World decide. If *I* were as *They*, my chief Endeavour should certainly be to batter down the *Examiner*, therefore I cannot but
approve their Design. Besides, they have indeed another Reason
55 for barking incessantly at this Paper: They have in their Prints
openly tax'd a most ingenious Person as Author of it; One who is
in great and very deserv'd Reputation with the World, both on
account of his Poetical Works, and his Talents for publick Business. They were wise enough to consider, what a Sanction it would
60 give their Performances, to fall under the Animadversion of such
a Pen; and have therefore us'd all the Forms of Provocation commonly practic'd by little obscure Pedants, who are fond of distinguishing themselves by the Fame of an Adversary. So nice a
Taste have these judicious Criticks, in pretending to discover
65 an Author by his Style and Manner of Thinking: Not to mention
the Justice and Candor of exhausting all the stale Topicks of
Scurrility in reviling a Paper, and then flinging at a venture
the whole Load upon One who is entirely innocent; and whose
greatest Fault, perhaps, is too much *Gentleness* towards a Party,
70 from whose *Leaders* he has receiv'd quite contrary Treatment.

46 *laying open*: 84.78.
56 *Person*: Addison was the first to associate Prior with *The Examiner*
when he identified him correctly as the author of *The Examiner*, No. 6, 7 September 1710 (*The Whig-Examiner*, 14 September 1710). More recently, as Swift
wrote to Stella on 9 February 1711, 'Prior was like to be insulted in the
street for being supposed the author of it; but one of the last papers cleared
him' (Swift, *Journal*, p. 185) (*E1922*, ix 168).
70 *Treatment*: Prior sent a copy of *An Ode, humbly Inscrib'd to the Queen.
On the glorious Success of Her Majesty's Arms* (1706), celebrating Marlborough's victory at Ramillies, to the Duke and received His Grace's 'particular
thanks' but nothing more. Prior's friends thought it would be 'strange if such
a performance should not meet with more than praise expressed by words' (HMC
Bath MSS, iii 435). For writing *The Campaign* (1705), celebrating Marlborough's
victory at Blenheim, Addison had been made an Under-Secretary of State.

The Concern I have for the Ease and Reputation of so deserving
a Gentleman, hath at length forc'd me, much against my Interest
and Inclination, to let these angry People know who is *not* the
Author of the *Examiner*. For, I observ'd, the Opinion began to
spread, and I chose rather to sacrifice the Honour I receiv'd by   75
it, than let injudicious People entitle him to a Performance, that
perhaps he might have Reason to be asham'd of: Still faithfully
promising, never to disturb those worthy Advocates; but suffer
them in quiet to roar on at the *Examiner*, if they or their Party
find any Ease in it; as Physicians say there is, to People in   80
Torment, such as Men in the Gout, or Women in Labour.

However, I must acknowledge my self indebted to them for one
Hint, which I shall now pursue, tho' in a different manner. Since
the Fall of the late Ministry, I have seen many Papers fill'd
with their Encomiums; I conceive, in imitation of those who write   85
the Lives of famous Men, where, after their Deaths, immediately
follow their Characters. When I saw the poor *Virtues* thus dealt
at random, I thought the Disposers had flung their Names, like
Valentines into a *Hat*, to be drawn as Fortune pleas'd, by the
J-nto and their Friends. There, *Crassus* drew *Liberality* and   90
Gratitude; *Fulvia, Humility* and *Gentleness*; *Clodius, Piety* and
Justice; *Gracchus, Loyalty* to his Prince; *Cinna, Love of his
Country and Constitution*; and so of the rest. Or, to quit this
Allegory, I have often seen of late, the whole Sett of discarded
Statesmen, celebrated by their judicious Hirelings, for those   95
very Qualities which their Admirers own'd they chiefly wanted.
Did those *Heroes* put off and lock up their *Virtues* when they came
into Employment, and have they now resum'd them since their Dis-
missions? If they wore them, I am sure it was *under* their *Great-
ness*, and without ever once convincing the World of their   100
Visibility or *Influence*.

90 *J-nto*] *J--n--to* ½° *Junta* 38 8°+12°

---

90 *Crassus*: Marlborough (E*1814*, iii 431).
91 *Fulvia*: Duchess of Marlborough (ibid.).
    Clodius: Wharton, 'whose profligacy was notorious' (ibid.).
92 *Gracchus*: Sunderland, whose rudeness to the Queen was notorious (Swift,
Prose, vii 9; viii 112, 118).
    Cinna: Probably Godolphin, whose 'predominant Passions were Love and
Play' (Swift, *Prose*, vii 9).

But why should not the present Ministry find a Pen to praise
them as well as the last? This is what I shall now undertake, and
it may be more impartial in me, from whom they have deserv'd so
105   little. I have, *without being called*, serv'd them half a Year in
quality of *Champion*, and by help of the Qu---- and a Majority of
Nine in Ten of the Kingdom, have been able to protect them
against a routed Cabal of hated Politicians, with a dozen of
Scriblers at their Head: Yet so far have They been from rewarding
110   me suitable to my Deserts, that to this Day they never so much as
sent to the *Printer* to enquire who I was; though I have known a
Time and a Ministry, where a Person of half my Merit and Consideration would have had fifty *Promises*, and in the mean time a
Pension settled on him, whereof *the first Quarter should be*
115   *honestly paid*. Therefore my Resentments shall so far prevail, that
in Praising those who are now at the Head of Affairs, I shall at
the same time take notice of their Defects.

Was any Man more eminent in his Profession than the present
L--d K----r, or more distinguish'd by his Eloquence and great
120   Abilities in the House of Commons? And will not his Enemies allow
him to be fully equal to the great Station he now adorns? But
then it must be granted, that he is wholly ignorant in the Speculative as well as practical Part of *Poligamy*: He knows not how to
metamorphose a Sober Man into a *Lunatick*: He is no *Free-thinker*
125   in Religion, nor has Courage to be *Patron* of an Atheistical Book,

105 I] *new paragraph* 38 12°   124 *Free-thinker*] *free-thinker* ½°

---

105   *half a Year*: *The Examiner* began on 3 August 1710, but Swift of course
did not start until 2 November 1710.
119   *L--d K----r*: Sir Simon Harcourt (1661-1727) managed the impeachment of
Somers in 1701 and defended Sacheverell in 1710. He succeeded Cowper, but
with the title of Lord Keeper, on 19 October 1710.
122-3 *Speculative ... Part of Poligamy*: 153.221-2.
123   *practical Part*: 67.28n.
124   *Man*: A commission of lunacy against Richard Wenman, 5th Viscount Wenman of Tuam in the Irish peerage, with an estate of £5,000 a year, was set
aside in February 1707 when Wenman was nineteen. After he married in 1709,
his brother-in-law, who was also his stepfather, sued in the court of chan-
cery for another commission of lunacy. Cowper granted the enquiry but the
jury found that Wenman was 'no ideot' (Luttrell, vi 136, 139, 450, 456, 470).
125   *Book*: John Clendon dedicated *Tractatus Philosophico-Theologicus de
Persona* (1710) to William Cowper, Lord High Chancellor of Great Britain.
Although the Lord Chancellor is indeed 'Keeper of the King's conscience'
(Beatson, i 227), the House of Commons in March 1710 ordered Clendon to be
prosecuted and the book to be burnt by the common hangman as 'a scandalous,

while he is Guardian of the Qu---'s Conscience. Though after all,
to speak my private Opinion, I cannot think these such mighty
Objections to his Character, as some would pretend.

The Person who now Presides at the Council, is descended from
a Great and Honourable Father, not *from the Dregs of the People*;   130
he was at the Head of the Treasury for some Years, and rather
chose to enrich his Prince than himself. In the Height of Favour
and Credit, he Sacrific'd the greatest Employment in the Kingdom
to his *Conscience* and *Honour*: He has been always firm in his
Loyalty and Religion, zealous for supporting the Prerogative of   135
the Crown, and preserving the Liberties of the People. But then,
his best Friends must own that he is neither *Deist* nor *Socinian*:
He has never convers'd with *T-l-nd*, to open and enlarge his
Thoughts, and dispel the Prejudices of Education; nor was he ever
able to arrive at that Perfection of Gallantry, *to ruin and im-*   140
prison the Husband, in order to keep the Wife without disturbance.

The present *L--d St---rd* has been always distinguish'd for his

seditious, and blasphemous, Libel ... [tending] to promote Atheism, Schism,
and Immorality' (*CJ*, xvi 385; Luttrell, vi 600).

129 *Person*: Laurence Hyde (1641-1711), Earl of Rochester (E*1738*), was the
second son of Edward Hyde, Charles II's Lord Chancellor. Rochester resigned
as Lord Treasurer in December 1686 rather 'than yield to the late King *James*'s
Sollicitations to turn Papist' (*A Letter from a Foreign Minister in England
to Monsieur Pettecum, containing the True Reasons of the late Changes in the
Ministry, and of the Calling a New Parliament: And therefore fit to be perus'd
by all the Electors*, London, for J. Baker, 1710, p. 13).

130 *Dregs*: Like the canard that Marlborough's grandfather was a 'Black-
smith near Dorchester' (*POAS*, Yale, vii 661), the belief that Somers's grandfather was a brickmaker (*POAS*, Yale, v 423) and his father 'a noted Rogue'
(Swift, *Prose*, v 258) were articles of Tory faith. For the facts, see William
L. Sachse, *Lord Somers. A Political Portrait*, Manchester, Manchester University Press, 1975, pp. 1-5.

137 *Deist*: Somers was called 'a Hobbist' and a Socinian (Vernon, iii 13,
156). He encouraged Toland to edit Milton's republican prose and to write a
life of Milton (1698) as preface (John Hughes, *The Works of Mr. Edmund Spen-
ser*, 6 vols., London, for Jacob Tonson, 1715, i, p. v). Somers was unmarried
but his mistress was Elizabeth, daughter of Sir Richard Fanshawe, married to
a minor government official named Blunt (*POAS*, Yale, v 427). *A Letter from
the Grecian Coffee-house, In Answer to the Taunton-Dean Letter*, London, 1701,
p. 7, mentions 'his L---p's ... keeping *Bl--t* in Jayle, while he lay with his
Wife'. 'I [have not seen] lord Somers ... since the first visit,' Swift told
Stella on 24 January 1711, 'for he has been a false deceitful rascal' (Swift,
Journal, p. 173).

142 *L--d St---rd*: John Sheffield, Duke of Buckingham and Normanby (1648-
1721), replaced the Duke of Devonshire as Lord Steward of the Household on
21 September 1710. He was Dryden's patron and Pope 'overlooked' an edition of
his works in 1723. Macky mentions his 'Learning, and good Natural Parts' and
Swift thought 'This Charact[e]r ... the truest of any' (*Prose*, v 257).

Wit and Knowledge; is of consummate Wisdom and Experience in Affairs; has continued constant to the true Interest of the Nation,
145 which he espous'd from the beginning, and is every way qualify'd
to support the Dignity of his Office: But in point of *Oratory*
must give Place to his Predecessor.

The D. of *Sh------y* was highly Instrumental in bringing about
the *Revolution*, in which Service he freely expos'd his Life and
150 Fortune. He has ever been the Favourite of the Nation, being
possess'd of all the amiable Qualities that can accomplish a
great Man; but in the agreeableness and fragrancy of his Person,
and the profoundness of his Politicks, must be allow'd to fall
very short of --------.

155   Mr. *H-----* had the Honour of being chosen Speaker successively
to three Parliaments; he was the first of late Years, that ventur'd to restore the forgotten Custom of treating his PRINCE with
Duty and *Respect*. Easy and disengag'd in private Conversation,
with such a weight of Affairs upon his Shoulders; of great Learn-
160 ing, and as great a Favourer and Protector of it; Intrepid by

151-2 all the amiable Qualities that can accomplish a great Man] many amiable
Qualities 38 8°+12°   156 that] who 38 8°+12°

---

147 *Predecessor*: William Cavendish, 2nd Duke of Devonshire (*c*.1673-1729),
succeeded his father as Lord Steward of the Household in September 1707. As
the Marquis of Hartington he was a Whig wheelhorse in the House of Commons
(November 1695-1707) and 'a bold Orator', but Swift put him down for 'A very
poor Understanding' (*Prose*, v 258) and Defoe includes a specimen of his Whiggish rhetoric in *The Dyet of Poland* (*POAS*, Yale, vii 106).
148 *Sh--------y*: Charles Talbot, 12th Earl and 1st Duke of Shrewsbury
(1660-1718), mortgaged his estates for £40,000 and joined William of Orange
at The Hague, landing with him at Torbay in November 1688. William, who called
him 'the *King of Hearts*', made him his Secretary of State (1689-90, 1695-8),
Privy Councillor, and Lord Chamberlain (1699-1700). In 1700 he was called 'le
Chef des Whigs' (BL MS Add. 30000D, f. 172), but his retreat to the continent
(1701-6) alienated the Junto and upon his return he became an ally of Harley.
In April 1710 he was again made Lord Chamberlain and a Privy Councillor 'by
the sole Interest of Harley' (BL MS Lansdowne 885, f. 67).
152 *fragrancy*: Henry Grey, Duke of Kent (1671-1740) 'was always violent
[for] the tory party and was never in any employment till he was made Lord
Chamberlain ... as [is] said for 10000 Pounds which he gave the Duchess of
Marlborough. He is one of a good estate, a very ugly figure, of but indifferent parts' (*Wentworth Papers*, p. 134). He was so malodorous that he was called
'The Bug' and 'his Stinkingness' (BL MS Add. 61459).
158 *Easy*: A rare glimpse of Harley *en pantoufles* is provided in [Jonathan
Smedley?,] *Dr. S---'s Real Diary; Being a True and Faithful Account of himself,
for that Week, wherein he is Traduc'd by the Author of a scandalous and malicious Hue and Cry after him: Containing, His entire Journal, from the Time he
left London, to his Settling in Dublin*, London, for R. Burleigh, 1715, sig. A3ᵛ.

Nature, as well as by the consciousness of his own Integrity, and
a despiser of Money; pursuing the true Interest of his PRINCE and
Country against all Obstacles. Sagacious to view into the remot-
est Consequences of Things, by which all Difficulties fly before
him. A firm Friend, and a placable Enemy, sacrificing his justest   165
Resentments, not only to Publick Good, but to commom Intercession
and Acknowledgment. Yet with all these Virtues it must be granted,
there is some Mixture of Human Infirmity: His greatest Admirers
must confess his Skill at *Cards* and *Dice* to be very low and
superficial: In *Horse-Racing* he is utterly Ignorant: Then, to   170
save a few Millions to the Publick, he never regards how many
worthy Citizens he hinders from making up their *Plumb*. And surely
there is one Thing never to be forgiven him, that he delights to
have his Table fill'd with *Black Coats*, whom he uses as if they
were *Gentlemen*.   175

My Lord *D--------* is a Man of Letters, full of good Sense, good
Nature and Honour, of strict Virtue and Regularity in Life; but
labours under one great Defect, that he treats his *Clerks* with
more Civility and good Manners, than others, in his Station,
have done the Qu---.   180

174 uses] useth 38 8°+12°   177 in Life] in his Life 38 8°+12°

---

169 *Cards and Dice*: 86.156.
170 *Horse-Racing*: Godolphin's dedication to the improvement of the breed
was so great that in April 1710, when Anne made her first move to bring down
his ministry, Godolphin was at the Newmarket races (Coxe, *Marlborough*, iii 61).
In August 1710 Anne's angry letter dismissing him was delivered by her groom
of the stables (Swift, *Corr.*, i 174).
172 *Plumb*: £100,000 (*OED*, s.v. plum).
174 *Black Coats*: clerics.
176 *D--------*: William Legge (1672-1750), educated at Westminster and
King's College, Cambridge, succeeded as 2nd Lord Dartmouth in October 1691.
As a 'Creature of Harley's' (BL MS Lansdowne 885, f. 66ᵛ), he was appointed
a Secretary of State in June 1710. 'He sets up for a Critick in Conversation,
makes Jests, and loves to laugh at them', was a contemporary judgement that
Swift characterized as 'right enough' (Swift, *Prose*, v 259). One of Dartmouth's Under-Secretaries was Swift's friend, Erasmus Lewis.
179 *Mariners*: Charles Spencer, 3rd Earl of Sunderland (1674-1722), married
Lady Anne Churchill, second daughter of the then Earl of Marlborough, in
January 1700. His 'rough way of treating his Sovereign' (Swift, *Prose*, vii 9)
offended Anne, but the Duke and Duchess of Marlborough wore down her resistance and in December 1706 Sunderland was appointed Secretary of State. Success, however, did not incline him to 'lay Aside the violence of his Temper'
(BL MS Add. 4291, f. 112). He treated the Queen 'with great rudeness and
neglect, and chose to reflect in a very injurious manner upon all princes,
before her, as a proper entertainment for her' (Burnet, 1833, vi 9 n.). Anne
was glad to dismiss him in June 1710.

Omitting some others, I will close this Character of the present
Ministry, with that of Mr. *S-------*, who from his Youth applying
those admirable Talents of Nature and Improvements of Art to publick Business, grew eminent in Court and Parliament at an Age
185 when the generality of Mankind is employ'd in Trifles and Folly.
'Tis to be lamented, that he has not yet procur'd himself a *busy,
important Countenance*, nor learn'd that profound Part of Wisdom,
to be *difficult of Access*. Besides, he has clearly mistaken the
true use of *Books*, which he has thumb'd and spoil'd with *Reading*,
190 when he ought to have multiplied them on his Shelves: Not like a
great Man of my Acquaintance, who knew a *Book* by the *Back*, better
than a *Friend* by the *Face*, though he had *never convers'd* with the
former, and often with the latter.

182 *S-------*: Henry St. John (1678-1751) began his political career as a
Tory Member for Wootton-Bassett (February 1701-1708), a Wiltshire borough to
which he was returned on the interest of his father, Sir Henry St. John of
Battersea, 4th baronet. In Parliament he attached himself to the New Country
Party of Harley and his brilliance as a speaker soon brought him success,
which included the post of Secretary of State in September 1710. From the
beginning Swift was fascinated with this brilliant rake, who is said to have
neglected 'his W----ng now and then, to toy with the Business of a N----n'
(Oldmixon, *The Life*, p. 356). In November 1711 Swift told Stella, 'I think
Mr. St. John the greatest young man I ever knew; wit, capacity, beauty, quick-
ness of apprehension, good learning, and an excellent taste; the best orator
in the house of commons, admirable conversation, good nature, and good manners; generous, and a despiser of money ... What truth and sincerity he may
have I know not: he is now but thirty-two, and has been secretary above a year.
Is not all this extraordinary?' (Swift, *Journal*, p. 401).
  189 *Books*: Sunderland was one of the great bibliophiles and collectors of
the period, 'A Peer to be deduc'd to future Ages, | For buying *Books*, and
reading *Title-Pages*' (*POAS*, Yale, vii 365).

No. 19 [Mainwaring and Oldmixon]   5 February 1711

The MEDLEY.

The Whigs the only good Churchmen.

Resistance a Tory-Principle.

Of the Examiner's *Modesty and Moderation.*

His Votes of Parliament.

A Character of the late Ministry, by the Lord Belhaven.

The Notion, that People are the Riches of a Nation, confuted.

THO the *Tories* have over and over again prov'd the *Whigs* to be
Republicans, they shall never make *Schismaticks* of them, nor shut
the *Ruin'd Party* out of the Pale of the Church: For there's nothing more plain than that the *Whigs* are good *Churchmen*, and as
little Occasional Conformists too, as the most stanch of 'em all;   5
nay, that their very Principles are *Primitive* and *Orthodox*: and
I shall prove it by such Authority, that no body shall have a
word to say against me. I grant the *Tories* have done great things
in the Church's name, as well as the *Whigs*: If the latter *abdicated* King *James*, and set King *William* on the Throne, which they   10
are always bragging of, the *Tories* routed the Junto; and that,
sure, is as great a piece of Service to the Church, considering
what Danger she was in, and how these sad Men were *sapping* and
undermining her. However, if I was a Tory, I wou'd not let the
Whigs have any share of the Honour of the Revolution, since   15
hardly any one but good Churchmen were concern'd in it, as may
be seen by the Bishop of *Rochester*'s Letters to the Earl of *Dorset*, printed in the Year 1689. *Twill be sufficient once for all*,
says that Prelate, *that the main Body of those who made so brave
a* Stand *were all of the Church of* England, *and the Principles on*   20
which they stood, were all Church-of-England *Principles. It was
by these Persons and these Principles that Popery was stopt in
its full Career, by these it was hinder'd from conquering, and
put in a condition to be shortly after conquer'd.* Again: *I know*,
says he, *it was formerly a popular Objection of divers misguided*   25
Dissenters from the Church of England, *that our Principles were
too* Monarchical, *and that we carry'd the Doctrine of Obedience
farther than might be consistent with the Safety of a Protestant
Church, or the Privileges of a Free-born People: But it is now*

13 these] those 12°   18 1689] 1688 ½°

---

2 *Republicans*: cf. 'the *Tories* call the *Whiggs Republicans*, and the *Whiggs*
call the *Tories Jacobites*' (*A Letter from a Foreign Minister in England to
Monsieur Pettecum*. 1710, p. 6).
13 *Danger*: 38.106-7.
13-14 *sapping and undermining*: cf. *A Collection of the Addresses*, i 21, 29,
40; ii 9.
18-32 *Twill ... countenance*: Thomas Sprat, *The Bishop of Rochester's
Second Letter to the Right Honourable the Earl of Dorset and Middlesex, Lord-
Chamberlain of His Majesty's Household*, [London], by Edward Jones, 1689, pp.
58, 53-4).

30   *to be hop'd that the strongest Argument of all others, which is*
     Experience from undoubted Matter of Fact, has put this Objection
     for ever out of countenance. What must the Bishop think of those
     that deny this *undoubted Matter of Fact*, and affirm there was no
     Resistance, no making a *Stand*? K. *James* himself drove this Argu-
35   ment too far, out of spite to the Church; and a Letter, publish'd
     by him on a certain occasion, charges the Preachers with leading
     their Hearers into *Disobedience, Schism,* and *Rebellion*, as he
     calls it: but we own no such thing. There was a Book publish'd in
     1688. licens'd by the President of the Council, in vindication of
40   the High Commission (of which two or three of the *Examiner*'s
     Friends now living were Members) wherein 'tis said, *His Majesty,*
     that he may convince the most obstinate Enemies to his Govern-
     ment, is resolv'd to proceed in the calmest way; and therefore

34 *Resistance*: The argument about what exactly happened in England between
November 1688 and April 1689 was inadvertently reopened by Offspring Blackall,
Bishop of Exeter, in a sermon preached before the Queen on 8 March 1709.
Blackall expounded the High Church doctrine that even a constitutional monarch
(like Anne) (1) 'has his Commission and Authority from God ... and *whosoever*
resisteth the Power, resisteth the Ordinance of God [*Romans* 13:2]' and (2) is
'not ... accountable to the People' (*The Divine Institution of Magistracy, and*
the Gracious Design of its Institution, London, for H. Hills, no date, p. 4).
Hoadly wrote a reply to the sermon, *Some Considerations humbly offer'd to the*
Right Reverend the Lord Bishop of Exeter (April 1709), and in his defence of
it Blackall said that 'K. *James* ... had withdrawn himself, and abdicated the
Government ... Whereupon the Parliament, finding no body in the Throne ...
fill'd it with Queen *Mary* his next Heir, joyning with her ... her Husband K.
William' (*The Lord Bishop of Exeter's Answer to Mr. Hoadly's Letter*, London,
1709, p. 14). This set off a fire-fight that eventually drew in everyone from
Swift's friend Will Pate, 'the learned Woollen-draper', to Tom o' Bedlam (*The*
Revolution No Rebellion: Or, Serious Reflections Offered to the Reverend Ben-
jamin Hoadly (1709); *Tom o' Bedlam's Answer to his Brother Ben Hoadly* (1709)).
Sacheverell added that William III 'solemnly *Disclaim'd* the Least Imputation
of *Resistance* in his *Declaration* [13 February 1689]; and that the *Parliament*
... did ... Unanimously condemn to the Flames, (as it justly Deserv'd) that
Infamous Libel [Charles Blount, *King William and Queen Mary, Conquerors*
(1693)], that would have *Pleaded* the *Title* of *Conquest*' (*The Perils of False*
Brethren, both in Church, and State, 1709, p. 13). It was this claim, in fact,
that became the first article of Sacheverell's impeachment: 'He, the said
Henry Sacheverell ... doth suggest and maintain ... *That his late Majesty, in*
his Declaration, disclaim'd the least Imputation of Resistance; and that to
impute Resistance to the said Revolution, is to cast Black and Odious Colours
upon his late Majesty, and the said Revolution' (*The Tryal*, pp. 8-9).
36-7 *leading ... Rebellion*: James II, *Directions concerning Preachers*,
London, by C. Bill *et al.*, 1685, pp. 3-5.
40 *High Commission*: 159.113.
41-54 *His ... Government*: [Henry Care,] *A Vindication of the Proceedings of*
His Majesties Ecclesiastical Commissioners, against the Bishop of London, and
the Fellows of Magdalen-College, London, Tho. Milbourn, 1688, pp. 77-8, 67,
69).

*notwithstanding the most undutiful and disloyal Reflections cast
on Majesty it self by some of the Church of* England, *'tis his*   45
*Royal Purpose that his Commissioners shall not exercise that
Severity against them, which they have against Protestant Dissenters, nor will his Majesty take those Advantages against their
Clergy which he might.* And *Instead of acting according to their*
quondam *avow'd Doctrine of Passive Obedience, they fly in the*   50
face of Authority, &c. He goes on, *When the Protestant Dissenters
went not half so far in their Disobedience to the Regal Authority, they cou'd not escape the Censure of being Enemies to the
Government.* Which shews that the Tories all this while are but
in jest, and believe no more of Passive Obedience and Non-   55
Resistance than other Folks, nor practise any more when they are
ever so little touch'd.

I have often observ'd, that my Friend the *Examiner* wou'd be
thought to write a State-Paper, and that to attack him is criminal. This is the best Argument he has on his side, and serves for 60
an Answer to all Objections. He assumes a superior Air, very useful and artful; and tho no Man in his wits can suppose the
Ministry wou'd own such a Tool as he, yet to fall upon him is, in
his way of speaking, to insult the Q---n, the Parliament, and
Ministers; and if he had a Law made to that purpose, he cou'd not 65
take more upon him. *I wish,* quoth he, *these Gentlemen wou'd compare the Liberty they take with what their Masters us'd to give,
how many Messengers and Warrants wou'd have gone out,* &c. Of
which his dear Friend *Lesley* is a famous Instance, who for six
or seven years wrote Treason thrice a week with impunity: So   70
inveterate and cruel was that Party, whom he and the *Examiner*
boast they have *ruin'd* by their Writings! Indeed we do take some
Freedoms with my Friend, and shall continue so to do, as long as
he so insolently treats the late Parliament and Ministry. Because
my Friend is so forward to charge others with the very thing he   75
is every week doing himself, the publishing *false, insolent,* and

75 my Friend] he 12°

66-8 *I ... out:* 194.54-6.
69 *Lesley:* Charles Leslie published *The Rehearsal* on Saturdays from 5
August 1704 to 6 April 1706 and on Wednesdays and Saturdays from 10 April 1706
to 26 March 1709.
76-7 *false ... Libels:* 193.42.

scandalous Libels; let us inquire into his last Paper a little,
and see how faithfully he draws the Picture of the late Parliament and Ministry: and then let any one judg what Censure he
80 deserves for so false, so insolent, and so scandalous an Invective.

The *Examiner's* Account of the late House of Commons and
Ministers, in his Votes of Parliament, *Numb.* 26.

*That they intended to bring in a Commonwealth, and sell every
Man's Birthright for a Shilling.*
85 *To pass an Act to qualify Atheists, Deists, and Socinians for
Places; which he appoints Mr.* Lechm--- *to bring in.*
*Another to forbid the Clergy to preach Religious Duties, as
Obedience,* &c.
Another to deprive Bishops of their Jurisdiction.
90 *Another to make a General for Life, and that the War shou'd
last as long as he liv'd.*
*Another to attaint two Dukes, one Earl, one Knight, two Squires,
and a marry'd Spinster, at a lump, for High Treason against the
Junto.*
95 *That they wou'd have declar'd the Original Contract to be a
Constitution of a Junto and a King or Queen; the Junto only to
have the Executive Power.*
*That they wou'd have pass'd an Act further to limit the Preroga-
tive.*

100 I shall say nothing of what he adds about the Merit of Elections, and deciding a Majority; for I verily believe he's asham'd
of it himself, and by this time wishes it out of his Libel, since,
to say Truth, he knows now as much of Majorities and Elections as
any body. I cannot but value my self a little on my Impartiality,
105 and even Friendship to the *Examiner*, being so much in love with
every thing he does, that you see I publish his very Scandal and
Sedition for him, and almost make my self as guilty as he is.
'Tis true, I do it in hopes he is in Favour, and that he would

84 *Birthright ... Shilling*: 195.76-7.
85-99 *To ... Prerogative*: 195.85-196.112.
93 *a marry'd Spinster*: 196.100.
100-1 *Elections*: 196.114.

not leave his Friend in the lurch, but take the whole Guilt on
himself, which indeed cannot be charg'd to me, but on his Account: 110
and thus much common Prudence oblig'd me to offer in my own Vindication; for doubtless such Calumny as that can never pass without a Day of Reckoning. After all this, what need is there of
mentioning his other intended Actions of the same Parliament and
Ministry, *as the cutting off all Hopes of a Peace, industriously* 115
involving the Nation in Debt, turning the Bishops out of the
House of Lords, selling their Lands, and setting up Presbytery?
which my Friend confidently affirms they wou'd have done if they
cou'd: And what's worse than all, have infallibly destroy'd the
Independency of the Clergy on the State, which he humourously   120
calls an *idle Claim*. But I don't think such things shou'd *be*
jested with, and I hope I shall not disoblige the Convocation, by
abhorring so as I do that *idle Claim* of his; an Expression as
much against good Manners as 'tis against Law. An unlucky Accident or two has happen'd, wherein my Friend has discover'd what   125
a strange Novice he is at Argument; about which, tho he has twice
or thrice made some Blunders, yet he has shewn too as much
Modesty as he cou'd. He once defy'd Mr. *Hoadley*: Nay, he wrote a
whole Paper against him, but drop'd him there for ever. He
threaten'd the *Management of the War*, but has not yet said a word 130
of it. That, 'tis true, I take to be a Fault of his Friends, and
not his own; they wou'd not let him expose himself, as they knew
he wou'd do, if he ventur'd upon it. Yet he pretends to answer
another Person, but finding the Force of Reason, and the Truth of
Fact against him, is so ingenuous as to own he did not know what   135
he said, and desires to be excus'd, because *he talk'd out of his*
Trade. An Excuse that, for ought I ever saw of his, he may lawfully make to every thing, except Fiction, Slander and Impudence.
His *Glocester* Story, which he has but half recanted; his Allusion
to *Verres*; his Votes, and a hundred other such Falsities, are   140

115-21 *the ... Claim*: 197.128-9, 133-6.
129 *Paper*: Atterbury, *The Examiner*, No. 13, 19-26 October 1710, 'a furious
polemic against Hoadly as the archpatron of the propagators of rebellion and
irreligion' (Bennett, p. 124).
130 *the Management of the War*: 169.200.
134 *Person*: 197.154-5.
136-7 *talk'd ... Trade*: 199.193.
139 *Glocester Story*: 152.205, 185.189.
140 *Verres*: 69.80-72.147.
        Votes: 195.81-196.124.

unquestionable Proofs of his being Master of his Trade in those
Matters. Very justly may that be apply'd to him, which *Plutarch*
says in the Life of *Pericles, Why shou'd one wonder at what such
Fellows say, who scurrilously reflect on other Mens Lives, and*
145   *daily, upon all Occasions, with their Reproaches and evil Speeches,*
sacrifice the Reputation of their Superiours, the Great and Good,
to the Envy and Spite of the Rabble, as to some evil Genius or
wicked Spirit? The *Examiner*'s excellent Talent at Panegyrick and
Satyr shines furiously in his last Paper, *Numb.* 27. one of the
150   merriest certainly which ever was publish'd, as I shall endeavour
to shew in my next; for I am always ready to do Justice to such
extraordinary Merit. To have a right Notion of his Inclination to
Scandal, in abusing the late Administration, 'twill be proper to
see some true Character of the then Ministers; and since mine
155   may be suspected, I'll give it the Reader from a Speech said to
be spoken by a *Scots* Lord, which was mightily cry'd up by the
Tories.

The Lord *Belhaven*'s Character of the late Ministry.

The Circumstances, says he, *of our Neighbours in* England *are*
160   *Great and Glorious; their Treaties are prudently manag'd both at*
Home and Abroad; their Generals brave and valorous; their Armies
successful and victorious; their Enemies subdu'd and routed; their
Strong-Holds taken; their Sieges reliev'd; Mareschals made
Prisoners; Provinces and Kingdoms are the Results of their Vic-
165   *tories; their Royal Navy is the Terror of* Europe; *their Trade*
and Commerce extended thro the Universe, incircling the whole
habitable World: And, *which is yet more than all these Things,*
the Subjects freely bestowing their Treasure upon their Sovereign:
And above all, these vast Riches, the Sinews of War, and without
170   *which all the Glorious Success had prov'd abortive; these Trea-*
sures are manag'd with such Faithfulness and Nicety, *that they*

163 *Strong-Holds*] *strong Holds* ½°

143-8 *Why ... Spirit*: Plutarch, *Life of Pericles*, xiii 11.
159-73 *The ... Distance*: John Hamilton, Lord Belhaven, *The Lord Beilhaven's
Speech in Parliament Saturday the Second of November* [*1706*], *on the Subject-
matter of an Union betwixt the Two Kingdoms of Scotland and England*, no place
of publication, 1706, pp. 15-16.

answer seasonably all their Demands, tho at never so great a
Distance.

Of all the popular Errors imbrac'd by Mankind, there's none
greater in my Mind, than that the Riches of a Nation consist in   175
the Number of the People. How can a Kingdom be the richer for a
parcel of Beggars, to eat the Bread out of one another's Mouths?
Sir *William Petty*, and other Dealers in Political Arithmetick,
pretend indeed, that every living Soul, Man, Woman and Child, is
worth the Publick at least 7 or 8 *l.* a year. A fine Notion that!   180
as if a poor *Palatine*, with a Wife and eight Children, was worth
80 *l.* a year to us, when we know we are 10 or 20 *l.* yearly out of
Pocket to maintain them. Thus 'tis very plain, the Number of
Inhabitants is rather the Poverty than Riches of a Nation; and
all wise Folks will keep themselves to themselves as much as they   185
can. Besides, we in *England* have a great many Reasons against
letting others come among us, which most other Kingdoms have not.
Foreigners, as soon as they land here, are bewitch'd by the
Whigs; and tho they come from a Popish, Arbitrary and Persecuting
Government, they immediately quit their Tory-Principles, vote   190
against the Church, fall to Trading as fast as they can, and grow
Enemies to the *Landed Interest*; which is by much the best we have,
unless it be, as *Old Double* says, the *Church-Interest*. The *Dutch*,
'tis true, are by some thought a pretty politick sort of People,
and yet they naturalize any body that will live with them. But   195

184 is] are ½°

---

176 *People*: This vulgar error was still the law of the land, for the Bill
to repeal the Act for a general Naturalization (194.75) passed the Commons
on 31 January but was thrown out by the Lords on 5 February 1711 (*LJ*, xix 215);
cf. 147.96.
178 *Petty*: 'Suppose the People of *England* be Six Millions in number, that
their expence at 7*l.* per Head be forty two Millions: suppose also that the
Rent of the Lands be eight Millions, and the profit of all the Personal Estate
be Eight Millions more; it must needs follow, that the Labour of the People
must have supplyed the remaining Twenty Six Millions, the which multiplied by
Twenty (the Mass of Mankind being worth Twenty Years purchase as well as Land)
makes Five Hundred and Twenty Millions, as the value of the whole People:
which number divided by Six Millions, makes above 80*l.* Sterling, to be valued
of each Head of Man, Woman, and Child' (Sir William Petty, *Political Arithme-*
tick, or A Discourse Concerning, the Extent and Value of Lands, People, Build-
ings, &c., London, for R. Clavel *et al.*, 1690, p. 32).

Sir *William Temple* tells us, *They do it out of Necessity, thro*
the multitude of People, which forces them to turn their Stock
into Trade. Now if they wou'd not naturalize so, they might have
less People, and that necessity of Trading wou'd be remov'd; so
200   that there's a great Inconvenience in having too many Inhabitants.
A Landed Interest is certainly as much more profitable, as 'tis
more genteel than a Trading. Are not the *Polanders* and *Lithu-*
anians the richest of all Nations? And how comes it about, d'ye
think? Why they have a landed Interest, and if it were not for
205   their Corn, we shou'd not know what to do sometimes. Are not the
Dutch, as the *Examiner* and the Tory-Writers represent them, a
despicable sorry People, *Herring-Curers*? And why, but because
they have a Trading Interest only; no Landed-Interest, no Church-
Interest, in which we have a great Advantage over them: Tho *Old*
210   *Double* says, they have thirty six Millions Sterling ready Cash
in the Bank of *Amsterdam*, four times as much as we have in all
Britain. But then our two other Interests are more than a Ballance for their one only, and I can't see why we shou'd be more
afraid of the War than they are, who are incumbred with so many
215   People, and so much Mony.

203 Nations? And] Nations; and ½°

─────

196 *Temple*: Sir William Temple, *Observations upon the United Provinces of*
the Netherlands, London, by A. Maxwell for Sa. Gellibrand, 1673, pp. 195,
203-4. Oldmixon is paraphrasing, not quoting, Temple's words.
201 *Landed Interest*: The Medley implies that Swift's fantasies about the
'decent hospitable' world of the landed gentry (130.98-9) are based on class
prejudice and chronological primitivism.
202-3 *Polanders and Lithuanians*: With the Grand Duchy of Lithuania in a
state of chronic revolt and the 'Landed Interest' barred from trade by considerations of honour, Poland was virtually bankrupt, so poor that 'a King of
Poland ... will scarcely ever be proof against fifty thousand Louis d'Or's'
(Bernard Connor, *The History of Poland*, 2 vols., London, by J.D. for Dan.
Brown *et al.*, 1698, i, p. vi, ii [2]35-8).
207 *Herring-Curers*: 130.95.
212 *two other Interests*: 225.193, 226.201.

No. 28 [Swift]   8 February 1711

The EXAMINER.

Caput est in omni procuratione negotii & muneris publici, ut avaritiæ
pellatur etiam minima suspicio.

THERE is no Vice which Mankind carries to such wild Extreams as
that of *Avarice*: Those two which seem to rival it in this Point,
are Lust and Ambition: But, the former is checkt by Difficulties
and Diseases, destroys it self by its own Pursuits, and usually
declines with Old Age: And the latter requiring Courage, Conduct   5
and Fortune in a high Degree, and meeting with a thousand Dangers
and Oppositions, succeeds too seldom in an Age to fall under common Observation. Or, is Avarice perhaps the same Passion with
Ambition, only placed in more ignoble and dastardly Minds, by
which the Object is chang'd from *Power* to *Money*? Or it may be,   10
that one Man pursues Power in order to Wealth, and another Wealth
in order to Power; which last is the safer way, tho' longer about,
and suiting with every Period as well as Condition of Life, is
more generally follow'd.

However it be, the Extreams of this Passion are certainly more   15
frequent than of any other, and often to a Degree so absurd and
ridiculous, that if it were not for their Frequency, they could
hardly obtain Belief. The *Stage*, which carries other Follies and
Vices beyond Nature and Probability, falls very short in the
Representations of *Avarice*; nor are there any Extravagances in   20
this Kind describ'd by ancient or modern Comedies, which are not
outdone by an hundred Instances, commonly told, among our selves.

I am ready to conclude from hence, that a Vice which keeps so
firm a Hold upon Human Nature, and governs it with so unlimited
a Tyranny, since it cannot be wholly eradicated, ought at least   25
to be confin'd to particular Objects, to Thrift and Penury, to
private Fraud and Extortion, and never suffer'd to prey upon the
Publick; And should certainly be rejected as the most unqualifying

Motto Cicero, *De Officiis*, ii 75: In every Employment, in public Office, it
is of the utmost Importance to keep free from even the least Suspicion of
Avarice.

Circumstance for any Employment, where Bribery and Corruption
30 can possibly enter.

If the Mischiefs of this Vice, in a publick Station, were confin'd to enriching only those particular Persons employ'd, the
Evil would be more Supportable; but it is usually quite otherwise. When a *Steward* defrauds his *Lord*, he must connive at the
35 *rest of the Servants*, while they are following the same Practice
in their several Spheres; so that in some Families you may observe a Subordination of Knaves in a link downwards to the very
Helper in the Stables, all cheating by Concert, and with Impunity:
And even if this were all, perhaps the Master could bear it with-
40 out being undone; But it so happens, that for every Shilling the
Servant gets by his Iniquity, the Master loses Twenty; the Perquisites of Servants being but small Compositions for suffering
Shop-keepers to bring in what Bills they please. It is exactly
the same Thing in a State: An avaricious Man in Office is in Con-
45 federacy with the whole *Clan* of his District or Dependance, which
in modern Terms of Art is call'd, *To Live, and let Live*, and yet
Their Gains are the smallest part of the Publick's Loss. Give a
Guinea to a Knavish *Land-Waiter*, and he shall connive at the
Merchant for cheating the Queen of an Hundred. A *Brewer* gives a
50 Bribe to have the Privilege of selling Drink to the *Navy*; but the
Fraud is ten times greater than the Bribe, and the Publick is at
the whole Loss.

Moralists make two kinds of Avarice; that of *Cataline, alieni*

41 loses] loseth 38 8°+12°   51 ten] a hundred 38 8°+12°

---

46 *To Live, and let Live*: cf. 'the Dutch proverb, Live and let others
live' (Tilley L380).
49 *Brewer*: 'A scandalous abuse [was] detected by a representation from the
victuallers of the navy, presented to the House of Commons. It was founded in
each seaman being allowed seven pints of beer per day; and although, when
ships were in port, it was usual for the captain to allow great part of the
crew to go ashore, the same quantity was charged to the government; the allowance of the absentees being held the perquisite of the purser, and through him
of the captain. The surplus beer was either sold to merchant vessels, or, what
was more common, it was never received from the brewer, who gave the purser a
sum of money in exchange for the difference between the quantity paid for by
the government, and that actually sent on board the vessel. By these collusory
contracts, the nation was defrauded of large sums. Thomas Ridge, Esq., a [Whig]
member of the House of Commons, was expelled the House, and ordered to be
prosecuted by the attorney-general for being accessory to such a fraud' (E*1814*,
iv 86).
53-4 *alieni ... profusus*: Sallust, *Bellum Catilinae*, v 4.

appetens, sui profusus; and the other more generally understood
by 'that Name; which is, the endless Desire of Hoarding: But I   55
take the former to be more dangerous in a State, because it
mingles well with Ambition, which I think the latter can not; for
though the same Breast may be capable of admitting both, it is
not able to cultivate them; and where the Love of heaping Wealth
prevails, there is not in my Opinion, much to be apprehended from   60
Ambition. The Disgrace of that sordid Vice is sooner apt to
spread than any other, and is always attended with the Hatred and
Scorn of the People: So that whenever those two Passions happen
to meet in the same Subject, it is not unlikely that Providence
hath placed *Avarice* to be a Check upon *Ambition*; and I have rea-   65
son to think, *some Great Ministers of State* have been of my
Opinion.

The Divine Authority of Holy Writ, the Precepts of Philosophers,
the Lashes and Ridicule of Satyrical Poets, have been all employ'd in exploding this insatiable Thirst of Money, and all   70
equally controll'd by the daily Practice of Mankind. Nothing new
remains to be said upon the Occasion, and if there did, I must
remember my Character, that I am an *Examiner* only, and not a
Reformer.

However, in those Cases where the Frailties of particular Men   75
do nearly affect the publick Welfare, such as a Prime Minister of
State, or a great General of an Army; methinks there should be
some Expedient contriv'd, to let them know impartially what is
the World's Opinion in the Point: Encompassed with a Crowd of
depending Flatterers, they are many degrees blinder to their own   80
Faults than the common Infirmities of Human Nature can plead in
their Excuse; Advice dares not be offer'd, or is wholly lost, or
return'd with Hatred: And whatever appears in Publick against
their prevailing Vice, goes for nothing; being either not applied,
or passing only for Libel and Slander, proceeding from the Malice   85
and Envy of a Party.

I have sometimes thought, that if I had lived at *Rome* in the
Time of the first *Triumvirate*, I should have been tempted to
write a Letter, as from an unknown Hand, to those three Great

65 *Avarice ... Ambition*: the leitmotiv for Marlborough.
71 *controll'd*: 'overruled; *arch.*' (*OED*).
89 *Letter*: 'The *Letter to Crassus* is the perfection of what Swift aimed at

90 Men, who had then usurp'd the Sovereign Power; wherein I would
    freely and sincerely tell each of them that Fault which I con-
    ceiv'd was most Odious, and of most Consequence to the Common-
    wealth: That, to *Crassus*, should have been sent to him after his
    Conquests in *Mesopotamia*, and in the following Terms.

95   *To* Marcus Crassus, *Health.*

    IF you apply as you ought, what I now write, you will be more
    oblig'd to me than to all the World, hardly excepting your Parents
    or your Country. I intend to tell you, without Disguise or Preju-
    dice, the Opinion which the World has entertain'd of you: And to
100 *let you see I write this without any sort of ill Will, you shall*
    first hear the Sentiments they have to your Advantage. No Man
    disputes the Gracefulness of your Person; You are allowed to have
    a good and clear Understanding, cultivated by the Knowledge of
    Men and Manners, though not by Literature. *You are no ill Orator*
105 *in the Senate; you are said to excel in the Art of bridling and*
    subduing your Anger, and stifling or concealing your Resentments.
    You have been a most successful General, of long Experience, great
    Conduct, and much Personal Courage. You have gain'd many impor-
    tant Victories for the Commonwealth, and forc'd the strongest
110 *Towns in* Mesopotamia *to surrender, for which frequent* Supplica-
    tions have been decreed by the Senate. Yet with all these Quali-
    ties, and this Merit, give me leave to say, you are neither
    beloved by the Patricians *or* Plebeians *at home, nor by the Offi-*
    cers or private Soldiers of your own Army abroad: And, do you
115 *know,* Crassus, *that this is owing to a Fault, of which you may*
    Cure your self, by one Minutes Reflection? What shall I say? You
    are the richest Person in the Commonwealth; You have no Male
    Child, your Daughters are all Married to wealthy Patricians; *you*
    are far in the decline of Life; and yet you are deeply stain'd
120 *with that odious and ignoble Vice of* Covetousness: *'Tis affirm'd,*
    that you descend even to the meanest and most scandalous Degrees
    of it; and while you possess so many Millions, while you are

    92 most] worst 38 8°+12°   103 *Knowledge*] *Knewledge* ½°   122 *Millions*]
    Million 38 8°

────

in his role of Examiner. The quiet intensity and restraint give his words a
quality of aloofness, as if beyond bias and passion' (Herbert Davis) (Swift,
Prose, iii, p. xvii).

daily acquiring so many more, you are sollicitous how to save a
single Sesterce, *of which a hundred ignominious Instances are*
produc'd, and in all Mens Mouths. I will only mention that Pas-   125
sage of the Buskins, *which after abundance of Persuasion, you*
would hardly suffer to be cut from your Legs, when they were so
wet and cold, that to have kept them on, would have endanger'd
your Life.

Instead of using the common Arguments to dissuade you from this   130
Weakness, I will endeavour to convince you, that   you are really
guilty of it, and leave the Cure to your own good Sense. For per-
haps, you are not yet persuaded that this is your Crime, you have
probably never yet been reproach'd for it to your Face, and what
you are now told, comes from One unknown, and it may be, from an   135
Enemy. You will allow your self indeed to be prudent in the
Management of your Fortune; You are not a Prodigal, like Clodius
or Cataline, *but surely that deserves not the Name of* Avarice. *I*
will inform you how to be convinced. Disguise your Person; go
among the Common People in Rome; *introduce Discourses about your*   140
self; inquire your own Character; do the same in your Camp, walk
about it in the Evening, hearken at every Tent, and if you do
not hear every Mouth Censuring, Lamenting, Cursing this Vice in
you, and even You for this Vice, conclude your self Innocent. If
you are not yet persuaded, send for Atticus, Servius Sulpicius,   145
Cato *or* Brutus, *they are all your Friends; conjure them to tell*
you ingenuously which is your great Fault, and which they would
chiefly wish you to correct; if they do not all agree in their
Verdict, in the Name of all the Gods, you are acquitted.

When your Adversaries reflect how far you are gone in this   150
Vice, they are tempted to talk as if we owed our Success, not to
Your Courage or Conduct, but to those Veteran *Troops you command,*
who are able to Conquer under any General, *with so many brave and*
experienc'd Officers to lead them. Besides, we know the Conse-
quences your Avarice hath often occasion'd. The Soldier hath   155

123 *daily*] *om.* 38 8°+12°   145 *are*] *be* 38 8°+12°   148 *all*] *om.* 38
8°+12°   151 *Success*] *Successes* 12° 38 8°+12°

---

137 *Clodius*: innuendo: Wharton (213.91).
155 *Soldier*: Complaints about Marlborough 'starving poor Soldiers, curtail-
ing their Bread' and 'sacrificing ... lives against stone walls' were common

been starving for Bread, surrounded with Plenty, and in an Ene-
mies Country, but all under **Sauf-guards** *and* **Contributions;** *which*
if you had sometimes pleas'd to have exchang'd for **Provisions,**
might at the Expence of a few **Talents** *in a Campaign, have so*
160 *endear'd you to the Army, that they would have desired you to*
lead them to the utmost Limits of **Asia.** *But you rather chose to*
confine your Conquests within the Fruitful Country of **Mesopotamia,**
where Plenty of Money might be rais'd. How far that fatal Greedi-
ness of Gold may have influenc'd you, in breaking off the Treaty
165 *with the old* **Parthian** *King* **Orodes,** *you best can tell; your Ene-*
mies charge you with it, your Friends offer nothing material in
your Defence; and all agree, there is nothing so pernicious,
which the Extreams of Avarice may not be able to inspire.

  The Moment you quit this Vice, you will be a truly Great Man;
170 *and still there will Imperfections enough remain to convince us,*
you are not a God. *Farewel.*

  Perhaps a Letter of this Nature, sent to so reasonable a Man as
Crassus, might have put him upon *Examining* into himself, and cor-
recting that little sordid Appetite, so utterly inconsistent with
175 all Pretences to a *Hero.* A Youth in the heat of Blood may plead
with some shew of Reason, that he is not able to subdue his Lusts;
An ambitious Man may use the same Arguments for his love of
Power, or perhaps other Arguments to justify it. But, Excess of
Avarice hath neither of these Pleas to offer; it is not to be
180 justified, and cannot pretend Temptation for Excuse: Whence can
the Temptation come? Reason disclaims it altogether, and it cannot be said to lodge in the *Blood,* or the *Animal Spirits.* So
that I conclude, *No Man of true Valour and true Understanding,*
upon whom this Vice has stollen unawares, when he is convinced he
185 *is guilty, will suffer it to remain in his Breast an hour.*

  161 *rather chose] chose rather* **38 12°**

(Leeds University MS Brotherton Lt.11, p. 160; Edmund Calamy, *An Historical
Account of My Own Life,* ed. John T. Rutt, 2nd edn., 2 vols., London, Colburn
and Bentley, 1829, ii 247).
  157 *Sauf-guards and Contributions:* **56.176.**
  164 *breaking off the Treaty:* 9.176. Cf. 'when Crassus had pitched his
camp at Nicephorium, ambassadors arrived from king Orodes with a message bid-
ding him remember the treaties ... Crassus, who coveted the royal treasures,
answered not a word' (Florus, i 46 4-5).

No. 20 [Mainwaring]   12 February 1711

The MEDLEY.

On a late Letter to Crassus.

Of Mens Ingratitude to their Country.

Of the Examiner's *being listed into the Service.*

His own False Account of it.

A Passage out of Archbishop Tillotson.

I Intended, in this Paper, to have consider'd the *Examiner's* late
Performance, *in praising those that are at the Head of Affairs,
and taking notice at the same time of their Defects,* to use his
own words; but he has relaps'd so soon into his Disease of Scandal, that I will defer what I had design'd upon the other Head,   5
that I may attend him at this time in his more dangerous Fit of
Defamation. Indeed he appears, by his last Paper, to be in so
desperate a Condition, that all his Friends should in good earnest look after him, lest, like the Weazle in the Fable, whilst he
endeavours *to bite the File, he shou'd happen to cut his own*   10
Tongue. Such is the common Fate of all impudent Dealers in
Calumny, who are justly expos'd in that Emblem. But of all that
ever made it their Business to defame, there never was such a
Bungler sure as my Friend. He writes a Letter now to *Crassus,* as
a Man mark'd out for Destruction, because that Hint was given   15
him six Months ago; and does not seem to know yet that he is
still employ'd, and that in attacking him, he affronts the Q---n,
and differs with his own Majority of Nine Parts in Ten of the

---

10 *File*] *Tile* ½° 12°

2-3 *in ... Defects*: 214.116-17.
9 *Fable: Centum et quinquaginta fabulae carminibus explicatae a Panta-
leone Candido,* Frankfurt, J. Rhodes, 1604, pp. 106-7; reprinted in Janus
Gruterus, *Delitiae Poetarum Germanorum,* 6 vols., Frankfurt, by Nicolaus Hoff-
mann for Jacob Fischer, 1612, ii 155-6; cf. L'Estrange, p. 46.
15 *Hint*: No 'Hint' of *The Examiner,* No. 28, is to be found in St. John's
Letter to The Examiner (August 1710), which says only that Anne's raising up
of Marlborough 'to the highest Degrees of Riches, of Power, and of Honour ...
Griev'd [some] of Her Subjects' (p. 12).
18 *Nine Parts in Ten*: 214.107 etc.

Kingdom, who all desire the Service of the General. Such an in-
20 corrigible Person is this *Examiner*! And yet we ought not to wonder at what he does, since he only follows Nature, and keeps up
to the heighth of his Genius. *Aristotle* says, There are some
Fishes that have Teeth upon their Tongues; one wou'd almost believe my Friend to be of the same Make, and that he cou'd not
25 move his Tongue but to bite. But what does he mean by throwing
away his Libels, where they never make the least Impression? If
what the Philosophers have held, be true, that it is an Honour to
receive Injuries, when we are not affected by them, because we
cannot otherwise shew the Firmness of our Minds; no body was ever
30 so much honour'd as our General has been by the *Examiner*. His
calm Contempt of such harmless Malice, puts me in mind of a Story
I have read of *Philip* the Second, King of *Spain*; who being told
that a certain Doctor had publickly defam'd him, and was put in
Prison for it, sent a Servant to the Man, to know *if he had done*
35 *him any Injury*. To which the Doctor answer'd, *Never in all his*
Life. This Report being made to the King, he order'd the Doctor
to be immediately set at Liberty. At which many People being surpriz'd, and desiring to know his Majesty's Reason for it; *I do it,*
said the King, *because the Man must be a Fool, for no body else*
40 *wou'd abuse so outrageously a Person that never injur'd him*; and
why shou'd I punish an Idiot? But this *Examiner* goes further; for
he not only falls upon one that never injur'd him, but upon one
that (if he will not own himself for *France* and Popery) has
actually done him, as well as all other *Englishmen*, signal Bene-
45 fits and Service. So that all he writes against this Great Man,
ought to be consider'd as the pure Effect of his Malice to our
Constitution; and all the Falshood and Poison that drops from

22 heighth] height 12°   47 drops] drop 12°

---

23 *Fishes ... Tongues*: Aristotle, *De hist*[*oria*] *Animal*[*ium*]. 1. 2. c. 17
(½° corrected).
    25 *bite*: A similar complaint was made of Swift's predecessors: the Examiner
'would have been more properly entitled the *Executioner*: At least, his Examination is like that which is made by the Rack and Wheel' (Addison, *The Whig-*
Examiner, 14 September 1710).
    31 *calm Contempt*: not reflected in Marlborough's threat to have some friend
break Tutchin's bones or in his complaints about 'the villanous way of printing, which stabes me to the heart' (HMC *Bath MSS*, i 105; *Marlborough-Godolphin*
Corr., p. 1662).
    32 *Philip the Second*: La Mothe le Vayer, i [1]54-5.

his Pen, shou'd meet with no more regard than the Raving of one
that is in a Phrenzy or a Feaver. The poor Man can't help it, it
is his Distemper; and it wou'd be wrong to shew Resentment   50
against one who has lost his Reason, who is carry'd away by the
Impetuosity of his own false Principles, and who was retain'd at
first to scribble against the Revolution, and hir'd to cry down
all those that contributed to it. But his scurrilous Reflections
on this General only, bring to my Thoughts a beautiful Comparison   55
in *Marcus Antoninus*; who says, A Person of true Merit and Vertue,
seems, in his Opinion, to resemble an agreeable Fountain, which
Men vainly endeavour to trouble and pollute, by throwing Filth
and Nastiness into it: The Water purges off immediately all such
Dregs and Dirt, and of it self grows clear again, and retains the 60
Purity of its Spring.

A good deal has been said of late concerning the Ingratitude of
a Country to those that have well deserv'd of it: Thus was *Rome*
ungrateful to the *Scipio's* to *Camillus*, to twenty more that might
be nam'd: Thus was *Athens* ungrateful to *Miltiades*, *Themistocles* 65
and others; *Lacedemon* to *Agis*; *Carthage* to *Hannibal* and *Hanno*:
and if it were reasonable to produce more modern Examples, other
Countries might be nam'd that were in a fair way of being as
illustrious for Ingratitude of this kind, as any of those above-
mention'd. But there is another kind of Ingratitude, of which   70
nothing has been said that I remember; which is the Vice of those
that are ungrateful to their Country. Now there are many ways of
being ungrateful in this sense, according to the Opinion of
Gyraldus: 'Men are ungrateful to their Country, says he, when
they stir up Sedition, Riots and Tumults in it: when they encour- 75
age Discord and Strife among the People: when they oppress them
with Poverty, or contrive any other Ways and Means, which may
lessen their Prosperity and Safety, and tend to the Ruin of their
Commonwealth. In all these Cases, that Author says, they are as
ungrateful to their Country, as if they invaded it with Fire and   80

58 vainly] in vain 12°

56-61 *A ... Spring*: Marcus Aurelius Antoninus, *Meditations*, viii 51.
74-85 *Men ... it*: [Giraldus] Paraen[eticus] advers[us] Ingrat[os]. [*Opera
omnia*, 1696, ii 697-8] (½°).

Sword, or made it subject to lawless Tyranny. But he adds, since
there are not only antient Examples of this matter, but some
very *fresh, and in every body's Memory*; and that it is a Subject
which has not only been handled by Famous Philosophers, but other
85   Authors *have collected Historical Accounts of it*: he therefore
thinks it unnecessary to say any more concerning it.'

I will follow the Opinion of this Author, and return to my
Friend the *Examiner*.

When that worthy Gentleman was first put upon writing his
90   Weekly Paper, it was presently given out by the Wags of his
Party, that *he was to maul the Whigs*: Scandal was the only thing
he pretended to; and knowing he had very little Good to say of
his Masters that employ'd him, he cou'd do no less than promise
to write a great deal of Ill of their Opponents. His Acquaintance
95   answer'd for him, that he had a Conscience exactly suted to such
an Undertaking, and a Complexion to carry him thro with it: That
he wou'd stick at nothing; but the highest Rank, the most con-
spicuous Merit wou'd be no Security against his Insolence. That
he wou'd never want Matter or Invention, having an inexhaustible
100 Fund of Malice and Calumny, which, according as he was paid, he
wou'd right or wrong apply to any Subject; and if his Image were
but foul enough, he wou'd not care for the Resemblance; but like
a common Dauber, wou'd write the Name of his Sign, which wou'd
serve as well as the Likeness with the Rabble for whom he was to
105 work. All this they promis'd for him; and that he shou'd maintain
an invincible Hatred to Truth, and never once submit to the
Drudgery of being Honest: That his Religion and Morality shou'd
consist entirely in his being One of the new *Godly Party*: That
he shou'd never have the least Remorse for any Injustice done to
110 Persons, or even to Vertue it self; and if he cou'd but escape
the Correction of others, that he shou'd never fall under the
severer Discipline of Conscience. We have lately heard very much
of False Brethren; and I had this Account from one of the
Examiner's, who was present when he enter'd into Articles. But
115 every body must do him the justice to say, he has taken care that

108   *the new Godly Party*: possibly a reference to Matthew Tindal, *New High-
Church Turn'd Old Presbyterian* (1709).

113   *False Brethren*: non-conformists. The sermon that precipitated Sacheverell's impeachment when it was published in November 1709 was preached at St.
Paul's and entitled *The Perils of False Brethren, both in Church, and State.*

his Securities shou'd run no hazard, by keeping up exactly to the
Terms of his Agreement. How applicable to my Friend is what a
French Author says on Defamatory Libellers? *The Pleasure they*
take in railing at and defaming those against whom they write,
makes these wretched Scribblers use all the Idea's and Expres-   120
sions a corrupt Imagination can furnish them with; and by their
Falshoods in Fact, they do as much Injury to the Truth of History,
as they give Offence to Modesty by the Leudness of their Pictures.
Whoever wou'd learn the Events of his own Time, in the Writings
of these Impostors, will not know the Persons that are named, so   125
different they appear there from what they are in themselves. The
Greatest Men are represented as without Merit and Honour, and the
most Unworthy adorn'd with their Characters.

Now you have seen this true Account of his being listed into
the Service, I will next present you with his own History of that   130
Matter; which is just of a piece with all his other Narratives.
First, he says he has serv'd the present Ministry half a year in
quality of *Champion*, without *being call'd*. And when I reflect on
his Abilities or Usefulness, I am amaz'd to think that this is
not true. But he goes on, with his usual Modesty: *And with the*   135
Help of the Q----, quoth he, *and a Majority of Nine in Ten of the*
Kingdom, I have been able to protect them against a routed Cabal.
What a Hero is this, with the Q----, and his Nine Parts in Ten
to support him! But what follows, is stranger still: Wou'd you
think it! says he, *These very M------rs that I have protected,*   140
and that all know me, and set me to work, *have been so far from*
rewarding me sutable to my Deserts, that to this day they never
so much as sent to the Printer to enquire who I was. When he gets
into a Vein of Merriment, there's no body can come up to him,
that's certain. These ungrateful M------rs that see him every   145
Morning, and give him his Cue, never think of finding him out.
But I can tell him, all the rest of the World find him out, and
see so plainly what he is, in every one of his Papers, that they
must have very little to do, if they shou'd make any further
Enquiry about him. But this was a Sally of his Wit; now you shall   150

118-28 *The ... Characters*: source unidentified.
132-3   *the ... call'd*: 214.102-6.
135-7   *And ... Cabal*: 214.106-8.
141-3   *have ... was*: 214.109-11.

have a Touch of his Cunning: He endeavours to disguise the Profits
of his Paper, values himself on the Frankness of his Service, and
plainly insinuates that he has neither *Place* or *Pension*. The first
I readily believe, it not occurring to me what Office he is most
155   fit for; but of the second, I dare say, the *first Quarter has
honestly been paid*: yet I can't answer how long it will be continu'd, *nor how long the Mony may be spar'd*. So that in a very
short time, 'tis possible my Friend may be as wrongfully accus'd
of being *mercenary* as my self: And we must both be satisfy'd with
160   the Pleasure of our several Employments; he, in writing Falshoods,
and I, in detecting them. If there were any hopes of him, I wou'd
yet give him one piece of Advice out of an Author of our own, who
of all I have yet quoted in any Language, I think the best; I
mean Archbishop *Tillotson*: But this Writer can have no Weight
165   with my Friend or his Party, who was the Object of their Slanders,
their Hatred, and Inventions; and who wou'd certainly have been
one of *the Ruin'd Party*, had he been still alive. However, I will
transcribe his Words: "Whatsoever Convenience may be thought to
be in Falshood, it is soon over; but the Inconvenience of it is
170   perpetual, because it brings a Man under an everlasting Jealousy
and Suspicion: so that he is not believ'd when he speaks Truth,
nor trusted, when perhaps he means honestly. When a Man has once
forfeited the Reputation of his Integrity, he is set fast, and
nothing will then serve his turn, neither Truth nor Falshood."
175   And in these happy Circumstances I will leave the *Examiner* for
the present.

153   *neither Place nor Pension*: 211.30.
155-6   *the ... paid*: 214.114-15.
160-1   *he ... them*: 212.45-51.
168-74   *Whatsoever ... Falshood*: John Tillotson, *Of Sincerity and Constancy
in the Faith and Profession of the True Religion*, ed. Ralph Barker, 4th edn.,
London, for Ric. Chiswell, 1704, p. 34.

No. 29 [Swift]   15 February 1711

The EXAMINER.

Inultus ut tu riseris Cotyttia?

An Answer to the Letter *to the* Examiner.

Sir,   *London, Feb. 15. 1710/11.*
THOUGH I have wanted Leisure to acknowledge the Honour of a
Letter you were pleas'd to write to me about six Months ago; yet
I have been very careful in obeying some of your Commands, and
am going on as fast as I can with the rest. I wish you had   5
thought fit to have convey'd them to me by a more private Hand,
than that of the *Printing-house*: For though I was pleas'd with a
Pattern of Style and Spirit which I propos'd to imitate, yet I
was sorry the World should be a Witness how far I fell short in
both.   10
    I am afraid you did not consider what an abundance of Work you
have cut out for me; neither am I at all Comforted by the Promise
you are so kind to make, that when I *have performed my Task,*
D-----n *shall blush in his Grave among the Dead,* W------le *among
the Living, and even* Vol----e *shall feel some Remorse.* How the   15
Gentleman in *his Grave* may have kept his Countenance, I cannot
inform you, having no acquaintance at all with the Sexton; but

Motto Horace, *Epodes*, xvii 56: Shall you Cotytto's Feasts deride, | Yet
safely triumph in your Pride?
    Subtitle: *Letter*: 74.36.
    6 *a more private Hand*: Even though St. John's *Letter to the Examiner* was
addressed to the pre-Swift Examiner, presumably Dr William King, it was a
source of annoyance to Swift for it provided evidence that *The Examiner* was
written under ministerial direction.
    13-15 *when ... Remorse*: St. John, *A Letter to the Examiner*, 1710, p. 6.
    14 *D----n*: John Dolben (1662-1710), the second son of John Dolben, Arch-
bishop of York, was a Whig Member of Parliament for Liskeard, Cornwall. As
'a great stickle[r] for Lord Treasurer', Dolben was 'the first Accuser' of
Sacheverell and chairman of the committee to impeach him. He died at Epsom on
29 May 1710 'at that *very Hour, eleven in the Forenoon*', when Sacheverell was
ordered to stand trial (*Wentworth Papers*, p. 73; *The Life and Adventures of
John Dolben, Esq;*, London, 1710, pp. 11, 12, 16).
    W----le: Robert Walpole, 'the invincible Brazen membr. of [King's] Lynn,
[Norfolk]' and a member of the committee to impeach Sacheverell, spoke 'very
abusively, and us'd Language worthy of himself' (*Etoniana*, ix (22 May 1907),
130; *POAS*, Yale, vii 436).
    15 *Vol---e*: Godolphin.

for the *other two*, I take leave to assure you, there have not yet
appear'd the least Signs of *Blushing* or *Remorse* in either, though
20 *some very good Opportunities* have offer'd, if they had thought
fit to accept them; so that with your Permission, I had rather
engage to continue this Work 'till *They* are *in their Graves* too,
which I am sure will happen much sooner than the other.

You desire I would collect *some of those Indignities offer'd*
25 *last Year to Her M-----y*. I am ready to oblige you; and have got
a pretty tollerable Collection by me, which I am in doubt whether
to publish by it self in a *large Volume in Folio*, or scatter them
here and there occasionally in my Papers. Tho' indeed I am sometimes thinking to stifle them altogether; because such a History
30 will be apt to give Foreigners a monstrous Opinion of our Country. But since it is your absolute Opinion, the World should be
inform'd; I will with the first Occasion pick out a few *choice*
Instances, and let them take their chance in the ensuing Papers.
I have likewise in my Cabinet certain Quires of Paper fill'd with
35 Facts of Corruption, Mismanagement, Cowardice, Treachery, Avarice,
Ambition, and the like, with an Alphabetical Table, to save
Trouble. And perhaps you will not wonder at the Care I take to
be so well provided, when you consider the vast Expence I am at;
I feed Weekly two or three *Wit-starv'd* Writers, who have no other
40 visible Support; besides several others that live upon my Offals.
In short, I am like a Nurse who Suckles Twins at one Time, and
has likewise one or two **Whelps** constantly to draw her Breasts.

I must needs confess, (and it is with Grief I speak it) that I
have been the innocent Cause of a great circulation of Dulness:
45 At the same time, I have often wondred ·how it has come to pass,
that these industrious People, after poring so constantly upon
the *Examiner*, a Paper writ with plain Sense, and in a tolerable

22 are] be 38 8°+12°   31 Opinion,] Opinion, that 38 8°+12°   34 like-
wise] also 38 8°+12°   40 that] who 38 8°+12°   42 likewise] besides,
38 8°+12°

24-5 *collect ... M-----y*: St. John, *A Letter to the Examiner*, 1710, p. 6.
36 *an Alphabetical Table*: 'Modern Wits are not to reckon upon the Infinity
of Matter ... What remains therefore, but that our last Recourse must be had
to large *Indexes*, and little *Compendiums*; *Quotations* must be plentifully
gathered, and bookt in Alphabet' (Swift, *Tale*, pp. 147-8).
47 *the Examiner*: cf. 'Yes, I do read the *Examiners*, and they are written
very finely, as you judge' (Swift, *Journal*, p. 208).

Stile, have made so little Improvement. I am sure it would have
fallen out quite otherwise with me; for, by what I have seen of
their Performances (and I am credibly inform'd they are all of a   50
Piece) if I had perused them 'till now, I should have been fit
for little but to make an Advocate in the same Cause.

You, Sir, perhaps will won er, as most others do, what End
these angry Folks propose, in writing perpetually against the
Examiner: It is not to beget a better Opinion of the late Mini-   55
stry, or with any Hope to convince the World that I am in the
Wrong in any one Fact I relate; they know all that to be lost
Labour; and yet their Design is important enough: They would fain
provoke me by all sort of Methods, within the length of their
Capacity, to answer their Papers; which would render mine wholly   60
useless to the Publick; for if it once came to Rejoinder and
Reply, we should be all upon a Level, and then their Work would
be done.

There is one Gentleman indeed, who has written three small
Pamphlets upon the *Management of the War*, and *the Treaty of*   65
Peace: These I had intended to have bestow'd a Paper in *Examin-*
ing, and could easily have made it appear, that whatevèr he says
of Truth, relates nothing at all to the Evils we complain of, or
controuls one Syllable of what I have ever advanc'd. No Body that
I know of did ever dispute the Duke of *M---------h*'s Courage,   70
Conduct or Success; they have been always unquestionable, and
will continue to be so, in spight of the Malice of his Enemies,
or, which is yet more, the *Weakness of his Advocates*. The Nation
only wished to see him taken out of ill Hands, and put into better. But, what is all this to the Conduct of the late *M-n-stry*,   75
the shameful Mismanagements in *Spain*, or the wrong Steps in the

71 Success;] ~, ½° 12°

64-5 *three small Pamphlets*: Since 11 January 1711 (169.200), Swift had seen
Hare's *The Negociations for a Treaty of Peace, in 1709. Consider'd in a Third
Letter to a Tory-Member* (1711). If he had seen 223.129-31, he ignores it.
69 *controuls*: 'overrules; arch.' (*OED*).
70-1 *M--------h's Courage, Conduct ... Success*: 'Lord Rivers, talking to
me the other day, cursed the paper called *The Examiner*, for speaking civilly
of the duke of Marlborough' (Swift, *Journal*, p. 195).
76 *Spain*: For two months in 1710 the Archduke Charles, called Carlos III as
the Habsburg pretender, sat on the throne of his ancestors in Madrid, but the
failure of supplies and reinforcements made the position untenable and the
retreat to Barcelona turned into disaster at Brihuega (145.52).

Treaty of Peace, the Secret of which will not bear the Light, and
is consequently by this Author very poorly defended? These and
many other Things I would have shewn, but upon second Thoughts
80 determin'd to have done it in a Discourse by it self, rather than
take up room here, and break into the Design of this Paper, from
whence I have resolved to banish Controversy as much as possible.
But the Postscript to his third Pamphlet was enough to disgust me
from having any Dealings at all with such a Writer; unless that
85 Part was left to some *Footman* he had pickt up among the Boys who

82 possible] possibly ½° 12°

77 *Treaty*: 9.176n.
80 *Discourse by it self*: This proliferated into two pamphlets, of which
the bibliography cannot be untangled until copies can be found of *An Examination of the First and Second Letters to a Tory Member, relating to the Management of the War*, 1711 (Morgan N264, apparently identical with Morgan N265),
and *An Examination of the Two Parts of the Management of the War*, 1711 (Morgan N267, almost certainly a ghost, the title being identical with the half-
title of Morgan N265). The pamphlets are: *An Examination of the Management of
the War. In a Letter to My Lord ****, London, J. Morphew, 1711 (Morgan N265)
and *An Examination of the Third and Fourth Letters to a Tory Member. Relating
to the Negociations for a Treaty of Peace in 1709. In a Second Letter to My
Lord ****, London, J. Morphew, 1711 (Morgan N266). The text of the Huntington
Library copy of *Remarks upon Dr. Hare's Four Letters to a Tory Member, concerning The Management of the War*, London, 1711 (Morgan N275) is identical
with that of Morgan N265.
83 *Postscript*: In a postscript Hare said: 'The *EXAMINER* is extremely mistaken, if he thinks I shall enter the Lists with so prostitute a Writer, who
can neither speak Truth, nor knows when he hears it. I shall not be mov'd
with the Ignorance and Malice of a Mercenary Scribler, who treats the D. of
M. and the Victorious Troops he has the Honour to Command, with so much Insolence, in so many of his Weekly Libels; and in one of them, *N. 4.* villanously
calls him *a Cataline at the Head of a Mercenary Army*: Words, which, I trust,
will not be easily forgotten. What I have said of the Management of the War,
will, I doubt not, support it self against all his Attacks; who, were he much
abler he is, has met with more than his Match, in the most Ingenious
Writer of the *MEDLEY*; and to his Correction I shall leave him' (*The Negociations for a Treaty of Peace, in 1709. Consider'd, in a Third Letter to a Tory-
Member*, 1711, p. 50). Catiline comes into *The Examiner*, No. 4, 24 August 1710
(not of course written by Swift), as the vehicle of a negative metaphor of
which the tenor is Queen Anne, not Marlborough: Anne is *not* like Catiline; to
suppose that the Queen would choose ministers who would repudiate the national
debt is 'a Wildness' without even a Roman analogue, except possibly Catiline,
who, if his mercenary legions had triumphed, might have repudiated the Government's debts. Hare's equation of Marlborough with Catiline reveals some unexpected reservations.
85 *Footman*: This precipitated both Mainwaring's *An Answer to the Examination of the Management of the War. Written by the Medley's Footman* (1711) and
*An Examination of the Third and Fourth Letters to a Tory Member. Relating to
the Negociations for a Treaty of Peace in 1709. In a Second Letter to My Lord
**** (1711). In the latter it is said that 'the Two pretended Persons [the
Medley and the Medley's footman] are the same; ... the Man is the Master, and
vice versa' (p. 40).

follow the Camp, whose Character it would suit much better than
that of the suppos'd Author. At least, the foul Language, the
idle impotent Menace, and the gross perverting of an innocent
Expression in the 4th *Examiner*, join'd to that Respect I shall
ever have for the Function of a *Divine*, would incline me to   90
believe so. But when he turns off his *Footman*, and disclaims
that Postscript, I will tear it out, and see how far the rest
deserves to be consider'd.

But, Sir, I labour under a much greater Difficulty, upon which
I should be glad to hear your Advice. I am worried on one side   95
by the *Whigs* for being too *severe*, and by the *Tories* on t'other
for being too *gentle*. I have formerly hinted a Complaint of this;
But having lately receiv'd two peculiar Letters, among many
others, I thought nothing could better represent my Condition,
or the Opinion which the warm Men of both Sides have of my Con-   100
duct, than to send you a Transcript of each. The former is
exactly in these Words.

To the EXAMINER.

Mr. Examiner,

BY your continual reflecting upon the Conduct of the late   105
M-n-stry, and by your Encomiums on the present, 'tis as clear as
the Sun at Noon-day, *that you are a* Jesuit *or* Nonjuror, *employed*
by the Friends of the Pretender, *to endeavour to introduce*
Popery, *and* Slavery, *and* Arbitrary Power, *and to infringe the*
sacred *Act of* Toleration *of* Dissenters. *Now, Sir, since the most*   110
ingenious Authors *who write Weekly against you, are not able to*
teach you better Manners, I would have you to know, that those
Great and Excellent Men, as low as you think them at present, do
not want Friends that will take the first proper Occasion to Cut
your Throat, *as all such Enemies to* Moderation *ought to be serv'd.* 115
'Tis well you have clear'd another Person from being Author of

---

110 *of* Toleration] for *Toleration* 38 8°+12°

88   *perverting*: cf. 'to adapt base Characters, at so vast a Distance, to any
peculiar Persons, is the worst of Defamation' (ibid., pp. 28-9).
97   *formerly*: 97.52-7.
109-10   *the sacred Act of Toleration*: mocking Tindal's phrase (*The Rights of*
the Christian Church Asserted, 4th edn., 1709, p. 144).
115   *Moderation*: 85.108.
116   *Person*: 212.56n.

your cursed Libels; tho' D--mme, perhaps after all, that may be a
Bamboozle *too. However, I hope we shall soon **Ferrit** you out. There-*
*fore I advise you as a Friend, to let fall your **Pen**, and retire*
120 *betimes; for our **Patience** is now at an end. 'Tis enough to lose*
*our **Power** and **Employments**, without setting the whole **Nation***
against us. Consider three Years is the Life of a **Party***; and*
D--mme, **every Dog** *has his* **Day,** *and it will be our Turn next;*
therefore take warning, and learn to **Sleep** *in a whole* **Skin,** *or*
125 *whenever we are uppermost, by G-d you shall find no Mercy.*

The other Letter was in the following Terms.

To the EXAMINER.

Sir,

I Am a Country Member, *and constantly send a dozen of your*
130 *Papers down to my* Electors. *I have read them all, but I confess*
not with the Satisfaction I expected. 'Tis plain you know a great
deal more than you write; why will you not let us have it all
out? We are told, That the Qu--- has been a long time treated
with Insolence by those She has most oblig'd; Pray, Sir, let us
135 *have a few good Stories upon that Head. We have been cheated of*
several Millions; why will you not set a Mark on the Knaves who
are guilty, and shew us what ways they took to rob the Publick at
such a rate? Inform us how we came to be disappointed of Peace
about two Years ago: In short, turn the whole Mystery of Iniquity
140 *inside-out, that every Body may have a View of it. But above all,*
explain to us, what was at the bottom of that same Impeachment:
I am sure I never liked it; for at that very Time, a Dissenting
Preacher in our Neighbourhood, came often to see our Parson; *it*
could be for no Good, for he would walk about the Barns and
145 *Stables, and desire to look into the Church, as who should say,*

144-5 *and Stables*] and the Stables 12° 38 8°+12°

---

118 *Bamboozle*: cf. 'certain Words invented by some *pretty Fellows*, such as
Banter, Bamboozle, Country Put, and *Kidney* ... I have done my utmost for some
Years past, to stop the Progress of *Mob* and *Banter*; but have been plainly
born down by Numbers, and betrayed by those who promised to assist me' (Swift,
Prose, ii 176).
123-4 *Dog ... Skin*: Both of these proverbial expressions (Tilley D464,
S530) are used here not as examples of folk wisdom but as mindless clichés.
139 *Mystery of Iniquity*: 2 Thess. 2:7.
141 *Impeachment*: 151.176.

These will shortly be mine; *and we all believed he was then contriving some Alterations against he got into Possession: And I
shall never forget, that a* Whig Justice *offer'd me then very high
for my* Bishop's *Lease.* I must be so bold to tell you, Sir, that
you are too favourable: I am sure, there was no living in quiet   150
for Us while they were in the Saddle. *I was turn'd out of the
Commission, and called a* Jacobite, *though it cost me a Thousand
Pound in joining with the Prince of* Orange *at the* Revolution. *The
Discoveries I would have you make, are of some Facts for which
they ought to be Hang'd; not that I value their Heads, but I*   155
would see them expos'd, *which may be done upon the* Owners Shoulders, *as well as upon a* Pole, &c.

These, Sir, are the Sentiments of a whole Party on one Side,
and of considerable Numbers on the other: However, taking the
medium between these Extreams, I think to go on as I have hither-   160
to done, though I am sensible my Paper would be more popular, if
I did not lean too much to the favourable Side. For nothing delights the People more than to see their Oppressors humbled, and
all their Actions, Painted with proper Colours, set out in open
View. *Exactos Tyrannos densum humeris bibit aure vulgus.*   165

But as for the *Whigs*, I am in some doubt whether this mighty
Concern they shew for the Honour of the late Ministry, may not be
affected, at least whether their Masters will thank them for their
Zeal in such a Cause. 'Tis I think, a known Story of a Gentleman
who fought another for calling him *Son of a Whore*; but the Lady   170
desired her Son to make no more Quarrels upon that Subject, *because it was true.* For pray, Sir, does it not look like a Jest,
that such a pernicious Crew, after draining our Wealth, and discovering the most Destructive Designs against our Church and
State, instead of thanking Fortune that they are got off safe in   175
their Persons and Plunder, shou'd hire these Bullies of the Pen
to defend their *Reputations*? I remember I thought it the hardest

153 *Pound*] Pounds 38 12°   170 the Lady] his Mother 38 8°+12°

---

165 *Exactos ... vulgus*: Horace, *Odes*, ii 13 31: the dense throng, shoulder to shoulder packed, drinks in ... with listening ear stories of tyrants
banished.
170-2 *Son of a Whore ... because it was true*: Francisco de Quevedo y
Villegas, *The Comical Works*, trans. Captain John Stevens, London, John Morphew, 1707, pp. 160-1.

Case in the World, when a poor Acquaintance of mine, having fallen
among Sharpers, where he lost all his Mony, and then complaining
180   he was cheated, got a good Beating into the Bargain, *for offering
to affront Gentlemen.* I believe the only Reason why these Pur-
loiners of the Publick, cause such a Clutter to be made about
their Reputations, is to prevent *Inquisitions*, that might tend
towards making them *refund*: Like those Women they call *Shop-*
185   *Lifters*, who when they are challenged for their Thefts, appear to
be mighty angry and affronted, for fear of being *Searched*.

I will dismiss you, Sir, when I have taken notice of one Particular. Perhaps you may have observ'd in the *tolerated* factious
Papers of the Week, that the E--- of R----- is frequently re-
190   flected on for having been *Ecclesiastical Commissioner* and *Lord
Treasurer* in the Reign of the late King *James*. The Fact is true;
and it will not be denied to his immortal Honour, that because
he could not comply with the Measures then taking, he resign'd
both those Employments; of which the latter was immediately sup-
195   ply'd by a Commission, compos'd of *two Popish Lords and the
Present E--l of* G--d--l--n.

179 *Sharpers*: 86.156. This is a good example of how easily Swift's style
falls into allegory: 'a poor Acquaintance' (the landed gentry made poorer by
the land tax) complain of being cheated by 'Sharpers' (Godolphin) and get
'a good Beating into the Bargain' (are stigmatized as Jacobites for complaining).
189 *R-----*: Two folio half-sheets, raking together all the known scandal
about Rochester, *The True Patriot Vindicated* (1701) and *An Inscription intended to be set up for the E--- of R---r, when by the Happy Effects of his
Ministry, the Chappel of St. Stephen's is become a Chappel of the Jesuites*
(1701), the latter widely attributed to Somers (PRO, PRO 31/3/189, f. 59),
were reprinted in *The History of King James's Ecclesiastical Commission* (1711).
196 *G-d-l---n*: Upon Rochester's resignation as Lord Treasurer James II put
the Treasury into commission. John Belasyse, Lord Belasyse, was First Lord,
and Henry Jermyn, Lord Dover, Godolphin, Sir John Ernle, and Sir Stephen Fox,
were members. Belasyse and Dover were Catholics. 'This malicious insinuation
being incontrovertible in point of its general truth, gave great uneasiness to
the whiggish papers' (E*1814*, iv 11).

No. 21 [Mainwaring and Oldmixon]   19 February 1711

The MEDLEY.

The Tories in a Combination with the Dissenters.
A History of High-Church Services to the Church and Clergy.
A Comparison therein between Them and Low-Church.
Some Remarks on the Examiner.

THE poor Whigs are every day so maul'd off by the Tories for
their *Fanaticism*, that one wou'd be apt to think there was something in what my Friend the *Examiner* and his Fellow-Writers of
that Faction tell us, That the Presbyterian Preachers began to
take Inventories of the Parsons *Barns and Stables, and to look*   5
into the Church, as who shou'd say these will shortly be mine:
if we did not know that not a word of Truth can come from 'em,
and that this same *Godly Party*, like that of 41, mean no more by
Church and *Orthodox*, than the other did by *Purity* and *Reformation*;
that they are alike acted by a furious and blind Zeal, the only   10
difference between them and the Puritans being, that the latter
were cunning enough to be Hypocrites, whereas our new *Godly Party*
usurp the Name without even the Form or Appearance. Yet every one
knows what use has been made of the word *Church* and *Churchmen*;
how the most constant and zealous of her Sons, as far as Zeal and 15
Constancy are to be shewn by Affection and Piety, are stigmatiz'd
as *Fanaticks* and *Schismaticks*; and how especially at all Elections,
the *Whigs* are branded as Sappers and Underminers of the *Church*
establish'd by *Law*. I shall therefore, to undeceive some unthinking People, who only can be impos'd upon by such a Pretence, give 20
a short History of some Facts, wherein High-Church distinguish'd
their Zeal, so much boasted of lately, in a very different manner,
and much to the scandal of all *True Churchmen*: which Facts I will
borrow from a Reverend Dignitary of the Church communicated to me
on this occasion.   25

4-6 *Preachers ... mine*: 244.143-245.146.
8 *Godly Party*: 236.108.
24 *Dignitary*: probably White Kennett, Dean of Peterborough and Mainwaring's
source in the Convocation (Oldmixon, *The Life*, p. 190).

Time was, when the known Patrons of the Dissenters were in a
strict Alliance with the Heads of the Tory-Interest; when
M-----ve and *S----ur* went hand in hand with them in all their
Counsels and Debates: But then such a Junction was not the least
30   discredit to the Cause of the *Church*, while they join'd in the
meritorious Work of perplexing the Affairs of King *William*, reducing the *Prerogative* of the Crown, and supporting *Presbyters*
against their *Bishops*; all which in other Men wou'd have been
call'd the proper Work of Republicans and Presbyterians. In the
35   first Year of the Q----, the Zeal of the Quakers for the Tory-
Interest stands upon Record, in *William Pen's* Circular Letter; a
Letter full of Concern for the then prevailing Power, and a lasting Testimony how little they shun the Company of Dissenters,
when they find them advance with a friendly Disposition. In their
40   own case only such Company is not in the least *Infectious*; in all
others 'tis next to *Pestilential*. There was a certain Peer, not

26 *Patrons*: Harley, Harcourt, Paul Foley, all with Presbyterian connections,
joined the leaders of the High Churchmen in the House of Commons, Sir Christopher Musgrave and Sir Edward Seymour, to form the New Country Party, which
brought down the Junto in 1698 and impeached three Junto leaders in 1701.
   31 *perplexing the Affairs of King William*: 'The Country-Party ... most of
whom the Court look'd upon as Disaffected, were such as never approved the
Methods by which the Revolution was accomplish'd; who always entertain'd a
Jealousie of King *William*, and therefore, upon several Occasions, endeavour'd
to cross his Designs' (Abel Boyer, *The History of King William the Third*, 3
vols., London, for A. Roper *et al.*, 1702-3, iii 289). Between 1697 and 1701
the New Country Party crossed William's designs (1) by reducing the standing
army to 7,000 men and officers and dismissing the Dutch Blue Guards regiment;
(2) by revoking William's grants of forfeited estates in Ireland; (3) by impeaching Somers, Halifax, Orford, and Portland for the partition treaties that
William himself had negotiated; (4) by passing the so-called Act of Settlement (An Act for further limitation of the Crown and for securing the rights
and liberties of the subject), which further limited the royal prerogative;
and (5) by lopping £100,000 from the budget of the royal household in 1701, and
other 'unreasonable & Extravagant things only to lessen the king' (BL MS Add.
7074, f. 15).
   32 *supporting Presbyters*: It was in the Convocation of March 1701 that the
'fatal and memorable Difference arose between both Houses ... upon the Question, Whether the Power of adjourning resides solely in the Archbishop, or
whether the Lower House have Power to Adjourn themselves' (Boyer, *The History
of King William the Third*, 1702-3, iii 472).
   36 *William Pen's Circular Letter*: This is an address from the general
assembly of Quakers in grateful acknowledgment of Anne's maintenance of the
Toleration Act, presented to the Queen some time after 25 March 1702, of
which no copy appears to have survived. The text is included in Charles F.
Holder, *The Quakers in Great Britain and America*, New York, Neuner, 1913,
pp. 228-9.
   41 *Peer*: Sir John Thompson of Gatton, Surrey, 1st baronet (*c.*1648-1710), a
Williamite before the Revolution, was created Lord Haversham in May 1696. But

more eminent for *Anniversary Speeches* than for Affection to the
Dissenters, and himself an *Occasional Conformist*: but for all
that, *High-Church* wou'd be much out of humour, shou'd we once
suggest that the Proceedings of the E. of *R*. and E. of *N*. are   45
against the High-Church, because the Lord *H----m* bore a great
part in the same Measures. All which is sufficient to prove what
a terrible Blow they give their own Friends, when they lay it
down for a Maxim at Elections of all kinds, That all Candidates,
Members, and their Adherents, if they vote with Dissenters, are   50
(however Orthodox themselves) *ipso facto* unchurch'd. For such is
the Virtue of the Name *Churchmen*, wherever they vouchsafe to fix
it, that it not only secures all that wear it against the Infec-
tion and Imputation of ill Company, not only wipes off all former Blemishes how unchurch-like soever, but it gives them a   55
future Right to use the Church and Clergy as ill as they please,
without the least danger of forfeiting their Title.

   Of pernicious consequence to the Church was the *Ecclesiastical
Commission* of King *James*, both in it self, and in the Intention
of that Unfortunate Prince; and so fatal must it apparently have   60
prov'd to the two great *Nurseries* of the *Church*, the *Universities*,
that one wou'd have hop'd whoever had been concern'd in that, had
forfeited his Reputation in the way of a *Churchman* for ever. And
yet (to see the Severity of these Gentlemen to some, and their
immoderate Clemency to others) all the Sins under a *Popish* Reign   65

when William neglected to appoint him First Lord of the Admiralty in December
1701, he bolted to the Tories. He was a 'very passionate and fiery' orator
who began the practice in 1704 of publishing his own state-of-the-nation
address, or '*Anniversary* Speech', as it came to be called (William Stephens,
A Letter to the Author of the Memorial of the State of England, London, 1705,
p. 17). But he was also 'a short red Faced Man' and a 'turbulent' Presbyterian
whose domestic arrangements were most entertaining (Macky, p. 104; *POAS*, Yale,
vii 157). So he proved to be an embarrassment to his new allies. Somers and
Mainwaring were certain that he could be bought back for £1,000 (*Private
Correspondence*, i 277).
   58-9 *the Ecclesiastical Commission*: The first act of the ecclesiastical
commission (159.113), in August 1686, was to suspend Henry Compton, Bishop of
London, for refusing to suspend John Sharp, rector of St. Giles-in-the-Fields,
for preaching anti-Catholic propaganda.
   61 *Universities*: 'The Thunder-bolts of the *Ecclesiastical Commission* fell
next on both Universities', first on Dr Peachell, Vice-Chancellor of Cambridge,
who was removed for refusing to grant an MA to one Alban Francis, a Benedic-
tine monk, and then on Charles Aldworth, the Vice-President, and the fellows
of Magdalen College, Oxford, all removed for refusing to admit Anthony Farmer,
a Roman Catholic, as President (*The History of King James's Ecclesiastical
Commission*, 1711, pp. 25-52).

are not only forgot and forgiven, but they cannot think the Church
in any degree of Safety under a *Protestant* one, till they see the
Administration in some of those very Hands which had the principal
Share in that illegal and destructive Commission. After the Revo-
70 lution, no two things were more freely reflected on as detrimen-
tal to the *Church*, than the *Act of Toleration* and the Commission
for *reviewing the Common-Prayer*. It was chiefly upon account of
this last, that many of the Bishops and Clergy cou'd never since
recover the Character of *Churchmen* among some of their own
75 Brethren, with whom notwithstanding, the E. of *N*'s Church-Title
has stood firm and unblemish'd from that day to this; tho it is
well known that Noble Hand usher'd the first into *Parliament*, and
the second into *Convocation*. We were told, in one of their Papers,
of a certain House of Commons, to whose *Zeal and Honesty it is*
80 *owing that the Church is enabled to weather the Faction*. Who are
meant there, is no Secret; but by what peculiar Services to the
Church they have merited that mighty Character, is a very great
one. And therefore a List of their good Offices in cases where
the Interest of the *Church* has been plainly and undeniably con-

68 *Hands*: Rochester succeeded Somers as Lord President of the council on
21 September 1710 and Buckingham, who had replaced Rochester on the ecclesiastical commission in October 1686, succeeded Devonshire as Lord Steward of
the Household on the same day.
71 *Toleration*: An Act for exempting their Majesties Protestant subjects
dissenting from the Church of England from the Penalties of certain Laws,
called the Toleration Act, received the royal assent on 24 May 1689. It extended freedom of public worship to all non-conformists but Roman Catholics,
Jews, and Unitarians. 'The Clergy began now to shew an implacable hatred to
the Nonconformists' (Burnet, ii 11).
    Commission: In September 1689 William III, by a special commission under
the great seal, empowered 'Ten Bishops and Twenty Divines ... to meet, and
prepare such Alterations, in the Book of Common-Prayer and Canons, as might be
fit to lay before the Convocation' (Burnet, ii 30). The alterations proposed,
Calamy said, 'would in all Probability have bro't in [to the Church of Eng-
land] Two Thirds of the *Dissenters* in *England*'. But the Convocation simply
adjourned 'without doing any Thing at all' (Edmund Calamy, *An Abridgement of
Mr. Baxter's History of His Life and Times*, 2nd edn., 2 vols., London, for
John Lawrence *et al.*, 1713, i 448, 452-5, 464).
77 *Hand*: Nottingham introduced the toleration bill into the House of Lords
on 28 February 1689 (*LJ*, xiv 134). On 4 December 1689 he brought 'The New
Commission ... to both Houses of *Convocation* ... and ... made an Eloquent
Speech ... wherein he exhorted them to lay aside all partial Prepossessions
and Animosities in their Proceedings' (Oldmixon, *The History*, p. 39). That
'partial Prepossessions' were not to be laid aside had already been signalled
by William Jane's acceptance speech as prolocutor of the Lower House, which
concluded with the fateful words, '*Nolumus Leges Angliae mutari*' (Kennett,
iii 591).
78 *one of their Papers*: unidentified.

cern'd, might have been very seasonable upon that head. But tho   85
they forget the Instances of their good Offices, we cannot forget
the Instances of some very ill ones, nor reconcile their Behaviour on certain Occasions, to that distinguishing Character of
Zeal for the Church and Clergy. In King *William*'s time Sir *J.*
J----, or at least some other stanch Whig, propos'd the excusing   90
all Livings under 40 *l. per ann.* but was oppos'd.by *M-----ve,*
B----y, &c. who took off even the Exemption from Livings of 30 *l.*
per ann. by a High-Church Majority; Sir *E---d S-----r* saying, in
the Debate, *He thought the Parsons did not behave themselves so*
well, as to deserve that Favour: But that is nothing from such a   95
Knight as he, *who thank'd God he had not been at Church for seven*
years. And so by these great Churchmen, poor Livings, that had
never before been tax'd, had the Load laid upon them.

In the present Reign the same Party (to shew their good Will to
Church-Power) past a Bill, to transfer the repairing of *Churches*   100
from the Ecclesiastical Court to the Justices of Peace, that is,
from the *Church* to themselves. 'Tis easily guess'd to what Condition such an Act, had not the Lords rejected it, wou'd have
reduc'd the *Chancels* of Impropriate Churches, when the same Person wou'd be frequently both *Party* and *Judg*. The Parliament some   105
years ago vested the Power in Justices of the Peace, to hear and

86 forget] forgot ½°

---

90 *J----*: In February 1704 the Queen sent a message to Parliament signifying her intent to apply the first fruits and tenths to the augmentation of
small benefices. 'When the Queen's Message was brought to the House of Commons, some of the Whigs, particularly Sir *John Holland* and Sir *Joseph Jekyll*,
moved that the Clergy might be entirely freed from that Tax, since they bore
as heavy a Share of other Taxes; and that another Fund might be raised of
the same Value, out of which small Benefices might be augmented: But this was
violently opposed by *Musgrave*, and other Tories, who said the Clergy ought to
be kept still in a Dependance on the Crown' (Burnet, ii 371).
92 *B----y*: William Bromley of Baginton, 'a flaming Tory'.
94-5 *He ... Favour*: Since these words are lacking in the unique account
of the debate of 3 February 1704 in Burnet (ii 371), they (and the next words
of Seymour) must have reached Mainwaring from oral sources.
100 *Bill*: A Bill for the more easy Recovery of Moneys for repairing
Churches passed the House of Commons in February 1703 but was defeated by the
Lords (*CJ*, xiv 17, 172; *LJ*, xvii 274). If it had passed, the parson's suit
for the repair of the chancel would frequently have been decided by a justice
of the peace who was also the holder of the impropriate tithes of the church
and not likely to decide against himself.

determine Causes about small *Tythes*; but reserv'd the Clergy the
Liberty of chusing their own Remedy, either this new one, or such
as the Law had provided before. But this Liberty the Quakers by
110 no means lik'd, and sollicited the Parliament to take it away;
and will it not seem incredible to the *Highfliers*, that the E. of
R. shou'd of all Mankind be the Promoter of such a Cause? Yet we
are told for certain, that his Lordship took upon him to manage
it for the Quakers, brought it into the House of Lords, and spar'd
115 no Pains to humble the Clergy to the Quakers. Her Majesty's Bounty
to the Clergy was first propos'd by the Bishop of *Salisbury* to
Queen *Mary*, who fully intended it, if she had liv'd; and that
Project was afterwards set on foot by a Great Minister in the last
Reign. It was then far advanc'd, and wou'd have been finish'd, had
120 he staid but a few Months longer in the Ministry. It is also very
well known, that when it was graciously renew'd by her Majesty,
some of the Persons imploy'd to bring it to bear were refer'd to
him for Assistance; and it was then promoted and carry'd on by
Members in the House of Commons, who were never so happy as to be
125 of the Tory-Party. Nay, they mov'd and endeavour'd to have the
Bill for confirming it made still more advantageous and beneficial
to the poorer Clergy, but cou'd not obtain it. They wou'd have had
all the *First-Fruits* and *Tenths*, as the last remaining Badg of
Popish Slavery, sunk for ever, and a Fund settled by Parliament

107 *small Tythes*: An Act for the more easie Recoverie of Small Tythes
(7 & 8 Gul. III. c. 6) received the royal assent on 13 February 1696 (Luttrell,
iv 17; *CJ*, xi 446). It provided that an action for the recovery of tithes not
in excess of 40*s*. could be brought before a justice of the peace, without preventing a subsequent action being brought in the court of exchequer or in the
ecclesiastical courts as before. This act was renewed in 1698 (10 Gul. III.
c. 21).
    109 *Quakers*: After passage of the second act in 1698 'the *Quakers*, to in-
duce the Legislature to take from the Clergy the legal Remedies which the two
... Acts leave them at full Liberty to pursue ... represented their Case in a
printed Paper', complaining that 'there have been prosecuted in the *Exchequer*,
Ecclesiastical, and other *Courts*, in *England* and *Wales*, for Demands recover-
able by the said *Acts*, above Eleven hundred of the People called *Quakers*, of
whom near Three hundred were committed to Prison, and several of them died
Prisoners' (*Papers Relating to the Quakers Tythe Bill*, London, J. Roberts,
1736, pp. 17, 4).
    112 *R.*: Rochester was in active opposition to the Junto in 1698, but no
other evidence that he supported the Quaker's 'Case' has been found.
    116 *Bishop of Salisbury*: 200.200.
    118-32 *Project ... Life*: quoted almost verbatim from Wotton, *The Case of
the Present Convocation Consider'd*, 1711, p. 23.
    118 *Minister*: Godolphin (Burnet, ii 370). Godolphin was forced to resign as
First Lord of the Treasury in December 1701.

in lieu of them, for the present Augmentation of small Livings;   130
whereas the other Fund was in a great measure anticipated by
Pensions for Life. The same Memoirs, from whence I took these,
furnish me with many more Instances of this nature; but I shall
conclude with the last, being what the Tories brag of most, and
boldly assume the Honour of it entirely to themselves, who it   135
seems had not the least share in it.

My Friend the *Examiner* is more mistaken than ever he was in his
Life, if he thinks I am angry with him, or take such notice of
him as I do, because I imagine he deserves it: But he may depend
upon it, as long as he takes the Liberty to write such notorious   140
Falshoods as he has done in every one of his Papers, so long
shall I continue to expose him. If he was capable of Improvement,
this faithful History would be a Lesson to him; but all I expect
from him, is, to brag of what he cou'd do if he wou'd, that he
does not write to the Whigs but to the Tories, or, as he pro-   145
fanely expresses himself, he makes *Meat for Babes*, an Allegory
he's extremely fond of; for in his very last Paper, he says, he's
a Nurse who suckles Whelps. A Week or two ago he was a *Champion*,
and now he's a *Nurse*. He cares not what he makes of himself, if
he has a Maggot to be malicious and mischievous: However, he is   150
not so weak, but he knows he has for these six Months been doing
what he can't answer, reviling the best Men, in Flattery to the
worst. He's doubtless asham'd or afraid of what he has done, and
therefore puts on all the Disguises his poor Imagination can
invent. His Friends too, for fear if he shou'd be found out   155
'twou'd be a Scandal to the Party, do their utmost to conceal
him; sometimes they insinuate he is a Poet, sometimes a Priest,

---

134-6 *Tories ... had not the least share*: What neither Mainwaring (nor
Burnet nor Wotton) say is that the Queen's message announcing her philanthropic
intention was brought to Parliament on 7 February 1704 by the Tory Secretary of
State, Sir Charles Hedges, and that four Tory members (Sir Simon Harcourt, William Bromley, John Sharpe, Thomas Conyers) and one 'High Church Courtier',
William Lowndes, were appointed to bring in a bill to enable the Queen to
realize her intention (*CJ*, xiv 332).
   146 *Meat for Babes*: 211.38.
   148 *a ... Whelps*: 240.41-2.
       Champion: 214.106.
   157-9 *Poet ... Priest ... Physician ... Academick ... Woman*: Mainwaring's
list—Prior ... Atterbury ... John Freind, MD ... William King, Senior Student
of Christ Church ... Delariviere Manley—is surprisingly accurate for the pre-
Swift *Examiners* and agrees closely with Swift's: 'St. John ... Atterbury ...
Prior ... Freind' (Swift, *Prose*, viii 123-4). But Mainwaring seems not yet to

sometimes a Physician, sometimes a silly Academick, and sometimes even an old Woman. But that won't do; no Man of common
160 Sense ever thought any body wrote the Paper but *Abel Roper*, or
some of his Allies, there being not one Quality in the *Examiner*,
which *Abel* has not eminently distinguish'd himself by since he
set up for a Political Writer. 'Tis true, *Abel* is the more modest
of the two, and it never enter'd into his Head to say as my
165 Friend does of his Paper, *'Tis writ with plain Sense, and in a*
tolerable Stile: For tho *Abel* is admir'd for that too by the
chief Politicians of his Party, he has never been so vain as to
value himself on his Excellence that way. An Expression dropt
indeed from the *Examiner* not long since, which looks as if he had
170 some knowledg of himself; for he says, *If he shou'd answer me, it*
wou'd render his Paper wholly useless, it being a very hard matter
for a Man, so often convicted of writing Falsities, to make any
Reply without becoming useless. His only way to keep up, is to do
what his Friends have enjoin'd him, Put a bold face on the matter,
175 and write on; to say as he does in his Thursday's Paper, *'Tis in*
vain to hope to convince the World he's wrong in one Fact, they
all know that to be lost Labour: and yet he has so just an
Opinion of himself, as to confess *the Design is important*. He's
so considerable a Person, if the Whigs cou'd once be too hard for
180 him, their Business wou'd be done. There's nothing so merry as

---

have had even an inkling of Swift himself. Of the 13 pre-Swift *Examiners*, No.
6 has been attributed to Prior, Nos. 10 and 13 to Atterbury, and Nos. 11 and
12 to King (Addison, *The Whig-Examiner*, 14 September 1710; *The Tatler*, 19 October 1710; Nichols, *Supplement*, pp. 62-3; Bennett, p. 124).
    160 *Roper*: Abel Roper (1665-1726) was born in Warwickshire but apprenticed
to a London printer. He set up for himself in a saddler's shop in Bell Yard
and had his first success publishing *Lilliburlero* (1688) (William Wagstaffe,
Some Memoirs of the Life of Abel, Toby's Uncle, London, for T. Warner, 1726,
p. 4). In Queen Anne's reign, however, he published *The Memorial of the Church
of England* (1705), *The Post-Boy* (May 1695-August 1714), the Tory counterpart
to Ridpath's *The Flying-Post*, and *The Supplement* (19 January 1709-30 July
1712) (*A Letter to the People of England Occasion'd by Defoe's Letter to the
Dissenters*, London, for John Oldisworth, 1714, p. 42. The Harley ministry
leaked stories to *The Post-Boy*, Swift wrote paragraphs for it, and Mainwaring
'believ'd *St. John* himself was sometimes [Roper's] *Assistant*' (Oldmixon, *The
Life*, p. 284).
    165-6 *writ ... Stile*: 240.47-241.48.
    170-1 *answer ... useless*: 241.60-1.
    176-7 *hope ... Labour*: 241.56-8.
    178 *Design is important*: 241.58.
    180 *their ... done*: 241.62-3.

what he says of his not answering the *Management of the War*, and
the *Treaty of Peace*: He cou'd, if he wou'd, have made it appear,
*The Management of the War Abroad did not relate to the Evils at
Home*. He can do any thing. He cou'd also prove there were *wrong
Steps* in the *Treaty* of *Peace*, the Allies wou'd have all; but he   185
won't do it, because he is treated like a *Footman*; and how shou'd
one know how to treat him but by his Writings? And where has he
by his Breeding given us reason to use him otherwise? 'Tis most
certain he never heard a word of the *Treaty* before, but what his
Coadjutor *Abel* told him; yet now the *Negotiations* are come out,   190
he assures us, the *Secret will not bear the Light*, and he wou'd
do Wonders if he might be us'd like a Man of Honour: but he's
more stupid than I take him to be, if he hopes to be so treated,
with such a Load of Infamy upon him.

181-3 *the ... Evils*: 241.65-8.
184-5 *wrong ... Peace*: 241.76-242.77.
186 *Footman*: 242.85.
188 *his Breeding*: cf. '*If, Sir, you have so much Learning, how came you to
have so little Manners?*' (Defoe, *Review*, 14 December 1710).
190 *come out*: (241.64-5n.).
191 *the ... Light*: 242.77.

No. 30 [Swift]   22 February 1711

The EXAMINER.

*Laus summa in fortunæ bonis, non extulisse se in Potestate, non fuisse in-
solentem in pecunia, non se prætulisse aliis propter abundantiam fortunæ.*

I Am conscious to my self that I write this Paper with no other
Intention but that of doing good: I never receiv'd Injury from
the late Ministry, nor Advantage from the present, further than
in common with every good Subject. There were among the former

Motto Cicero, *De Oratore*, ii 342: In the Goods of Fortune it is the highest
Commendation to say, that he was not elated in Power, insolent in Riches, or
contemptuous amidst the overflowing of Fortune.
2-3 *never ... Ministry*: cf. 'I am already represented to Harley as a discontented person, that was used ill for not being Whig enough' (Swift, *Journal*, p. 36).

5   one or two, who must be allow'd to have possess'd very valuable
    Qualities; but Proceeding by a System of Politicks, which our
    Constitution could not suffer; and discovering a Contempt of all
    Religion, but especially of that which hath been so happily esta-
    blish'd among us ever since the Reformation, they seem to have
10 been justly suspected of no very good Inclinations to either.
        'Tis possible, that a Man may speculatively prefer the Consti-
    tution of another Country, or an *Utopia* of his own, before that
    of the Nation where he is born and lives; yet from considering
    the Dangers of Innovation, the Corruptions of Mankind, and the
15 frequent impossibility of reducing Idea's to Practice, he may
    join heartily in preserving the present Order of Things, and be
    a true Friend to the Government already settled. So in Religion;
    a Man may perhaps have little or none of it at Heart; yet if he
    conceals his Opinions, if he endeavours to make no Proselites,
20 advances no impious Tenets in Writing or Discourse: If, according
    to the common Atheistical Notion, he believes Religion to be only
    a contrivance of Politicians for keeping the Vulgar in Aw, and
    that the present Model is better adjusted than any other to so
    useful an End: Though the Condition of such a Man as to his own
25 future State be very deplorable; yet Providence, which often
    works Good out of Evil, can make even such a Man an Instrument
    for contributing towards the Preservation of the Church.
        On the other side, I take a State to be truly in danger, both
    as to its Religion and Government, when a Set of Ambitious Politi-
30 cians, bred up in a Hatred to the Constitution, and a Contempt for
    all Religion, are forc'd upon exerting these Qualities in order to
    keep or encrease their Power, by widening their Bottom, and taking
    in (like *Mahomet*) some Principles from every Party, that is any
    way discontented at the present Faith and Settlement; which was

---

    8 but] *om.* 38 8°+12°   19 conceals] conceal 38 8°+12°   endeavours]
    endeavour 38 8°+12°   20 advances] advance 38 8°+12°

---

        5 *one or two*: Somers, to whom Swift had dedicated *A Tale of a Tub* (1704),
    and of whom he continued to speak in superlatives—'this extraordinary Genius'
    (*Prose*, vii 7), is certainly one of these. But since 1704 Swift had come to
    suspect that Somers was a deist (215.137) and a republican (*Prose*, vii 5).
        21 *common Atheistical Notion*: 'Atheists ... suppose Religion to be a Poli-
    tick Device, contriv'd on purpose for the better regulating of human Societys'
    (Tindal, *The Rights of the Christian Church Asserted*, 4th edn., 1709, p. 13;
    cf. Swift, *Prose*, ii 34).

manifestly our Case. Upon this Occasion I remember to have ask'd   35
some considerable Whigs, whether it did not bring a Disreputa-
tion upon their Body, to have the whole Herd of Presbyterians,
Independants, Atheists, Anabaptists, Deists, Quakers and Socinians, openly and universally Listed under their Banners? They
answer'd, That all this was absolutely necessary, in order to   40
make a Ballance against the *Tories*, and all little enough: For
indeed, it was as much as they could possibly do, tho' assisted
with the absolute Power of disposing every Employment; while the
Bulk of *English* Gentry kept firm to their old Principles in
Church and State.   45

But notwithstanding whatever I have hitherto said, I am inform'd, several among the *Whigs* continue still so refractory,
that they will hardly allow the Heads of their Party to have
entertain'd any Designs of ruining the Constitution, or that they
would have endeavour'd it, if they had continu'd in Power. I beg   50
their Pardon if I have discover'd a Secret; but who could imagine
they ever intended it should be One, after those *Overt-Acts* with
which they thought fit to conclude their *Farce*? But perhaps they
now find it convenient to deny vigorously, that the Question may
remain; *Why was the old Ministry changed?* Which they urge *on*   55
without ceasing, as if no Occasion in the least had been given,
but that all were owing to the Insinuations of crafty Men, Practicing upon the Weakness of an easy Pr---e. I shall therefore
offer, among a hundred, one Reason for this Change, which I think
would justify any Monarch that ever Reign'd, for the like Pro-   60
ceeding.

'Tis notorious enough, now highly Princes have been blamed in
the Histories of all Countries, particularly of our own, upon the
Account of *Minions*; who have been ever justly odious to the
People, for their Insolence and Avarice, and engrossing the   65
Favour of their Masters. Whoever has been the least conversant
in the *English* Story cannot but have heard of *Gaveston*,

---

59 offer,] ~ ½°   60 that] who 38 8°+12°   63 own,] ~; ½° 0^{ab} L CtY
TxU CSmH CLU-C^   ~ ½° 0^C LU NjP PU 12°   64 Account of] Account of their
38 8°+12°

---

52 *Overt-Acts*: 178.10-179.18.
67 *Gaveston*: 'Piers Gaveston, Earl of Cornwall, the favourite of Edward II'
(E*1922*, ix 191).

the *Spencers*, and the Earl of *Oxford*; who by the Excess and Abuse
of their Power, cost the Princes they serv'd, or rather govern'd,
70 their Crowns and Lives. However, in the Case of *Minions*, it must
at least be acknowledg'd that the Prince is pleased and happy,
though his Subjects be aggriev'd; and he has the Plea of Friendship to excuse him, which is a Disposition of generous Minds.
Besides, a wise *Minion*, tho' he be haughty to others, is humble
75 and insinuating to his Master, and cultivates his Favour by Obedience and Respect. But *Our* Misfortune has been a great deal worse:
We have suffer'd for some Years under the Oppression, the Avarice
and Insolence of those, for whom the Qu--n had neither Esteem nor
Friendship; who rather seem'd to snatch their own Dues, than
80 receive the Favour of their Sovereign, and were so far from returning Respect, that they forgot common good Manners. They impos'd on their Prince, by urging the Necessity of Affairs of their
own creating: They first rais'd Difficulties, and then offer'd
them as Arguments to keep themselves in Power. They united them-
85 selves against Nature and Principle, to a Party they had always
abhorred, and which was now content to come in upon any Terms,
leaving Them and their Creatures in full Possession of the Court.
Then they urg'd the formidable Strength of that Party, and the
Dangers which must follow by disobliging of it. So that it seems
90 almost a Miracle, how a Prince, thus Besieged on all Sides, could
alone have Courage and Prudence enough to extricate Herself.
    And indeed there is a Point of History relating to this Matter,

68 the Earl of *Oxford*] some others 38 8°+12°   89 of] *om.* 38 8°+12°

---

68 *the Spencers*: 'Hugh le Despencer, Earl of Winchester, and his son of
the same name, both favourites of Edward II., and both hanged in 1326' (E*1922*,
ix 191).
    Oxford: 'Robert de Vere, Earl of Oxford, favourite of Richard II' (E*1922*,
ix 191).
78 *those*: Marlborough and Godolphin, who lost the Queen's 'Esteem [and]
Friendship' in February 1708 (260.128n.).
82-3 *Affairs of their own creating*: cf. 'It has been indeed one great Art
by these men to create a necessity & then to use it to justify their enormous
Practices' (Harley, 'Plaine English', p. 104). The Act of Union is one example
(102.175n.).
85 *Party*: the Whig Junto. In return for their support for the Union with
Scotland, Marlborough and Godolphin were forced to take three more members of
the Junto into the Government: Somers as Lord President of the council (November 1708), Wharton as Lord-Lieutenant of Ireland (December 1708), and Orford
as First Lord of the Admiralty (November 1709).

which well deserves to be consider'd. When Her M-----y came to
the Crown, she took into Favour and Employment, several Persons
who were esteem'd the best Friends of the old Constitution; among   95
whom none were reckon'd further gone in the *High Church* Principles
(as they are usually called) than two or three, who had at that
Time most Credit, and ever since, till within these few Months,
possessed all Power at Court. So that the first Umbrage given to
the Whigs, and the Pretences for clamoring against *France* and   100
the *Pretender*, were derived from Them. And I believe nothing
appear'd then more unlikely, than that such different Opinions
should ever incorporate; that Party having upon former Occasions
treated those very Persons with Enmity enough. But some L--ds
then about Court, and in the Qu---'s good Graces, not able to   105
endure those growing Impositions upon the Prince and People, presum'd to interpose, and were consequently soon removed and disgraced: However, when a *most exorbitant Grant* was propos'd,
antecedent to any visible Merit, it miscarry'd in Parliament, for
want of being Seconded by those who had most Credit in the House,   110
and who having always oppos'd the like Excesses in a former Reign,
thought it their Duty to do so still, to shew the World that the
Dislike was not against Persons but Things. But this was to cross
the *Oligarchy* in the tenderest Point, a Point which outweigh'd
all Considerations of Duty and Gratitude to their Prince, or   115
Regard to the Constitution. And therefore after having in several
private Meetings concerted Measures with their old Enemies, and
granted as well as receiv'd Conditions, they began to change
their Style and their Countenance, and to put it as a Maxim in
the Mouths of their Emissaries, That *England must be saved by the*   120
Whigs. This unnatural League was afterwards cultivated by another

93 deserves] deserveth 38 8°+12°   101 believe] belive ½°   120 the]
om. 12° 38 8°+12°

---

97 *two or three*: Marlborough and Godolphin, who were Tories at the time of
Anne's accession.
104 *some L--ds*: Rochester, Anne's first Lord-Lieutenant of Ireland, was
dismissed in February 1703, and Nottingham, her first Secretary of State, in
April 1704.
108 *Grant*: Anne's desire to settle £5,000 a year on Marlborough in December
1702, 'before the duke had commenced his brilliant career', was defeated in
the Commons by Seymour, Musgrave, and other Tories. This 'may be supposed
still farther to have alienated the Duke of Marlborough from that party' (*CJ*,
xiv 85, 87; Luttrell, v 247; E*1814*, iv 16).

Incident; I mean the *Act of Security*, and the Consequences of it,
which every Body knows; when (to use the Words of my Correspondent) *the Sovereign Authority was parcelled out among a Faction,*
125   *and made the Purchase of Indemnity for an offending M------r:*
Thus the *Union* of the two Kingdoms improv'd That between the
Ministry and the *J-nto*, which was afterwards cemented by their
mutual Danger in that Storm they so narrowly scaped about three
Years ago; but however was not quite perfected till the Prince's
130   Death; and then they went lovingly on together, both satisfied
with their several Shares, at full Liberty to gratify their pre-
dominant Inclinations; the first, their Avarice and Ambition;
the other, their Models of Innovation in Church and State.

Therefore, whoever thinks fit to revive that baffled Question,
135   *Why was the late Ministry changed?* May receive the following
Answer; That it was become necessary by the Insolence and Avarice
of some about the Qu---, who in order to perpetuate their Tyranny
had made a monstrous Alliance with those who profess Principles
destructive to our Religion and Government: If this will not suf-
140   fice, let him make an Abstract of all the Abuses I have mention'd
in my former Papers, and view them together; after which if he
still remains unsatisfy'd, let him suspend his Opinion a few
Weeks longer. Though after all, I think the Question as trifling
as that of the Papists, when they ask us, *where was our Religion*

---

124 *a] the* 12° 38 8°+12°   127 *J-nto] J--n--to* ½° 12°   *Junta* 38 8°+12°
129 the Prince's] Prince *George*'s 38 8°+12°   142 remains] remain 38 8°+12°

---

122   *Act of Security*: 102.175n.
124-5   *the ... M------r*: St. John, *A Letter to the Examiner*, 1710, p. 12,
cf. *Review*, 8 March 1711.
128   *Storm*: In February 1708 Harley, then Secretary of State, had Anne's
support for his plan to replace Godolphin, retaining Marlborough in his
commands and bringing more Tories into the Government. The duumvirs drew
together, however, and frightened Anne into dismissing Harley (Swift, *Corr.*,
i 69-70; Addison, *Letters*, pp. 91-2; cf. *POAS*, Yale, vii 297-9).
129-30   *the Prince's Death*: Anne's consort, Prince George of Denmark, 'had
long conceived an incurable aversion for [the Whig] party' (Swift, *Prose*, viii
112). He died on 28 October 1708. The Junto took advantage of the Queen's grief
to force two of its members, Wharton and Somers, into ministerial posts (Henry
L. Snyder, *HLQ*, xxxv (1971-2), 326-7; Gregg, p. 283).
132   *Avarice and Ambition*: 229.65.
144-5   *where was our Religion before Luther?*: The answer: 'Where it *is, viz.*
in *England*' (Robert Sanderson, *A Discourse concerning the Church*, London, by
T. B. for R. Taylor, 1688), p. 22).

before Luther? And indeed, the Ministry was chang'd for the same   145
Reason that Religion was reform'd, because a thousand Corruptions
had crept into the *Discipline* and *Doctrine* of the *State*, by the
Pride, the Avarice, the Fraud, and the Ambition of those *who
administred to us in Secular Affairs.*

I heard my self censur'd t'other Day in a Coffee-House, for   150
seeming to glance in the Letter to *Crassus*, against a great Man,
who is still in Employment, and likely to continue so. What if I
had really intended that such an Application should be given it?
I cannot perceive how I could be justly blam'd for so gentle a
Reproof. If I saw a handsome young Fellow going to a Ball at   155
Court with a great *Smut* upon his Face, could he take it ill in me
to *point out the Place*, and desire him with abundance of good
Words to pull out his Handkerchief and *wipe it off*; or bring him
to a *Glass*, where he might plainly *see it with his own Eyes.* Does
any Man think I shall suffer my Pen to inveigh against Vices,   160
only because they are charged upon Persons who are no longer in
Power? Every Body knows, that certain Vices are more or less
pernicious, according to the Stations of those who possess them.
For Example, Lewdness and Intemperance are not of so bad Consequences in a Town Rake as in a Divine. Cowardice in a Lawyer is   165
more supportable than in an Officer of the Army. If I should find
Fault with an Admiral because he wanted *Politeness*, or an Alderman for not understanding *Greek*; That indeed would be to go out
of my way, for an Occasion of Quarrelling; but excessive *Avarice*
in a *G-----l*, is I think the greatest Defect he can be liable to,   170
next to those of Courage and Conduct, and may be attended with
the most ruinous Consequences, as it was in *Crassus*, who to that
Vice alone ow'd the Destruction of himself and his Army. 'Tis the
same Thing in praising Mens Excellencies, which are more or less
valuable, as the Person you commend has occasion to employ them.   175

157 *point*] point ½° 12° 38 8°+12°   159 *see*] see ½° 12° 38 8°+12°
165 Rake as in] Rake as ½° 12°

---

148 *Avarice ... and ... Ambition:* 229.65.
151 *Letter to Crassus:* 230.95.
153 *Application:* ''twas applicat: ɔn made the Ass' (*Some Memoirs of the Life
of Abel, Toby's Uncle,* 1726, p. 19).
156 *Smut:* Swift himself becomes 'SMUT ... the Wittiest Knave' in Dr Hermo-
dactyl's [i.e. Harley's] troupe of mountebanks (*The Enigmatical Court: Or, A
Key to the High-German Doctor,* Dublin, for G. Risk, 1714, p. 15).

A Man may perhaps *mean Honestly*, yet if he be not able to *Spell*,
he shall never have my Vote for a *Secretary*: Another may have Wit
and Learning in a Post where Honesty, with plain common Sense,
are of much more Use: You may praise a Soldier for his Skill at
180 *Chess*, because it is said to be a Military Game, and the Emblem
of drawing up an Army; but this to a *Tr------r* would be no more
a Compliment, than if you call'd him a *Gamester* or a *Jockey*.

   P. S. I receiv'd a Letter relating to Mr. *Greenshields*; the
Person who sent it may know, that I will say something to it in
185 the next Paper.

177 for] to be 38 8°+12°

---

182 *a Gamester or a Jockey*: 217.169, 170.
183 *Greenshields*: James Greenshields graduated MA from Glasgow in 1687. In
1694 he was ordained by 'a Depos'd *Non-Juror*' (*Review*, 17 March 1711), James
Ramsay, the exauctorate Bishop of Ross, and presented with the cure of Tynan,
county Armagh, in Ireland. He returned to Edinburgh in 1709 and began to conduct services according to the Book of Common Prayer in a rented house in the
Canongate, opposite St. Giles. Continuing to preach in defiance of the Presbytery of Edinburgh and the local magistracy, he was imprisoned in the Tolbooth
in September 1709 and found guilty by the Court of Session of introducing
dangerous innovations in the church service. In December 1709, still in jail,
Greenshields appealed to the House of Lords, as he was entitled to do by the
Act of Union (1707).

No. 22 [Mainwaring and Oldmixon]   26 February 1711

The MEDLEY.

The Loyalty of High-Church to the Q---n.
Their Affection to the Union.
Some Remarks on the Examiner.
The Tories the Hypocrites.

HAVING in my last given some Account of the Services of the
Tories to the *Church* and *Clergy*, I shall now take a short View
of their Duty and Respect to the Q---n, which they boast of as
much, as if they verily believ'd what their Great Apostle Bishop

Sanderson has asserted, That Subjects must not *resist* to save   5
their own Souls, nor the Souls of all Mankind. And my Friend the
Examiner has more than once vouch'd for them, *That they have the*
most profound Veneration for Royalty and Crown'd Heads, and al-
ways spoke of her most Sacred Majesty with the utmost Submission:
Which wou'd have very great weight with it, coming from such a   10
Pen, if the matter of Fact, as it generally happens with him, was
not quite contrary. But 'tis the way of their Writers, to say
Things which all the World knows to be *false*, with as good an Air
as if they were as well known to be *true*. They have so much of
Popery in them, that they wou'd put a Force on our Faith, in   15
opposition to our Reason, and even to our Senses. They were indeed pretty mannerly a year or two, when they hop'd to be as
Arbitrary in the *Administration*, as they are in their *Principles*;
but as soon as they found the Q---n wou'd not go the Lengths they
wou'd have had her, that she was for *Union* and *Moderation*, there   20
was nothing bold and undutiful which they did not say and do, to
vent their Malice, and animate their Faction. Did they not revive
the Clamour of the *Church's Danger*, tho her Majesty had declar'd,

6 *nor*] *and* 12°

5-6 *not ... Mankind*: Oldmixon (or Mainwaring) may be quoting from memory
a Whig treatise attributed to Sir John St. Leger in which Robert Sanderson,
Bishop of Lincoln (1660-3), is quoted as follows: 'defensive Arms [against
established authority] are *de toto genere* unlawful, and may not be taken up
by any Man, at any time, in any Case, upon any Colour, or Pretension whatsoever, not for the Defence of Religion; nor for the Preservation of a Church,
or State, no, nor yet, if that could be imagin'd possible, for the Salvation
of a Soul, no, not for the Redemption of the whole World' (*The Managers Pro*
and Con: Or, An Account of what is said at Child's and Tom's Coffee-Houses for
and against Dr. Sacheverell, 3rd edn., London, A. Baldwin, 1710, p. 17).
7-9 *have ... Submission*: Atterbury, *The Examiner*, No. 10, 5 October 1710.
17 *a year or two*: 1702-4, before the Tories in Anne's first government
were dismissed (259.104n.).
20 *Union and Moderation*: In her speech at the opening of Parliament in
November 1703 Anne made a plea for 'perfect Peace and Union' among her subjects and urged them to avoid 'any Heats or Divisions' that might 'give Encouragement to the common Enemies of our Church and State' (*CJ*, xiv 211).
23 *Church's Danger*: On 6 December 1705 the cry that the Church was in
danger was picked up by Rochester in the House of Lords, whereupon both Houses
passed a resolution that 'the Church ... is now, by God's Blessing, under the
happy Reign of Her Majesty, in a most safe and flourishing Condition; and
that whoever goes about to suggest and insinuate, that the Church is in Danger
under Her Majesty's Administration, is an Enemy to the Queen, the Church, and
the Kingdom' (*LJ*, xviii 43; *CJ*, xv 58; cf. Clyve Jones, *Historical Journal*,
xix (1976), 759-61).

None but Her and the Kingdom's Enemies wou'd endeavour to raise
25 *such groundless Distrusts and Jealousies?* Did they not continue
it with the same Impudence and Virulency till the *Impeachment?*
What was their *Tack* but a Defiance of the Court? What their
Memorial, but a flagrant Libel against the Q---n and Government?
What the Sermons of their Clergy, but Declamations of Disgust
30 and Sedition? What car'd they that the Parliament voted all Reports and Insinuations of that kind *malicious and scandalous*,
that the Queen her self pronounc'd them *seditious and malicious?*
Did it put a stop to their Cry, or end in any thing but silencing
their Doctor, and the Mutinies and Changes which follow'd? Did
35 not the E. of *R.* tell the House of Lords, *He compar'd the full*
Expressions in the Queen's Speech, to the Law in King Charles *the*
Second's time, to make it Treason to call the King a Papist; for
which very Reason he always thought him so? And her Majesty being
present, was it not, as my Friend characterizes the *Tories*, to
40 *approach the Throne with the most dutiful Awe and Reverence?*
Wou'd not one have thought the *Church* to have been in as much
Peril, as when the *High-Commission* was in the Zenith of its

24-5 *None ... Jealousies*: *LJ*, xviii 8.
27 *Tack*: 89.41n. As Somers reported, 'the court exerted themselves in that
matter ... and brought such a number to join with the whigs, that the attempt
was baffled by a very great majority' (*Shrewsbury Corr.*, pp. 646-7).
28 *Memorial*: *A Memorial of the Church of England, Humbly Offer'd to the*
Consideration of all True Lovers of our Church and Constitution (July 1705)
raised the cry of the Church in danger, 'the drift of it pretending to shew
that the lord treasurer [Godolphin], dutchesse of Marlborough, &c. are undermining the church, by encouraging the whiggs, and putting them into places'
(Luttrell, v 574). Marlborough was outraged: 'the most impudent and scarolous
thing I ever read' (*Marlborough-Godolphin Corr.*, i 475), but Godolphin was
'very near weeping' (Thomas Sharp, *The Life of John Sharp, D.D.*, 2 vols.,
London, C. & J. Rivington, 1825, i 366). The Queen, 'with a little more
Warmth' than usual, noticed the work in her speech opening her second Parliament on 1 November 1705: 'there have not been wanting', she said, 'some, so
very malicious, as even in Print to suggest, the Church of *England*, as by Law
established, to be in danger at this Time' (*CJ*, xv 7).
31 *malicious and scandalous*: The actual phrase was 'seditious and scandalous' (*CJ*, xv 65).
32 *seditious and malicious*: In her speech proroguing Parliament on 5 April
1710 Anne made pointed reference to 'wicked and malicious Libels ... [that]
insinuate that the Church is in any Danger from My Administration' (*LJ*, xix
145).
34 *Doctor*: On 23 March 1710 Sacheverell was sentenced not to preach for
three years and his sermons were ordered to be burnt by the common hangman
(*LJ*, xix 118).
35-8 *He ... so*: Boyer, *Annals*, 1706, p. 203.
40 *approach ... Reverence*: Atterbury, *The Examiner*, No. 10, 5 October 1710.
42 *High-Commission*: 159.113n.

Tyranny? And hardly will it be believ'd it was possible for any
Member of that Court in King *James*'s Reign, to have so much real
Concern for the Safety of the Church in Queen *Anne*'s. Was it not   45
a most remarkable Instance of the Respect and Duty of these Loyal
Subjects, when Dr. *Aldr----* and Dr. *A-------y* left the Bishops
abruptly, and wou'd not hear the Queen's Letter to the Convocation read, of which a learned Prelate said at that time, *It was
the greatest Piece of Insolence he ever saw*? Have they since the   50
famous *Tryal*, which her Majesty call'd *a necessary Prosecution*,
forborn to condemn it as illegal and impious, or in their Libels
and Addresses paid the least Deference to the Judgment of the
Q---n and Parliament? Yet their *Submission* is without *Reserve*,
their *Loyalty* without *Limits*; and they are so wondrous full of   55
Respect, that the *Examiner* assures us, they are *afraid of addressing her Majesty, lest the occasion shou'd be too trifling*. 'Tis
true, their *Majority* in the Convocation about five years ago,
refus'd to sign the *Address* of the *Upper House*: Was it, d'ye
think, that they were afraid of disturbing the Q---n, or knew   60
themselves so well, they were asham'd to subscribe to this Part

---

47 *Aldr---- ... A-------y*: 'On the first day of *March* [1706] the Upper
House of Convocation being sat in the *Jerusalem*-Chamber, the Bishop of *Norwich* sent for Dr. *Bincks*, Dean of *Litchfield*, and Prolocutor of the Lower-
House, who attended with some other Members. As the Bishop was about Reading
the Queen's Letter, Dr. *A*[*tterbur*]*y*, taking the Prolocutor by the Sleeve,
desired him to be gone, adding, They had no Business there. Hereupon the
Bishop of *S*[*aru*]*m* rising from his Seat, and stepping to them, told them, *'Twas
the greatest Piece of Insolence he ever saw, thus to refuse to hear the Queen's
Orders* ... Dr. *Bincks* being made Sensible of his Duty, staid and heard part of
the Queen's Letter Read. In the mean time Dr. *A*[*tterbur*]*y*, Dr. *A*[*ldridg*]*e*, and
some others, return'd to the Lower-House, and Dr. *Bincks* being come there
also, they adjourn'd themselves to the *Wednesday* following' (Boyer, *Annals*,
1706, p. 267).
51 *Tryal*: In her speech proroguing Parliament on 5 April 1710 Anne expressed her 'great Concern, that you have had so necessary an Occasion of
taking up a great Part of your Time towards the latter End of this Session'
(*LJ*, xix 145).
52 *illegal and impious*: 151.178.
56-7 *addressing ... trifling*: Atterbury, *The Examiner*, No. 10, 5 October
1710.
57-67 *'Tis ... Word*: Kennett, *An Account of the Proceedings in the Convocation Which began, Oct. 25. 1705*, London, 1706, p. 15.
59 *Address*: In November 1705 the Lower House of Convocation refused either
to concur with the Upper House in an address to the Queen or to put their
objections in writing. 'The Majority inclining to some other Opinion about
the Danger of the Church, seem'd very unwilling to come into this Address; So
they rejected another Motion for having it read over Paragraph by Paragraph'
(Lambeth Palace MS Conv. I/2/10, ff. 8-13^V; ibid., p. 16).

of it? *'Tis no new thing for designing Men to prostitute the
venerable Name of the Church to the Service of their own private
Ends; yet we think it very strange that any shou'd be so ex-*
65 *tremely weak and undutiful as to be deluded by these groundless
Clamours, when they have been so often and so publickly confuted
by your Royal Word*, &c. Their many scurrilous Invectives as well
in the Pulpit as out of it, during the late Administration,
shou'd, methinks, have put an end for ever to their Pretences to
70 *Superlative* Obedience; for tho they have lately been wonderfully
jealous of the Reputation of the Ministers, yet such was then
their Duty to the Q---n, that her *Court* was almost always represented by them as full of *Treachery* and *Corruption*, and the
Calumnies now collected by my Friend were then spread about with
75 as little Caution and Discretion. 'Twas to no purpose that the
whole Body of the Clergy had, in another Address, return'd her
Majesty their humble Thanks *for the wise Management of her
Treasury, Fleets and Armies, for the free Course of the Law, the
Security of Liberty and Property, and the Support and Incourage-*
80 *ment of a Flourishing Church*: All under a Ministry, which, like
my Friend, they have treated as if *neither God nor Man cou'd
endure them.*

The Thing her Majesty express'd to have most at heart was the
Union; and who were the Men that oppos'd it so warmly in *England*
85 and *Scotland*? Did not the D. of *A*. protest against it, as *contrary
to the Honour, Interest, Fundamental Laws and Constitutions of*
Scotland, &c. The M. of *A*. as *contrary to the Birthright of the
Peers, the Rights and Privileges of the Barons, the Claim of
Right, the Property and Liberty of the Subject*, &c.? What share

73 *Treachery and Corruption*: 240.35.
74 *collected*: 240.34.
77-80 *for ... Church*: This is from the address of both Houses of Convocation
to the Queen on 7 December 1706 (Boyer, *Annals*, 1707, p. 390).
81-2 *neither ... them*: 52.75. Oldmixon also quotes these 'hard Words' in
A Letter to the Seven Lords of the Committee, Appointed to Examine Gregg,
London, J. Baker, 1711, p. 22.
85-7 *contrary ... Scotland*: John Murray, Duke of Atholl, was a violent
Jacobite who 'much affected Popularity'. He may have opposed the Union simply
in opposition to Queensberry (Lockhart, pp. 64, 66; Boyer, *Annals*, 1707,
p. 357; P.W.J. Riley, *The Union of England and Scotland*, Manchester University
Press, Manchester, 1978, pp. 46-7, 49, 61-3).
87-9 *contrary ... Subject*: Boyer, *Annals*, 1707, pp. 368-9. It was the loss
of William Johnstone, Marquess of Annandale's post as Secretary of State that
'induced him to oppose the Union' (Lockhart, p. 180).

the D. of *H.* had in the Obstacles it met with at *Edinburgh,* is   90
not yet forgotten by every body. We all know who they were that
put the Lord *H-----m* on his *Annual* Speeches; and how zealously he
spoke against it is still in our Remembrance. *That Authority,*
said he, speaking of the Q---n's Approbation, *tho it be the*
strongest Motive to incline the Will, is the weakest Argument to   95
convince the Understanding. 'Tis the *Argument the Church of* Rome
makes use of for their superstitious Worship, where there are ten
Ave Mary's to one Pater Noster: *as if ten times the Application*
and Address were made to a She-Favourite, *as to the Person of the*
Sovereign; which is a kind of State-Idolatry. The *Tories,* you   100
see; are the most short-sighted Creatures upon earth: They look
no further than to day; and if a Thing makes for 'em now, they
don't care what it does a month hence, being alike incapable of
Conviction or Shame. The same Lord who said *the Union was made*
up of so many mismatch'd Pieces, of such jarring incongruous   105
Ingredients, that if ever it took effect, he fear'd we shou'd
want a Standing Army to keep us from breaking in pieces; wou'd
now without blushing have rejoic'd in the happy Effects of it,
and term'd it, as her Majesty did, *the solid Foundation of last-*
ing Peace, the Security of Religion, Liberty, and Property: and   110
our Scots Brethren had been as much in their mouths, as they
were in their *Puritan* Ancestors. Tho both *Tories* and *Jacobites,*
when 'twas in Agitation, not only wrote and rail'd, but preach'd
and pray'd against it, as a *Mongrel-Union,* to use the Doctor's
Phrase, intended to introduce *Presbytery* and a *Commonwealth.* And   115
yet such ill Judges were they, the Whigs were all the while doing
'em a piece of Service; which if it was possible for them to be
grateful, they wou'd now own to be the best that has been done

---

90 *H.*: James Douglas, 4th Duke of Hamilton, led the opposition to the
treaty of Union with England. He voted against every article for which a division list is recorded and adhered to every protest (*APS*, xi 315-405).
    92 *H-----m*: 248.41n.
    93-100 *That ... State-Idolatry*: Boyer, *Annals*, 1707, p. 443.
    104-7 *Union ... pieces*: ibid.
    108 *Effects*: Harley's carefully selected Scots lords provided him with a
small majority in the upper house (BL MS. Add. 61461, f. 154).
    109-10 *the ... Property*: Boyer, *Annals*, 1707, p. 336.
    114 *Mongrel-Union*: The phrase is Sacheverell's, but he used it to describe
the comprehension of all sects into the Church of England (*The Perils of False*
Brethren, both in Church, and State, 1709, p. 10).

'em these Twenty Years.

120   Nothing in the World is so aukward as a Dull Fellow who pretends to be witty, of which the *Examiner* has lately given us two
or three lively Instances; but knowing he had no Fund of his own,
he steals from his very Adversarys. The *Tatler* had told him he
liv'd upon him; and my Friend, to be as like him as he can, some-
125   times says *he'll take the Bread out of our Mouths*, and won't
write a word more; at other times, that he feeds two or three
Authors a week *upon his Offals*: for now and then he calls things
by their right Name, without thinking of it. The worst of it is,
when he has filch'd any thing he's fond of, he does not know how
130   to conceal the Theft. The old Cheat of writing Letters to one's
self, practis'd by several of his Brother-Writers, was very
serviceable to him in his Paper, *Numb. 29*. where he so naturally
imitates a Presbyterian Epistle: *D-mme that's a Bambouzle: D-mme
every Dog has his Day, and by G-d you shall find no Mercy*: being
135   so plain as to own in another of his Papers, *he's no Reformer,
but an Examiner*. And to shew how fast his Stock already increases,
he informs us he has in his Cabinet Quires of Papers fill'd with
*Corruption, Mismanagement, Cowardice, Treachery, Avarice, Ambi-
tion*: which is hardly credible, considering People have not yet
140   had much time to shew themselves; and if he has got any such Collection, no doubt but he'll *stifle* it, for very good Reasons
which he and I know, if no body else does. One thing I can't help
blaming him for; and that is, his making a Tory desire him *to
turn the Mystery of Iniquity inside out*: because 'tis what the
145   poor Creatures have been expecting these six months; and some of
'em are so saucy, as to grumble as if there was now as much
Mystery as ever. I ask'd an honest Freeholder of *Surry*, why he
was such a Blockhead as not to vote for Sir *Richard*? *Lord!* says

---

123 *Tatler*: 'numberless vermin ... feed upon this Paper, and find their
Sustenance out of it: I mean, the small Wits and Scribblers that every Day
turn a Penny by nibbling at my Lucubrations ... I have been *Annotated, Re-
tattled, Examined*, and *Condoled*' (Addison, *The Tatler*, 23-6 September 1710).
  125 *take ... Mouths*: 96.45.
  126-7 *feeds ... Offals*: 240.39-40.
  133-4 *D-mme ... no Mercy*: 244.117-25.
  135-6 *no ... Examiner*: 229.73-4.
  137-9 *in ... Ambition*: 240.34-6.
  141 *stifle*: 240.29.
  144 *turn ... out*: 244.139-40.
  148 *Sir Richard*: Sir Richard Onslow, the Whig Member for Surrey (1689-

he, *they told me there shou'd be no more Taxes, but they wou'd
carry on the War by Fines and Resumptions.* A Livery-Man of *Wap-*   150
ping being check'd for giving his Vote for the *Colonel*; *In troth,*
quoth he, *I had not done it, but they said the Seamen shou'd be
all paid off by* Candlemas, *and Navy-Bills be better than Par.*
I put such another Question to a West-Country *Land-Jobber: Why
truly,* says he, *I shou'd have voted right, but that I hate the*   155
Funds, and they swore they wou'd raise all the Money in the Year.
A Jolly Parson of *Kent* being ask'd why they us'd Mr. *P-------l* so
ill, reply'd roughly, *Faith! we thought the Conventicles wou'd
have been shut up by this time, and the Barns put to their true
Use.* Now since Matters are not so manag'd, it shou'd be a Lesson   160
to some not to promise, to others not to believe too much. If the
Evils and Difficulties of the Times are to be charg'd upon the
Ministers, there will be but an ill prospect for some, whom the
Examiner has done what he can to set off by his Flattery, as much
as he endeavours to blacken others by his Falshoods. Mony and   165
good Words have a strong Influence upon such Writers as my Friend;
'twill make 'em sacrifice Truth, Reason, and even Common Sense,
to the Humour of a Faction. By this means we are so entertain'd
with his *Panegyrick* and *Scandal.* As for his *Encomiums,* they are
so ridiculous, 'twou'd be a jest to take notice of 'em: but his   170
Slander is of a kind, that it shou'd be remember'd for ever.
'Twas a great piece of Honesty in him, to own the E. of

153 *Navy*] *Nvay* ½°

1708, 1713-16) and Speaker of the House (1708-10), came third in a poll won
by two Tories in the general election of October 1710, but found refuge in
the safe borough of St. Mawes, Cornwall. Oldmixon is responding to the
Examiner's claim that the court influence was not deployed in the election.
    151 *the Colonel*: John Cass(e) or Cash was involved in a plot to assassinate
William III in 1696. In the next reign he was elected a Member of Parliament
for London (November 1710-1715) and, after two defeats, an alderman for Port-
soken ward in January 1711. He was knighted in June 1712. His commission,
unknown to Dalton, was in a City regiment (*A Letter to the People of England,
Occasion'd by the Letter to the Dissenters,* London, for John Oldsworth, 1714,
p. 58; Luttrell, vi 654, 681; Shaw, ii 277).
    155-6 *the Funds*: 4.76.
    157 *Mr. P-------l*: David Polhill, the Whig Member for Kent (11 January-
October 1710), came bottom of the poll in the general election won by two
Tories. He was one of the five Kentish Petitioners who demanded war with
France in May 1701 and was immortalized in verse by Defoe and in a fine en-
graving by Robert White (*POAS,* Yale, vi 334).
    169 *Panegyrick and Scandal*: 214.116-17.

R. was one of the *Ecclesiastical Commissioners*: for tho the Commission is in Print, as also the Bishop of *London*'s Tryal, where
175   we find that Name more than once mention'd; yet if he had deny'd
it, 'twou'd have been no more than he has done already by Facts
every whit as true. And in this Case tho he has not told a downright Falshood, 'tis so near one, that it deserves the same Correction. He tells us his Commission in the T-------y was *supply'd*
180   *by the E. of* G. *and two Popish Lords*: Whereas he might have said
with as much truth, 'twas supply'd by my Lord *G-------* and two
Protestant Knights, Sir *Stephen Fox* and Sir *John Ernle*; but then
he cou'd not have shewn his Good-Will to his Lordship, which he
does as well as he can in every Paper. A sign by his overdoing
185   it, why 'tis done, and who set him to work. He is not content to
brand the late Ministers, *Numb.* 29. as *Knaves, Fools, Cowards,
Traitors, Misers, Tyrants, a pernicious Crew that drein'd our
Wealth, and conspir'd to destroy both Church and State.* He pretends he knows a *great deal more than he writes*; which is one of
190   the truest things he ever spoke in his life, and his Friends
wou'd soon take his Office from him, if he shou'd *let us have all.*
      The Whigs have lately pretended to have a great Aversion to

173 *R.*: 246.189. Rochester's record in Compton's trial (249.58-9) was not
good. 'The Earl [of Rochester], and Bishop of *Rochester*, and the Lord Chief
Justice *Herbert*, were for acquitting him. There was not so much as a colour
of law to support the sentence: So none could be given [cf. Luttrell, i 385].
But the King was resolved to carry this point, and spoke roundly about it to
the Earl of *Rochester*. He saw he must either concur in the sentence, or part
with the White Staff [of the Lord Treasurer]. So he yielded' (Burnet, i 677),
and Compton was suspended by a 4:2 vote.
174 *Print*: *The History of King James's Ecclesiastical Commission* (1711) and
two accounts of Compton's trial: *An Exact Account of the whole Proceedings
against the Right Reverend Father in God, Henry Lord Bishop of London, before
the Lord Chancellor, and other Ecclesiastical Commissioners* (1688) and *A True
Narrative of all the Proceedings against the Lord Bishop of London, in the
Council-Chamber at White-hall, by the Lords Commissioners Appointed by His
Majesty to inspect Ecclesiastical Affairs* (1689). None of these, however, includes the story of Rochester's sell-out.
178-80 *supply'd ... Lords*: 246.195-6.
182 *Fox*: Except for July-September 1684 and April 1689-March 1690, Sir
Stephen Fox was a commissioner of the Treasury from 1679 to 1702. He became a
Protestant hero in 1685 when he refused a peerage from James II on condition
that he become a Catholic (William Pittis, *Memoirs of the Life of Sir Stephen
Fox*, London, for J. Sackfield and sold by J. Roberts, 1717, p. 114).
      Ernle: Sir John Ernle served Charles II and James II as Chancellor of
the Exchequer. As a Member of Parliament for Marlborough, Wiltshire (1685-
95), he appears to have been a High Church courtier.
186-8 *Knaves ... State*: 240.35-6, 245.173-5.
189-91 *knows ... all*: 244.131-2.

Hypocrisy; as if *all*, as my Friend says, *was owing to the Insinu-*
ations of Crafty and Practising Men. The new *Godly Party*, like
the old one, are charg'd by them with *Dissimulation* and *Disguise*;   195
tho the truth is, the *Tories* as to that are as .open downright
Persons as one cou'd wish, and either out of Negligence or Stupidity are as wicked, while they have nothing but *God* and the
Church in their mouths, as if, like their late Patron, they
visited it but once in a Prenticeship. Now I all along thought   200
this was a *Whiggish* Sham, and that the *High-Church* were not half
so *Hypocritical*; till the *Examiner*, who is always blundering,
declar'd truly that 'tis a very common thing among them: *A Man*,
says he, *Numb.* 30. *may perhaps have little or no Religion at*
heart, may believe it to be only a Contrivance of Politicians to   205
keep the Vulgar in awe; yet Providence can make such a Man an
Instrument for contributing towards the Preservation of the
Church. He has so many Friends of this Character, I do not know
which he means by it. But the *Church*, which was lately in such
danger, being at this time so very safe, is a strong Proof on his   210
side; and that Folks may have no Religion at all, may have a mean
Opinion of it, and yet in the *modern* Acceptation of the Phrase be
very good *Churchmen*: A Point I will rather give up to him, than
have any Dispute with him; because indeed I am not so good a Judg
of these things as he is.   215

193-4 *all ... Men*: 257.57.
199 *Patron*: 251.93-7. Seymour died on 17 February 1708.
203-8 *A ... Church*: 256.17-27.

No. 31 [Swift]   1 March 1711

The EXAMINER.

Quæ enim domus tam Stabilis, quæ tam firma civitas est, quæ non odiis atq;
   discidiis funditus possit everti?

Motto Cicero, *De Amicitia*, vii 23: What Family so established? What Society
so firmly united, that it cannot be broken and dissolved by intestine Quarrels
and Divisions?

IF we Examine what Societies of Men are in closest Union among
themselves, we shall find them either to be those who are engag'd
in some *evil Design*, or who labour under one *common Misfortune*:
Thus the Troops of *Banditti* in several Countries abroad; the
5 knots of *High-Way Men* in our own Nation, the several Tribes of
Sharpers, *Thieves* and *Pick Pockets*, with many others, are so
firmly knit together, that nothing is more difficult than to
break or dissolve their several *Gangs*. So likewise those who are
Fellow-Sufferers under any *Misfortune*, whether it be in Reality
10 or Opinion, are usually contracted into a very strict Union; as
we may observe in the *Papists* throughout this Kingdom, under
those real Difficulties which are justly put on them; and in the
several Schisms of *Presbyterians*, and other Sects, under that
grievous *Persecution* of the Modern kind, call'd *Want of Power*.
15 And the Reason why such Confederacies are kept so sacred and inviolable, is very plain, because in each of those Cases I have
mentioned, the whole Body is mov'd by one common Spirit, in pursuit of one general End, and the Interest of Individuals is not
cross'd by each other, or by the whole.
20   Now, both these Motives are join'd to unite the *High-flying*
Whigs at present: They have been always engag'd in an *evil Design*,
and of late they are faster riveted by that terrible *Calamity*,
the Loss of Power. So that whatever Designs a mischievous Crew of
dark Confederates may possibly entertain, who will stop at no
25 Means to compass them, may be justly apprehended from these.
On the other side, those who wish well to the Publick, and
would gladly contribute to its Service, are apt to differ in
their Opinions about the Methods of promoting it, and when their
Party flourishes, are sometimes envious at those in Power, ready
30 to over-value their own Merit, and be impatient till it is rewarded by the Measure they have prescrib'd for themselves. There

15 Confederacies] ~, ½°   30 till ... is] untill ... be 38 8° until ...
be 38 12°   31 prescrib'd] ptescrib'd ½°

---

14 *Want of Power*: cf. '*Liberty* is the Cry, but the Chace is after *Power*'
(Abel Roper, *The Moderator*, 26-9 May 1710).
31 *the Measure ... prescrib'd for themselves*: cf. 'the justest Method
would be ... to tax those Qualities ... for which Men chiefly value themselves;
the Rate to be ... according to the Degrees of excelling; the Decision whereof
should be left entirely to their own Breast' (Swift, *Prose*, xi 173).

is a further Topick of Contention, which a Ruling Party is apt to
fall into, in relation to *Retrospections*, and *Enquiry* into past
Miscarriages; wherein *some* are thought too warm and zealous;
others too cool and remiss; while in the mean time these Divi-   35
sions are industriously fomented by the discarded Faction; which
though it be an old Practice, hath been much improv'd in the
Schools of the *Jesuits*, who when they despair'd of perverting this
Nation to *Popery*, by Arguments or Plots against the State, sent
their Emissaries to subdivide us into Schisms. And this Expedi-   40
ent is now with great Propriety taken up by our Men of *incensed*
Moderation, because they suppose themselves able to attack the
strongest of our Sub-divisions, and so subdue us one after
another. Nothing better resembles this Proceeding, than that
famous Combat between the *Horatii* and *Curiatii*, where two of the   45
former being kill'd, the third, who remain'd entire and untouch'd,
was able to kill his three wounded Adversaries, after he had
divided them by a Stratagem. I well know with how tender a Hand
all this should be touched; yet at the same Time I think it my

---

35 cool] cruel 38 8°+12°

---

33 *Retrospections*: The October Club was formed in January 1711 when a dozen
country squires who were also Tory Members of Parliament began to meet at the
Bell Tavern in King street, Westminster. By 5 February, when they made known
their presence in the House of Commons, there were between seventy and eighty
members, whose motto, 'We will not be Harl'd', announced their dissatisfaction
with Harley (SRO GD 220/5/808/15). Before long there were 159 members, all men
of 'good Estate and not one in the Government' (Boyer, *The Political State*,
2nd edn., iii 117-22; John Rylands Library MS Legh of Lyme, F. Legh to P. Legh,
20 February 1711). 'The October-club ... declared, upon all occasions, their
desire of ... a strict enquiry into former mismanagements' (Swift, *Prose*,
viii 125).
35 *others*: Swift thought it was Harley's 'over-moderate proceedings' that
gave rise to the October Club (ibid.).
38 *Jesuits*: By an irony that is as unconscious as it is revealing of his
assessment of Harley, Swift describes Harley's method of dealing with the
October Club in exactly the same Jesuitical terms: 'dividing them among themselves, and rendering them jealous of each other' (ibid.). The fear that the
Jesuits manipulated the non-conformists originated during the Popish Plot:
'Jesuits ... mingle amongst Anabaptists, Quakers, and other Sectaries, and are
their Teachers' (Dryden, *His Majesties Declaration Defended: In a Letter to
a Friend*, London, for T. Davies, 1681, p. 17).
40 *Schisms*: cf. 'The ministry ... stand like an Isthmus between the Whigs
on one side, and violent Tories on the other' (Swift, *Journal*, p. 206).
41-2 *incensed Moderation*: 85.108.
45 *Horatii and Curiatii*: Livy, i 24-6.

50 Duty to *warn* the Friends as well as *expose* the Enemies of the
    Publick Weal, and to begin preaching up *Union* upon the first Sus-
    picion that any Steps are made to disturb it.

    But the two chief Subjects of Discontent, which, in most great
    Changes, in the management of publick Affairs, are apt to breed
55 Differences among those who are in Possession, are what I have
    just now mention'd; a Desire of punishing the Corruptions of for-
    mer Managers; and the rewarding *Merit*, among those who have been
    any way instrumental or consenting to the Change. The first of
    these is a Point so nice, that I shall purposely wave it. But the
60 latter I take to fall properly within my District: By *Merit* I
    here understand that Value which every Man puts upon his own
    Deservings from the Publick. And I believe there could not be a
    more difficult Employment found out, than that of *Pay-Master
    General* to this sort of *Merit*; or a more noisy, crowded Place,
65 than a Court of *Judicature*, erected to settle and adjust every
    Man's Claim upon that Article. I imagine, if this had fallen into
    the Fancy of the antient Poets, they would have drest it up after
    their Manner into an agreeable Fiction, and given us a Genealogy
    and Description of *Merit*, perhaps not very different from that
70 which follows.

    A Poetical Genealogy and Description of MERIT

    THAT *true Merit*, was the Son of *Virtue* and *Honour*; but that
    there was likewise a spurious Child who usurp'd the Name, and
    whose Parents were *Vanity* and *Impudence*. That, at a distance,
75 there was a great Resemblance between them, and they were often
    mistaken for each other. That the *Bastard Issue* had a *loud shrill
    Voice*, which was perpetually employ'd in *Cravings* and *Complaints*;
    while the other never spoke louder than a *Whisper*, and was often
    so bashful that he could not speak at all. That in all great

    53 in] upon 38 8°+12°   66 Article] Artcle ½°   71 *A* ... MERIT] *om.*
½° 0ᵃᵇ TxU   72 THAT] That, ½° 0ᵃᵇ TxU THAT, 38 8°+12°   79 all great]
great 38 8°+12°

---

    50 *Friends*: Even though it is not reflected in the *Journal to Stella* or his
    letters, Swift's 'first Suspicion' of antagonism between Harley and St. John
    must have occurred in February 1711.
    57 *rewarding Merit*: 'They have not enough [places] to satisfy all expec-
    ters, and so they keep them all in hopes, that they may be good boys in the
    mean time' (Swift, *Journal*, p. 226).

Assemblies, the *false Merit* would step before the *true*, and stand   80
just in his Way; was constantly at Court, or great Mens *Levees*,
or whispering in some *Minister's* Ear. That the more you fed him,
the more hungry and importunate he grew. That he often pass'd for
the *true* Son of *Virtue* and *Honour*, and the Genuine for an *Impos-*
tor. That he was born *distorted* and a *Dwarf*, but by force of Art   85
appear'd of a handsome Shape, and *taller* than the usual size; and
that none but those who were *wise* and *good*, as well as *vigilant*,
could discover his *Littleness* or *Deformity*. That the *true Merit*
had been often forc'd to the Indignity of applying to the *false*,
for his Credit with those in Power, and to keep himself from   90
Starving. That he fill'd the *Anti-chambers* with a Crew of his
Dependants and *Creatures*, such as *Projectors, Schematists, Occa-*
sional Converts to a Party, prostitute Flatterers, starvling
Writers, Buffoons, shallow Politicians, empty Orators, and the
like, who all own'd him for their *Patron*, and grew discontented   95
if they were not immediately fed.

   This Metaphorical Description of *false Merit*, is, I doubt, calculated for most Countries in *Christendom*; and as to our own,
I believe it may be said with a sufficient Reserve of Charity,
that we are fully able to reward every Man among us according to   100
his *real Deservings*. And I think I may add, without suspicion of
Flattery, that never any Prince had a Ministry with a better
Judgment to distinguish between false and real *Merit*, than that
which is now at the Helm; or whose Inclination as well as Interest it is to encourage the latter. And it ought to be observ'd,   105
that those great and excellent Persons we see at the Head of
Affairs, are of the Qu---'s *own Personal voluntary Choice*; not
forc'd upon Her by any *insolent, overgrown Favourite*, or by the
pretended *Necessity* of complying with an *unruly Faction*.

   Yet these are the Persons whom those Scandals to the Press, in   110
their Daily Pamphlets and Papers, openly revile at so ignominious

   91 he] the false Merit 38 8°   the false Merit he 38 12°   97 This] The
½° 0^{ab} TxU   99 be] *om.* ½°

   80-91 *the false Merit ... with a Crew*: innuendo: Godolphin and the moneyed
men (6.98n., 7.112n.).
   111 *Pamphlets*: Defoe interpreted this to be 'a hint of ... Laying a Tax
upon publick Prints and Pamphlets' (*Review*, 29 March 1711), which was actually
done in August 1712.

a Rate, as I believe was never Tolerated before under any Government. For surely no lawful Power derived from a Prince, should be
so far Affronted, as to leave those who are in Authority expos'd
115   to every scurrilous Libeller. Because in this Point I make a
mighty Difference between those who are *in*, and those who are *out*
of Power; not upon any Regard to their Persons, but the Stations
they are placed in by the Sovereign. And if my Distinction be
right, I think I might appeal to any Man, whether if a Stranger
120   were to read the Invectives which are Daily Publish'd against the
present Ministry, and the outragious Fury of the Authors against
me for censuring the *last*; he would not conclude the *Whigs* to be
at this Time in full possession of Power and Favour, and the
Tories entirely at Mercy? But all this now ceases to be a Wonder,
125   since the Qu--- Her self is no longer spared; witness the Libel
Publish'd some Days ago under the Title of *A Letter to Sir* J---b
B--ks, where the Reflections upon Her Sacred Majesty are much
more plain and direct, than ever the *Examiner* thought fit to publish against the most obnoxious Persons in a *M------y*, discarded
130   for endeavouring the Ruin of their Prince and Country. *Cæsar*
indeed threaten'd to hang the *Pirates* for presuming to disturb
him while he was their Prisoner aboard their Ship. But it was
Cæsar who did so, and he did it to a Crew of *Publick Robbers*; and
it became the Greatness of his Spirit, for he lived to execute
135   what he had threaten'd. Had *They* been in his Power, and sent such
a Message, it could be imputed to nothing but the Extreams of
Impudence, Folly or Madness.

I had a Letter last Week relating to Mr. *Greenshields* an *Episco-*

126-7 *A Letter to Sir* J---b B--ks: Swift mentioned this pamphlet by William
Benson in his letter of 19 February 1711 to Peterborough: 'shewing that the
liberty of Sweden was destroyed by the principle of passive obedience ... the
piece is shrewdly written: and in my opinion, not to be answered, otherwise
than by disclaiming that sort of passive obedience which the Tories are
charged with' (Swift, *Corr.*, i 212). Benson began early to earn his place in
The Dunciad as 'bold *Benson*' by insinuating, by means of Swedish analogues,
that Anne 'was a *Papist in her Heart*' (pp. 10-11). This pamphlet also provided Swift with the subject of *The Examiner*, No. 34, 22 March 1711 (E*1814*,
iv 25).

130 *Cæsar*: Plutarch, *Life of Cæsar*, ii.

138-69 *I ... Tyranny*: quoted in the *Review*, 17 March 1711. While acknow-
ledging that the Examiner 'has Treated *Scotland* with something more Candor
and Justice, than any of our Modern Writers on that Side, in the Case of Mr.
Greenshields', Defoe points out that the Examiner is 'altogether uninform'd
in the Particulars' of the case, as the Examiner himself admits (277.148).

138 *Letter*: 262.183.

pal Clergyman of *Scotland*, and the Writer seems to be a Gentleman
of that part of *Britain*. I remember formerly to have read a   140
printed Account of Mr. *Greenshields*'s Case, who has been Prosecuted and Silenc'd for no other reason beside reading Divine Service, after the manner of the Church of *England*, to his own
Congregation, who desir'd it: though, as the Gentleman who writes
to me says, there is no Law in *Scotland* against those Meetings;   145
and he adds, that the Sentence pronunc'd against Mr. *Greenshields*
will soon be affirm'd, if some Care be not taken to prevent it.
I am altogether uninform'd in the Particulars of this Case, and
besides to treat it justly, would not come within the Compass of
my Paper; Therefore I could wish the Gentleman would undertake it 150
in a Discourse by it self; and I should be glad he would inform
the Publick in one Fact, whether *Episcopal* Assemblies are freely
allow'd in *Scotland*? 'Tis notorious that abundance of their Clergy

144 who ... though] which ... although 38 8°+12°   146 pronunc'd] pronounced 12° 38 8°+12°   *Greenshields*] ~, ½°

---

141 *printed Account*: There were at least three such accounts. The one Swift
read may have been *A True State of the Case of the Reverend Mr. Greenshields,
now Prisoner in the Tolbooth in Edinburgh, for reading Common-prayer in an
Episcopal Congregation there, tho' qualify'd by taking the Oaths and praying
for the Queen and Princess Sophia* (1710).
144 *Congregation*: Greenshields told White Kennett that his Episcopal congregation was the only one of seven or eight in Edinburgh that used the Book
of Common Prayer (which required prayers for Queen Anne and Princess Sophia)
(BL MS Lansdowne 1024, f. 236).
145 *no Law ... against those Meetings*: 'Not Fact', Defoe insisted (*Review*,
17 March 1711), but Swift's source was right. The Lords of Session decided
that 'there needs no law condemning the English service, for the introducing
the Presbyterian worship explodes it as inconsistent' (*Decisions of the Lords
of Council and Session, from June 6th, 1678, to July 30th, 1712*, ed. Sir
John Lauder of Fountainhall, Edinburgh, for G. Hamilton and J. Balfour,
1761, ii 523).
147 *affirm'd*: The sentence was in fact reversed on 1 March 1711 (*LJ*, xix
240) (E*1922*, ix 200).
153 *allow'd*: Since the General Assembly defined toleration as 'establishing
Iniquity by a Law', there was no Act of Toleration in Scotland (*A True State
of the Case of the Reverend Mr. Greenshields*, London, for Jonah Bowyer, 1710,
pp. 9, 10). 'If you mean ... *Allow'd by the Law*,' Defoe replied, 'Why then
are so many Pushes made at a Toleration in *Scotland*? or why do you, Sir, complain in the same Paragraph for want of it?' (*Review*, 22 March 1711). Although
not '*Allow'd by the Law*', Episcopal services were generally 'Allow'd by
Connivance'.
153-7 *abundance ... us*: Defoe quotes these lines and confirms what the
Examiner says: 'In these Tumults [1688-9], many of the Parish Ministers in
... the West Country were violently driven away ... Now it may not be unlikely, that the Episcopal Clergy thus driven away by the Mob, might come to
England, as the *Examiner* says, *as from a Persecution*' (*Review*, 5 April 1711).

fled from thence some Years ago into *England* and *Ireland*, as
155   from a Persecution; but it was alledg'd by their Enemies, that
they refused to take the Oaths to the Government, which however
none of them scrupled when they came among us. It is somewhat
extraordinary to see our *Whigs* and *Fanaticks* keep such a stir
about the *Sacred Act of Toleration*, while their *Brethren* will not
160   allow a *Connivance* in so near a Neighbourhood; especially if what
the Gentleman insists on in his Letter be true, that nine Parts
in ten of the Nobility and Gentry, and two in three of the *Com-*
mons, be *Episcopal*; of which one Argument he offers, is the
present Choice of their Representatives in both Houses, tho'
165   oppos'd to the utmost by the *Preachings*, *Threatnings* and *Ana-*
thema's of the *Kirk*. Such Usage to a *Majority* may, as he thinks,
be of dangerous Consequence; and I entirely agree with him. If
these be the Principles of *High Kirk*, God preserve at least the
Southern Parts from their Tyranny!

166 *Majority*] ∼, ½°

---

156 *Oaths*: 'In not one in ten of [the Episcopal congregations] through the
Nation do the Ministers either take the Oaths to the Government, or pray for
her Majesty ... and some openly and avowedly [pray] for the *King*, and the
Pretender by Name' (*Review*, 22 March 1711).
159 *the ... Toleration*: Tindal, *The Rights of the Christian Church*
Asserted, 4th edn., 1709, p. 144.
161-3 *nine ... Episcopal*: cf. 'The Nobles and Gentry are generally Episcopal, and so the People especially Northward' (Thomas Morer *et al.*, *An Account*
of the Present Persecution of the Church in Scotland, in Several Letters,
London, for S. Cook, 1690, p. 2).
164 *Representatives*: Swift's correspondent is right, both about the sixteen Scottish representative peers, who apparently voted *en bloc*, and about
the forty-five Scottish Members, of whom 'the Court could perhaps count wholly
on twenty-three to twenty-five' (P.W.J. Riley, *The English Ministers and Scot-*
land 1707-1727, London, Athlone Press, 1964, p. 157). A contemporary account
puts the last figure at thirty-one (*A True and Exact List of those Worthy*
Patriots who, to their Eternal Honour, have, in One Session, detected the
Mismanagements of the Late M-----ry (1711)).
168-9 *God preserve ... the Southern Parts*: This was one point where Swift
and Mainwaring could agree; cf. Mainwaring, 'And grant Presbytery may stay,
| And all the canting Breed, | For ever, and also for ay, | On t'other side
the *Tweed*.' (*POAS*, Yale, vii 14).

No. 23 [Mainwaring and Steele]   5 March 1711

The MEDLEY.

Of Envy and Emulation.
A Story of a Ball at Wapping.
A Comparison between the Examiner *and his Brother* Abel.

THERE are no Affections of the Mind that seem at first sight more
nearly related to one another than Envy and Emulation. Yet if we
consider them attentively, we shall find that there are none more
different. Both indeed arise from the Comparison of our selves
with those above us; but in these Comparisons, Envy repines at   5
superiour Merit in another, Emulation bewails the want of it in
our selves. The business therefore of the envious Man is to
vilify and disparage, as it is the nature of the Emulous to endeavour after those Perfections which they behold in Men more
excellent than themselves. The Design of both is to place them-   10
selves upon a level with those above them: but as to this end one
of them practises all the little Arts of Detraction, Defamation,
and Calumny, to pull down their Superiours to their own Condition; the other makes use of Industry, Vigilance, and Application, the Instruments of an honest and active Ambition, to raise   15
himself up to that pitch of Reputation which he admires in Men
above him.

   As every Passion is more useful or pernicious according to the
Circumstances of the Person in whom it reigns; what makes Men of
a private Character disagreeable, makes those in a publick Sta-   20
tion pernicious. In order to equal those who have serv'd their
Country with Glory in the same Stations, they derogate from every
Action that is confessedly Great, and give the worst Interpretation to every thing that can appear doubtful. Thus when they
despair of rising to the Perfections of their Predecessors, they   25
keep themselves in countenance by endeavouring to deface them.

   I cannot forbear repeating on this occasion the Story of a
merry Rake, who was giving an account of a Ball which he had seen

18-19 *every ... reigns*: 261.162-3.

at a Musick-House in *Wapping*. The Men concern'd in it were made
30 up of a Crew of Sailors and Colliers. The Colliers, who came in
last, observing the Sailors, contrary to their Expectation, to be
spruc'd up in their best Clothes, withdrew into another Room to
wash their Faces and brush themselves; when the Head of the Col-
liery, who was more cunning than the rest, said to them: *Look ye,*
35 *Lads, it is all fruitless pains; if you will be rul'd by me, let*
us go into the great Room, and justle among the Sailors for their
Places: and I'll engage, tho we cannot make our selves as clean
as they are, we shall quickly make them as black as our selves.

    I make a Present of this short Story to my Friend the *Examiner*,
40 in return for his polite Simile of a Man of Quality going to a
Ball with Smut upon his Forehead.

    Were any such Persons as are above describ'd at the head of
Affairs at any time, how happy wou'd they be in such a Tool as
the *Examiner*? such an Inventor of groundless Falshoods, such a
45 Reviver of confuted Calumnies, who has no regard to the Dictates
of Truth, nor even the Sentiments of common Humanity; that takes
upon him the infamous Task of libelling and reviling every one
that has done service to his Country for these ten Years, and of
cherishing in the Minds of the Ignorant a Spirit of Bitterness
50 and Prejudice. Slanderous and reproachful Libels were formerly
the Weapons of the Party that was out of power, which they made
use of as the Means, tho they were very base Means, to reinstate
themselves. One cannot however but reflect, that Adversaries must
be very formidable, and have uncommon Merit, when there is a
55 necessity for defaming them even in their Adversity.

    This kind of Ribaldry passes for Wit and Humour among the Under-
lings of the Party; who, when the Author is very foul-mouth'd, are
taught to believe that he is very satyrical; and when he appears
scurrilous in an extraordinary degree, smile upon one another, and
60 whisper, the *Examiner* is *Devilish severe to day*. Thus plain
Calumnies, and downright matter of Scandal, without any of those

---

40 *Simile*: 261.154-9.
55 *defaming*: Steele may appear to score heavily here with an appeal to
good sportsmanship and not hitting a man when he is down. But Swift knew
better that successful propaganda requires a scapegoat, and that ignoring the
Whigs would by no means be so effective as dehumanizing them, converting
multivalent historical figures into single-character freaks: L'Avare Marlborough, Sid Hamet Godolphin, Defecator Wharton, Will Bigamy Cowper.

nice Glances or Strokes of Wit that are admir'd in other Writers
of this kind, are here receiv'd as fine Raillery and Invective.
Nay I have known some so very silly, as to admire him for the
boldness of his Sentiments, tho every one knows that he deserves   65
too ill to be in Danger. 'Tis true, he himself has suggested to
us, that his Paper is an *Orthodox* Libel, where he calls those of
his Adversaries, *The Tolerated Papers of the Week*.

There is indeed a great resemblance between his Brother *Abel*
and himself; and I find a great Dispute among the Party, to which   70
of them to give the Preference. They are both News-Writers, as
they utter things which no body ever heard of but from their
Papers: They are equally keen and pleasant in their Sarcasms:
They have both fallen into the same Expedient of being witty.
When *Abel* wou'd effectually lessen a Great Person, he Prints his   75
Name in a *small* Character. When the *Examiner* rises to a Pun, he
distinguishes the Point of Wit in a *dark* Letter. When *Abel* lashes
the Republicans, he tells you that several of them, in some distant Hamlet or Borough, drank Confusion to the Church with a Vol-
ley of Oaths and Curses. When the *Examiner* exposes the same Party,   80
he writes a Letter to himself, under the name of one of them, in
which he cries *G-d D--m me*, and *by G-d*. They differ however in
this: The *Examiner* utters Falshoods that are altogether stale and
exploded; whereas *Abel* serves them up fresh and fresh. If the
Examiner sometimes does shew himself the better Scholar, *Abel*   85
must be allow'd to know the World better.

I have in former Papers remark'd, that the *Examiner*, whoever
has enjoy'd that Post for some Weeks, has so much towards a Wit,
that he has very little Discretion: For a proof of this I need go
no further than his last Thursday's Paper. Wou'd any Man have   90
told us, that there were *one or two who seem to have been justly*
suspected of no very good Inclinations to the Reformation; and

---

68 *The ... Week*: 246.188-9.
77 *dark Letter*: 117.160, 132.122, 124, 240.42. The pun to which Mainwaring
objects is at 131.116.
82 *G-d ... G-d*: 244.123-5. Another point where Swift and Mainwaring could
agree was their hatred of profanity (Swift, *Journal*, p. 273; Oldmixon, *The*
Life, p. xvii).
87 *whoever*: Although he was 'always inclin'd to think [Prior] had the
greatest hand in it' (ibid., p. 157), Mainwaring did not know in January 1711
who wrote *The Examiner*.
91-2 *one ... Inclinations*: 256.5-10.

not have expected to be ask'd, whether one of these two had been
bred a Presbyterian, or either of them had been a Papist? Wou'd
95 any Man have confess'd, all that is contended for by his Adversary, that a Man without Religion may be a *good Churchman*, and
that the name of a Churchman, as us'd by his Friends, does not
imply a Zeal for *Religion*, but a *Party*? as he has wisely acknowledg'd in the following words: ''Tis possible that a Man may have
100 little or no Religion at Heart; yet if he conceals his Opinions,
if he endeavours to make no Proselytes, advances no impious
Tenets in Writing, or Discourse: If, according to the common
Atheistical Notion, he believes Religion to be only a Contrivance
of Politicians, for keeping the Vulgar in awe, and that the
105 present Model is better adjusted than any other to so useful an
end; tho the Condition of such a Man, as to his future State, be
very deplorable; yet Providence, which often works Good out of
Evil, can make even such a Man an Instrument for contributing
towards the Preservation of the Church.'
110 Wou'd any Man in his Wits have spoken of his Sovereign in the
following words? 'Why was the old Ministry chang'd? Which they
urge on without ceasing, as if no occasion in the least had been
given; but that all were owing to the Insinuations of crafty Men,
practising upon the Weakness of an easy Pr---e.'
115 I must confess I shou'd not have ventur'd to quote this Sentence, had I not taken it out of a *Protected* Paper; but whether
after this it ought to be a *Tolerated* one, I shall leave the
World to judg, unless the Patrons of it take care to have it
supervis'd before it is publish'd.
120 Again, whom does he aim at by that Expression? 'A Man may perhaps mean honestly; yet if he be not able to spell, he shall
never have my Vote for a Secretary.' I believe no body ever heard
of above *one* Secretary that cou'd not spell.

115 quote] have quoted ½° 89

99-109 *a ... Church*: 256.17-27.
111-14 *Why ... Pr---e*: 257.55-8. Mainwaring scores here because there is
too much truth in Harley's craftiness and Anne's 'Weakness'. 'Crafty' in fact
was one of Mainwaring's epithets for Harley (Oldmixon, *The Life*, pp. 129,
149). Oldmixon quoted part of this at 271.193-4, but failed apparently to
see the applicability to Harley.
117 *Tolerated*: 246.188.
120-2 *A ... Secretary*: 262.176-7.

Sometimes indeed he is not quite so impudent as he is at others:
and tho he observes no Measures with those *that are out*, he en-   125
deavours to be civil at any rate to those *that are in*; for he
assures us, nothing was done *by the necessity of complying with
an unruly Faction*: Which Saying of his will have a very good
Effect with those who are so willing to believe every thing he
says as I am.   130

125 *Those ... out*: 276.116.
127-8 *by ... Faction*: 275.108-9.

No. 32 [Swift]   8 March 1711

The EXAMINER.

Garrit aniles

Ex re fabellas.

I Had last Week sent me by an unknown Hand a Passage out of *Plato*,
with some Hints how to apply it. That Author puts a Fable into
the Mouth of *Aristophanes*, with an Account of the Original of
Love. That, Mankind was at first created with four Arms and Legs,
and all other Parts double to what they are now; 'till *Jupiter*,   5
as a Punishment for his Sins, cleft him in two with a Thunder-
bolt, since which Time we are always looking for our *other Half*;
and this is the Cause of *Love*. But *Jupiter* Threatned, that if
they did not mend their Manners, he would give them t'other Slit,
and leave them to hop about in the shape of Figures in *Basso*   10
relievo. The Effect of this last Threatning, my Correspondent
imagines, is now come to pass; and that as the first *splitting*
was the Original of *Love*, by inclining us to search for our
t'other Half, so the second was the cause of *Hatred*, by prompting

13 search] search out 38 8°+12°

Motto Horace, *Satires*, ii 6 77: Never fails | To chear our Converse with
his pithy Tales.
1 *Passage*: Plato, *The Symposium*, 189-92.

15 us to fly from our *other side*, and dividing the same *Body* into
    two, gave each Slice the Name of a Party.
        I approve the Fable and Application, with this Refinement upon
    it. For *Parties* do not only *split* a Nation, but every Individual
    among them, leaving each but *half* their Strength, and Wit, and
20 Honesty, and good Nature; but one Eye and Ear for their Sight
    and Hearing, and equally lopping the rest of the Senses: Where
    Parties are pretty equal in a State, no Man can perceive one bad
    Quality in his own, or good one in his Adversaries. Besides,
    Party being a dry disagreeable Subject, it renders Conversation
25 insipid or sowr, and confines Invention. I speak not here of the
    Leaders, but the insignificant Crowd of Followers in a *Party*, who
    have been the Instruments of mixing it in every Condition and
    Circumstance of Life. As the *Zealots* among the *Jews* bound the
    Law about their Foreheads, and Wrists, and Hems of their Garments;
30 so the *Women* among us have got the distinguishing Marks of *Party*
    in their *Muffs*, their *Fans*, and their *Furbelow's*. The *Whig*-Ladies
    put on their *Patches* in a different manner from the *Tories*. They
    have made *Schisms* in the *Play-House*, and each have their particu-
    lar sides at the *Opera*: And when a Man changes his *Party*, he must
35 infallibly count upon the Loss of his *Mistress*. I ask'd a Gentle-
    man t'other day, how he liked such a *Lady*? but he would not give
    me his Opinion, 'till I had answer'd him whether she were a *Whig*
    or a *Tory*. Mr. ----- since he is known to visit the present
    M-----ry, and lay some time under Suspicion of writing the *Exami-*
40 *ner*, is no longer a Man of *Wit*; his very *Poems* have contracted a
    Stupidity many Years after they were Printed.
        Having lately ventur'd upon a Metaphorical Genealogy of *Merit*;
    I thought it would be proper to add another of *Party*, or rather,

---

    16 gave] give 38 8°+12°   17 the Fable] the Table ½° of the Fable 38
    8°+12°   26 Crowd] Brood 38 8°+12°   34 changes] changeth 38 8°+12°
    38 a] *om*. 38 8°+12°

---

    18 *Parties*: cf. 'I am apt to think this schism in politics has cloven our
    understandings, and left us but just half the good sense that blazed in our
    actions' (Swift, *Corr*., i 211).
    28 *bound*: see *OED*, s.v. *Phylactery*.
    32 *Patches*: Addison devoted *The Spectator*, 2 June 1711, to this conceit
    (E*1922*, ix 203).
    38 -----: Prior (E*1814*, iv 28).
    39-40 *Examiner*: 212.56.

of *Faction*, (to avoid Mistake) not telling the Reader whether it
be my own or a Quotation, 'till I know how it is approv'd; but   45
whether I Read or Dream'd it, the Fable is as follows.

LIberty, *the Daughter of* Oppression, *after having brought forth
several fair Children, as* Riches, Arts, Learning, Trade, *and many
others, was at last delivered of her youngest Daughter, called*
FACTION; *whom* Juno, *doing the Office of the Midwife, distorted in*   50
its Birth, out of Envy to the Mother, from whence it derived its
Peevishness *and* Sickly Constitution. *However, as it is often the
Nature of Parents to grow most fond of their youngest and dis-
agreeablest Children, so it happen'd with* Liberty, *who doated on
this Daughter to such a Degree, that by her good Will she would*   55
never suffer the Girl to be out of her Sight. As Miss Faction
*grew up, she became so Termagant and Froward, that there was no
enduring Her any longer in* Heaven. Jupiter *gave Her warning to be
gone; and her Mother rather than forsake her, took the whole
Family down to* Earth. *She landed at first in* Greece, *was expell'd* 60
*by degrees through all the Cities by her Daughters ill Conduct;
fled afterwards to* Italy, *and being banish'd thence, took shelter
among the* Goths, *with whom she passed into most Parts of* Europe;
*but driven out every where, she began to lose Esteem, and her
Daughter's Faults were imputed to her self. So that at this Time,*   65
*she has hardly a Place in the World to retire to. One would won-
der what strange Qualities this Daughter must possess, sufficient
to blast the Influence of so divine a Mother, and the rest of her
Children:* She *always affected to keep mean and scandalous Company; valuing no Body, but just as they agreed with her in every*   70
*capricious Opinion she thought fit to take up; and rigorously
exacting Compliance, though she changed her Sentiments ever so
often. Her great Employment was to breed* Discord *among Friends
and Relations, and make up monstrous Alliances between those
whose Dispositions least resembled each other. Whoever offer'd to*   75
*contradict her, though in the most insignificant Trifle, she
would be sure to distinguish by some ignominious* Appellation, *and
allow them to have neither Honour, Wit, Beauty, Learning, Honesty
or common Sense. She intruded into all Companies at the most unseasonable Times, mixt at Balls, Assemblies, and other Parties of*   80

50 *the Midwife*] *Midwife* 38 8°+12°   62 *fled afterwards*] *she fled after-*
wards 38 8°   *she afterwards fled* 38 12°   *64 but*] *but being* 38 8°+12°

Pleasure; haunted every Coffee-house and Booksellers Shop, and by
her perpetual Talking filled all Places with Disturbance and Con-
fusion. She buzzed about the Merchant *in the Exchange, the* Divine
in his Pulpit, and the Shopkeeper *behind his Counter. Above all,*
85 *she frequented* Publick Assemblies, *where she sate in the shape of*
an obscene, ominous Bird, *ready to prompt her* Friends *as they*
spoke.

   If I understand this Fable of *Faction* right, it ought to be
apply'd to those who set themselves up against the true Interest
90 and Constitution of their Country; which I wish the *Undertakers*
for the late *M-----y* would please to take notice of; or tell us
by what Figure of Speech they pretend to call so great and *un-*
forc'd a Majority, with the Qu--- at the Head, by the Name of *the*
Faction: Which is not unlike the Phrase of the *Nonjurors,* who
95 dignifying one or two deprived Bishops, and half a score Clergymen of the same Stamp, with the Title of the *Church of England,*
exclude all the rest as *Schismaticks*; or like the *Presbyterians,*
laying the same Accusation, with equal Justice, against the *Esta-*
blished Religion.
100   And here it may be worth inquiring what are the true Character-
isticks of a *Faction*, or how it is to be distinguish'd from that
great Body of the People who are Friends to the Constitution? The
Heads of a *Faction*, are usually a set of *Upstarts*, or Men ruin'd
in their Fortunes, whom some great Change in a Government, did at
105 first, out of their Obscurity, produce upon the Stage. They associate themselves with those who dislike the old Establishment,
Religious and Civil. They are full of new Schemes in Politicks
and Divinity; they have an incurable Hatred against the old
Nobility, and strengthen their Party by Dependents raised from
110 the lowest of the People; they have several ways of working themselves into Power; but they are sure to be *called* when a *corrupt*
Administration wants to be supported, against those who are endeavouring at a *Reformation*; and they firmly observe that celebrated Maxim of preserving *Power* by the same Arts it is attain'd.
115 They act with the Spirit of those who believe their *Time is but*
short; and their first Care is to heap up immense Riches at the

   94 *Faction*: 68.50n.
   114 *Power*: cf. 'The same *Arts* that did *gain* | A *Pow'r* must it *maintain'*
(Marvell, *An Horatian Ode upon Cromwel's Return from Ireland* (1678), 119-20).

Publick Expence; in which they have two Ends, beside that common
one of insatiable Avarice; which are, to make themselves Necessary, and to keep the Commonwealth in Dependance: Thus they hope
to compass their Design, which is, instead of fitting their Prin-   120
ciples to the Constitution, to alter and adjust the Constitution
to their own pernicious Principles.

'Tis easy determining by this Test, to which Side the Name of
Faction most properly belongs. But however, I will give them any
System of Law or Regal Government, from *William* the Conqueror to   125
this present time, to try whether they can *tally* it with their
late *Models*; excepting only that of *Cromwell*, whom perhaps they
will reckon for a *Monarch*.

If the present Ministry, and so great a Majority in the Parlia-
ment and Kingdom be only a *Faction*, it must appear by some   130
Actions which answer the Idea we usually conceive from that Word.
Have they abus'd the Prerogatives of the Prince, or invaded the
Rights and Liberties of the Subject? Have they offer'd at any
dangerous Innovations in Church or State? Have they broached any
Doctrines of Heresy, Rebellion or Tyranny? Have any of them   135
treated their Sovereign with Insolence, engross'd and sold all
Her Favours, or deceived Her by base, gross Misrepresentations of
Her most faithful Servants? These are the Arts of a *Faction*, and
whoever has Practis'd them, they and their Followers must take up
with the *Name*.   140

It is usually reckon'd a *Whig* Principle to appeal to *the People*;
but that is only when they have been so wise as to poison their
Understandings before-hand: Will they now stand to this Appeal,
and be determin'd by their *Vox Populi*, to which Side their Title
of *Faction* belongs? And that the *People* are now left to the   145
natural Freedom of their Understanding and Choice, I believe our
Adversaries will hardly deny. They will now refuse this *Appeal*,
and it is reasonable they should; and I will further add, that if

131 answer] answers ½° 12°   132 Prerogatives] Prerogative 38 8°+12°

---

132 *Prerogatives*: Although Swift himself favoured increasing the royal
prerogative (318.129-31), he is on dangerous ground here, for the Act of
Settlement (June 1701), which imposed serious limitations on the royal veto
and was 'the first statutory encroachment on royal control of foreign policy',
was the work of Harley and the New Country Party (Ogg, iii 468; Swift, *Discourse*, p. 138).

our *People* resembled the old *Grecians,* there might be danger in
150   such a Tryal. A Pragmatical Orator told a great Man at *Athens,*
that whenever the *People* were *in their Rage,* they would certainly
tear him to Pieces; yes, says the other, and they will do the
same by you, whenever they are *in their Wits.* But God be thanked,
our Populace is more merciful in their Nature, and *at present*
155   under better Direction; and the *Orators* among us have attempted
to confound both *Prerogative* and *Law,* in their *Sovereign's*
Presence, and before the *highest Court of Judicature,* without any
Hazard to their Persons.

153 by] to 12° 38 8°+12°

_____

150 *Orator*: Demosthenes (Plutarch, *Life of Phocion,* ix 5).
156 *confound both Prerogative and Law*: Swift may imply that Sacheverell's
impeachment by the House of Commons invaded Anne's prerogative under the Act
of Supremacy (176.197n.); cf. 151.178n.

No. 24 [Mainwaring and Oldmixon]   12 March 1711

The MEDLEY.
The Growth of Deism and Immorality, of Tory Origin.
Of the Freedom of the Will, and a Voluntary Choice.
False Merit and Faction consider'd.
More Remarks on the Examiner.

IF it were worth while to argue with the Tories, one wou'd endeavour by the Force of Reason and Facts to make 'em asham'd of the
absurd and ridiculous Notions they have lately reviv'd, and the
notorious Falshoods they are continually broaching. But what
5   wou'd it all signify? They know very well their Business is not
to be done by Truth and Argument? 'Tis enough for them to pretend
to Loyalty and Zeal, to make a great Noise and look big, to
assert and deny boldly; if the World won't believe 'em, they
can't help it. 'Tis all they have to persuade 'em to it. If they
10   will, they'l push it as far as it will go, and they have often
carry'd their Point by it. They were all along in King *Charles*

the Second's Reign for *Passive-Obedience* and *Non-Resistance*: At
the Revolution they ran in to the Prince of *Orange*: In King *William*'s Time they were as much for Non-Resistance and Passive-
Obedience as any body: In Queen *Anne*'s they murmur'd, mutiny'd   15
and rebel'd; and on a sudden they cry'd out for their old exploded Tenets as loud as ever. The Church was, besides, over-run
with *Atheism, Blasphemy*, and *Schism*, and that was intolerable.
They did not care in whose Hands Affairs were, provided the
Church was safe, and a stop put to the Deluge of Infidelity that   20
had like to have overwhelm'd us; in order to which they did what
they cou'd to blacken the *Reformation of Manners*. They ridicul'd
it, misrepresented it, wrote against it, preach'd against it, and
did their utmost to ruin the Design, as savouring of *Schism* and
Fanaticism, which are with them the worst sort of *Atheism* and   25
Deism. I have in former Papers observ'd how ill-grounded their
Pretences to Zeal and Loyalty are, how they have abandon'd the
Church, how they have insulted their Sovereign; and now I will
enquire into their *Morals* and *Doctrine*, and see whether the
Growth of Deism and Immorality is not of *Tory* Origin. An Inquiry   30
which wou'd seem very vain and superfluous, if we had not to do
with People who will deny to morrow what they did yesterday, with
as good a Grace as they did it. They have forgot that the Court
of King *Charles* the Second was almost always Tory, and yet *Atheism, Deism* and *Irreligion* were more publickly profess'd and prac-   35
tis'd there than in all the Courts of *Europe*: That their Great
Champion *Dodwell* has by a new System destroy'd the Immortality
of the Soul: That *Hickes, B----s*, &c. have advanc'd more Heterodox

20-1 *Deluge ... us*: 131.117.
22 *blacken the Reformation of Manners*: 176.201. Swift favoured the idea
of societies for the reformation of manners, but he heard that they had
'dwindled into factious Clubs, and grown a Trade to enrich little knavish
Informers of the meanest Rank' (Swift, *Prose*, ii 49, 57).
27 *Pretences to Zeal and Loyalty*: 247.8-24.
    abandon'd: 249.58-253.136.
28 *insulted*: 262.1-268.119.
37 *Dodwell*: 155.40n.
38 *Hickes*: George Hickes (1642-1715), the antiquarian, graduated BA from
Magdalen College, Oxford, in February 1663. In February 1690 he was deprived
of the deanery of Worcester. In May 1693 he was received by James II at Saint-
Germain, and upon his return was secretly consecrated Bishop of Thetford by
William Sancroft, the deprived Archbishop of Canterbury. Hickes's heterodoxies
included his belief in 'the Illegality of the *Revolution*, and the Usurpation
of King *William* and Queen *Mary*' (Kennett, iii 614), but what particularly

[*Notes to line* 38 *cont. on next page*].

Notions than all the Whig-Writers. But what's all this to them?
40 They don't think themselves oblig'd to look into the Rise and
Causes of Things. If they did, all their Clamour wou'd return on
themselves, and the *Whigs* have Schism only to answer for. I will
therefore put 'em in mind of what a famous Judg Sir *Matthew Hale*,
who had nothing of *Whig* about him, but Charity, Integrity and
45 Piety, says on this occasion: *When Men see so much Religion plac'd*
by Professors of Christianity, in those Things which every intel-
ligent Man values but as Forms or Inventions, or Modes or Arti-
fices, and yet as great Weight laid upon them, as great Fervour
and Animosity us'd for or against them, as almost for any Points
50 *of Christian Religion; they are apt presently to censure and throw*
off all Religion, and reckon all of the same Make. How these
Forms, Inventions, Modes and Artifices have since been stickled
for, every one knows, and who they are that have thence given
occasion to the Growth of *Atheism* and *Deism*, to the *throwing off*
55 *all Religion*, and *reckoning all of the same Make.* But the Behaviour of the *High-Church* Clergy to King *William* and Queen *Anne*,
has perhaps had worse Consequences in this Case than that. I will
not impose my own Sentiments on the Reader, but give him those of
a noted Author on this Head, in a Treatise publish'd not long
60 since, where he introduces a Deist speaking thus to his Friend,

offended Oldmixon was *A New Catechism, with Dr. Hickes's Thirty Nine Articles*
(1710), '*So fruitful of Contradictions, Blasphemy and Treason*' (Oldmixon, *The*
Life, p. 111).
    38 *B----s*: William Binckes (*c.*1653-1712) graduated BA from St. John's Col-
lege, Cambridge, in 1674 and proceeded DD in 1699. His heterodoxies include
contumacy and something very close to blasphemy. On 30 January 1702, while
proctor of the diocese of Lichfield, he preached a sermon to the Lower House
of Convocation in which he elaborated a 'Blasphemous Parallel, to shew that
the Indignities and Sufferings of King *Charles* [I] exceed[ed] those of Jesus
Christ' (Defoe, *A New Test of the Church of England's Loyalty: Or, Whiggish*
Loyalty and Church Loyalty Compar'd, 1702, p. 12). The House of Lords resolved
that these 'Expressions ... give just Scandal and Offence to all Christian
People' (*LJ*, xvii 132) and ordered Binckes to be reprimanded. Instead he was
appointed Dean of Lichfield in May 1703 and elected prolocutor of the Convocation in 1705 (Luttrell, v 298, 609). In the latter capacity he allowed the
Lower House to continue sitting after the Archbishop had prorogued the Convocation. This brought an action of contumacy in April 1706 that was only
dropped after Binckes had made a formal submission to the Archbishop (Boyer,
Annals, 1707, pp. 485-6).
    45-51 *When ... Make*: *The Judgment of the late Lord Chief Justice Sir*
Matthew Hale, Of the Nature of True Religion, the Causes of its Corruption,
and Churches Calamity, by Mens Additions and Violences, ed. Richard Baxter,
London, for B. Simmons, 1684, p. 16.

who wou'd have converted him if he cou'd: *Have you not,* says he,
for many years heard them preach up the Divine Right and Inde-
feasible Authority of Kings, together with Passive-Obedience, as
the chief distinguishing Doctrines by which their Church approv'd
it self Apostolick beyond all other Churches? Nay, were not the   65
Doctrines of Loyalty to the King insisted on more than Faith in
Christ? And yet, when their particular Interest requir'd it, the
whole Stream of Loyalty was turn'd from the King to the Church,
the Indefeasible Right was superseded by a miraculous Conquest
without Blood, the Oath of Allegiance to the divinely rightful   70
King James *had its Force allay'd by another Oath of the same Im-*
portance made to the de facto *King* William *and* Queen Mary; *and*
all this is sanctify'd by the name of the Church, i.e. *their own*
Party and Interest, for the sake of which it is done: Rem rem
quocunque modo rem. And how far such Prevarications and Practices   75
have contributed to the Discredit of Religion; how far the Lives
of these Genuine Sons of the Church have dishonour'd their Mother;
how far their boasted Zeal is downright Hypocrisy, is too apparent to admit of any further Animadversion, either now or hereafter; and I shall have done with them on this Article, the   80
Subject of which brings to my Memory a Passage in the Chancellor
de l'Hopital's Will, which I read in *Brantome: Those who got me*
remov'd out of my Place, did it under the Colour of Religion,
while they were themselves without Piety and without Religion.
'Tis true, these things are always to be expected, for the Man-   85
ners and Merit of People are not much consider'd in the Disposition of Favours. 'Tis the Side, the Interest: *Cæsar,* as errant a
Tory as ever liv'd, told such as blam'd him for advancing worth-
less Fellows, *If Robbers and Assassins had help'd him to mount to*
his present Dignity, he wou'd do the same by them.   90
     I have had a great Mind to puzzle my Friend the *Examiner* with
Metaphysicks, and write a short Essay on the *Freedom of the Will,*
because the Tories would make us as great Fools in that as in

65 *Nay*] *nay* ½°

61-75 *Have* ... *rem*: William Stephens, *An Account of the Growth of Deism in*
England, London, 1696, pp. 10-11.
82-4 *Those* ... *Religion: Memoires de Mre. Pierre de Bourdeille, Seigneur*
de Brantome, 10 vols., Leyden, Jean Sambix, 1665-1722, vii 100.
89-90 *If* ... *them*: Suetonius, *Divus Iulius,* lxxii.

every thing else. King *James*'s Abdication was, say they, a Deser-
95   tion, an *Act of Volition*, without any manner of Resistance or
Constraint. Some Alterations that happen'd afterwards were a *personal voluntary Choice*, without any foreign Influence, as Sermons,
Libels, Tumults, Riots, &c. If I did not consider I have something else to do, and shou'd soon tire the Reader, my Friend's
100 Example is sufficient to fright any Man from such a Scholar-like
Attempt; for the more learned and serious he pretends to be, he
is always the more foolish and impertinent: However I will venture to tell him, Mr. *Lock* lays it down as a Principle, That
Uneasiness, and not any positive Good, determines the Will. After
105 which he shews us how we come to chuse Ill: I will trouble the
Reader with part of it, tho he will have a terrible Leap from Mr.
Lock to the *Examiner*. *There is a Case wherein a Man is at liberty
in respect of* Willing; *and that is, the chusing a remote Good as
an End to be pursu'd. Here a Man may suspend the Act of his*
110 *Choice from being determin'd for or against the thing propos'd,
till he has examin'd whether it be really of a nature in it-self
and Consequences to make him happy or no. For when he has chosen
it, and thereby it is become part of his Happiness, it raises
Desire; and that proportionably gives him Uneasiness, which deter-*
115 *mines his Will, and sets him at work in pursuit of his Choice on
all Occasions that offer. And here we may see how it comes to
pass that a Man may justly incur Punishment, tho it be certain
that in all the particular Actions that he wills, he does, and
necessarily does will that which he then judges to be good. For*
120 *tho his* Will *be always determin'd by that which is judg'd good by
his Understanding, yet it excuses him not: because by a too hasty
Choice of his own making, he has impos'd on himself wrong Measures
of Good and Evil; which, however false and fallacious, have the
same influence on all his future Conduct, as if they were true*
125 *and right. He has vitiated his own Palate, and must be answerable
to himself for the Sickness and Death that follows from it.*
    I don't believe there is a Man living so apt to speak Truth of

---

    104 *Uneasiness ... Will*: The Medley quotes the fifth edition (ii 21 31),
An Essay concerning Humane Understanding, London, for Awnsham and John Churchill and Samuel Manship, 1706, p. 159.
    107-26 *There ... it*: ibid., pp. 171-2. The passage (ii 21 56) was intro-
duced in Pierre Coste's French translation (1700) and is not found in any of
the English editions before Locke's death (1704).

himself and others, as the *Examiner*; but then 'tis when he does
not intend it, and always with a Blunder. After he has been railing with as much Rancour and Scurrility as he cou'd against the   130
late Ministry, he confesses he *never receiv'd any Injury from
them*. Now one wou'd have thought they had impeach'd him at least,
by the Treatment they have met with from him: but he says as ill
things of his Friends too, *Nor Advantage from the present*. A bold
way of writing! which, was it design'd, wou'd be very much to his   135
Honour. He sets up lately for a most impartial Author; and after
the great things that have been done, vouchsafes to own *one or
two* of the late *Ministers possess'd of very valuable Qualities*:
and he has not a word to say against them, but that being for the
Revolution and Toleration, they are Enemies to the Constitution   140
in Church and State. 'Tis plain his Eulogies are not for Men who
deserve them; and his Panegyrick will be always lame, if there's
no room for Flattery. But there are some Men of such shining
Worth, that neither Malice nor Envy can help speaking well of 'em.
'Twas of such *Cicero* said, *He had rather err with* Plato, *than*   145
speak or think justly in following the Opinion of others. And
again: Cato *cou'd sooner make Drunkenness honourable, than Drunkenness dishonour* Cato. There are others of so scandalous a Character,
that if they have a good Talent 'tis sully'd by their Vices; every
thing they do disgusts and offends. It is very hard to meet with   150
a *Cato* in our days; and I don't know one Politician but what
Drunkenness wou'd make a Sot of. I am ready in all cases to favour
my Friend even to a fault, and I shall certainly then never omit
doing him Justice: He has a pretty Tale of *Merit*, in one of his
last Papers, *which he takes to fall properly within his District*,   155
as indeed it does, considering how he places it. And wou'd any
Man of common Sense have given such a Description of *False Merit*
as cou'd agree with no Faction in the World but his own? for put
Torism instead of it, and it fits exactly in all its Parts. *'Tis
the Child of Vanity and Impudence, has a loud and shrill Voice,*   160

131-2 *never ... them*: 255.2-3.
134 *Nor ... present*: 255.3.
137-8 *one ... Qualities*: 256.5-6; cf. 281.90-91.
145-6 *He ... others*: Cicero, *Tusc. Disp.*, i 17 39.
147-8 *Cato ... Cato*: Seneca, *De tranquillitate animi*, xvii 9.
155 *he ... District*: 274.59-60.
160-9 *Child ... &c.*: 274.71-275.96.

which is perpetually employ'd in Cravings and Complaints. It steps
before True Merit in all great Assemblies, and stands just in its
way. 'Tis constantly at Court, at Great Mens Levees, or whisper-
ing in some Minister's Ear. The more you feed it, the more hungry
165 *and importunate it grows. 'Twas born distorted and a Dwarf, but*
by Force of Art appears of a handsom Shape, and taller than the
usual Size. Its Dependants and Creatures are Schematists, Occasional Converts to a Party, starveling Writers, shallow Politicians, and empty Orators, &c. What can be more natural than the
170 whole? but the latter part of his Description is as plain as if
he had been as honest as I, and written the *true* Name over his
Sign. His other Fable of *Faction* too is entirely his own: so that
by this time the Party see, sure, he is not to be trusted with
such things as Tales and Fables; for Mischief comes of it as
175 often as he attempts it, and the *Tories* are the Sufferers. This
second *Bastard* of his is *distorted, peevish, sickly, termagant*
and froward. She always affects the Company of the Rabble, and
values no body but just as they agree in every capricious Opinion
she thinks fit to take up; to which she rigorously exacts Confor-
180 *mity. Her great Employment is to breed Discord among Friends and*
Relations, and make up monstrous Alliances between those whose
Dispositions least resemble each other. She intrudes into all
Companies, haunts Coffee-Houses, and fills all Places with Dis-
turbance and Confusion. She buzzes about the Merchant at the
185 *Exchange, the Divine in his Pulpit, and the Shopkeeper behind his*
Counter. Above all, she frequents publick Assemblies, where she
sits in the shape of an obscene ominous Bird, ready to prompt her
Friends as they speak. He loves to end smartly! And now I leave
it to all Mankind to judg, whether the *Tories* are not mad, to let
190 the *Examiner* deal in Descriptions and Images. For having a narrow
Invention of his own, he's forc'd always to copy after some Original: and if his Enemies won't sit to him, his Friends shall. I
have warn'd them of this before; but the truth on't is, they are
the worst People in the world to to take warning, or having been
195 so often baffled in their Politicks, they wou'd not have set up

    166 *of a*] *of as* ½°

176-88 *distorted ... speak:* 285.50-286.87.
193 *warn'd ... before:* 142.160-1.

for Statesmen any more. In King *Charles*'s time they cou'd never
hold it above a year or two; and whenever they have it in a better Reign, their own must for certain be much shorter. Till he
can calculate better, and find out that his Nine in Ten are not,
as he assures us, in *Scotland* for High-Church too, he will no   200
more frighten People with his Majorities, than he convinces 'em
by his Arguments, or entertains 'em with his Wit. As for his
Schisms at the Play-house, I wonder how he cou'd offer to impose
on his Readers so. The Ladies of both Parties have never distinguish'd themselves by any thing but their Faces: And even Credit   205
has not been more constant to the *Ruin'd one*, than Beauty. The
Fair ever sided with the Brave, Witty, and Rich. The very Principles of the Tories are enough to deform their Persons as well
as their Minds. And the Graces and Furies may as soon agree as
Tories and Beauty.   210

What he says in behalf of his Friend *Carvel*, is very extraordinary, for the Frankness of the Confession: *His very Poems have
contracted a Stupidity many years after they were printed.* And
why is it? because *he lay under the suspicion of writing the*
Examiner: At which he seems to be strangely surpriz'd, as if such   215
a Suspicion was not enough to ruin the Reputation of the best
Poet in *Britain*. Nay, he puts the thing further, and tells us he
visits the Present M-------; which, whatever it may do for other
things, will never make the World have the better opinion of his
Wit. Besides, 'tis no such great matter for a Man's Works to con-   220
tract a Stupidity many years after they are printed. And tho the
Tories cry up my Friend now for such a topping Writer, yet if his
Works do not even with them contract the very same thing within
this Twelvemonth, I am as ill a Guesser as himself, or they are
duller than I take 'em to be. If my Friend was not oblig'd to   225
fall upon the late Ministers, as he does in every one of his

198 *shorter*: The last two Tory administrations lasted, respectively, less
than a year (1701) and barely two (1702-4).
199-200 *Nine in Ten ... for High-Church*: Oldmixon scores here, for Swift's
informant was wrong (278.160-2). Defoe's estimate that only one-sixth of the
Scottish parishes remained episcopal in 1688 is closer to the truth (Thomas
Maxwell, *Scottish Church History Society Records*, xiii (1957-9), 25-37).
203 *Schisms at the Play-house*: 284.33.
206 *Ruin'd one*: 207.156.
211 *Carvel*: Prior, from Prior's delightful facetia, *Hans Carvel* (1701).
212-15 *His ... Examiner*: 284.39-41.
218 *visits ... M-------*: 284.38-9.

Papers, I believe he has heard so much of it, that tho perhaps he
is not the modestest Person that ever was, yet he cou'd not but
have some shame in him. He must do it, or there wou'd be an end
230   of his Paper. In the last he is so civil to her Majesty and then,
that he declares he can compare their Administration to nothing
but the Usurper *Cromwell*'s. He is not a very good Historian, or
if he was, he wou'd not care for that, he'd say what he pleas'd.
Every body knows *Cromwell*'s was an Arbitrary *Tory* Reign; that he
235   rul'd by a Standing Army, dispens'd with the Laws, and set up
Will and Pleasure against them. There is another thing, I think,
he shou'd not so soon have charg'd the Whigs with; and that is,
appealing to the People. He shou'd have let it alone till some
late Occurrences were forgotten. But the pleasantest of all is,
240   that now the Doctrines of *Hereditary Right* and *Protestant Succession, Revolution* and *Non-Resistance* are advanc'd together, and
one must alike give Assent to all of 'em on pain of Sedition:
yet, quoth he, *the People are now left to the natural Freedom of
their Understanding*. If what he says were true, they must either
245   have very little, or have made a very ill use of it.

232   *Cromwell*: 287.127.
238   *appealing to the People*: 287.145-7.
238-9   *some late Occurrences*: 154.9n.
243-4   *the ... Understanding*: 287.145-6.

No. 33 [Swift]   15 March 1711

The EXAMINER.

*Non est ea medicina, cum sanæ parti corporis scalpellum adhibetur, atq;
integræ; carnificina est ista, & crudelitas. Hi medentur Reipublicæ qui
exsecant pestem aliquam, tanquam strumam Civitatis.*

I Am diverted from the general Subject of my Discourses, to reflect upon an Event of a very extraordinary and surprizing Nature:

Motto Cicero, *Pro P. Sestio*, 135: To apply the Knife to a sound and healthy
Part of the Body is Butchery and Cruelty; not real Surgery: These are the true
Physicians and Surgeons of a State, who cut off the Pests of Society, like
Wens from the human Body.

Entred in y.e Hall-book &c.   F. Hoffman Inv. & scu

If any Masquerader, take in hand
A spritely Partner, late from Swisserland,
Let him take up her Linnen: if the Creature
Prove Femme, t'will end i' th' Masquerade of Nature
But if You find a Devil of Guiscard's Gender,
This is your Warrant; seize, on the Pretender.

Sold by Edward Lewis   in Flower-de-luce Court Fleetstreet   pr. 6.d

The French Assassin Guiscard . . . [London], sold by Edward Lewis, [1711]

A great Minister, in high Confidence with the Queen, under whose
Management the Weight of Affairs at present is in a great measure
supposed to ly; sitting in Council, in a Royal Palace, with a   5
dozen of the Chief Officers of State, is stabbed at the very
Board, in the Execution of his Office, by the Hand of a *French
Papist* (Fig. VI), then under Examination for High Treason. The

4 *Management*: cf. 'in the House of Commons ... [Harley] is the great mover'
(Swift, *Journal*, p. 249); 'He was the first spring of all our motion by his
credit with the queen' (*The Works of the late Right Honourable Henry St. John,
Lord Viscount Bolingbroke*, 5 vols., London, David Mallet, 1754, i 16).
7-8 *French Papist*: Antoine de Guiscard (1658-1711) was a younger son of one
of the most ancient families in France, with estates at Quercy in Guienne. He
was educated in the seminary at Sedan, where his father was governor, and
instituted to the abbey of Bonnecombe in the province of Rouergue, and made
prior of Dreu-en-Souvienne (Bayle, *Dictionary*, ii 1512-14). But the abbé de la
Bourlie, as he called himself, soon gained a reputation as one of the most
'illustrious Debauchées' in Paris. His vicious exploits forced him to flee,
first to the Cevennes in 1702, where he failed to raise an insurrection of the
Catholic provinces of Quercy and Rouergue in support of the Protestant Camisars, and then to Lausanne in December 1703, where he had the good fortune to
meet Richard Hill, the new British ambassador to the court of Savoy. Hill recruited him to command a task force of 450 French Protestant refugees who
sailed from Nice in June 1704 to make a landing on the coast of Languedoc to
reinforce the Camisars. The operation was a total failure (Hill, *Corr.*, i 306,
375, 431). Thereafter, the marquis de Guiscard, as he now called himself, sur-
faced at The Hague in November 1704, where he interested Heinsius and Marlborough in another plan to reinforce the Camisars, this time from the west,
at Barcelona in November 1705, where he gained the attention of Charles III,
the Habsburg pretender, and Charles Mordaunt, the Earl of Peterborough, and
at London in February 1706, where his credit finally ran out (300.69-301.70). In
October 1706 he was back in The Hague (*Marlborough-Godolphin Corr.*, pp. 715,
735) and in March 1707 it was rumoured that he was to lead an invasion of
Languedoc from Catalonia. But in the meantime he was running out of money. The
Dutch had cut off his pension, but he managed to sell his colonelcy in August
1708 even though his regiment was destroyed at Almansa and not reformed. In
December 1708 he was again at The Hague, trying to sell Marlborough 'un proiet
pour faire un grand coup contre la France' that he had stolen from another
refugee in Brussels (*Marlborough-Heinsius Corr.*, p. 414). In October 1709 he
was 'oblig'd to lay down his Coach ... pawn his Plate, and run into Debt to
keep ... from Starving'. His friend Henry St. John kept him from starving by
petitioning the Queen in December 1710 for an annual pension of £500, which
Harley had frugally reduced to £400 (*CTP 1708-1714*, p. 231). But his 'Pension
... did not answer his Expence', as Burnet (ii 566) observed, and early in
1711 he allowed himself to be recruited into the French intelligence service
and began a treasonable correspondence with one M. Moreau, a banker in Paris,
which was discovered almost immediately. St. John issued a warrant for his
arrest on 8 March and he was brought to St. John's office in the Cockpit to
be interrogated by a committee of the Privy Council. He returned evasive
answers to St. John's questions, but when Harley confronted him with his last
letter to Moreau and asked him if he recognized the handwriting, Guiscard
realized that he had been discovered (BL MS Add. 17677EEE, f. 117^V; HMC *Third
Report*, Appendix, p. 276; HMC *Mar & Kellie MSS*, i 488). He asked to speak
privately with St. John and when this was denied he said, 'Voilà qui est dur,
pas un mot!' and approached Harley as if to speak to him. 'J'en veux donc à

Assassin redoubles his Blow, to make sure Work; and concluding
10 the *Chancellor* was dispatched, goes on with the same Rage to murder a Principal Secretary of State: And that whole Noble Assembly
are forced to rise, and draw their Swords in their own Defence,
as if a wild Beast had been let loose among them.

This Fact hath some Circumstances of Aggravation not to be
15 parallel'd by any of the like kind we meet with in History.
Cæsar's Murder being performed in the *Senate*, comes nearest to
the Case; but That was an Affair concerted by great Numbers of
the chief Senators, who were likewise the Actors in it, and not
the Work of a *vile, single Ruffian*. *Harry* the Third of *France* was
20 stabbed by an Enthusiastick *Fryer*, whom he suffered to approach
his Person, while those who attended him stood at some distance.
His Successor met the same Fate in a Coach, where neither He nor
his Nobles, in such a Confinement, were able to defend themselves.
In our own Country we have, I think, but one Instance of this
25 sort, which has made any Noise, I mean that of *Felton*, about
fourscore years ago: But he took the opportunity to stab the Duke
of *Buckingham* in passing through a dark Lobby, from one Room to
another: The Blow was neither seen nor heard, and the Murderer
might have escaped, if his own Concern and Horror, as it is usual
30 in such Cases, had not betray'd him. Besides, that Act of *Felton*
will admit of some Extenuation, from the Motives he is said to

toy', he said, and stabbed Harley in the chest with a knife used by the clerks
to cut quills that he had picked up in the outer office. The knife struck the
breastbone and broke off half an inch from the handle, so the second blow
produced only a shallow wound and a contusion. Guiscard then turned on St.
John, but by this time the councillors had drawn to protect themselves. Guiscard failed to wrest a sword from one of them and was run through by St. John
and Newcastle. He was finally secured by the Queen's messengers. He boasted
that the blow was intended for Marlborough, who had insulted him, and begged
Ormond to give him the *coup de grâce* (BL MS Add. 17677EEE, f. 118; *Wentworth
Papers*, p. 186). Amid all the confusion, with St. John crying '*The Villain has
kill'd Mr.* Harley' and running off to tell the Queen, Harley was 'the only
Person unconcern'd at the Accident that had befallen him'. Guiscard died of
his wounds nine days later in Newgate and his body was pickled and shown for
a penny (Boyer, *The Political State*, i 273-328).

    19 *Harry the Third*: 'Henri III. was assassinated by Jacques Clément, a
Dominican friar, August 1st, 1589' (E*1922*, ix 208).

    22 *Successor*: 'Henri IV. was assassinated by François Ravaillac, May 14th,
1610' (E*1922*, ix 208); cf. Swift, *Tale*, pp. 163-4.

    27 *Buckingham*: 'George Villiers, [first] Duke of Buckingham, was stabbed by
Lieut. John Felton, August 23rd, 1628' (E*1922*, ix 208).

    31 *Motives*: The House of Commons had voted on 11 June 1628 that 'the exces-
sive Power of the Duke of *Buckingham*, and the Abuse of that Power, are the
chief Cause of ... Evils and Dangers to the King and Kingdom' (*CJ*, i 911).

have had. But this Attempt of *Guiscard* seems to have outdone them
all in every heightning Circumstance, except the difference of
Persons between a King and a great Minister: For I give no Allowance at all to the difference of *Success* (which however is yet   35
uncertain and depending) nor think it the least Alleviation to
the *Crime*, whatever it may be to the *Punishment*.

I am sensible, it is ill arguing from Particulars to Generals,
and that we ought not to charge upon a Nation the Crimes of a few
desperate Villains it is so unfortunate to produce: Yet at the   40
same time it must be avowed, that the *French* have for these last
Centuries, been somewhat too liberal of their *Daggers*, upon the
Persons of their greatest Men; such as the Admiral *de Coligny*,
the Dukes of *Guise*, Father and Son, and the two Kings I last mentioned. I have sometimes wondred how a People, whose Genius seems   45
wholly turned to Singing and Dancing, and Prating, to Vanity and
Impertinence; who lay so much Weight upon *Modes* and *Gestures*;
whose Essentialities are generally so very superficial; who are
usually so serious upon Trifles, and so trifling upon what is
serious, have been capable of committing such *solid Villanies*;   50
more suitable to the Gravity of a *Spaniard*, or Silence and
Thoughtfulness of an *Italian*: Unless it be, that in a Nation
naturally so full of themselves, and of so restless Imaginations,
when any of them happen to be of a morose and gloomy Constitution, that huddle of confused Thoughts, for want of evaporating,   55

Immediately after the assassination Felton said 'that ... reading the Remon-
strance of the house of Parliament it came into his mind, that in committing
the Act of killing the Duke, hee should doe his Country great good service'
(*Original Letters Illustrative of English History*, ed. Sir Henry Ellis, 3
vols., 1st Series, 2nd edn., London, Harding *et al.*, 1825, iii 258).

38 *from Particulars to Generals*: Abel Boyer, a French *émigré*, objects to
the Examiner's '*unfair and unjust Argument from Particulars to Generals*'
(Boyer, *The Political State*, i 317-18).

43 *Coligny*: '[Gaspard] de Coligny was assassinated August 23rd, 1572'
(*E1922*, ix 209).

44 *Guise*: 'François de Lorraine, Duc de Guise, was shot in 1563. His son
and successor (Henri le Balafré) was killed December 23rd, 1588' (*E1922*,
ix 209).

46 *Singing and Dancing*: Boyer calls this a '*very merry Strain*' of national
prejudice (Boyer, *The Political State*, i 317).

55 *evaporating*: Swift reverts to his theory of vapours (*Tale*, pp. 163-6).
Dartmouth concluded that Guiscard was 'lightheaded' (Burnet, 1833, vi 44) and
it is difficult to read *Mémoires du marquis de Guiscard, dans les quels est
contenu le Récit des entreprises qu'il a faites dans le roiaume et hors de
roiaume de France pour le recouvrement de la liberté de sa patrie* (Delft,

usually terminates in Rage or Despair. *D'Avila* observes, that
Jacques Clement was a sort of Buffoon, whom the rest of the Fryers
used to make Sport with: But at last, giving his Folly a serious
Turn, it ended in Enthusiasm, and qualified him for that desperate
60   Act of Murdering his King.

But in the *Marquis de Guiscard* there seems to have been a Complication of Ingredients for such an Attempt: He had committed
several Enormities in *France*, was extremely prodigal and vicious;
of a dark melancholy Complexion, and cloudy Countenance, such as
65   in vulgar Phisiognomy is call'd an *Ill Look*. For the rest, his
Talents were very mean, having a sort of inferior Cunning, but
very small Abilities; so that a great Man of the late M-----ry,
by whom he was invited over, and with much Discretion raised at
first Step from a profligate *Popish Priest* to a Lieutenant-General,

56 *D'Avila*] *D'avila* ½°

F. Arnaud, 1705), in which he takes full and exclusive credit for raising the
insurrection of the Camisars in 1702, without coming to the same conclusion.
    56 *D'Avila*: '[Enrico Caterino] Davila was the author of *Historia delle
Guerre Civili di Francia* [Venetia, T. Baglioni] (*c.*1630)' (E*1922*, ix 209).
Swift owned *The Historie of the Civill Warres of France*, trans. William Ayles-
bury and Sir Charles Cotterell, 2 vols. in 1, London, by R. Raworth for W. Lee
et al., 1647-8 (*Swift's Library*, p. 15): 'There was in Paris one *Jacques
Clement*, a Frier of the Order of *St. Dominick* ... a young man about two and
twenty yeers of age, and always thought by his fellow-Friers ... to be a half-
witted fellow, and rather a subject of sport, then to be feared, or that any
serious matter of consequence was to be hoped for from him' (p. 815).
    63 *Enormities*: These are retailed in Delariviere Manley, *A True Narrative
of what pass'd at the Examination of the Marquis De Guiscard at the Cock-Pit,
The 8th of March, 1710/11*, London, for John Morphew, 1711, pp. 7-9, and in
Boyer, *The Political State*, i 276-8.
    67 *Abilities*: 'the most tedious, trifling talker, I ever conversed with'
(Swift, *Prose*, viii 127).
         great Man: Godolphin.
    68 *invited*: Swift is the only source for the claim that Guiscard came to
England at Godolphin's invitation and Swift does not repeat the claim in his
later accounts of the affair (*Prose*, viii 126, 145). But it may be true none
the less. After Guiscard's failure to land in Languedoc in June 1704, Hill
wrote to Godolphin: 'I can make no more use of him; but if your Lordship has
any consideration concerning him, you will please to let me receive your commands' (Hill, *Corr.*, i 424). There is much evidence that Godolphin did take
'consideration concerning him': he enthusiastically supported Guiscard's plan
for a landing in Guienne, he paid him, and handled him as his agent while he
was in England (*Marlborough-Godolphin Corr.*, pp. 874, 1071, 1166; Luttrell,
vi 153).
    69-70 *Lieutenant-General, and Colonel*: Guiscard's plan for a landing in
Guienne to reinforce the Camisars came closest to realization in July 1706.
An invasion fleet of 150 sail was assembled at Portsmouth under the joint command of Sir Cloudesley Shovel and Richard Savage, Earl Rivers, for a descent

and Colonel of a Regiment of Horse, was forced at last to drop   70
him for Shame.

   Had such an Accident happened under that M----try, and to so
considerable a Member of it, they would have immediately charged
it upon the whole Body of those they are pleased to call *the Fac-*
tion. This would have been Styled a *High Church Principle;* the   75
Clergy would have been accused as Promoters and Abettors of the
Fact; Com------s would have been sent to promise the Criminal his
Life, provided they might have Liberty to *direct and dictate his*
Confession: And a *Black List* would have been printed of all those

upon Blaye on the Gironde, in the province of Guienne (HMC *Bath MSS*, i 84).
As a Roman Catholic Guiscard could not legally be commissioned in the British
army. But with nothing more from the Queen than an *'Order to be obey'd as a*
Lieutenant General, in Case of a Descent upon France' (Boyer, *The Political*
State, i 291), he was put in command not only of one regiment, Guiscard's
French Dragoons (HMC *Lords MSS*, new series, x 47) but also of six regiments
of foot on the Irish establishment, all recruited from French Protestant refu-
gees, and promised a commission as Lieutenant-General 'but not to be acknowledged ... till the fleet [was] at sea' (Luttrell, vi 70; *Marlborough-Godolphin*
Corr., p. 623). Major-General Frederic William de Roye de la Rochefoucauld,
Earl of Lifford, resigned his commission as colonel of one of the six regiments
of foot rather than serve under Guiscard (Luttrell, vi 47). Before joining the
fleet Guiscard published in French and English a *Manifeste adressé aux*
François for distribution after the landing, urging the populace to join the
invaders to pull down Louis XIV and restore the states general, in which may
be heard distant rumblings of the French Revolution (Boyer, *Annals*, 1707, pp.
[2]74-81). Rivers found something amiss in the manifesto and in the first council of war aboard the flagship he uncovered Guiscard's ignorance of military
matters and lack of credible intelligence sources within France. The descent
on Blaye was abandoned, the fleet was ordered to proceed directly to Lisbon,
and Guiscard was recalled to London (Boyer, *The Political State*, i 291-2;
Tindal, iii 761-2).
   71 *Shame*: Godolphin persisted until the end of 1708 in his delusion that
Guiscard might be useful and dropped him not 'for Shame' but because good
intelligence sources warned him in April 1709 that Guiscard was dangerous
(*Marlborough-Godolphin Corr.*, pp. 1166, 1169; HMC *Eighth Report*, Appendix, pp.
36, 37).
   72 *Had ... M----try*: Oldmixon quotes these lines and asks rhetorically,
'What do your Lordships think of this Passage? does not this *State Writer*
charge you with intending to take away [Harley's] Life, by the basest of
Subornations?' (*A Letter to the Seven Lords of the Committee, Appointed to*
Examine Gregg, 1711, pp. 2-3), to which the noble lords could only answer,
'Aye, by the basest'.
   77 *Com---s*: 39.127. The parallel with the Lords' committee to examine
Greg may have been suggested by St. John, who told Swift 'several particulari-
ties of [Harley's] accident' on 9 March (Swift, *Journal*, p. 212). St. John
told one of his correspondents that when the attack on Harley was reported in
the House of Lords, 'they left their seats; and since they could not hang Mr.
Harley, they were resolved to shew no resentment to Guiscard for stabbing him'
(Bolingbroke, *Letters*, i 103).
   79 *Black List*: The Whigs published 'a scandalous Paper, called the Black
List' before the general election of November 1701. Special attention was

80 who had been ever seen in the Murderer's Company. But the present
Men in Power hate and despise all such detestable Arts, which
they might now turn upon their Adversaries with much more plausibility, than ever these did their Honourable *Negotiations* with
Greg.
85   And here it may be worth observing how unanimous a Concurrence
there is between *some Persons* once in great Power, and a *French
Papist*; both agreeing in the great End of taking away Mr. *Harley*'s
Life, tho' differing in their Methods: The first proceeding by
Subornation, the other by *Violence*; wherein *Guiscard* seems to
90 have the Advantage, as aiming no further than His *Life*; while the
others designed to destroy at once both *That* and His *Reputation.*
The Malice of both against this Gentleman seems to have risen
from the same Cause, his discovering Designs against the Government. It was Mr. *Harley* who detected the Treasonable Correspon-
95 dence of *Greg*, and secured him betimes; when a *certain Great Man
who shall be Nameless*, had, out of the depth of his Politics,
sent him a Caution to make his Escape; which would certainly have
fixed the Appearance of Guilt upon Mr. *Harley*: But when that was
prevented, they would have enticed the condemned Criminal with
100 Promise of a Pardon, to *Write* and *Sign* an Accusation against the
Secretary. But to use *Greg*'s own Expression, *His Death was nothing near so ignominious, as would have been such a Life that must
be saved by prostituting his Conscience.* The same Gentleman lies
now Stabbed by his *other Enemy*, a Popish Spy, whose Treason he
105 has discovered. God preserve *the Rest* of Her Majesty's Ministers

86 great] high 38 8°+12°

---

called to those who had been seen in the company of Jean Baptiste Poussin, a
French agent who was declared *persona non grata* in September 1701 (Swift,
Discourse, pp. 77-9).
    95 *Great Man*: 'such villainous Suggestions as were publish'd in the
Examiner of *Thursday* last, and the *Post-Boy* of *Saturday* last [17 March]
against the Lord *S---* ... certainly come within the reach of the Case *De
Libellis famosis*' (*The Observator*, 17-21 March 1711). Somers and Somerset,
who were members of the select committee to examine Greg, are possibilities,
but the most likely candidate is Sunderland, who was chairman (Boyer, *The
History*, p. 332; Luttrell, vi 252).
    101-3 *His ... Conscience*: [dh title] *A True Copy of the Paper Left by Mr.
William Gregg, who suffered for High-Treason the 28th Day of April, 1708,*
London, for J. Morphew, 1708.

from such *Protestants*, and from such *Papists*!

I shall take Occasion to hint at some Particularities in this surprizing Fact, for the sake of those at distance, or who may not be thorowly informed. The Murderer confessed in *Newgate*, that his chief Design was against Mr. *Secretary St. John*, who happened   110
to change Seats with Mr. *Harley*, for more Convenience of examining the Criminal: And being asked what provoked him to Stab the *Chancellor*? he said, that not being able to come at the *Secretary*, as he intended, it was some satisfaction to Murder the Person whom he thought Mr. *St. John* loved best.   115

And here, if Mr. *Harley* has *still* any Enemies left, whom his Blood spilt in the Publick Service cannot reconcile, I hope they will at least admire his *Magnanimity*, which is a Quality esteemed even in an Enemy: And I think there are few greater Instances of it to be found in Story. After the Wound was given, he was ob-   120
served neither to change His Countenance, nor discover any Concern or Disorder in his Speech: He rose up, and walked along the

106 *such Protestants*: Greg was a Scot and on the scaffold he said, 'the Religion in which I was brought up, and do now Die ... is the Protestant' (ibid.; cf. *The Whole Life and Conversation, Birth, Parentage and Education of Mr. William Gregg, Who was Executed on Wednesday the 28th of April 1708 for High Treason*, London, for J. Rogers, 1708).
110 *chief Design was against ... St. John*: The source of this detail, both here and in other accounts (*Wentworth Papers*, p. 186), is St. John himself, but Swift decided later that St. John was 'either mistaken or misinformed'. Harley's son complained that the statement was 'senseless' and Harley's brother admired 'with what industry Secretary St. John took care to have it published' in *The Examiner* (BL MS Portland Loan 29/66/3; 29/52/8). St. John read Swift's copy before it was printed 'but made no alteration in that passage'. Swift saw too late that 'if it were true, the consequence must be, that Mr. St. John had all the merit, while Mr. Harley remained with nothing but the danger and the pain'. Oldmixon crowed: 'He has Repented of that Passage: He cannot blot it out, but denies the Consequence' (*A Letter to the Seven Lords of the Committee, Appointed to Examine Gregg*, 1711, p. 4). Although Swift wrote later that 'the first misunderstanding between Mr. Harley and Mr. St. John ... took it's rise' during Harley's long and difficult convalescence in March and April (Swift, *Prose*, viii 128), his 'first Suspicion' of antagonism occurred in February 1711 (274.51-2).
113-15 *he ... best*: This romantic detail was widely reported (BL MS Add. 17677EEE, f. 123^V; Boyer, *The Political State*, i 307) but it has all the staleness of an afterthought and may be another fabrication of St. John.
116-24 *And ... Confusion*: St. John must be Swift's source for the details of these lines. Although St. John was beginning to hate him, he could not conceal his admiration for Harley's composure: 'It is impossible to express to you', he wrote, 'the ... magnanimity which Mr. Harley showed upon this surprising occasion: I, who have always admired him, never did it so much; the suddenness of the blow, the sharpness of the wound, the confusion which followed, could neither change his countenance, nor alter his voice' (Bolingbroke, *Letters*, i 102-3).

Room while He was able, with the greatest Tranquility, during the
midst of the Confusion. When the Surgeon came, he took him aside,
125   and desired he would inform Him freely whether the Wound were
Mortal, because in that Case, he said, he had some Affairs to
settle, relating to his Family. The Blade of the Penknife, broken
by the violence of the Blow against a Rib, within a quarter of an
Inch of the Handle, was dropt out (I know not whether from the
130   Wound, or his Cloaths) as the Surgeon was going to dress him; He
ordered it to be taken up, and wiping it himself, gave it some
body to keep, saying, he thought *it not ; oper j belonged to Him*.
He shewed no sort of Resentment, or s٦oke one violent Word against
Guiscard, but appeared all the while the least concerned of any in
135   the Company. A State of Mind, which in such an Exigency, nothing
but Innocence can give, and is truly worthy of a *Christian* Philosopher.

If there be really so great a difference in Principle between
the *High-flying Whigs*, and the Friends of *France*, I cannot but
140   repeat the Question, how come they to join in the Destruction of
the same Man? Can his Death be possibly for the Interest of *Both*?
or have they *Both* the same Quarrel against Him, that he is perpetually discovering and preventing the treacherous Designs of
our Enemies? However it be, this great Minister may now say with
145   St. *Paul*, that he hath been *in Perils by his own Countrymen, and
in Perils by Strangers*.

In the midst of so Melancholly a Subject, I cannot but congratulate with our own Country, that such a Savage Monster as the *Marquis de Guiscard*, is none of her Production; A Wretch perhaps
150   more detestable in his own Nature, than even this barbarous Act
has been yet able to represent Him to the World. For there are
good Reasons to believe, from several Circumstances, that he had
Intentions of a *deeper Dye*, than those he happened to Execute

132 *belonged*] *belonging* ½° 12°

---

127 *Blade*: Harley later gave it to Swift (Swift, *Journal*, p. 215).
145-6 *in ... Strangers*: 2 Cor. 11:26. Whether deliberately or not, Swift
recalls the sermon, *The Perils of False Brethren, Both in Church, and State*
(1709), that was the occasion as well as the main evidence for the impeachment of Sacheverell (*The Tryal*, pp. 8-10).
153 *Intentions*: The suspicion that Guiscard intended to assassinate the
Queen (Swift, *Journal*, p. 217; Delariviere Manley, *A True Narrative of what*

I mean such as every good Subject must tremble to think on. He
hath of late been frequently seen going up the *Back-Stairs* at   155
Court, and walking alone in an outer Room adjoyning to Her
Ma----y's Bedchamber. He has often and earnestly pressed for some
time to have *Access* to the Qu---, even since his Correspondence
with *France*; and he has now given such a Proof of his Disposition, as leaves it easy to guess what was before in his Thoughts,   160
and what he was capable of attempting.

It is humbly to be hoped, that the *Legislature* will interpose
on so Extraordinary an Occasion as this, and direct a Punishment
some way Proportionable to so execrable a Crime.

> *Et quicunque tuum violavit vulnere corpus,*   165
> *Morte luat merita ------*

pass'd at the Examination of the Marquis De Guiscard, at the Cock-Pit, The 8th
of March, 1710/11, 1711, p. 31; Burnet, ii 566) was rightly dismissed as groundless (BL MS Add. 17677EEE, f. 119; Boyer, The Political State, i 313). Dartmouth
must have misunderstood what the Queen said to him (Burnet, 1833, vi 43-4n.).

162 Legislature: The House of Commons obliged on 14 March 1711 by bringing
in a bill to make an attempt on the life of a Privy Councillor a felony without benefit of clergy (CJ, xvi 548; LJ, xix 300) (E1922, ix 213).

165-6 Et ... merita: Virgil, Aeneid, xi 848: For whoso hath with wound
profaned thy limbs shall pay the debt of death.

No. 25 [Mainwaring and Oldmixon]   19 March 1711

The MEDLEY.

Of Resumptions.
The True Story of the Marquiss de Guiscard.
Some Remarks upon him and the Examiner.

I Who in former Papers discours'd of *Credit* and *Funds*, and have
seem'd to incline a little to the common Error that they were
both somewhat sunk in their Reputation, cannot do better than
inquire how matters may be mended; and in my mind there's no

1 *Credit and Funds*: 46.120-49.192, 200.1-205.126.

 5 likelier way than by a *Resumption*. I have heard several foolish
    Reasons against it; particularly, That such sort of Acts cannot
    be made without breaking into so many *private Contracts, Marriage-*
    Settlements, Jointures, Mortgages, and Sales for valuable Con-
    siderations, that there is hardly any Tax which probably the
10 *People wou'd not consent to, rather than bring so vast a Disorder*
    and Ruin upon such a Number of private Families. I don't take
    that to be any Argument at all: For what's the Interest of Private
    Families to the Pleasure of the Publick? I'm told prodigious Sums
    of Mony might be rais'd, to clear off the Debts of the Navy, and
15 all other Debts whatsoever. Those that question whether it wou'd
    answer or not, do not remember what was done in *Ireland* six or
    seven years ago; how Mony came tumbling into the Exchequer there,
    besides about some Twenty two thousand Pounds a year to those
    honest Gentlemen the Commissioners, who cou'd not have had it
20 without a *Resumption*. The most ridiculous Objection of all is,
    that such Acts are not usual. They must be sorry Historians that

    8-9 *Considerations*] *Consideration* ½°

    ⎯⎯⎯⎯

    5 *Resumption*: Leave was given on 1 March 1711 to three Tories, two of them
    Jacobites: Thomas Strangeways, Jr., William Shippen, and George Lockhart of
    Carnwath, to bring in a bill appointing commissioners to examine the value of
    all lands granted by the Crown since February 1689 in order to resume these
    grants and apply them to the use of the public (*CJ*, xvi 529).
        6-11 *cannot ... Families*: On 16 April 1711 Commissioners for Examining the
    Value of Lands granted by the Crown since 13 February 1689 were elected. Old-
    mixon may be quoting oral reports of the Commons debate. The resumption bill
    was rejected by the Lords two weeks later (Boyer, *The Political State*, i
    427-8).
        16 *Ireland*: Early in 1700, against fierce opposition from the court Whigs
    that was only overcome by tacking it to a money bill, Harley's New Country
    Party secured passage of a bill resuming the grants that William III had made
    of forfeited estates of Irish Jacobites and vesting the properties in thirteen
    trustees. The estates were to be auctioned before 24 June 1703 in Dublin with
    the proceeds to be applied towards reducing Government debts contracted in the
    Irish war of 1689-90 (Simms, pp. 110-20).
        17 *Mony*: Since the political purpose of the resumption bill was to insult
    the King and discredit the Junto, estimates of the value of William's grants
    were greatly exaggerated. As a result, not half of the estimated value,
    £1,547,792, was returned to the Exchequer (Simms, p. 108).
        19 *Commissioners*: The thirteen trustees (whom Oldmixon calls commissioners)
    received £1,500 a year, or £19,500 (Simms, p. 119). A contemporary account
    estimated that in salaries, management costs, '*Discoverers Shares* ... and
    Rewards' the trustees spent £200,000 in three years (*A Letter from a Gentle-*
    man to the Trustees of the Irish Forfeitures, London, 1704, p. 16).

do not know how many of our Monarchs of Blessed Memory have done
the same thing: as *William Rufus*, King *Stephen*, *Edward* II.
Richard II. *Henry* VI. *Henry* VII. *&c.* Indeed we read of no Resumption in the Reigns of *Edward* III. or *Henry* V. But they were so   25
proud of conquering *France*, they wou'd give away what they
pleas'd to reward their Ministers and Generals, who serv'd them
bravely and faithfully in their Conquests. And there were some
who thought such Rewards were very allowable: Of these was that
Great Lawyer Sir *John Fortescue*, who says this in a Treatise *de*   30
Dominio Regali, &c. And some of the same Lands, Tenements, and
Rents his good Grace has given to such as have serv'd him so
notably; that as their Renown will be eternal, so it befits the
King's Magnificence to make their Rewards everlasting in their
Heirs, to his Honour and their perpetual Memory. And for Lack of   35
Mony, 'twas reasonable his Grace shou'd reward them with Land.
All this does not make against *Resumptions*. *France* is not quite
conquer'd, and there's no excuse for giving away *Crown-Lands* for
Lack of Mony. Besides, Cases may so alter, that what was reckon'd
good Service at *one* time, may at *another* be thought rather to   40
deserve a *Fine* than a *Grant*. So that what has been done by so
many of our Kings, will not admit of any dispute, but shou'd be
universally approv'd of. Some Persons are very well satisfy'd of
this; and yet they are for no *Partial* Resumptions, as they call
'em. They are for going back, I don't know how far. Thus when   45
the *Irish* Resumption was afoot, the Whigs to puzzle it, wou'd

22 *Monarchs*: Resumptions of grants by all the kings whom Oldmixon mentions
are included in Davenant, *A Discourse upon Grants and Resumptions, Showing*
How our Ancestors have Proceeded with such Ministers As have Procured to
Themselves Grants of the Crown-Revenue; And that the Forfeited Estates ought
to be Applied towards the Payment of the Publick Debts, London, for James
Knapton, 1700, pp. 106-7, 107-8, 116-19, 119-27, 149-80, 232-8.
22-3 *have done the same thing*: 'have had the same thing done to them'(?).
24-5 *no Resumption*: ibid., pp. 119, 148.
31-6 *And ... Land*: 'The Manuscript is in the *Bodleian* Library at *Oxford*;
'tis intituled, Sir *John Fortescue's* Treatise *De Dominio Regali*, and *De*
Dominio Regali Politico [Bodl. MS Digby 145, f. 133]' (ibid., p. 256).
44 *no Partial Resumptions*: ''Tis probable That up will rise some Arrogant Man ... and cry ... *Did not the Ministers in King* Charles*'s Reign give*
away the Crown Lands; Recal those Grants, and we are ready to surrender ours.
Resume all or none' (ibid., p. 28). Mainwaring probably refers to the bill
that was ordered to be brought in on 7 February 1698 to resume all of William's
grants of Irish estates made since 13 February 1689. At the same time, however, other bills were ordered to include grants of English estates and to
push back the date to 1660 (*CJ*, xii 90), so all of them were dropped.
46 *Whigs*: 'we are willing to Resume, provided you will go far enough back-

have had all King *Charles* II's and King *James*'s Grants revok'd
too: to which several such good Answers were given, that they
were forc'd to submit. And it was plainly made out, that the best
50   thing in the World wou'd be to resume just from the Thirteenth of
February 1688. and to prevent any Inconveniences which might
arise to *good Churchmen*, to have saving Clauses, which were common heretofore, and for that reason must be very fair. There were
no less than an Hundred and Eighty Five *Savings* in one such Act
55   in *Henry* the Sixth's time; wherein the *Lancaster* Faction then
uppermost took care of themselves: and others shou'd do the same
now. The only thing that seems to me to be against a *Resumption*,
is the ill Consequences it had in *Sweden* much about the time that
the People lost their Liberty: For the Learned Bishop of *B----l*
60   tells us, *It destroy'd all Publick Faith.* But he shews in the
same Book, that instead of it, the People got the true Belief of
*Jure Divino, Uncontroulable Power in Princes, and Passive Obedi-
ence in Subjects*: And therefore no body sure will say they were
Losers by such a Bargain.
65   The *Examiner* and I are at last agreed in one thing; which is,
that the Marquiss *de Guiscard* is a *Villain*, and that such a rash
and wicked Attempt is hardly to be parallel'd in Story. I confess
I heard of it with Horrour; and had my Friend himself receiv'd
the Wound, I shou'd have been concern'd for him, tho he has so
70   often been the *Assassin* of the Reputation of so many Persons of
Honour. I did not doubt but he wou'd do just as he has done, and

55 Sixth's] Seventh's 12°

---

*wards: We shall join in it if you will take in all the Grants since the
Restoration of King* Charles *the Second.* But ... such as are for making their
Resumption so large, desire none at all' (Davenant, *A Discourse upon Grants*,
1700, p. 431).
    50-1 *Thirteenth of February 1688*: 'All the Premisses consider'd, perhaps it
will appear to any unbiass'd Person ... That, to follow the greatest Number of
Presidents ... the Bill ought to look no farther backwards than this ... Reign
[which began 13 February 1688/9, when the crown was offered to William and
Mary]' (ibid., pp. 444-5).
    54 *Act*: 28 Hen. VI c. 53 (ibid., pp. 154-78).
    60 *destroy'd ... Faith*: [John Robinson,] Bishop of B[risto]l, *Account of*
Sweden [1694], *pag.* 125 (½°).
    62-3 *Jure ... Subjects*: 'to reunite to the Crown all such Lands, as by for-
mer Kings had been alienated by way of Donation ... [provided] an opportunity
to lay the Foundations of as *Absolute a Sovereignty*, as any Prince in *Europe*'
(ibid., pp. 94, 97).

in his fair and candid way insinuate that the Whigs are not without blame for the *Frenchman*'s Villany. *Abel* began the Scandal,
talk'd of *Gregg*, and Great Men. The *Examiner* cou'd not let such
a notable Hint escape him: *Gregg* is had up again, he says all he   75
knows of the matter, and that the *late Ministry invited* Guiscard
over; which is as true as the rest. He came into *England* first
about the year 1703: If the Ministry was then in *Whig*-Hands,
which I will not allow, it does not follow that they sent for him,
or that they did not take him on the Recommendation of some of   80
our Allies. But be that as it will, however he came hither, the
Ministers I find got rid of him in a very little time; for he was
in *Spain* two years after, and wanted a new Recommendation to *Eng-*
land, which he had from the King of *Spain*, as appears by a Letter
from that Prince to her Majesty in 1705, wherein are these Ex-   85
pressions.

The Marquiss de Guiscard *having acquainted me that he receiv'd*
about two years ago Commissions from the late Emperor, my most
honour'd Father, and that even your Majesty was graciously pleas'd
to entrust him with your Ships and Troops, in order to make some   90
Attempts upon Languedoc; *I thought in following the very Schemes*

72 *Whigs*: 304.138-41.
73 *Abel*: 'Seven Great and Excellent Men are to meet at a House near Charing-
Cross, and ... will find Witnesses to prove, that notwithstanding Mr. H----y
discovered this Treason, as he did likewise that of Mr. Greg, yet ... he was
an Accomplice of the Man, who wou'd have Murder'd him' (Abel Roper, *The Post*
Man, 8-10 March 1711).
75 *Gregg*: 302.85-103.
76-7 *the ... over*: 300.68n.
77 *England*: Boyer is the only source for this 'Journey [Guiscard] made some
Years before [i.e. before February 1706] into *England*', where 'he had particularly been known' to the Duke of Devonshire (Boyer, *The Political State*,
i 289). If Guiscard had been in England and had been 'particularly ... known'
to the great Duke of Devonshire before he met Hill in Lausanne in December
1703 (297.7-8n.), he would certainly have said so, for this would have greatly
enhanced his bona fides. Instead, he told Hill that he had fled to Lausanne
'for having endeavoured to raise the province of Rovergue' against Louis XIV
(Hill, *Corr.*, i 430). Mainwaring himself partly confirms the truth of Guiscard's statement: '*Guiscard* ... went first upon making his Escape from *France*,
to the Court of *Savoy*' (311.126-7).
83 *in Spain two years after*: 298.7-8n.
87-97 *The ... Opinion*: Boyer, *The Political State*, i 288.
88 *Commissions*: Guiscard's commission from Leopold II as *mareschal de camp*
(lieutenant-general) was signed by Prince Eugene and countersigned by the Duke
of Savoy. For the descent upon Languedoc he also had a commission as colonel
signed by the Queen (Hill, *Corr.*, i 431; i 319).

of your Majesty and the Emperor, I could not refuse him my Pro-
tection, and to pray your Majesty to grant him yours, being per-
suaded there is no fitter Person than he, in several Respects, to
95 *render this Enterprize successful. All the Inhabitants of this*
Province wish it passionately; my Lord Peterborough *and Mr.* Crow
seem to be of the same Opinion. Here are the Emperor, King
Charles, the *Catalans,* my Lord *Peterborough,* &c. acting and
speaking in behalf of him; and yet the *Examiner* wou'd have a
100 great Man accountable for advancing him. All the World knows that
one Great Man always look'd upon him as a *Trifler,* and abridg'd
him in the Pension his Recommendations procur'd him. Whether his
Poverty made him desperate, or that 'tis possible for a Rogue, as
all Spies must be, to sacrifice his Life for his Master's Service,
105 I shall not enquire. Such a Wretch is a proper Subject only for
the *Examiner,* who argues better upon it than he has done upon any
other. He seems fond of it, and reasons about *Frenchmen* most
philosophically. *When any of them happen to be of a morose and*
gloomy Constitution, that huddle of confus'd Thoughts, for want
110 *of evaporating, usually terminates in Rage and Despair.* Can any
thing be more deep and clear? 'Twas very odd in him, when he was
reckoning up all the *Assassination-Plots,* not to mention that
against King *William*; but no doubt he can tell why 'twas omitted.

96 *Peterborough*: Charles Mordaunt, third Earl of Peterborough (1658-1735),
began his political career as Shaftesbury's collaborator and was the first to
press the Prince of Orange 'to undertake the business of *England*' (Burnet,
i 762). He was 'brave and generous' but 'always in Debt, and very poor', and
'his natural Giddiness, in running from Party to Party', eventually cost him
the favour of 'all honest Men' (Macky, pp. 64-6). In November 1705, however,
Peterborough was at the top of his career. In September he had accomplished
the impossible by capturing Barcelona and enabling the Archduke to march in
and be proclaimed Carlos III, King of Spain.
        Crow: Mitford Crow(e) (?-1718) began his political career as a Tory
Member of Parliament for the borough of Southampton (January 1701-1702). He
was a special diplomatic representative in Genoa (May-October 1705), whence he
was sent to Barcelona as an envoy extraordinary to Carlos III (*CTB 1706-7,*
p. 80). By the time that Swift became acquainted with him in 1711 he was the
'late governor of Barbados', having cleared himself of the charges of bribery
for which he had been removed (Noble, ii 176; Horn, pp. 73, 128; Luttrell,
vi 653, 664; Swift, *Journal,* p. 272).
    100 *great Man*: Godolphin (300.67).
    101 *one Great Man*: Presumably Mainwaring refers to Godolphin again, but in
apparent contradiction of the facts. It was Harley who 'abridged' Guiscard's
pension (297.7-8n.) and, coincidentally, Swift who discovered what a *'Trifler'*
Guiscard was (300.67n.).
    108-10 *When ... Despair*: 299.54-300.56.
    113 *William*: Robert Charnock, Sir William Parkyns, and other Jacobites,
conspired to assassinate William III in February 1696.

The Tories don't love to hear of it, and indeed I can't discommend them: For *Charnock* and *Parkins*, I won't say *Friend*, were as   115
much Assassins as *Clement* and *Ravillac*, tho they did not accomplish their execrable Design. I was surpriz'd to see him so very
civil to *Felton*, who butcher'd the Duke of *Buckingham*; *that Act*,
says he, *will admit of some Extenuation*: For at that rate *Ravillac*
and *Clement* are much more entitled to his good Word. *Felton* said,   120
he did it for the good of the *State*; and the *French* Assassins,
for the good of the *Church*. There's no Comparison. The *Extenuation* certainly lies all on the side of the *Fryars*: And let my
Friend himself be Judg, I am sure he will be of that mind upon
second Thoughts.   125

   The true Story of *Guiscard* is this: He went first, upon making
his Escape from *France*, to the Court of *Savoy*; that Prince living
near, knew his Character, and having Information of whatever
passes within his Dominions, found that he had got an exact Plan
made of *Turin*: However he parted with him civilly, but sent a   130
Messenger after him to seize him upon the Frontier of the Country, search his Papers, and take away the Plan; which was done
accordingly. From hence he went to *Vienna*, where with his great
Promises he succeeded better, and had a Regiment given him under
King *Charles* in *Spain*. Thus prefer'd and recommended, he came   135
hither to sollicite Affairs for King *Charles*, and to undertake
great Matters on the Coast of *France*. He never had any Commission
here, nor cou'd have any, being still an avow'd Papist, and only
a Malecontent in *France*. And at last, when he went with Earl
Rivers, he had a Commission from the Emperor to be Lieutenant-   140

---

   115 *Friend*: Sir John Friend, although he had a secret commission from
James II to raise a Jacobite regiment, refused to join the conspiracy to
assassinate William III. But he was found guilty of high treason and executed
along with Sir William Parkyns in April 1696.
   118-19 *that ... Extenuation*: 298.30-1.
   121 *good of the State*: 298.31n.
   130-3 *sent ... accordingly*: Boyer, *The Political State*, i 280.
   133 *Vienna*: 'He did not go to Vienna, as the Author of the Medley (Number
25) pretends' (ibid., i 280, sidenote).
   134 *Regiment*: non-existent.
   137 *Commission*: for Guiscard's commissions on the English establishment,
see 300.69-301.70.
   140 *Rivers*: Guiscard did not sail with Rivers (300.69-301.70). When the descent upon Blaye was abandoned, command of Guiscard's regiment fell to Lieutenant-
Colonel François La Fabreque. 'The splendid charge of La Fabreque's Dragoons,
towards the close of the battle [of Almansa], was one of the redeeming features of that fatal engagement' (Dalton, v 194).

General, and there was nothing more from the Queen than an Order,
that in case the Troops shou'd land in *France*, he shou'd be
obey'd by them as such.

Such a notorious Villain and Lyar is the *Examiner*, who says,
145 *he was invited over by the late Ministry*, prefer'd to a Regiment,
and made Lieutenant-General, when there is an Act of Parliament
against Papists being so. And the first thing I wou'd beg of this
vile Slanderer, is to make out what he affirms of his *being invited over*. If he wou'd but prove that one Particular, I wou'd
150 forgive him all his Lyes past, and yet to come; for on the contrary, the most zealous Friend he ever had was one mention'd in
the same Paper, such black Enmity seldom arising but from the
Disappointment of a former Friendship. Notwithstanding all which
the *Examiner* says, *It is worth observing what a Concurrence there
155 is between some Persons once in Power, and a* French *Papist, both
agreeing in the great end of taking away Mr.* H----*y's Life*. And
now that the Reader has seen that remarkable Passage, I will
present him with another Paragraph out of the same Paper: *The
Murderer confess'd in* Newgate, *that his chief Design was against
160 Mr. Secretary* St. John, *who happen'd to change Seats with Mr.*
Harley. Thus, when this most frontless Wretch had charg'd the
whole late Ministry with the Design of murdering Mr. *H----y*, the
very next thing he tells you, is, That truly there was no Design

---

144 notorious Villain and Lyar] ½° TxU   vile Slanderer Σ   148 vile Slan-
derer] ½° TxU Libeller Σ

141-3 *nothing ... such*: Boyer, *The Political State*, i 291.
145 *invited*: 300.68.
151 *Friend*: St. John escorted Guiscard to Portsmouth in July 1706 with a
guard of horse grenadiers 'upon apprehension that some French emissaries might
way lay him' (Luttrell, vi 70), but there can be little doubt that both of
them were less interested in 'the Fall ... | Of Foreign Tyrants [than] of
Nymphs at home'. In Paris Guiscard was rated among the *'Petits Maîtres*, or
Rakes of Quality', and St. John was equally notorious in London. Despite
a quarrel 'about ... a child, which neither of them would own', St. John
secured Guiscard a pension, and only ten days before the attack on Harley
Swift was 'interceding with the Secretary, in [Guiscard's] Behalf' (Boyer,
The Political State, i 276; *CTP 1708-1714*, p. 231; Swift, *Corr.*, i 215-16).
154-6 *It ... Life*: 302.85-8.
158-61 *The ... Harley*: 303.109-11.
163-4 *no Design ... against Mr.* H----*y*: 303.109-11; cf. 'The *Examiner* has
spoil'd his own Story ... for he says *Guiscard's* chief Design was against Mr.
Secretary *St. John*, and that he only stab'd Mr. *Harley* because he miss'd the
other; so that the Whigs could not be in a Concert with *Guiscard* against Mr.
Harley' (*The Observator*, 14-17 March 1711). Swift admitted the blunder
(320.187-8).

at all against Mr. *H----y*; and that the *Criminal being ask'd what provok'd him to stab the Chancellor, he said, That not being able to come at the Secretary, as he intended, it was some Satisfaction to murder the Person whom he thought Mr. St. J--- lov'd best.* See what a dangerous thing it might have prov'd to be so dearly lov'd by this great M------r. But not to trifle upon so odious a Subject, I will conclude this Paper with a fair Challenge to the whole World, to shew me in any one Libel such an Instance of Malice and Stupidity at once, as that which I have now fairly stated out of this incorrigible Slanderer and most abandon'd Scribler.

165

170

173 Slanderer] ½° TxU Blunderer Σ

164-7 *the ... best*: 303.112-15.

No. 34 [Swift]   22 March 1711

The EXAMINER.

De Libertate retinenda, qua certe nihil est dulcius, tibi assentior.

THE Apologies of the ancient Fathers are reckoned to have been the most useful Parts of their Writings, and to have done greatest Service to the Christian Religion, because they removed those Misrepresentations which had done it most Injury. The Methods these Writers took, was openly and freely to discover every Point of their Faith, to detect the Falshood of their Accusers, and to charge nothing upon their Adversaries but what they were sure to make good. This Example has been ill followed of later Times; the *Papists* since the Reformation using all Arts to palliate the Absurdities of their Tenets, and loading the Reformers with a

5

10

Motto Cicero, *Ad Atticum*, xv 13: I agree with you in Respect to your Sentiments for preserving our Liberty, than which nothing can be more pleasing to a human Mind.
1 *Apologies*: Justin Martyr, *Apologia* (AD 150), Minucius Felix, *Octavius*, Tertullian, *Apologeticus ad gentes* (AD 197), Lactantius Firmianus, *Divinarum Institutionum* (AD 311), and the like; copies of the last two were in Swift's library at his death (*Swifts's Library*, pp. 10, 15).

thousand Calumnies; the Consequence of which has been only a more various, wide, and inveterate Separation. It is the same thing in Civil Schisms: A *Whig* forms an Image of a *Tory*, just after the thing he most abhors, and that Image serves to represent the
15 whole Body.

   I am not sensible of any material Difference there is between those who call themselves the *Old Whigs*, and a great majority of the present *Tories*; at least by all I could ever find, from Examining several Persons of each Denomination. But it must be
20 confessed that the present Body of *Whigs*, as they now constitute that Party, is a very odd mixture of Mankind, being forced to enlarge their Bottom by taking in every Heterodox Professor either in Religion or Government, whose Opinions they were obliged to encourage for fear of lessening their Number; while
25 the Bulk of the Landed Men and People were entirely of the old Sentiments. However, they still pretended a due Regard to the *Monarchy* and the *Church*, even at the Time when they were making the largest Steps towards the Ruin of both: But not being able to wipe off the many Accusations laid to their Charge, they en-
30 deavoured, by throwing of Scandal, to make the *Tories* appear blacker than themselves, so that the People might join with *Them*, as the smaller Evil of the two.

   But among all the Reproaches which the *Whigs* have flung upon their Adversaries, there is none hath done them more Service than
35 that of *Passive Obedience*, as they represent it, with the Conse-quences of *Non-resistance, Arbitrary Power, Indefeasible Right, Tiranny, Popery*, and what not? There is no Accusation which has passed with more Plausibility than this, nor any that is supported with less Justice. In order therefore to undeceive those who have
40 been misled by false Representations, I thought it would be no improper Undertaking to set this Matter in a fair Light, which I think has not yet been done. A *Whig* asks whether you hold *Pas-sive Obedience*? You affirm it: He then immediately cries out, You are a *Jacobite*, a *Friend* of *France* and the *Pretender*; because he

14 serves] serveth 38 8°+12°   31 so that] that so ½° 12° 38 8°+12°

---

17 *Old Whigs*: 'Well over 30' Whig Members of Parliament retained office in the Harley administration (Holmes, p. 380).
20 *Whigs*: New Whigs, followers of the Junto.

makes You answerable for the Definition he has form'd of that   45
Term, however different it be from what you understand. I will
therefore give two Descriptions of *Passive Obedience*; the first
as it is falsly charged by the *Whigs*; the other as it is really
professed by the *Tories*, at least by nineteen in twenty of all
I ever conversed with.   50

Passive Obedience as charg'd by the WHIGS.

THE Doctrine of Passive Obedience *is to believe, That a King,*
even in a limited Monarchy, holding his Power only from God, is
only answerable to Him. That such a King is above all Law, that
the cruellest Tirant must be submitted to in all Things; and if   55
his Commands be ever so unlawful, You must neither fly nor resist,
nor use any other Weapons than Prayers *and* Tears. *Though he should*
force your Wife or Daughter, murder your Children before your
Face, or cut off five hundred Heads in a Morning for His Diver-
sion, You are still to wish him a long prosperous Reign, and to   60
be patient under all His Cruelties, with the same Resignation as
under a Plague or a Famine; because to resist Him would be to
resist God in the Person of his Vicegerent. If a King of England
should go through the Streets of London, *in order to murder every*
Man he met, Passive Obedience *commands them to submit. All Laws*   65
made to limit him signify nothing, though passed by his own Con-
sent, if he thinks fit to break them. God will indeed call Him to
a severe Account, but the whole People, united to a Man, cannot

67 *thinks*] think 38 8°+12°

---

47 *two Descriptions*: cf. 'I think I cannot take a more sincere, open, and
compendious way ... than by drawing forth a *double Character* of a *Papist*: The
one expressing a *Papist* in those very Colours as he is painted in the *imagina-*
tion of the *Vulgar, Foul, Black,* and *Antichristian*; with the chief *Articles* of
his *imagined Belief,* and *reputed Principles* of his Profession. The *other*
representing a *Papist*, whose *Faith* and exercise of his *Religion*, is according
to the *Direction* and *Command* of *his Church*' (John Gother, *A Papist Mis-*
represented and Represented: or, A Twofold Character of Popery, no place of
publication, 1685, sigs. A3^V-A4^r). The double-entry form of Swift's argument
may 'have been drawn up in imitation' of this work, as Walter Scott suggested,
but it is clear that Swift borrowed nothing else (E*1814*, iv 47).
56 *Commands*: cf. 'A *Sacheverellite* saith, That *no Subjects* must question
the Legality of the King's *Command*' (*Chuse which you Please: Or, Dr. Sachever-*
ell, and Mr. Hoadley, Drawn to the Life. Being a Brief Representation of the
Respective Opinions of each Party in Relation to Passive Obedience and Non-
Resistance, London, 1710, p. 4).

presume to hold His Hands, or offer him the least active Disobedi-
70 ence. *The People were certainly Created for Him, and not He for
the People. His next Heir, though worse than what I have described,
though a Fool or a Madman, has a divine undefeasible Right to succeed Him, which no Law can disannul; nay though he should kill his
Father upon the Throne, he is immediatly King to all Intents and*
75 *Purposes, the Possession of the Crown wiping off all Stains. But
whosoever sits on the Throne without this Title, tho' never so
peaceably, and by Consent of former Kings and Parliaments, is an*
Usurper, *while there is any where in the World another Person
who hath a nearer Hereditary Right, and the whole Kingdom lies*
80 *under mortal Sin 'till that Heir be restored; because He has a*
Divine *Title which no Human Law can defeat.*

     This and a great deal more hath, in a thousand Papers and Pamph-
lets, been laid to that Doctrine of *Passive Obedience*, which the
Whigs are pleased to charge upon us. This is what they perpetually
85 are instilling into the People to believe, as the undoubted Principles by which the present Ministry, and a great Majority in Parliament, do at this time proceed. This is what they accuse the
Clergy of delivering from the Pulpits, and of preaching up as Doctrines absolutely necessary to Salvation. And whoever affirms in
90 general, That *Passive Obedience* is due to the Supream Power, he is
presently loaden by our candid Adversaries with such Consequences
as these. Let us therefore see what this Doctrine is, when stript
of such Misrepresentations, by describing it as really taught and
practiced by the *Tories*, and then it will appear what Grounds our
95 Adversaries have to accuse us upon this Article.

     85 Principles] Principle 38 8°+12°   88 Doctrines] a Doctrine 38 8°+12°

---

     78 *another Person*: innuendo: the Pretender; cf. 'A *Sacheverellite* ...
believe[s] *ten Thousand* Acts of *Parliament* can't divest him of *either* of those
two Titles to the Crown [hereditary and divine right]' (ibid.).
     82-3 *Papers and Pamphlets*: Temple Scott lists eight (E*1922*, ix 217).
     92-5 *Let ... Article*: cf. 'I'll endeavour therefore to seperate those
Calumnies and *Scandals*, from what is *really* the *Faith* and *Doctrine* of that
Church; I'll take off the *Black* and *Dirt*, which has been thrown upon her; and
setting her forth in her *genuine* complection, let the World see how much
fairer she is, than she's *painted*; and how much she's *unlike* that *Monster*
which is shewn for her' (Gother, *A Papist Mis-represented and Represented*,
1685, sig. A3V).

Passive Obedience, as professed and practiced
by the TORIES.

THey think that in every Government, whether Monarchy or Repub-
lick, there is placed a supream, absolute, unlimited Power, to
which Passive Obedience *is due. That wherever is entrusted the*   100
Power of making Laws, that Power is without all Bounds, can re-
peal or enact at pleasure whatever Laws it thinks fit, and justly
demands Universal Obedience and Non-resistance. That among us, as
every Body knows, this Power is lodged in the King or Queen, to-
gether with the Lords and Commons of the Kingdom; and therefore   105
all Decrees whatsoever, made by that Power, are to be actively or
passively obeyed. That the Administration or Executive Part of
this Power is in England *solely intrusted with the Prince, who in*
administring those Laws, ought to be no more resisted than the
Legislative Power it self. But they do not conceive the same abso-   110
lute Passive Obedience *to be due to a limited Prince's Commands,*
when they are directly contrary to the Laws he has consented to,
and sworn to maintain. The Crown may be sued as well as a private
Person; and if an arbitrary King of England *should send his Offi-*
cers to seize my Lands or Goods against Law, I can lawfully resist   115
them. The Ministers by whom he acts are liable to Prosecution and
Impeachment, tho' his own Person be Sacred. But if he interposes
his Royal Authority to support their Insolence, I see no Remedy,
'till it grows a general Grievance, or 'till the Body of the
People have Reason to apprehend it will be so; after which it be-   120
comes a Case of Necessity, and then I suppose à free People may
assert their own Rights, yet without any Violation to the Person
or lawful Power of the Prince. But although the Tories *allow all*

101 *Power*: cf. 'An *Hoadleian* believes *that* to be the *Supreme* Power in every
Kingdom and Commonwealth, *which* hath the *Authority* of *making* and *repealing*
Laws, and that *this Power* is by our Constitution lodg'd in *Queen, Lords*, and
Commons in Parliament *assembled*; and that the Queen, who by our Law is vested
with the sole Executive Power, is in that very Capacity bound by the Legislative ... And therefore an *Hoadlean* believes, That ... *Passive Obedience*, and
Non Resistance, is a *Duty* to be paid to *this Power* by all Subjects ... And ...
that the *Authority* (that is) the *Legal* Power of the Crown ought not to be
resisted in any Case whatsoever' (*Chuse which you Please*, 1710, p. 4).
119 *general Grievance*: cf. 'An *Hoadlean* saith, That ... if the *Oppression*
be not *general*, the *Body* of the People will *not* be *affected*, and consequently
will not be induced to rise in Arms' (ibid., p. 5).
121 *Necessity*: 5.92.

this, and did justify it by the Share they had in the Revolution,
125   *yet they see no Reason for entring upon so ungrateful a Subject,*
      or raising Controversies upon it, as if we were in daily Appre-
      hensions of Tirany, *under the Reign of so excellent a Princess,*
      and while we have so many Laws of late Years made to limit the
      Prerogative; when according to the Judgment of those who know our
130   *Constitution best, Things rather seem to lean to the other Ex-*
      tream, which is equally to be avoided. As to the Succession; the
      Tories *think an Hereditary Right to be the best in its own Nature,*
      and most agreeable to our old Constitution; yet at the same time
      they allow it to be defeasible by Act of Parliament, and so is
135   Magna Charta *too, if the Legislature thinks fit; which is a Truth*
      so manifest, that no Man who understands the Nature of Govern-
      ment, can be in doubt concerning it.

      These I take to be the Sentiments of a great Majority among the
      Tories, with respect to *Passive Obedience*: And if the *Whigs*

129-31 *Prerogative; when ... avoided.*] Prerogative. 38 8°+12°

---

124 *Revolution*: The signers of the invitation to William of Orange in June
1688 included only two Tories, Henry Compton, Bishop of London, and Danby, but
it had become a commonplace that the Revolution was made 'almost entirely' by
Tories (*The Whigs Appeal to the Tories. In a Letter to Sir T--- H---* (London,
for S. Popping, 1711, p. 7).
129 *Prerogative*: 'The Act declaring the Rights and Liberties of the Subject and settling the Succession of the Crown [the Bill of Rights] (1 Gul. &
Mar. Sess. 2. c. 2), and the Act for the Further Limitation of the Crown and
better securing the Rights and Liberties of the Subject [the Act of Settle-
ment] (12 & 13 Gul. III. c. 2) [287.132n.], limited the power of the Crown'
(E1922, ix 219). The Triennial Act, which William vetoed in March 1693,
limited the power of the Crown to summon and prorogue Parliament. The Act of
Settlement, drafted in anticipation of yet another non-English monarch, was
particularly limiting: 'this Nation [shall] be not obliged to ingage in any
Warr for the Defence of any Dominions or Territories which do not belong to
the Crown of England without the Consent of Parliament ... no Person who shall
hereafter come to the Possession of this Crown shall go out of the Dominions
of England Scotland or Ireland without Consent of Parliament ... no Person
born out of the Kingdoms of England Scotland or Ireland or the Dominions there-
unto belonging ... shall be capable ... to enjoy any Office or Place of Trust
either Civill or Military ... no Pardon under the Great Seal of England be
pleadable to an Impeachment by the Commons in Parliament' (*Statutes of the
Realm*, vii 637). In Anne's reign the prerogative was further limited only in
the most minor way. An Act for the better Support of Her Majesties Houshold
and of the Honour and Dignity of the Crown (1 Ann. c. 1) placed further limitations upon grants of Crown land.
135 *Magna Charta*: cf. 'the Legislature may ... turn out Christianity if
they think fit' (Swift, *Prose*, ii 105).

insist, from the Writings or common Talk of warm and ignorant Men,   140
to form a Judgment of the whole Body, according to the first Account I have here given, I will engage to produce as many of
their Side, who are utterly against *Passive Obedience* even to the
Legislature; who will assert the last Resort of Power to be in
the People, against those whom they have chosen and trusted as   145
their Representatives, with the Prince at the Head; and who will
put wild improbable Cases to shew the reasonableness and necessity of resisting the Legislative Power, in such imaginary Junc-
tures. Than which however nothing can be more idle; For I dare
undertake in any System of Government, either Speculative or   150
Practick, that was ever yet in the World, from *Plato*'s Republick
to *Harrington*'s *Oceana*, to put such Difficulties as cannot be
answered.

All the other Calumnies raised by the *Whigs* may be as easily
wiped off; and I have Charity to wish they could as fully answer   155
the just Accusations we have against Them. *Dodwell, Hicks*, and
Lesley, are gravely quoted, to prove that the *Tories* design to
bring in the *Pretender*; and if I should quote Them to prove that
the same Thing is intended by the *Whigs*, it would be full as
reasonable, since I am sure they have at least as much to do with   160
Non-jurors as we. But our Objections against the *Whigs* are built
upon their constant Practice for many years, whereof I have produced a hundred Instances, against any single one of which no
Answer hath yet been attempted, tho' I have been curious enough
to look into all the Papers I could meet with that are writ   165
against the *Examiner*; such a Task as I hope no Man thinks I would
undergo for any other End, but that of finding an Opportunity to
own and rectify my Mistakes; as I would be ready to do upon Call
of the *meanest* Adversary. Upon which Occasion, I shall take leave
to add a few Words.   170

I flattered my self last *Thursday*, from the Nature of my Subject

163 one of] one; to 38 8°+12°

---

144 *Power*: Swift had once held this republican opinion himself (Swift,
Discourse, p. 83), but since 1701 he had come to believe that it is 'the
Legislative Power' that is 'the supream Power' (41.185) in a mixed monarchy.
156 *Dodwell*: 155.40.
    Hicks: 289.38.
157 *Lesley*: 35.23.

and the inoffensive manner I handled it, that I should have one
Week's Respite from those merciless Pens, whose Severity will
some time break my Heart; but I am deceived, and find them more
175   violent than ever. They charge me with two Lies and a Blunder.
The first Lie is a Truth, that *Guiscard* was invited over: But it
is of no Consequence; I do not tax it as a Fault; such sort of
Men have often been serviceable: I only blamed the Indiscretion
of raising a profligate Abbot, at the first Step, to a Lieutenant-
180   General and Colonel of a Regiment of Horse, without staying some
reasonable time, as is usual in such Cases, 'till he had given
some Proofs of his Fidelity, as well as of that Interest and
Credit he pretended to have in his Country: But that is said to
be another Lie, for he was a *Papist*, and could not have a Regi-
185   ment. However this other Lie is a Truth too; for a Regiment he
had, and paid by us, to his Agent Monsieur *Le Bas*, for his Use.
The third is a *Blunder*, that I say *Guiscard*'s Design was against
Mr. *Secretary St. John*; and yet my Reasonings upon it, are, as if
it were personal against Mr. *Harley*. But I say no such Thing, and
190   my Reasonings are just; I relate only what *Guiscard* said in *Newgate*, because it was a Particularity the Reader might be curious
to know (and accordingly it lies in a Paragraph by it self, after
my Reflections) but I never meant to be answerable for what *Guiscard* said, or thought it of Weight enough for me to draw Conclu-
195   sions from thence, when I had the Address of both Houses to
direct me better; Where it is expresly said, *That Mr.* Harley*'s
Fidelity to her Majesty, and Zeal for Her Service, have drawn
upon Him the Hatred of all the Abettors of Popery and Facti∩n.*
This is what I believe, and what I shall stick to.
200   But alas, these are not the Passages which have rais'd so much

176   *Guiscard ... invited*: 300.68n.
185   *Regiment*: 301.69-70n.
186   *Le Bas*: Charles Le Bas was the recruiting agent and paymaster for
Guiscard's French Dragoons (*CTB 1710*, pp. 286-7).
187   *Blunder*: 312.163. As Walter Scott supposed, it was the impossibility of
pleasing both Harley and St. John on 'this nice point' (*E1814*, iv 39) that
caused Swift to leave the full account of the Guiscard incident to Delariviere
Manley. 'I was afraid of disobliging Mr. Harley or Mr. St. John in one critical
point', he explained to Stella, 'and so would not do it myself' (Swift, *Journal*, p. 245).
196-8   *That ... Faction*: *CJ*, xvi 541. Cf. 'The *Examiner* knows *you* [the
seven Whig lords of the committee to examine Greg] are as much intended by
Faction, as *Guiscard* was by *Popery*' (Oldmixon, *A Letter to the Seven Lords of
the Committee, Appointed to Examine Gregg*, 1711, p. 6).

Fury against me. One or two Mistakes in Facts of no Importance,
or a single Blunder, would not have provoked them; they are not
so tender of my Reputation as a Writer. All their Outrage is occasion'd by those Passages in that Paper, which they do not in the
least pretend to answer, and with the utmost Reluctancy are   205
forc'd to mention. They take abundance of Pains to clear *Guiscard*
from a Design against Mr. *Harley*'s Life, but offer not one Argument to clear their other Friends, who in the Business of *Greg*,
were equally guilty of the *same Design* against the *same Person;*
whose Tongues were very Swords, and whose *Penknives* were *Axes.*   210

208 *other Friends*: Oldmixon identifies these as 'your Lordships certainly'
(ibid., p. 5) and the Yale copy of ½° is annotated with the names of the
seven members of the committee.
210 *whose ... Axes*: cf. 'a very elegant Expression; but the *English* of it
is, that your Lordships would by *Subornation* [of William Greg] have taken away
the Life of Mr. *H.*' (ibid., p. 7).

No. 26 [Oldmixon]   26 March 1711

The MEDLEY.

Of Good Giving.
Part of a Scene out of Beaumont *and* Fletcher.
Gregg's *Business.*
Some Remarks on the Examiner.

PEOPLE may very well wonder how such a stale Story as that of
Diego and his *Will* shou'd come into my Head at this time of day;
for, truly, I was surpriz'd at it my self, seeing it cou'd have
no manner of relation to the political *Topicks* I am us'd to treat
of. But the Name and Nature of my Paper are such, that Connection   5
wou'd be a Vice in it. I have declar'd against Form and Order,
and at first assum'd a Liberty to ramble as I pleas'd. I will not
pretend to give the whole History of this *Spaniard*, but it appears

1 *Story*: from Beaumont and Fletcher, *The Spanish Curate*. Oldmixon apparently quotes from memory or from rough notes, for his text is neither that of
the folios of 1647 and 1679 nor of Tonson's edition of 1711.
7 *ramble*: 105.42.

by it that he was of the most *giving* Humour in the World; which
Disposition of his one wou'd think cannot in the least relate to
10   the Age we live in. However we may be mistaken too; other Nations
may have their *Diego*'s as well as *Spain*, those being always the
most liberal who have the least *to give*. If a Man has not much,
he does not think it worth keeping: If nothing, let him be as
bounteous as he will, he can't lose by it. And this has often
15   made People affect a generous Air, who had they been rich, wou'd
have been errant Misers. Riches are apt to contract the Mind, and
have a craving Quality, and are hard to be parted with. Poverty
out of Spite puts on another Face, and wou'd be thought open-
hearted, acquiring Reputation at a cheap rate, which she is sure
20   not to suffer by. Those that *give* away what they have not, or
what is not their own, have generally lavish Hands: While such as
have good Bottoms will be more *sparing*, because they are not to
pay with *Words* only. We had a wicked Fellow in *England* some time
since, who in the Agony dispos'd of Lands and Tenements that were
25   none of his; for his true *Fund* wou'd not have purchas'd a Shroud
for the Carcase, which in a few hours after wanted it. He knew he
shou'd soon be *dissolv'd*, and did not care who made good his
Donations, provided he had the Credit of giving them while he was
yet in being. *Diego* had play'd the same Prank, and thence *Beau-*
30   *mont* and *Fletcher* took the Hint of one of the pleasantest Scenes
in all their Comedies. His Design was to impose on a credulous
Lawyer, who took him for a Man of vast Wealth, believ'd every
word he said, and swore to see his Testament executed; which is
an Advantage abundance of *Givers* can never hope for. But I shou'd
35   spoil the Story by endeavouring to refine upon it, and shall
therefore give it the Reader in the Poets Language. The *Spaniard*
had before made very large Gifts, Sums after Sums had been put
down to fill up his *Will*, which ended in this merry manner; and
'tis remarkable that the Itch of *Giving* comes upon Men most vio-
40   lently when they are nearest their End. The Play is the *Spanish*
Curate, and the Persons

Diego, Lopez, *and* Bartolus.

Diego.] I give Five Hundred Crowns to buy a Church-yard, A spa-
cious Church-yard to lay Thieves and Knaves in.
45   *Lopez.*] Are ye not weary?

Diego.] Never of well-doing.

Bartolus.] These are mad Legacies.

Diego.] They were got as madly, I have no Heirs.

Bartolus.] This cannot be, 'tis monstrous. You have made me full
     Executor.   50

Diego.] Full, full and total: Wou'd I had more to give ye: But
     these may serve an honest Mind.

Bartolus.] Ye say true. A very honest Mind, and make it rich too;
     Rich, wondrous rich: but where shall I raise these Monies?
     Where shall I find these Sums?   55

Diego.] *Ev'n where you please, Sir.* You are wise and provident,
     and know Business: Ev'n *raise 'em where you shall think
     good.* I am reasonable.

Bartolus.] Think good! Will that raise Thousands? Where I please?
     This is pack'd sure to disgrace me.   60

Diego.] Ye are just and honest, and are sworn to do it: I know
     you will, and that's my dying Comfort, *Ev'n where you
     please.* For you know where the Wealth is.

Bartolus.] I am abus'd, betray'd, *&c.*

'Tis pleasant enough to see what Work *Abel* and my Friend the   65
Examiner make with *Gregg* every day. I did not mind it much at
first, knowing they mean nothing, only take thence an Opportunity
to abuse those who hang'd him. But I find the Party talk now of
it as if there was really something in it, and that the House of
Lords were nor better nor worse than the first Actors in the Plot   70
against Mr. *H-----. Their Tongues,* says my worthy Friend, *were
very Swords, and their Penknives were Axes*: which made me resolve
to enquire into that Business, and 'twas upon this Inquiry I
found that all the Scandal with which those two Scriblers have
aspers'd the late Ministry on this occasion, is properly thrown   75
at the House of Peers, who took cognizance of that Affair, and
appointed a Committee to examine *Gregg* in *Newgate.* Accordingly
they took his Examination, and laid it before the House, which
was very long. It was printed, and every one may see it, as well

70 nor better] not 12°

71-2 *Their ... Axes*: 321.210.

80   as the Address that follow'd upon it. *Gregg* confess'd, among
     other things,

       'That the rough Draught of the Queen's Letter to the Emperor,
     as it was alter'd by the Lord Treasurer, was left in the publick
     Book of the Office, to be enter'd the same Night it was to be
85   sent away: There *Gregg* said he found it and transcrib'd it, and
     any other Clerk of the Office might have done it as well as he.
       'All the Books in the Office lie in a Press, the Key is always
     in the Door; and not only the Clerks, but the Chamber-Keepers may
     have Access.
90   'All Letters, except those wrote to the Duke of *Marlborough*,
     are enter'd in the Books; but those are only copy'd in loose
     Sheets. *Gregg* said he had copy'd many of those. He own'd he sent
     the Copy of the Queen's Letter to Mr. *Chamillard*, the same night
     the Queen's Letter was dispatch'd to the Emperor.'

95   From this Examination my Friend justly concludes, That the Late
     Ministry had the same Design of murdering Mr. *H-----* that *Guis-*
     card had; who, he says afterwards, had no Design of murdering Mr.
     H----- at all: in which alone I believe the late Ministers and
     that Villain ever agreed. But whatever Conspiracy there was
100 against that Secretary, the House of Lords must answer for it:

82-94 *the ... Emperor*: *The Humble Address of the Right Honourable the*
Lords Spiritual and Temporal in Parliament Assembled, with the Reports therein
Contained, and the Several Examinations Annexed, Presented to Her Majesty on
Munday the Two and twentieth Day of March, 1707, London, by Charles Bill *et*
al., 1708, pp. 6-7.
    82 *Letter*: cf. 'The Author of the *Medley* having, in his Paper of Yesterday,
endeavour'd maliciously to insinuate, that there was a great Carelessness and
Neglect in suffering Greg to see a Letter from the Queen to the Emperor; we
think it necessary to let the Publick know, that it appears by the Report of
the Lords, that that Letter was communicated to Greg by Mr. Man, now living,
in the Family of the Earl of Godolphin; and that the said Mr. Man was a very
diligent Clerk, and not in the least guilty of any Fault, in shewing the said
Letter to Greg, who had then given no body any just Cause, to suspect him; so
that the scandalous Author of the Medley, has done great wrong to Mr. Man,
who has further to alledge in his Justification, that the Contents of that
Letter were no matter of Secret; for it has been since printed, and the Subject of it was only to desire the Emperor to send Prince Eugene to command in
Spain, which was mention'd 6 Weeks before the date of this Letter, in Eigh-
teen News Papers printed in London; in Fourteen printed in Holland, besides
other Gazettes publish'd at Vienna, Berlin, Paris, Milan, and Hamburgh' (*The*
Post-Boy, 24-7 March 1711).
    96 *same Design*: 321.207.
    97 *no Design*: 320.187.

For there's no colour of throwing it on the Ministry, let there
be what there will in it. And this will appear by the Address the
Lords presented to her Majesty, wherein is this Paragraph:

'It is your Majesty's Glory, and the Happiness of *Europe*, that
you are at the Head of one of the greatest Confederacies that   105
ever was known in History; and it is the common Concern of the
whole Alliance, that your Counsels shou'd be kept with the strictest Secrecy: But in the Papers now laid before You, your Majesty
will be pleas'd to observe that some of your Resolutions of the
greatest moment, and that requir'd the utmost Secrecy, have been   110
sent to your Enemies, by the same Post they were dispatch'd to
the Allies: That all the Papers in Mr. Secretary *Harley*'s Office
have for a considerable time been expos'd to the View even of
the meanest Clerks in that Office; and that the Perusal of all
the Letters to and from the *French* Prisoners was chiefly trusted   115
to *Gregg*, a Person of a very suspicious Character, and known to
be extremely indigent. It is not easily to be known what ill Consequences may have attended such Negligence; but we depend upon
it, that these Matters being thus plainly laid open to your
Majesty, we shall be secur'd against any Dangers of this nature   120
for the future, *&c.*'

To which her Majesty was pleas'd to return this most gracious
Answer:

The Examples you lay before me, will, I do not doubt, be a suf-
ficient Warning to keep all Matters of Importance as secret as   125
may be, and to employ such only as there shall be good Grounds to
believe will be faithful, &c.

104-21 *It ... future*: The *Humble Address of the Right Honourable the Lords
Spiritual and Temporal*, 1708, p. 19.
118 *Negligence*: Defoe had warned Harley of the poor security in his office
more than three years before the Greg case: 'I have been in the Secretarys
Office of a Post Night when Had I been a French Spye I could ha' Put in my
Pockett my Lord N[ottingha]ms Letters Directed to Sir Geo: Rook and to the
Duke of Marlebro' Laid Carelessly on a Table for the Doorkeepers to Carry to
the Post Office' (Defoe, *Letters*, pp. 38-9).
124-7 *The ... faithful*: The *Humble Address of the Right Honourable the
Lords Spiritual and Temporal*, 1708, p. 19.

As the *Examiner* has it, *'tis with the utmost Reluctancy* we are
forc'd to mention these Passages: We had rather look forwards
130   than backwards, and have an Abhorrence for all Innuendo's that
hurt the Reputation of Great Men. But how was it possible for any
good *Englishman* to be passive, and see two such profligate Writers
continually insult the Greatest Assembly in the World, the House
of Peers, with their false and scurrilous Imputations? as if that
135   August Body cou'd be guilty of as base a Villany as a *French*
Priest, or attempt the Life of a Person who was not in their
favour: It being plain that all that Affair was manag'd by the
House of Lords, and not by the Ministers; and that there's no
more in't than what I have related. If my Friend can prove any
150   thing more, as well as he has done the Lyes I charg'd him with,
he shall always find me as ready to *rectify my Mistakes* as he can
be. But in all these Cases I am for *Records* only; and the Legend
is in as good Credit with me, as *Abel* and his Brother.

If every body did not by this time know my Friend, some might
155   take him by his last Paper to be one of the most impartial Authors that ever wrote. So willing is he to own his Errors, he
reads what's written against him for no other end. But it happens he is so infallible, he can't be convicted of one. Indeed
the Falsities laid to his charge in the last *Medley* were so
160   notorious, he cou'd not help taking notice of them, and doing
what he cou'd to clear himself; which is, by being guilty of two
or three more. *The first Lye,* says he, *is Truth*; Guiscard *was invited over*. Now, was ever any thing better made out? You have his
word for it, and that's all. He does not add a Syllable more to
165   prove it, tho he had so much Encouragement; being promis'd to
have all the Lyes he has told, and shall tell, forgiven him, if
he cou'd do it. Instead of this, he wou'd have me take an Excuse
for Evidence: *It is of no consequence*, he says, *he does not tax
it as a Fault*; which is extremely kind in him. But I suppose the
170   main Reason may be, for that he knows e'er this, who were most

128-9 *with ... Passages*: 321.204-6.
151 *rectify my Mistakes*: 319.168.
159 *Falsities*: 311.126-313.169.
162-3 *The ... over*: 320.176.
165 *being promis'd*: 312.149-50.
168-9 *It ... Fault*: 320.176-7.
170 *who*: Rumours 'that Mr. H--- and Mr. St. J--- were those who chiefly
countenanced' Guiscard had already reached Dublin (Swift, *Corr.*, i.216).

fond of the Renegade, and on whom the Reflection wou'd turn.

As to the other Lye, the Fact is this: The Emperor gave him a
Regiment in *Spain*, and made him a Lieutenant General; he cou'd
not have any such Command by an *English* Commission, the Laws
being against it: And yet my Friend positively affirm'd *he was*   175
made a Lieutenant General and a Colonel of Horse by the late
Ministry: which he sticks to, is no Lye; and so he has got off
that too, as he did the other. 'Twill be impossible to fix any
thing upon him. *Guiscard* receiv'd Mony here, and that doubtless
was for the Regiment the Ministers gave him in the Emperor's Army: 180
tho if that Regiment was paid here, it was no more than a great
many others were, that had Commissions from some of our Allies.

The *Blunder* he does not much matter, and contents himself with
protesting he says no *such thing, and that his Reasonings are*
just. If there were any Truth in what he says, it wou'd be a hard   185
Case that we shou'd have fal'n upon him the only time they cou'd
be so call'd. But you'll see how *just* his *Reasonings* are presently.
He said *'twas worth observing that the late Ministry concur'd with*
a French *Papist in the great End of killing Mr. H-----*: And afterwards, that *the Murderer confess'd his Design was against Mr. St.*   190
John. These are his *just Reasonings*; and tho we can't say he ever
reason'd more *justly*, yet it does not therefore follow that this
is not as great a Blunder as we made it: and 'tis left to the
Reader, thus fairly stated as it is, to determine between us.
What he adds in his own Vindication a line or two lower, is a   195

172 *Fact*: Oldmixon repeats 311.134 and 309.88 but offers no evidence for
either.
174 *English Commission*: Guiscard is reported to have sold his commission
as colonel of Guiscard's French Dragoons in August 1708, before it was decided
in April 1709 not to reform the regiment (HMC *Portland MSS*, iv 500; *CTB 1709*,
ii 140).
175-7 *he ... Ministry*: 300.67-301.71, 320.186.
179 *Guiscard receiv'd Mony*: Payments to Guiscard that were made through
Charles Le Bas probably came from secret service funds, but after he sold his
commission, payments to him made out of the civil list are duly recorded in
The Calendar of Treasury Books, 1708-11. In all this there is no evidence of
a regiment in the imperial army, but Guiscard's French Dragoons on the English
establishment continued to require attention as late as 1714: the accounts
could not be made up because the muster rolls were wanting (HMC *Lords MSS*,
new series, x 470).
183 *Blunder*: 320.187.
184-5 *says ... just*: 320.189-90.
188-91 *'twas ... St. John*: 302.85-8, 303.109-11.

little more to the purpose: *It was a Particularity the Reader*
might be curious to know, but he never meant to be answerable for
it. True or False, if it touch'd the Reader's Curiosity, 'twas
enough with him; he'll answer for nothing: and thinks it strange,
200   that we who have known him so long, *shou'd be provok'd at one or*
two Mistakes in Facts, or a single Blunder: which, 'tis true,
are, in his way of writing, Trifles, and what must always be expected from him.

196-8   *It ... it*: 320.190-3.
200-1   *shou'd ... Blunder*: 321.201-2.

No. 35 [Swift]   29 March 1711

The EXAMINER.

Sunt hic etiam sua præmia laudi;
Sunt lachrymæ rerum, & mentem mortalia tangunt.

I Begin to be heartily weary of my Employment as *Examiner*; which
I wish the M-----ry would consider, with half so much Concern as
I do, and assign me some other with less Pains, and a larger
Pension. There may soon be a Vacancy, either on the Bench, in the
5   Revenue, or the Army, and I am *equally* Qualify'd for each: But
this Trade of *Examining*, I apprehend may at one time or other go
near to sowr my Temper. I did lately propose that some of those
ingenious Pens, which are engag'd on the other Side, might be
employ'd to succeed me, and I undertook to bring them over for
10   *t'other Crown*; but it was answer'd, that those Gentlemen do much
better Service in the Stations where they are. It was added, that
abundance of Abuses yet remain'd to be laid open to the World,
which I had often promised to do, but was too much diverted by

3 larger] *om.* 38 8°+12°

Motto Virgil, *Aeneid*, i 462:   ... See | The Palm that Virtue yields! in
scenes like these | We trace Humanity, and Man with Man | Related by the
Kindred Sense of Woe.
10   *t'other Crown*: 'in my t'other Hose' is proverbial (Tilley H723).
12   *Abuses*: 84.90.

other Subjects that came into my Head. On the other side, the
Advice of some Friends, and the Threats of many Enemies, have put   15
me upon considering what would become of me if *Times should alter*.
This I have done very maturely, and the Result is, that I am in
no manner of Pain. I grant, that what I have said upon Occasion,
concerning the late Men in Power, may be call'd Satyr by some
unthinking People, as long as that Faction is down; but if ever   20
they come into Play again, I must give them warning before-hand,
that I shall expect to be a *Favourite*, and that those pretended
Advocates of theirs, will be Pilloried for *Libellers*. For I appeal
to any Man, whether I ever charg'd that Party, or its Leaders,
with one single Action or Design, which (if we may judge by their   25
former Practices) they will not openly profess, be proud of, and
score up for Merit, when they come again to the Head of Affairs?
I said, they were Insolent to the Qu---; Will they not value themselves upon That, as an Argument to prove them bold Assertors of
the Peoples Liberty? I affirm'd they were against a Peace; will   30
they be angry with me for setting forth the Refinements of their
Politicks, in pursuing the *only* Method left to preserve them in
Power? I said, they had involved the Nation in Debts, and engross'd much of its Mony; they go beyond me, and boast they have
got it *all*, and the *Credit* too. I have urg'd the Probability of   35
their intending great Alterations in Religion and Government: If
they destroy both at their next Coming, will they not reckon my
foretelling it, rather as a Panegyrick than an Affront? I said,
they had formerly a Design against Mr. *H----y*'s Life: If they
were now in Power, would they not immediately cut off his Head,   40
and thank me for justifying the Sincerity of their Intentions? In
short, there is nothing I ever said of those worthy Patriots,
which may not be as well excused; Therefore, as soon as They
resume their Places, I positively design to put in my Claim; and,
I think, may do it with much better Grace, than many of that Party 45
who now make their Court to the present M-----ry. I know two or
three great Men, at whose Levees you may Daily observe a Score

28 *Insolent to the Qu---*: 217.179-80.
30 *against a Peace*: 9.176.
33 *involved the Nation in Debts*: 7.121-2.
34 *Mony*: 208.186-7.
36 *Alterations*: 245.174.
39 *Design*: 321.207.

of the most forward Faces, which every Body is asham'd of, except
those that wear them. But I conceive my Pretensions will be upon
50   a very different Foot: Let me offer a paralell Case. Suppose,
King *Charles* the First had entirely subdued the Rebels at *Naseby*,
and reduc'd the Kingdom to His Obedience: Whoever had gone about
to Reason, from the former Conduct of those *Saints*, that if the
Victory had fallen on Their side, they would have murdered their
55   Prince, destroy'd Monarchy and the Church, and made the King's
Party compound for their Estates as Delinquents; would have been
call'd a false, uncharitable Libeller, by those very Persons who
afterwards glory'd in all this, and call'd it the *Work of the
Lord*, when they happen'd to succeed. I remember there was a Person
60   Fin'd and Imprison'd for *Scandalum Magnatum*, because he said the
Duke of *York* was a Papist; but when that Prince came to be King,
and made open Profession of his Religion, he had the Justice immediately to release his Prisoner, who in his Opinion had put a
Compliment upon him, and not a Reproach: And therefore Colonel
65   *Titus*, who had warmly asserted the same Thing in Parliament, was
made a Privy Councellor.

By this Rule, if that which, for some Politick Reasons, is now
call'd Scandal upon the late M-----ry, proves one Day to be only
an Abstract of such a Character as they will assume and be proud
70   of; I think I may fairly offer my Pretensions, and hope for their
Favour. And I am the more confirm'd in this Notion by what I have
observ'd in those Papers, that come Weekly out against the *Examiner*. The Authors are perpetually telling me of my Ingratitude to
my Masters, that I *blunder*, and betray the Cause; and write with

49 that] who 38 8°+12°   68 proves] prove 38 8°+12°

---

59 *Person*: Charles Gerard, styled Lord Brandon until he succeeded his
father as 2nd Earl of Macclesfield in January 1694, and a strongly Exclusion-
ist Member for Lancashire (March 1679-January 1694), was a member of the
Middlesex grand jury that presented the Duke of York as a popish recusant.
He was arrested during the Rye House Plot, but pardoned by James II in August
1697 (Luttrell, i 421).
65 *Titus*: 'Silas [Silius] Titus, author of the celebrated tract against
Oliver Cromwell, entitled, "Killing no Murder," and a zealous supporter of
the bill for excluding the Duke of York from the crown, was, nevertheless,
sworn privy counsellor to James II., on the 6th July 1688' (E*1814*, iv 55).
'In his notes on Burnet Swift says: "Titus was the greatest Rogue in England"
[Swift, *Prose*, v 266]' (E*1922*, ix 224).
73-4 *Ingratitude to my Masters*: 237.139-43.
74 *blunder*: 327.183.

more Bitterness against those that hire me, than against the   75
Whigs. Now I took all this at first only for so many Strains of
Wit, and pretty Paradoxes to divert the Reader; but upon further
thinking I find they are Serious. I imagin'd I had complimented
the present Ministry for their dutiful Behaviour to the Queen;
for their Love of the old Constitution in Church and State; for   80
their Generosity and Justice, and for their Desire of a speedy,
honourable Peace: But it seems I am mistaken, and they reckon all
this for Satyr, because it is directly contrary to the Practice
of all those whom they set up to defend, and utterly against all
their Notions of a good Ministry. Therefore I cannot but think   85
they have Reason on their side: For suppose I should write the
Character of an *Honest*, a *Religious*, and a *Learned* Man; and send
the first to *Newgate*, the second to the *Græcian Coffee House*, and
the last to *White's*; would they not all pass for *Satyrs*, and
justly enough, among the Companies to whom they were sent?   90

Having therefore employ'd several Papers in such sort of
Panegyricks, and but very few on what they understand to be
Satyrs; I shall henceforth upon Occasion be more Liberal of the
latter, of which they are like to have a Taste, in the remainder
of this present Paper.   95

Among all the Advantages which the Kingdom hath receiv'd by the
late Change of Ministry, the greatest must be allow'd to be the
calling of the present Parliament, upon the Dissolution of the
last. It is acknowledg'd, that this excellent Assembly hath entirely recover'd the Honour of P--------ts, which had been unhap-   100
pily prostituted for some Years past by the Factious Proceedings

75 that] who 38 8°+12°   97 to be] to 12° *om.* 38 8°+12°

---

75 *Bitterness*: 294.192.
88 *Newgate*: the chief jail for the City of London and the county of Middlesex.
       Græcian: An Unbelieving Club, of which Anthony Collins was a member, is
said to have met at the Grecian Coffee House in Devereux Court near Temple
Bar (Asgill, *A New Project, Dedicated neither to the Q---n nor the Lord
T------r, nor any of the Houses of P-------nt, but to the Unbelieving Club
at the Grecian*, London, 1712; James H. Monk, *The Life of Richard Bentley, D.D.*,
London, C.J.G. and F. Rivington, *et al.*, 1830, p. 268).
89 *White's*: White's Chocolate House in St. James's Street had become a
gambling club. Swift called it 'the common Rendezvous of infamous Sharpers,
and noble Cullies' (Swift, *Prose*, xii 50).

of an *unnatural Majority*, in Concert with a most corrupt Administration. 'Tis plain, by the present Choice of Members, that the
Electors of *England*, when left to themselves, do rightly under-
105 stand their true Interest. The Moderate *Whigs* begin to be convinc'd that we have been all this while in wrong Hands, and that
Things are now as they should be. And as the present House of
Commons is the best Representative of the Nation that hath ever
been summoned in our Memories; so they have taken care in their
110 first Session, by that noble Bill of *Qualification*, that future
Parliaments should be compos'd of Landed Men, and our Properties
lie no more at Mercy of those who have none themselves, or at
least only what is *transient* or *imaginary*. If there be any Gratitude in Posterity, the Memory of this Assembly will be always
115 Celebrated; if otherwise, at least we, who share in the Blessings
they derive to us, ought with grateful Hearts to acknowledge them.

I design, in some following Papers, to draw up a List (for I
can do no more) of the great Things this Parliament hath already
perform'd, the many Abuses they have detected; their Justice in
120 deciding Elections without regard of Party; their Chearfulness

102 *unnatural Majority*: This idea, to which the Examiner so frequently
recurs (256.27-257.39, 314.19-23), was also St. John's: 'You may observe your-
self', he said, 'what a difference there is between the truth strength of this
nation and the fictitious one of the Whigs. How much time, how many lucky
incidents, how many strains of power, how much money must go to create a
majority of the latter'. (Bolingbroke, *Letters*, i 16).
104 *Electors*: cf. 180.40-1.
110 *Bill*: 'The qualification required by this act [An Act for securing the
Freedom of Parliaments by the farther qualifying the Members to sit in the
House of Commons (9 Ann. c. 5), which received the royal assent on 26 February 1711] is some estate in land [£600 a year for knights of the shire and
£300 a year for burgesses], either in possession or certain reversion; a provision avowedly intended for the security of the landed against the monied
interest' (E*1814*, iv 57).
113 *transient or imaginary*: 'Alluding to the funds' (E*1814*, iii 430).
119 *Abuses*: Harley's 'first Regulation was that of the Exchequer-Bills,
which to the great Discouragement of publick Credit, and Scandal to the Crown',
circulated only at a discount. He 'procured an Act of Parliament, by which the
Bank of *England* should be obliged in consideration of five and fourty thousand
Pounds, to accept and circulate those Bills without any Discount. He then proceeded to stop the Depredations of those who dealt in Remittances of Money to
the Army, who by unheard-of Exactions in that kind of Traffick had amassed
prodigious Wealth' (Swift, *Prose*, vii 75-6).
120 *deciding Elections*: The general election of October 1710 'for sheer
bitterness and fury was never equalled in the eighteenth century' (Holmes,
p. 48). The same bitterness produced an unusually large number (seventy-five)
of petitions to the Committee of Privileges and Elections to settle controverted elections and double returns. Of the forty-eight of these that pitted

and Address in raising Supplies for the War, and at the same time
providing for the Nations Debts; their Duty to the Queen, and
their Kindness to the Church. In the mean time I cannot forbear
mentioning two Particulars, which in my Opinion do discover, in
some Measure, the Temper of the present Parliament; and bear   125

Whig against Tory, thirty-eight were decided against the Whig. On balance, the
Tories added about thirty-six votes to their majority by this means. The numbers, however, make the matter seem a great deal simpler than it actually was.
Two cases will show something of the complexity of the politics. Col. Samuel
Gledhill, an unsuccessful Tory candidate for Carlisle, petitioned on 4 December 1710 against the return of the Whig incumbent, Sir James Montagu, late
Attorney-General and younger brother of Halifax, charging falsification and
bribery (*CJ*, xvi 414). Harley, however, who was trying to win Halifax's support, 'spoke very warmly for Sr James' and after a long debate on 14 March
1711 the House decided that Gledhill had failed to make good his charges (SRO
GD 220/5/808/10/8a; *CJ*, xvi 548). At Lymington, Hants, two Tories were put up
against the Whig patron, Paul Burrard, and Lord William Powlett, the Duke of
Bolton's brother and 'Head of the Pack' that hunted Sacheverell to earth
(*POAS*, Yale, vii 398). After their defeat the Tories petitioned, charging
'many illegal Practices' (*CJ*, xvi 407), but, despite a huge Tory majority in
the House, the return of Burrard and Lord William was upheld. This is the kind
of vote 'without Regard of Party' that Swift had in mind, but the numbers are
against him.

121 *Supplies*: On 30 November 1710, in the first week of the session, the
House undertook, in an address to the Queen, 'to grant the necessary Supplies,
for a vigorous Prosecution of the War in all its Parts, and especially in
Spain', and did so before Christmas (*CJ*, xvi 406 ff.).

122 *Nations Debts*: Harley had introduced his plan for funding the entire
national debt by incorporating the creditors into a Company for Trading to
the South Seas, 'without entring into Particulars', when 'a sudden Stop was
put to this Affair' by Guiscard's knife (Swift, *Prose*, vii 76).

Duty to the Queen: The phrase appears in an address to the throne of
30 November 1710 (*CJ*, xvi 406; cf. 217.179n).

123 *Church*: 'The minister and churchwardens of Greenwich aplied to the
House of Commons on February 14th, 1710/1, for aid in the rebuilding of their
church. The House referred the application to a committee. On February 28th
the lower house of Convocation sent a deputation to the Speaker expressing
their satisfaction at what had been done. On his reporting this to the House
on the following day, they expressed their readiness to receive information.
The lower house of Convocation prepared a scheme and presented it to the
Speaker on March 9th; this was referred to the committee on the 10th. Acting
on a hint received from the court, the bishops and clergy presented an
Address to the Queen on March 26th, and this was followed by a Message from
Her Majesty, on the 29th, to the House of Commons, recommending that Parliament
should undertake "the great and necessary work of building more churches." On
April 9th the House of Commons replied in an Address, promising to make provision, and resolved, on May 1st, to grant a supply for building fifty new
churches in or about London and Westminster. On May 8th it fixed the amount at
a sum "not exceeding £350,000." In pursuance of this a Bill was introduced on
May 18th, which received the Royal Assent on June 12th (9 Ann. c. 17). This
Bill granted £350,000 (to be raised by a duty on coals) for building fifty new
churches in London and Westminster. In this connection it is interesting to
remember that Swift, two years before, had recommended the building of more
churches as part of his suggestions for "the Advancement of Religion" [Swift,
Prose, ii 61]' (E*1922*, ix 278).

Analogy to those Passages related by *Plutarch*, in the Lives of
certain great Men; which, as himself observes, *Though they be not
of Actions that make any great Noise or Figure in History, yet
give more Light into the Characters of Persons, than we could*
130   *receive from an Account of their most Renown'd Atchievements.*

Something like this may be observ'd from two late Instances of
Decency and *good Nature*, in that Illustrious Assembly I am speaking of. The first was, when after that inhuman Attempt upon Mr.
Harley, they were pleas'd to Vote an Address to the Queen, wherein
135   they express their utmost Detestation of the Fact, their high
Esteem and great Concern for that able Minister, and justly impute his Misfortunes to that Zeal for Her Majesty's Service,
which had *drawn upon him the Hatred of all the Abettors of Popery
and Faction*. I dare affirm, that so distinguishing a Mark of
140   Honour and good Will from such a Parliament, was more acceptable
to a Person of Mr. *H----y*'s generous Nature, than the most *bounti-
ful Grant* that was ever yet made to a Subject; as Her Majesty's
Answer, fill'd with gracious Expressions in his Favour, adds more
to his *real Glory*, than any *Titles* She could bestow. The Prince
145   and Representatives of the whole Kingdom, join in their Concern
for so important a Life. These are the true Rewards of Virtue,
and this is the Commerce between noble Spirits, in a Coin which
the *Giver* knows where to bestow, and the *Receiver* how to value,
tho' neither *Avarice* nor *Ambition* would be able to comprehend its
150   Worth.

The other Instance I intended to produce of *Decency* and *good
Nature*, in the present House of Commons, relates to their most
worthy *Speaker*; who having unfortunately lost his *eldest Son*, the

127 observes, *Though*] observeth, *Although* 38 8°+12°   128 that] which
12° 38 8°+12°

127-30 *Though ... Atchievements*: Plutarch, *Life of Alexander*, i 2.
134 *Address*: *CJ*, xvi 541; cf. 320.196-8. Temple Scott observes that Swift
'somewhat strengthens' the language of the address (E*1922*, ix 226). But the
words that Swift quotes are quoted exactly and the rest is paraphrased very
much in the style of the original, which is heavy with outrage and superla-
tives: 'most barbarous ... most deeply affected'.
138-9 *drawn ... Faction*: 320.197-8.
143 *Answer*: Anne's reply emphasizes Harley's 'known Opposition to Popery
and Faction' (*CJ*, xvi 548).
153 *Speaker*: 'Mr. Bromley's son died of the small-pox, and the House

Assembly, mov'd with a generous Pity for so sensible an Afflic-
tion, adjourn'd themselves for a Week, that so good a Servant of   155
the Publick, might have some Interval to wipe away a *Father's*
Tears: And indeed that Gentleman has too just an Occasion for his
Grief, by the Death of a *Son*, who had already acquir'd so great
a Reputation for every amiable Quality, and who might have liv'd
to be so great an Honour and an Ornament to his antient Family.   160

Before I conclude, I must desire one Favour of the Reader, that
when he thinks it worth his while to peruse any Paper writ against
the *Examiner*, he will not form his Judgment by any mangl'd Quotation out of it which he finds in such Papers, but be so just to
read the Paragraph referr'd to; which I am confident will be   165
found a sufficient Answer to all that ever those Papers can object. At least I have seen above fifty of them, and never yet
observ'd one single Quotation transcrib'd with common Candor.

adjourned for a week, that he might wipe off his tears. "I think," says Swift
to Stella, "it is very handsomely done. But I believe one reason is, that
they want Mr. Harley so much" [Swift, *Journal*, p. 221]' (E*1814*, iv 59).
163-4 *mangl'd Quotation*: Defoe notices this: 'nor can he say my Quotation is
not just, as I find he complains of others' (*Review*, 5 April 1711).

No. 27 [Oldmixon]   2 April 1711

The MEDLEY.

The Tories argue like the Papists.
A Proof of it out of Bishop Stillingfleet.
The True High-Church Doctrine of Passive Obedience.
The Conditions on which the Examiner *may turn Whig.*

I Shou'd have been extremely taken with the *Examiner* of the 22d
of *March*, if my Friend were not so unlucky that he can't help

1-10 I ... that] Tho the late Marquiss of *Hallifax* was of Opinion, *That it
wou'd be Ingratitude in some Men to turn Honest, when they owe all they have
to their Knavery*: yet I shou'd have been extreamly taken with the *Examiner* of
22d March in which my Friend discover'd so good a Disposition to be one of our
Party, if 12°
_____
1-2 *the Examiner of the 22d of March*: Oldmixon calls this the '*Whiggish*
Examiner' (355.184).

spoiling all he does, by some *Falsity* or other. One wou'd hope
'tis rather his *Fate* than his *Inclination*, since he then dis-
5 cover'd so good a Disposition to be one of our *Party*. The Marquiss
of *Hallifax* says, *In truth it wou'd be Ingratitude in some Men to
turn Honest, when they owe all they have to their Knavery*. As to
the Ingratitude of it, I know my Friend and the *Faction* he was
quitting don't mind that: But I wish he wou'd not have confounded
10 things so; and that when he was order'd to declare himself a *Whig*,
he wou'd have acted like one, been honest and spoke his mind, and
not have call'd *Revolution-Principles* by a *Tory* Name. He knows
every word of the Charge about *Passive Obedience*, even as he has
put it down for the Whigs, is true against the Tories; and by the
15 falling off of his Patrons, they wou'd become so inconsiderable,
that he needed not be afraid of 'em. He might have maul'd 'em as
much as he wou'd; and he and I being well agreed, we shou'd soon
be too hard for the stoutest *Club* of 'em all; and let 'em be as
restiff as they will, can have Mony enough, I'll warrant ye. Only
20 I must caution my Friend not to make such a *Blunder*, as to write

11 honest] ∼, ½°   14-22 and ... for] But instead of frankly confessing
it, he has done one of the most ridiculous things that ever he was guilty of,
in writing after the Copy of his Friends the Papists, in the Days of King
James the second. A true Account being then given of Popish Principles and
Practices: Hold, said the Papist, this is all wrong; and then was publish'd
their famous Pamphlet call'd *A Papist Represented and Misrepresented*. In like
manner, we having given some Account of Tory Principles, out comes this ingenious Writer with his *TORIES REPRESENTED AND MISREPRESENTED*; as if he had not
enough imitated the Papists already, but were resolv'd to follow them in every
thing. And 12°

5 *Disposition*: alluding to the Examiner's Whiggish definition of passive
obedience (317.98-318.137).
6-7 *In ... Knavery*: George Savile, Marquis of Halifax, *Some Cautions
offered to the Consideration of Those who are to Chuse Members to Serve in
the Ensuing Election*, London, 1695, p. 8.
12 *Revolution-Principles*: Is the 'Tory Name' 'a Case of Necessity'
(317.120-1)?
20-1 *write as the Papists did*: Too ill to write *The Medley* himself, Mainwaring gave instruction to Oldmixon: '*The* Examiner *gives a better handle
against himself than ever, this Morning* [22 March 1711], *by writing as the*
Papists *did: You know their first Book in King* James's *time, was a Papist misrepresented and represented* [315.47]. *Answer'd by Bishop* Stillingfleet, *in the
End of his sixth Volume, where doubtless, you may find good Hints; and this is
a better Subject, than that of the* Republicans. Davenant *is not worth meddling
with: The Marquiss of* Hallifax, *was not a steady Tory; besides, some Notice
should be taken of the* Examiner's *persisting in his Lyes, and some further
Justification might be made of the* Lords *concern'd in* Gregg's *Business*' (Oldmixon, *The Life*, p. 201).

as the Papists did in King *James*'s time. He copies them too
closely in his Tories *misrepresented* and *represented*; for as he
has manag'd it, nothing can be more justly apply'd to him, and
his Description of the *Whig*-Charge and *Tory*-Principles, than what
Bishop *Stillingfleet* writes in his Answer to that Popish Pamphlet. 25
'Tho the *Father of Lyes be the Author of misrepresenting*, yet
we have no reason to think, but that if he were to plead his own
Cause to Mankind, he wou'd very much complain of being *misrepresented* by them. The great *Instruments* he hath made use of in
deceiving and corrupting Mankind, have been as forward as any to   30
complain of being *misrepresented*. The true Reason is, because no
great Evil can prevail in the World unless it be *represented*
otherwise than it is; and all Men are not competent Judges of the
Colours of Good and Evil. Therefore *when the Designs of those who
go about to deceive* begin to be laid open, they then betake them-   35
selves to the fairest *Representatation* they can make of themselves, and hope that many will not see thro their Pretences.'
One Method which that Learned Prelate us'd to convince his
Adversaries, was to shew that the Misrepresentations which it was
pretended the Protestants made of Popery, were supported by the   40
best Romish Authors, who gave the like accounts of their own
Faith. The same Course I shall now take with my Friend, and shew
him that his Scheme of Passive Obedience, as charg'd by the Whigs,
is no other than what the chief Writers of his Party have maintain'd: And I will make my Quotations out of no less a Book than   45
the Tryal of *Sacheverel*; for the exquisite Management of which,
the Council have been highly applauded, and two of them been most
worthily made Lord Chan------s, and abundance of People are apt

23 it] the matter 12°   25 writes] writ then 12°

26-37 *Tho ... Pretences*: Stillingfleet, *The Doctrines and Practices of the
Church of Rome Truly Represented; In Answer to a Book Intituled, A Papist
Misrepresented, and Represented, &c.*, London, for W. Rogers, 1686, pp. 6-7.
46 *the Tryal of Sacheverel*: All of Oldmixon's quotations of High Church
divines, and his references to the original sources, are taken from this
work. They were offered in evidence that Sacheverell's principles had always
been those of the Church.
47 *two*: Two of Sacheverell's lawyers had places in Harley's ministry: Sir
Simon Harcourt was made Lord Keeper on 19 October 1710 and Constantine Phipps
was appointed Lord Chancellor of Ireland on 22 January 1711.

to murmur that poor *Dunc-n D--* is so long neglected. My Friend
begins his Account of Passive Obedience, as charg'd by the Whigs,
thus:-----*The Doctrine of Passive Obedience is to believe that a
King, even in a Limited Monarchy, holding his Power only from
God, is only answerable to him,* &c. (for I will not tire the
Reader with transcribing the whole.) Now let us see what their
Authors say: and I will quote none but those that are either
avow'd to have been High-Churchmen, or that now flourish under
that happy Denomination.

'For a Man to take up Arms (Offensive or Defensive) against a
lawful Sovereign, being a thing in its nature unlawful, may not
be done by any Man, at any Time, in any Cases, upon any Colour or
Pretence whatsoever; not for the Maintenance of the Lives or
Liberties either of our selves or others; nor for the Defence of
Religion, nor for the Preservation of a Church or State; no nor
yet, if that cou'd be imagin'd possible, for the Salvation of a
Soul; no not for the Redemption of the whole World.'

'Subjects must obey *passively*, where they can't obey actively;
otherwise Government would be precarious. Nor is this only a
State-Doctrine, but the Doctrine also of Jesus Christ, and that
a necessary and indispensable one too, as sufficiently appears
from these famous Words of St. *Paul, Rom.* 13. 1,2. which are so
plain, that they need no Comment; so that so long as this Text
stands in our Bibles, the Doctrine of Non-Resistance or Passive
Obedience must be of Obligation to all Christians.'

Decree of the University of Oxford, July 21. 1683. *against such
damnable Doctrines as these.*

'That if lawful Governors become Tyrants, or govern otherwise

53 for] *om.* 12°   70 2] 3 12°

---

49 *Dunc-n D--*: Another of Sacheverell's lawyers remained neglected until
7 January 1714 when he was appointed to the commission of appeals in the
excise (*CTB*, xxviii 79).
51-3 *The ... him*: 315.52-4.
58-65 *For ... World*: [Robert] Sanderson, [*XXXVI Sermons*, London, for
B. Tooke *et al.*, 1686], p. 552 (½° corrected) (*The Tryal*, p. 235).
66-73 *Subjects ... Christians*: 'Archbishop of York's Sermon before the House
of Lords in 1700' (½°) (*The Tryal*, pp. 216, 243).
76-89 *That ... State*: [*The Judgment and*] Decree of the University of Oxford

than by the Laws of God and Man they ought to do, they forfeit
the Right they had unto their Government.

'Birthright and Proximity of Blood give no Title to Rule or
Government; and it is lawful to preclude the next Heir from his   80
Right and Succession to the Crown.

'There lies no Obligation upon Christians to Passive-Obedience,
when the Prince commands any thing against the Laws of our Country.

'It is not lawful for Superiours to impose any thing in the
Worship of God, that is not antecedently necessary.   85

'We decree, judg and declare all and every of these Propositions
to be false, seditious and impious, and most of them to be also
heretical and blasphemous, infamous to Christian Religion, and
destructive of all Government both in Church and State.'

'The Wrath of God shall as certainly fall upon those that rise   90
up against the King, as upon those that fight against God. And no
wonder that the Punishment should be the same, when the Fault is
the same: For he that fights against his King, fights against God
himself, who hath invested him with that Power and Authority to
govern his People, representing his own glorious Majesty before   95
them.

'Upon this Ground it is, that I believe the Wickedness of a
Prince cannot be a sufficient Plea for the Disobedience of his
Subjects.'

'What else means St. *Paul*, when in so many words he declares,   100
That whosoever resisteth the Power, resisteth the Ordinance of
God; and they that resist, shall receive to themselves Damnation?
Rom. 13.2. Out of all doubt he there speaks of the Temporal
Power, and of Eternal Damnation to ensue upon resisting it; than
which what more grievous Punishment could have been inflicted,   105
had they immediately resisted God himself?

[*Past in their Convocation*] *July 21. 1683, Against* [*certain Pernicious Books*
and] *Damnable Doctrines* [*Destructive to the Sacred Persons of Princes, their*
State and Government, and of all Humane Society. Rendred into English, and
Published by Command, Oxford, 1683, pp. 3-7] (½°) (*The Tryal*, pp. 236, 237,
238).
    90-9 *The ... Subjects*: '*Bishop* Beveridge*'s Private Thoughts*' (½°) (*The*
Tryal, p. 241).
    100-14 *What ... resisting*: '*Bishop of* Rochester*'s Sermon before the Artil-*
lery Company, 1692. pag. 25, 26' (½°) (*The Tryal*, p. 246).

'And recollect, I intreat you, the time when this was so positively pronounc'd by St. *Paul*; it must have been written under
the Reign of *Claudius* or *Nero*. So that 'tis evident, all that
110   resisted them were, without Repentance, in a damnable State. Can
there be then any Colour so specious, any Cause so just, in
which, instead of Damnation, a Christian Subject may justly expect to receive to himself Salvation, on the account of resisting?'

115   'Is he not the Vicegerent of God? Wherever therefore his Sovereign the Almighty has not prevented him by any precedent Commands, there he has a Right and Liberty to put forth his; in
these Cases to expect an active chearful Obedience, and that we
should *in no Case, and for no Reason, resist*.
120   'The Church, of which we have the Blessing to be Members,
where she can't obey, is ready to endure, expecting her Reward
in Heaven.'

'Nay, tho the Laws of our Earthly Governors should in some Instances be contrary to the Divine Laws (upon which Supposition
125   the Magistrate does certainly exceed the Bounds of his Commission) yet this does not void their Authority, they are the Ministers of God for all this; or else there were none that were so,
there were none that could be call'd so when the Apostle wrote
this Epistle: and there is a Duty lying on Subjects even in this
130   Case, *viz. Not to oppose nor resist the Power*, but *quietly* and
patiently to *suffer the Penalty* of those Laws, which they can't,
without sinning against God, yield an active Obedience to.'

Let the Reader now judg whether all these Great Men, and true
Churchmen, do not maintain as much upon this Head, as any Whig
135   ever charg'd upon them; but I would be glad to see a Quotation
out of any one of this Party, to justify that Account of Passive-
Obedience, which my Friend says is profess'd and practis'd by
the Tories, and which he will be oblig'd to recant if there be

115-22 *Is ... Heaven*: '*Bishop of* Bath *and* Wells's *Sermon before the King,*
Novemb. 5. 1681. *pp.* 11, 19' (½°) (*The Tryal,* p. 248).
123-32 *Nay ... to*: '*Bishop of* Exeter's *Sermon before her Majesty on her*
Accession to the Throne, p. 13, 14' (½°) (*The Tryal,* p. 250).

not a speedy Change of Measures. Did ever any stanch Tories believe a word of what this worthy Author has printed as a Summary   140
of their Faith? I confess I shou'd never have enter'd upon this
Argument, had it not been to set my Friend right, finding him
lately in so hopeful a way. If I cou'd once get him cur'd of his
Itch of *Scandal* and *Fiction*, he would be towardly enough. And
seeing it is impossible for Matters to go as we would have them   145
in Tory-Hands, I should be as forward as any body to desire they
may be shifted: and I expect the Trouble I have given my self to
shew the Tories in their true Colours, should have its Merit with
him; since I do it to inform him, and make him a thorow Convert.
It was matter of Comfort to me to observe, that some of his   150
Friends began to find the necessity of returning to their old
Principles. 'Tis true, they should have had a little more mercy
than to have put him upon writing a Paper contradicting all his
former, since the poor Man must write what they will have him.
But that being now passed, if they should think it their Interest   155
to make him go back to his Tory-Principles again, tho he'll do
it with all his Heart; yet he has so lost his Credit with good
Churchmen, that they'll never hearken to him, and the Design of
his Paper is ruin'd for ever.

    Therefore tho he threatens again to fall upon the last Ministry, 160
and to display his Talent of *Satyr*, I should hope that for the
future there will be no danger of his *Relapse*, which depends entirely on the Instructions that are given him. But as well as we
are with one another, there are several Conditions I shall exact
of him before the Agreement is quite made: He must renounce all   165
Pretences to *Favour* from the old Ministers, for the Obligations
he told us last Thursday he has laid on them: He must learn to
cast Account better, and not make One in Five Hundred to be Nine
in Ten, as he did in the City-Election, nor One in a Thousand to

---

142-9 finding ... inform him] *om.* 12°   154 former,] ~. 12°   since ...
him] *om.* 12°   162 *Relapse*,] ~. 12°   162-3 which ... him] *om.* 12°
165-7 renounce ... must] *om.* 12°   168 make] to make 12°

---

151 *Friends*: 248.26.
161 *Satyr*: 331.93.
169 *City-Election*: Oldmixon refers again to the fact that the Whig John
Ward lost by only sixteen votes, roughly one in every 500 votes cast (209.212).

170 be Nineteen in Twenty, as he did when he affirm'd so many of the
     Tories were of *Whig* Principles. He must never compare the House
     of Lords and the *French* Villain *Guiscard*, as he has often done in
     the Case of Mr. *H-----*, and still stands to it. He must not be-
     lieve there's no way of complementing the present Ministers, but
175 by vilifying the late ones. He must not say the latter were
     against a Peace, because they were for having *Spain*; nor term the
     last Parliament an *Unnatural Majority*, because they were for the
     Revolution and *Toleration*. He must never say arbitrarily *This
     House* is best, or *That House* is best, without giving good Reasons
180 for't; nor pretend to give us his own Word against her Majesty's
     frequent Declarations from the Throne. He must never brag of a
     Bill, till he sees the Event of it; nor depend on the Gratitude
     of Posterity, till he is sure the next Age will be wiser than
     this. He must not commend People by halves; nor for the sake of
185 a *Qualification*-Act forget the *French* Bill, which promises so
     many Blessings and Advantages. These and many other Conditions
     will be requir'd of him to confirm his Conversion, or he must
     still herd with the Reprobate.

> 170-1 *Nineteen in Twenty ... Tories*: 315.49-50.
> 173 *stands to it*: 321.207-9.
> 176 *against a Peace*: 329.30.
> 177 *Unnatural Majority*: 332.102.
> 185 *Qualification-Act*: 332.110.
>   *French Bill*: A Bill for repealing the Act of the 3d and 4th Years of
> her Majesty's Reign, entitled An Act for prohibiting all Trade and Commerce
> with France; so far as it relates to the prohibiting the Importation of French
> Wines, passed the House of Commons and was sent up to the Lords on 10 March.
> 'The Expectation of good Wine being, of itself, a powerful Recommendation,
> their Lordships gave their Concurrence to it' and it received the royal assent
> on 17 March 1711 (*The History and Proceedings of the House of Commons*, iv 193,
> 199).

No. 36 [Swift]   5 April 1711

The EXAMINER.

Nullo suo peccato impediantur, quo minus alterius peccata demonstrare
possint.

I Have been considering the Old Constitution of this Kingdom,
comparing it with the Monarchies and Republicks whereof we meet
so many Accounts in ancient Story, and with those at present in
most Parts of *Europe*: I have considered our Religion, established
here by the Legislature soon after the Reformation: I have like-   5
wise examined the Genius and Disposition of the People, under
that reasonable Freedom they possess: Then I have turned my Reflections upon those two great Divisions of *Whig* and *Tory*,
(which, some way or other, take in the whole Kingdom) with the
Principles they both profess, as well as those wherewith they   10
reproach one another. From all this, I endeavour to determine,
from which Side Her present M-----y may reasonably hope for most
Security to Her Person and Government, and to which She ought, in
Prudence, to trust the Administration of Her Affairs. If these
two Rivals were really no more than *Parties*, according to the   15
common Acceptation of the Word, I should agree with those Politicians who think, a Prince descends from his Dignity by putting
himself at the Head of either; and that his wisest Course is, to
keep them in a Balance; raising or depressing either as it best
suited with his Designs. But when the visible Interest of his   20
Crown and Kingdom lies on one Side, and when the other is but a
Faction, raised and strengthned by Incidents and Intrigues, and
by deceiving the People with false Representations of Things; he
ought, in Prudence, to take the first Opportunity of opening his
Subjects Eyes, and declaring himself in favour of those, who are   25
for preserving the Civil and Religious Rights of the Nation,
wherewith his own are so interwoven.

17 descends] descendeth 38 8°+12°

Motto Cicero, *In Q. Caecilium Divinatio*, xxxiv: No Fault or Crime in themselves hinders them from searching into and pointing out the Faults of others.

This was certainly our Case: For I do not take the Heads, Advocates, and Followers of the *Whigs*, to make up, strictly speaking,
30 a *National Party*; being patched up of heterogeneous, inconsistent
Parts, whom nothing served to unite but the common Interest of
sharing in the Spoil and Plunder of the People; the present Dread
of their Adversaries, by whom they apprehended to be call'd to an
Account, and that general Conspiracy, of endeavouring to overturn
35 the Church and State; which, however, if they could have com-
passed, they would certainly have fallen out among themselves,
and broke in pieces, as *Their Predecessors* did, after they destroyed the Monarchy and Religion. For, how could a *Whig*, who is
against all *Discipline*, agree with a *Presbyterian*, that carries
40 it higher than the *Papists* themselves? How could a *Socinian*
adjust his Models to either? Or how could any of these cement
with a *Deist* or *Free-thinker*, when they came to consult upon
settling Points of Faith? Neither would they have agreed better
in their Systems of Government, where some would have been for a
45 King, under the Limitations of a Duke of *Venice*; others for a
Dutch Republick; a third Party for an *Aristocracy*, and most of
them all for some new Fabrick of their own contriving.
   But however, let us consider Them as a *Party*, and under those
general Tenets wherein they agreed, and which they publickly
50 owned, without charging them with any that they pretend to deny.
Then let us *Examine* those Principles of the *Tories*, which their
Adversaries allow them to profess, and do not pretend to tax them
with any Actions contrary to those Professions: After which, let
the Reader judge from which of these two Parties a Prince hath
55 most to fear; and whether Her M-----y did not consider the Ease,
the Safety and Dignity of Her Person, the Security of Her Crown,

---

39 that] who 38 8°+12°   43 settling] *om.* 12° 38 8°+12°   45 a Duke]
the Duke 38 8°+12°

---

29 *Whigs*: 257.37-9, 314.20-3.
39 *Discipline*: 'generally, the system by which the practice of a church,
as distinguished from its doctrine, is regulated. *spec.* ... The ecclesiastical
polity of the Puritan or Presbyterian party' (*OED*).
40 *Socinian*: The 'amicable *Agreements* ... and comfortable Communion'
reached by the Socinians and Presbyterians in 1689 after more than a century
of conflict (*A Brief History of Presbytery and Independency, from their first
Original, to this Time*, London, for Edward Faulkner, 1691, p. 27), lasted only
until 1693.

and the transmission of Monarchy to her Protestant Successors,
when She put Her Affairs into the present Hands.

Suppose the Matter were now entire; the Qu--- to make Her
Choice, and for that end, should order the Principles on both   60
Sides to be fairly laid before Her. First, I conceive the *Whigs*
would grant, that they have naturally no very great Veneration
for *Crowned Heads*; that they allow, the Person of the Prince may,
upon many Occasions, be resisted by Arms; and that they do not
condemn the War raised against King *Charles* the First, or own it   65
to be a Rebellion, though they would be thought to blame his
Murder. They do not think the *Prerogative* to be yet sufficiently
limited, and have therefore taken care (as a particular Mark of
their Veneration for the Illustrious House of *Hannover*) to clip
it closer against the next Reign; which, consequently, they would   70
be glad to see done in the present: Not to mention, that the
Majority of them, if it were put to the Vote, would allow, that
they prefer a Commonwealth before a Monarchy. As to *Religion*;
their universal, undisputed Maxim is, That it ought to make no
Distinction at all among *Protestants*; and in the Word *Protestant*   75
they include every Body who is not a *Papist*, and who will, by an
Oath, give Security to the Government. Union in Discipline and
Doctrine, the offensive Sin of Schism, the Notion of a Church and
a Hierarchy, they laugh at as Foppery, Cant and *Priestcraft*. They
see no necessity at all that there should be a National Faith;   80
and what we usually call by that Name, they only style the *Reli-*
gion of the Magistrate. Since the Dissenters and we agree in the
Main, why should the Difference of a few Speculative Points, or
Modes of Dress, incapacitate them from serving their Prince and
Country, in a Juncture when we ought to have all Hands up against   85
the common Enemy? And why should they be forced to take the
Sacrament from our Clergy's Hands, and in our Posture, or indeed
why compelled to receive it at all, when they take an Employment
which has nothing to do with Religion?

   59 now] not 38 8°+12°   70 the] *om.* ½° 12°

---

   64 *resisted*: 5.92n., 317.120-3.
   67 *Prerogative*: 318.129.
   81-2 *the Religion of the Magistrate*: 143.15.
   83-5 *why ... Country*: Swift is speaking 'in *Tindal*'s Phrase' (Swift, *Prose*,
ii 115).

90   These are the Notions which most of that Party avow, and which
        they do not endeavour to disguise or set off with false Colours,
        or complain of being misrepresented about. I have here plac'd
        them on purpose, in the same Light which themselves do, in the
        very Apologies they make for what we accuse 'em of; and how in-
95   viting even these Doctrines are, for such a Monarch to close with,
        as our Law, both Statute and Common, understands a King of *Eng-
        land* to be, let others decide. But then, if to these we should
        add other Opinions, which most of their own Writers justify, and
        which their universal Practice has given a Sanction to, they are
100   no more than what a Prince might reasonably expect, as the
        natural Consequence of those avow'd Principles. For when such
        Persons are at the Head of Affairs, the low Opinion they have of
        Princes, will certainly tempt them to violate that Respect they
        ought to bear; and at the same time, their own want of Duty to
105   their Sovereign is largely made up, by exacting greater Submis-
        sions to themselves from their Fellow-Subjects: It being undis-
        putably true, That the same Principle of Pride and Ambition makes
        a Man treat his Equals with Insolence, in the same Proportion as
        he affronts his Superiors; as both Prince and People have suffi-
110   ciently felt from the late M-----ry.
        Then from their confess'd Notions of Religion, as above related,
        I see no reason to wonder, why they countenanced not only all
        sorts of Dissenters, but the several *Gradations* of *Free-thinkers*
        among us (all which were openly enroll'd in their Party); nor
115   why they were so very averse from the present establish'd Form of
        Worship, which by prescribing Obedience to Princes from the
        Topick of Conscience, would be sure to thwart all their Schemes
        of Innovation.
        One thing I might add, as another acknowledg'd Maxim in that
120   Party, and in my Opinion, as dangerous to the Constitution as any
        I have mention'd; I mean, That of preferring, on all Occasions,
        the *Monyed* Interest before the *Landed*; which they were so far
        from denying, that they would gravely debate the Reasonableness
        and Justice of it; and at the rate they went on, might in a little

    94 'em] them 38 8°+12°   103 tempt] lead 38 8°+12°   114 nor] or 38
    8°+12°
    _____
    95 *close*: 'To come to terms or agreement (with ...)' (*OED*).

time have found a Majority of Representatives, fitly qualified to   125
lay those heavy Burthens on the rest of the Nation, which themselves would not touch with one of their Fingers.

However, to deal impartially, there are some Motives which
might compel a Prince, under the Necessity of Affairs, to deliver
himself over to that Party. They were *said* to possess the great   130
Bulk of Cash, and consequently of Credit in the Nation, and the
Heads of them had the Reputation of presiding over those
Societies who have the great Direction of both: So that all Appli-
cations for Loans to the Publick Service, upon any Emergency,
must be made thro' them; and it might prove highly dangerous to   135
disoblige them, because in that Case, it was not to be doubted,
that they would be obstinate and malicious, and ready to obstruct
all Affairs, not only by shutting their own Purses, but by endeavouring to sink *Credit*, tho' with some present imaginary Loss
to themselves, only to shew, it was a *Creature* of their own.   140

From this Summary of *Whig-Principles* and Dispositions, we find
what a Prince may reasonably fear and hope from that Party. Let
us now very briefly consider, the Doctrines of the *Tories*, which
their Adversaries will not dispute. As they prefer a well-
regulated Monarchy before all other Forms of Government; so they   145
think it next to impossible to alter that Institution here, without involving our whole Island in Blood and Desolation. They
believe, That the Prerogative of a Sovereign ought, at least, to
be held as sacred and inviolable as the Rights of his People, if
only for this Reason, because without a due share of Power, he   150
will not be able to protect them. They think, that by many known
Laws of this Realm, both Statute and Common, neither the Person,
nor lawful Authority of the Prince, ought, upon any Pretence whatsoever, to be resisted or disobey'd. Their Sentiments, in relation
to the Church, are known enough, and will not be controverted,   155
being just the Reverse to what I have deliver'd as the Doctrine
and Practice of the *Whigs* upon that Article.

126 lay] leave 38 12°   136 that] this 38 8°+12°

---

133 *Societies*: The power of the Bank of England and the East India Company to manipulate the Government and Parliament through their monopoly of
lending to the government had been noticed before (*Remarks upon the Bank of
England, With Regard more Especially to our Trade and Government*, London, for
A. Baldwin, 1705, pp. 27-39); cf. 5.78n.

But here I must likewise deal impartially too, and add one Principle as a Characteristick of the *Tories*, which has much dis-
160 courag'd some Princes from making use of them in Affairs. Give
the *Whigs* but Power enough to insult their Sovereign, engross his
Favours to themselves, and to oppress and plunder their Fellow-
Subjects; they presently grow into good Humour and good Language
towards the Crown; profess they will stand by it with their Lives
165 and Fortunes; and whatever Rudenesses they may be guilty of in
Private, yet they assure the World, that there never was so
gracious a Monarch. But to the shame of the *Tories*, it must be
confess'd, that nothing of all this hath been ever observ'd in
them; in or out of Favour, you see no Alteration, further than
170 a little cheerfulness or cloud in their Countenances; the highest
Employments can add nothing to their Loyalty, but their Behaviour
to their Prince, as well as their Expressions of Love and Duty,
are, in all Conditions, exactly the same.

Having thus impartially stated the avow'd Principles of *Whig*
175 and *Tory*; let the Reader determine, as he pleases, to which of
these two a wise Prince may, with most Safety to himself and the
Publick, trust his Person and his Affairs; and whether it were
Rashness or Prudence in Her M-----y to make those Changes in the
Ministry, which have been so highly extoll'd by some, and con-
180 demn'd by others.

175 pleases] pleaseth 38 8°+12°

No. 28 [Oldmixon]   9 April 1711

The MEDLEY.

The Late Ministry vindicated by the Q---n and Parliament.
The Examiner *against the Addresses.*
Popery and Faction charged upon the Tories.

MATCHIAVEL, on the *Decades* of *Livy*, says, *Accusations of the*

1-21 *MATCHIAVEL ... own*] *om.* 12°
_____

1 *MATCHIAVEL: Discourses*, i 8.

Great ought to be incourag'd, Calumny detested and punish'd. The
Examiner, who is of all Men the most guilty of this Vice, sets
up for a Paper of *State*; and whether his Presumption in that does
not add to his Crime, let the World judg. Who it is he affronts   5
in so doing, is too obvious to need any Remark; and those who
suffer his Scandal, are without doubt Sharers in the Guilt of it.
The abovemention'd Author adds in the same Book: *Indeed under a*
good Prince you will find the happy Golden Age, where each is at
liberty to have and sustain the Opinion which pleases him. But   10
sure he does not mean that every leud Writer may with Impunity
affirm all the Falsitys he *pleases* of the *Best* and *Greatest* of
Men. For my part I pity the Fortune of a Faction, which cannot
maintain it self without such base Shifts and wretched Advocates.
Common Policy should methinks oblige them to silence such   15
Scriblers as *Abel* and his Brother: For unless they are Men of
more Foresight than Monsieur *De Wit* was, whose Sentiments of the
Vicissitude of *English* Councils I have formerly mention'd, they
may well imagine the People will be the same three years hence
they were three years ago, and then what a Present will a Set of   20
Examiners be? I own I don't see any reason why one Parliament is
not as good as another: Their Acts have the same Force; and if
the Laws of One that is *dissolv'd* are liable to be repeal'd, are
not the Laws of One that is in *being* subject to the same Fate?
I can't find out wherein the Infallibility of one more than   25
another consists; and the *Declarations* of the *Past* are with me
as sacred as those of the *Present*. 'Tis true, those who deal in
Scandal, like my Friend, have the Advantage upon a *Dissolution*.
However one wou'd think, that the Authority of the Legislature
being always the same, the *Present* are for their own sakes con-   30
cern'd to vindicate the Honour of the *Past*; since, they may

21 don't] Never cou'd 12°

----

5 *Who*: innuendo: the Queen.
8 *same Book*: *Discourses*, i 10.
16 *Abel*: 254.160.
17 *De Wit*: 81.227-9.
21 *Parliament*: Oldmixon begins with an apparent retort to 'the great Things
this Parliament hath ... perform'd' (332.118-19).
23 *repeal'd*: The Examiner had failed to mention that the Bill to repeal the
Act for a general Naturalization (194.75-195.76) passed the Commons but was
thrown out by the Lords on 5 February 1711 (*LJ*, xix 215).

depend upon it, their own Actions will be as rudely censur'd, if
ever they meet with such rude Censurers as he is. What is it that
he has not said against the late Ministers? His and my Papers are
35   full of his Fictions and Insolence. That *neither God nor Man*
could endure them, is one of the tenderest of his *Reflections*.
Has he not accus'd them of Tyranny, Treachery, Corruption, and
all the Vices his wicked Imagination could invent? Has he not now
laid *Murder* to their Charge? And yet *His* is still one of the
40   *tolerated* Papers of the Week. I shall not pretend to write a formal Vindication of those Great Men; the plain History of their
Administration, which is in all our Memories, as it will be the
brightest Part of the *British Annals* of our Times, so it will be
for ever preserv'd to the Confusion of those who have vilify'd
45   them, and those who have incourag'd it. I shall content my self
with giving the Reader the very words of both *Lords and Commons*,
in their Addresses upon the *Pretender's* Invasion, and begin with
that of the *Commons*.

'There can be nothing so dangerous or fatal to the Safety of
50   your Royal Person, and the Security of the present Establishment,
as those Persons who endeavour to create Divisions and Animosities among your faithful Subjects, or by any artful Methods
lessen the just Esteem your Majesty has for those who have so
eminently, and in so distinguishing a manner commanded your
55   Armies, *and manag'd your Treasure*, to the Honour and Glory of
your Majesty Abroad, and the entire Satisfaction of your People
at Home: We therefore humbly beg leave to beseech your Majesty to
discountenance all such Persons and Designs, in the most remarkable Manner.'

60   *Her Majesty's most Gracious Answer.*

'I think all who endeavour to make Divisions among my faithful

---

35-6 *neither ... them*: 52.74-5.
39 *Murder*: 321.210.
39-40 *the ... Week*: 246.188-9.
41 *the plain History*: 'Godolphin managed the national finances with great
care and skill' (Dickson, p. 59).
49-59 *There ... Manner*: This is from the Commons' reply to the Queen's
address of 11 March 1708 informing Parliament that the Pretender had sailed
from Dunkirk that morning at the head of a French invasion fleet (*CJ*, xv 608).
61-5 *I ... Services*: *CJ*, xv 611.

Subjects, must be mine and the Kingdom's Enemies; and I shall
never countenance any Persons who would go about to lessen the
just Esteem which I have for those who have done, and continue to
do me the most eminent Services.'   65

Who those Persons were whom her Majesty declar'd had so *eminently* serv'd her, we all know; and notwithstanding this Declaration, shall see presently how they have been insulted and revil'd
by the *Examiner*, assuming all the while an *authoritative* Air, as
if what he has done was meritorious.   70

The Lords Address at the same Time.

'We most humbly offer it to your Majesty as our Opinion, That
your Majesty should principally depend upon, and encourage those
who have been ever since the Revolution most steddy, and firm to
the Interest of the late King, and of your Majesty during your   75
happy Reign.'

To which her Majesty was pleas'd to Answer.

'As I cannot but wish there were not the least occasion of Distinction among my Subjects; so I must always place my *chief Depen-
dence* upon those, who have given such repeated Proofs of the   80
greatest Warmth and Concern *for the Support of the Revolution*,
Security of my Person, and of the Protestant Succession.'

If I should take upon me to insinuate who they were whom the
Commons understood in their Address to be *discountenanc'd in the
most remarkable manner*: What were the *artful Methods* they made   85
use of: What their Designs, and how they were then disappointed
as well as the *Pretender*; am I sure I should not be cry'd out
against as an *Abettor of Faction*? And yet was it not the Address

70 was] were 12°   72 most] must ½° 12°   87 cry'd out] exclaim'd 12°

72-6 *We ... Reign*: LJ, xviii 508.
78-82 *As ... Succession*: LJ, xviii 511.
88 *Abettor of Faction*: 334.139.

of a House of Commons, who had the Glory and Interest, the Safety
90   and Peace of *Great Britain* as much at heart as ever any *Represen-*
tatives had? Is there not as great a Sanction in what they *said*,
as will be in the *Sayings* of This House Three Years hence? Is not
her Majesty *Semper Eadem*? Are not her Sentiments of the *Eminent*
Services of those Ministers the best Panegyrick? And how daring
95   must be the Impudence of such Libellers, as, contrary to these
authentick Evidences of their Merit, load their Characters with
the vilest and falsest Slanders? The *Examiner* falls upon them, in
his last Paper but one, with more Fury than ever; and because he
pretends his Quotations are mangled, I assure the Reader, who
100 perhaps wou'd on no account be at the drudgery to examine him,
that there is not a word quoted out of him in this Paper, but
what is his own, and made much stronger by his *Amplifications*.
'I grant, says this honest and witty Writer, that what I have said
upon occasion concerning the late Men in Power, may be call'd
105 Satyr by some unthinking People, as long as that Faction is down.
I said they were insolent to the Queen; I affirm'd they were
against a Peace; I said they had involv'd the Nation in Debts;
I have urg'd the Probability of their intending great Alterations
in Religion and Government; I said they had form'd a Design
110 against Mr. *H----y*'s Life, *&c.*' A great deal more to the same
purpose, may be found in that *Examiner*; but here's enough to give
a Taste of his Modesty and Fair-dealing. In the same Paper there's
a Passage which not only shews what a good Opinion my Friend had
of King *James*, but also what a fine Notion he and the Tories have
115 of *Justice*. 'A Person, says he, was fin'd and imprison'd for
Scandalum Magnatum, because he said the Duke of *York* was a Papist;
but when that Prince came to be King, he had the Justice immediately to release his Prisoner.' Is not that very extraordinary?
He suffer'd him to rot *unjustly* in Jail four or five Years, and
120 then was so just as to let him out. What a great loss we had in

90-1 *Representatives*] *Representative* ½°   95 as,] who 12°

----

93 *Semper Eadem*: 'Always the same', adopted by the Queen on 31 December
1702, 'it being the same that had been us'd by her Predecessor Queen *Elizabeth*,
of glorious Memory' (Boyer, *Annals*, 1703, p. 162).
99 *Quotations ... mangled*: 335.167-8.
103-10 *I ... Life*: 329.18-39, with large omissions.
115-18 *A ... Prisoner*: 330.59-63.

a Prince of such righteous Principles?

In my last *Medley* I was at the pains to bring the University of
Oxford and several good *Church*-Bishops to prove that the Tories
cannot without Apostacy forsake their Doctrines of *Passive Obedience* and *Non-Resistance*; since which I wonder'd why I went so   125
far out of the way, when the late Addresses are full of nothing
else: and 'tis very well known, the Addressers are too wise to
have given themselves so much needless trouble, had it not been
to have asserted those Doctrines against the Impeachment, which
was likely to have lessen'd their Credit; and their Leaders   130
thought it the best Card they cou'd play, to recover their lost
Power. Yet tho the Addresses have had so good an effect, the
Examiner and his Friends are afraid People will not long be impos'd on by exploded Principles, and have ungratefully left the
Addressers in the lurch, as I ever believ'd they wou'd do. For   135
they are not such Fools, but they see the general Bent of the
Nation is for the Doctrines that secur'd their *Liberty* at the
Revolution. Nevertheless I can't help thinking it hard, that my
Friend shou'd be so ill us'd, and be made to say and gainsay at
the Pleasure of every Crafty Courtier. How can it be hop'd that   140
his Writings shou'd live till the next Year, if he's forc'd to
change his Principles three or four times in this? Indeed they
have got a Man for their purpose: He'll be a Tory or a Whig, a
Jacobite or a Republican, any thing at as cheap a rate as they
can wish; yet 'tis barbarous to expose him so as they do, and   145
make him write so madly, that every body may perceive he cares
not what he says or does, if those that set him to work like it,
as doubtless they tell him they do, if that's all he has for it,
which I cannot think. I shan't repeat what he alledges is

122 *Medley*] Paper 12°   125 since ... went] but I needed not to have
gone 12°   126 when] since 12°   128-30 had ... Credit] *om.* 12°
130 and] if 12°   131 thought ... play] had not thought those Doctrines
most likely 12°   135 in the lurch] *om.* 12°   139 gainsay] unsay 12°
146 madly,] ~. 12°   146-9 that ... think.] *om.* 12°

126 *Addresses*: 209.211.
134-5 *left the Addressers*: The Examiner contradicted the High Church addressers in his Whiggish definition of passive obedience (317.98-318.137), which
acknowledges the Revolution principles of the right of rebellion in 'Case of
Necessity' and the right of Parliament to alter the succession.

150 believ'd by Nineteen Tories in Twenty; which if it were true,
    wou'd make errant Whigs of 'em; but see what the Addressers say
    on that Head, and in my choice of them take only those that were
    remarkable for being well drawn up, presented, and introduc'd; as
    that from the Men of *Radnor*, who promise Obedience according to
155 the 12th of *Charles* the Second, and against Papists and Republi-
    cans. Now the 12th of *Charles* the Second, is a High-Church Act,
    and forbids Resistance on any account whatsoever; which Law, tho
    not repeal'd, was extremely weaken'd by the Abdication. The
    Coventry Clergy tell her Majesty, they will still preach up the
160 *good old Doctrines of Passive Obedience and Non-Resistance*: And
    there were more Abhorrers of Resistance in 1710. than of Peti-
    tions in 1683. when High-Church flourish'd almost as much as she
    does now. The Chief Men of *Worcester* call the condemn'd Doctor's
    Prosecution for those *good old Doctrines*, the *Tryal of the Church.*
165 I will not rake farther into such Rubbage, referring the Reader
    to the *History of Addresses* lately publish'd, which will convince
    my Friend of his Inadvertency, in making the Tories to believe
    and practise what they there so solemnly abhor and renounce.
        In turning over those Addresses, I found that *Popery* and *Fac-*
170 *tion* were no new Terms, which I took 'em to be: They were, on the
    contrary, made use of a good while ago in a *Church*-Sense. Resis-
    tance is call'd a *Factious and Jesuitical Principle,* a *Popish and*

153 presented, and introduc'd] introduc'd, and presented 12°
169-71 *Popery ... ago*] the Whigs are now charg'd with *Popery* and *Faction* 12°

---

150 *Nineteen ... in Twenty*: 315.49-50.
154 *Radnor*: The address for Radnorshire was presented to the Queen by
Harley. It cited An Act for Safety and Preservation of His Majesties Person
and Government against Treasonable and Seditious practices and attempts (13
Car. II. Stat. I. c. 1) as a legal basis for the doctrine of passive obedience and non-resistance.
159-60 *the ... Non-Resistance*: A *Collection of the Addresses*, ii 1.
161-2 *Abhorrers ... of Petitions in 1683*: 90.46n. 1683 is presumably a slip
for 1680.
164 *Tryal*: A *Collection of the Addresses*, ii 35.
166 *the History of Addresses*: Oldmixon published the first volume of *The
History of Addresses. By One very near a Kin to the Author of a Tale of a Tub*
in 1709 and the second in 1711.
172-3 *Factious ... Assertion*: A *Collection of the Addresses*, ii 1, 2. These
phrases and others linking together the Church's enemies of the right and left
recur so frequently in the addresses of April-November 1710 as to support
Mainwaring's claim (209.211n.) that some of them were written from 'Patterns'
sent down from London (*A Collection of the Addresses*, i 3, 6, 19, 21, 30, 38,
41, 42, 43; ii 1, 2, 3, 19, 37, 38, 39, 40).

Fanatical Assertion, &c. Yet I am of the Opinion, that 'tis not
in the power of the *Examiner* to make it cleverly out, as dextrous as he is at making out things, that *Popery* and *Faction* do   175
not properly belong to the *Tories*. Not to go so far back as Dr.
Laud and his Clergy, every one knows that no longer ago than
King *Charles* the Second's Reign, the Papists and Tories were in
one Interest, and it will be a hard matter to make it separate
now. If I shou'd say *Hickes* has advanc'd several notorious Popish   180
Doctrines; that another of 'em, *Lesley*, has written for a Recon-
ciliation with the Popish *French* Church; my Friend wou'd excuse
it, by calling 'em *warm* or *ignorant* Writers, as he did in his
Whiggish Examiner. I shall therefore prove Popery upon them by
better Authority. When the Dutchess of *York* turn'd *Papist*, she   185
publish'd her Reasons, in which she tells the World, *She spake*
severally to Sheldon *Archbishop of* Canterbury, *and* Blandford
Bishop of Worcester, *who both told her there were many things in*
the Roman *Church, which it were much to be wish'd we had kept; as*
Confession, which was no doubt commanded of God: That praying for   190
the Dead was one of the antient things in Christianity: That for
their parts they did it daily, tho they wou'd not own it. And
afterwards pressing Blandford *very much upon the other Points, he*
told her that if he had been bred a Catholick, he wou'd not change
his Religion.   195
    As to *Faction*, do we not all remember the Æra of the *Memorial*;
the Sermons of the Stamp of that at St. *Paul*'s; the Tumults, Riots,

174 cleverly] clearly 12°   175 making] the making 12°   186 World,]
~; ½°   196 Æra] date 12°

---

180 *Hickes*: 289.38.
181 *Lesley*: Charles Leslie, *The Case of the Regale and of the Pontificat*
Stated, no place of publication, 1700, pp. 259-98.
183 *warm or ignorant*: 319.140.
185 *Dutchess of York*: Anne Hyde, Duchess of York, was converted to Roman
Catholicism in August 1670 (Kennett, iii 319-20).
186-95 *She ... Religion*: *The Works of* [*that Eminent and most Learned Prelate,*
Dr. Edw.] *Stillingfleet, [Late Lord Bishop of Worcester*, 6 vols., London, by
J. Heptinstall for H. Mortlock, 1710, vi 657] (½° corrected).
196 *Memorial*: *The Memorial of the Church of England* (July 1705) (264.28n.).
precipitated an unusually acrimonious debate early in the next session of
Parliament.
197 *Sermons*: 236.113n.
     Riots: 154.9n. Spencer Cowper pointed out during the trial that
Sacheverell's sermon 'had produced an Actual Rebellion' (Yale MS Osborn Files:
Sacheverell, 'Account of the Trial', ff. 19ᵛ-20).

Rebellions and Progresses, that attended and follow'd the Tryal
of *Sacheverel*? And even now the very Person who escap'd the Pil-
200 lory for printing the *Memorial*, thro the Mercy of the Court only,
has insolently reprinted it, with the Names and Eulogies of the
Authors; and I do not yet hear whether he is to be rewarded or
punish'd.

201 Eulogies] Praises 12°   202-3 rewarded or punish'd] punish'd, or rewarded 12°

---

198 *Progresses*: Immediately after he was sentenced (264.34n.), Sacheverell
was presented to a parsonage in Selattyn, Shropshire, worth £200 a year
(Hearne, ii 368, 384). In June 1710 he left London and proceeded westward to
receive, 'as his due, the homage and adoration of multitudes' (*Private Correspondence*, ii 135) in the market towns and private estates through which he
passed.
199 *Person*: The printer of *The Memorial of the Church of England* (1705),
David Edwards of Nevils Alley, Fetter Lane, who had absconded, surrendered
upon a written promise from Harley that he should be pardoned for naming the
author (Boyer, *The History*, p. 221). This he confessed he was unable to do,
but he testified that bundles of copies had been sent to three privileged
Tory Members of Parliament: Henry Pooley, John Ward, and Sir Humphrey Mack-
worth (*Parl. Hist.*, vi 512). He did not mention Dr James Drake, whom 'The
Town' knew to be the author (*The Observator*, 11-15 August 1705; BL MS Add.
4291, f. 41). He is presumably not the writer (but may be the printer) of 'An
Introductory Preface' to the 1711 edition, in which Drake, who had died in
March 1707, is eulogized.

No. 37 [Swift]   12 April 1711

The EXAMINER.

Tres species tam dissimiles, tria talia texta
Una dies dedit exitio

I Write this Paper for the Sake of the *Dissenters*, whom I take
to be the most spreading Branch of the *Whig-Party*, that *profes-
seth Christianity*, and the only one that seems to be zealous for
any particular System of it; the Bulk of those we call the *Low*
5 *Church*, being generally indifferent, and undetermin'd in that
Point; and the other Subdivisions having not yet taken either the

Motto Lucretius, *De Rerum Natura*, v 94: Such different Forms of various
Threads combin'd, | One Day pull'd down in common Ruin join'd.

Old or New Testament into their Scheme. By the *Dissenters* therefore, it will easily be understood, that I mean the *Presbyterians*,
as they include the Sects of *Anabaptists*, *Independents*, and
others, which have been melted down into them since the *Restora-*   10
tion. This Sect, in order to make it self National, having gone
so far as to raise a Rebellion, murder their King, destroy
Monarchy and the Church, was afterwards broken in pieces by its
own Divisions; which made way for the King's Return from his
Exile. However, the Zealous among them did still entertain Hopes   15
of recovering the *Dominion of Grace*; whereof I have read a remarkable Passage, in a Book Publish'd about the Year, 1661, and written by one of their own side. As one of the Regicides was going
to his Execution, a Friend ask'd him, *Whether he thought the*
Cause would Revive? He answer'd, *The* Cause *is in the Bosom of*   20
Christ, and as sure as Christ rose from the Dead, so sure will
the Cause *revive also.* And therefore the *Nonconformists* were
strictly watch'd and restrain'd by Penal Laws, during the Reign
of King *Charles* the Second; the Court and Kingdom looking on them
as a *Faction*, ready to join in any Design against the Government   25
in Church or State: And surely this was reasonable enough, while
so many continued alive, who had Voted, and Fought, and Preached
against both, and gave no Proof that they had chang'd their
Principles. The *Nonconformists* were then exactly upon the same
Foot with our *Nonjurors* now, whom we double Tax, forbid their   30
Conventicles, and keep under Hatches; without thinking our selves
possess'd with a Persecuting Spirit, because we know they want
nothing but the Power to Ruin us. This, in my Opinion, should
altogether silence the *Dissenter*'s Complaints of Persecution
under King *Charles* the Second; or make them shew us wherein they   35
differ'd, at that time, from what our *Jacobites* are now.

16 *Dominion of Grace*: cf. Swift, *Tale*, p. 201.
19-22 *Whether ... also*: 'It is recorded in *The Speeches and Prayers of some*
of the Late King's Judges, viz. Major General Harrison, Octob. 13. ..., 1660
[p. 13], and in *Rebels no Saints*, 1661, that at the execution of John Carew,
on October 15th, 1660: "One asked him if he thought there would be a resurrection of the cause? He answered, he died in the faith of that, as much as he
did that his body should rise again"' (E*1922*, ix 235).
30 *Nonjurors*: However much they contributed to 'the True Church of England',
as they called it, the non-jurors were still required by ancient prescription
to pay tithes to the parish church. Toland complained that 'the impolitick
Device of *Double Taxes* ... [was] of no *use* to the Crown' (*The Memorial of*
the State of England, 1705, p. 92).

Their Inclinations to the Church were soon discovered, when
King *James* the Second succeeded to the Crown, with whom they
unanimously join'd in its Ruin, to revenge themselves for that
40   Restraint they had most justly suffered in the foregoing Reign;
not from the Persecuting Temper of the Clergy, as their Clamors
would suggest, but the Prudence and Caution of the Legislature.
The same Indulgence against Law, was made use of by them and the
Papists, and they amicably employ'd their Power, as in Defence
45   of one Common Interest.

But the Revolution happening soon after, serv'd to wash away
the Memory of the Rebellion; upon which, the Run against *Popery*,
was, no doubt, as just and seasonable, as that of *Fanaticism*,
after the Restoration: And the Dread of *Popery*, being then our
50   latest Danger, and consequently the most fresh upon our Spirits,
all Mouths were open against That; the *Dissenters* were rewarded
with an Indulgence by Law; the Rebellion and King's Murder were
now no longer a Reproach; the former was only a Civil War, and
whoever durst call it a *Rebellion*, was a *Jacobite*, and *Friend* to
55   *France*. This was the more unexpected, because the Revolution
being wholly brought about by Church of *England* Hands, they hoped
one good Consequence of it, would be the relieving us from the
Incroachments of *Dissenters*, as well as those of *Papists*, since
both had equally Confederated towards our Ruin; and therefore,
60   when the Crown was new settled, it was hoped at least that the
rest of the Constitution would be restored. But this Affair took
a very different Turn; the *Dissenters* had just made a shift to
save a Tide, and join with the Prince of *Orange*, when they found
all was desperate with their *Protector* King *James*. And observing

---

42 *Legislature*: the Cavalier Parliament, which enacted the Clarendon Code
—the Corporation Act (1661), the Act of Uniformity (1662), the Conventicle
Act (1664), the Five Mile Act (1665)—and the Test Act (1673).
43 *Indulgence*: 126.23-4n.
52 *Indulgence by Law*: An Act for Exempting their Majestyes Protestant Subjects dissenting from the Church of England from the Penalties of certaine
Lawes (1 Gul. & Mar. c. 18) received the royal assent on 24 May 1689. Although
the word 'toleration' nowhere occurs in it, the law is called the Toleration
Act. High Churchmen, however, tended to use the word 'indulgence' ([Hoadly,]
A Collection of Several Papers Printed in the Year 1710, 1718, p. 19). So,
when the Queen in her address from the throne at the opening of Parliament on
29 November 1710 said, 'I am resolved ... to maintain the Indulgence, by Law
allowed to scrupulous Consciences' (*CJ*, xvi 403), 'Bank-Stock fell that very
Day 3 *per Cent*' (Boyer, *The Political State*, i 40; Burnet, ii 558).
55 *Revolution*: 318.124n.

a Party, then forming against the old Principles in Church and   65
State, under the Name of *Whigs* and *Low-Churchmen*, they listed
themselves of it, where they have ever since continu'd.

It is therefore, upon the Foot they now are, that I would apply
my self to them, and desire they would consider the different
Circumstances at present, from what they were under, when they   70
began their Designs against the Church and Monarchy, about
seventy Years ago. At that Juncture they made up the Body of the
Party, and whosoever join'd with them from Principles of Revenge,
Discontent, Ambition, or Love of Change, were all forc'd to shelter under their Denomination; united heartily in the Pretences of   75
a further and purer Reformation in Religion, and of advancing the
great Work (as the *Cant* was then) *that God was about to do in
these Nations*, receiv'd the Systems of Doctrine and Discipline
prescrib'd by the *Scots*, and readily took the *Covenant*; so that
there appear'd no Division among them, 'till after the common   80
Enemy was subdu'd.

But now their Case is quite otherwise, and I can hardly think
it worth being of a *Party*, upon the Terms they have been receiv'd
of late Years; for suppose the whole *Faction* should at length
succeed in their Design of destroying the Church; are they so   85
Weak to imagine, that the new Modelling of Religion, would be
put into their Hands? Would their Brethren, the *Low-Churchmen* and
Free-thinkers, submit to their *Discipline*, their *Synods* or their
Classes, and divide the Lands of Bishops, or Deans and Chapters,
among Them? How can they help observing that their Allies, in-   90
stead of pretending more Sanctity than other Men, are some of
them for levelling all Religion, and the rest for abolishing it?
Is it not manifest, that they have been treated by their

77 to] *om.* ½°   84 of] *om.* 38 8°+12°

---

76 *Reformation*: 'By a *farther Reformation* they mean a more strict Prohibi-
tion of the Use of the *Book of Common-Prayer*' (*The Moderator*, 4-7 August 1710).
   76-7 *the great Work*: cf. 'finish the good Work ... begun in the Reformation
of the Church' (*Fanatic Blunders, Faithfully Collected from their Books, Sermons, and Prayers, Containing a Gallimaufry of Enthusiastick Zeal, Farce, and
Nonsense*, London, J. Howe and J. Baker, 1710, p. 11).
   79 *the Covenant*: 'The Scotch General Assembly approved the "Solemn League
and Covenant" [establishing a national church on the Presbyterian model] on
August 17th, 1643; it was publicly taken by the House of Commons at St. Mar-
garet's, Westminster, on September 25th' (*E1922*, ix 236).
   88 *Discipline*: 344.39.

Confederates, exactly after the same manner, as they were by King
95   *James* the Second, made Instruments to ruin the Church, not for
their Sakes, but under a pretended Project of universal Freedom
in Opinion, to advance the dark Designs of those who employ them?
For, excepting the *Antimonarchical Principle*, and a few false
Notions about *Liberty*, I see but little Agreement betwixt them;
100 and even in these, I believe, it would be impossible to contrive
a Frame of Government, that would please them all, if they had it
now in their Power to try. But however, to be sure, the *Presbyterian* Institution would never obtain. For, suppose, they should in
imitation of their Predecessors, propose to have no King but our
105 Saviour Christ, the whole Clan of *Free-thinkers* would immediately
object, and refuse his Authority. Neither would their *Low-Church*
Brethren use them better, as well knowing what Enemies they are
to that Doctrine of unlimited Toleration, where-ever they are
suffer'd to Preside. So that upon the whole, I do not see, as
110 their present Circumstances stand, where the *Dissenters* can find
better Quarter, than from the Church of *England*.

Besides, I leave it to their Consideration, whether, with all
their Zeal against the Church, they ought not to shew a little
Decency, and how far it consists with their Reputation, to act in
115 concert with such Confederates. It was reckon'd a very infamous
Proceeding in the present most *Christian King*, to assist the *Turk*
against the *Emperor*: Policy, and Reasons of State, were not
allow'd sufficient Excuses, for taking Part with an *Infidel*
against a *Believer*. It is one of the *Dissenters* Quarrels against
120 the Church, that She is not enough reformed from Popery; yet they
boldly enter'd into a League with *Papists* and a *Popish Prince*, to
destroy Her. They profess much Sanctity, and object against the
wicked Lives of some of our Members; yet they have been long, and
still continue, in strict Combination with *Libertines* and *Atheists*,
125 to contrive our Ruin. What if the *Jews* should multiply, and become a formidable Party among us? Would the *Dissenters* join in
Alliance with them likewise, because they agree already in some
general Principles, and because the *Jews* are allow'd to be a

108   *Toleration*: 278.159n.
116   *King*: Louis XIV's active subvention of the infidel was frequently noticed in the news prints (Luttrell, iii 387-8, 433, 450 ff.).
120   *Church ... not enough reformed*: 127.41n.
124   *Libertines and Atheists*: innuendo: Wharton and Somers.

stiff-necked and rebellious People?

It is the Part of Wise Men to conceal their Passions, when they   130
are not in Circumstances of exerting them to Purpose: The Arts of
getting Power, and preserving Indulgence, are very different. For
the former, the reasonable Hopes of the *Dissenters*, seem to be at
an end; their Comrades, the *Whigs* and *Free-thinkers*, are just in
a Condition proper to be forsaken; and the Parliament, as well as   135
the Body of the People, will be deluded no longer. Besides, it
sometimes happens for a Cause to be exhausted and worn out, as
that of the *Whigs* in general, seems at present to be: The Nation
has had enough of it. It is as vain to hope restoring that decay'd
Interest, as for a Man of Sixty to talk of entring on a new Scene   140
of Life, that is only proper for Youth and Vigor. New Circumstances and new Men must arise, as well as new Occasions, which
are not like to happen in our Time. So that the *Dissenters* have
no Game left, at present, but to secure their *Indulgence*: In
order to which, I will be so bold to offer them some Advice.   145

First, That until some late Proceedings are a little forgot,
they would take Care not to provoke, by any Violence of Tongue
or Pen, so great a Majority, as there is now against them, nor
keep up any longer that Combination with their broken Allies, but
disperse themselves, and lie dormant against some better Opportu-   150
nity: I have shewn, they could have got no Advantage if the late
Party had prevail'd; and they will certainly lose none by its
Fall, unless thro' their own Fault. They pretend a mighty Veneration for the Queen; let them give Proof of it, by quitting the
ruin'd Interest of those who have used Her so ill; and by a due   155
Respect to the Persons she is pleas'd to trust at present with
her Affairs: When they can no longer hope to Govern, when strugg-
ling can do them no good, and may possibly hurt them, what is
left but to be Silent and Passive?

Secondly, Though there be no Law (beside that of God Almighty)   160
against *Occasional Conformity*, it wou'd be Prudence in the

139 has had] hath felt 38 8°+12°   146 are] be 38 8°+12°
_____

129 *stiff-necked ... People*: Exod. 32:9.
148 *Majority*: In Parliament the Tory majority was 2:1 (464.25n.). In the
country at large Atterbury(?) estimated that the dissenters 'do not make
a Tenth of the Nation' (*The Examiner*, 24 August 1710).
161 *against Occasional Conformity*: 90.45-6n., 89.41n. Swift was in London
in December 1703 when the second bill to prevent occasional conformity passed

Dissenters to use it as tenderly as they can: For, besides the
infamous Hypocrisy of the Thing it self, too frequent Practice
would perhaps make a Remedy necessary. And after all they have
165   said to justify themselves in this Point, it still continues hard
to conceive, how those Consciences can pretend to be scrupulous,
upon which an Employment has more Power than the Love of Unity.

In the last place, I am humbly of Opinion, That the *Dissenters*
would do well to drop that *Lesson* they have learn'd from their
170   Directors, of affecting to be under horrible Apprehensions, that
the *Tories* are in the Interests of the *Pretender*, and would be
ready to embrace the first Opportunity of inviting him over. It
is with the worst Grace in the World, that they offer to join in
the Cry upon this Article: As if those, who alone stood in the
175   Gap against all the Encroachments of *Popery* and *Arbitrary Power*,
are not more likely to keep out both, than a Set of *Schismaticks*,
who to gratify their Ambition and Revenge, did, by the meanest
Compliances, encourage and Spirit up that unfortunate Prince, to
fall upon such Measures, as must, at last, have ended in the Ruin
180   of our Liberty and Religion.

I wish those who give themselves the trouble to write to the
Examiner, *would consider whether what they send be proper for such*
a Paper to take notice of: I had one Letter last Week, written, as
I suppose, by a Divine, to desire I would offer some Reasons
185   *against a Bill now before the Parliament for* Ascertaining the
Tythe of Hops: *from which the Writer apprehends great Damage to*
the Clergy, *especially the poorer* Vicars: *If it be, as he says,*
(and he seems to argue very reasonably upon it) the Convocation
now sitting, will, no doubt, upon due Application, represent the
190   *Matter to the House of Commons; and he may expect all Justice and*

the House of Commons by a huge majority, 223:140 (*CJ*, xiv 246). His new Whig
friends 'mightily urged' him to write against the bill, but Swift procrasti-
nated. 'I know not what to think', he said, 'and therefore shall think no more'
(Swift, *Corr.*, i 39). The bill was defeated in the House of Lords, 71:59, with
fourteen Low Church bishops making up the majority (*Parl. Hist.*, vi 171), and
by this time Swift knew what to think.

163 *Hypocrisy*: 'Occasional Hypocrisy' was what High Churchmen called it
(*A Collection of the Addresses*, i 42); 'there is a vast Differences between
eating and drinking to remember the Death of Christ, and to qualifie our
selves for a Place in the *Civil Government*. Nay, Men have been driven to it to
obtain a Licence to sell Ale' (C.H., *A Letter from a Gentleman in Scotland to*
his Friend in England, against the Sacramental Test; as inconsistent with the
Union, 3rd edn., London, Benj. Bragg, 1709, p. 7).

Favour from that Great Body, *who have already appear'd so tender
of their* Rights.

*A Gentleman, likewise, who hath sent me several Letters, relat-
ing to Personal Hardships he received from some of the late Ministry; is advised to publish a Narrative of them, they being too   195
large, and not proper for this Paper.*

No. 29 [Oldmixon]   16 April 1711

The MEDLEY.
*A View of the Practices of High-Church, as to
Passive-Obedience and Non-Resistance.
Of the* Memorial.
Remarks on the Examiner.

THE *Tories* are certainly the merriest of all Mortals. They tell
you they are for *Non-Resistance* and *Passive-Obedience*, and yet
brag that we owe the *Revolution* to them. They tell you they are
for the Church, and yet most of them seldom trouble it. Are not
these fine Men to be argu'd with? 'Twou'd be just as if I shou'd   5
go about to prove the *Examiner* has been guilty of a Lye, when
there is not a Paper of his without one. I must own I know no way
of dealing with 'em, but to do as they do, be bold and positive,
assert and deny at pleasure. However, as the Whigs are not us'd
to such Reasoning, but are so foolish as to oppose Reason to Non-   10
sense, and Argument to Contradiction, I shall look a little into
the *Practices* of the *Tories*, to see how they answer their Principles. Not that I expect, after I have prov'd 'em to be the most
Antimonarchical People that ever were in *England*, they shou'd be
asham'd of their *Libels*, *Sermons*, and *Addresses*; since, it seems, 15
'tis a Prerogative of theirs to profess or abhor any Doctrine or
Opinion, as it serves a present Turn or Humour. Neither do I hope

5-9 'Twou'd ... pleasure.] *om.* 12°   9-11 as ... Contradiction,] *om.* 12°
11-22 I ... *Incorrigible*] *om.* 12°

---

3 *Revolution*: 358.55-6.

they will be asham'd of their late Pretences to *Obedience with-*
out Reserve. I don't believe 'tis possible to put 'em out of
20   countenance: And after what has been said and done within these
few months, he must be a sorry *Observer* of Men and Things, who
does not perceive they are *Incorrigible.* Only I wou'd not have
them lay these Hardships upon our Understanding and Senses, without letting 'em know we are not so weak, as not to see when they
25   wou'd impose on us: and that they themselves, while they are
preaching up *Hereditary, Irresistible,* and *Indefeasible Right,*
have been always most forward to act quite contrary, ever since
the *Reformation*; I will make use of none but good *Church-*
Authorities, and such as cannot lie under the least suspicion of
30   abetting Faction, or, which is all one, of *favouring Presbytery.*

  All the World knows, that the Reformation in its Infancy was
charg'd with breaking in upon the *Divine Right* of *Succession*:
That the Princess *Mary* was set aside, and the Lady *Jane* proclaim'd
Queen; whose Title that truly Orthodox Bishop and Martyr Dr.
35   *Ridley* own'd and vindicated, preaching at St. *Paul*'s Cross against
Queen *Mary*; tho he was so far from being a Presbyterian Bishop,
that he had a famous Contest with Bishop *Hooper* in defence of the
Habits and *Ceremonys* of the *Church.*

  When Sir *Thomas Wyat resisted* that *Popish Queen, Heylin* says,
40   *The Restitution of the Reform'd Religion was the matter princi-*
pally aim'd at; and Dr. Poynet, *Bishop of* Winchester *in King*
Edward's *days, was not only of Council in the Plot, but put him-*
self into his Camp. Again, *All they that wish'd well to the*
Reformation, were hook'd in to approve his Design.

  21 months] monthts ½°   24 are ... to] *om.* 12°   25 wou'd] *om.* 12°
30 of] *om.* ½°

  18-19 *Obedience without Reserve*: In a fine frenzy of Tory rhetoric, the
burgesses of Salisbury imagine 'throwing ourselves at Your Royal Feet, with
Hearts knowing no *Bounds* in *Loyalty*, nor *Reserve* in *Obedience*' (*A Collection
of the Addresses*, i 27).
  26 *Hereditary ... Right*: Nearly all of the Tory addresses emphasize Anne's
'*Hereditary Right*', and one of them acknowledges 'Your Majesty's Hereditary
Title and Irresistible Authority', but none of them uses 'indefeasible' (ibid.,
ii 29, 36).
  35 *Ridley*: [Peter] Heylyn, [*Ecclesia Restaurata. The*] *History of the Refor-*
m[*ation of the Church of England*, 3rd edn., London, by R.B. for H. Twyford
et al. and sold by Thomas Randes, 1674, pp. 151-62]. (½°).
  37 *Hooper*: ibid., p. 53.
  40-4 *The ... Design*: ibid., pp. 204-5.

In Queen *Elizabeth*'s Reign, the Clergy granted a Subsidy for   45
the *Laudable Enterprize of* France, as 'twas worded, and as it was
indeed, for the Assistance of Admiral *Coligny* and his *Protestant*
Army against their *Popish* King's, who had provok'd them to Arms
by Oppression and Massacres. About the same time the Clergy tax'd
themselves for the *Charges of the Low-Country Wars*: that is, for   50
Succours to the *Netherlanders* against their Sovereign *Philip* II.
of *Spain*: and Dr. *Whitgift*, Archbishop of *Canterbury*, his Brother
of *York*, the Bishops of *London, Winchester,* &c. were of the Committee appointed to consider of the Motion of the Commons in
favour of the *Netherlanders*. The Parliament was so far from being 55
puritanically inclin'd, that this very Assembly made a Law to
inflict Death or Banishment on those who absented themselves a
Month from the Service of the Church, and exercis'd those *Whole-*
som Severitys so highly extol'd by the condemn'd Doctor and the
modern Tories.   60
What need we add the Assistance King *James* I. gave the *Dutch*
and *French* Protestants, or the *Fast* appointed in King *Charles* I's
Reign, and the Form of Prayer for the Success of the *Rochellers,*
bravely resisting the Tyranny of *Lewis* XIII? The two unfortunate
Expeditions to assist those Citizens, are enough to prove that   65
King *Charles the Martyr* was not always of opinion that Subjects
must be *passively Obedient.*

61 add] ∼, ½°

---

49 *Clergy*: In March 1585 the House of Commons requested the Lords to join
with them in support of Leicester's expedition to the Lowlands. The Spiritual
Lords resolved to contribute two shillings in the pound of their temporalities
towards armed resistance against Philip II of Spain ([Sir Simon] D'Ewes, *The*
Journal[s of All the Parliaments during the Reign of Queen Elizabeth, ed. Paul
Bowes, London, for John Starkey, 1682, pp. 386-7]) (½°).
58-9 *Wholesom Severitys*: Sacheverell, *The Perils of False Brethren, both in*
Church, and State, 1709, p. 19.
62 *Fast*: A *Forme of Prayer, Necessary to bee used in these dangerous times*
of Warre: Wherein we are appointed to Fast, according to His Maiesties Procla-
mation; For the preservation of His Maiestie, and His Realmes, and all re-
formed Churches, London, by Bonham Norton and John Bill, 1628 (STC 16547).
63 *Rochellers*: 'for the reliefe of some of our distressed brethren, our
Gracious Sovereigne [Charles I] ... is mooved ... to send foorth a Fleete to
Sea for their reliefe' (*A Prayer to bee publiquely used at the going forth of*
the Fleete this present yeere, 1628, [London, by Bonham Norton and John Bill,
1628] (STC 16546). '[Charles I's] Opinion ... about *Subjects defending their*
Religion and Liberties by Force of Arms, appear'd in the business of *Rochell'*
(James Welwood, *Memoirs*, London, for Tim. Goodwin, 1700, p. 79).

     As to the Practices of the Tories in K. *Charles* II's time, they
had no opportunity to shew how they approv'd of Resistance, but
70 in assisting the House of *Braganza* against that of *Austria*, who
had the *Divine Right* to the *Portugal* Succession; and in owning
Don *Pedro*, who had depos'd his elder Brother Don *Alphonso*, to be
King. The want of Occasion to do otherwise, made 'em pretend the
more Zeal for their Doctrine of Non-Resistance; and they hardly
75 preach'd any other all that Reign, and as much of the next as was
favourable to them. But when the Prince of *Orange*, by their Invitation, came hither to *resist* King *James*, one wou'd have thought
such a strange Principle had never been heard of in *England*. At
Nottingham 'tis declar'd, *To* Resist *a Tyrant, that makes his Will*
80 *his Law, they justly esteem no Rebellion, but a necessary Defence,*
And her Royal Highness, under the Guard of the Bishop of *London*,
joining with the Gentlemen who made this *Declaration*. If the
Tories were capable of Modesty, they wou'd never have nam'd a
Doctrine again, which is so plainly against all that was done
85 there and elsewhere to advance the Revolution; as the Associations

   80 *Defence,*] ~. ½° 12°   82 *Declaration.* If] ~; if ½° 12°

---

     68 *Charles II*: With the aid of English regiments sent by Charles II the
Portuguese defeated Don John of Austria at Ameixial in June 1663 and secured
the throne for the new Bragança dynasty. ([John Colbatch], *An Account of the
Court of Portugal, under the Reign of the present King Dom Pedro II*, London,
for Thomas Bennet, 1700, pp. [2]126-36).
     72 *Don Pedro*: The English envoy, Sir Robert Southwell, took an active part
in the *coup d'état* of October 1667 by which Dom Pedro deposed and imprisoned
his incompetent elder brother, Afonso VI (ibid., pp. 89-101, [2]153-9).
     79-80 *To ... Defence*: 'Declaration of the Assembly at Nottingham to assist
the Prince of Orange', 22 November 1688 (*A Collection of State Tracts, Publish'd on Occasion of the Late Revolution in 1688*, 3 vols., London, [John
Darby,] 1705-7, i 80).
     81 *her Royal Highness*: The Princess Anne took flight from London on the
night of 25 November 1688, during her father's absence. She fled first to the
hiding place of the suspended Bishop of London, Henry Compton, who had been
a soldier before he was ordained, and she rode into Nottingham on 1 December
'attended by that noble Prelate in his Buff-Coat, and ... other Military
Accoutrements' at the head of about forty deserted troopers (Echard, iii 921).
     84 *Doctrine*: 220.34n.
     85 *Associations*: From the landing at Torbay William of Orange marched his
army to Exeter, where 'Sir *Edward Seymour* sent for Dr. *Burnet*, and ask'd him,
Why they were a Rope of Sand, why they had not an ASSOCIATION?' One was drawn
up binding the signers 'to stick firm' to the cause 'till our *Religion, Laws*
and *Liberties* are so far secured to us in a Free Parliament, that they shall
be no more in Danger of falling under *Popery* and *Slavery* ... This *Association*
was sent and sign'd in many Places, and particularly by many in the University
of *Oxford*' (Echard, iii 912-13).

at *Exeter* and other places, especially that of the University of *Oxford*.

I will not further tire the Reader with Things to fresh in his memory. 'Tis sometimes the Boast of *High-Church*, that they did all before the *Convention* sat. *The Revolution was wholly brought*   90 *about by Church-of*-England *Hands*, says the *Examiner*. And what did they do then? Why they were for *Desertion*, and not *Abdication*; as the E. of *N.* said in the Debate at the famous Conference about the word *Abdicate*. They were for *securing the Nation against the Return of King* James *into this Kingdom, and the Lords wou'd*   95 *therefore concur with the Commons in any Act that shou'd be thought necessary to prevent such his Return.* All that the Tories can object to this, is, That as he went away, so he might be kept out without any *Resistance.* I shall conclude what I have to say of their Practices, with the Testimony of Dr. *Atterbury*, in his   100 *Rights of an* English *Convocation*; wherein he urges, among other things, *That the Convocation sitting with the Parliament, might be useful to the State as well as to the Church, that so they may be in heart, and always at hand to stand up with them in behalf*

89 *Boast*: 'what is to be remember'd is, That the chief Actors were all Church of *England* Men, and proceeded, as Bishop *Sprat* terms it, *upon Church of* England *Principles*' (ibid., iii 920).
90-1 *The ... Hands*: 358.55-6.
93 *Conference*: On 4 February 1689, during the debate on the bill sent down from the Commons that became the Act of Settlement, the Lords substituted the word 'deserted' for 'abdicated' and struck out the clause declaring the throne to be vacant. The next day, at a conference in the Painted Chamber, 'the first that spoke on the Lords Side was the Earl of *Nottingham*, who alledg'd, "That the main Reason of the Change of the Word *Abdicate*, was upon the Account of the Consequences drawn in the Conclusion of the Vote of the Commons, *That the Throne is thereby Vacant*; by which Expression the Commons seem'd to mean that the Throne was so Vacant as to null the Succession in the Hereditary Line, and so all the Heirs to be cut off, which the Lords said wou'd make the Crown *Elective*".' Ultimately the Lords had to give way on both of these amendments (ibid., iii 966; *LJ*, xiv 115-18; Eveline Cruickshanks *et al.*, *Bulletin of the Institute of Historical Research*, liii (May 1980), 59-65).
94-7 *securing ... Return*: Since no account of the free conference of 5 February 1689 was printed, Oldmixon must be quoting from one of the 'Written Copies ... of no good Authority' that were 'dispersed about the Town' (Edmund Bohun, *The History of the Desertion, or An Account of all the Publick Affairs in England, from the beginning of September 1688. to the Twelfth of February following*, London, for Ric. Chiswell, 1689, p. 125; cf. *LJ*, xiv 117).
102-6 *the ... Tyranny*: Atterbury, *The Rights, Powers, and Privileges of an English Convocation*, 2nd edn., 1701, pp. 136-7. The first clause is paraphrased: what Atterbury wrote was 'the *Commons Spiritual* think it very Proper and Reasonable, that they should ... have a Recourse to the *Commons Temporal*; whose Interests in the State ... parallel ... Theirs in the Church'.

105   *of Liberty, when it shall be attack'd, and to* resist *a growing
      Tyranny,* &c. I might have fill'd many Papers with the like In-
      stances; but this sure is sufficient to convince any Man of
      Common Sense, that all the Tories profess of *Passive-Obedience*
      and *Non-Resistance*, is Affectation and Grimace, and that we shall
110   make a very pretty Figure in Story, for having so stale a Cheat
      so often impos'd on us by them.

         What I am going to mention, is not that I am at all surpriz'd,
      but the Extravagance of it at this time is not to be past by,
      because the Tories are the Persons who set up for *Unlimited*
115   *Loyalty*; while the poor *Whigs*, who for six years had serv'd the
      Queen and Country with so much Zeal and Success, are branded with
      Faction. Those that will run over the History of the *Memorial*,
      will soon see who are the truly factious, which, as I hinted in
      the last, is now insolently reprinted, with the names of the
120   Authors, and a vile Panegyrick on them, after her Majesty and the
      Parliament had declar'd it to be a seditious and scandalous Libel.
      It comes out now with the Boast of a new and glorious *Æra, the
      Flourishing Year of the Church*; which is a Proof of the Deference
      they pay to her Majesty's Opinion and Pleasure. I shall not take
125   notice of the Vote of the Lords and Commons, that the Church was
      in a most safe and flourishing Condition five years ago, when
      that Libel was first publish'd, nor of their Address upon it, for
      *punishing the Authors and Spreaders of those seditious and scan-
      dalous Reports*: For my Friend and his Party will tell me, they

   112-13 that ... not] *om.* 12°   119-20 with ... them] *om.* 12°
   122 *Æra*] Date 12°   125 Vote] Votes 12°

   ───────

   117 *Faction*: 343.22.
        the History of the Memorial: Within a few days of the publication of
   The Memorial of the Church of England (July 1705), the author, printer, and
   publisher were ordered to be apprehended (Hearne, i 4). In August 1705 it was
   presented as a false, scandalous, and traitorous libel by the grand jury of
   Middlesex county and ordered to be burnt by the common hangman (Luttrell,
   v 588). In December, after Parliament had resumed, it was voted a seditious
   and scandalous libel and rewards of £250 were offered for the apprehension of
   the author and printer (*LJ*, xviii 44; Steele, i 523). In spite of all this a
   second edition of 'that nasty pamphlet' was advertised in *The Examiner*, 29
   March 1711, and published two days later with the following imprint: 'Printed
   in the flourishing Year of the Church. M.DCC.XI' (HMC *Portland MSS*, iv 316;
   355.196n.).
        126 *in ... Condition*: 263.23n.
        128-9 *punishing ... Reports*: *LJ*, xviii 49.

are now no Parliament, and they care for none but the present.   130
Wherefore I shall put them in mind of her Majesty's Sentiments
of that Pamphlet, to which her Speech in Parliament at the opening of that Session had Reference in this *Paragraph.*

*I mention this with a little more Warmth, because there have
not been wanting some so very malicious, as even in Print to sug-*   135
gest the Church of England, *as by Law establish'd, to be in
Danger,* &c.

And her Royal Proclamation afterwards speaks more directly to
this Point:

Whereas the said seditious and scandalous Reports have been   140
*greatly promoted and spread, by the Printing and Publishing of
a malicious and seditious Libel, intitled,* The Memorial of the
Church of *England,* &c. Notwithstanding which, the *Faction* have,
with an Insolence that is not to be parallel'd, again publish'd
this very Libel, and as yet with Impunity. Now let any one judg   145
who are the *Factious,* who are those that deal disrespectfully by
the Queen, and to whom the Charge laid by the *Examiner* and his
Brethren against the Whigs, does properly belong. If I should
mention the Libel's having been burnt by the Hangman, on the
Presentment of the Grand Jury at the *Old Bailey,* who had the   150
Thanks of that Court for it, wou'd not the Tories presently cry
out, They were *Fanaticks and Schismaticks*; which is a short
Answer with them to any thing? But the Sense of that Jury is so
just, I can't help repeating part of their *Presentment: We, with*

---

142 *intitled*] iutitled ½°   143-4 have, ... parallel'd,] have 12°
146 are those] those ½° 12°

134-7 *I ... Danger*: *LJ*, xviii 8.
140-3 *Whereas ... England*: *CJ*, xv 57; Steele, i 523.
146 *Factious*: 331.101.
147 *Queen*: 329.28.
151 *that Court*: the court of quarter-sessions.
154-60 *We ... Libel*: While these words do appear in *The Presentment of the
Grand Jury* (Boyer, *Annals*, 1706, pp. 175-6) there is no other evidence that
James Drake was fined and pilloried for libel. *The History of the Last Parliament* (1702) was presented for libel but Drake was acquitted (*LJ*, xvii 122-3;
Luttrell, v 389). His 'Prefatory Dedication' to *Historia Anglo-Scotica* (1703)
was ordered by the Scottish Parliament to be burnt by the common hangman
(*APS*, xi 66; cf. Defoe, *The History of the Union between England and Scotland*,
London, for John Stockdale, 1786, p. 75). He was never officially discovered
to be the author of *The Memorial of the Church of England* (1705), but in October 1706 he was arrested for some paragraphs in his paper, *Mercurius Politicus,*

155 *the utmost Indignation and Resentment, do present one Book lately*
     printed by a notorious Criminal (convicted in this Court for
     Printing and Publishing a seditious and treasonable Libel, for
     which he was fin'd and pillory'd, and is now fled from Justice)
     intitled, The Memorial of the Church of *England,* &c. *to be a*
160 *false, scandalous and traitorous Libel.* It stole into the World
     at first, disown'd by the very Fathers of it, and had nothing
     after all to recommend it but Falshoods and Impudence; and it
     should never have been mention'd here, were it not to shew what
     dutiful Subjects they are, how free from any Imputations of Sedi-
165 tion, and how ready to punish all those, who, in defiance of her
     Majesty's Commands, dare print and publish so villanous and
     treasonable a Libel.

     When the *Examiner* told us in his Paper three Weeks ago, the
     Tories were of Opinion, That *as the Crown may be su'd, so the*
170 *King's Officers may be lawfully resisted*; I was sure he had gone
     too far: and tho some of his Patrons might perhaps, from the
     prejudice of Education, approve of his *Republican* Tenets; yet
     I thought it impossible for such Doctrine as that to go down with
     a Primitive and Orthodox *Convocation.* Accordingly he was forc'd
175 to recant immediately, and to tell us a Paper or two after, *The*
     Prince ought not to be resisted or disobey'd upon any Pretence

     166 villanous and] *om.* 12°

No. 29, 18 September 1705. He was tried in the Guildhall before Lord Chief
Justice Holt, but a flaw was found in the information and Drake was acquitted
(Hearne, i 186, Luttrell, vi 16, 43, 105). Sir James Montagu, the Attorney-
General, lodged a writ of error in the House of Lords, however, but Drake died
before the appeal could be heard (Luttrell, vi 121, 145).
   161 *Fathers*: Oldmixon believed that *The Memorial of the Church of England*
was 'written by Dr. *Drake*, with the Assistance of Mr. *Pooley* in Matters of Law,
and one of the discarded Ministers in Matters of Politicks' (Oldmixon, *The
Life*, p. 104). The discarded minister is Buckingham, who had been removed as
Lord Privy Seal some three months before the publication of *The Memorial of
the Church of England* (July 1705). Henry Pooley or Poley (*c.*1653-1707) was a
Tory Member for Eye (1689-95), West Looe (1703-5), and Ipswich (1705-7). 'He
was a Man of a very despicable Presence, being deform'd to the Highest Degree.
But ... he was accounted one of the best common Lawyers in England, & for that
reason suspected to have had a Hand in Penning *The Memorial of the Church of
England*' (Hearne, i 203).
   169-70 *the Crown ... resisted*: 317.113-16.
   175-7 *The ... whatsoever*: 347.152-4. Oldmixon scores here not only because the Examiner appears to contradict himself but also because there are
real contradictions in Swift's role of High Church Whig: 'Of all *Whigs* a Whig-
Clergyman is the greatest Monster, as the Abuse of the best Things is always

whatsoever; which was a little too much to come from the same Pen
in a Fortnight's time; but this is nothing. If he is bid to write
for the Toleration, he'll do it; if for the Statute *de Hæret.*
Comburend. 'tis all one. For I must do him the Justice to own   180
I have been strangely mistaken in him, and that in his way he's
one of the most impartial Writers upon Earth. He'll write for or
against any Party, he cares not which, according as he has Instructions from those that make use of him.

I could not help laughing at the Simplicity of my Friend, when   185
with a grave Air he refers it to the Reader to determine, whether
a *wise* Prince ought not to trust the *Tories* with his *Person and*
Affairs. Who can suspect that those Hands, which ruin'd all that
ever trusted them, are not preferable to all others, when recommended by so honest and judicious a Person as the *Examiner? Who*   190
has compar'd our Constitution with the Monarchies and Republicks,
whereof we meet with so many Accounts in antient Story, and with
those at present too: Who has consider'd our Religion; who has
likewise examin'd the Genius and Disposition of the People, and
turn'd his Reflections upon those two great Divisions of Whig and   195
Tory. He says all this with as much Assurance, as if he had really
been reading these seven or eight Months; whereas, in truth,
there's never a Book in *English*, wherein his History or Politicks
are to be met with. He comes by both at a cheaper rate, having
all from his own Invention, or that of his Friends. I will desire   200
but one Favour from him for the many Obligations he has receiv'd
from me, and that is, to put this Question to the first Man he

182-4 He'll ... him.] *om.* 12°   185 I] *no paragraph* But I 12°
190 Person as the *Examiner*?] Person? 12°   196 says ... Assurance,] goes
further on with the same Assurance. 12°   196-200 as if ... Friends] *om.* 12°
200-1 I ... him] But instead of transcribing any more from him, I will only
desire one favour 12°   202 and that] which 12°   202-3 to put ... meets]
That he will please in his next to answer this Question, fairly 12°

---

the worst' (*The Character and Principles of the Present Set of Whigs*, London,
for John Morphew, 1711, p. 31). On the crucial issue of resistance Swift's
view is impeccably Whiggish (5.92), but on the question of conformity Swift
is as rigid as Sacheverell (147.93-4). Oldmixon enforces his point by omitting
the words 'neither the Person, nor lawful Authority of', before 'the Prince'.
   179-80 *de Hæret. Comburend.*: This statute (2 Hen. IV c. 15), by which Lol-
lards were publicly burned, was repealed and replaced by another (25 Hen. VIII.
c. 14), by which Protestants were burned in the reign of Mary (1553-8).
   186-8 *a ... Affairs*: 348.175-7.
   191-6 *compar'd ... Tory*: 343.2-8.

meets, stated in his own words: *Which is the Faction that has
rais'd and strengthen'd it self by Incidents and Intrigues, and
205   by deceiving the People with false Representations?* I will not
insinuate who is meant, and yet I dare promise my self the Answer
from any one would be to the Confusion of my Friend, if he was
not so harden'd as he is, and the best Reply I could make to his
last *Examiner* but one: For as I have often observ'd, when he
210   writes ill of any body, he certainly brings his Friends in, as a
Blunderer will always do; and I shall begin to think some People
not half so cunning as they make themselves, if they imploy him
much longer.

Having before paid his Compliment to the Whigs, he now aukardly
215   cajoles the Dissenters, as if he hop'd to make such Monsters of
them as the new City Projector, an *Anabaptist Tory*; which however is not the wildest of his *Chimeras*. To shew you how well he
is learned in the Doctrines and Definitions of our *Sects*, he says,
by the *Dissenters* he *means the Presbyterians, as they include the*
220   *Anabaptists*, there having been always so great an Agreement between them. To let us see what an Historian he is, he affirms the
Presbyterians murder'd the King; tho as it generally happens with
him, the quite contrary is entirely true, and none but he ever
did or ever will deny, that the Presbyterians not only voted but
225   fought against it; that Thousands of them dy'd in that Quarrel,
and that to them, in a great measure, was owing the *Restoration*
of the Prince, who in return, as my Friend writes himself,
strictly watch'd and restrain'd them by Penal Laws, looking on
them as a Faction ready to destroy the Government they had them-
230   selves *restor'd.* This is the History and Argument we are to have
from him. Just like what he says, when he would prove to us, that
the *Presbyterians*, who brought in King *Charles*, were on the same

---

206-42 I will ... Mind] *om.* 12°   215-16 such ... as] ½°0 IU^a them
like ½°L IU^b TxU   *om.* 12°   216 an *Anabaptist Tory*] ½°0 IU^a *om.* ½°L
IU^b TxU 12°

203-5 *Faction ... Representations*: 343.22-3.
216 *Projector*: Sacheverell was 'very rudely treated' when he appeared in
the City to vote for the Tory candidates for directors of the Bank (*The Post-
Boy*, 19 April 1711; 380.20n.).
219-20 *Presbyterians ... Anabaptists*: 357.8-9.
222 *Presbyterians ... King*: 357.8-12.
228-9 *strictly ... Government*: 357.23-5.
232-3 *the same ... Nonjurors*: 357.29-30.

foot in that Reign, as the *Nonjurors* are, who would bring in the
Pretender in this. The Reader has seen how more than once he has
represented himself as a Man that cannot lye, and yet in his very   235
last Paper he asserts, that the Dissenters *unanimously join'd*
with the Papists to ruin the Church in King *James*'s time. A very
pious and learned Prelate, in a late Speech, does indeed make
honourable mention of them, for their hearty *joining with* the
Church in *opposing* the Measures of that *Popish* Court; but the   240
Examiner thinks his word will go farther with his Party than the
best Bishop's in *England*, and truly I am of his Mind.

236-7 *unanimously ... Church*: Oldmixon patches together three phrases to
produce this 'mangl'd Quotation' (358.39, 44, 360.95).
238 *Prelate*: William Wake (*The Bishop of Lincoln's and the Bishop of Norwich's Speeches in the House of Lords, March the 17th [1710]*, London, for John
Morphew, 1710, p. 36).

No. 38 [Swift]   19 April 1711

The EXAMINER.

Semper causæ eventorum magis movent quam ipsa eventa.

I Am glad to observe, that several among the *Whigs* have begun
very much to change their Language of late. The Style is now
among the reasonable part of them, when they meet a Man in Business, or a Member of Parliament; *Well, Gentlemen, if you go on as*
you have hitherto done, we shall no longer have any Pretence to   5
Complain. They find, it seems, that there have been yet no Overtures made to bring in the *Pretender*, nor any preparatory Steps
towards it. They read no enslaving Votes, nor Bills brought in to
endanger the Subject. The Indulgence to scrupulous Consciences,

Motto Cicero, *Ad Atticum*, ix 5: We are always more moved at the Causes of
Events than at the Events themselves.
7 *Pretender*: Swift did not know that the Pretender at this time was bringing the strongest pressure to bear on the Queen, his half-sister, to invite
him to England as her successor. Nor did Swift know either that Harley was in
communication with Saint-Germain or that what Harley communicated was recognized to be nothing but 'pump and banter', 'only ... fair words' (Macpherson,
Original Papers, ii 218-27; HMC *Stuart MSS*, i 277).
9 *Indulgence*: 22.66.

10 is again confirm'd from the Throne, inviolably preserv'd, and not
the least Whisper offer'd that may affect it. All Care is taken
to support the War; Supplies chearfully granted, and Funds readily
subscrib'd to, in spight of the little Arts made use of to discredit them. The just Resentments of some, which are laudable in
15 themselves, and which at another Juncture it might be proper to
give way to, have been soften'd or diverted by the Calmness of
others. So that upon the Article of present Management, I do not
see how any Objection of Weight can well be rais'd.

However, our Adversaries still alledge, that this great Success
20 was wholly unexpected, and out of all probable View. That in publick Affairs, we ought least of all others, to judge by Events;
That the Attempt of changing a Ministry, during the Difficulties
of a long War, was rash and inconsiderate: That if the Qu---
were disposed by Her Inclinations, or from any Personal dislike,
25 for such a Change, it might have been done with more Safety, in
a Time of Peace: That if it had miscarried by any of those Incidents, which in all Appearance might have intervened, the Consequences would perhaps have ruined the whole Confederacy; and
therefore, however it hath now succeeded, the Experiment was too
30 dangerous to try.

But this is what we can by no means allow them. We never will
admit Rashness or Chance to have produc'd all this Harmony and
Order. 'Tis visible to the World, that the several Steps towards
this Change were slowly taken, and with the utmost Caution. The
35 *Movers* observ'd as they went on, how Matters would bear, and
advanc'd no farther at first, than so as they might be able to
stop or go back, if Circumstances were not Mature. Things were
grown to such a Height, that it was no longer the Question,
whether a Person who aim'd at an Employment, were a *Whig* or a
40 *Tory*, much less, whether he had Merit or proper Abilities for

14 Resentments] Resentmens ½°

---

12 *Supplies*: 333.121n.
Funds: cf. 'all this Noise and Clamour of the Funds falling, and the
danger of credit, was nothing but a Stock-jobbing Business' (Davenant, *Sir
Thomas Double at Court, and in High Preferments*, 1710, p. 85; Hill, pp. 407-
11).
13 *Arts*: 193.43n.
14 *some*: innuendo: the October Club (273.33n.).
34 *Change*: 2.29n.

what he pretended to: He must owe his Preferment only to the
Favourites; and the Crown was so far from *Nominating*, that they
would not allow it a *Negative*. This, the Qu--- was resolv'd no
longer to endure, and began to break into their *Prescription*, by
bestowing one or two Places of Consequence, without consulting   45
Her *Ephori*; after they had fix'd them for others, and concluded
as usually, that all their Business was to signify their Pleasure
to Her M-----y. But tho' the Persons the Qu--- had chosen, were
such as no Objection could well be rais'd against upon the score
of Party; yet the *Oligarchy* took the Alarm; their Sovereign   50
Authority was, it seems, called in Question; they grew into Anger
and Discontent, as if their undoubted Rights were violated. All
former Obligations to their Sovereign now became cancell'd; and
they put themselves upon the Foot of People, who were hardly us'd
after the most eminent Services.   55

   I believe all Men, who know any thing in Politicks, will agree,
that a Prince thus treated, by those he has most confided in, and
perpetually loaded with his Favours, ought to extricate himself
as soon as possible; and is then only blameable in his choice of
Time, when he defers one Minute after it is in his Power; because,   60
from the monstrous Encroachments of exorbitant Avarice and Ambition, he cannot tell how long it may continue to be so. And it
will be found, upon enquiring into History, that most of those
Princes, who have been ruin'd by Favourites, have owed their Misfortune to the neglect of early Remedies; deferring to struggle   65
'till they were quite Sunk.

   The Whigs are every Day cursing the ungovernable Rage, the
haughty Pride, and unsatiable Covetousness of a *certain Person*,
as the Cause of their Fall; and are apt to tell their Thoughts,

42 *Crown*: 17.179n.
44 *Prescription*: cf. 144.44.
46 *Ephori*: 'The *Ephori* in *Sparta* were at first only certain Persons deputed
by the Kings to judge in Civil Matters, while *They* were employ'd in the Wars.
These Men, at several times, usurp'd the absolute Authority, and were as cruel
Tyrants as any in their Age' (Swift, *Discourse*, p. 86).
50 *Alarm*: 'Upon the fall of that great minister and favourite [Godolphin],
that whole party ... seemed to expect the worst' (Swift, *Prose*, viii 118)
(E*1922*, ix 242).
61-2 *Avarice and Ambition*: innuendo: Marlborough.
68 *Person*: 'The Duchess of Marlborough, whose haughty conduct to the queen
occasioned the rupture betwixt her majesty and the administration formed under
the duchess's influence, and composed chiefly of her allies'(E*1814*, iv.77).

70 that *one single Removal* might have set all things right. But the
    Interests of that single Person, were found, upon Experience, so
    complicated and woven with the rest, by *Love*, by *Awe*, by *Marriage*,
    by *Alliance*, that they would rather confound Heaven and Earth,
    than dissolve such an Union.

75   I have always heard and understood, that a King of *England*,
    possess'd of his People's Hearts, at the Head of a Free Parlia-
    ment, and in full Agreement with a great Majority, made the true
    Figure in the World that such a Monarch ought to do, and pursued
    the real Interest of Himself and his Kingdom. Will they allow Her
80 M-----y to be in those Circumstances at present? And was it not
    plain by the Addresses sent from all Parts of the Island, and by
    the visible Disposition of the People, that such a Parliament
    would undoubtedly be chosen? And so it prov'd, without the Court's
    using any Arts to influence Elections.

85   What People then, are these in a corner, to whom the Constitu-
    tion must truckle? If the whole Nations Credit cannot supply
    Funds for the War, without humble Application from the entire
    Legislature to a few *Retailers* of Mony, 'tis high time we should
    sue for a Peace. What new Maxims are these, which neither We nor
90 our Forefathers ever heard of before, and which no wise Institu-
    tion would ever allow? Must our Laws from henceforward pass the
    Bank and *East-India* Company, or have their *Royal Assent* before
    they are in force?

        To hear some of these worthy Reasoners talking of *Credit*, that
95 she is so nice, so squeamish, so capricious; you would think they
    were describing a Lady troubl'd with Vapors or the Cholick, to be

---

    70 *Removal*: Although she had been estranged from the Queen since September
1708, the Duchess was not forced to resign her offices (53.107n., 57.198n.) until 17 January 1711.
    74 *Union*: Harley's animadversions on 'the family' who 'share amongst them
the wealth of the nation' may be reflected here (Harley, 'Plaine English',
p. 105). Swift believed that the Duchess was related to Godolphin by 'Love'
(Swift, *Prose*, viii 111), to Marlborough by 'Marriage', to Godolphin by
'Alliance' (the marriage of her eldest daughter, Henrietta, to Francis, Lord
Ryalton, Godolphin's only son), and to Sunderland by 'Alliance' (his marriage
to her second daughter, Ann, 'the little Whig').
    81 *Addresses*: 181.86n.
    84 *Elections*: 181.85n.
    88 *Retailers of Mony*: 347.133n.
    96 *troubl'd with Vapors*: After the failure of *The Whig-Examiner* in Octo-
ber 1710 Addison had 'resolved to observe an exact Neutrality between the
Whigs and Tories' in *The Spectator*, but broke his resolve to support the Whigs

only removed by a *Course of Steel*, and *swallowing a bullet*. By
the narrowness of their Thoughts, one would imagine they conceiv'd the World to be no wider than *Exchange Alley*. 'Tis probable they may have such a sickly Dame among them, and 'tis well   100
if she has no worse Diseases, considering what Hands she passes
through. But the *National Credit* is of another Complexion; of
sound Health, and an even Temper, her Life and Existence being a
Quintessence drawn from the Vitals of the whole Kingdom. And we
find these *Mony-Politicians*, after all their Noise, to be of the   105
same Opinion, by the Court they paid Her, when she lately appear'd
to them in the form of a *Lottery*.

As to that mighty Error in Politicks, they charge upon the
Qu---, for changing Her Ministry in the Heighth of a War, I suppose, it is only look'd upon as an Error under a Whigish Admini-   110
stration; otherwise, the late King has much to answer for, who
did it pretty frequently. And it is well known, that the late
Ministry of *Famous Memory*, was brought in during this present War,
only with this Circumstance, that two or three of the Chief, did

97 and] or 38 8°+12°   109 War,] ~. ½°   111 has] had 38 8°+12°
113 this] the 38 8°+12°

---

in *The Spectator*, No. 3, 3 March 1711, on 'the Decay of Publick Credit', which
includes this phrase.
97 *Steel*: Iron or steel filings taken internally was one of the quack
medicines of the day. Sir Richard Blackmore prescribed 'spa-water and ... tincture of steel daily' for the Revd John Shower. Swift tried the same course for
his headaches, but gave away the spa water and took only the 'nasty steel
drops' (Swift, *Journal*, p. 622).
    bullet: Is this an early form of 'to bite the bullet' (to behave cour-
ageously), of which the first occurrence in *OED Supplement* is 1891?
100 *sickly*: cf. 'POOR CREDIT! ... I hardly knew her she was so lean, so
pale; look'd so sickly' (*Review*, 1 February 1711).
107 *Lottery*: 'The lottery bill received the royal assent on the 6th March,
and advertisement was made, that payments would begin to be received on Tues-
day the 13th. But when the receivers met for this purpose on the morning of
that day, it was found that £.27,000 had been subscribed at the Bank of England above the first payment of the whole sum of £.1,500,000. So that the
lottery was more than full before the books were opened. But such a cry was
raised against the directors of the bank and stock-jobbers, for having en-
grossed the fund to the disappointment of the public, that they found themselves obliged to give up one-fifth part of the tickets purchased. As these
monied men were chiefly Whigs, Swift's sarcasm is easily understood' (E*1814*,
iv 79; cf. Dickson, pp. 71-4; Hill, p. 408).
113 *Ministry*: War was declared on France on 4 May 1702 and 'The Queen
appointed a ministry with Lord Godolphin as lord treasurer in ... May-July
1702' (E*1922*, ix 244).
114 *two or three*: 259.97n. '"Godolphin's Ministry" ... began in 1702 almost
entirely Tory, and ended in 1710 almost wholly Whig' (Trevelyan, i 187).

115 first change their own Principles, and then took in suitable Companions.

But however, I see no reason why the *Tories* shou'd not value
their Wisdom by Events, as well as the *Whigs*. Nothing was ever
thought a more precipitate rash Counsel, than that of *altering*
120 *the Coin* at the Juncture it was done; yet the Prudence of the
Undertaking was sufficiently justify'd by the Success. Perhaps it
will be said, that the Attempt was necessary, because the whole
Species of Mony, was so grievously Clip'd and Counterfeit. And,
is not Her Majesty's Authority as Sacred as Her Coin? and has not
125 that been most scandalously *Clip'd* and *Mangl'd*, and often *Counter-
feited* too?

It is another grievous Complaint of the Whigs, that their late
Friends, and the whole Party, are treated with abundance of
Severity in Print, and in particular by the *Examiner*. They think
130 it hard, that when they are wholly depriv'd of Power, hated by
the People, and out of all hope of re-establishing themselves,
their Infirmities should be so often display'd, in order to render them yet more odious to Mankind. This is what they employ
their Writers to set forth in their Papers of the Week; and it is
135 Humersome enough to observe one Page taken up in railing at the
Examiner for his Invectives against a discarded Ministry; and the
other side fill'd with the falsest and vilest Abuses, against
those who are now in the highest Power and Credit with their
Sovereign, and whose least Breath would scatter them into Silence
140 and Obscurity. However, tho' I have indeed often wondred to see
so much Licentiousness taken and connived at, and am sure it
would not be suffer'd in any other Country of Christendom; yet I
never once invok'd the Assistance of the *Goal* or the *Pillory*,
which upon the least Provocation, was the usual Style during their
145 Tyranny. There hath not pass'd a Week these twenty Years without

120 *Coin*: 'The clipping of coin had become so widespread that it was absolutely imperative that steps should be taken to readjust matters. It was resolved, therefore, in 1695, to call in all light money and recoin it. The
matter was placed in charge of the then chancellor of the exchequer, Charles
Montague, afterwards Earl of Halifax, and he, with the assistance of Sir Isaac
Newton, successfully accomplished the very arduous task. It cost the nation
about £2,200,000, and a considerable inconvenience owing to lack of coins'
(*E1922*, ix 245).
   134 *Writers*: Mainwaring, Oldmixon, Ridpath, and de Fonvive are the chief
ones.
   141 *Licentiousness*: 275.110-276.113.

some malicious Paper, scatter'd in every Coffee-House by the
Emissaries of that Party, whether it were *down* or *up*. I believe,
they will not pretend to object the same thing to Us. Nor do I
remember any constant Weekly Paper, with Reflections on the late
Ministry or J-nto. They have many weak, defenceless Parts, they   150
have not been us'd to a regular Attack, and therefore it is that
they are so ill able to endure one, when it comes to be their
Turn. So that they complain more of a few Months Truths from us,
than we did of all their Scandal and Malice, for twice as many
Years.   155

I cannot forbear observing upon this Occasion, that those
worthy Authors I am speaking of, seem to me, not fairly to represent the Sentiments of their Party; who in disputing with us, do
generally give up several of the late M-----ry, and freely own
many of their Failings. They confess the monstrous *Debt upon the*   160
Navy, to have been caused by most scandalous Mismanagement; they
allow the Insolence of *some*, and the *Avarice* of *others*, to have
been insupportable: But these Gentlemen are most liberal in their
Praises to those Persons, and upon those very Articles, where
their wisest Friends give up the Point. They gravely tell us,   165
that *such a one* was the most faithful Servant ever any Prince
had; *another* the most dutiful, a third the most generous, and a
fourth of the greatest Integrity. So that I look upon these Champions, rather as retain'd by a *Cabal* than a *Party*, which I desire
the reasonable Men among them would please to consider.   170

150 J-nto] J--n--to ½° Junta 38 8° *Junta* 38 12°   154 Scandal and
Malice,] Scandal and Malice 12° Lies, and 38 8°+12°

146 *Paper*: William Pittis was forced to abandon *Heraclitus Ridens* in March
1704 to avoid prosecution for libel and James Drake died in March 1707 during
libel proceedings against *Mercurius Politicus*. The widely read Tory paper,
John Dyer's weekly newsletter, survived by circulating only in handwritten
copies. But Swift forgets *The Rehearsal*, of which Leslie turned out 398 numbers from August 1704 to March 1709.
160-1 *Debt upon the Navy*: On 30 September 1710 the debt upon the Navy exceeded £6,000,000 (*CJ*, xvi 415) and with six per cent Navy bills trading at
discounts of 26-30 per cent, City bankers, who held £4,000,000 of them, were
clamouring for payment (Dickson, pp. 64, 362-3).
162 *Insolence of some*: innuendo: Sunderland.
    Avarice of others: innuendo: Marlborough.
166 *such a one*: the Duchess of Marlborough (74.31-2).
167-8 *another ... a third ... a fourth*: innuendo: Sunderland, Marlborough,
and Wharton?

No. 30 [Mainwaring and Oldmixon]   23 April 1711

The MEDLEY.

Of the City's Recovery from the late Phrensy.
A proper Punishment for the Incendiary that occasion'd it.
Some Instructions for the Examiner.
Whether the Whigs are hated by the People.

THE Philosopher *Bias* being ask'd, *What is hard to bear couragi-*
ously? answer'd, *A Change, when it proves to be for the worse.*
It is not my Intention to inlarge upon that Subject now, but to
entertain the Reader with something more agreeable, I mean, *a*
5   *Change for the better,* or rather *a perfect Recovery,* which is the
present happy Condition of our Great and Flourishing City.
    I have often thought it very ridiculous in me, and such other
able Authors, to go about to prove seriously that Plenty is a
Blessing; and yet this is what the *Tories* are every day putting
10 upon us. They require us to make out, That *Liberty* increases
Happiness, That *Trade* is *Riches,* and *Riches* the *Strength* of a
Nation; sweetly intimating at the same time, that they think
Liberty is Rebellion, *Trade* Artifice and Tumult, and *Riches* the
Ruin of the *Landed Interest.* What they said of Liberty was
15 answer'd by so many Writers, that I wou'd not concern my self in
that Dispute; but I cou'd never help making some Remarks on the
great Indifference they shew'd for *Trade* and *Mony,* which they
always treated like Philosophers, and seem'd to look down upon
with the utmost Contempt. At last the Secret is come out; for by
20 their late impotent Struggle to *usurp* the *Direction* of the two

1-2 *What ... worse*: Diogenes Laertius, *Life of Bias,* i 5 86.
19 *Contempt*: 129.84-130.95.
20 *impotent Struggle*: 'At the beginning of the parliamentary session of
1710-11 there had been noisy threats from the crowded Tory back benches that
"the power of the House of Commons" would be used to eject the existing
directors [of the Bank of England] before the end of their term. But Harley
knew better than to lend any official encouragement to so arbitrary an action:
"if that should happen", wrote Arthur Mainwaring, "the Bank wou'd fall to
forty the next day". The prime minister recognised that if change was to come
it must come from within. And so in [April] 1711 each political party for the
first time submitted its own list of 24 proposed directors to the share-
holders. The Tories ... resorted to feverish house-to-house canvassing, and

Great Bodies in the City, 'tis plain, that Trade and Mony are
both against the *Tories*. That Party was therefore in the right to
declare War against Trade and Mony; yet upon this occasion, no
Arts nor Industry were wanting to gain an *unnatural Majority*, as
my Friend the *Examiner* has it upon another Subject. Some thought-   25
less *Whigs* were got over to their Party; their own small Stocks
were *split* and subdivided; several indirect Practices were us'd;
and above all, great Care was taken that their *Fool*, who had
rais'd such a Ferment last year, and carry'd all before him,
should appear in full Lustre at these Elections. But alas! to the   30
never-ceasing Grief of his Friends and Patrons, his Reception did
not answer the measure of their Hopes and Expectations; for which
I refer you to the melancholy Account of honest *Abel* himself.

'On Thursday and Friday last (being the Days appointed for
chusing Governors and Directors for the *Bank* of *England*) Dr.   35
Sacheverel was very rudely treated at the aforesaid Place, altho
the Doctor had as much Right to appear there, and give his Vote,
as any other Member of that Court.'

The Doctor rudely treated! What a Change is here! But this is
no more than I always expected. And, as I take him to be the last   40
Man of the whole Order that will ever be prefer'd, under any
Ministry; so I am much deceiv'd, if some signal Punishment does
not yet overtake him. I remember, when he was infatuating the
Nation, it was an Expression we frequently met with, That in any
other Country, such a *Fellow would have been boil'd in Oil*: But   45
I have thought of a cooler Punishment, which is the worst that
I wish may ever be inflicted on him; the *Muscovites* have a way of
punishing Offenders, by placing them under a Spout of cold Water,
which falls from a great height upon them without ceasing. I

30 But] ~, ½°

---

even ... recruited the assistance of Sacheverell, who bought £500 of Bank
stock to qualify for a vote' (Holmes, p. 173). But not one Tory candidate was
elected.
   24 *unnatural Majority*: 332.102.
   34-8 *On ... Court*: *The Post-Boy*, 19 April 1711 (½°).
   45 *Fellow ... Oil*: The more common fate imagined for Sacheverell was roasting, as reflected in the title, *The Roasting of a Parson*, and first line 'If
you have a fat Parson that's fleshy and new', of two popular songs of 1710.

50   should be glad to see this flaming Divine under such an Execution;
      the rather, because it would bear some relation to the Nature of
      his Offence, which was inflaming the Nation, intoxicating the
      Rabble, and setting our Women all a madding. For such a Criminal
      as this, no Correction can be properer than *Cooling*.
55   But this is only hinted by the By: In the mean time I wou'd now
      advise the *Examiner* to return peaceably to his Panegyricks on the
      Landed Interest, and to propagate the Division between *Land* and
      Mony, as if we were not yet sufficiently divided. Instead of say-
      ing, The *Church* has nine Parts in ten of our *Mony* and *Trade*, and
60   that nineteen in twenty of our wealthy Citizens are *stanch* Tories;
      he has nothing now to do but to cry up his *Church Interest*, and
      his *Land-Interest*: And let him repeat those words as often as he
      will, and make the most of them. Let him give into the Opinion of
      a famous Senator of his Party, who being inform'd that the *Turky*
65   Fleet were lost in a Storm, swore, *D---- him, he was glad of it;*
      for the Citizens grew so proud, there wou'd be no humbling of
      them till they were poor: or of another Leading Man among them,
      who being sollicited by the *West-India* Merchants and Planters to
      favour them in an Affair they had depending in Parliament, curs'd
70   them and their Plantations, swearing, *He wish'd them all at the*
      Devil, for they were good for nothing but to be a Receptacle for
      Fanaticks. And while he thus sticks to the *Church* and the *Land*,
      let him never fear the Reflection of *Macchiavel*, who says fool-
      ishly and rudely, That *Gentlemen are a sort of People who are*
75   *useless Members of Society, and the Plagues of Princes or Common-*
      wealths. This Saying of his is a Proof to me, that he was not the
      Politician he was taken for; unless you can suppose he confin'd

    53 *Women*: Sacheverell was so popular with women that they lined up at West-
minster Hall every morning at seven to secure seats for the trial (*Wentworth*
Papers, p. 113).
    59 *nine Parts in ten*: 68.51-2, 82.27, etc.
    60 *nineteen in twenty*: 315.49.
    65-7 *D--- ... poor*: The reference may be to the Great Storm of November
1703, in which the losses to the merchant fleet were so great that they were
not even estimated (Trevelyan, i 308), but the cynical Tory remains unidentified.
    70-2 *He ... Fanaticks*: The Tory leader is unidentified; cf. 'The most
material Objections to our Colonies in *America* are ... That they are a retreat
to Men of Notions opposite to the Religion of their Country' (Davenant, *Dis-*
courses on the Publick Revenues, 1698, ii 195).
    74-6 *Gentlemen ... Commonwealths*: Machiavelli, *Discourses*, i 55 (½° cor-
rected).

his Reflections to his own pitiful Republick of *Pisa*. But then to
be so blunt, so positive and general, is what he will always be
blam'd for in good Hereditary Monarchies, and with very just
reason: For why shou'd any poor *Pisan* of *Italy* pretend to give   80
the Character of a ruddy *Octobrian* of *West-Saxony*? Such *Gentlemen* ought not to fall under the Lash of rude Pens; and I hope my
Friend will vindicate them from such Aspersions. *They, the useless Members of Society! They, the Plagues of Princes or Commonwealths*! Here let my Friend display his Eloquence: Let him shew,   85
That they who are possess'd of the *Landed Interest*, are the only
Support of Government; That the rest are all Mechanicks, and as
he himself observes, *frame Rules for the Administration, with the
Spirit of Shop-keepers*; That a Man, who has a single Life in a
Copy-hold of 300 *l. per ann.* is fitter to be trusted than one   90
worth 30000 *l.* in Mony: That considering the natural Disadvantages
we lie under as to Commerce; how we are straiten'd for want of
Ports, how poor in Manufactures and Minerals, how bare of Timber
for Ship-building; how ignorant in that Art, and in Navigation;
how safe without Fleets, in our Militia; Trade is of all others   95
the thing we ought least to be concern'd for: That we ought to
leave the Trouble of it to any People that will take it, except
our Enemies the *Dutch*, and not be plagu'd with so mean and impertinent a thing our selves: And lastly, That we ought to employ our
whole Thoughts to keep up Corn at 10 *s.* a Bushel, and oblige other 100
Folks to fetch it as fast as we would have them. What can we in
Great Britain do better? This would make it needless to fight any
more for *Spain* in hopes of getting some Silver, since we shou'd
soon have enough of our own: and this wou'd for ever silence the
Whigs, who still are clamouring against the *Land-Interest*; and   105
wou'd so effectually unite that with the *Church-Interest*, that
they wou'd soon be more than a Match for all the other *Interests*

81 *Octobrian of West-Saxony*: a member of the October Club (273.33n.) from
Wessex, or the West Country.
87 *Support of Government*: cf. 'We are plagued here with an October Club,
that is, a set of above a hundred parliament-men of the country, who drink
October beer at home, and meet every evening at a tavern near the parliament,
to consult affairs, and drive things on to extreams against the Whigs, to call
the old ministry to account, and get off five or six heads ... The ministry is
for gentler measures' (Swift, *Journal*, pp. 194-5).
88-9 *frame ... Shop-keepers*: 130.92.
100 *Corn*: The price of wheat in nine market towns in March 1711 ranged
from 4*s.*3*d.* to 6*s.*4*d.* a bushel (*The Post-Boy*, 22-4 March 1711).

in the Universe.

In the mean time, while my Friend is proving all this, I hope
110 the poor Whigs, who are said by him (*Exam. Numb.* 38.) *to be wholly
depriv'd of Power, hated by the People, and out of all Hope of re-
establishing themselves*; may be allow'd to pursue their true Interest, and that of their Country, as far as they are capable of
knowing it. Whether they will ever *regain Power*, is more than I
115 can tell; but 'tis plain by the *Elections* already mention'd, and
by the late Choice of an Alderman in one of the City-Wards, which
had been long in Tory Hands, that they are not *hated by the
People*: And therefore my Friend, according to custom, took an ill
time to blunder upon that Expression. But he can't help it; and
120 I easily forgive him that, and every thing he has said, except
this one Sentence in the same Paper: *They complain more of a few
months TRUTHS from us, than we did of all their Scandal*, &c.
Truths from him! This is surely enough to make any Man merry and
sick at once. It is well known, that the first eight years of her
125 M-----y's Reign were so glorious, that there is no Parallel to be
found for them in History. At home we enjoy'd Safety and Plenty,
and a most miraculous Credit: Abroad, a continu'd Series of Victory and Success; yet the whole Business of this Teller of Truths
has been to prove that those Ministers *were hated by God and Man*,
130 by whom the greatest things had been done that are recorded in
any History. This is what he has over and over affirm'd; and now
when in the Course of almost forty Papers, he is known by all
impartial Readers, never to have advanc'd one true Fact, he decently concludes, that the Whigs are offended at his *TRUTHS*. Well!
135 I wish him long Life, as one does any Rarity in Nature, the like
of which one expects to see no more; and I desire him at his
leisure to think of the late wonderful Change in the City, and
then to remember one of his own Jests (*Exam. Numb.* 25) when he

110 him] ~, ½°

110-12 *wholly ... themselves*: 378.130-1.
116 *Alderman*: In the City election of 13 April 1711 Sir Henry Furnese, a
Whig, was elected alderman of the ward of Bridge-Within, which had been held
since 1700 by the infamous Tory, Sir Charles Duncombe (*POAS*, Yale, vi 261-3,
301-8).
121-2 *They ... Scandal*: 379.153-4.
129 *hated by God and Man*: 52.75.

laughs at the *Ruin'd Party, for hoping, that* some late Things that
have happen'd were *only occasion'd by a short Madness of the*   140
People, from which they will recover. I beg the favour of him to
reflect seriously upon this Passage; and as he must needs be
a Person of exquisite Judgment, I beseech him to weigh attentively
whether this Wit of his be as good now, as it was six months ago.

139-41 *the ... recover*: 178.9-22.

No. 39 [Swift]   26 April 1711

The EXAMINER.

Indignum est in eâ civitate, quæ legibus continetur, discedi a legibus.

I Have been often considering how it comes to pass, that the Dexterity of Mankind in Evil, should always outgrow, not only the
Prudence and Caution of private Persons, but the continual Expedients of the wisest Laws contriv'd to prevent it. I cannot imagine
a Knave to possess a greater share of natural Wit or Genius, than   5
an honest Man. I have known very notable Sharpers at Play, who
upon all other Occasions, were as great Dunces, as Human Shape
can well allow; and I believe, the same might be observ'd among
the other Knots of Thieves and Pick-pockets, about this Town. The
Proposition however is certainly true, and to be confirm'd by an   10
hundred Instances. A Scrivener, an Attorney, a Stock-jobber, and
many other *Retailers of Fraud*, shall not only be able to over-
reach others, much wiser than themselves, but find out new Inventions, to elude the Force of any Law made against them. I suppose,
the Reason of this may be, that as the *Aggressor* is said to have   15
generally the Advantage of the *Defender*; So the Makers of the Law,
which is to defend our Rights, have usually not so much Industry
or Vigour, as those whose Interest leads them to attack it.

Motto Cicero, *Pro Cluentio*, 146: It is shameful and unworthy in a State,
whose Support and Preservation is founded on Laws, that the Laws should be
rendered useless, and evaded.

Besides, it rarely happens that Men are rewarded by the Publick
20 for their Justice and Virtue; neither do those who act upon such
Principles, expect any Recompence 'till the next World: Whereas
Fraud, where it succeeds, gives present Pay; and this is allow'd
the greatest Spur imaginable both to Labour and Invention. When
a Law is made to stop some growing Evil, the Wits of those, whose
25 Interest it is to break it with Secrecy or Impunity, are immediately at Work; and even among those who pretend to fairer Characters, many would gladly find means to avoid, what they would not
be thought to violate. They desire to reap the Advantage, if
possible, without the Shame, or at least, without the Danger.
30 This Art is what I take that dextrous Race of Men, sprung up soon
after the Revolution, to have Study'd with great Application ever
since, and to have arriv'd at great Perfection in it. According
to the Doctrine of some *Romish* Casuists, they have found out *Quam
prope ad peccatum sine peccato possint accedere.* They can tell
35 how to go within an Inch of an Impeachment, and yet come back
untoucht. They know what degree of Corruption will just forfeit
an Employment, and whether the Bribe you receive be sufficient to
set you right, and put something in your Pocket besides. How much
to a Peny, you may safely cheat the Qu--n, whether forty, fifty
40 or sixty *per Cent.* according to the Station you are in, and the
Dispositions of the Persons in Office, below and above you. They
have computed the Price you may securely take or give for a Place,
or what part of the Salary you ought to reserve. They can dis-
creetly distribute Five Hundred Pounds in a small Burrough, with-
45 out any Danger from the Statutes, against bribing Elections. They
can manage a Bargain for an Office, by a third, fourth or fifth
Hand, so that you shall not know whom to accuse; and win a Thousand Guineas at Play, in spight of the Dice, and send away the
Loser satisfy'd: They can pass the most exorbitant Accounts,
50 overpay the Creditor with half his Demands, and sink the rest.
It would be endless to relate, or rather indeed impossible to

47 and] they can 38 8°+12°

---

19 *rewarded*: cf. 'these People [the Lilliputians] thought it a prodigious
Defect of Policy among us, when I told them that our Laws were enforced only
by Penalties, without any Mention of Reward' (Swift, *Prose*, xi 43).
30 *that dextrous Race*: 6.98n., 7.112n.
33-4 *Quam ... accedere*: Rushworth, iv 185.

discover, the several Arts which curious Men have found out to
enrich themselves, by defrauding the Publick, in defiance of the
Law. The Military Men, both by Sea and Land, have equally cultivated this most useful Science: Neither hath it been altogether   55
neglected by the other Sex; of which, on the contrary, I could
produce an Instance, that would make ours blush to be so far outdone.

  Besides, to confess the Truth, our Laws themselves are extremely
defective in many Articles, which I take to be one ill Effect of   60
our best Possession, Liberty. Some Years ago, the Ambassador of
a great Prince was Arrested, and Outrages committed on his Person
in our Streets, without any possibility of Redress from *West-*
minster-Hall, or the Prerogative of the Sovereign; and the Legislature was forc'd to provide a Remedy against the like Evil in   65
Times to come. A Commissioner of the Stamp'd Paper was lately
discovered to have notoriously cheated the Publick of great Sums
for many Years, by Counterfeiting the Stamps, which the Law had
made Capital. But the Aggravation of his Crime, prov'd to be the
Cause that sav'd his Life; and that additional heightning Circum-   70
stance of betraying his Trust, was found to be a legal Defence.

  57 *an Instance*: innuendo: the Duchess of Marlborough. She remarked that
'Women signify nothing unless they are the mistress of a Prince or a first
Minister'. And she herself, who 'had long been [Godolphin's] Mistress', con-
ducted the 'Sale of Offices and Places of Trust' in the Godolphin ministry
(*The Opinions of Sarah Duchess-Dowager of Marlborough Published from Original
MSS.*, Edinburgh, 1788, p. 120; Swift, *Prose*, viii 111; Pittis, *The Case of the
Church of England's Memorial Fairly Stated*, London, 1705, p. 36; *An Account of
the Conduct*, p. 122).
  61 *Ambassador*: 'In September 1707, [Andrei Artemonowitz] Matveof, the
Russian ambassador, having taken leave at court, one Morton, a laceman, with
some of his other creditors, fearing he was about to leave the kingdom without satisfying their claims, had him arrested in the open street, and forced
to a spunging house. Czar Peter the Great was violent and inexorable in his
demand of satisfaction for this indignity; nor was it possible for a long
time to convince him that the creditors had, however imprudently, only
availed themselves of the means of recovering their debts allowed them by the
laws of the country; and that, therefore, no legal punishment could be inflicted on them. At length, in 1709, the Czar consented to rest satisfied with
the queen's formal excuses, on account of the insufficiency of the laws; and
an act [7 Ann. c. 12] was past to secure the persons, equipages, and effects,
of ambassadors, from such indignities in future' (E*1814*, iv 85).
  66 *Commissioner of the Stamp'd Paper*: 'He was a justice of the peace
[for Middlesex], and worth twenty thousand pounds. His name was [Richard]
Dyet. His trial took place at the Old Bailey 13 January 1710-11. See *Journal
to Stella*, 3d October, 1710' (E*1814*, iv 85). Although he stole £100,000 and
was indicted for a felony, 'he was acquitted of the indictment, it being only
a breach of trust' (Luttrell, vi 678).

I am assur'd, that the notorious Cheat of the Brewers at *Portsmouth*, detected about two Months ago in Parliament, cannot by any Law now in Force, be punished in any Degree, equal to the Guilt
75 and Infamy of it. Nay, what is almost incredible, had *Guiscard* surviv'd his detestable Attempt upon Mr. *Harley*'s Person, all the inflaming Circumstances of the Fact, would not have sufficed, in the Opinion of many Lawyers, to have punish'd him with Death; and the Publick must have lain under this *Dilemma*, either to Condemn
80 him by a Law, *ex post Facto* (which would have been of dangerous Consequence, and from an ignominious Precedent) or undergo the Mortification to see the greatest Villain upon Earth escape unpunished, to the infinite Triumph and Delight of *Popery* and *Faction*. But even this is not to be wondred at, when we consider,
85 that of all the Insolences offer'd to the Qu--- since the Act of Indemnity, (at least, that ever came to my Ears) I can hardly instance above two or three, which, by the Letter of the Law could amount to High Treason.

From these Defects in our Laws, and the want of some discre-
90 tionary Power safely lodg'd, to exert upon Emergencies; as well as from the great Acquirements of able Men, to elude the Penalties of those Laws they break, it is no wonder, the Injuries done to the Publick, are so seldom redress'd. But besides, no Individual Suffers, by any wrong he does to the Commonwealth, in proportion
95 to the Advantage he gains by doing it. There are seven or eight Millions who contribute to the Loss, while the whole Gain is sunk among a few. The Damage suffer'd by the Publick, is not so immediately or heavily felt by particular Persons, and the Zeal of

74 any] a 38 8°+12°   92 wonder,] wonder that 38 8°+12°

---

72 *Brewers*: 228.49n.
75 *Guiscard*: 'It being the Opinion of many Lawyers, That if Mr. *de Guiscard* surviv'd his barbarous Attempt upon Mr. *Harley*, all the heightning Circumstances of that horrid Fact would not have been sufficient to punish him with Death; it was at first design'd to supply that Defect in our Laws, by inserting in the Bill before-mention'd [an Act to make an Attempt on the Life of a Privy Councellor in the Execution of his Office to be a Felony without Benefit of Clergy (9 Ann. c. 21)], a Clause to attaint him; but he dying of his Wounds, it was thought fit to leave out that Clause: Which how just soever in itself, would have been a dangerous Precedent, to punish a Man by a Law, *ex post facto*' (Boyer, *Annals*, 1711, p. 344).
83-4 *Popery and Faction*: 320.198.
85 *Insolences*: 217.179n.
85-6 *Act of Indemnity*: 72.153n.

Prosecution is apt to drop and be lost among Numbers.

But imagine a Set of Politicians for many Years at the Head of   100
Affairs, the Game visibly their own, and by Consequence acting
with great Security: May not these be sometimes tempted to forget
their Caution, by length of Time, by excess of Avarice and Ambition, by the Insolence or Violence of their Nature, or perhaps by
a meer Contempt for their Adversaries? May not such Motives as   105
these, put them often upon Actions directly against the Law, such
as no Evasions can be found for, and which will lay them fully
open to the Vengeance of a prevailing Interest, whenever they are
out of Power? 'Tis answer'd in the Affirmative. And here we cannot refuse the late M-----y their due Praises, who foreseeing a   110
Storm, provided for their own Safety, by two admirable Expedients,
by which, with great Prudence, they have escap'd the Punishments
due to pernicious Councils and corrupt Management. The first, was
to procure, under Pretences hardly specious, a general Act of
Indemnity, which cuts off all Impeachments. The second, was yet   115
more refin'd: Suppose, for Instance, a Counsel is to be pursu'd,
which is necessary to carry on the dangerous Designs of a prevailing Party, to preserve them in Power, to gratify the unmeasurable
Appetites of a few *Leaders*, Civil and Military, though by hazard-
ing the Ruin of the whole Nation: This Council, desperate in it   120
self, unpresidented in the Nature of it, they procure a Majority
to form into an Address, which makes it look like the Sense of
the Nation. Under that Shelter they carry on their Work, and lie
secure against After-reckonings.

I must be so free to tell my Meaning in this, that among other   125
Things, I understand it of the Address made to the Qu--- about

123 their] the 38 8°+12°

103-4 *Avarice and Ambition*: innuendo: Marlborough.
116-24 *Suppose ... After-reckonings*: These lines are quoted in *A Letter to
the People of England, Occasion'd by the Letter to the Dissenters*, London, for
John Oldsworth, 1714, pp. 74-5.
126 *Address*: 'The Address of both Houses to the Queen, presented on December 23rd, 1707, urged: "That ... no peace can be honourable or safe ... if
Spain, the West Indies, or any part of the Spanish Monarchy, be suffered to
remain under the power of the House of Bourbon" [*LJ*, xviii 398-9]. The resolutions as carried in the House of Lords on December 19th [*LJ*, xviii 395] did
not include the words "or any part of the Spanish Monarchy"; these words
were introduced on a motion by Somers who was in the chair when the Select
Committee met on December 20th to embody the resolutions in proper form. The

three Years ago, to desire that Her M-----y would not consent to
a Peace, without the entire Restitution of *Sp--n*. A Proceeding,
which to People abroad, must look like the highest Strain of
130 Temerity, Folly, and Gasconade. But we at Home, who allow the
Promoters of that Advice to be no Fools, can easily comprehend
the Depth and Mystery of it. They were assur'd by this Means, to
pin down the War upon us, consequently to encrease their own Power
and Wealth, and multiply Difficulties on the Qu--- and Kingdom,
135 'till they had fix'd their Party too firmly to be shaken, whenever they should find themselves dispos'd to reverse their Address,
and give us leave to wish for a Peace.

If any Man entertains a more favourable Opinion of this monstrous Step in Politicks; I would ask him what we must do, in Case
140 we find it impossible to recover *Spain*? Those among the *Whigs* who
believe a GOD, will confess, that the Events of War lie in his
Hands; and the rest of them, who acknowledge no such Power, will
allow, that *Fortune* hath too great a share in the good or ill Success of Military Actions, to let a wise Man reason upon them, as
145 if they were entirely in his Power. If Providence shall think fit
to refuse Success to our Arms, with how ill a Grace, with what
Shame and Confusion, shall we be oblig'd to recant that precipitate Address, unless the World will be so Charitable to consider,
that Parliaments among us, differ as much as Princes, and that by
150 the fatal Conjunction of many unhappy Circumstances, it is very
possible for our Island to be represented sometimes by those who
have the least Pretensions to it. So little Truth or Justice there
is in what some pretend to advance, that the Actions of former
Senates, ought always to be treated with Respect by the latter;
155 that those Assemblies are all equally Venerable, and no one to be

138 entertains] entertain 38 8°+12°   152 Pretensions to it.] Pretensions?
38 8°+12°

---

altered resolution was quickly hurried through the Lords and agreed to by the
Commons ... By this bold move Somers prolonged the war indefinitely' (E*1922*,
ix 251-2).
130 *Temerity, Folly, and Gasconade*: Mainwaring mocks this phrase in *Reflections upon the Examiner's Scandalous Peace*, London, for A. Baldwin, 1711, p.
17) (which was pirated(?) as *A Few Words upon the Examiner's Scandalous Peace*,
with no publisher's imprint) and in *A Letter to a Member of the October-Club:
Shewing, That to yield Spain to the Duke of Anjou by a Peace, wou'd be the
Ruin of Great Britain*, London, for A. Baldwin, 1711, pp. 55, 60.
149-56 *Parliaments ... another*: This may reply to 349.21-7.

preferr'd before another: By which Argument, the Parliament that
began the Rebellion against King *Charles the First*, voted his
Trial, and appointed his Murderers, ought to be remembred with
Respect.

But to return from this Digression; 'tis very plain, that con-   160
sidering the Defectiveness of our Laws, the variety of Cases, the
weakness of the Prerogative, the Power or the Cunning of ill-
designing Men, it is possible, that many great Abuses may be
visibly committed, which cannot be legally Punish'd: Especially
if we add to this, that some Enquiries might probably involve   165
those, whom upon other Accounts, it is not thought convenient to
disturb. Therefore, it is very false Reasoning, especially in the
Management of Publick Affairs, to argue that Men are Innocent,
because the Law hath not pronounc'd them Guilty.

I am apt to think, it was to supply such Defects as these, that   170
Satyr was first introduc'd into the World; whereby those whom
neither Religion, nor natural Virtue, nor fear of Punishment,
were able to keep within the Bounds of their Duty, might be with-
held by the Shame of having their Crimes expos'd to open View in
the strongest Colours, and themselves rendred odious to Mankind. 175
Perhaps all this may be little regarded by such harden'd and abandoned Natures as I have to deal with; but, next to taming or binding a Savage-Animal, the best Service you can do the Neighbourhood,
is to give them warning, either to Arm themselves, or not come in
its way.   180

Could I have hoped for any Signs of Remorse from the Leaders of
that Faction, I should very gladly have chang'd my Style, and forgot or pass'd by their Million of Enormities. But they are every
Day more fond of discovering their impotent Zeal and Malice: witness their Conduct in the City about a Fortnight ago, which had   185
no other End imaginable, beside that of perplexing our Affairs,
and endeavouring to make Things desperate, that Themselves may
be thought Necessary. While they continue in this frantick Mood,
I shall not forbear to treat them as they deserve; that is to
say, as the inveterate, irreconcilable Enemies to our Country and 190
its Constitution.

185 *Conduct*: 381.34-8.

No. 31 [Mainwaring]   30 April 1711

The MEDLEY

A Prayer of Timoleon, *about Freedom of Speech.*
The Torys *for a new Partition-Treaty.*
The Whigs *mad to look after their Interest.*
Why the Torys *are against Liberty and Property.*

WE read in the Life of *Timoleon*, that when he was extremely rail'd
at by *Demænetus*, he said, *He had at length obtain'd his Desire;*
for he had always beg'd of the immortal Gods, that they wou'd
restore the People to a State of Freedom, in which every Man might
5 *safely say what he pleas'd of any body else.* Such a State of Freedom it must be own'd, we happily enjoy: and as this *Demænetus* was,
in all likelihood, a saucy, bold, inventing Wretch, of the Character of our *Examiner*; so *Timoleon*, the Person he abus'd, was one,
that by his Great Actions had preserv'd his Native Country from
10 Ruin and Slavery. In the last Paper of this most hardned Scribler,
notice being *taken of the Address made to the* Q---- *about three*
Years ago, to desire that her M------ *wou'd not consent to a*
Peace without the entire Restitution of Spain; he adds, That *we*
at Home, who allow the Promoters of that Advice to be no Fools,
15 *can easily comprehend the Depth and Mystery of it: They were*
assur'd by this means, to pin down the War upon us, consequently
to encrease their own Power and Wealth, and multiply Difficulties
in the Q---- *and Kingdom.* If one did not know the *Examiner*, one
wou'd conclude from this, that the Address he mentions, had been
20 contriv'd and carry'd on by that Person chiefly of the late Ministry, whom he so often accuses of a Design *to perpetuate the War:*

7 **Wretch**] Author 12°   10 **most hardned Scribler**] Author 12°

2-5 *He ... else*: Corn[elius] Nep[os, *Timoleon*, v 3] (½°).
11-18 *the Address ... Kingdom*: 389.126-390.134.
20 *that Person*: Godolphin, whom Mainwaring can defend against designing
'to perpetuate the War' (116.140) because the Lord Treasurer only learned of
Somers' 'No Peace without Spain' clause when it was reported out of committee
(389.126n.).
21 *to perpetuate the War*: 9.173-4, 116.140.

Whereas, in truth, that Minister knew nothing of it, till it was
over; which his Friends complain'd of, and thought him not well
us'd. And, I believe, it will be found upon enquiry, that the
chief Promoter of it was not so much as one of the Ministry: yet   25
after all the Reasonings of this vain Writer, it will be hard to
convince any impartial Man, that this was *so monstrous a Step in
Politicks*; or that it appear'd so impossible a Thing at that time
to recover all *Spain*, as I am afraid it is grown to be now. Whatever this Author may invent and impose upon the World, Mankind   30
will still have their Thoughts at liberty, and all indifferent
Persons will make their own Conclusions, whether if there had been
no Change any where of Measures and Councils, we had not before
this been in the full Possession of *Spain*.

    There is another Paragraph in the same Paper, which 'tis impos- 35
sible to pass over without some Remark: He is outragious against
the *Leaders of a certain Faction, for discovering their impotent
Zeal and Malice in their Conduct in the City about a Fortnight
ago*, which, he says, had no *other End imaginable beside that of
perplexing* OUR Affairs. I do believe indeed that what happen'd   40
lately in the City, *did perplex the Affairs* of some People, and
broke a very hopeful Scheme for overturning all Business and
Credit: Yet how those honest Citizens happen'd to be ʼguilty of
Malice, that harmlessly voted according to their Opinions; or how
their Zeal can be said to be *Impotent*, which carry'd the Elec-   45
tions by a Majority of Two to one, is past my discovering. But
the *Examiner* says, *While they continue in this frantick Mood,
he shall not forbear to treat them as they deserve; that is to
say, as the inveterate, irreconcilable Enemies to our Country
and its Constitution*. What he means by their *continuing in this*   50
frantick Mood, I can no more find out than what I mention'd
before; unless he reckons Men mad, that look after their Estates.
But in his next Paragraph he fully explains his own Meaning,

    28 *Politicks*;] ∼. 12°   28-9 or ... now.] *om.* 12°

---

    25 *Promoter*: Somers, who had no position in the Godolphin ministry until
25 November 1708, when he was appointed Lord President of the council.
    27-8 *monstrous ... Politicks*: 390.138-9.
    37-40 *the ... Affairs*: 391.181-6.
    40-1 *what happen'd lately in the City*: 380.20.
    47-50 *While ... Constitution*: 391.188-91.

where he boldly calls them the *inveterate Enemies of their*
55 *Country*; for which most impudent Slander and Calumny, I have
more Charity than to wish that this Hireling *shou'd be treated
as he deserves*. I wou'd only for his Punishment have that one
Condition added to the Liberty we now enjoy, of speaking or
writing what we think; I mean, that we shou'd not be allow'd
60 that Privilege, but in what *we believe to be the Truth*. Some
may say, that wou'd be too severe, and amount to no less than
silencing the Gentleman: since all that ever he will be order'd
to write, will be as much against the Conviction of his own
Conscience, as what he publish'd last Week, of the *Whigs* being
65 *Enemies to their Country*. I grant the Force of that Objection;
and yet must still think it were better that he, or any body
were silenc'd, than that there shou'd come out. as if it were
by Authority, a printed Weekly Libel, insolently sporting with
Truth, Justice and Honour; and reviling the Best Men, and the
70 Best Cause that ever any Realm was bless'd with. They that have
extol'd the rare Happiness of Times, *when every Man might speak
or write what he shou'd think*; did not foresee that there ever
wou'd be such a Time, when under the Shelter of this Liberty,
a Man shou'd be hir'd *to write what he did not think*. This is the
75 only thing I complain of: If my Friend would only *write what he
thinks*, I shou'd wish him good Luck, and many courteous Readers:
nay, knowing his Composition, I cou'd allow him *to think* more out
of the way, and more absurdly and falsly, than ever any Mortal
thought before him. But to have him put upon us eternally down-
80 right Contradictions and notorious Falshoods in Point of Fact;
things that neither he, nor any of his Disciples can think, and
that his Masters can't impart to him without either laughing or
blushing; this, I say, is shameful and intolerable: and if he
can't be cur'd of this vile Prostitution, I don't see how it is
85 possible for him and me to continue *Friends* much longer.

55 most impudent] *om*. 12°   56-7 that this Hireling] he 12°   62 less]
~, ½°

71-2 *when ... think*: Mainwaring quotes the same unknown source in an unpublished dialogue (BL MS Add. 61462, f. 80).

I don't wonder the *Tories* are against Liberty and Property;
'tis because they can never make any thing of them. They have
always had so little care of Liberty, and so little Interest in
Property, we must expect they shou'd never give 'em a good Word,
nor name 'em, but to make a Jest of them. My Friend, the *Exami-*   90
ner, will not deny this, but tell you, as to Liberty, 'tis the
most ruinous thing we can desire. Last *Thursday* he told us, That
the reason why *Publick Injuries are so seldom redress'd, is for
want of Arbitrary Power*. Which is like his usual way of blundering: for tho his Patrons may think nothing else can do their   95
business, yet after we have been at about One hundred and forty
Millions Expence to secure us against that Power, which, to
soften, he calls *discretionary*; he will do his Party no more Service in writing for't, than he has done in pleading for the Duke
of *Anjou*, and a Partition of *Spain*.   100
They take the same freedom with Property as they have done with
Liberty; and for no other reason, but that they can't make themselves Masters of it without his *Discretionary Power*. The *Examiner*
says he wou'd have forgotten no less *than a Million of Enormities*,
and have *chang'd his Stile*, if the *Whigs* wou'd have trusted the   105
Tories with their Stocks too. This is indeed one of the ill
Effects of Liberty: This comes of free Votes, and Elections: And

86-9 I ...'em] There are few things to which he is more a declar'd Enemy
than to Liberty: He never names it 12°   90-1 them ... 'tis] it; and he
seems to think it 12°   94 *Power*.] Power: which, to soften, he call'd
discretionary. 12°   94-5 Which ... blundering] But if he had been wise,
he wou'd have conceal'd his Thoughts upon that Subject 12°   95 his
Patrons] some Men perhaps 12°   96 been at] spent 12°   97 Expence] *om.*
12°   97-8 which ... *discretionary*;] *transferred to line 94 above* 12°
98 Party] Friends 12°   100 and] and for 12°   101-34 They take ...
Credit;] *om.* 12°

---

86 *Liberty*: 387.61.
93-4 *Publick ... Power*: 388.89-93. Oldmixon makes the same point in *Re-*
flections on Dr. Swift's Letter to the Earl of Oxford, about the English
Tongue, London, A. Baldwin, [1712,] p. 9: 'The reason *why Publick Injuries are*
so seldom redress'd, is for want of Arbitrary Power; he calls it *Discretionary*,
'tis true, and if I have wrong'd him, by putting *Arbitrary* in its Place, I ask
his Pardon.'
100 *Partition of Spain*: The Examiner nowhere advocates a partition of Spain.
Mainwaring evidently construes entertaining the impossibility of recovering
Spain for the Habsburgs (390.139-40) as pleading for the duke of Anjou.
104-5 *Million ... Stile*: 391.182-3.

you have seen how he threatens 'em for daring to assert their
Right, and how well he wou'd have spoken of 'em, had they aban-
110 don'd it. But as he has hitherto manag'd his Panegyricks, I'm
afraid he'll never find another Market for 'em.

If the *Examiner* was in such Reputation that any body upon
Earth wou'd be pleas'd to know who he is, his last Paper but one
wou'd have put me upon guessing at him, which I confess I shou'd
115 have done before now; but his Writings have given me such an Idea
of him, I was afraid of finding him out lest he shou'd be so
inconsiderable, that the Pains I took about him wou'd be a Jest
upon me. He is such an admirable Historian, that I was inclin'd
to think, those who told me, the Author of the *Barcelona* History
120 writ it, knew something of the Matter; and had I not known better
things, this Information wou'd have seem'd probable enough, because in that *Examiner* he affects to shew he is as well vers'd in
the *Faculty* as he is in History. He describes Credit to be in as
languishing a Condition as if she was his Patient, and eaten up
125 with the *Vapours* and *Cholick*: but this crazy Dame belongs, he
assures us, to *Exchange-Alley*; and all the Cure he has for her,
is the true Tory *Catholicon, Bullets* and *Steel*.

There's another *Credit* that has nothing to do with *Trade* and
Business; but, as if she was in a *Consumption*, thrives best by
130 following the *Plough*. By this means, tho she has not a Penny in
her Purse, she looks jolly; but that jolly look of hers is the
same which many Ladys in her Condition have carry'd to their
Graves with them. To this rustick Nymph he gives the Name of
National Credit; and, instead of placing her on so unstable a
135 *Foundation* as the Pillars of the *Exchange*, he has given her the
solid *Base* of a *Lottery*.

Men make mad Work when they meddle with things they don't under-

134 and,] And therefore 12°   on] upon 12°   136 *Base*] *Basis* 12°
137-8 Men ... understand.] The same mad Work he makes Whenever he meddles
with Trade and Stocks: 12°

119 *Author*: John Freind, *An Account of the Earl of Peterborow's Conduct
in Spain, Chiefly since the Raising the Siege of Barcelona,* London, for Jonah
Bowyer, 1707.
123 *Faculty*: the medical profession (*OED*), of which Freind, MD Oxford,
1707, was a member.
123-7 *Credit ... Steel*: 376.94-377.97.
134-6 *National Credit ... Lottery*: 377.102-7.

stand. The *Tories*, I say again, have nothing to do with *Trade* and
Mony. The Bank and the *East-India* Companies are, says my Friend,
but *Retailers of Mony*, not worth minding by such substantial Per-   140
sons as they are: and I wonder the *Examiner* should give himself
the trouble to take so much notice of 'em. There, it seems, he
has no Vote; and by the value he sets on them, one would imagine
that to have one, was worth no more than a Vote at a Vestry or
St. *Peter*'s. Indeed he represents the State of the City-*Credit*   145
to be such, that the Stir some Folks make about it is very ridiculous, *she has so many Diseases, and passes thro such Hands.*
Which is not the only Compliment she and her *Directors* must expect from this worthy Author.

  The *Examiner*, from the very beginning, wou'd fain have had us   150
believe, he writes for the State; and has all along taken a very
odd way to make his Court to the M--------, by laying all the
Falshood and Scandal he has been guilty of, at their Door, as if
it had been only to do them a Service. As little as I know of
them, I cannot give into this, nor suppose they will take such   155
a Charge upon themselves; it being impossible for so scandalous
a Libel to be carry'd on so, but it must, some time or other,
come to an unlucky End. In his Paper, No. 38. he threatens, That
he has not yet summon'd the Government to his Aid: *He has not*

  138-9 The ... *Mony*] *om.* 12°   139-41 The ... are:] He says, the Bank and
the *East-India* Company are no better than *Retailers of Mony*; not worth the
care of substantial Landed Persons. 12°   141-2 and ... 'em.] And indeed
I don't wonder he shews such Contempt for those Places; 12°   142 There]
½° O L TxU They are Places where ½° IU^{ab}   142-3 There ... and] since
12°   143 on] upon 12°   143-5 one ... *Peter*'s] 'tis plain he has no
Vote in *either* 12°   145 Indeed he represents the State] But his Description 12°   146-7 to ... ridiculous,] is still more ridiculous: He says she
is *in a languishing Condition*; And he observes, that 12°   147-9 *Hands* ...
Author.] hands, that her Case seems to him to be dangerous and uncertain: 12°
lines 134-6 *follow here in* 12°   150-8 The ... End.] But all these fine
strokes of his Fancy are not sufficient to keep him in good Humour: 12°
158 he] he grows very sullen and revengeful: 12°   158-60 That ... &c.] all
his Opponents, and gives them to understand, *that he has not yet invok'd*, &c.
nor summon'd the Government to his Aid. 12°

  140 *Retailers of Mony*: 347.133.
  143 *Vote*: Stockholders of less than £500 had no voting rights; cf. Swift,
Journal, pp. 74, 135.
  145 *St. Peter's*: St. Peter's is Westminster Abbey, where the Convocation
sat.
  147 *she ... Hands*: 377.100-2.
  159-60 *not invok'd*: 378.142-3.

160 *invok'd*, &c. He is so apt to forget himself, that he does not
know where he is. One wou'd think, he took this *flourishing Year
of the Church* to be four or five and twenty Years backwards, when
the *Ministers* reign'd, and not the *Law*; which, as powerful as he
is, and as much a *Tory*, neither he nor his dead-doing People, who
165 *with the least Breath can scatter Folks into Silence and Obscurity*, will ever be able to bring about.

He says, he does not *remember any constant weekly Paper against
the late Ministers*. He never heard of *Lesley*. He has a very
treacherous Memory, when it makes against him. At other times he
170 can remember things back as far as *Forty-One*. He is very industrious to have it thought, that whatever is said to vindicate those
Ministers, when he has slander'd and abus'd them, is little less
than Treason. He matters not that they are Men of the highest
Quality and Fortune, and possest of more even of his Land-Inter-
175 est, than the whole Set of his Patrons. He boldly affirms, *the
falsest and vilest Abuses* are written of those now in the *highest
Power and Credit*; that is, because we say he is guilty of the
same Faults against Men of the highest Worth and Esteem, whom he
knows he has *falsly and vilely* abus'd in ev'ry one of his *Exami-
180 ners*: Whereas, I defy him to give a single Instance of a false
thing said in this Paper, for or against any Man, in or out of

160 not] not seem to 12°   161 is] lives 12°   162 four or] *om*. 12°
163-4 *Law; ... Tory*] *Law*: For till that golden Age returns 12°
164-7 People, ... says,] People will be able to bring about what he threatens;
nor *to scatter Folks* with their *least Breath into Silence and Obscurity*. But
12°   167 *remember*] *remember that* 12°   *Paper*] Paper *was written* 12°
168 He] Poor Man! he 12°   *Lesley. He has*] *Lesley*: having at some times 12°
169 when ... him.] *om*. 12°   At other times] tho at others 12°   170 He is]
And he is still 12°   171 those] *those late* 12°   173-80 He ... Whereas,]
As all things that are observ'd of *Those now in the Highest Power and Credit,*
he boldly affirms are *the falsest and vilest Abuses*. I have no body to answer
for but my self. But 12°

161-2 *this flourishing Year of the Church*: 368.126n.
165-6 *least ... Obscurity*: 378.139-40.
167-8 *not ... Ministers*: 379.148-50.
168 *Lesley*: 379.146n. It is strange that neither Swift nor Mainwaring
remember the Examiner's 'Brother', Abel Roper, for *The Post-Boy* survived even
Roper's death in February 1726.
170 *Forty-One*: 359.72.
175-7 *the ... Credit*: 378.137-8.
180 *defy him to give a single Instance*: The Examiner did not rise to the
bait.

Credit and Power. The Paper before mention'd, has hardly a Paragraph without the Q---n and *Government* in it. He has no Respect
for her Majesty's Sacred Character. Her Name, he hopes, will,
without any Warrant, justify his Insolence; and that's another   185
of his Impositions upon the Reason of Mankind: As if any Man of
common Sense could not perceive that, as he says of his Adversaries, he is *retain'd by a Cabal* only; and that there can be no
greater Affront to her Majesty, than to vilify so basely those
Ministers with whose Service she so frequently and solemnly de-   190
clar'd herself well pleas'd. That she does not employ them now,
is no excuse for his reviling them as he does: if it were, their
Successors wou'd have but a melancholy Prospect of it; since her
Royal Prerogative is the same as it was, and her Favour too dif-
fusive to be always confin'd to a Party.   195

  182 The ... a] Whereas he has not only defam'd Men of the highest Worth and
Quality, but in his Paper above mention'd, there is hardly one 12°
184 Character. ... hopes,] Character; but he hopes her Name 12°   185 and
that's] which is 12°   186 As if any] But every 12°   187 common] *om.*
12°   could not] must 12°   187-8 as ... that] *om.* 12°   192 as he
does] *om.* 12°   193 of it] *om.* 12°

  188 *retain'd by a Cabal*: 379.169.

No. 40 [Swift]   3 May 1711

The EXAMINER.

Quis tulerit Gracchos de seditione querentes?

THERE have been certain Topicks of Reproach, liberally bestow'd
for some Years past, by the *Whigs* and *Tories*, upon each other.
We charge the former with a Design of destroying the *Establish'd
Church*, and introducing *Fanaticism* and *Free-thinking* in its stead.
We accuse them as Enemies to Monarchy; as endeavouring to under-   5
mine the present Form of Government, and to build a Commonwealth,
or some new Scheme of their own, upon its Ruins. On the other
side, their Clamors against us, may be summed up in those three

  Motto Juvenal, *Satires*, ii 24: in Vain | Gracchi of Sedition must complain.
3-7 We ... *Ruins*: cf. 344.34-47.

formidable words, *Popery, Arbitrary Power*, and the *Pretender*. Our
10 Accusations against them we endeavour to make good by certain
Overt-Acts; such as their perpetually abusing the whole Body of
the Clergy; their declared Contempt for the very Order of Priesthood; their Aversion for Episcopacy; the publick Encouragement
and Patronage they gave to *Tindall, Toland*, and other Atheistical
15 Writers; their appearing as professed Advocates, retained by the
Dissenters, excusing their Separation, and laying the Guilt of it
to the Obstinacy of the Church; their frequent Endeavours to
repeal the Test, and their setting up the Indulgence to scrupulous Consciences, as a Point of greater Importance than the
20 Establish'd Worship. The Regard they bear to our *Monarchy*, hath
appeared by their open ridiculing the Martyrdom of *King Charles
the First*, in their Calves-head Clubs, their common Discourses
and their Pamphlets: Their denying the unnatural War rais'd
against that Prince, to have been a Rebellion; their justifying
25 his Murder in the allow'd Papers of the Week; their Industry in
publishing and spreading Seditious and Republican Tracts; such as
Ludlow's Memoirs, *Sidney* of Government, and many others; their

13 for] against 38 8°+12°

---

9 *Popery, Arbitrary Power, and the Pretender*: '*Popery*' and 'the *Pretender*'
occur but once or twice in *The Medley*. Swift is reacting to Mainwaring's
deliberate misquotation of 'discretionary Power' (388.89-90) as '*Arbitrary
Power*' (395.98).
14 *Toland*: Harley, who had patronized Toland in 1700-1, must have been
amused at this sally (Swift, *Discourse*, pp. 36-42).
18 *repeal the Test*: The Whigs had agitated for repeal of the Test Act
(1673-8) ever since 1678, most intensively in the 1706-7 session of the English Parliament (Hearne, i 324; Luttrell, vi 137) and in the 1707 session of
the Irish Parliament (James S. Reid, *History of the Presbyterian Church in
Ireland*, 3rd edn., 3 vols., London, Whittaker and Co., 1853, iii 28, 33, 43;
Swift, *Prose*, ii 118).
Indulgence: 358.52.
22 *Calves-head Clubs*: These clubs, of which John Milton is supposed to have
been one of the founders, met on 30 January to perform a kind of republican
black mass to celebrate the execution of Charles I on 30 January 1649. The
ceremonies are said to include the singing of republican hymns and 'a Calfs
head served up in a dish like St. John Baptists head in a charger' (Edward
Ward, *The Secret History of the Calves-Head Club*, 5th edn., 1705, pp. 27-72;
HMC *Hope-Johnstone MSS*, p. 116; *POAS*, Yale, vii 560-9).
27 *Ludlow ... Sidney*: 'These works can hardly be called "tracts." Algernon
Sidney's *Discourses concerning Government* (1698), is a portly folio of 467
pages, and Ludlow's *Memoirs* (1698-9) occupy three stout octavo volumes'
(*E1922*, ix 256). Volume iii of the latter, with marginalia in Swift's hand,
was in his library at his death (*Swift's Library*, p. [2]16). On the 'Industry'

endless lopping of the Prerogative, and mincing into nothing Her
M-----y's Titles to the Crown.

What Proofs they bring for our endeavouring to introduce   30
Popery, *Arbitrary Power*, and the *Pretender*, I cannot readily tell,
and would be glad to hear; however, those important Words having
by dextrous Management, been found of mighty Service to their
Cause, though apply'd with little Colour, either of Reason or
Justice; I have been considering whether they may not be adapted   35
to more proper Objects.

As to *Popery*, which is the first of these, to deal plainly, I
can hardly think there is any Set of Men among us, except the
Professors of it, who have any direct Intention to introduce it
among us: But the Question is, whether the Principles and Prac-   40
tices of Us, or the *Whigs*, be most likely to make way for it?
'Tis allow'd, on all Hands, that among the Methods concerted at
Rome, for bringing over *England* into the Bosom of the Catholick
Church; one of the chief was, to send Jesuits and other Emissaries, in Lay-Habits, who Personating Tradesmen and Mechanicks, 45
should mix with the People, and under the Pretence of a further
and purer Reformation, endeavour to divide us into as many Sects
as possible, which would either put us under the Necessity of
returning to our old Errors, to preserve Peace at Home; or by
our Divisions make way for some Powerful Neighbour, with the   50
Assistance of the Pope's Permission, and a consecrated Banner, to
Convert and Enslave us at once. If this hath been reckon'd good
Politicks (and it was the best the Jesuit-Schools could invent)
I appeal to any Man, whether the *Whigs*, for many Years past, have
not been employ'd in the very same Work? They profess'd on all   55
Occasions, that they knew no Reason why any one System of
Speculative Opinions (as they term'd the Doctrines of the Church)
should be establish'd by Law more than another; or why Employments

40 among us] here 38 8°+12°

---

of publishing republican propaganda, see Edmund Ludlow, *A Voyce from the Watch
Tower*, Part Five: 1660-1662, ed. A.B. Worden, Camden fourth series, vol. xxi,
London, Royal Historical Society, 1978, pp. 19-39.
  55 *They professed*: In this sentence and the next Swift paraphrases Tindal,
*An Essay concerning the Power of the Magistrate, and the Rights of Mankind in
the Matters of Religion*, London, by J.D. for Andrew Bell, 1697, pp. 16, 168;
cf. Swift, *Prose*, ii 115.

should be confined to the Religion of the Magistrate, and that
60 called the Church Established. The grand Maxim they laid down,
was, That no Man, for the sake of a few Notions and Ceremonies,
under the Names of Doctrine and Discipline, should be deny'd the
Liberty of serving his Country: As if Places would go a begging,
unless *Brownists, Familists, Sweet-Singers, Quakers, Anabaptists*
65 and *Muggletonians*, would take them off our Hands.

I have been sometimes imagining this Scheme brought to Perfection, and how diverting it would look to see half a dozen *Sweet-
Singers* on the Bench in their Ermins, and two or three *Quakers*
with their white Staves at Court. I can only say, this Project is
70 the very Counter-part of the late King *James*'s Design, which he
took up as the best Method for introducing his own Religion,
under the Pretext of an universal Liberty of Conscience, and that
no difference in Religion, should make any in his Favour. Accordingly, to save Appearances, he dealt some Employments among Dis-
75 senters of most Denominations; and what he did was, no doubt, in
pursuance of the best Advice he could get at Home or Abroad; and
the Church thought it the most dangerous Step he could take for
her Destruction. 'Tis true, King *James* admitted *Papists* among the
rest, which the *Whigs* would not; but this is sufficiently made
80 up by a material Circumstance, wherein they seem to have much
out-done that Prince, and to have carried their Liberty of Conscience to a higher Point, having granted it to all the Classes
of *Free-thinkers*, which the nice Conscience of a Popish Prince
would not give him leave to do; and was therein mightily over-
85 seen; because it is agreed by the Learned, that there is but a
very narrow Step from *Atheism*, to the other Extream, *Superstition*.

76 and] but 38 8°+12°

---

59 *Religion of the Magistrate*: 143.15n.
64 *Familists, Sweet-Singers*: Addison and Steele describe 'a Show ... *carried* up and down in *Germany*, which represents all the Religions of *Great
Britain* in Wax-work'. The group turning their backs upon the rest 'called
themselves the *Philodelphians*, or the Family of Love. In the opposite Corner
there sat another little Congregation of strange Figures, opening their Mouths
as wide as they could gape, and distinguished by the Title of the *Sweet Singers
of Israel*' (*The Tatler*, 28-30 November 1710).
69 *Staves*: The Lord High Steward, the Comptroller of the Household, the
Lord Treasurer, and the Lord Chamberlain, upon appointment to office were presented with a white staff which was broken when the appointment ended; cf.
POAS, Yale, vii 475 and illustration.

So that upon the whole, whether the *Whigs* had any real Design of
bringing in Popery or no, 'tis very plain, that they took the
most effectual Step towards it, and if the Jesuits had been their
immediate Directors, they could not have taught them better, nor   90
have found apter Scholars.

Their second Accusation is, That we encourage and maintain
Arbitrary Power in Princes, and promote enslaving Doctrines among
the People. This they go about to prove by Instances, producing
the particular Opinions of certain Divines in King *Charles the*   95
Second's Reign; a Decree of *Oxford*-University, and some few
Writers since the Revolution. What they mean, is the Principle
of *Passive-Obedience* and *Non-Resistance*, which those who affirm,
did, I believe, never intend should include Arbitrary Power. However, tho' I am sensible that it is not reckon'd Prudent in a   100
Dispute, to make any Concessions without the last Necessity; yet
I do agree, that in my own private Opinion, some Writers did
carry that Tenet of *Passive-Obedience* to a height, which seem'd
hardly consistent with the Liberties of a Country, whose Laws can
be neither Enacted nor Repealed, without the Consent of the whole   105
People. I mean not those who affirm it due in general, as it certainly is to the Legislature, but such as fix it entirely in the
Prince's Person. This last has, I believe, been done by a very
few; but when the *Whigs* quote Authors to prove it upon us, they
bring in all who mention it as a Duty in general, without apply-   110
ing it to Princes, abstracted from their Senate.

96 *Decree*: 'On July 21st, 1683, the University of Oxford passed a decree
condemning as "false, seditious, and impious," a series of twenty-seven propositions, among which were the following: "All civil authority is derived originally from the people [cf. Swift, *Discourse*, p. 83]. The King has but a co-
ordinate power, and may be over-ruled by the Lords and Commons. Wicked kings
and tyrants ought to be put to death. King Charles the First was lawfully put
to death." The decree was reprinted in 1709/10 with the title, *An Entire Con-*
futation of Mr. Hoadley's Book, of the Original of Government. It was burnt
by the order of the House of Lords, dated March 23rd, 1709/10' (E*1922*, ix 258).
103-4 *height ... Country*: Swift agrees with Hoadly, who called passive
obedience a 'Doctrine of Servitude' (*The Revolution no Rebellion*, London, for
Jonah Bowyer, no date, p. 12), a phrase quoted by Swift's friend, William Pate
(*The Divine Rights of the British Nation and Constitution Vindicated*, London,
for J. Baker, 1710, p. 89).
105-6 *the whole People*: cf. 'in all Government there is an absolute unlimited Power, which naturally and originally seems to be placed in the whole
Body' (Swift, *Discourse*, p. 83).
107 *Legislature*: Swift is thinking of the formula, 'King, Lords and Commons in Parliament assembled'; cf. 'the Legislature ... may turn out Christianity if they think fit' (Swift, *Prose*, ii 105).

By thus freely declaring my own Sentiments of *Passive-Obedience*,
it will at least appear, that I do not write for a Party: Neither
do I, upon any Occasion, pretend to speak their Sentiments, but
115   my own. The Majority of the two Houses, and the present Ministry
(if those be a Party) seem to me in all their Proceedings, to
pursue the real Interest of Church and State: And if I shall happen to differ from particular Persons among them, in a single
Notion about Government, I suppose they will not, upon that
120   Account, explode me and my Paper. However, as an Answer once for
all, to the tedious Scurrilities of those idle People, who affirm,
I am hired and directed what to write; I must here inform them,
That their Censure is an Effect of their Principles: The present
M------y are under no Necessity of employing prostitute Pens;
125   they have no dark Designs to promote, by advancing Heterodox
Opinions.

But (to return) suppose two or three private Divines, under
King *Charles the Second*, did a little overstrain the Doctrine of
Passive-Obedience to Princes; some Allowance might be given to
130   the Memory of that unnatural Rebellion against his Father, and
the dismal Consequences of Resistance. 'Tis plain, by the Proceedings of the Churchmen before and at the Revolution, that this
Doctrine was never design'd to introduce Arbitrary Power.

I look upon the *Whigs* and *Dissenters* to be exactly of the same
135   Political Faith; let us, therefore, see what share each of them
had in advancing Arbitrary Power. 'Tis manifest, that the

113 least] last 38 8°+12°

---

113 *I do not write for a Party*: cf. 'no Man [is] great enough to set me
on Work' (Swift, *Prose*, iii 194).
122 *hired*: 394.84. Swift was outraged when Harley sent him a banknote for
£50 on 5 February 1711 and refused to see him until Harley apologized (Swift,
Journal, pp. 181-2, 191, 193, 208, 322).
124 *employing prostitute Pens*: Swift himself deployed the pens of his
'Understrappers', Delariviere Manley, Abel Roper, and 'little Harrison', who
succeeded Steele as writer of *The Tatler* in January 1711 (Swift, *Journal*,
p. 162). But Defoe enjoyed an entirely different status, presumably unknown
to Swift. Harley had procured him a pension on the civil list (which was
chronically in arrears) and left him 'at full Liberty to Persue [his] Own Reason and Principle' in the *Review*, for which he was 'Neither Employ'd, Dictated
to, or Rewarded for' (Defoe, *Letters*, pp. 287, 315, 332, 379-80).
133 *Arbitrary Power*: 395.94n.; cf. 'it is obvious, that in joining the
Tories, Swift reserved to himself the right of putting his own interpretation
upon the speculative points of their political creed' (E*1814*, iv 96).

Fanaticks made *Cromwell* the most absolute Tyrant in *Christendom*:
The *Rump* abolished the House of Lords; the Army abolished the
Rump; and by this Army of *Saints*, he Governed. The *Dissenters*
took Liberty of Conscience and Employments from the late King   140
James, as an acknowledgement of his dispensing Power; which makes
a King of *England* as absolute as the *Turk*. The *Whigs*, under the
late King, perpetually declared for keeping up a standing Army,
in Times of Peace; which has in all Ages been the first and great
Step to the Ruin of Liberty. They were, besides, discovering   145
every Day their Inclinations to destroy the Rights of the Church;
and declared their Opinion, in all Companies, against the Bishops
sitting in the House of Peers: Which was exactly copying after
their Predecessors of Forty One. I need not say their real Intentions were to make the King Absolute, but whatever be the Designs   150
of innovating Men, they usually end in a Tyranny: As we may see
by an hundred Examples in *Greece*, and in the later Commonwealths
of *Italy*, mentioned by *Machiavel*.

    In the third place, the *Whigs* accuse us of a Design to bring
in the *Pretender*; and to give it a greater Air of Probability,   155
they suppose the *Qu---* to be a Party in this Design; which

    137 Tyrant] Power 38 8°+12°   142 a] the 38 8°+12°   150 the King]
King 38 8°+12°

---

   139 *Dissenters*: 126.20n.
   143 *standing Army*: 'The business of the standing Army', Toland said, 'became the very test ... of Whig and Tory' in the session of Parliament that
began in December 1697. But the roles of the two parties were reversed. The
Whigs, who had opposed a standing army commanded by Charles II or James II,
defended one for William III. Harley's New Country Party 'labour'd to represent it as absolutely destructive to the Constitution of the *English* Government' (*A Collection of Several Pieces of Mr. John Toland*, ed. Pierre Des
Maizeaux, 2 vols., London, J. Peele, 1726, ii 341; Kennett, iii 741).
   147 *Bishops*: During the debate on the bill of attainder of Sir John Fenwick, Charles Lord Spencer, then Member of Parliament for Tiverton (1695-1702)
and later 3rd Earl of Sunderland and a member of the Junto, boldly proposed
that bishops be excluded from voting (Vernon, i 69).
   151 *Tyranny*: cf. 'although most Revolutions of Government in *Greece* and
Rome began with the Tyranny of the People, yet they generally concluded in
that of a Single Person; so that an usurping Populace is its own *Dupe*; a meer
Underworker, and a Purchaser in Trust for some Single Tyrant' (Swift, *Discourse*, p. 116).
   153 *Machiavel*: *The History of Florence*, iv 1-3.
   156 *Qu---*: Although the claim was certainly made in private by Richard
Steele and others (Hamilton, pp. 42, 44), it seems unlikely to have been published and 'there is no valid reason to believe that the queen ... intended
in any way to contravene the Hanoverian settlement' (Gregg, p. 364).

however, is no very extraordinary Supposition in those who have
advanced such singular Paradoxes concerning *Greg* and *Guiscard*.
Upon this Article, their Charge is general, without ever offer-
160 ing to produce an Instance. But I verily think, and believe it
will appear no Paradox, that if ever he be brought in, the *Whigs*
are his Men. For, first, it is an undoubted Truth, that a Year or
two after the *Revolution*, several Leaders of that Party had their
Pardons sent them by the late King *James*, and had entered upon
165 Measures to restore him, on account of some Disobligations they
receiv'd from King *William*. Besides, I would ask, whether those
who are under the greatest Ties of Gratitude to King *James*, are
not at this Day become the most zealous *Whigs*? And of what Party
those are now, who kept a long Correspondence with St. *Germains*?
170   It is likewise very observable of late, that the *Whigs* upon all
Occasions, profess their Belief of the *Pretender*'s being no Impostor, but a real Prince, born of the late Queen's Body: Which
whether it be true or false, is very unseasonably advanc'd, considering the Weight such an Opinion must have with the Vulgar, if
175 they once throughly believe it. Neither is it at all improbable,
that the *Pretender* himself puts his chief Hopes in the Friendship
he expects from the *Dissenters* and *Whigs*, by his choice to invade

---

158 *Paradoxes*: The paradox concerning Greg is that Harley was 'conniving at
Mr. *Greg*'s treasonable Practices' (Swift, *Corr.*, i 70; Boyer, *The History*,
p. 321; cf. Oldmixon, *The History*, p. 397). The paradox concerning Guiscard
is that Harley 'was an Accomplice of the Man who would have murder'd him'
(Abel Boyer, *The Post Boy*, 8-10 March 1711; cf. Swift, *Journal*, p. 236n.).

164 *Pardons*: 'James II. sent a Declaration to England, dated April 20th,
1692, in which he promised to pardon all those who should return to their
duty', but he specifically excluded Churchill 'until he should efface the
memory of his ingratitude by some eminent service' (E1922, ix 260).

166 *those*: James II raised John Churchill to the English peerage as Baron
Churchill of Sandridge (May 1685) and commissioned him colonel of the third
troop of horse guards (August 1685). James appointed Lord Godolphin, one of
his most trusted advisers, chamberlain to Queen Mary (February 1685), commissioner of the Treasury (January 1686), and keeper of Cranborne Chase (in
Windsor Forest) (July 1688).

171 *Pretender*: The argument that the Whigs came to believe in the Preten-
der's legitimacy in order to emphasize the necessity for resistance in the
Revolution, seems to have been started by Charles Leslie: 'in all the *Last
Reign*, [the Whigs] gave the *Pretender* no other Name but that of *Perkin* and
Impostor: But now *Observators*, *Reviews*, and all are Turn'd about, and Plead
for his *Birth* and own it' (Leslie, *The Good Old Cause, Further Discuss'd*,
1710, p. 7; cf. *The Character and Principles of the Present Set of Whigs*,
London, for John Morphew, 1711, p. 20).

177 *invade*: On 9/20 March 1708, less than a month after Harley's resignation had forced Godolphin to turn to the Junto for support, the pretended

the Kingdom when the latter were most in Credit: And he had Reason to count upon the former, from the gracious Treatment they
receiv'd from his suppos'd Father, and their joyful Acceptance   180
of it. But further, what could be more consistent with the *Whiggish* Notion of a *Revolution*-Principle, than to bring in the *Pretender?* A *Revolution*-Principle, as their Writings and Discourses
have taught us to define it, is a Principle perpetually disposing
Men to *Revolutions*: And this is suitable to the famous Saying of   185
a great *Whig, That the more Revolutions the better*; which how
odd a Maxim soever in appearance, I take to be the true Characteristick of the Party.

A Dog loves to turn round often; yet after certain *Revolutions*,
he lies down to *Rest*: But Heads, under the Dominion of the Moon,   190
are for perpetual Changes and perpetual *Revolutions*: Besides, the
Whigs owe all their Wealth to Wars and *Revolutions*; like the Girl
at *Bartholomew* Fair, who gets a Peny by turning round a hundred
times, with Swords in her Hands.

To conclude, the *Whigs* have a natural Faculty of bringing in   195
Pretenders, and will therefore probably endeavour to bring in the
Great One at last: How many *Pretenders* to Wit, Honour, Nobility,
Politicks, have they brought in these last Twenty Years? In short,
they have been sometimes able to procure a majority of *Pretenders*
in Parliament; and wanted nothing to render the Work compleat,   200
except a *Pretender* at their Head.

---

178 were] was 38 8°+12°

James III sailed from Calais with 'about 5000 men ... and large summs of
money' to seize the throne of Scotland (Luttrell, vi 277).

185 *the famous Saying*: The 'great *Whig*' may be Benjamin Hoadly, whose argument that the only claim to the throne of future English monarchs in the
Protestant line will be the '*Revolution-Title*' was interpreted to mean that
'all our future Princes, are to succeed by so many Revolutions' (Hoadly, *The
Voice of the Addressers*, London, sold by A. Baldwin, 1710, p. 8; *The Vindication and Advancement of our National Constitution and Credit*, London, printed
for Jonah Bowyer, 1710, p. 13).

191 *perpetual Revolutions*: cf. 'perpetual turning' (Swift, *Tale*, p. 70).

192 *Girl*: 'The next Figure ... was a Youthful Damsel ... having disarm'd
most of the ... Men in the Room, she ... began to handle them [the swords]
... dextrously ... putting her-self into a Circular Dance, wherein she turn'd
as Merrily Round as a Gig ... shifting her Swords, to all parts of her Face
and Breast, to the very great amazement of Countrey Fools, and the very little
danger of her own Carcase' (Edward Ward, *The London Spy. For the Month of
September, 1699. Part XI*, London, J. How, p. 9) (E*1814*, iv 98).

No. 32 [Mainwaring]   7 May 1711

The MEDLEY.

A Letter from an unknown Hand concerning the Year 1688.
The Examiner *exhorted to the Study of Truth.*
That it is absolutely necessary in all Praises and Panegyricks.
And that Censures or Reflections are of no Effect without it.

HAVING observ'd that other Weekly Authors print the Letters that
are sent to them, which are very well receiv'd by their Courteous
Readers; I have resolv'd for the future to take the same course:
So that whoever has any thing to communicate for the Benefit or
5 Instruction of the Publick, may expect to see it as fairly publish'd, as this following Letter, which I have receiv'd from an
unknown Person, who appears to be very young, by one Paragraph in
his Letter; but writes extremely well for one of his Age.

SIR,

10 'SO many fatal Misfortunes having happen'd to this Nation since
that unhappy Year 1688. I wonder our Friend the *Examiner* and his
Masters, of whose unerring Judgments in State-Affairs we have had
in some late Instances most convincing Proofs, have not yet taken
more of them into their Consideration, and made it appear by un-
15 doubted Matter of Fact (as most certainly cou'd with great Ease
and Plainness be done) that the Work of that Year has been the
Origin and principal Cause of all the Sufferings of this Nation,
with regard both to Church and State, for about these two and
twenty Years last past. As for our Friend, I suppose the Reason
20 of his not having consider'd them before, is, his not having
receiv'd Orders from the Persons whom he serves: but that any

7 in] ½° 89 of 12°

---

7 *unknown Person*: Anthony Henley (*c.*1666-1711) was the well-known Whig wit
to whom Garth dedicated *The Dispensary* (1699). He was a Member of Parliament
for Andover (1698-1700) and for Weymouth and Melcombe Regis (1702-11), a member of the Kit-Cat Club, and a friend and correspondent of Swift—'that dog
Henley' (Oldmixon, *The Life*, p. 194; Swift, *Journal*, p. 113; Burnet, 1833,
ii 476n.).

Noble Patriots shou'd omit a thing, which wou'd be so beneficial
to their Country, in opening the Eyes, and rectifying the Understandings of prejudic'd and misguided Men; this, I say, can by
impartial Thinkers be attributed to nothing, but their present   25
Engagement in Politicks and Projects for the carrying on this so
necessary a War, and in Concerns of the next Consequence to that.
Nor is it to be doubted, but that after the confus'd Posture, in
which Affairs were left by some late M------rs, is with due Care
and Trouble regulated, this so great a piece of Service to the   30
Publick will not be look'd upon as deserving any longer Neglect.
But tho more urgent Business hath hitherto employ'd those inde-
fatigable Politicians, so as to occasion their Omission in this
Point; yet I hope it may be lawful for Friends thus privately to
anticipate together the Satisfaction and Joy, which all *British*   35
Minds must and will receive from the effecting such a good (and
I had almost said grateful) Work.

   'For my part, I often bless my Good-Fortune, that I had not my
Being in those dismal Days. Thankful, with reason thankful, I am,
that I have not seen a rebellious People rising in Arms against   40
their Prince, upon the slight occasion of his endeavouring to
subvert their establish'd Religion and Laws, the Consequence of
which wou'd at the most have been but Popery and miserable
Slavery. And had their Fury ended here, it might have been in
some measure pardonable; but, for nothing more than the Security   45
of their Religion and State, to depose, nay, even drive out of
the Kingdom their lawful Sovereign; and upon the Throne from
which was depuls'd the mighty, *inalienable, indefeasible Jure*
Divino Title, to place a weak (the *tolerated Examiner* wou'd say
usurp'd) *Parliamentary one*; this certainly was the height of Mad-   50
ness, push'd on by a foolish Zeal for the best of Religions and
inestimable Liberty. Many other Facts, scarce less heinous than

---

   24 *misguided Men*: 83.58-61, 85.109-10, 211.38, 314.40.
   38-9 *had not my Being*: It is impossible to say what the joke is about.
Henley may be writing in the person of his eldest son, also Anthony (1704?-
48), who was indeed 'very young' in 1688 (Romney Sedgwick, *The House of Com-*
mons 1715-1754, 2 vols., New York, for the History of Parliament Trust by
Oxford University Press, 1970, ii 126).
   49 *tolerated*: Henley adds *The Examiner* to 'the tolerated factious Papers of
the Week' (246.188-9).
   50 *usurp'd*: Nowhere does the Examiner call William's title usurped; cf.
Swift, *Poems*, 6-10.

what has been mention'd, have made that Antimonarchical Year an
ever-memorable Epocha to this Nation. Of what Evils then can, nay
55 must it not have been the Cause? If I had not good Authority on
my side, I shou'd not venture to affirm, that since that Year
have been given all the unreasonable Grants now in force: In our
Historians, indeed, we find Accounts of a great many bestow'd on
undeserving Persons, even Pimps, Flatterers, and Mistresses; all
60 which, after what we have lately seen and heard, we may suppose
were granted since the unlucky 1688. Nor with less reason did a
Sagacious and Learned Divine move in the Convocation, that that
Year shou'd be voted the Spring of *Atheism, Deism*, and *Immorality*,
which have so much pester'd this Nation of late. So that every
65 body must be persuaded, that all the Atheistical Rubbige which
was reviv'd, or rather made famous not long ago in the Tryal of
the Church, proceeded originally from the Revolution. And I wou'd
ask any impartial Man, what else but the Revolution cou'd possibly have been the Cause of the great Wind which happen'd some
70 years ago? Can we impute to any other thing the Loss of so many
Trees, Houses and Church-Steeples, which were then blown down?
I presume also every body will allow that Year to have been the
Cause of the late Attempt of a villainous *French* Priest upon the
Person of a Great Minister of State. But you will excuse me, Sir,
75 if I omit (as to my knowledg I do) a numerous Train of Evils too
long to be here recited, and which may be better represented in
their deserv'd Colours by the skilful Pen of the *Examiner*, to
whom it more properly belongs, and who is so excellent an Artist
in libellous Scandal, which in this Case is very requisite: It
80 will be a Satisfaction to me, if this puts him in mind of his
great Neglect: And for the promoting so good a Work, no Pains
shall ever be thought too great by,

                                        SIR,

                                        Your unknown humble Servant.

57 *Grants*: The bill to resume all grants made since February 1689 (306.5n.)
was thrown out by the Lords on 3 May 1711 (*LJ*, xix 287). Henley defends this
action by arguing that not all 'unreasonable' grants had been made since that
date and citing Charles II's grants to 'Pimps' etc.
   66-7 *Tryal of the Church*: i.e. Sacheverell's trial.
   69 *the great Wind*: the Protestant east wind of November 1688 that blew
William of Orange and his army into Torbay (*POAS*, Yale, iv 295).
   73 *French Priest*: 297.7-8.

I shall make no Remarks upon this Letter, but recommend it to   85
my Friend the *Examiner*, that he may pursue the Hints there given
him, rather than amuse the World with such monstrous Absurdities
as are contain'd in his last Paper: *I verily think*, says he, *that
if the Pretender be ever brought in, the* Whigs *are his Men*. He is
a pretty *Thinker*, that's certain: And those Men that carry'd the   90
Abdication, and settled the *Succession*, are just as likely to
bring in the Pretender, as some others, that shall be nameless,
are to keep him out. But I have often wonder'd why he will not be
persuaded once, for Curiosity-sake, to write a Paper with some
Truth in it, or at least some Probability. He that is a great   95
Scholar, as every one may see by his Motto's, must needs know,
that all the antient Authors who laid down the Rules of Writing,
unanimously agree, that nothing of that kind can ever please, or
be of any Consequence, if it has not a Foundation of Truth.

I will instance only in two *common Topicks* of Writing or Dis-   100
course, I mean those of *Praise* and *Censure*, which I chuse out of
all the rest, because it only concerns the *Examiner* to be well
instructed in them, he having no other Business but to flatter
the New M-------, and abuse the Old.

In the first place, Whenever any body would praise another, all   105
he can say will have no Weight or Effect, if it be not True or
Probable. If therefore, for Example, my Friend shou'd take it
into his head to commend a Man, *for having been an Instrument of
Great Good to a Nation*, when in Truth that very Person had brought
that same Nation under great Difficulties, to say no more; such   110
ill-chosen Flattery would be of no use or moment, nor add the
least Credit to the Person so commended. Or if he shou'd take that
occasion to revive any false and groundless Calumny upon other
Men, or another Party of Men; such an Instance *of Impotent but*

88-9 *I ... Men*: 406.160-2.
91 *Abdication*: 367.92.
    Succession: 41.176n.
108-9 *an ... Good*: a phrase from the Speaker's congratulatory address upon
the occasion of Harley's resumption of his seat in the House on 26 April 1711
(*CJ*, xvi 616; 414.6).
113-4 *other Men*: innuendo: the seven Whig lords appointed to the committee
to examine Greg in February 1708, whom Swift found 'equally guilty' with Guiscard (321.208).
114-5 *Impotent ... Malice*: another phrase from Bromley's address of 26
April 1711: 'God be thanked [that Harley's enemies] have been hitherto disappointed, and have not been able to accomplish, what their inveterate, but

115 *Inveterate Malice*, wou'd make him still appear more vile and contemptible. The Reason of all which is, that what he said was
neither Just, Proper, nor Real, and therefore must needs want
the force of true Eloquence, which consists in nothing else but
in well representing Things as they really are. I advise there-
120 fore my Friend, before he praises any more of his Heroes, to
learn the common Rules of writing; and particularly to read over
and over a certain Chapter in *Aristotle*'s First Book of Rhetorick,
where are given very proper and necessary Directions, *For praising a Man who has done nothing that he ought to be prais'd for.*
125   But the Antients did not think it enough for Men to speak what
was true or probable, they requir'd further that their Orators
shou'd be heartily in earnest; and that they shou'd have all
those Motions and Affections in their own Minds which they endeavour'd to raise in others. *He that thinks*, says *Cicero, to*
130 *warm others with his Eloquence, must first be warm himself.* And
Quintilian says, *We must first be affected our selves, before we
can move others.* This made *Pliny*'s Panegyrick upon *Trajan* so well
receiv'd by his Hearers, because every body knew the wonderful
Esteem and Affection which he had for the Person he commended:
135 And therefore, when he concluded with a Prayer to *Jupiter*, that
he wou'd take care of the Life and Safety of that Great and Good
Man, which he said contain'd in it all other Blessings; tho the
Expression was so high, it pass'd very well with those that heard
him, as being agreeable to the known Sentiments and Affection of
140 the Speaker. Whereas, if my Friend should be known to bear ill-

119-20 advise therefore] therefore advise 12°

---

impotent, Malice had designed against [his] person and reputation' (*CJ*, xvi
615).
  119 *representing Things as they really are*: This is the Quest, impelled
by the thrust of the new science, in which all the major Augustans from Dryden to Samuel Johnson were engaged.
  123-4 *For ... for*: Aristotle, *The Art of Rhetoric*, i 9 38-9.
  129-30 *He ... himself*: *Ardeat, qui vult incendere* (½°), apparently quoting
from memory *quae possit incendi, nisi ipse inflammatus ad eam et ardens
accesserit* (Cicero, *De Oratore*, ii 45 190).
  131-2 *We ... others*: *Prius afficiamur ipsi, ut alios afficiamus* (½°),
again quoting from memory, *adficiamurque antequam adficere conemur* (Quintilian,
Institutio Oratoria, vi 2 28).
  140 *Speaker*: Bromley (135.197n.) had adequate reason to 'bear Ill-will'
toward Harley, who had lobbied 'knavishly' and successfully against his election as Speaker in October 1705 (*POAS*, Yale, vii 111, 133-41).

will to another Person, or to have an extream bad Opinion of him,
or to think him an Obstructer of those fine Measures he would
bring about, and should yet in one of his Panegyricks pray to
God for the continuance of that very Person's Life, as *an
invaluable Blessing*; such a fulsom piece of Insincerity would   145
only expose him to shame and derision.

   In the next place, whoever wou'd blame or condemn any other Person, shou'd take care that there be some ground or reason for his
Accusation, if he means it shou'd have any effect: for such Cen- ·
sures, private or publick, as contradict the general Knowledge and 150
Experience of the World, turn always to the Disgrace of those that
pass them, and to the Honour of those that are so censur'd. *Lucian*
lays it down for a Maxim, That Calumny it self can do no harm, unless it reports such things as seem at least to be true: For he
says, That the Goddess Truth, who is Mistress of all other things, 155
can only be subdu'd by an Enemy resembling her self. It was in vain
therefore that the Senate of *Athens* impeach'd *Aristides* upon the
Subject of his *Accounts*, and condemn'd him for wasting the Publick Treasure, when in the course of his long Services, he had
given such convincing Proofs of his Innocence, Justice and Vir-   160
tue: His Character was not at all blemish'd by that groundless
Accusation: He had still the glorious Distinction of being call'd
Aristides the Just: And he was afterwards, in a very few Years,
recall'd to the Service of his Country. And all that the prevailing Faction gain'd by their unjust Sentence was the Loss of their 165
Credit at that time, and the Reproach of History ever since; in
which they still stand branded upon Record for a violent unruly
Multitude, without Sense of Honour, of Merit, or of Justice.

   For these and a thousand other Reasons, I wou'd feign exhort
my Friend to the Study and Love of Truth, that his Writings   170

---

142 *Obstructer*: innuendo: Harley. William Stephens supposed that Harley was
capable '(through his skill in the Rules and Methods of the House of Commons)
to obstruct and defeat all Motions which were not of his own making' (*A Letter
to the Author of the Memorial of the State of England*, 1705, p. 31). This was
currently the October Club's complaint against Harley.
   145 *invaluable*: Another phrase from Bromley's address of 26 April 1711, in
which he invoked Providence to 'continue still to preserve so invaluable a
Life' (*CJ*, xvi 616).
   152 *Lucian*: *Calum. non tem. cred.* [*Lucian*, edd. A.M. Harmon *et al.*, 8 vols.,
Loeb Classical Library, London, Heinemann, 1913-67, i 375] (½°).
   157 *Aristides*: Plutarch[, *Life of Aristides*, iv 3, vii 2, viii 1]; Cor[ne-
lius] Nep[os, *Aristides*, 1] (½°).

might pass better in the World: but I am afraid 'tis labour lost,
and I might as well give him quite over.

No. 41 [Swift]   10 May 1711

The EXAMINER.

Dos est magna parentium virtus.

I Took up a Paper (Fig. VII) some Days ago in a Coffee-House; and
if the Correctness of the Style, and a superior Spirit in it, had
not immediately undeceiv'd me, I should have been apt to imagine,
I had been reading an *Examiner*. In this Paper, there were several
5   Important Propositions advanced. For Instance, That *Providence*
rais'd up Mr. H----y to be an Instrument of great Good, in a very
critical Juncture, when it was much wanted. That, *His very Ene-*
mies acknowledge his eminent Abilities, and distinguishing Merit,
by their unwearied and restless Endeavours against His *Person and*
10   *Reputation*: That *they have had an inveterate Malice against both*:
That he *has been wonderfully preserv'd from SOME unparalell'd*
Attempts; with more to the same Purpose. I immediately computed
by Rules of Arithmetick, that in the last cited Words there was
something more intended than the Attempt of *Guiscard*, which I
15   think can properly pass but for *One* of the *SOME*. And, tho' I dare
not pretend to guess the Author's Meaning; yet the Expression
allows such a Latitude, that I would venture to hold a Wager,
most Readers, both *Whig* and *Tory*, have agreed with me, that this
Plural Number must in all Probability, among other Facts, take in
20   the Business of *Greg*.

Motto Horace, *Odes*, iii 24 21: The Lovers for their Dowry claim | The happy
Mother's spotless Fame.
  1 Paper: [dh title] *The Congratulatory Speech of William Bromley, Esq;*
Speaker of the Honourable House of Commons, to the Right Honourable Robert
Harley, Esq; Chancellor of Her Majesty's Exchequer, upon his Attending the
Service of the House of Commons, on Thursday the 26th of April 1711. Together
with the Chancellor of the Exchequer's Answer, London, for S. Keble and Henry
Clements, 1711 (E*1922*, ix 262). Swift may be suspected to have written this
work, which the Commons ordered to be published, for Bromley's literary talent
was very modest (*POAS*, Yale, vii 111-12). At least two editions were required.
  20 *Greg*: 39.127n.

The *Congratulatory* SPEECH *of* William Bromley, *Esq; Speaker of the Honourable* House *of* Commons, *to the Right Honourable* Robert Harley, *Esq; Chancellor of Her* MAJESTY's *Exchequer, upon his Attending the Service of the* House *of* Commons, *on* Thursday *the* 26th *of* April, 1711. *Together with the Chancellor of the Exchequer's* ANSWER.

Mercurij 11. *die Aprilis,* 1711.

Resolved, Nemine Contradicente,

THAT *when the Right Honourable* Robert Harley, *Esq; Chancellor of Her Majesty's* Exchequer, *Attends the Service of this House, the Speaker do, in the Name of this House, congratulate the said Mr.* Harley's *Escape and Recovery, from the barbarous and villanous Attempt made upon him by the Sieur* De Guiscard.

Veneris 27. *die Aprilis,* 1711.

Ordered,

THAT *Mr. Speaker be desired to print his Congratulatory Speech to Mr. Chancellor of the* Exchequer, *yesterday, with the Answer of Mr. Chancellor of the* Exchequer *to the same.*

Mr. Chancellor of the Exchequer.

HEN *the barbarous and villanous Attempt made* upon you *by the Sieur* De Guiscard, *a French Papist,* was communicated to this House, they immediately declared, *they were most deeply affected to find such an Instance of inveterate Malice* against you. And observing, how you have been treated by some Persons, they concluded, they had Reason to believe, *That your Fidelity to Her Majesty, and Zeal for Her Service, had drawn upon you the Hatred of all the Abettors of Popery and Faction.*

In this Opinion they must be abundantly confirmed, since the LORDS and the QUEEN have concurred with them.

Sir. If your *Fidelity to Her Majesty, and Zeal for Her Service,* could ever be doubted, and wanted any Testimonials to prove them, you have now the most Honourable, the most Ample, and the most Undeniable, that can be given ; and after these, it would be an unpardonable Presumption in me, to imagine I could add to them, by saying any thing of your Faithful Discharge of those great Trusts you have been honoured with. To which your eminent Abilities at first recommended you, and your distinguishing Merits have since justified Her Majesty's wise Choice.

Your very Enemies, Sir, acknowledge this, by their unwearied, and restless Endeavours against your Person and Reputation.

God be thanked, they have been hitherto disappointed, and have not been able to accomplish what their *Inveterate,* but impotent, *Malice,* had designed against both.

A   And

(Above and facing). The Congratulatory Speech of William Bromley, Esq; Speaker of the Honourable House of Commons, to the Right Honourable Robert Harley, Esq; . . . London, for Samuel Keble and Henry Clements, 1711, folio half sheet

And may the same Providence, that has wonderfully preserved you from some unparallelled Attempts; and that has raised you up to be an Instrument of Great Good in a very critical Juncture, when it was much wanted, continue still to preserve *so invaluable a Life*, for the Perfecting of what is so happily begun; that we may owe to your Counsels, and to your Conduct (under Her Majesty) the Maintenance and Firm Establishment of our Constitution in Church and State.

These Expectations, Sir, have filled this House with an inexpressible Satisfaction for your *Escape and Recovery*, which they have unanimously commanded me to congratulate. I do therefore, *in the Name of this House, congratulate your Escape and Recovery from the barbarous and villanous Attempt made upon you by the Sieur De Guiscard.*

The Chancellor of the *Exchequer's* ANSWER.

MR. SPEAKER,

THE Honour this House has done me, which You have expressed in so obliging a Manner, is a sufficient Reward for the greatest Merit. I am sure, it so far exceeds my Deserts, That all I can do or suffer for the Publick, during the whole Course of my Life, will still leave me in Debt to Your Goodness.

By the Acceptance You have vouchsafed my Poor Service, How Noble an Encouragement, Worthy of You, has this House given all our Fellow-Subjects, to exert themselves in the Glorious Cause of Preserving the Constitution in Church and State, and in Loyalty to the Best of SOVEREIGNS?

This, without Doubt, was Your View; And this may convince all who are not designedly obstinate, how dear the True Interest of the Nation is to this Honourable *Assembly.*

SIR, The undeserved Favour I have received this Day, is deeply imprinted in my Heart; and whenever I look upon my Breast, it will put me in Mind of the Thanks due to GOD, my Duty to the QUEEN, and that Debt of Gratitude and Service I must always owe to this Honourable House, *to You,* MR. SPEAKER, *and to every Particular Member.*

BY Virtue of an Order of the House of Commons, *I do appoint Samuel Keble and Henry Clements to Print this Speech and Answer; And that no other Person presume to Print the same.*

W. BROMLEY *Speaker.*

LONDON: Printed for *Samuel Keble* at the *Turk's Head* in *Fleetstreet*, and *Henry Clements* at the *Half-Moon* in S. *Paul's* Church-yard. 1711.

(*Price Two Pence.*)

See now the Difference of Styles. Had I been to have told my
Thoughts on this Occasion; instead of saying how Mr. *H----y was
treated by some Persons*, and *preserved from some unparalell'd
Attempts*; I should with intolerable Bluntness and ill Manners,
have told a formal Story, of a Com----ee sent to a Condemn'd   25
Criminal in *Newgate*, to bribe him with a Pardon, on Condition he
would Swear High Treason against his Master, who discovered his
Correspondence, and secur'd his Person, when *a certain grave
Politician* had given him Warning to make his Escape: And by this
means I should have drawn a whole swarm of Hedge-writers to ex-   30
haust their Catalogue of Scurrilities against me as a Lyar, and
a Slanderer. But with Submission to the Author of that foremen-
tion'd Paper, I think he has carry'd that Expression to the utmost it will bear: For after all this Noise, I know of but *two
Attempts* against Mr. *H----y*, that can really be call'd *unpara-* 35
lell'd, which are those aforesaid of *Greg* and *Guiscard*; and as to
the rest, I will engage to *parallel* them from the Story of *Cataline*, and others I could produce.

However, I cannot but observe, with infinite Pleasure, that a
great Part of what I have charged upon the late prevailing Fac-   40
tion, and for affirming which, I have been adorn'd with so many
decent Epithets, hath been sufficiently confirm'd at several
times, by the Resolutions of one or t'other House of Parliament.
I may therefore now say, I hope, with good Authority, that *there
have been some unparalell'd Attempts against Mr.* HARLEY. That the   45
late Ministry were justly to blame in some Management, which

23 *from*] by 38 8°+12°   36 and] For, 38 8°+12°

25-7 *a Com---ee ... Master*: Oldmixon explains that the Examiner 'meant to
say in plain *English, that there was a Committee of Seven Lords, sent to a
Condemn'd Criminal in* Newgate, *to bribe Him with a Pardon, on Condition he
would swear High Treason, against His Master*' (*A Letter to the Seven Lords of
the Committee, Appointed to Examine Gregg*, 1711, p. 9).
28 *Politician*: Sunderland? (302.95n.). The word retained something of its
original pejorative meaning: 'a shrewd schemer; a crafty plotter or intriguer'
(*OED*).
43 *one or t'other House*: cf. 'He does, with his own Impudence, and with
the Malice of a *Devil*, bring in *Both Houses* of P--- to say and mean the same
thing, and afterwards (upon another Occasion) this very Honourable *Gentleman*
[William Bromley], to strengthen his security' (Oldmixon, *A Letter to the
Seven Lords of the Committee, Appointed to Examine Gregg*, 1711, p. 10) (*E1922*,
ix 264).

occasion'd the unfortunate Battel of *Almanza*, and the disappointment at *Toulon*. That the Publick has been grievously wrong'd by
most notorious Frauds, during the *Whig* Administration. That those
50 who advis'd the bringing in the *Palatines*, were Enemies to the
Kingdom. That the late Managers of the Revenue have not duly
pass'd their Accounts, for a great Part of Thirty Five Millions,
and ought not to be trusted in such Employments any more. Perhaps
in a little time, I may venture to affirm some other Paradoxes of
55 this kind, and produce the same Vouchers. And perhaps also, if it
had not been so busy a Period, instead of one *Examiner*, the late
Ministry might have had above Four Hundred, each of whose little
Fingers would be heavier than my Loins. It makes me think of

---

47 *Almanza*: In April 1707 'the allies having besieged Villena, the duke of
Berwick march't to it's relief, and they drawing off mett him in the plain of
Almanza [sixty miles south-west of Valencia], where, after an hours engagement, the allies had 8000 men killed, a great number made prisoners', and
Spain was 'quite lost' (Luttrell, vi 167; *POAS*, Yale, vii 289). When it was
discovered in January 1708 that of the 29,395 English troops provided for
service in Spain and Portugal only 8,660 were actually there, the Tories were
able to pass a vote of censure which scared Godolphin out of his wits (*CJ*,
xv 520, 525; *Faults on both Sides*, 1710, p. 30).

48 *Toulon*: The major effort of the allies in 1707 was to have been the
capture of Toulon, the naval base from which the French fleet harried Dutch
and English shipping in the Mediterranean. The siege was opened on 15/26 July
and London bookmakers were offering 3:10 that Toulon would fall before the end
of October (Luttrell, vi 204). On 11/22 August the siege was abandoned. Failure was 'attributed to the not following prince Eugene's council, who was for
attacking the French intrenchments ... before they were finish't, but the duke
of Savoy, &c. were against it' (ibid., vi 208). Actually, it was the duke of
Savoy who had ordered the attack and Prince Eugene who refused to obey the
orders (Burnet, ii 477; Trevelyan, ii 307-9). 'The news of Toulon', Godolphin
wrote to Harley, 'is extremely dejecting, and I dread the consequences of it'
(HMC *Bath MSS*, i 179).

49 *Frauds*: So far only 'Abuses' had been unearthed (332.119n.); discovery
of the great frauds awaited investigation of Marlborough (54.113n.) (Godfrey
Davies, *HLQ*, xv (1951-2), 21-44).

50 *Palatines*: The Commons resolved on 14 April 1711 'That the inviting,
and bringing over, into this Kingdom the poor *Palatines*, of all Religions, at
the publick Expence, was an extravagant and unreasonable Charge to the Kingdom, and a scandalous Misapplication of the publick Money ... and of dangerous Consequence to the Constitution in Church and State ... [and] That whosoever advised the bringing over the poor *Palatines* into this Kingdom, was an
Enemy to the Queen, and this Kingdom' (*CJ*, xvi 598)(E*1922*, ix 264).

51 *Managers*: Of whom Mainwaring, as auditor of the imprest, was one.

52 *Thirty Five Millions*: The Commons resolved on 24 April 1711 'that of the
Moneys, granted by Parliament, and issued for the publick Service, to *Christmas*, 1710, there are Thirty-five millions ... for a great Part whereof no
Accounts have been laid before the Auditors, and the rest not prosecuted by
the Accomptants, and finished' (*CJ*, xvi 613).

Neptune's Threat to the Winds: *Quos ego----- sed motos præstat componere fluctus.* Thus when these Sons of *Æolus*, had almost sunk 60
the Ship with the Tempests they rais'd, it was necessary to smooth
the Ocean, and secure the Vessel, instead of pursuing the Offenders.

But I observe the general Expectation at present, instead of
dwelling any longer upon Conjectures who is to be Punish'd for 65
past Miscarriages, seems bent upon the Rewards intended to those,
who have been so highly instrumental in rescuing our Constitution
from its late Dangers. 'Tis the Observation of *Tacitus*, in the
Life of *Agricola*, that his eminent Services had rais'd a general
Opinion of his being design'd, by the Emperor, for *Prætor* of 70
Britain. Nullis in hoc suis sermonibus, sed quia par videbatur;
And then he adds, *Non semper errat Fama, aliquando & eligit.* The
Judgment of a wise Prince, and the general Disposition of the
People, do often point at the same Person; and sometimes the
popular Wishes, do even foretel the Reward intended for some 75
superior Merit. Thus among several deserving Persons, there are
Two, whom the publick Vogue hath in a peculiar Manner singled
out, as design'd very soon to receive the choicest Marks of the
Royal Favour. *One* of them to be placed in a very high Station,
and *Both* to encrease the number of our Nobility. This, I say, is 80
the general Conjecture; for I pretend to none, nor will be chargeable if it be not fulfill'd; since it is enough for their Honour,

60 these] the 38 8°+12°   75 foretel] fortel ½° 38 12°   79 *One*] One
½°Oab L NjP   80 *Both*] both ½°Oab L NjP

59-60 *Quos ... fluctus*: Virgil, *Aeneid*, i 135: Whom I—but it is better to
calm the troubled waves.
71-2 *Nullis ... eligit*: Tacitus, *Agricola*, 9: Not because any word from
him contributed thereto, but simply because he was judged competent ... Rumor
is not always wrong; sometimes it even chooses the winner.
79 *One*: Swift had been predicting since 10 April that Harley was to succeed
as Lord Treasurer, an office that only seven men have held since 1660 (GEC,
x 264), and on 22 April he told Stella, 'I believe Mr. Harley must be lord
treasurer; yet he makes one difficulty which is hard to answer: he must be
made a lord, and his estate is not large enough' (Swift, *Journal*, pp. 239,
249).
80 *Both*: Walter Scott's gloss is 'Harley and Harcourt' (E*1814*, iv 102).
Harley was created Earl of Oxford in 23 May 1711 and Harcourt, the Lord
Keeper, was created Baron Harcourt of Stanton Harcourt on 3 September 1711.
But Swift may have had in mind St. John, whose elevation to the peerage as
Viscount Bolingbroke was delayed to 7 July 1712 because 'they want him still
in parliament', as Swift explained (Swift, *Journal*, p. 451).

that the Nation thinks them worthy of the greatest Rewards.

85   Upon this Occasion I cannot but take notice, That of all the
Heresies in Politicks, profusely scatter'd by the Partisans of
the late Administration, none ever displeased me more, or seem'd
to have more dangerous Consequences to Monarchy, than that pernicious Talent so much affected, of discovering a Contempt for
Birth, Family, and *ancient Nobility.* All the Threadbare Topicks
90   of Poets and Orators were display'd to discover to us, that *Merit*
and *Virtue* were the only *Nobility*; and that the Advantages of
Blood, could not make a Knave or a Fool either Honest or Wise.
Most popular Commotions we read of in Histories of *Greece* and
Rome, took their Rise from unjust Quarrels to the *Nobles*; and in
95   the latter, the *Plebeians* Encroachments on the *Patricians,* were
the first Cause of their Ruin.

Suppose there be nothing but Opinion in the Difference of
Blood; every Body knows, that *Authority* is very much founded on
Opinion. But surely, that Difference is not wholly imaginary. The
100 Advantages of a liberal Education, of chusing the best Companions
to converse with; not being under the Necessity of practicing
little mean Tricks by a scanty Allowance; the enlarging of Thought,
and acquiring the Knowledge of Men and Things by Travel; the
Example of Ancestors inciting to great and good Actions. These
105 are usually some of the Opportunities, that fall in the way of
those who are born, of what we call the better Families; and
allowing *Genius* to be equal in them and the Vulgar, the Odds are
clearly on their side. Nay, we may observe in some, who by the
appearance of Merit, or Favour of Fortune, have risen to great
110 Stations, from an obscure Birth, that they have still retain'd

88-9 *Contempt for ... Nobility*: 'While he was Member of the House of Commons, [Sunderland] would often among his familiar Friends refuse the Title of
Lord; [and] swear that he ... hoped to see the Day, when there should not be
a Peer in *England.*' Lemuel Gulliver was a 'great Admirer of old illustrious
Families', but his experience in Glubbdubdrib 'inclined [him] a little to
abate of that profound Veneration' (Swift, *Prose,* vii 9; xi 182, 184).
91 *Virtue ... the only Nobility*: cf. 'For Fame of Families is all a
Cheat, | *'Tis Personal Virtue only makes us great*' (Defoe, *The True-Born
Englishman* (1701) (*POAS,* Yale, vi 309).
93 *Commotions*: 'Dissentions between the *Nobles* and *Commons,* with the Consequences of them, in *Greece* and *Rome,* wherein the latter were the Aggressors', is the subject of Swift's *A Discourse of the Contests and Dissentions*
(1701), and he concludes that 'this entire Subversion of the *Roman* Liberty
and Constitution, was altogether owing to those Measures which had broke the
Balance between the *Patricians* and *Plebeians*' (Swift, *Discourse,* pp. 91, 110).

some sordid Vices of their Parentage or Education, either *insatiable Avarice*, or *ignominious Falshood* and *Corruption*.

To say the Truth, the great neglect of Education, in several Noble Families, whose Sons are suffer'd to pass the most improveable Seasons of their Youth, in Vice and Idleness, have too much 115 lessen'd their Reputation: But even this Misfortune we owe, among all the rest, to that *Whiggish* Practice of reviling the *Universities*, under the Pretence of their instilling *Pedantry, narrow Principles*, and *High-Church Doctrines*.

I would not be thought to undervalue *Merit* and *Virtue*, wherever 120 they are to be found; but will allow 'em capable of the highest Dignities in a State, when they are in a very great degree of Eminence. A Pearl holds its Value tho' it be found in a Dunghil; but however, that is not the most probable Place to search for it. Nay, I will go farther, and admit, that a Man of Quality without 125 *Merit*, is just so much the worse for his Quality; which at once sets his Vices in a more publick View, and reproaches him for them. But on the other side, I doubt, those who are always undervaluing the Advantages of *Birth*, and celebrating Personal Merit, have principally an Eye to their own, which they are fully satis- 130 fy'd with, and which no Body will dispute with them about; whereas they cannot, without Impudence and Folly, pretend to be Nobly born: Because this is a Secret too easily discovered. For no Mens Parentage is so nicely inquir'd into, as that of assuming Upstarts; especially when they affect to make it better than it is, as they 135 often do, or behave themselves with Insolence.

But whatever may be the Opinion of others upon this Subject, whose Philosophical Scorn for *Blood* and *Families*, reaches even to those that are *Royal*, or perhaps took its Rise from a *Whiggish* Contempt of the latter; I am pleas'd to find *Two* such Instances 140

---

121 'em] ½°0^ab L NjP them Σ   127 reproaches] reproacheth 38 8°+12°
133 discovered.] ½°0ab NjP ~: Σ   138 reaches] reacheth 38 8°+12°
140 *Two*] *two* ½°0ab NjP 12° 1738 8°+12°

---

112 *Avarice*: innuendo: Marlborough.
    Corruption: innuendo: Godolphin.
117-18 *Universities*: cf. 'Awkardness, Stiffness, Pedantry and wrangling Temper, for which those [bred in the universities] ... are so remarkable' (Tindal, *The Nation Vindicated from the Aspersions cast on it in a late Pamphlet, intitled A Representation of the Present State of Religion*, London, for A. Baldwin, 1711, p. 33).

of extraordinary Merit, as I have mention'd, join'd with ancient
and honourable Birth, which whether it be of real or imaginary
Value, hath been held in Veneration by all wise, polite States,
both Ancient and Modern. And, as much a Foppery, as Men pretend
145   to think it, nothing is more observable in those who rise to
great Place or Wealth, from mean Originals, than their mighty
Solicitude to convince the World that they are not so low as is
commonly believ'd. They are glad to find it made out by some
strain'd Genealogy, that they have some remote Alliance with bet-
150   ter Families. *Cromwel* himself was pleas'd with the Impudence of
a Flatterer, who undertook to prove him descended from a Branch
of the Royal Stem. I know a *Citizen*, who adds or alters a Letter
in his Name with every *Plumb* he acquires. He now wants but the
change of a Vowel, to be allied to a Sovereign Prince in *Italy*;
155   and that perhaps he may contrive to be done, by a *Mistake* of the
Graver upon his Tombstone.

     When I am upon this Subject of Nobility, I am sorry for the
Occasion given me, to mention the Loss of a Person who was so

153 acquires.] ½°0^{ab} NjP ~: Σ   but] only 38 8°+12°

---

149 *strain'd Genealogy*: The most celebrated example in the reign, Harley's claim of descent from the de Veres and the Mortimers, provided another
'Handle' that *The Medley* failed to seize.
     150 *Cromwel*: Cromwell's mother, Elizabeth Steward, was said to have been
related to the Scottish royal family by common descent from Banquo (Mark
Noble, *Memoirs of the Protectorate-House of Cromwell*, 2 vols., Birmingham,
Pearson and Rollason, 1784, ii 231-5).
     152 *Citizen*: Sir Henry Furnese (1658-1712), the son of a bankrupt butcher,
began his career as 'apprentice to a Stockin-seller in the exchange ... [and]
traded in poynt to Flanders by which it is said he gott an estate' (*Le Neve's
Pedigrees of the Knights*, ed. George W. Marshall, London, Harleian Society,
1873, p. 436). He was one of the original directors of the Bank of England in
1694 and served as receiver for the £2,000,000 loan which the New East India
Company made to the Government in 1696. His first attempt to secure election
to Parliament ended in expulsion in February 1699, but 'Equipt with Leudness,
Oaths, and Impudence' (Defoe, *Reformation of Manners* (1702) [*POAS*, Yale,
vi 406]), he was elected Sheriff of London the following year. His second
attempt to secure a seat in Parliament also ended in expulsion in February
1701, but in November 1701 he was finally elected for Sandwich and served
until his death, delivering a Whig vote in all recorded divisions. In July
1707 he was created the first baronet of Great Britain and the following year
his success was sealed by his election to the Kit-Cat Club (*Private Correspondence*, i 279). 'In the official *Return of Names of Members [of Parlia-
ment]*, the name is given successively as, Furnace, Furnac, Furnice, Furnise,
Furness and Furnese' (*E1922*, ix 268).
     153 *Plumb*: 217.172.
     158 *Person*: Rochester died on 3 May 1711. 'He is a great loss to us', Swift
said (Swift, *Journal*, p. 260).

great an Ornament to it, as the late Lord President; who began
early to distinguish himself in the Publick Service, and pass'd   160
through the highest Employments of State, in the most difficult
Times, with great Abilities and untainted Honour. As he was of
a good old Age, his Principles of Religion and Loyalty had
receiv'd no Mixture from *late Infusions*, but were instill'd into
him by his illustrious Father, and other noble Spirits, who had   165
expos'd their Lives and Fortunes for the Royal Martyr.

Pulcherrima proles,
Magnanimi Heroes nati melioribus annis.

His first great Action was, like *Scipio*, to defend his Father,
when oppress'd by Numbers; and his Filial Piety was not only re-   170
warded with long Life, but with a Son, who upon the like Occasion,
would have shewn the same Resolution. No Man ever preserv'd his
Dignity better when he was out of Power, nor shew'd more Affabi-
lity while he was in. But I must here break off, however abruptly,
not pretending in the narrow Compass of this Paper, to draw so   175
great a Character; which I leave to abler Pens.

174-6 But ... Pens.] ½°0^{ab} NjP To conclude: His Character (which I do not
here pretend to draw) is such, as his nearest Friends may safely trust to the
most Impartial Pen; nor wants the least of that Allowance which, they say, is
required for those who are Dead. Σ

---

165 *Father*: Rochester was the second son of Edward Hyde, Earl of Clarendon,
Charles II's Lord Chancellor and historian of the Civil War.
167-8 *Pulcherrima ... annis*: Virgil, Aeneid, vi. 648: family most fair,
high-souled heroes born in happier years.
169 *Scipio*: Livy, xxi 46 6-8: the consul was wounded and was only saved
from danger by the intervention of his son, who was just reaching manhood.
This is the youth who will have the glory of finishing this war, and be sur-
named Africanus, from his famous victory over Hannibal and the Phoenicians.
defend his Father: Charles II sacrificed his Lord Chancellor to win
favour with the House of Commons, which instituted impeachment proceedings
against Clarendon in November 1667. 'When the tumultuous perplex'd charge of
accumulated Treasons was preferr'd against him by the *Commons*; his son *Lawrence*, then a member of that house, stept forth with this brave defiance to
his Accusers, that, if they cou'd make out any proof of any *one* single
article, he wou'd, as he was authoriz'd, join in the condemnation of his
father' (John Burton, *The Genuineness of Ld Clarendon's History of the Rebellion Printed at Oxford Vindicated*, Oxford, for James Fletcher, sold by
M. Cooper, 1744, p. 111) (E*1814*, iv 106).

No. 33 [Mainwaring]   14 May 1711

The MEDLEY.

*How Fortune comes to have so great a share in the Government of Kingdoms
    and States.*
The Examiner *turn'd Whig again.*
Why the Tories can never succeed in the Management of State-Affairs.
The Examiner *goes beyond a* French *Jesuit.*
A Law in Plato *concerning Modesty and Justice.*

THE Campaign being now begun, my Friend turns his Thoughts that
way, and gives you his Opinion of Warlike Matters: *Fortune*, he
says, *has too great a share in the good or ill Success of Military
Actions.* This is a Maxim which he advanc'd to lessen, as much as
5 in him lies, the Merit of a certain General's past Services, and
the Hopes we have of his future; and it plainly shews, that his
Good-will to him still continues. I will not pretend to say at
this time how much our wonderful Successes have been owing to his
Conduct and Valour; but since the *Examiner* will have it, that
10 Fortune is so powerful, I will only wish she may be as kind as
she has been, and not presume to suppose she has no share in our
Actions Abroad, since it is evident to all *Europe* what Wonders
she performs at Home:

$$Ludum\ insolentem\ ludere\ pertinax,$$
15 $$Transmutat\ incertos\ Honores.$$

Socrates, who was the wisest Man that ever the World saw, till
the *Examiner* appear'd in it, gives the Reason why Chance has so
much to do with Human Affairs: he says, 'tis because bold Men are
suffer'd to meddle with what they do not understand; whereas, if
20 People had more Steddiness, Constancy and Prudence, we should not

---

1 *Campaign*: Marlborough's last campaign began on 19/30 April 1711 when he
joined the confederate army at Orchies and moved out the next day towards
Valenciennes (Boyer, *Annals*, 1712, p. 9).
2-4 *Fortune ... Actions*: 390.144-5.
14-15 *Ludum ... Honores*: Horace, *Odes*, iii 29 50-1: [Fortune] stubborn to
pursue her wanton sport, shifts her fickle favours.

be so much expos'd to Fortune. But I will translate his own
words: Having been invited by a King to take care of him, and his
Kingdom, he writ a Letter to him, some of which was to this effect: 'You offer me part of your Kingdom, and invite me to it,
not as to another Government, but to rule both your Subjects and   25
your self; but I confess I have not learn'd to command, and
would no more undertake to rule, not knowing how, than to play at
Dice, having never been taught. And doubtless if other Men were
of the same Mind, there would be fewer Troubles in Life: Whereas,
now the Confidence of such as are ignorant, undertaking Things   30
they do not understand, occasions these many Disturbances. Hence
it is that People make Fortune greater than she is, and by their
own *Folly* increase her Power.'

If my Friend therefore thinks that Fortune has a greater share
in Business now than she had some time ago, he will do well to   35
find out some better Reason for it than this is.

But I know not what has come into his Head, that all of a sudden he has a mind to turn Whig again: *I do agree,* quoth he, *that
in my own private Opinion, some Writers did carry that Tenet of
Passive-Obedience to a height, which seem'd hardly consistent*   40
*with the Liberties of a Country, whose Laws can neither be
enacted nor repeal'd without the Consent of the whole People.*
This I repeat, that the Tories may perceive he is not the Man
they took him for. They thought he would have done and said any
thing they requir'd of him, and have stood to it also; and indeed   45
he has perform'd pretty well. But alas! he is too apt to be
frighted at every idle Rumour, and when they want him in earnest,
they may by this observe, he will as surely leave them in the
lurch, as they left King *James*; when by crying up Passive-
Obedience and Non-Resistance, they had tempted him to put their   50
Loyalty to the Tryal. Because, forsooth, there is a noise of
several new Promotions, and no body is yet nam'd out of the hot-
test Rank of Tories; therefore this ungrateful Person, forgetting
all the sweet Advantages he has receiv'd from the extravagant
Rage of his Party, is growing, beyond all Expectation, to be a   55

24-33 *You ... Power*: Stanley, p. 100.
38 *turn Whig again*: 336.9-11.
38-42 *I ... People*: 403.102-6.
52 *Promotions*: 417.78, 80.

very civil moderate Churchman. And if it shou'd be thought proper
to take in any of the *Ruin'd Party*, I make no doubt but this very
Friend of mine wou'd soon be answering all his own Papers, falling upon all the Bishops and other Writers *that have carry'd that*
60 *Tenet of Passive Obedience to a height*, &c. and reviling even the
Homilies, the *Convocation-Book*, and the dear *Oxford Decree*, with
the same Fury which he once exerted in behalf of them.

   And after all, it is not impossible, but such a day as this may
come; for I know not how it happens, that nothing cou'd ever
65 succeed that was trusted to the Management of this unfortunate
Set of Men, call'd Tories: Which puts me in mind of a late Rant
of one that passes for a Great Man at present; who speaking of
that Party, apply'd not improperly some Verses out of a Play. The
Tories, said he, are only to us

70 　　　　　　*The Steps on which we tread to rise and reach*
　　　　　　Our Wish; and that obtain'd, Down with the Scaf-
　　　　　　　　folding.
　　　　　　------------------*They've serv'd their End,*
　　　　　　And are like Lumber, *to be left and scorn'd.*

75 But I hope this was no more than a sudden Flight, without ground
or reason; and that after their signal Services, Riots and In-
surrections, they will not so soon be made *Lumber* and *Scaffolds*.
Some of them at least will surely be more civilly treated; and
they have generally such admirable Talents for Business, and have

---

   58 *answering*: The Examiner threatened on 14 December (96.45) to answer him-
self and carried out the threat in *The Examiner*, No. 23, 4 January 1711.
   60-1 *the Homilies*: The Book of Homilies mentioned in the 35th Article of
Religion of the Church of England is in two volumes, *Certayne Sermons, or
Homelies, appoynted by the Kynges Maiestie, to be declared and redde, by all
Persones, Vicars, or Curates, every Sondaye in their Churches, where they have
Cure* (1547) and *The Second Tome of Homelyes* (1563), written by Thomas Cranmer,
Hugh Latimer, John Jewel, Edmund Grindal, and others.
   61 *the Convocation-Book*: presumably Atterbury, *The Rights, Powers, and
Privileges of an English Convocation, Stated and Vindicated* (1701), quoted
above (367.102-368.106).
   　Oxford Decree: 403.96.
   66 *Set*: Mainwaring mocks the Examiner with one of his favourite words
(6.98, 38.125, 256.29, etc.).
   67 *Great Man*: St. John(?); cf. 74.36n.
   69 *us*: innuendo: Jacobites.
   70-4 *The ... scorn'd*: Congreve, *The Mourning Bride. A Tragedy*, London, for
Jacob Tonson, 1697, pp. 24-5.

Principles so well fitted to our Constitution, that People will   80
be mightily pleas'd to see them employ'd; for they must needs
make a most wonderful figure. 'Tis true, there will be great
danger, that the Whigs will get the better of them in time;
because, after all the ill things that have been said of their
Doctrines and Practices, they have this advantage over those of   85
the Tories, that they happen to be founded upon Truth and Reason:
And since those are the two Enemies which that Party fight against,
it is not strange if the Principles of the Whigs prove too hard
for them, as they ever have been for all kinds of Opposers: Nor
will any body else be in fault, if this shou'd happen; the Tories   90
will have nothing else to blame but themselves and their own
Principles, which have the misfortune to be inconsistent not only
with Reason or Truth, but with the Revolution too, on which the
present Government is founded.

What the *Examiner* says of Nobility in general, and of the two   95
Coronets he has bespoke, is so very mysterious and extraordinary,
that it must be refer'd to my next. But I can't help taking notice of a former Passage of his, before he last turn'd Whig. It
had been urg'd on the other side, that as much regard was due to
the Acts of former Parliaments, as to those of the present; and   100
something civil had been said of those two black Whig Parliaments
that sat before and after the Union: Upon which, quoth my Friend,
*By the same Argument the Parliament that began the Rebellion
against King* Charles *the First, voted his Tryal, and appointed
his Murderers, ought to be remember'd with respect.* I beg the   105
Reader to consider attentively this Paragraph, because there is
not one more extraordinary in all my Friend's Works. First, he
plainly insinuates that those two Parliaments before-mention'd
deserve no more Honour than that which murder'd the King: And
next, he expresly and boldly affirms, that the Parliament which   110

100 Acts] Act ½°

---

95 *Nobility*: 418.84-420.156.
99 *urg'd*: 349.21-7.
101 *something civil had been said*: 350.40-351.82.
103-5 *By ... respect*: To score here Mainwaring omits Swift's antecedent,
which is Oldmixon's foolish argument that 'one Parliament is ... as good as
another' (349.21-2). By Oldmixon's argument it is indeed true that the Rump
'ought to be remembered with Respect', as Swift says.

began the Rebellion, was the same with that which committed the
Murder. This was so surprizing an Assertion, that remembring a
French Jesuit had writ a History of those Times, I cou'd not help
looking into it, to see if my Friend had not borrow'd this Pas-
115 sage from him. But alas! the *French* Priest durst not injure so
much his Conscience and his Cloth, to write any thing like it:
For speaking of that Murder and the Murderers, he calls them
*Forty Villains, the Scum of the Kingdom, who made void all that
the Parliament had been doing*: And he says, very honestly, *The
120 Thing they call'd a Parliament, was then only a monstrous Gang,
much differing from the Majesty of an Assembly formerly compos'd
of so many Great Men.* Thus we see how far the *Examiner* can outdo
even the errantest *French* Priest; who tho employ'd and rewarded
by King *James*, and instructed to fix any Infamy on our Parlia-
125 ments, yet had too much Modesty and Justice to publish so known
a Falshood.

There is a Law mention'd by *Plato*, which *Jupiter* is said to
have enacted in his own name; That if any Man appear'd plainly to
be incapable of Modesty or Justice, he shou'd immediately be
130 knock'd o'th' Head as a common Pestilence. The Account he gives
of it, is this.

He is describing the first State of Human Society: How Mankind
built Towns to defend themselves from Beasts; and how in a more
than brutal manner they afterwards fell upon one another; and at
135 last he says, *Jupiter* justly fearing that the whole Race wou'd
be destroy'd, order'd *Mercury* to go to them, and to carry along
with him Modesty and Justice, as the best Support and Ornament
of their new-built Cities, and the firmest Bond of their own
mutual Friendship. *Mercury* upon this occasion ask'd *Jupiter* in
140 what manner he shou'd bestow Justice and Modesty upon Mankind:
Whether, said he, as the Arts are divided, shall I also divide
these Vertues (which indeed are of two kinds) and shall I give to

111 *same*: The Long Parliament 'which began the Rebellion' cannot be the
same as the Rump 'which committed the Murder' of Charles I, because the large
majority in the Long Parliament opposed to the trial of Charles I were for-
cibly excluded from the House of Commons on 6-7 December 1648 (Clarendon,
The History of the Rebellion, iii 183-4).
118-22 *Forty ... Men*: Pierre Joseph d'Orleans, *The History of the Revolutions in England under the Family of the Stuarts from the Year 1603 to 1690*,
2nd edn., London, for E. Curll *et al.*, 1722, pp. 124, 132.
132-53 *How ... Republick*: Plato, *Protagoras*, 322B-D.

some Men one, to some the other; as we see by experience, that
one skilful Physician is sufficient for a great many of the
Ignorant, and so of other Arts and Professions: Or shall I so   145
divide them among the whole Race of Mankind, as that every single
Person may have a share of them? Divide them in that manner,
says *Jupiter*, and let all Mankind be Partakers of them: For if
these Vertues were only convey'd to a few, as the Arts and
Sciences are given, it wou'd be impossible for any Cities to sub-   150
sist. Therefore I wou'd have you go further and establish a Law
in my Name, That whoever can't be made to partake of Modesty and
Justice, shall be destroy'd as a Plague of the Republick.

   I have often thought how very short-liv'd my Friend had been,
if he had happen'd to live under such a Law as this.   155

No. 42 [Swift]   17 May 1711

The EXAMINER.

Quem cur distringere coner,   ·
Tutus ab infestis latronibus?

I Never let slip an Opportunity of endeavouring to convince the
World, that I am not Partial, and to confound the idle Reproach
of my being hired or directed what to write in Defence of the
present Ministry, or for detecting the Practices of the former.
When I first undertook this Paper, I firmly resolv'd, that if   5
ever I observ'd any gross Neglect, Abuse or Corruption in the
publick Management, which might give any just Offence to reasonable People, I would take notice of it with that innocent Boldness which becomes an honest Man, and a true Lover of his Country;
at the same time preserving the Respect due to Persons so highly   10
entrusted by so wise and excellent a Queen. I know not how such

   9 becomes] becometh 38 8°+12°

   Motto Horace, *Satires*, ii 1 41: Safe it lies | Within the Sheath, 'till
Thieves and Villains rise.
   3 *hired*: 404.122.

a Liberty might have been resented; but I thank God there has
been no Occasion given me to exercise it; for I can safely affirm,
that I have with the utmost Rigour, examin'd all the Actions of
15 the present Ministry, as far as they fall under general Cognizance, without being able to accuse them of one ill or mistaken
Step. Observing indeed some time ago, that Seeds of Dissention
had been plentifully scatter'd from a *certain Corner*, and fearing
they began to rise and spread, I immediately writ a Paper on the
20 Subject; which I treated with that Warmth I thought it required:
But the Prudence of those at the Helm soon prevented this growing
Evil; and at present it seems likely to have no Consequences.

I have had indeed for some time a small Occasion of Quarrelling,
which I thought too inconsiderable for a formal Subject of Com-
25 plaint, though I have hinted at it more than once. But it is
grown at present to as great a Height, as a Matter of that Nature
can possibly bear; and therefore I conceive it high time that an
effectual stop should be put to it. I have been amaz'd at the
flaming Licentiousness of several Weekly Papers, which for some
30 Months past, have been chiefly employ'd in barefac'd Scurrilities
against those who are in the greatest Trust and Favour with the
Qu---, with the first and last Letters of their Names frequently
Printed; or some Periphrasis describing their Station, or other
Innuendo's, contriv'd too plain to be mistaken. The Consequence

26 a Height] Height 38 8°+12°

---

17 *Dissention*: Passage of the Woollen Act (1699) and the Resumption Acts
(1699-1701) made Harley's New Country Party of 'Wiggs mescontents et Tories'
(248.26) vastly unpopular in Ireland. And when impeachment proceedings were
opened against the leaders of the preceding ministry, Somers, Orford, and
Charles Montagu, it appeared to Swift, 'that the same manner of proceeding, at
least as it appeared ... from the views we received of it in Ireland, had
ruined the liberties of Athens and Rome, and that it might be easy to prove it
from history. Soon after I went to London [April 1701]; and, in a few weeks,
drew up a discourse, under the title of [*A Discourse of*] *the Contests and Dissentions of the Nobles and Commons in Athens and Rome, with the Consequences
they had upon both those States*. This discourse I sent very privately to the
press' (Swift, *Prose*, viii 119).
19 *Paper*: A *Discourse* was published in October 1701 (Swift, *Discourse*,
p. 176).
21 *the Prudence of those at the Helm*: Somers and Orford came to trial before the Lords and were acquitted when the Commons failed to appear to argue
its case against them. The other two cases, Montagu and Portland, were then
dismissed. Swift gives credit now to the Speaker for aborting the proceedings,
but Harley's role is ambiguous (ibid., p. 145).

of which is, (and it is natural it should be so) that their long   35
Impunity hath render'd them still more Audacious.

At this time I particularly intend a Paper call'd the *Medley*;
whose indefatigable, incessant Railings against me, I never
thought convenient to take notice of, because it would have
diverted my Design, which I thought was of Publick Use. Besides,   40
I never yet observ'd that Writer, or those Writers, (for it is
every way a *Medley*) to argue against any one material Point or
Fact that I had advanced, or make one fair Quotation. And after
all, I knew very well how soon the World grows weary of Controversy. 'Tis plain to me, that three or four Hands at least have   45
been join'd at times in that worthy Composition; but the Out-
lines as well as the Finishing, seem to have been always the
Work of the same Pen, as it is visible from half a score Beauties
of Style inseparable from it. But who these *Medlers* are, or where
the judicious Leaders have pick'd them up, I shall never go about   50
to Conjecture. Factious Rancour, false Wit, abandon'd Scurrility,
impudent Falshood, and servile Pedantry, having so many Fathers,
and so few to own them, that Curiosity her self would not be at
the pains to guess. It is the first time I ever did my self the
Honour to mention that admirable Paper: Nor could I imagine any   55
Occasion likely to happen, that would make it necessary for me to
engage with such an Adversary. This Paper is Weekly Publish'd,
and as appears by the Number, has been so for several Months, and
is next to the *Observator*, allow'd to be the best Production of
the Party. Last Week my Printer brought me that of *May* 7, Numb.   60

40 thought was] intended to be 38 8°+12°   46 that] this 38 8°+12°
50 Leaders] Leader 38 8°+12°   60 the] that 38 8°+12°

---

37 *the Medley*: 'Many People wonder'd why it was so long before the *Examiner*
did me the honour to take notice of me; but I ... was surpriz'd at his ever
naming me at all, because it oblig'd him to vindicate himself' (*The Medley*,
16 July 1711).

43 *Quotation*: 335.163-4.

45 *Hands*: During Mainwaring's illness (January-April 1711) he received
major help from Oldmixon and minor assistance from White Kennett, Henley, and
Steele (Oldmixon, *The Life*, pp. 190, 193).

48 *the same Pen*: Even during his illness Mainwaring sent 'Hints' to Oldmixon and revised or corrected his work (ibid., pp. 192, 193, 201).

54 *the first time*: This is the Examiner's first mention of *The Medley* but
the third or fourth reference to *The Medley* (49.18n., 68.49n., 113.69n., 390.
149-56n.).

59 *the Observator*: 35.21n.

32. where there are two Paragraphs relating to the *Speaker* of the
House of Commons, and to Mr. *Harley*; which, as little as I am
inclin'd to engage with such an Antagonist, I cannot let pass,
without failing in my Duty to the Publick: And if those in Power
65 will suffer such infamous Insinuations to pass with Impunity,
they act without Precedent from any Age or Country of the World.

I desire to open this Matter, and leave the *Whigs* themselves to
determine upon it. The House of Commons resolv'd, *Nemine Contra-*
dicente, that the *Speaker* should congratulate Mr. *Harley*'s Escape
70 and Recovery in the Name of the House, upon his first Attendance
on their Service. This is accordingly done; and the Speech, together with the Chancellor of the *Exchequer*'s, are Printed by
Order of the House. The Author of the *Medley* takes this Speech to
task the very next Week after it is Publish'd, telling us, in the
75 aforesaid Paper, That *the* Speaker's *commending Mr.* Harley, *for*
being an Instrument of great Good to the Nation, *was ill-chosen*
Flattery; because Mr. Harley *had brought the Nation under great*
Difficulties, to say no more: He says, *that when the* Speaker *tells*
Mr. Harley, that Providence has wonderfully preserv'd him from
80 some unparallel'd Attempts (for that the *Medley* alludes to) *he*
only revives a false and groundless Calumny upon other Men; which
is an Instance of impotent, but inveterate Malice, that makes him
[the *Speaker*] *still appear more vile and contemptible*. This is an
Extract from his first Paragraph. In the next this Writer says,
85 *That the* Speaker's *praying to God for the continuance of Mr.*
Harley's *Life, as an invaluable Blessing, was a fulsom piece of*
Insincerity, which exposes him to Shame and Derision; because he
is known to bear ill Will to Mr. Harley, *to have an extream bad*
Opinion of Him, and to think him an Obstructor of those fine
90 *Measures he would bring about.*

87 *exposes*] *exposeth* 38 8°+12°

---

61   *two Paragraphs*: 411.105-413.146.
68-70 *The ... House*: *CJ*, xvi 590, 615-16, 617.
75-8 *commending ... more*: 411.108-10.
78-80 *He ... Attempts*: Temple Scott points out that *The Medley* does not
'mention ... Providence having wonderfully preserved [Harley] from some un-
paralleled attempts' (E*1922*, ix 273). But this clause in Bromley's speech,
with its slur on the seven Whig lords of the committee to interrogate Greg
(*CJ*, xvi 615), is clearly the clause that *The Medley* alludes to at 411.113-14.
81-3 *revives ... contemptible*: 411.112-412.116.
85-90 *praying ... about*: 412.140-413.146.

I now appeal to the *Whigs* themselves, whether a great Minister
of State, in high Favour with the Qu---, and a *Speaker* of the
House of Commons, were ever Publickly treated after so extraordinary a Manner, in the most licentious Times? For this is not a
clandestine Libel stolen into the World, but openly Printed and   95
Sold, with the Bookseller's Name and place of Abode at the Bottom. And the Juncture is admirable, when Mr. *H----y* is generally
believ'd upon the very Point to be made an *Earl*, and promoted to
the most important Station of the Kingdom: Nay, the very Marks of
Esteem he hath so lately received from the whole Representative   100
Body of the People, are call'd *ill-chosen Flattery, and a fulsom
Piece of Insincerity, exposing the* Donors *to Shame and Derision.*

Does this intrepid Writer think he has sufficiently disguis'd
the Matter, by that stale Artifice of altering the Story, and
putting it as a suppos'd Case? Did any Man who ever saw the   105
Congratulatory Speech, read either of those Paragraphs in the
Medley, without Interpreting them just as I have done? Will the
Author declare upon his great Sincerity, that he never had any
such Meaning? Is it enough, that a Jury at *Westminster-Hall*
would, perhaps, not find him guilty of defaming the *Speaker* and   110
Mr. *Harley* in that Paper? Which however, I am much in doubt of
too; and must think the Law very defective, if the Reputation of
such Persons must lie at the Mercy of such Pens. I do not remember to have seen any Libel, suppos'd to be writ with Caution and
double Meaning, in order to prevent Prosecution, deliver'd under   115
so thin a Cover, or so unartificially made up as this; whether
it were from an Apprehension of his Reader's Dulness, or an Effect
of his own. He hath transcrib'd the very Phrases of the *Speaker*,
and put them in a different Character, for fear they might pass
unobserv'd, and to prevent all possibility of being mistaken.   120
I shall be pleas'd to see him have recourse to the old Evasion,
and say, that I who make the Application, am chargeable with the
Abuse: Let any Reader of either Party be Judge. But I cannot forbear asserting, as my Opinion, that for a M-----ry to endure such

98 *made an Earl, and promoted*: 417.80n.
101-2 *ill-chosen ... Derision*: 411.111, 413.145-6.
112 *Law ... defective*: 387.59-60.
121 *the old Evasion*: i.e. ''twas Application made the Ass'; cf. *Some
Memoirs of Abel, Toby's Uncle*, 1726, p. 19.

125 open Calumny, without calling the Author to Account, is next to
deserving it. And this is an Omission I venture to charge upon
the present M-----ry, who are too apt to despise little Things,
which however have not always little Consequences.

When this Paper was first undertaken, one Design, among others,
130 was, to *Examine* some of those Writings so frequently Publish'd
with an evil Tendency, either to Religion or Government; but I
was long diverted by other Enquiries, which I thought more immediately necessary; to animadvert upon Mens Actions, rather than
their Speculations; to shew the Necessity there was of changing
135 the Ministry, that our Constitution in Church and State might be
preserv'd; to. expose some dangerous Principles and Practices
under the former Administration, and prove by many Instances,
that those who are now at the Helm, are entirely in the true Interest of Prince and People. This I may modestly hope, hath in
140 some Measure been already done, sufficient to answer the End
propos'd, which was to inform the Ignorant and those at distance,
and to convince such as are not engag'd in a Party, from other
Motives than that of Conscience. I know not whether I shall have
any Appetite to continue this Work much longer; if I do, perhaps
145 some Time may be spent in exposing and overturning the false
Reasonings of those who engage their Pens on the other side, without losing time in vindicating my self against their Scurrilities,
much less in retorting them. Of this sort there is a certain
humble Companion, A *French Maitre des Langues*, who every Month

142 from other] from no other 38 8°+12°   149 *Maitre*] *Maitres* 12° 38
8°+12°

---

125 *calling the Author to Account*: This reflects Harley's opinion: 'I ...
wil always be ready to contribute the utmost I can to ... allaying those
heates and animositys which are greatly encreasd by the many scandalous
Lying Pamphlets which are dayly propagated by designing Knaves', he wrote to
the archbishop of Canterbury in January 1702, and he enclosed the draft of a
bill 'to have a Printer or Author answerable for every thing which is pub-
lishd' (Lambeth Palace MS 930, f. 25).
144 *continue*: 328.1.
149 *A French Maitre des Langues*: Abel Boyer (1667-1729) was a Frenchman,
born in Castres, Languedoc, and educated at the Protestant university of
Franeker in Friesland. He arrived in England in 1689 and 'fell into great
poverty' (David E. Baker, *Biographia Dramatica*, 3 vols. in 4, London, Longman *et al.*, 1812, i. 1 53). But he became 'a voluminous compiler of Annals,
Political Collections, &c.' (*The Dunciad*, ii 381n.), performed 'some Services'
for Harley (Boyer, *Annals*, 1712, p. 264), and grew rich. In 1705 Boyer took

Publishes an Extract from Votes, News-Papers, Speeches and Procla- 150
mations, larded with some insipid Remarks of his own; which he
calls *The Political State of* Great Britain: This ingenious Piece
he tells us himself, is constantly translated into *French*, and
Printed in *Holland*, where the *Dutch*, no doubt, conceive most
noble Sentiments of us, convey'd through such a Vehicle. 'Tis   155
observable in his Account for *April*, that the Vanity, so predomi-
nant in many of his Nation, has made him more concern'd for the
Honour of *Guiscard*, than the Safety of Mr. *H----y*: And for fear
we should think the worse of his Country upon that *Assassin*'s
Account, he tells us, there have been more Murders, Paracides and 160
Villanies, committed in *England*, than any other part of the World.
I cannot imagine how an illiterate Foreigner, who is neither
Master of our Language, or indeed of common Sense, and who is
devoted to a Faction, I suppose, for no other Reason, but his
having more *Whig*-Customers than *Tories*, should take it into his 165
Head to write Politick Tracts of our Affairs. But I presume, he
builds upon the Foundation of having been call'd to an Account
for his Insolence in one of his former Monthly Productions, which
is a Method that seldom fails of giving some Vogue to the foolish-
est Composition. If such a Work must be done, I wish some toler-   170
able Hand would undertake it; and that we would not suffer a
little whiffling *Frenchman* to neglect his Trade of teaching his
Language to our Children, and presume to instruct Foreigners in
our Politicks.

  150 Publishes] publisheth 38 8°+12°

---

over *The Post-Boy* and kept up a running battle with 'Drunken P[*itti*]*s*' until
Boyer gave over in August 1709 (Dunton, ii 432). In October 1710 he provided
some effective propaganda for the new Government: *A Letter from a Foreign
Minister in England to Monsieur Pettecum* and *An Essay towards the History of
the Last Ministry and Parliament* (Henry L. Snyder, *HLQ*, xxxiii (1970), 148-9).
But, failing to secure the post of gazetteer (HMC *Portland MSS*, iv 615),
Boyer went into opposition and wrote *The Protestant Post-Boy* from September
1711 to August 1712 (*N&Q*, ccxx (1975), 489).
  156 *Account*: Boyer quotes 299.39-300.56 and, after disclaiming that 'It is
altogether foreign to my present Design to apologize for the *French* Nation', he
apologizes for the French nation. Then he quotes 299.38-9 and, after retorting
upon Swift the fallacy of premature generalization, he argues that 'no foreign
Records can afford a greater Number of *Murtherers, Parricides*, and ... *solid
Villainies*, than our *English* History' (Boyer, *The Political State*, i 318;
Luttrell, vi 198-9).

No. 34 [Mainwaring]   21 May 1711

The MEDLEY.

The Examiner's *Ingratitude to the Writer of this Paper.*
Some few Remarks upon his Last.

DIOGENES said to a Man that slander'd him, *None will believe you*
when you speak Ill of me, no more than they wou'd believe me if
I shou'd speak Well of you. I know not whether it is not come to
the same pass with the *Examiner* and me, in our important Contro-
5 versy about Whig and Tory: He has said much Ill of me in his last
Paper, which I hope no body will believe; and I have upon many
occasions spoke extremely well of him, and endeavour'd to use him
like a Friend: yet it looks, after all, as if he scarce believ'd
me himself. What abundance of Time and Pains have I lost! But
10 I never took any thing so ill of him as his last Piece of Ingratitude, of which I will give a short account, and let the Reader be
Judg between us. I had observ'd long ago this great Defect in all
his Papers, that they were neither *True* nor *Probable*; and having
always found that even the profess'd Writers of Romances endea-
15 vour'd to give an Air of Truth to their Fictions, I had many
melancholy Reflections to see that of all the Authors I ever
read, my Friend was the only Man that had no regard to Truth or
Decency. Mov'd by this true Concern for his Good and Improvement,
I study'd hard a whole Day, and with the help of *Aristotle*,
20 shew'd him the absolute Necessity of going upon those Foundations,
if he intended his Works shou'd please: And as a charitable
Supplement to that Instruction, I laid down some of the common
Rules for *Praising* and *Accusing*, of which my Friend seem'd extremely ignorant, tho they were the two chief Subjects on which

1-3 *None ... you*: Stanley, p. 289.
5 *said much Ill*: 429.37-432.128.
7 *spoke extremely well*: Mainwaring and Oldmixon had ironically praised the
Examiner's wit (78.161), authoritative air (120.42-3), truthfulness (292.127),
and dexterity in argument (355.174-5).
11-12 *I ... us*: Mainwaring may be mocking 430.67-8; cf. 344.53-4, 348.175.
13 *neither True nor Probable*: 411.93-5, 106-7.
19 *Aristotle*: 412.122-4.
23 *Rules*: 412.125-414.172.

he employ'd his Pen. One wou'd have thought a Design like this,   25
conceiv'd in so friendly a manner, and executed to the best of my
small Abilities, wou'd have had his Pardon at least, if not his
Thanks; but on the contrary, I find, to my infinite surprize,
there is a most malicious and ungrateful Return given in his last
Paper, to this my good-natur'd Intention. My most necessary Hints   30
for improving his Panegyricks upon the Great, he says are downright Reflections upon them; as if he thought it a Scandal to be
decently and reasonably commended: And if this be true, I confess
he is very free from any Scandal of that kind. But I was so far
from naming any particular Person, or so much as directing him   35
whom he shou'd commend, that I was only giving general Rules for
the Exercise of his Talents that way. And tho he complains now a
second time of *bare-fac'd Scurrilities against Those who are in
the greatest Trust and Favour with the Qu---, with the first and
last Letters of their Names frequently printed*; if he can find   40
any such thing in my poor Papers, from the Beginning to the End
of them, I desire he wou'd quite throw me off, and never more own
me for his Friend. Yet he rails at me beyond measure, and calls
upon *Those in Power* to correct me, talks of *Westminster-Hall*, of
Juries and the Law; and all this, for no more than for two or   45
three common Rules of Rhetorick, intended only for the Benefit of
School-boys and himself. Well, 'tis an ungrateful World we live
in! And whoever has the least Experience or Knowledg of it, wou'd
never do a Curtesy. The late *Obadiah Walker* publish'd a whole
Book of Rhetorick, even after he turn'd Papist; and I never heard   50

---

34 from] from having ever given 12°

38-40 *bare-fac'd ... printed*: 428.30-3.
  41 *any such thing*: Scurrilities against Harley (43.30; 411.109-110) and the
first and last letters of his name (312.156, 162; 313.164) both occur in *The
Medley*, but not together.
  44 *Those in Power*: 430.64. It must have been at this time that Mainwaring
learned of Harley's inquiry whether several unspecified numbers of *The Medley*
were actionable. The Attorney-General, Sir Edward Northey, advised Harley
that they were not (p. lxi above). 'Mr. *Harley* readily acquiesced in his Judgment, and that threatning Storm blew over' (Oldmixon, *Memoirs*, pp. 11-12).
  44-5 *Westminster-Hall ... Juries and the Law*: 431.109, 112.
  49 *Walker*: Obadiah Walker (1616-99) was the Master of University College
who was converted to Roman Catholicism (*c.*1678), became the eager collaborator of James II in the Romanization of Oxford, and narrowly escaped conviction
on charges of high treason (June 1690) (Luttrell, ii 10-11, 14, 50). In his
disgrace he published *Some Instructions in the Art of Grammar* (1691).

he was call'd to account for it. Yet my Friend says, *If those in Power will suffer me to pass with Impunity, they act without Precedent from any Age or Country of the World.*

55 Thus am I to be silenc'd in a little time, and that perhaps in good Company; for he himself says, *He knows not whether he shall have any Appetite to continue his Work much longer.* But immediately after there is a word of Comfort: *If I do*, says he, *perhaps some time may be spent in overturning the false Reasonings of those that engage on the other side.* Now as ill as he has us'd me

60 for my last kind Advice, I can't resist giving him some more, to revive and *continue his Appetite to his Work.* It is certain he might make his Paper more comprehensive, and *find time to overturn more false Reasonings than he does*, if he wou'd alter and correct his Stile, which is too loose and diffus'd in all Con-

65 science: So that when I read him some times for a good while together, tho I go on very evenly and smoothly, I find it difficult to recollect what I have been doing, and whether I have been reading or sleeping. My present Advice to him therefore is, that he wou'd study *Tacitus*, and such other Politicians as say much in

70 few words: And if he obstinately persists in the same Childish Fondness for his Stile, which he has so often express'd in his Papers, I will make an Epitome of one of them, and send it to him, that he may see in how small a Compass the whole Substance may be contain'd. All this vile Drudgery will I submit to for his

75 sake, yet behold what Returns he makes me.

The Philosopher before-mention'd being ask'd, *What is best among Men*; reply'd, *Freedom of Speech*: But my Friend is so far from allowing me this Liberty, that he denies me the Freedom of our Language, and forbids me the use of certain *Words* and *Phrases*;

80 because, he says, they have been us'd by a certain *Great Man*. This is a Piece of Tory Hardship, that was not impos'd on us in former Reigns: They did not then offer to engross any part of the *English* Tongue; but knowing they cou'd not do much with it themselves, they left it to the Whigs to use and improve it as they

51-3 *If ... World*: 430.64-6.
55-6 *knows ... longer*: 432.143-4.
57-9 *If ... side*: 432.144-6.
71 *Fondness for his Stile*: 240.47-241.48.
76-7 *What ... Speech*: Stanley, p. 288.
79 *Phrases*: 431.118.

pleas'd. And notwithstanding all that my Friend has said, I am   85
still of Opinion, that the Alphabet is our own, and that we may
make use of any of the four and twenty Letters as we think fit,
if we do nothing which is forbidden by our Law. But there is one
Favour I beg of him with the greatest Earnestness, That when no
Persons are nam'd in any manner whatsoever, he will for the   90
future give me leave *to mean* for my self: For as well as I love
him, he may be assur'd, that of all Men I shall not allow him to
mean for me.

But I am surpriz'd, that it shou'd ever enter into his Head to
set the Ministry against me for an Offence, which he confesses   95
with great Simplicity, he only is guilty of himself. Why shou'd
he fancy I had any other *Meaning*, than to teach him how to flatter better, since I had so often complain'd of his *Method* of
doing it? which indeed was so gross and so slovenly, it us'd to
put me in mind of a Saying of *Antisthenes, That it was better to*   100
fall among Crows than Flatterers; for those only devour the Dead,
these the Living. My Friend seem'd to *devour* his Patrons with his
Praises: And I had a mind he shou'd touch them more gently. But
let him be as base and ungrateful as he will, and do his worst
against me, he will never be able, under this Administration, to   105
charge People with the Guilt of *Meanings* which others find out
for them, tho I can't discommend him for endeavouring to get the
Government on his side: where there is neither Strength of Reason,
nor Force of Truth, Power and Authority are extremely necessary.

But to be serious with him once in my Life, I can't help   110
repeating what I have already told him, that he mistakes the
Reign we live in. We have a Queen who will not suffer any of her
Subjects to be insulted in Weekly Libels, without giving others
the Liberty of the Law to vindicate their Characters against the

110 Life,] ~. ½° 12°

---

91 *mean for my self*: 431.108-9.
95-6 *an Offence ... he ... is guilty of himself*: 'that innocent Boldness
which becomes an honest Man'(?) (427.8-9).
100-2 *it ... Living*: Stanley, p. 279.
106 *Meanings*: Mainwaring may refer to the rule of pleading in libel cases
that wherever the words sued on are susceptible of two meanings, it is for the
jury and no one else to decide which meaning was in fact conveyed to the
readers (*Law Reports, Appeal Cases*, London, Wm. Clowes and Sons, 1882,
vii 741).

115 Malice and Insolence of their Enemies. It was this that gave
    Birth to the *Medley*: And the Author of it observing how boldly
    and basely *another Person* vilify'd the late Ministry, the *Scots*
    Nation, and the Union, the Trading and Mony'd Interest of *Great*
    Britain, the moderate Clergy and Laity of our Church, the Dis-
120 senters, and the whole Whig-Party, her Majesty's most loyal and
    faithful Subjects, thought he might lawfully undertake to answer
    the Calumnies and Falshoods of so notorious a Libeller; and this
    Design he shall pursue as long as that *other Gentleman's Appetite*
    to abuse and revile them *continues*. But whenever that shall cease,
125 the *Examiner* will have no more occasion to complain of the Author
    of the *Medley*; and he may well imagine it can be no pleasant Task
    for a Man of any Principles or Integrity to rake every Week into
    such a Heap of Slander and Scurrility as is to be met with in his
    Papers. He will then soon perceive that my Views were more gener-
130 ous than his own: That I had no private Interest to promote, nor
    Prejudice to gratify; but an honest Intention to speak well of
    Vertue in any Circumstances, while he was the servile Adorer of
    Power.

        Cou'd any true Lover of his Country hear our General call'd *a*
135 Catiline *at the Head of a Mercenary Army*, without saying a word
    in his Defence, whose Sword has been so often and so gloriously
    drawn in Defence of our Nation and of *Europe*? Cou'd he hear our
    Archbishop and the greater part of our Bishops treated as Apos-
    tates and Betrayers of the Church, and not have something at
140 least to speak in behalf of those Prelates, who had spoken and
    done so much for our Religion and Liberty? Were the most Excel-
    lent and Worthy Persons of the Kingdom to be represented as Athe-
    ists and Traitors, and given up to the Rage of a malicious and
    mutinous Faction? Or must those that never sold an Office, or
145 took a Bribe, be represented as Robbers and Cheats, and must none
    dare to do Justice to their Merit? This cou'd never be suppos'd
    in a Government, where the Laws are so freely and equally distri-
    buted; where Juries are not to be pack'd, nor Judges to be

    116 *observing*: Mainwaring may be mocking 428.17-19.
    132 *Vertue*: Mainwaring fails to score here. He wraps himself in 'Vertue'
    with even less conviction than the Examiner hides behind the throne (399.183-
    5), and for less reason.
    134 *General*: 242.83n.
    138 *Bishops*: 134.169-135.192.

influenc'd; and where the Tories must despair of reviving their
cruel Practices, which made them so terrible heretofore, and so   150
contemptible ever since. It is under the Protection of those Laws
that this Paper is now publish'd: To them it shall never give
Offence, nor to any Man whose Conscience is not first his Accuser.

151 *Laws*: The Licensing Act of 1662 (14 Car. II. c. 33), by which James II
had been able to maintain an effective censorship of all opposition, was
allowed to expire in May 1695. Thereafter, until May 1712, when an Act for
laying severall Duties upon certain printed Papers, Pamphlets, and Advertise-
ments (10 Ann. c. 18) received the royal assent, the only restraints on the
press were the laws against blasphemy, libel, and treason.

No. 43 [Swift]   24 May 1711

The EXAMINER.

Delicta majorum immeritus lues,
Romane; donec templa refeceris,
Ædesq; labentes deorum;

SEveral Letters have been lately sent me, desiring I would make
Honourable mention of the pious Design of building Fifty Churches,
in several parts of *London* and *Westminster*, where they are most
wanted; occasion'd by an Address of the *Convocation* to the Queen,
and recommended by Her Majesty to the House of Commons; who im-   5
mediately promis'd, they *would enable* Her *to accomplish so excel-*
lent a Design, and are now preparing a Bill accordingly. I thought
to have deferr'd any Notice of this important Affair 'till the
end of this Session; at which time I propos'd to deliver a particular Account of the great and useful Things already perform'd   10

Motto Horace, *Odes*, iii 6 1-3:
                    Though guiltless of your Father's Crimes,
                    Roman, 'tis thine, to latest Times
                    The Vengeance of the Gods to bear,
                    'Till thou their lawful Domes repair.
  2 *Fifty Churches*: 333.123n. Only twelve were actually built (Bennett, p. 134).
  5 *House of Commons*: After hearing the Queen's address of 29 March 1711, the
Commons resolved to 'enable her Majesty to make an effectual Provision for the
carrying on so good and necessary a Work' (*CJ*, xvi 567). The words 'to accomplish so excellent a Design' are quoted here and below (440.30-1) from the
Commons' address of 9 April 1711 (440.28).

by this present Parliament. But in compliance to those who give
themselves the Trouble of advising me; and partly convinced by
the Reasons they offer; I am content to bestow a Paper upon a
Subject, that indeed so well deserves it.

15   The Clergy, and whoever else have a true Concern for the Constitution of the Church, cannot but be highly pleas'd with one Prospect in this new Scene of Publick Affairs. They may very well
remember the Time, when every Session of Parliament, was like a
Cloud hanging over their Heads; and if it happen'd to pass with-
20   out bursting into some Storm upon the Church, we thank'd God, and
thought it an happy Escape 'till the next Meeting; upon which we
resum'd our secret Apprehensions, tho' we were not allow'd to
believe any Danger. Things are now alter'd; the Parliament takes
the Necessities of the Church into Consideration, receives the
25   Proposals of the Clergy met in Convocation, and amidst all the
Exigencies *of a long expensive War*, and *under the Pressure of
heavy Debts*, finds a Supply for erecting Fifty Edifices for the
Service of God. And it appears by the Address of the Commons to
Her Majesty upon this Occasion (wherein they discover'd a true
30   Spirit of Religion) that the applying the Mony granted *to accomplish so excellent a Design*, would, in their Opinion, be the most
effectual way of carrying on the War: That it would (to use their
own Words) *be a Means of drawing down Blessings on Her Majesty's
Undertakings, as it adds to the number of those Places, where the
35   Prayers of Her devout and faithful Subjects, will be daily offer'd
up to God, for the Prosperity of her Government at Home, and the
Success of Her Arms Abroad.*

        I am sometimes hoping, that we are not naturally so bad a
People, as we have appear'd for some Years past. *Faction*, in

14 deserves] deserveth 38 8°+12°   27 for the] to the 38 8°+12°

---

23 *Danger*: 38.107n.
28 *Address*: 'In their Address, on April 9th, 1711, the House of Commons
said: "Neither the long expensive war, in which we are engaged, nor the pressure of heavy debts, under which we labour, shall hinder us from granting to
your Majesty whatever is necessary, to accomplish so excellent a design, which,
we hope, may be a means of drawing down blessings from Heaven on all your
Majesty's other undertakings, as it adds to the number of those places, where
the prayers of your devout and faithful subjects will be daily offered up to
God, for the prosperity of your Majesty's government at home, and the success
of your arms abroad"' (E*1922*, ix 279-80).

order to support it self, is generally forc'd to make Use of such 40
abominable Instruments, that as long as it prevails, the Genius
of a Nation is over-press'd, and cannot appear to exert it self:
But when That is broke and suppress'd, when Things return to the
old Course, Mankind will naturally fall to act from Principles of
Reason and Religion. The *Romans*, upon a great Victory, or escape 45
from publick Danger, frequently built a Temple in Honour of some
God, to whose peculiar Favour they imputed their Success or
Delivery: And sometimes the *General* did the like, *at his own Ex-*
pence, to acquit himself of some pious Vow he had made. How little
of any thing resembling this hath been done by us after all our 50
Victories! and perhaps for that Reason, among others, they have
turn'd to so little Account. But what could we expect? We acted
all along as if we believ'd nothing of a God or His Providence;
and therefore it was consistent to offer up our Edifices only to
Those, whom we look'd upon as *Givers of all Victory*, in his stead. 55

I have computed, that Fifty Churches may be built by a Medium,
at Six Thousand Pound for a Church; which is somewhat *under* the
Price of a *Subject's Palace*: Yet perhaps the Care of above Two
Hundred Thousand Souls, with the Benefit of their Prayers for the
Prosperity of their Queen and Country, may be almost put in the 60
Balance with the Domestick Convenience, or even Magnificence of
any *Subject* whatsoever.

Sir *William Petty*, who under the Name of Captain *Graunt*, Publish'd some Observations upon Bills of Mortality about five Years
after the *Restoration*; tells us, the Parishes in *London*, were 65
even then so unequally divided, that some were Two Hundred times
larger than others. Since that Time, the encrease of Trade, the
frequency of Parliaments, the desire of living in the Metropolis,

54 *Edifices*: These included Holywell House in St. Albans, the Ranger's
Lodge in Windsor Forest, Marlborough House in Pall Mall, and Blenheim Palace.
58-9 *Two Hundred Thousand Souls*: On the basis of figures supplied by the
Convocation, the select committee concluded that there were in London '240,500,
of the Communion of the Church of *England*, for whom no Churches are provided'
(*CJ*, xvi 542, 583).
66-7 *Two Hundred times larger*: *Natural and Political Observations ... upon*
the Bills of Mortality. By John Graunt, London, by Tho. Roycroft *et al.*, 1662,
p. 53. The figures that Atterbury presented to the Speaker were even more
revealing: St. Andrew Holborn, one church and a chapel of ease for 30,000
people; St. Giles Cripplegate, one church and a chapel of ease for 42,600
people; the Seven Tower Hamlets in Stepney, one church for 86,598 people (*CJ*,
xvi 542).

together with that Genius for Building, which began after the
70   *Fire*, and hath ever since continu'd, have prodigiously enlarg'd
this Town on all Sides, where it was capable of Encrease; and
those Tracts of Land built into Streets, have generally continu'd
of the same Parish they belong'd to, while they lay in Fields; so
that the Care of above Thirty Thousand Souls, hath been sometimes
75   committed to one Minister, whose Church wou'd hardly contain the
Twentieth part of his Flock: Neither, I think, was any Family in
those Parishes oblig'd to pay above a Groat a Year to their Spiritual Pastor. Some few of those Parishes have been since divided;
in others were erected Chapels of Ease, where a Preacher is main-
80   tain'd by general Contribution. Such poor Shifts and Expedients,
to the infinite Shame and Scandal, of so vast and flourishing a
City, have been thought sufficient for the Service of God and
Religion; as if they were Circumstances wholly indifferent.

This Defect, among other Consequences of it, hath made *Schism*
85   a sort of necessary Evil, there being at least Three Hundred
Thousand Inhabitants in this Town, whom the Churches would not be
able to contain, if the People were ever so well dispos'd: And in
a City not overstock'd with Zeal, the only way to preserve any
Degree of Religion, is to make all Attendance upon the Duties of
90   it, as easy and cheap as possible: Whereas on the contrary, in
the larger Parishes, the Press is so great, and the Pew-keeper's
Tax so exorbitant, that those who love to save Trouble and Mony,
either stay at home, or retire to the *Conventicles*. I believe
there are few Examples in any *Christian* Country of so great a
95   Neglect for Religion; and the Dissenting Teachers have made their
Advantages largely by it, *Sowing Tares among the Wheat while Men
slept*; being much more expert at procuring Contributions, which
is a Trade they are bred up in, than Men of a liberal Education.

And to say Truth, the Way practic'd by several Parishes in and
100 about this Town, of maintaining their Clergy by voluntary Sub-

73 in Fields] in the Fields 38 8°+12°   79 in] and 38 8°+12°   98 a
liberal] liberal 38 12°

85-6 *Three Hundred Thousand Inhabitants*: The select committee estimated
that there were 'about 342,000 ... Souls for whom no Churches are as yet provided ... But ... *French* Protestants and Dissenters ... do amount to about
101,500' (*CJ*, xvi 582-3).
96-7 *Sowing ... slept*: Matt. 13:25.

scriptions, is not only an Indignity to the Character, but hath
many pernicious Consequences attending it; such a precarious
Dependance, subjecting a Clergyman, who hath not more than ordinary Spirit and Resolution, to many Inconveniences, which are
obvious to imagine: But this Defect will, no doubt, be Remedied   105
by the Wisdom and Piety of the present Parliament; and a Tax laid
upon every House in a Parish, for the Support of their Pastor.
Neither indeed can it be conceiv'd, why a House, whose Purchase
is not reckon'd above one Third less than Land of the same Yearly
Rent, should not pay a Twentieth Part annually (which is half   110
Tyth) to the Support of the Minister. One Thing I could wish,
that in fixing the Maintenance to the several Ministers in these
new intended Parishes, no determinate Sum of Mony may be nam'd,
which in all Perpetuities ought by any means to be avoided; but
rather a Tax in Proportion to the Rent of each House, tho' it be   115
but a Twentieth or even a Thirtieth part. The contrary of this,
I am told, was done in several Parishes of the City after the
Fire; where the Incumbent and his Successors were to receive for
ever a certain Sum; for Example, one or two hundred Pounds a
Year. But the Lawgivers did not consider, that what we call at   120
present, One Hundred Pounds, will, in process of time, have not
the intrinsick value of Twenty; as Twenty Pounds now are hardly
equal to Forty Shillings, Three Hundred Years ago. There are a
thousand Instances of this all over *England*, in reserv'd Rents
apply'd to Hospitals, in old Chiefries, and even among the Clergy   125
themselves, in those Payments which, I think, they call a *Modus*.

As no Prince had ever better Dispositions than her present
Majesty, for the advancement of true Religion, so there was
never any Age that produc'd greater Occasions to employ them on.
'Tis an unspeakable Misfortune, that any Designs of so excellent   130
a Queen, shou'd be check'd by the Necessities of a long and
ruinous War, which the Folly or Corruption of *Modern Politicians*

107 their] the 38 12°   122 as] and 38 8°+12°

---

125 *Chiefries*: 'The dues belonging to the chief ... of an [Irish] clan or
district; the analogous payment of ... rent to the lord superior' (*OED*).
126 *I think*: Swift remembers that the Examiner, a country squire, is
'talking out of [his] Trade' again (66.16-67.29, 199.193).
   Modus: 'An abbreviation of *modus decimandi*, a composition in lieu of
payment of tithes' (E*1922*, ix 282).

have involv'd us in, against all the Maxims whereby our Country
flourish'd so many Hundred Years. Else Her Majesty's Care of
135 Religion would certainly have reach'd even to Her *American* Plantations. Those noble Countries, stock'd by Numbers from hence,
whereof too many are in no very great Reputation for Faith or
Morals, will be a perpetual Reproach to us, 'till some better
Care is taken for cultivating *Christianity* among them. If the
140 Governours of those several Colonies were obliged, at certain
Times, to transmit an exact Representation of the State of Religion, in their several Districts; and the Legislature here would,
in a time of Leisure, take that Affair under their Consideration,
it might be perfected with little Difficulty, and be a great Addi-
145 tion to the Glories of Her Majesty's Reign.

But to wave further Speculations upon so remote a Scene, while
we have Subjects enough to employ them on at Home; it is to be
hop'd, the Clergy will not let slip any proper Opportunity of
improving the pious Dispositions of the Queen and Kingdom, for
150 the Advantage of the Church; when by the Example of Times past,
they consider how rarely such Conjunctures are like to happen.
What if some Method were thought on towards repairing of Churches?
For which there is like to be too frequent Occasions, those ancient *Gothick* Structures, throughout this Kingdom, going every
155 Year to decay. That Expedient of repairing or rebuilding them by
charitable Collections, seems in my Opinion not very suitable,
either to the Dignity and Usefulness of the Work, or to the
Honour of our Country; since it might be so easily done, with
very little Charge to the Publick, in a much more Decent and
160 Honourable Manner, while Parliaments are so frequently call'd.
But these and other Regulations must be left to a Time of *Peace*,

133 *Maxims*: According to the traditional wisdom, the War of the Spanish
Succession (1) should have been declared against Spain, not against France—
'The Earl of *Rochester* observed, it was a Saying of old Duke *Schomberg*'s, that
the attacking *France* in the *Netherlands*, was like taking a Bull by the Horns';
(2) should have been fought at sea, not on land; and (3) should have engaged
England as 'a Second', not as 'the Principal' (*The History of the Life and
Reign of her late Majesty Queen Anne*, London, 1740, p. 251; Anon., p. 470;
Swift, *Prose*, vi 8).
154 *Gothick Structures*: Almost all the churches in the southern half of
England were damaged in the great storm of November 1703. The following is
typical of dozens of petitions received by Parliament in March-April 1711:
the parish church of St. George the Martyr in Southwark 'is very ruinous, and
much out of Repair; and the Roof thereof is decayed and rotten, so that the
same is in Danger of falling' (*CJ*, xvi 568).

which I shall humbly presume to wish may soon be our Share, however offensive it may be to any, either *abroad* or *at home*, who
are Gainers by the War.

164   *abroad or at home*: innuendo: Marlborough in Flanders and Sir Henry
Furnese in the City, through whose hands passed all payments to the armed
forces in Flanders (Hill, p. 401).

No. 35 [Mainwaring]   28 May 1711

The MEDLEY.

Proofs from the Examiner's *last Paper*.
That what he says is neither True *nor* Probable.
That he's guilty of Profaneness or Blasphemy.

HAVING already shewn, to the Satisfaction of impartial Readers,
the *Examiner*'s base Ingratitude for my last Favour; it remains
for me to shew likewise, that he was in extreme want of such a
Friend; and that I was neither impertinent nor officious in
offering him my Counsel, and sending him my Instructions. This   5
can only be done by giving undeniable Proofs, that a great deal
of what he has publish'd to the World, is neither *True* nor *Probable*, for that is the Proposition which I pretended to demonstrate. But it is not enough for me to affirm it, unless I can
also make it good. And tho I have two very strong Objections   10
against undertaking this Labour: One is, That my Friend will
appear still more black and immoral, when it shall be shewn what
a necessary Benefit I design'd him: The other is, That the setting forth these Proofs will engage me in the nauseous Work of
reviewing his former Papers; yet to do him Service, I can almost   15
submit to any thing: And he has sav'd me the Trouble of looking
far for my Proofs at this time; since in his very last Paper (N^o.
43.) he has furnish'd me with more than is necessary for my
present purpose: His words are these, 'The Clergy, and whoever

2 *Ingratitude*: 434.10-435.25.
7-8 *neither True nor Probable*: 434.13.
19-27 *The ... Danger*: 440.15-23.

20 else have a true Concern for the Constitution of the Church,
    cannot but be highly pleas'd with one Prospect in this new Scene
    of publick Affairs. They may very well remember the time, when
    every Session of Parliament was like a Cloud hanging over their
    Heads; and if it happen'd to pass without bursting into some
25 Storm upon the Church, we thank'd God, and thought it an happy
    Escape, till the next Meeting; upon which we resum'd our secret
    Apprehensions, tho we were not allow'd to believe any Danger.'
        Now I appeal to the Reader, whether what my Friend here says be
    either *True* or *Probable*. First, Is it true in Fact, that at any
30 time, since her M-----y's most happy Reign, the Church has been
    in the perilous Condition here describ'd? Does any body remember
    such *Clouds hanging over it*, or *such Storms coming upon it*? Does
    any body remember such a Session of Parliament, in which *it had
    so happy an Escape, that there was reason to thank God for it*?
35 I remember indeed a Time, when a very bold Attempt was made upon
    the Civil and Religious Rights of our Fellow-Subjects, by certain
    Men call'd *Tackers* or High-Churchmen, which only ended in their
    own Confusion, as their Designs will always end: But I can't call
    to mind one single Instance of any Attempt that has been made or
40 threaten'd against the Church. I remember also a very great
    Bounty which her Majesty bestow'd upon the Clergy, when she had
    the Misfortune to have no better Advisers than the poor late
    Ministers, who my Friend says are *so hated both by God and Man*.
    Nor have I forgot her most Gracious Declaration then publish'd,
45 That *she thought it in a safe and flourishing Condition, and that
    those who endeavour'd to spread other Reports were her own and
    the Kingdom's Enemies*. Yet my modest and ingenious Friend, who
    from spreading such Reports, is now, if you will believe him, a
    State-Writer, gives us still an Account of his *own secret Appre-*
50 *hensions* at that time, tho *he was not allow'd to believe any*

        36 *Rights*: Burnet (ii 337) thought it was 'The Toleration itself' that was
    'aimed at' in the three bills to prevent occasional conformity.
        37 *Tackers*: 89.41n.
        38 *Confusion*: Besides splitting the Tory party, the Tackers themselves
    fared very badly in the next general election. Of the 134 of them, forty-four
    were not returned in May 1705 (Speck, *Tory and Whig*, p. 108).
        41 *Bounty*: 129.79n.
        43 *so ... Man*: 52.74-5.
        45-7 *in ... Enemies*: 263.23n.
        49-51 *secret ... Danger*: 440.22-3.

Danger. And from his Description of Times past, and his ravishing
Prospect in this new Scene of Affairs, one wou'd think we had
hitherto liv'd under the Reign of some wicked Prince; that the
Laws had been all just breaking, and the Government overturning;
and that the forlorn and weeping Church had narrowly escap'd a   55
most severe and bitter Persecution.

He has often complain'd of his Words being quoted by halves,
and carp'd at unjustly; for which Reason I have now taken the
Pains to transcribe them entire, and must leave it to others to
determine whether I have put any wrong Construction upon them.   60

But there is not less *Truth* in this Assertion of his, than
there is *Probability*. How is it *probable* that under her present
M-----y, who sees with her own Eyes, and hears with her own Ears,
who looks narrowly and impartially into all Affairs her self, and
has the Interest of our Church at heart, preferable to all other   65
Cares or Concerns; how is it *probable*, I say, or even possible,
that under such a Q----, such *Clouds* and *Storms* shou'd be gathering about the Church, without being seen for so many Years together? How is it *probable* that she shou'd sit so long in Council
with a Set of Men, who, if my Friend may be believ'd, are Enemies   70
to all Religion, without sooner disovering their Principles and
Practices, and conceiving a just Abhorrence of them? Nay, how is
it *probable*, that the Blessing of Heaven shou'd have attended so
remarkably our Affairs both at Home and Abroad, if the Men, that
were all this while employ'd, had been plotting and contriving   75
the Destruction of God's Church? For it must be consider'd, That
all those Years in which my Friend supposes our Church in so much
danger, the Successes of her M-----y's Arms, and the Reputation
of her Government, were greater than ever they were under any of
her Predecessors: And I only wish for the sake of the new   80
M------rs, who, my Friend will have it, are so much better Friends
to the Church, That every thing may go as well under their Administration.

To conclude therefore this Article, I will now presume boldly
to affirm, That in the whole Paragraph above-written, which I have 85
fairly transcrib'd out of the last *Examiner*, there is not one

57 *quoted by halves*: 335.163-4, 429.43.
67 *Clouds ... Storms*: 440.19-20.
73-4 *Blessing ... Abroad*: 440.33-7.

Sentence or Word that is either *True* or *Probable*; but that the
whole is an ill-made Story, for which he ought rather to be corrected than rewarded; and that it is libellous and scandalous in
90 the highest degree, insolently reflecting on her M-----y's Wisdom and Goodness, on the Archbishops and Bishops of our Church,
and upon all other Persons employ'd for so many Years, whether in
Offices Ecclesiastical or Civil.

And yet I wish this were the worst Passage that were to be
95 found in his last Paper: But there is another still more extraordinary, which I am almost afraid to copy. He is speaking of a
Custom among the *Romans, upon a great Victory to build a Temple,*
&c. and then adds these words: 'How little of any thing resembling this hath been done by us after all our Victories! and per-
100 haps for that reason among others, they have turn'd to so little
account. But what cou'd we expect? We acted all along as if we
believ'd nothing of a God or his Providence; and therefore *it
was consistent to offer up our* EDIFICES *only to those whom we
look'd upon as Givers of all* VICTORY IN HIS STEAD.' I have not
105 often read *Blasphemy*, and therefore can't tell exactly whether
this comes up to it or not; but sure I am, it is the highest
Reflection that ever I met with, where, of all other places, it
ought least to have been made. *We have acted*, says he, *all along,
as if we believ'd nothing of a God or his Providence.* I beg of
110 him to be inform'd who it is that has so acted. Her M-----y upon
every great and signal Victory has appointed a Day of Thanksgiving to be paid to Almighty God for it: And she has gone upon
that solemn Day in a most decent religious Procession at the head
of her faithful Parliaments, and with the Acclamations of her
115 People, to return her Praises and Acknowledgments in the chief
Cathedral of her Kingdom. Is this acting as if *nothing were believ'd of a God or his Providence*? It is confess'd also, that to
reward the eminent Services of our General, and particularly his
March to the *Danube*, for which he was rais'd to a Principality in

115 Acknowledgments] Acknowledments ½°

---

97 *the ... Temple*: 441.45-6.
98-104 *How ... STEAD*: 441.49-55.
111-12 *Thanksgiving*: In doing so, Anne revived a custom of her great Tudor
predecessor, Elizabeth I.

a foreign Empire, her M-----y was pleas'd to build for him a very   120
noble Palace: But shall my impious Friend be suffer'd to call
this, *An offering up of our Edifices only to Those, whom, instead*
of Providence, we look upon as Givers of all Victory? This is
such a Point as I dare no longer touch upon. My Hand trembles as
I write, and I must leave the Reader to make his own Reflections.   125
    I wonder what Atonement his Patrons and Superiors will exact
from him for this Crime, and what effect it will have upon his
own harden'd Mind. I have read of *a certain Italian* in the fif-
teenth Century, one more learned as well as unfortunate than my
Friend, who having committed an Offence like this, and spoken   130
some blasphemous Words, cou'd never be comforted afterwards, but
left the Town he liv'd in; and retiring like a Savage to the
Woods, there pass'd the Remainder of his days in great Misery,
avoiding all human Society. I hope my Friend will not quite turn
Savage, and that the World is not to lose him for this Offence;   135
yet I can't but wish he may be touch'd with a due sense of it.
And since our Saviour gives him some words of Comfort, and says,
That *even Blasphemy shall be forgiven unto Men*; I hope his Repentance and Contrition will be sutable to the Heinousness of his
Guilt, and sufficient to obtain his Pardon.   140
    What he says with respect to Building of Churches, and the new
Tythe which he intends to lay upon the People, being in the same
profane audacious Strain with what is here mention'd, I shou'd
(to use his own words) *be negligent of my Duty to the Publick*, if
I did not make some Remarks upon them. But those must be defer'd   145
till the next.

128 *a certain Italian*: Ant. [Codrus] Urceus (Bayle, *Dict[ionary*, iv 2999]
(½°).
138 *even ... Men*: Matt. 12:31.
144 *negligent ... Publick*: 430.64.

No. 44 [Swift]   31 May 1711

The EXAMINER.

Scilicet, ut posses curvo dignoscere rectum.

HAving been forc'd in my Papers to use the Cant-words of *Whig* and
Tory, which have so often vary'd their Significations, for twenty
Years past; I think it necessary to say something of the several
Changes those two Terms have undergone since that Period; and
5   then to tell the Reader what I have always understood by each of
them, since I undertook this Work. I reckon that these sorts of
conceited Appellations, are usually invented by the Vulgar; who
not troubling themselves to examine through the Merits of a Cause,
are consequently the most violent Partisans of what they espouse;
10   and in their Quarrels, usually proceed to their beloved Argument
of *calling Names*, 'till at length they light upon one which is
sure to stick; and in time, each Party grows proud of that Appellation, which their Adversaries at first intended for a Reproach.
Of this kind were the *Prasini* and *Veneti*, the *Guelfs* and
15   *Gibelines*, *Huguenots* and *Papists*, *Round-heads* and *Cavaliers*, with
many others, of ancient and modern Date. Among us of late there
seems to have been a Barrenness of Invention in this Point; the

Motto Horace, *Epistles*, ii 2 44: That hence you may distinguish Right from
Wrong.
7 *conceited*: 'strained or far-fetched' (*OED*).
14 *Prasini and Veneti*: 'There were four factions, or parties, distinguished by their colours, which contended in the ancient circus at Constantinople. The white and the red were the most ancient. In the sixth century the
dissension between the green (or Prasini) and the blue (or Veneti) was so
violent, that 40,000 men were killed, and the factions were abolished from
that time. See also Gibbon ... chap. xl' (E*1922*, ix 284). Gibbon explains that
the colours, used originally to distinguish the chariot drivers in the circus,
not only divided the Roman people but in Constantinople 'produced two strong
and irreconcileable factions, which shook the foundations of a feeble government' (*The History of the Decline and Fall of the Roman Empire*, 4 vols.,
London, A. Strahan and T. Cadell, 1788, iv 62).
14-15 *Guelphs and Gibelines*: 'The Guelfs were the Papal and popular party
in Italy, and the Ghibellines were the imperial and aristocratic. It is said
that these names were first used as war cries at the battle of Weinsberg in
1140' (E*1922*, ix 284).
15 *Round-heads and Cavaliers*: 'These terms came into use about 1641' (E*1922*,
ix 284) to describe an 'adherent of the Parliamentary party' and 'those who
fought on the side of Charles I' in the Civil Wars (*OED*).

Words *Whig* and *Tory*, though they are not much above thirty Years
Old, having been press'd to the Service of many Successions of
Parties, with very different Idea's fastened to them. This Dis-   20
tinction, I think, began towards the latter part of King *Charles*
the Second's Reign; was dropt during that of his Successor, and
then revived at the *Revolution*; since which it has perpetually
flourish'd, though apply'd to very different kinds of Principles
and Persons. In that Convention of Lords and Commons, some of   25
both Houses were for a *Regency* to the Prince of *Orange*, with a
Reservation of Style and Title to the absent King, which should
be made use of in all Publick Acts. Others, when they were brought
to allow the Throne vacant, thought the Succession should immediately go to the next Heir, according to the Fundamental Laws   30
of the Kingdom, as if the last King were actually dead. And tho'
the Dissenting Lords (in whose House the chief Opposition was)

18 though ... are] although ... be 38 8°+12°

---

18 *Whig and Tory*: '*Whig-a-more* was a nick-name given to the western
peasantry of Scotland, from their using the words frequently in driving
strings of horses. Hence, as connected with calvinistical principles in religion, and republican doctrines in policy, it was given as a term of reproach
to the opposition party in the latter years of Charles II. These retorted
upon the courtiers the word *Tory*, signifying an Irish freebooter, and particularly applicable to the Roman Catholic followers of the Duke of York. At
length, both parties acknowledged, and prided themselves on the distinctions,
originally meant to convey reproach and disgrace' (*E1814*, iv 124). By the
1690s both words had found their way into a dictionary: '*Tories*, Zealous
Sticklers for the Prerogative and Rights of the Crown, in behalf of the
Monarchy; also Irish-thieves, or *Rapparies*. *Whiggs*, the Republicans or
Common-wealths-men, under the Name of Patriots, and Lovers of Property; originally the Field-conventiclers in the West of *Scotland*' (B.E., *A New Dictionary
of the Terms Ancient and Modern of the Canting Crew*, London, for W. Hawes,
[1690?], not paginated; cf. Robert Willman, *The Historical Journal*, xvii
(1974), 247-64.
18-19 *thirty Years Old*: 'At this time [March 1681] the distinguishing names
of *Whig* and *Tory* came to be the denominations of the parties' (Burnet, i 499)
(*E1922*, ix 285).
20 *different Idea's*: When the Whigs became a court party for the first
time in 1694-9, they abandoned many of their earlier policies (405.142-3); cf.
Swift, *Discourse*, p. 5.
25 *Convention*: 'The Convention was summoned by the Prince of Orange in
December, 1688. After a lengthened debate they resolved, on February 12th,
1688/9, that the Prince and Princess of Orange should "be declared King and
Queen." The Sovereigns were proclaimed on February 13th, and on the 20th the
Convention was voted a Parliament' (*E1922*, ix 285).
26 *Regency*: A large minority in the House of Lords and about a third of
the Commons was for a regency, 'in opposition to those who were for setting
up another King' (Burnet, i 810-11).
32 *Dissenting Lords*: 367.93n.

did at last yield both those Points, took the Oaths to the new
King, and many of them Employments, yet they were look'd upon
35 with an evil Eye by the warm Zealots of the other side; neither
did the Court ever heartily favour any of them, though some were
of the most eminent for Abilities and Virtue, and serv'd that
Prince, both in his Councils and his Army, with untainted Faith.
It was apprehended, at the same time, and perhaps it might have
40 been true, that many of the Clergy would have been better pleas'd
with that Scheme of a *Regency*, or at least an uninterrupted
lineal Succession, for the sake of those whose Consciences were
truly *Scrupulous*; and they thought there were some Circumstances,
in the Case of the depriv'd Bishops, that look'd a little hard,
45 or at least deserv'd Commiseration.

These, and other the like Reflections did, as I conceive, revive the Denominations of *Whig* and *Tory*.

Some time after the Revolution the Distinction of *High* and *Low*-
Church came in, which was rais'd by the Dissenters, in order to
50 break the Church Party, by dividing the Members into *High* and
Low; and the Opinion rais'd, That the *High* join'd with the
Papists, inclin'd the *Low* to fall in with the Dissenters.

And here I shall take leave to produce some Principles, which

41 that] the 38 8°+12°

---

35 *Zealots of the other side*: Whigs.
40 *many of the Clergy*: 'The greatest part of the Clergy' declared themselves for a regency (Burnet, i 811).
44 *the depriv'd Bishops*: 'The bishops who were deprived for refusing to
take the oath of allegiance to King William were [William] Sancroft, the Archbishop of Canterbury; [Thomas] Ken, Bishop of Bath; [Thomas] White, Bishop of
Peterborough; [Francis] Turner, Bishop of Ely; [Robert] Frampton, Bishop of
Gloucester; and [William] Lloyd, Bishop of Norwich' (E1922, ix 286). Swift
expressed his 'Commiseration' and his sense of outrage in his unfinished
Pindaric *Ode to Dr. William Sancroft, Late Lord Archbishop of Canterbury*,
which remained unpublished until 1789 (Swift, *Poems*, p. 33).
48-9 *High and Low-Church*: Although the earliest occurrences in print date
from 1702 (*OED*), Kennett (iii 779) believed that the terms became current in
1699. From the beginning the distinction was abusive: '*Terms of factious Jargon*', 'raisd on Design to distract us yet more', as Burnet complained (Swift,
Prose, ii 72; William Pittis, *The Proceedings of Both Houses of Parliament in
the Years 1702, 1703, 1704, Upon the Bill to prevent Occasional Conformity*,
London, for J. Baker, 1710, p. 39). Sacheverell's scurrilous *The Character of
a Low-Church Man* (1702), which achieved at least three or four editions, gave
wide currency both to the author and to the term. *The Distinction of High-
Church and Low-Church* (1705), a more temperate work, has been attributed to
John Norris of Bemerton (William Atwood, *The Scotch Patriot Unmask'd*, 1705,
p. 29).

in the several Periods of the late Reign, serv'd to denote a Man
of one or t'other Party. To be against a Standing Army in Time of   55
Peace, was all *High-Church, Tory* and *Tantivy*. To differ from a
Majority of B----ps was the same. To raise the Prerogative above
Law for serving a Turn, was *Low-Church* and *Whig*. The Opinion of
the Majority in the House of Commons, especially of the Country-
Party, or Landed Interest, was *High-flying* and *rank Tory*. To   60
exalt the King's Supremacy beyond all Precedent, was *Low-Church,
Whiggish* and *Moderate*. To make the least Doubt of the pretended
Prince being Supposititious, and a Tyler's Son, was, in their

55 *Standing Army*: 405.143.

56 *Tantivy*: An equestrian term of obscure origin meaning 'at full gal-
lop, in great haste', took on political meaning in 1680 when a woodcut was
published showing a number of churchmen, booted and spurred, mounted upon the
Church of England and riding tantivy to Rome, with the motto, 'They must goe
[when] the Devill Drives: Tantivy Tantivy Tantivy' (*POAS*, Yale, ii, opposite
p. 370). Thereafter High Churchmen and Tories were Tantivies. Swift was called
'an ambitious Tantivy' in *The Protestant Post-Boy*, 25 September 1711 (Swift,
Journal, p. 381) (E*1922*, ix 286).

57 *B----ps*: 134.172n.

Prerogative: The reference is almost certainly to the two treaties (September 1698 and February 1700) whereby William III and Louis XIV partitioned
the Spanish Empire among France, the Empire, and the Netherlands. In negotiating these treaties the King's prerogative of *ius pacis et belli* was
pushed to the limit. No English ministers were involved in the secret negotiations of the first treaty, for which the King at Loo simply ordered Somers to
send him a blank commission under the Great Seal to record the terms. Negotiations for the second were not secret but again involved no English ministers
(Swift, *Discourse*, pp. 28-32). Swift's vagueness here may be deliberate. For
by defending the 'Lords Partitioners' in *A Discourse of the Contests and Dissentions* (1701) he was by implication defending the Partition Treaties and
William's manner of negotiating them, which he here puts down as 'above Law'.

60 *High-flying*: '[making] or [supporting] lofty claims on behalf of ... the
Church' (*OED*). The earliest quotation in the *OED* is 1680 and it was a pejora-
tive term from the beginning. The high-flyers were 'the *Grumbletonians* of K.
William's Reign ... who fretted and foam'd upon the Bit, because they were not
allow'd to *Tyrannize* over their Neighbours, as in other Reigns' (John Dunton,
A Satyr upon K. William, 2nd edn., London, 1703, p. 74).

61 *Supremacy*: If there is a specific reference to the Calvinist King's
exercise of his power as supreme head on earth of the Church of England, it
may be to William's refusal to summon a Convocation between 1689 and 1699.

63 *Prince*: According to 'the absurd legend of the warming pan' (Ogg, iii
201), when Queen Mary miscarried, another child was provided and 'delivered'
by Judith Wilkes, the Queen's midwife, on Sunday morning, 10 June 1688 (*POAS*,
Yale, iv 256-72).

a Tyler's Son: In a later elaboration of the absurd legend, which became Whig orthodoxy, the Prince's wet-nurse, 'one Cooper, a tilemaker's wife'
(Luttrell, i 453), was conflated with the child's 'real' mother, and the Prince
for whom Dryden wrote *Britannia Rediviva* (1688) and whose godfather was Pope
Innocent XI became 'a Tyler's Son'. The name of the child's 'real' mother was
supplied by Thomas Fuller, *The Evidence: A Brief Discovery of the True Mother
of the Pretended Prince of Wales known by the Name of Mary Grey* (1696).

Phrase, *Top and Top-gallant*, and perfect *Jacobitism*. To resume
65   the most exorbitant Grants, that were ever given to a Set of
profligate Favourites, and apply them to the Publick, was the
very Quintessence of *Toryism*; notwithstanding those Grants were
known to be acquir'd, by Sacrificing the Honour and the Wealth of
England.
70   In most of these Principles, the two Parties seem to have
shifted Opinions, since their Institution under King *Charles* the
Second, and indeed to have gone very different from what was expected from each, even at the Time of the *Revolution*. But as to
that concerning the *Pretender*, the *Whigs* have so far renounc'd
75   it, that they are grown the great Advocates for his Legitimacy:
Which gives me the Opportunity of Vindicating a Noble D--- who
was accus'd of a Blunder in the House, when upon a certain Lord's
mentioning the *Pretended Prince*, his G---- told the Lords, He
must be plain with them, and call that Person, not the Pretended
80   *Prince, but the Pretended Impostor*: Which was so far from a Blunder in that Polite L--d, as his ill-willers give out, that it was
only a refin'd way of delivering the avow'd Sentiments of his
whole Party.
     But to return, This was the State of Principles when the Qu---

64   *Top and Top-gallant*: 'short for *topsail* and *top-gallant sail*; hence
fig. ... with all sail set, in full array or career' (*OED*).
     65   *Grants*: The size of William's grants of Irish land to his favourites
was indeed regal: 135,820 acres to Willem Bentinck, Earl of Portland; 108,633
acres to Henri de Massue de Ruvigny, Earl of Galway; 26,480 acres to Godard
van Reede, Baron de Ginkel and Earl of Athlone; 95,649 acres, 'all the Private
Estate of the late King James', to Elizabeth Villiers, formerly William's mistress and now married off to James Hamilton, Earl of Orkney. The grants were
resumed by Harley's New Country Party in April 1700 (306.16).
     75   *Advocates for ... Legitimacy*: cf. 406.171n. Charles Leslie noticed
that Stanhope's speech in the Sacheverell trial 'openly *Avow'd* the *Birth* of
the *Pretender*' (*The Good Old Cause, Further Discuss'd. In a Letter to the
Author of the Jacobite's Hopes Reviv'd*, 1710, sig. E2[V]) and a current Whig
toast was said to be 'Health to all those that *believe neither in the BRICK-
LAYER's NOR IN THE CARPENTER's SON*' (Trapp, *The Character and Principles of
the Present Set of Whigs*, 2nd edn., 1711, p. 47). In May 1710 an address from
Totnes confirmed that 'Popish Doctrines are revived and enforced by Republicans, and even the Legitimacy of the Pretender maintain'd, in Opposition to
Your Majesty's Undoubted and Hereditary Right to the Throne' (*A Collection of
the Addresses*, i 41). Finally, in February 1711, the Whigs republished *The
several Declarations, together with the several Depositions made in the Council on Monday, the 22d of October, 1688, concerning the Birth of the Prince
of Wales* (London, J. Baker), by which James II established the Prince's legitimacy (Boyer, *The Political State*, i 376).
     76   *D---*: unidentified.

came to the Crown; sometime after which, it pleas'd *certain great*   85
Persons, who had been all their Lives in the Altitude of *Tory*-
Profession, to enter into a Treaty with the *Whigs*, from whom they
could get better Terms than from their old Friends, who began to
be resty, and would not allow Monopolies of Power and Favour; nor
consent to carry on the War intirely at the Expence of this   90
Nation, that they might have Pensions from Abroad; while another
People, more immediately concern'd in the War, Traded with the
Enemy as in times of Peace. Whereas, the other Party, whose Case
appear'd then as desperate, was ready to yield to any Conditions
that would bring them into Play. And I cannot help affirming,   95
That this Nation was made a Sacrifice to the unmeasurable Appetite of Power and Wealth in a *very few*, that shall be Nameless,
who in every Step they made, acted directly against what they had
always profess'd. And if His Royal Highness the Prince had died
some Years sooner (who was a perpetual Check in their Career)   100
'tis dreadful to think how far they might have proceeded.

Since that Time, the bulk of the *Whigs* appears rather to be
link'd to a certain Set of *Persons*, than any certain Set of
Principles: So that if I were to define a Member of that Party,
I would say, he was one *who Believed in the late M-----ry*. And   105
therefore, whatever I have affirm'd of *Whigs* in any of these
Papers, or objected against them, ought to be understood either
of those who were Partisans of the late Men in Power, and privy
to their Designs; or such who join'd with them, from a Hatred to
our Monarchy and Church, as Unbelievers and *Dissenters* of all   110
Sizes: Or Men in Office, who had been guilty of much Corruption,
and dreaded a Change; which would not only put a stop to further
Abuses for the future, but might, perhaps, introduce Examinations
of what was past. Or those who had been too highly oblig'd, to
quit their Supporters with any common Decency. Or lastly, the   115

97 that] who 38 8°+12°   102 appears] appeareth 38 8°+12°

---

86 *Persons*: innuendo: Marlborough and Godolphin.
91 *Pensions from Abroad*: Marlborough's £10,000 a year as Commander-in-Chief
of the Dutch forces, plus the income from Mildenheim (Hearne, i 162; 53.104-5n.).
91-2 *another People*: innuendo: the Dutch.
93 *other Party*: innuendo: the Whigs.
97 *a very few*: innuendo: Marlborough and Godolphin.
99 *the Prince*: 260.129-30n.
103 *Set*: 424.66n.

Mony-Traders, who could never hope to make their Markets so well of *Præmiums* and Exorbitant Interest, and high Remittances, under any other Administration.

Under these Heads, may be reduc'd the whole Body of those whom
120 I have all along understood for *Whigs*: For I do not include within this Number, any of those who have been misled by Ignorance, or seduc'd by plausible Pretences, to think better of that sort of Men than they deserve, and to apprehend mighty Danger from their Disgrace: Because, I believe, the greatest Part of
125 such well-meaning People, are now thorowly converted.

And indeed, it must be allow'd, that those two fantastick Names of *Whig* and *Tory*, have at present very little Relation to those Opinions, which were at first thought to distinguish them. Whoever formerly profess'd himself to approve the *Revolution*, to be
130 against the *Pretender*, to justify the Succession in the House of *Hannover*, to think the *British* Monarchy not absolute, but limited by Laws, which the Executive Power could not dispense with, and to allow an Indulgence to Scrupulous Consciences; such a Man was content to be called a *Whig*. On t'other side, whoever asserted
135 the Queen's Hereditary Right; that the Persons of Princes were Sacred; their lawful Authority not to be resisted on any Pretence; nor even their Usurpations, without the most extream Necessity: That Breaches in the Succession were highly dangerous; that *Schism* was a great Evil, both in it self and its Consequences;
140 that the Ruin of the *Church*, would probably be attended with that of the *State*; that no Power should be trusted with those who are not of the Establish'd Religion; such a Man was usually call'd a *Tory*. Now, tho' the Opinions of both these are very consistent, and I really think are maintain'd at present by a great Majority
145 of the Kingdom; yet, according as Men apprehend the Danger greater, either from the *Pretender* and his Party, or from the Violence and Cunning of *other Enemies* to the Constitution; so their common Discourses and Reasonings, turn either to the first

117 under] by 38 8°+12°   118 Administration.] ~, ½°   123 Danger]
Dangers 38 8°+12°   126 those] the 38 8°+12°

---

117 *Præmiums*: 6.107n.
127 *Whig and Tory*: cf. Swift to Peterborough: 'Whig and Tory have quite
altered their meanings' (Swift, *Corr.*, i 227).
147 *other Enemies*: innuendo: the Whigs.

or second Set of these Opinions I have mention'd, and are consequently styl'd either *Whigs* or *Tories*. Which is, as if two   150
Brothers Apprehended their House would be set upon, but disagreed
about the Place from whence they thought the *Robbers* would come,
and therefore would go on different sides to defend it. They
must needs weaken and expose themselves by such a *Separation*;
and so did we, only our Case was worse: For in order to keep off   155
a *weak*, *remote Enemy*, from whom we could not suddenly apprehend
any Danger, we took a *nearer* and a *stronger* one into the *House*.
I make no Comparison at all between the two Enemies: *Popery* and
Slavery are without doubt the greatest and most dreadful of any;
but I may venture to affirm, that the Fear of these, have not, at   160
least since the *Revolution*, been so close and pressing upon us,
as that from *another Faction*; excepting only one short Period,
when the Leaders of that very Faction, invited the abdicating
King to return; of which I have formerly taken notice.

Having thus declared what sort of Persons I have always meant,   165
under the Denomination of *Whigs*, it will be easy to shew whom I
understand by *Tories*. Such whose Principles in Church and State,
are what I have above related; whose Actions are derived from
thence, and who have no Attachment to any Set of *Ministers*, further than as these are Friends to the Constitution in all its   170
Parts, but will do their utmost to save their Prince and Country,
whoever be at the Helm.

By these Descriptions of *Whig* and *Tory*, I am sensible those
Names are given to several Persons very undeservedly; and that

162 *another Faction*: innuendo: the Whigs.
163 *Leaders*: About twenty-nine Lords Spiritual and Temporal who happened
to be in London in December 1688 formed themselves into a kind of committee
of safety, meeting daily in the council chamber at Whitehall. On 11 December
they signed a Declaration inviting the Prince of Orange, who was approaching
London at the head of his army, to rescue them from 'Popery and Slavery', but
not inviting him to London (Robert Beddard, *The Historical Journal*, xi (1968),
403-20). Two days later they invited James II, who had fled to Feversham, to
return to his palace at Whitehall. 'The Prince expressed his displeasure with
the officiousness of those who had prevented the King from going off' to
France (Dalrymple, ii [2]219; Edmund Bohun, *The History of the Desertion, or,
An Account of all the Publick Affairs in England, from the Beginning of September 1688. to the Twelfth of February following* (1689), p. 100; John Sheffield, Duke of Buckingham, *The Works*, 2 vols., London, for John Barber, 1723,
i 85-8).
164 *notice*: There is no explicit earlier reference in *The Examiner* to this
invitation, but it might have been part of the projected 'Piece of *Secret
History*' (40.153).

175   many a Man is call'd by one or t'other, who has not the least
       Title to the Blame or Praise I have bestow'd on each of them
       throughout my Papers.

No. 36 [Mainwaring]   4 June 1711

                             The MEDLEY.
                Of Building of Churches.
                Of the Examiner's *New Tythe.*
                His Care of America.
                A Dissertation about a Latin *Word,* [Peculatus].

THERE can be nothing so good and commendable in it self, that
does not seem to lose its Quality when the *Examiner* takes it in
hand. One wou'd have thought it impossible for so pious a Design
as that of Building of Churches to be so ill represented, as he
5   has done it in his Paper, *Numb.* 43. yet he says, *Several Letters*
have been sent him, desiring he wou'd make honourable mention of
that Design. If all he writes were as diverting as that Paragraph,
what a Pleasure shou'd we take in reading it! *He is desir'd to*
mention a certain Design, in order to do it Honour: Which is just
10   as if *Abel Roper* shou'd be desir'd to print a Piece of News, in
order to have it pass for Truth. But indeed it is exceeding
strange, that any Men shou'd write Letters to him on such a Subject, knowing his irregular and extravagant way of Thinking.
They must doubtless be very worthy Persons, or they wou'd not be
15   his Correspondents; and 'tis easy enough to guess what their
Profession is, by his Paper, there being above a Column on the
Tythe and Income of the Ministers, and hardly a Line of the Advantage that from these new Churches may accrue to Religion.
   But he says, *There are at least Three Hundred Thousand Souls,*

   5-7 *Several ... Design*: 439.1-2.
   16 *Paper*: By this time Mainwaring could have learned that 'The reputed
Author [of *The Examiner*] is Dr. S---t, with the assistance, sometimes of Dr.
Att---y, and Mr. P---r' (John Gay, *The Present State of Wit, In a Letter to a*
Friend in the Country [before 14 May] 1711, p. 10).
   19 *There ... Souls*: 442.85-7.

for whom there wants Church-room; tho the Act of Parliament says   20
they are but One Hundred Seventy five Thousand: What cares he for
that? He is resolv'd to make the Number almost as many more, and
to correct our Senators for building but fifty Churches, when
there is occasion for near a hundred; especially since it appears
by his long Paragraph against Schism, that he intends to shut up   25
the Doors of all the Conventicles, except those of the Papists
and Nonjurors, which never seem to be included in his Descriptions of Schism or Faction.

But he is the first Man that ever made an Objection to the new
Scheme for Building Churches, or dislik'd as insufficient the   30
Provision made for it by Parliament. He must be meddling with
every thing, tho always sure to blunder. All the rest of Mankind
rejoic'd at the Undertaking, and approv'd of it. They were
pleas'd with every thing that her M-----y takes pleasure in; or
they wou'd have no pretence left for a vain Excuse in not coming   35
to Church for want of Elbow-room; or they flatter'd themselves it
wou'd empty all the Meeting-houses, tho there are a hundred
Conventicles in the City, where there are a hundred Churches, and
but fifty in the Suburbs, where there are not half so many
Churches; or lastly, they thought it wou'd make the Town more   40
beautiful, and that we shou'd resemble the old *Romans* in the Number of our Churches, as well as in that of our Victories and
Triumphs. Thus every body but my Friend had his Reason for
applauding the Design.

But he had a much greater matter at heart than this: His chief   45
Concern is, that any of the Clergy shou'd receive Contributions
of the Laity; which, he says, *is an Indignity to their Character,
and subjects them to a Dependance*: And I confess any Dependance
is very improper for his Churchmen, who pretend to be Independent

20 *Act*: 9 Ann. c. 17 supplies no demographic statistics (*Statutes of the Realm*, ix 473-5); cf. 442.85-6n.
25 *Paragraph against Schism*: 442.84-98.
29 *Objection*: Since the Examiner pronounces himself 'highly pleased' with the prospect (440.16), it is difficult to imagine what Mainwaring construes to be an objection.
38 *Conventicles ... Churches*: There were seventy-five Presbyterian, Ana-baptist, Independent, and Quaker meeting-houses and forty-six Anglican churches and chapels in the twenty-seven parishes of London, Westminster, and the suburbs (*CJ*, xvi 542).
47-8 *is ... Dependance*: 443.101-3.
49 *Churchmen*: 161.167n.; but see 197.136n.

50 on the State. But with his usual Modesty, he instructs the Parliament how this Inconvenience may be remedy'd: *'Tis but laying a
Tax upon every House in a Parish for Support of the Pastor*, and
the thing is done. A twentieth or even a thirtieth part of the
annual Rent of all Houses, wou'd in his opinion serve the Turn.
55 This, according to the lowest Computation, wou'd amount to a very
large Income for every particular Minister; and wou'd effectually
relieve his Friends from the many Inconveniences arising from
their Dependance: They might then say or do what they pleas'd,
without being afraid of losing by it, and no Parish shou'd be
60 able to get rid of them, tho they rais'd as many Riots as
Sacheverel. See what glorious Times we are to enjoy, if ever
these Men shou'd get Power, and what reason the People have to be
fond of supporting High Churchmen: For behold here is a new Tax
and a new Tythe already projected by him, and these he will have
65 all our poor Housekeepers hereafter bear the weight of, who are
not to be sav'd so cheaply as they have been.

    In this audacious manner my Friend directs the Parliament: Nor
are his Cares confin'd to our own Country, but extend to the
American Islands. In vain was a Society erected for propagating
70 the Gospel in those Colonies; he is ready to take the Business
out of their Hands, and wou'd fain oblige all the Governors to

    71 fain] feign ½°

    51-2 *laying ... Pastor*: 443.106-7.
    69 *Society*: Henry Compton, Bishop of London and ex-officio bishop of the
English colonies, learned in 1676 that there were 'scarce four ministers of
the Church of England in all the vast tract of America'. But it was Compton's
appointment of Thomas Bray, a poor parish priest, as his 'superintendent,
commissary or suffragan' to the province of Maryland in 1696 that eventually
got results. In June 1701 Bray received from William III a charter for a corporation for the propagating the Gospel in the English plantations. The
Society for the Propagation of the Gospel was a success from the start. It
raised £1,537 in its first year and sent out as one of its first missionaries
George Keith, a convert from Quakerism, whose mission to America in 1702-4
was a phenomenal success: 'There are now Thirteen Ministers in the Northern
Parts of *America*,' he reported, 'all placed within these two Years last past,
and generally Supported and Maintained by the *Honourable Society for the
Propagation of the Gospel in Foreign Parts*' (Keith, *A Journal of Travels from
New-Hampshire to Caratuck, On the Continent of North-America*, London, by
Joseph Downing for Brab. Aylmer, 1706, p. 88).
    71 *Governors*: 444.140). What the Examiner proposed had in fact already been
done. One of the first acts of the SPG was to send out questionnaires to the
colonial governors and two of them, Colonel Lewis Morris of New Jersey and
Colonel Joseph Dudley of New England, were in London in 1702 providing first-

transmit to him an Account of Church-Affairs within their several
Governments. I am only afraid that all these Accounts wou'd not
equally please him; as for Instance, when he shou'd receive a
State of Religion from *Jamaica*, and another from *New-England*, as   75
I doubt not but he wou'd make a fine Panegyrick on the former for
being so Primitive and Orthodox, so I suspect we shou'd have as
great an Invective on the latter for being Schismatical and Factious: And therefore, upon the whole, I think the less he knows
of that Matter the better; for he wou'd certainly do those *Ameri-*   80
cans more Harm than Good, being of all Men that ever I met with
the bitterest Enemy to Trade.

The mentioning of these Churches leads me to explain the meaning of a certain *Latin* word, which has occasion'd much Discourse
of late, and which, among other great Crimes, has been sometimes   85
us'd to signify *the Robbing of a Church*; I mean the word *PECU-*
LATUS. There having been a Paper industriously spread about in
Latin, in which it is affirm'd, that once upon a time this Crime
rag'd among us like any Plague; the Unlearned in the *Latin* Tongue
were very curious to know what the Nature of that Crime was, and   90
what that Word signify'd. And because there have been often

.

hand evidence (H.P. Thompson, *Into All Lands. The History of the Society for
the Propagation of the Gospel in Foreign Parts, 1701-1950*, London, SPCK, 1951,
p. 21). In 1708 Swift was 'thought of for bishop of Virginia' (Nichols,
Supplement, p. 742).
75 *Jamaica*: 'In 1704 [Major General Thomas] Handasyde reported that the
Church was in a bad way. There were sixteen parishes and only five parsons,
the rest being all dead or left' (Frank Cundall, *The Governors of Jamaica in
the First Half of the 18th Century*, London, The West India Committee, 1937,
p. 34).
  New-England: Transported felons and refugees from the persecutions of
the Church of England did not require many Anglican churches in New England.
In 1711 there was one, King's Chapel in Boston.
82 *Enemy to Trade*: 129.84-131.102.
87 *Paper*: Harley was created Earl of Oxford on 23 May. His patent of nobility, in Latin and English, was published by Morphew as *The Reasons which
induc'd Her Majesty to Create the Right Honourable Robert Harley, Esq; a Peer
of Great Britain. The Latin Preamble by Dr. John Freind* (1711) and immediately pirated by Edmund Curll with Morphew's imprint. John Nichols surmised
that it was 'originally written in English by [Swift], and from thence translated by Dr. *Freind*' (Nichols, *Supplement*, p. 30). But when Swift tells Stella
that he had 'read the preamble to Mr. Harley's [patent], full of his praises',
there is no hint that he is reading his own work (Swift, *Journal*, p. 265).
91 *that Word*: In the preamble *peculatus* occurs in the following context:
'*Ærarij nostri curam Quaestor sustinuit, late grassanti peculatus pesti
coercendae ... laborantibus Fisci* (he bore the Weight of Our *Exchequer* as
Chancellor, and thereby prevented the further Plundering the Nation ... by
Rescuing Public Credit' (pp. 4, 7)). It was interpreted as 'a vile Reflection

heretofore Complaints of the Misapplication of Mony, or of the
employing it to other Services than those it was originally design'd for, these unlearned Persons generally suppos'd that the
95 Word imply'd no more than such a Misapplication.

But every Man that knows any thing of *Latin* will agree, that
this Word cannot possibly bear so mild an Interpretation, having
been always us'd by the most approv'd Authors of that Language,
to signify one of these three things, and nothing else; *Stealing*
100 *the Publick Mony, Adulterating the Coin*, or *Robbing some Holy*
Place or Church. Since therefore it is said that this Crime in
times past did spread it self over the Nation, one wou'd be apt
to think the meaning of *Peculatus* in modern *Latin*, is the same as
'twas in the antient, and then it must be, *That the Publick*
105 *Treasury was rob'd*, or *the Coin was spoil'd*, or *the Churches were*
broke open and pillag'd: And consequently this wou'd be the State
of any Land or Nation whenever it is thus visited; one of these
Plagues at least must afflict the People, or how can it be said
that this Crime rages among them? Wherefore if it shou'd be
110 affirm'd, that at a time when the publick Treasury was well
manag'd, when the Coin was all true Sterling, and when the
Churches were free from Sacrilege, a Nation under these happy
Circumstances was over-run with the Crime above-mention'd; and
that all this had happen'd under the Management and Direction of
115 an honest disinterested Person, who was never suspected for having
cheated the Publick, nor will ever be accus'd for keeping any
Mony for himself; on whom must such a Reflection turn? And wou'd
it not put People in mind of the Story of *Lucius Scipio*, a famous
Roman, who suffer'd under the same Accusation?
120 This Good and Virtuous Person, ally'd to the greatest Men of
Rome, was, after long and faithful Services done to his Country,
accus'd of this very Crime. Neither his Merits nor his small
Estate cou'd protect him from the Violence of some Tribunes of
the People; who being convinc'd (without Inquiry) that he had

on the Lord *Godolphin*, inserted in the Preamble to his Successor's Patent,
where the preceding Administration in the Treasury, was charg'd with Pecula-
tion or Plundering' (Oldmixon, *The Life*, p. 196).
  99-101 *Stealing ... Church*: Lex Julia (½°); Justinian, *Corpus iuris
civilis*, 1663, xlviii 13 1, 4.
  115 *Person*: innuendo: Godolphin.
  118 *Lucius Scipio*: Livy, xxxviii 55 4-5.
  123-4 *Tribunes of the People*: innuendo: the Commissioners for taking,

embezel'd the publick Treasure, immediately condemn'd him for it,   125
laid a Fine upon him, and confiscated his Goods to pay it. But
when the publick Officers came to take possession of them, then
at last it appear'd how falsly he had been accus'd. The Historian
says, there were *no Footsteps of those immense Sums which he was*
said to have stoln from the Publick; nor cou'd he have paid his   130
Fine, if his Kindred and Friends had not contributed to it; and
yet he had enjoy'd some Legacies, and was always a Man of a very
moderate Expence. But the Author ends this Book with observing,
That *the Accusers of this just Person, and all that were con-*
cern'd in his Condemnation, were abhor'd for it ever after; and   135
that the Weight and Disgrace of so wicked a Sentence turn'd at
last upon the Men that procur'd it.

examining, and stating the publick accounts of the Kingdom, seven Tories (including two members of the October Club and two Jacobites), who were elected
in March 1711 (*CJ*, xvi 562). This was the committee that promulgated the Tory
legend of the unaccounted-for £35,000,000 (416.52). If Mainwaring alludes to
Swift's *Discourse*, reprinted in *Miscellanies in Prose and Verse* (27 February
1711), he scores heavily, for '*Tribunes of the People*' was Swift's hieroglyph
for the New Country Party leaders in the fourth Parliament of William III
(1698-1700), 'the most mischievous Parliament that has ever sat at Westminster'
(Sir John William Fortescue, *A History of the British Army*, 13 vols. in 14, New
York, Macmillan, 1910-35, i 389). 'By these Tribunes', Swift said, 'the People
were grosly imposed upon to serve the Turns and Occasions of revengeful or ambitious Men, and to commit such Exorbitances as could not end, but in the Dissolution of the Government' (Swift, *Discourse*, pp. 102-3).
    129-31 *no ... it*: Livy, xxxviii 60 8-9.
    132 *Legacies*: As the third son of Sir Francis Godolphin, who had to com-
pound for his estates in 1647, Godolphin was 'far from being rich' (*Private*
Correspondence, i 365). If he had not inherited £4,000 a year from his eldest
brother in August 1710 (Luttrell, vi 623), he might have taxed the charity of
his friends.
    134-7 *the ... it*: Livy, xxxviii 60 10.

464

The EXAMINER.

Magna vis est, magnum nomen, unum & idem Sentientis Senatus.

WHoever calls to mind the Clamour and the Calumny, the artificial
Fears and Jealousies, the shameful Misrepresentation of Persons
and of Things, that were rais'd and spread by the Leaders and
Instruments of a *certain Party*, upon the Change of the last Mini-
5   stry, and Dissolution of Parliament; if he be a true Lover of his
Country, must feel a mighty Pleasure, though mix'd with some Indignation, to see the Wishes, the Conjectures, the Endeavours of
an inveterate Faction intirely disappointed; and this important
Period wholly spent, in restoring the Prerogative to the Prince,
10   Liberty to the Subject, in reforming past Abuses, preventing
Future, supplying old Deficiencies, providing for Debts, restoring the Clergy to their Rights, and taking Care of the Necessi- .
ties of the Church: And all this unattended with any of those
Misfortunes which some Men *hoped* for, while they pretended to
15   *fear*.

For my own part, I must confess, the Difficulties appear'd so
great to me, from such a noise and shew of Opposition, that I
thought nothing but the absolute Necessity of Affairs, could ever
justify so daring an Attempt. But, a wise and good Prince, at the
20   Head of an able Ministry, and of a Senate freely chosen; all
united to pursue the true Interest of their Country, is a Power,
against which, the little inferior Politicks of any Faction, will
be able to make no long Resistance. To this we may add one additional Strength, which in the Opinion of our Adversaries, is the
25   greatest and justest of any; I mean the *Vox Populi*, so indisput-
ably declarative on the same Side. I am apt to think, when these

9 Prince,] Prince, and 38 8°+12°   26 think] believe 38 8°+12°

Motto Cicero, *Philippics*, iii 32: Great is the Name and Authority of a
Senate unanimous in Opinion and undivided in their Sentiments.
14-15 *hoped for, while they pretended to fear*: 178.9-179.22, 183.113-15.
25 *Vox Populi*: The election of October 1710 is said to have returned twice
as many Tories as Whigs (Speck, *Tory and Whig*, p. 110).

discarded Politicians begin seriously to consider all this, they
will think it proper to give out, and reserve their Wisdom for
some more convenient Juncture.

It was pleasant enough to observe, that those who were the   30
chief Instruments of raising the Noise, who started Fears, bespoke Dangers, and form'd ominous Prognosticks, in order to scare
the *Allies*, to spirit the *French*, and fright ignorant People at
Home; made use of those very Opinions themselves had broach'd,
for Arguments to prove, that the Change of Ministers was danger-   35
ous and unseasonable. But if a House be *Swept*, the more Occasion
there is for such a Work, the more *Dust* it will raise; if it be
going to *Ruin*, the *Repairs*, however necessary, will *make a Noise*,
and *disturb the Neighbourhood* a while. And as to the Rejoicings
made in *France*, if it be true, that they had any, upon the News   40
of those Alterations among us; their Joy was grounded upon the
same Hopes with that of the *Whigs*, who comforted themselves, that
a Change of Ministry and Parliament, would infallibly put us all
into Confusion, increase our Divisions, and destroy our Credit;
wherein, I suppose, by this time they are *equally* undeceiv'd.   45

But this long Session, being in a manner ended, which several
Circumstances, and one *Accident*, altogether unforeseen, have
drawn out beyond the usual Time; it may be some small piece of
Justice to so excellent an Assembly, barely to mention a few of
those great Things they have done for the Service of their QUEEN   50
and Country; which I shall take notice of, just as they come to
my Memory.

The Credit of the Nation began mightily to suffer by a Discount
upon *Exchequer Bills*, which have been generally reckon'd the
surest and most sacred of all Securities. The present Lord   55

30 was] is 38 8°+12°   47 unforeseen] unforseen ½°

---

28 *give out*: desist (*OED*).
39-40 *Rejoicings ... in France*: 3.41.
46 *Session ... ended*: 'The session did not actually close till June 12th'
(E*1922*, ix 292).
50 *great Things*: 'I design, in some following Papers, to draw up a List ...
of the great Things this Parliament hath already perform'd' (332.117-19).
54 *Exchequer Bills*: 'The House of Commons had resolved on January 16th,
1710/1, to provide for converting all non-specie exchequer bills into specie'
(E*1922*, ix 293). The 'Method' was to pay the Bank of England £45,000 to
accept them at par (*CJ*, xvi 457-8; Dickson, pp. 374-5; Hill, pp. 406-8).

Treasurer, then a Member of the House of Commons, propos'd a
Method, which was immediately comply'd with, of raising them to
a *Par* with *Specie*; and so they have ever since continu'd.

The *British* Colonies of *Nevis* and St. *Christophers*, had been
60   miserably Plunder'd by the *French*, their Houses burnt, their Plantations destroy'd, and many of the Inhabitants carried away
Prisoners: They had often, for some Years past, apply'd in vain
for Relief from hence; 'till the present Parliament, considering
their Condition as a Case of Justice and Mercy, voted them One
65   Hundred Thousand Pound by way of Recompence, in some Manner, for
their Sufferings.

Some Persons, whom the Voice of the Nation authorises me to
call her *Enemies*, taking Advantage of the general Naturalization
Act, had invited over a great Number of Foreigners of all Reli-
70   gions, under the Name of *Palatines*; who understood no Trade or
Handicraft, yet rather chose to Beg than Labour; who besides in-
festing our Streets, bred Contagious Diseases, by which we lost
in *Natives*, thrice the Number of what we gain'd in *Foreigners*.
The House of Commons, as a Remedy against this Evil, brought in
75   a Bill for repealing that Act of general Naturalization, which,
to the Surprize of most People, was rejected by the L--ds. And
upon this Occasion, I must allow my self to have been justly
rebuk'd by one of my Weekly Monitors, for pretending in a former
Paper, to hope that Law would be repeal'd; wherein the Commons
80   being disappointed, took care however to send many of the

65 Pound] Pounds 38 8°+12°   67 authorises] authorizes 12°   authorizeth
38 8°+12°

---

59 *Nevis and St. Christophers*: 'The Act for licensing and regulating hack-
ney coaches, etc. (9 Ann. c. 16) provided that a sum of £103,003 11s. 4d.
should be distributed among those proprietors and inhabitants of Nevis and St.
Christopher's who had suffered "very great losses by a late invasion of the
French" [*CJ*, xvi 620, 692]' (E*1922*, ix 293).
70 *Palatines*: 129.85-6n. A petition of the minister and parishioners of St.
Olave's in Southwark presented to the Commons in January 1711 a complaint that
200 Palatines had re-entered the parish, 'supposed from *Ireland*', raising fears
of 'contagious Distempers' and that 'they ... are likely to become chargeable,
to the utter Ruin of the said Parish [*CJ*, xvi 456, 596-8]' (E*1922*, ix 293).
75 *Bill*: 194.75n. The Bill to repeal the Act for a general Naturalization
was thrown out by the Lords on 5 February 1711 (*LJ*, xix 215). It 'was, however, again brought in, and passed next session in both houses' (E*1814*, iv 133).
78-9 *former Paper*: 194.75; cf. *The Observator*, 16 June 1711.

Palatines away, and to represent their being invited over, as a
pernicious Council.

The *Qualification*-Bill, incapacitating all Men to serve in
Parliament, who have not some Estate in Land, either in Possession or certain Reversion, is perhaps the greatest Security that   85
ever was contriv'd for preserving the Constitution, which otherwise might, in a little time, lye wholly at the Mercy of the
Mony'd Interest: And since much the greatest part of the Taxes
is paid, either immediately from Land, or from the Productions
of it; 'tis but common Justice, that those who are the Proprie-   90
tors, should appoint what Portion of it ought to go to the Support of the Publick; otherwise, the engrossers of Money, would be
apt to lay heavy Loads on others, which themselves never touch
with one of their Fingers.

The Publick Debts were so prodigiously encreas'd, by the Negli-   95
gence and Corruption of those who had been Managers of the
Revenue; that the late M------rs, like careless Men, who run out
their Fortunes, were so far from any Thoughts of Payment, as they
had not the Courage to state or compute them. The Parliament
found that Thirty Five Millions had never been accounted for; and   100
that the Debt on the Navy, wholly unprovided for, amounted to
Nine Millions. The late Chancellor of the *Exchequer*, suitable to
his transcendent Genius for Publick Affairs, propos'd a Fund to
be Security for that immense Debt, which is now confirm'd by a

83 all] *om.* 12° 38 8°+12°   89-90 the Productions of it] its Productions
38 8°+12°   98 as] that 38 8°+12°

---

81 *Palatines*: 'On the invitation of [the Earl of Wharton] the lord lieutenant [and the Irish Privy Council] 3,000 Palatines were sent into Ireland
in August, 1709, and 800 in the following February. Many of them subsequently
returned to England [466.70n.] in the hope that they would be sent to Caro-
lina ... The government spent £22,275 in transporting 3,300 of them to New
York' (E*1922*, ix 294).
83 *Qualification-Bill*: 332.110n.
87-8 *the Mony'd Interest*: 5.78.
100 *Thirty Five Millions*: 416.52.
101 *Debt on the Navy*: 379.160-1n. Swift evidently refers to the £3.5 million in 'Accounts' lying before the Auditors' *plus* the £6.7 million in 'Accounts under the Examination of the Navy Board' in the audit submitted to
Parliament on 24 April 1711 (*CJ*, xvi 612). These sums are included in the £35
million unaccounted for.
102 *Chancellor of the Exchequer*: From Chancellor of the Exechequer Harley
succeeded as Lord Treasurer on 23 May 1711.

105 Law, and is likely to prove the greatest Restoration and Establishment of the Kingdom's Credit. Nor content with this, the
Legislature hath appointed Commissioners of Accompts, to inspect
into past Mismanagements of the publick Mony, and prevent them
for the future.

110   I have, in a former Paper, mention'd the Act for building Fifty
new Churches in *London* and *Westminster*, with a Fund appropriated
for that pious and noble Work. But while I am mentioning Acts of
Piety, it would be unjust to conceal my Lord High Treasurer's
Concern for Religion, which have extended even to another King-
115 dom: His Lordship having some Months ago, obtain'd of Her Majesty
a Remission of the First Fruits and Tenths to the Clergy of *Ire-*
land, as he is formerly known to have done for that Reverend Body
in this Kingdom.

    The Act for carrying on a Trade to the South-Sea, propos'd by
120 the same great Person, whose Thoughts are perpetually employ'd,
and always with Success, on the good of his Country, will, in all
probability, if duly executed, be of mighty Advantage to the Kingdom, and an everlasting Honour to the present Parliament.

    I might go on further, and mention that seasonable Law against
125 excessive Gaming; the putting a stop to that scandalous Fraud of

---

116 a Remission of] *om.* 38 8°+12°   117 formerly known to have] known to
have already 38 8°+12°   118 in this Kingdom] here 38 8°+12°   121 al-
ways] ever 38 8°+12°

---

105 *Law*: On 2 May 1711 Harley proposed a bill to fund all public and
national debts by exchanging them for stock yielding six per cent in the South
Sea Company with a monopoly to trade to South America which 'will yearly bring
vast Riches from Peru and Mexico into Great-Britain' (*The History and Pro-*
ceedings of the House of Commons, iv 208). The bill was introduced on 17 May
and on 12 June the royal assent was received for an Act for making good Deficiencies and satisfying the public Debts and for erecting a Corporation to
carry on a Trade to the South Seas (9 Ann. c. 15), an extremely long and com-
plex piece of legislation.
    107 *Commissioners of Accompts*: An Act for the taking examining and stating
the publick Accounts of the Kingdom (9 Ann. c. 18) received the royal assent
on 16 May (*CJ*, xvi 668).
    111 *Churches*: 439.2.
    116 *Remission*: It had been decided that the Duke of Ormond was to have the
honour of announcing the Queen's remission of the first fruits and tenths
(that Swift had negotiated with Harley in October 1710) in his speech opening
the Irish Parliament in July 1711 (Swift, *Journal*, p. 291; *Corr.*, i 241).
    124 *Law*: 'A Bill for the better preventing of Excessive and Deceitful
Gaming, was introduced January 25th, 1710/1, passed April 11th, and obtained
the Royal Assent, May 16th (9 Ann. c. 19)' (*E1922*, ix 296).

false Musters in the Guards; the diligent and effectual Enquiry
made by the Commons into several gross Abuses. I might produce
many Instances of their impartial Justice in deciding controverted Elections, against *former Example*, and great Provocations
to retaliate. I might shew their chearful Readiness in granting   130
such vast Supplies; their great Unanimity, not to be broken by
all the Arts of a malicious and cunning Faction; their unfeigned
Duty to the QUEEN; and lastly, that Representation made to Her
Majesty from the House of Commons, discovering such a Spirit and
Disposition in that noble Assembly, to redress all those Evils,   135
which a long Male-Administration had brought upon us.

'Tis probable, that trusting only to my Memory, I may have
omitted many Things of great Importance; neither do I pretend
further in the compass of this Paper, than to give the World some
general, however imperfect Idea, how worthily this great Assembly   140
hath discharg'd the Trust of those who so freely chose them; and
what we may reasonably hope and expect from the Piety, Courage,
Wisdom, and Loyalty of such excellent Patriots, in a Time so
fruitful of Occasions to exert the greatest Abilities.

129 Elections] Election ½° 12°

---

126 *false Musters in the Guards*: 'The officers [connived] at tradesmen, and
others, who enlisted merely for the purpose of securing their persons from
their creditors, and, as they did no duty, were contented that the officers
should draw their pay. These inefficient recruits were called *Romans*, because
they served their country without pay' (E*1814*, iv 135). 'A clause was inserted in the Recruiting Bill to remedy this evil (10 Ann. c. 12 §39), and
the House [of Commons] passed a strong resolution against the practice, on
May 26th [*CJ*, xvi 680]' (E*1922*, ix 296). One of the principals was Lieutenant-
Colonel Francis Charteris, a company commander in the first regiment of foot
guards, whose infamies are noticed in Pope's verse and Hogarth's engravings.
127 *Abuses*: On 4 June 1711 the Commons voted an address to the Queen complaining of 'the Imprest Accomptants, the public Debts, the Arrears of Taxes,
the Abuses of the Victualing Office, the bringing over the *Palatines*, and the
Charter imposed upon the Corporation of *Bewdley*, in the County of *Worcester*'
(*CJ*, xvi 683-5). It was this address that reported £35,302,107 unaccounted
for.
128-9 *deciding controverted Elections*: 332.120n.
131 *Supplies*: 333.121n. During the entire session the Parliament voted the
unprecedented sum of £14,000,000 (*The History and Proceedings of the House of
Commons*, iv 178-99).
133 *that Representation*: *CJ*, xvi 683-5.
135 *Evils*: The unspoken evil in the 'Representation' was that lots of Whigs
remained in places of profit (314.17), and the address concludes by begging
the Queen to employ none but those who 'have given good Testimonies of their
Duty to your Majesty, and of their Affection to the true Interest of your
Kingdom' (*CJ*, xvi 685).

145   And now I conceive the main Design I had in writing these
Papers, is fully executed. A great Majority of the Nation is at
length thorowly convinc'd, that the Qu--- proceeded with the
highest Wisdom, in changing Her Ministry and Parliament. That
under a former Administration, the greatest Abuses of all kinds
150 were committed, and the most dangerous Attempts against the Constitution for some time intended. The whole Kingdom finds the
present Persons in Power, directly and openly pursuing the true
Service of their QUEEN and Country; and to be such whom their
most bitter Enemies cannot tax with Bribery, Covetousness, Ambi-
155 tion, Pride, Insolence, or any pernicious Principles in Religion
or Government.

For my own Particular, those little barking Pens which have so
constantly pursu'd me, I take to be of no further Consequence to
what I have writ, than the scoffing Slaves of old, placed behind
160 the Chariot, to put the General in mind of his Mortality; which
was but a Thing of Form, and made no Stop or Disturbance in the
Shew. However, if those perpetual Snarlers against me, had the
same Design, I must own they have effectually compass'd it; since
nothing can well be more mortifying, than to reflect that I am of
165 the same Species with Creatures capable of uttering so much Scurrility, Dulness, Falshood and Impertinence, to the Scandal and
Disgrace of Human Nature.

145 *Design*: 'As for the *Examiner*, I have heard a whisper, that after that
of this day [7 June 1711], which tells what this parliament has done, you will
hardly find them so good. I prophecy they will be trash for the future; and
methinks in this day's *Examiner* the author talks doubtfully, as if he would
write no more, so that if they go on, they may probably be by some other hand,
which in my opinion is a thousand pities; but who can help it?' (Swift, *Journal*, p. 291).
159-60 *scoffing Slave ... Mortality*: Tertullian, *Apologeticus*, xxxiii 4.
164 *mortifying*: cf. 'This was Matter of ... Mortification to my self. For
now I could no longer deny, that I was a real *Yahoo*, in every Limb and Feature' (Swift, *Prose*, xi 251).

No. 37 [Mainwaring]   11 June 1711

The MEDLEY.

An entire Paragraph out of the last Examiner, *with some Notes upon it.*
A Letter from an unknown Hand concerning the late Act of Indemnity.

THERE is one Paragraph in the last *Examiner* so very extraordinary,
that I hope the Reader will forgive me, if I can't help transcribing it entire.

'For my own Particular, those little barking Pens which have so
constantly pursu'd me, I take to be of no further Consequence to   5
what I have writ, than the scoffing Slaves of old, plac'd behind
the Chariot, to put the General in mind of his Mortality; which
was but a thing of Form, and made no Stop or Disturbance in the
Shew. However, if those perpetual Snarlers against me had the
same Design, I must own they have effectually compass'd it; since   10
nothing can well be more mortifying, than to reflect that I am of
the same Species with Creatures capable of uttering so much Scurrility, Dulness, Falshood and Impertinence, to the Scandal and
Disgrace of Human Nature.'

If my Friend will shew me such another *scurrilous, dull, false*   15
and *impertinent* Paragraph in any Writer Antient or Modern, I will
hereafter believe him upon his own bare word, which is the greatest Promise that was ever made to Mortal.

In the first place, having occasion to compare himself to some
body, who shou'd he pitch upon but a very Great Conqueror? A   20
little Hireling Scribler, *pursu'd*, as he admirably expresses it,
by barking Pens, has wonderfully the Air and Resemblance of a
Roman Hero in his Triumph. But this is according to his usual way
of Thinking, and just as well apply'd as any thing he ever
meddled with. Every body knows a *Roman* Triumph was the greatest   25
Honour that cou'd be decreed to any Mortal. When great Actions
had been perform'd in War, great Numbers of the Enemy subdu'd,

4-14   *For ... Nature*: 470.157-67.
27-8   *subdu'd ... Provinces*: 54.119, 55.130.

new Provinces acquir'd, or mighty Spoils brought Home; this was
the Reward of such high and publick Service. Now comes my Friend,
30   and he acquaints you, that truly *the main Design he had in Writing
is fully answer'd*; And therefore what does he, but immediately
put himself in the Seat of one of these Conquerors, and away he
rides in the Triumphal Chariot, placing all that reflect upon him
in the room *of scoffing Slaves, to put him mind of his Mortality.*
35   What a Hero is here brought upon the Stage in a Farce of his own
making, and what an Image must it give us of a *Roman* Triumph, to
suppose such a *Harlequin* plac'd in the chief Seat of the Chariot!
     In the next Place there are several Particulars in this Account
worth remarking: For *if his Design be*, as he says, *fully executed*,
40   it ought to occasion very melancholy Reflections in every honest
Man; his Design being, as he himself has set it forth, to flatter
the new Ministers, to invent Calumnies against the old, to vilify
our General, abuse our Bishops, insult our late Parliaments,
affront our Allies, and revile the Union, with other worthy In-
45   tentions of the like Tendency. And tho perhaps in Wit and Learning it may easily be prov'd that *Lesley* has the Advantage of him,
yet I am not sure that the *Air of Authority* he gave himself, his
insipid Mirth, and bold Assertions, did not impose for some time
upon easy credulous People. It was therefore necessary for me and
50   others to prepare an Antidote for his Poison, which I believe is
almost work'd off; for sure 'tis impossible that *Britain* shou'd
long be deluded by a Man who can write nothing that is either
True or *Probable*, as I have often prov'd, and shall continue
still to demonstrate.
55   For even in this Account of a General in his Triumph, there are
almost as many Errors as Words; there were no *scoffing* Slaves of
old plac'd in a Triumphal Chariot, nor was any body plac'd there
to put the General in mind of his Mortality, which wou'd not have
been a very proper Office for a scoffing Slave. There was indeed

---

30-1 *the ... answer'd*: 470.145-6.
37 *Harlequin*: The first reference is to The Examiner/Blunderer, but there
is also a slur at Harley, whose nickname this is (*POAS*, Yale, vii 324).
47 *Air of Authority*: 351.69; cf. 'by assuming to himself an Air of Authority, and speaking in the Person of one employ'd by the Ministry, he sometimes
gives a kind of weight to what he says, so as to make Impressions of Terrour
upon honest Minds' (Mainwaring, *Reflections upon the Examiner's Scandalous
Peace*, London, for A. Baldwin, 1711, p. 3).
53 *often prov'd*: 411.93-5, 106-7; 434.13.
56 *Errors*: Mainwaring fails to score here (470.159-60n.).

one Man plac'd there, whose Business was to bear the Triumphal   60
Crown, and he was sometimes a Slave, but oftner the Common Hangman. And *Pliny* tells us, That the Image of the God *Fascinus* being
always hung up in the Chariot, this Slave or Hangman frequently
whisper'd the General to look back upon the God, that Envy might
have no power to sully his Triumph, and *Fortune might be appeas'd*, 65
who can't easily bear too much Glory.

But tho there were no Scoffers in the Chariot, a good Author
informs us, 'That in the middle of the Harpers and Pipers, there
always went a Fellow half-mad, who made a great many sensless
Jests.' And an Historian describing the Triumph of *Scipio*, says,   70
'Among the rest of the Pomp and Ceremony, there was a Troop of
Singers and Musicians in a short tuck'd up Dress; and a Man went
among them in a Coat down to his Ancles, cover'd over with ridiculous Fringes and Bracelets, who by his various Gestures *insulted
the Conquer'd Enemies*, and occasion'd great Laughter in the Multi- 75
tude.'

Here is now *the scoffing Slave* that my blundering Friend plac'd
behind the Chariot. He had heard there was one somewhere, and
sure he might set him where he pleas'd: And indeed I never knew
him come so near the Truth in my life. Therefore, I wish with all 80
my heart that a Triumph were decreed for his Reward. I shou'd be
glad *to see him* any where; who is the greatest Curiosity that
Nature has yet brought forth. If he cou'd not get into the *Chief
Place of the Chariot*, it is certain he wou'd extremely well become the *Seat behind*: And if our General, who has so long and so 85
justly deserv'd a Triumph, were, as he says, *to be put in mind of
his Mortality*, my Friend wou'd upon all accounts be the fittest
Man to sit at his Elbow; tho I am sensible that most People wou'd

77 now] 12° not ½° (*erratum noted in* The Medley, *No. 38*)

61-2 *the Common Hangman*: Rosinus, [*Antiquitatum Romanarum*, Geneva, Jacob
Stoer, 1641, p. 1043] lib. 10. c. 29, Paralipom. (½°).
62-6 *Fascinus ... Glory*: Pliny, [*Natural History*,] xxviii 7 (§39) (½° corrected).
65 *Fortune ... appeas'd*: Exorata a tergo Fortuna (½°).
68-70 *That ... Jests*: Alexand[ri] ab Alexand[ro, *Iurisperiti Neapolitani*,
genialium dierum libri sex, Paris, apud Ioannem de Lastre, 1679, f. 332] lib.
6. c. 6 (½°).
69 *a Fellow half-mad*: Quispiam pene delirus (½°).
71-6 *Among ... Multitude*: Appian. Libycis. [ix 66] (½°).
74-5 *insulted ... Enemies*: Hostibus de victis insultans (½°).

rather place him among *the Singers and Pipers*, where, as the
90   *Roman* Buffoon *insulted the Conquer'd Enemies*, he might insolently
scoff and insult the *Ruin'd Party*.

Either of these Under-Places in the Triumph my Friend wou'd fill
most admirably; and I wou'd not have the World wonder why I
trouble my self so much about him. When I first enter'd into his
95   Friendship, I oblig'd my self to admonish him of all the Blunders
and Falshoods he shou'd publish, and to cure him, if it was possible, of his intolerable Aversion to Truth, and natural Hatred
to Modesty; therefore 'tis easy to imagine how much work is still
upon my hands, and what pains are yet to be taken with him; of
100 which I shall give another Instance in this Paper. The Tories
have frequently given out most dreadful Declarations what they
wou'd do against the late Ministry, if their Hands had not been
tied up by an Act of Indemnity, which these crafty Persons procur'd to shelter themselves against the Law. Nothing was so com-
105 mon in their Mouths and Libels as this: Not only the *Examiner*,
but his Patrons, affirm'd it, with equal regard to Conscience and
Humanity, tho the last knew every word of it to be groundless and
invented. But with them I have nothing to do: I may say of them
as *Catullus* did of *Cæsar, I know not of what Colour their Hair is*;
110 yet I was just going, in pursuance of my Promise and Obligation,
to correct my Friend for publishing so gross a Fiction, when I
receiv'd from an unknown Hand the following Letter.

   SIR,

THE Examiner *in his Paper of the 26th of* April *has these words*:
115 'And here we can't refuse the late Ministry their due Praises,
who foreseeing a Storm, provided for their own Safety by two admirable Expedients, by which, with great prudence they have
escap'd the Punishments due to pernicious Counsels and corrupt
Management: The first was to procure, under Pretences hardly spe-
120 cious, a general Act of Indemnity, which cuts off all Impeachments.'

   91 *the Ruin'd Party*: 207.156n.
   95 *Blunders*: 106.79, 122.108, 327.183, 459.32.
   103 *Act of Indemnity*: 72.153n.
   109 *I ... is*: Catullus 93.
   115-21 *And ... Impeachments*: 389.109-15.

This gave me occasion to look into the Act, where I find the
following Exceptions.

'And also excepted out of this Pardon all and every the Sums of
Mony and Duties following, and the Concealment and wrongful De-   125
tainment thereof; that is to say, &c. or any other Tax, Assessment, Duty, Imposition, Debt, or Sum of Mony whatsoever to the
Queen's Majesty, given or levyable by any Act of Parliament, *or*
otherwise due or belonging to the *Queen's Majesty,* &c. *and all*
Corruption and Misdemeanours of any Officer or Minister of or   130
concerning the same, and *all Accounts* and Suits whatsoever to be
had, made, or prosecuted for the same; and also excepted all and
singular *Accounts* of all and every Collector and Collectors, Commissioners, *Treasurers,* Receivers or other Officers, or other
Accomptants whatsoever, who have receiv'd or collected, or are   135
any other way accountable to her Majesty for any Subsidy, &c.'

If you think proper some way to take notice of this Matter, you
will undeceive a very great number of Persons, who by misunder-
standing a late Vote of the House of Commons, apprehend that a
great part of Thirty Five Millions has been converted by the late   140

124-32 *And ... same:* 7 Ann. c. 22 §34 (*Statutes of the Realm,* ix 99).
132-6 *and ... Subsidy:* 7 Ann. c. 22 §37 (ibid.). Mainwaring scores heavily
here, for Swift appears to have been ignorant of the terms of the Act of Indemnity. Mainwaring followed up his advantage by inserting in *The Medley* of
2, 9, 16, and 23 July 1711 the following advertisement: '*The next time the*
Examiner, *according to his usual Method, goes about to blast the Reputation*
of the most worthy Gentlemen in Britain, *by the most villanous Forgery that*
ever any Knight of the Post lost his Ears for, he is advis'd so to contrive
Matters, that his Lye may not be disprov'd; as it was in the Case of the late
Ministry, when he charg'd them with getting an Indemnity to cover their cor-
rupt Management; since all such Crimes are particularly excepted in that Act.'
'I have been with two men at dinner', he wrote to the Duchess of Marlborough,
'And one of them say'd, he had seen Dr. Atterbury lately, who own'd that the
Advertisement in the Medley about the Act of Indemnity, had quite sunk the
Examiner, and that he never wou'd recover it' (BL MS Add. 61461; cf. *The*
Grand Accuser the Greatest of all Criminals, 1735, p. 30).
140 *Thirty Five Millions:* The report of £35,000,000 unaccounted for (467.
100) was the product of 'a stage-managed and harmless inquiry' undertaken to
satisfy Tory demands for Whig scapegoats. No evidence of impeachable mismanagement was found. 'The report did not mention any of Godolphin's senior
colleagues except the Paymaster of the Forces Abroad, James Brydges, and did
not investigate the reasons for Brydges' failure to submit his accounts.
Brydges continued, in defiance of the Commons' recommendation [that he be
dismissed], to be employed in his office and protected by Harley' (Hill,
p. 409).

Ministry to their private Use; and that the only reason why they
are not impeach'd for it, is because, as the Examiner *says,* all
Impeachments are cut off by the General Act of Indemnity procur'd
by them for that purpose. *I am,* &c.

145   Behold what Care the late Ministry took to protect themselves
from the Law, and how sensible they were of their *Plunderings* and
Depredations! My worthy Friend has often protested that there is
not one Lye in all his Papers; and therefore I hope the Reader
will be satisfy'd with this new Taste of his Veracity, and by
150   this Instance form a true Judgment of him, if he has not done it
already. If my Arguments were all Demonstrations, I know the
Examiner wou'd except against my *Authority*, which is a thing he
claims wholly to himself: And for that reason I have now shewn
him what opinion others have of him; and to what pains he puts
155   People to undeceive themselves, after he has taken so much to
deceive them. But what can one think of such a Man as this, who
durst assert so notorious a Falshood, of which it was so easy to
convict him? Is there such another Scandal and Disgrace of *Human*
Nature? Is it not mortifying to be of the *same Species with such*
160   *a Creature*? to use his own words. And yet this honest Gentleman
has more than once declar'd, and will again declare, that neither
I, nor any of the *barking Pens* have ever *disprov'd him in any one*
material Point in Fact; which now I submit to Judgment, and join
issue with him upon this Article, for the World to determine
165   between us.

146 *Plunderings*: 348.162. 'Depredations' seems not to be Swift's word.
158-60 *Scandal ... Creature*: 470.163-7.
162 *barking Pens*: 470.157.
162-3 *any ... Fact*: 429.42-3.

No. 46 [Swift and Manley]   14 June 1711

The EXAMINER.

Melius non tangere Clamo.

WHEN a General has conquer'd an Army, and reduc'd a Country to
Obedience, he often finds it necessary to send out small Bodies,
in order to take in petty Castles and Forts, and beat little
straggling Parties, which are otherwise, apt to make Head and
infest the Neighbourhood: This Case exactly resembles mine; I   5
count the main Body of the *Whigs* entirely subdu'd; at least,
'till they appear with new Reinforcements, I shall reckon them as
such; and therefore do now find my self at leisure to *Examine* inferior Abuses. The Business I have left, is, to fall on those
Wretches that will be still keeping the War on Foot, when they   10
have no Country to defend, no Forces to bring into the Field, nor
any thing remaining, but their bare good-will towards *Faction* and
Mischief: I mean, the present Set of Writers, whom I have suffer'd, without Molestation, so long to infest the Town. Were
there not a concurrence from Prejudice, Party, weak Understand-   15
ing, and Misrepresentation, I should think them too inconsiderable in themselves to deserve Correction: But as my Endeavour

5 exactly] *om.* 38 12°   10 that will be still] who would still be 38°
8°+12°   14-15 Were there] If there were 38 8°+12°

Motto Horace, *Satires*, ii 1 45: But he who hurts me (nay, I will be heard)
| Had better take a Lion by the Beard.
   1 *General*: The metaphor may have been suggested by *The Medley*: 'what does
he, but immediately put himself in the Seat of one of these Conquerors, and
away he rides in the Triumphal Chariot' (472.31-3).
   2 *small Bodies*: Delariviere Manley, who took over *The Examiner* with this
number, was 'very fat' (Swift, *Journal*, p. 474). Writing on 22 June 1711,
Swift said 'Yesterday's was a sad *Examiner*, and last week was very indifferent, though some little scraps of the old spirit, as if he had given some
hints' (Swift, *Journal*, pp. 474, 296). The hints must have been left with Mrs
Manley before 9 June 1711, when Swift departed London to spend ten days with
Henry Petty, Lord Shelburn, at High Wycombe (Swift, *Journal*, p. 293).
   13-14 *Set of Writers ... suffered, without Molestation*: *The Examiner*, Swift
said, was 'not intended for the Management of Controversy', for 'if it once
came to Rejoinder and Reply, we should be all upon a Level' (200.205, 241.60-
2). So, with only one exception (429.37-432.128), Swift did not waste time
answering the Whig journalists.

hath been to expose the gross Impositions of the *Fallen Party*,
I will give a Taste, in the following Petition, of the Sincerity
20 of these their *Factors*, to shew how little those Writers for the
Whigs were guided by Conscience or Honour, their Business being
only to gratify a prevailing Interest.

To the Right Honourable the present M-----ry, the humble Petition
of the Party-Writers to the late M-----ry.

Humbly Sheweth,
25 *THAT your Petitioners have serv'd their time to the Trade of*
Writing Pamphlets *and* Weekly Papers, *in defence of the* Whigs,
against the Church of England, *and the Christian Religion, and*
Her Majesty's Prerogative, and Her Title to the Crown: That since
the late Change of Ministry, and meeting of this Parliament, the
30 *said Trade is mightily fallen off, and the Call for the said*
Pamphlets and Papers, much less than formerly; and 'tis fear'd,
to our further Prejudice, that the Examiner *may discontinue Writ-*
ing, whereby some of your Petitioners will be brought to utter
Distress, forasmuch as thro' false Quotations, noted Absurdities,
35 *and other legal Abuses, many of your Petitioners, to their great*
Comfort and Support, were enabled to pick up a weekly Subsistance
out of the said Examiner.

That your said poor Petitioners, did humbly offer your Honours
to write in Defence of the late Change of Ministry and Parliament,
40 *much cheaper than they did for your Predecessors, which your*
Honours were pleas'd to refuse.

Notwithstanding which Offer, your Petitioners are under daily
Apprehension, that your Honours will forbid them to follow the

20 these] *om*. 38 8°+12°   22 prevailing] private 38 8°+12°

---

23 *Petition*: Swift apparently had drafted this mock petition to the ministry six months before (83.50-2). It closely parodies the legal jargon and
obsequious tone of petitions to the Queen, the Privy Council, the ministry,
and the Parliament in every session. The poor insolvent debtors in the Fleet
prison or the several maltsters in the town of Andover depose that they are
reduced to the last extremity and must inevitably perish unless relieved in
the premises by the honourable etc. (*CJ*, xvi 445, 462).
26 *Writing Pamphlets*: cf. 'Four-score and eleven Pamphlets have I written
under three Reigns, and for the Service of six and thirty Factions' (Swift,
Tale, p. 70).
34 *false Quotations*: 335.163-4.
36 *weekly Subsistance*: 240.39.

said Trade any longer; by which your Petitioners, to the number
of Fourscore, with their Wives and Families, will inevitably   45
starve, having been bound to no other Calling.

Your Petitioners desire your Honours will tenderly consider
the Premisses, and suffer your said Petitioners to continue
their Trade (those who set them at Work, being still willing
to employ them, tho' at lower Rates) and your said Petitioners   50
will give Security to make use of the *same Stuff*, and dress it
in the *same Manner*, as they always did, and no other.

> *And your Petitioners*, &c.

'Tis a certain Sign a Man is in the right, when he raises all
the Scriblers against him: I have sometimes had it in my Head, to   55
write a particular History of Abuses and Corruptions. As I find
my self at leisure this Summer, I shall pursue the Design; where,
besides enumerating the gross Defect, not only of Duty and
Respect to the most Gracious QUEEN that ever Reign'd: I propose
to shew, in every Article, how wrong Things were manag'd under   60
the late M-----ry, how right they are now, and according to the
Constitution. Such a History would be the best Means, not only
to expose those who were the principal Actors in it, but the
Persons who defend them by their Writings: Which are so notoriously disingenuous, so distant from Matter of Fact, so short of   65
that Spirit and Entertainment which too often mingle with such
Pens as dip only in Falsities; that were I to rake into their
particular Absurdities (an Attempt which they are secured from
by their excessive Dulness) during that Employment, I should have
reason to look upon my Sufferings little short of the Merit of   70

---

51 it] *om.* 12°   54 Sign] Sign, that 38 8°+12°   raises] raiseth 38
8°+12°   60 wrong] wrong all 38 8°+12°   63 those who were] *om.* 38 8°+
12°   Actors in it,] Actors; 38 8°+12°   64 Persons ... Which] Weekly
Hirelings who toil in their Defence: Who 38 8°+12°   65 disingenuous] disingenuous ½°0^b L   67 were I] if I were 38 8°+12°   69 Dulness) during
that Employment,] Dulness;) 38 8° Dulness; 38 12°

---

54 *a certain Sign*: cf. 'When a true Genius appears in the World, you may
know him by this infallible Sign; that the Dunces are all in Confederacy
against him' (Swift, *Prose*, i 242).

the *Decii*, who sacrific'd themselves meerly for the Good of their Country.

I have been often wondering how it comes to pass, that the late Men in Power should be so ill provided with Writers: Considering at what full Leisure the Heads and Leaders of them are, and I hope will ever be, they might certainly have made a wiser and more judicious Collection. If, as some imagin, their own Hands have dipt in Ink, and that they themselves have a share in dressing up the *Medley* and *Observator*; it is a plain discovery, that their Speculations are as mean and low as their Practices: For how can we conceive that the Politeness and sound Judgment of *One*, should ever descend to *Billingsgate*-Pedantry and Nonsense? Or that a *Second*, who either *stole* or borrow'd his Reputation of Wit, can of a sudden find himself so well provided, as to be able to spare so much, of what they call Wit, to his Neighbours; any more than that he should every Day make his Court officiously to a certain Great Minister, and yet once a Week so clumsily abuse him in his Writings. When I consider the factious Spirit (if any Spirit they have) of these Papers, I can hardly look for the Author of them in one, who by what means soever better convinc'd, had once so much of that sort of Loyalty, as to profess himself a

---

71 the *Decii* ... their] that *Roman*, who by leaping into a bottomless Gulph, sacrificed his Life to preserve his 38 8°+12°   83-6 either ... much, of what they call Wit, ... he] either ... much of what they call Wit ... he ½°0^b L owes his Reputation of Wit, to his Neighbours; 38 8°+12°   90 convinc'd,] ~ ½°

---

71 *the Decii*: Livy, viii 9 2-8.

82 *One*: innuendo: Somers, whose 'Judgment' and 'Politeness' are mentioned in the Dedication to him of *A Tale of a Tub* (Swift, *Tale*, pp. 23, 25).

83 *a Second*: innuendo: Halifax. Oldmixon took this to mean that the Examiner suspected that Somers and Halifax 'had been assisting in writing the *Medley*' (Oldmixon, *The Life*, p. 198).

86 *make ... Court*: After dining with Halifax on 28 November 1710 Swift reported to Stella, 'I know he makes court to the new men, although he affects to talk like a Whig' (Swift, *Journal*, p. 106; cf. Angus McInnes, *Robert Harley, Puritan Politician*, London, Gollancz, 1970, p. 119n.).

90 *one*: innuendo: Mainwaring. Mainwaring assumed that Swift wrote this slur on his Jacobite past (*The Yearbook of English Studies*, xi (1981), 50-3), but it was probably Mrs Manley. Oldmixon observes that Mainwaring 'cou'd not properly be call'd a Nonjuror, because he had never been put to the Tryal, whether he wou'd take the Oaths to King *William* and Queen *Mary* or not. He had been in no Station that made it requisite for him to take them, and he took them as soon as he was call'd to it [in November 1701]' (Oldmixon, *The Life*, p. 199). But if Mainwaring neglected to be called to the bar to avoid taking the oaths, it amounts to the same thing.

Nonjuror.

With humble Submission to worse Judgments, I must determine,
that the Author of the *Medley*, is a Dunce out of his Element,
pretending to intermeddle with *Raillery* and *Irony*, wherein he has   95
no manner of Taste or Understanding: His Topick of Raillery may
be all reduc'd under those two Words *QUOTH HE*, which he seldom
fails in any one of his Papers, to be arch with. His *Irony* consists of the Words *MY FRIEND*, though sometimes reliev'd with an
Epithet. Does he think that when he says, my *impious Friend*, my   100
stupid Friend, and the like; says it in every Paper, and often a
dozen times in one, that this is either Wit, Humour, or Satyr? If
I were *impious* or *stupid*, I should really hope to be his Friend,
and think he spoke in earnest. *Irony* is not a Work for such
groveling Pens, but extream difficult, even to the best; 'tis   105
one of the most beautiful Strokes of *Rhetorick*, and which asks a
Master-hand to carry on and finish with Success: But when a Bungler attempts beyond his Skill; what was at first only mishapen,
with awkard polishing becomes entirely deform'd: As the false
Beauty of Paint upon a Lady's Face is less desirable than no   110
Beauty at all; and the Pertness of a shallow Fop, more disagreeable than his Silence.

I should not have descended so much below the Dignity of this
Paper, as to regard the course of these muddy Writers, did not
the Heads of the late Faction still endeavour to corrupt the   115
Minds of weak People, who are at distance from the Metropolis,
by their Diligence and Liberality in circulating these weekly
Poisons *gratis*. Great numbers are constantly sent into the Country, to prepossess the Reader against the *Examiner*; for no other
Reason, but because they would still mislead and prevent their   120
being set right in Facts, that they might not see how well People
did to assist the Church and QUEEN: To this end, they have been
forc'd to make use of gross Falsities, without the least Appearance of Truth: But however, those more modest of their Party here,
may blush and wonder at the Assurance of their Friends; it serves   125
their Design in the Country, where Truth arrives late; and since
the Mercy of the Government, or rather a just Contempt, still
suffers these Writers to continue their Efforts, it is not doubted

121 well] well the 38 8°+12°   128 their] these 38 8°+12°

there, but what they deliver is, at least, free from notorious
130 Falshood. But those Clouds of Ignorance, will certainly fly before that Light, which now shines throughout the Nation from the
Representation offer'd to Her Majesty, by the best House of
Commons that ever sate; who come the nearest our happy Constitution, both in the Freedom of their Elections, and that True
135 *English* Spirit, which have unanimously carried the Majority of
them *through*, to the end of this memorable Sessions. In which
Representation, the People may be convinced, that five parts in
six of what the *Examiners* have charg'd on the late M-----ry and
Faction is right: Which is so glorious, so unanswerable a Justi-
140 fication of these Papers, that any longer to declaim against them
(like Midnight Curs barking at the Moon) will be as vain and insignificant, as it has always been a ridiculous Endeavour.

   133 nearest] nearest to 38 8°+12°   139 is right] are true 38 8°+12°
141 (like ... Moon)] *om.* 38 8°+12°

No. 38 [Mainwaring]   18 June 1711

The MEDLEY.

The Examiner *beaten out of his Politicks.*
Grown distracted upon it.
Fancies himself still a General.
And imitates Isaac Bickerstaff.

All Authors but One *Nonjurors.*

I Have new Occasions of Complaint against my Adversary the *Examiner* (for he will not let me call him *my Friend* any more:) He
excepts against my Skill in Irony when I use that name; but I
fear I shall not be thought to have improv'd my self in the use
5   of that Figure, when I call such a Writer an Adversary. It is
indeed a Jest to hold him for an Opponent, who so shamefully

   3 *Irony*: 481.94-9.

evades the Question before us, and implicitly acknowledges his
Guilt in reviling innocent Men, whom he had accus'd of procuring
an Act of Indemnity to cover their Crimes against their Country.
A plain Recital of *the Clause wherein all are excepted who have*   10
had to do with the Publick Treasure, has confounded all he cou'd
possibly invent further on that Subject; and he is now forc'd to
leave off his Politicks, and write a Paper on Thursday last, in
which he had no End imaginable, but to be as witty and angry as
was possible.   15

But as Great as he is, he can't hinder me from being *his Friend*;
and I will be so, in spite of him, as long as I think fit. And
indeed he is more friendly to me upon one occasion, than I believe he is aware of; for whenever I want any rude Expressions,
he is always ready to supply them: I only dip into one of his   20
Papers, and strait I find plenty for all Uses, which I beg the
Reader to observe, and to remember that whatever of this kind
appears in my Papers, is always in my Friend's own words. For
instance, 'His Writings are so notoriously disingenuous, so distant from Matter of Fact, so short of that Spirit and Entertain-   25
ment which too often mingle with such Pens as dip only in
Falsities; that were I to rake into their particular Absurdities,
my Sufferings,' *&c.* wou'd be intolerable. This is exactly my
Sense of his Writings, and how cou'd I better have express'd it
than in *these his own words*, fairly copy'd out of his last Paper?   30

Now, he will say the next Week, that this is a *Billingsgate
Paragraph*, and quite forget that it is his own. But how come any
words to be *Billingsgate* in my Papers, and to be Courtly and
Ministerial in his? Or if they are *Billingsgate* Words, pray whose
Words are they? They had never been written by me, if I had not   35
found them us'd by so great a Master of Style. And how comes it
to pass, that my Friend is so highly enrag'd, when only his own
Expressions are turn'd against himself? How comes it to pass,
that whenever he pleases to call me a *Lyar*, he provokes me no
more than if he call'd me a *Tory*; whereas, if I happen at any   40
time to accuse him of Falshood, it has a terrible Effect upon his
Reason? Plain simple Readers will be apt to guess from this, that
I am not conscious of having that ill Quality, but defy him to

10 *Clause*: 475.132-6n.
24-8 *Writings ... Sufferings*: 479.64-70.

prove any Falshood upon me: And that he is too sensible of his
45 natural Infirmity, and of the Proofs that have been made against
him.

But if I had thought there had been the least Danger of his
present Misfortune, I wou'd neither have been so *merry* nor so
serious with him as I have been. I thought it was as impossible
50 for him to lose any part of his Understanding, as to acquire more;
and this made me boldly go on to *detect* him: Indeed I was apprehensive that such Discoveries wou'd gall him a little, and make
People read him with less patience, and perhaps quite spoil the
Design of employing him; but I cou'd not possibly foresee he
55 wou'd take it so much to heart, and go out of his Senses upon it.
Now, as all People in that Condition rave most of their last
Whimsies, you have him again, in the beginning of his Paper,
fancying himself *a General, who has conquer'd an Army, reduc'd a*
Country to Obedience, and routed the main Body of the Whigs: That
60 is to say, all who love the Revolution, the Toleration, the
Protestant Succession, Liberty, Trade and Mony. And this great
Service being over, *he finds it necessary to send out small*
Bodies, in order to take in petty Castles and Forts, and beat
little straggling Parties. Does not all this put one in mind of
65 some Inhabitants of a certain Place, who are often heard making
War alone in their dark Rooms? And this Freak is no sooner over,
but behold him in another Fit; other Business crouds on his victorious Hands, and *he finds himself at leisure to subdue the*
present Set of Writers, whom he has suffer'd without Molestation
70 *so long to infest the Town.*

This way of Fighting he has learn'd from being beaten by One
who was very lucky in it; I mean the late *Isaac Bickerstaff*, who
under the fantastical Notion of a Censor, and a Man of Gravity
and Learning, mix'd with something ridiculous in his manner of
75 possessing those Qualities, had the Skill to talk in a superior
Air to his Opponents, and support himself in it, by giving him-

---

54 *Design*: 470.145.
58-9 *a ... Whigs*: 477.1-6.
62-4 *he ... Parties*: 477.2-4.
65 *a certain Place*: Bethlehem Hospital for the insane.
68-70 *finds ... Town*: 477.8, 13-14.
72 *the late Isaac Bickerstaff*: The last number of *The Tatler* appeared on
2 January 1711. Steele said it had become 'an irksome Task ... to personate
Mr. *Bickerstaff* any longer'.

self a comical Figure at the same time. Without this Subtlety or
Carelesness of himself, the *Tatler* had been the most insupport-
ably arrogant of any Writer that ever appear'd in the World.

Now this *Bungler* the *Examiner*, this *Dunce out of his Element*,   80
observing that the Jest of the Thing carry'd the Reputation of
that Paper to a great height, and that by the Force of it he us'd
his Adversaries as he thought fit; I say, this *Dunce out of his
Element* resolves upon the same way, and without any previous
notice that he design'd to be witty, assumes an aukward Grandeur   85
and Superiority to all that pretend to oppose him. *The Business
I have left*, quoth he, *is to fall on those Wretches that will be
still keeping the War on foot, when they have no Country to
defend, no Forces to bring into the Field, nor any thing remaining, but their bare Good-Will towards Faction and Mischief*. He   90
goes on to represent the Sincerity of the Writers, whom he calls
Factors to the Whigs, after the manner of the abovesaid *Bickerstaff*, by forming a Petition for them to blank Letters: And the
whole Humour consists in the *Tatler*'s old Jest of saying, That
other Writers gain'd a Subsistence out of him. Here is now   95
another Symptom of his Distemper! If he had continu'd in his Wits,
he wou'd never have thought he cou'd have imitated the *Tatler*.

The insipid Petition I have mention'd is follow'd by an impertinent Commendation, which is as great an Addition of Glory to
the Sacred Person he mentions, as it is that her most Gracious   100
Speech is printed in *Abel*'s *Post-boy*. But we have liv'd to see
the Day, wherein every thing that is Great and Illustrious among
Men, is treated with an unbecoming Familiarity. When Matters are
come to this pass, that the *Examiner* shall prate as if he were
in the Secret of the Government, and the *Post-boy* licentiously   105
print, among the Trash of his Paper, a Speech from the Throne;
all Orders of Men must expect to be huddled into the vile Multitude, and us'd as if they had not Sense of Glory or Infamy.

80 *Bungler*: *Examiner*, *Numb*. 46 ($\frac{1}{2}°$ corrected) (481.107-8).
    Dunce out of his Element: 481.94. Mainwaring is simply retorting the
Examiner's words.
   86-90 *The ... Mischief*: 477.9-13.
   92 *Factors ... Whigs*: 478.20-1.
   94 *the Tatler's old Jest*: 268.123n.
   101 *Speech*: The Queen's speech proroguing Parliament on 12 June was printed
verbatim in *The Post-Boy*, 12-14 June 1711.

During the *Examiner*'s Leisure *to examine inferior Abuses*, he
110   imploys some part of it in wondering the Whigs have not better
Writers; and then raises a Suspicion that a Person *of Politeness
and sound Judgment descends to* Billingsgate *Pedantry and Nonsense*;
and that another, who has *borrow'd a great deal of Wit, shou'd
abuse a Man clumsily*. It is sometimes impossible to make any
115   tolerable Guesses whom this *Bungler* intends by his Hints; but I
that have had much to do with him, am so far let into his manner
of Writing and Thinking, that wherever he throws a Calumny, I
take it for a Sign of superior Merit in the Person he calumniates.
When he mentions therefore these two Persons, I know he means to
120   wound in the one a Man whom all Parties allow to have the most
consummate Wisdom and Abilities; and in the other, whom he aptly
calls a *Borrower*, a Person of the most prompt and ready Faculties,
either in Business or Conversation, of any Man living. As to his
Third, whom he describes by the word Nonjuror, I am utterly at a
125   loss to know whom he means, having no Acquaintance with any Person that ever was a Nonjuror. If he speaks of him with relation
to his Party, there can be nothing so inconsistent as a Whig and
a Nonjuror: And if he talks of him merely as an Author, all the
Authors in the World are Nonjurors, but the ingenious Divine who
130   writ *the Tale of a Tub*. He, I say, is the only Writer in the

109 *Leisure ... Abuses*: 477.8-9.
111 *a Person*: Somers (480.82).
113 *another*: Halifax (480.83-8).
120 *a Man*: Somers.
121 *the other*: Halifax.
124 *Third*: Mainwaring (480.90-481.92).
130 *Tale of a Tub*: A few months later Mainwaring stated his objection more
explicitly: 'that Author who writ the *Tale of a Tub* ... to please the very
worst Men among us, the *Deists, Socinians*, and *Free-Thinkers*, made a Satyr
upon Religion' (Mainwaring, *Remarks upon the Present Negotiations of Peace
Begun between Britain and France*, London, 1711, p. 23). This had become a
critical commonplace: 'we see by Experience, that *Socinianism, Arianism,
Deism*, and the Ridiculing of all reveal'd Religion, with the like Damnable
Errors, such as those of *Asgil, Coward, Swift, Burnet, Sherlock*, &c. have been
discover'd to be, and are daily more and more found among the profess'd Members of the Church of *England*' (*Brief Remarks on the Late Representation of
the Lower House of Convocation; as the same respects the Quakers only*, London,
1711, p. 13); 'there is a certain Clergy-Man who has publickly ridicul'd the
most Sacred Mysteries, and represented the Religion, both of the Presbyterians,
Papists, and Church-Men, as nothing else but a *Tale of a Tub*' (John Withers,
*The Whigs Vindicated, the Objections that are commonly brought against them
Answer'd, and the Present Ministry prov'd to be the best Friends to the Church,
the Monarchy, the Lasting Peace, and real Welfare of England*, 8th edn., London, for John Clark, 1715, p. 17). But the observations of the Grubaean Sage

World who is not a Nonjuror; for he is the first Man who introduc'd those Figures of Rhetorick we call Swearing and Cursing in
Print: and as the *Examiner* is an Enemy to Nonjurors, and takes
upon him to set up for an Ecclesiastical Jurisdiction among us,
I wou'd advise him to subjoin to the next Invective he makes   135
against the *Whigs*, this short Anathema of *Peter*'s in that religious Tale,—If you will not comply in all and singular the
Premises, *G-d damn you, and all your Posterity; and so we bid
you heartily farewel.*

---

upon the founders of new religions (Swift, *Tale*, p. 162) apply as well to
Jesus as to John Knox and 'some proper mystical Number' was as sacred to the
imaginations of Anglican Churchmen as to that of Papists, a fact attested by
the Trinitarian Controversy (1690-6), of which Swift could not have been un-
aware when he was writing *A Tale of a Tub*.
   132 *Swearing and Cursing*: 281.82n.
   138-9 *G-d ... farewel*: Mainwaring may be quoting from memory: '*G— d--mn
You and Yours to all Eternity. And so we bid you heartily Farewel*' (Swift,
Tale, p. 113).

INDEX

THE commentary is indexed as well as the main text. Noblemen are referred to by title rather than family name, with cross-references from the latter where necessary. Acts of Parliament are grouped together under one entry. The reader is advised to distinguish carefully between l (roman *fifty*) and 1 (arabic *one*).

Owen, James 176
Oxford, Robert de Vere, Earl of 258
Oxford, Robert Harley, Earl of
xxiff., 2, 196, 216-17: accused
of Jacobitism, French sympathy,
lx, 25; acrostic on 58-9; and Act
of Settlement 287; admitted to
Middle Temple 64; ancestry 420; as
Aristophanic character 63ff.;
assassination attempt upon 297ff.,
308ff., 323-4, 327, 329, 334, 350,
352, 388, 410, 411-12, 414, 430;
attempt to displace Junto 260; as
Claude Barbin 27, 29, 30, 32;
borrows to fund Marlborough's
campaigns 50; and Clement xxiv-
xxv; 'crafty' 282; criticized by
Medley 435; and Defoe xxiv, 404;
'destructive smile' 61; disliked
119; on the Dutch 9; and Earl of
Nottingham 100-1, 145; and David
Edwards 356; effigy of shot at 116;
elevation to peerage 417, 425, 431,
461; empirical politics of lxii;
and *Essay upon Publick Credit* 201;
and the *Examiner* 34, 43, 139; and
Faults on both Sides 8, 205;
financial measures of 332-3, 380,
467-8; friends in the Church 119;
and Godolphin xxvii; and James
Greenshields xxxii; and Greg
xxviii, 302, 406, 414; and Antoine
de Guiscard xxix, 297ff., 310, 320,
406; and Halifax 333; as 'Honest
Gentleman' 86, 119; as an intendant
63; and Ireland 428; and the Junto
xxvii; learned 216; on libellous
pamphlets 432; as Machiavelli 31;
and Marlborough's command 52, 260;
and Mrs Masham 122; a moderate 34,
273; 'moderation' his election
slogan 22; and *The Moderator* xxiv-
xxv; nicknamed 'Harlequin' 472; as
'obstructor' 413; and October Club
273; 'old' Whig xxvii, 205; peace
negotiations with France xxix;
praised 414-15; Presbyterian connections 248; and Pretender 373;
propagandist xlvi; and Queen Anne
122, 297; and Queen Anne's Bounty
200; quoted 8; removal advocated by
Sunderland 97-8; resigns 51, 260;
and resumption of Irish land grants
306, 454; retains Whigs and Tories
in office 2; and St. John 274, 303;
sends £50 to Swift 404; and Spanish
campaign 145; sponsors *The Review*
35; succeeds as Lord Treasurer 467;

and suggested repudiation of
national debt 40; supports William
of Orange xxvi, 37; and Swift
xxiff.; and Toland 149, 400; and
Treasury 2, 7; uncommunicative
xxix-xxx; and Wharton xxx-xxxi
Oxford University: and Exeter Association 366-7; grant to Sir Roger
L'Estrange 156; and passive obedience 338-9, 353, 403, 424; Romanization of 435

Pakington, Sir John lvii, 135
Palatines, the lvii, 129-30, 144,
225, 416, 466-7, 469
Paleotti, Andrea, marchese of Bologna
33
Pall Mall 53
Palmer, Roger: *see* Castlemaine, Earl
of
panegyrics 122, 224, 236, 293, 331,
352, 368, 382, 396, 413, 435, 461;
see also Pliny the Younger
paper-credit 202ff.
Papists: *see* Catholicism
parasites: *see* flattery; Medius
Parker, Benjamin 170
Parker, Samuel 158
Parker, Sir Thomas 146, 151
Parkyns, Sir William 310-11
Parliament 3, 7, 9: as 'asserter'
(of William III and the Revolution) 60; and declaration of war
114; dissolved 2, 9, 51, 179;
moderates in 22; one as good as
another 349-50; qualification for
332, 342; and Queen Anne's letter
on Convocation 132ff.; vote commending Marlborough 61-2
parliamentary committee on Greg 39
Parmenio 111
Partition Treaties 248, 453
passive obedience 6, 104, 112, 221,
276, 289, 291, 314ff., 336ff., 353,
354, 363ff., 370-1, 403-4, 432-4;
see also arbitrary power
patches 284
Pate, William 220, 403
Paterson, William 7
patricians 418
Patrick, Simon, Bishop of Chichester
157, 159
patriotism 86
patronage, crisis of (1710) 100
Peachell, Dr. John, Vice-Chancellor
of Cambridge University 249
peculatus 461-2
Pedro II (of Portugal) 366

the Devil 20; and Greg 39; as
'Immorality and Irreligion' 184;
and Lambert 71; as 'libertine' 360;
Lord-Lieutenant of Ireland 20, 68,
71, 91-2, 147, 258; and lying 23;
Mainwaring's feeble defence of lvi;
member of Junto 38-9; and Palatines
467; profligacy 21; and Sacheverell
151-2; and sacramental test 147;
and swearing 24; Swift's philippic
against xxx-xxxi, lv, 69, 151; as
Verres 69ff., 91-2, 152; and
William III 151-2
'whifflers' 96
Whig-Examiner, The liii-liv, 68, 69,
376-7
Whigs, the xxvii, 22: appeal to the
people 287, 296; bad poets 63;
change in meaning of word 314,
450ff.; 456; and Charles I 345,
400; and Church 219, 247, 314, 399;
and clergy 126, 134, 370-1, 400;
and constitution (Defoe) 119;
and 'credit' 40, 49, 179, 347;
'declining' party 1; difficulty of
maintaining majority 25; and disputed elections 25, 99, 332-3; and
dissenters 247, 257, 314, 344, 359,
361, 404-5; and Duchess of Marlborough 375-6; and *Examiner* 97; and
general election (1710) 178; and
hypocrisy 270-1; 478; and James II
219, 406; lack of support of landed
gentry 25; and letter to Elector of
Bavaria 141-2; and loss of power
272; and lottery 377; and mismanagement 84; and 'moderation' 22,
85; and monarchy 314, 345-6, 375,
399-400; object to criticism of
William III's campaigns 61; 'old'
and 'new' xxvii, 205, 209, 314;
and passive obedience 314ff.; and
Pretender 406-7, 411, 454; propaganda 12, 52; and Queen Anne's
title to throne 41, 401, 478; and
republicanism 219, 345; retained by
Harley in office 2; and revolution
47, 407, 456; 'ruined party' 3,
49, 92, 96, 142, 178, 207-8, 210-
11, 219, 238, 295, 361, 385, 424,
474, 478; and standing army 405;
success 119; threaten constitution
192; and Toleration Act 278; unite
in adversity 272; an 'unnatural'
majority 332; vanity of 58; and
William III 37, 52, 61, 219; and
wit 58; *see also* Junto, the
White, Robert 269

White, Thomas, Bishop of Peterborough
452
White's Chocolate House 331
Whitgift, Dr John, Archbishop of
Canterbury 365
Wildman, Major John 128
Wilkes, Judith 453
Wilkins, John 88
will, freedom of 291-2
Will Bigamy: *see* Cowper, William
(Earl Cowper)
William III (of England), Prince of
Orange 5, 245, 289, 409: Assassina-
tion Plot and 31, 161, 269, 310-11;
as 'asserter' (of liberty) 60; and
Book of Common Prayer 250; changes
ministers in wartime 377; and the
Church 134, 141, 152, 452-3, 460;
declared king 220, 451-2; and
dissenters 358; and Duke of Shrewsbury 31, 216; and Exeter Association 366; Harley and xxvi; invitation to rescue from 'popery and
slavery' 318, 457; land grants in
Ireland 306, 454; Mainwaring on
xlix-l; military defeats 61; and
New Country Party 248; and nonjurors 127; and Nottingham declaration 366; and partition of Spanish
Empire 453; political support for
37, 366; and standing army 405;
Swift supports xxvi, lvi; Torbay
landing 366; Tories under 289;
vetoes Triennial Act 318; and
Wharton 151-2; and Whigs 52, 128,
219, 405
William the Conqueror 287
William of Orange: see William III
(of England), Prince of Orange
William Rufus 112, 307
Willis, Richard 135
Winchester, Hugh le Despencer, Earl
of [two of the same name] 258
windows in the breast (in fable) 140
Windsor Park 53, 88
wit: of the *Examiner* 81, 82; lack of
in news-writers 36; of Tories 58;
of Whigs 58
Withers, John 486
Woburn Abbey 144
'wolf' (cry of) 40
women in finance 105
Wood, Thomas lvii
Woodstock 53
Woodward, Josiah 171
Wooton (hundred of) 53
Worcester, address from 354
Wotton, William: answers *Examiner*